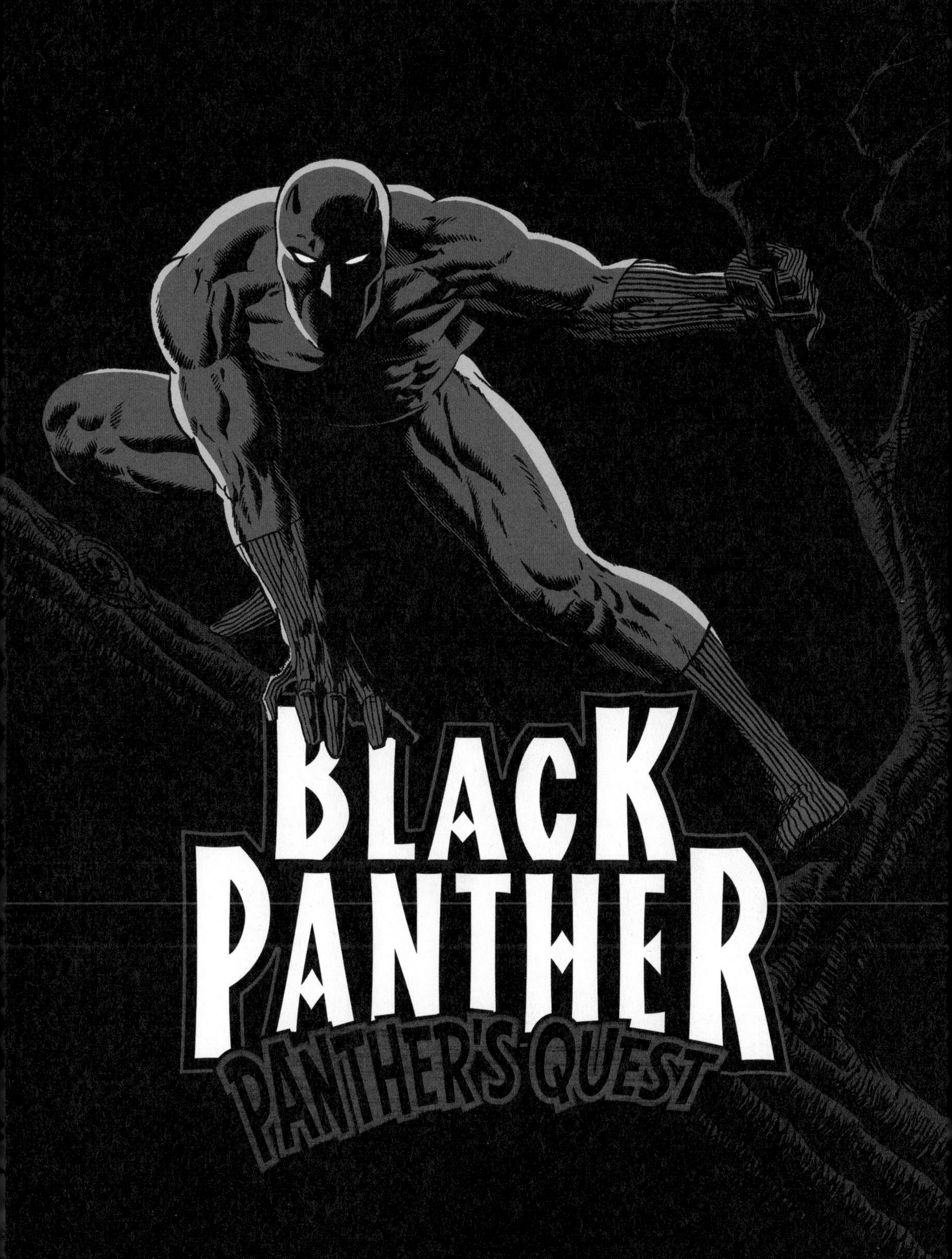
BLACK PANTHER
PANTHER'S QUEST

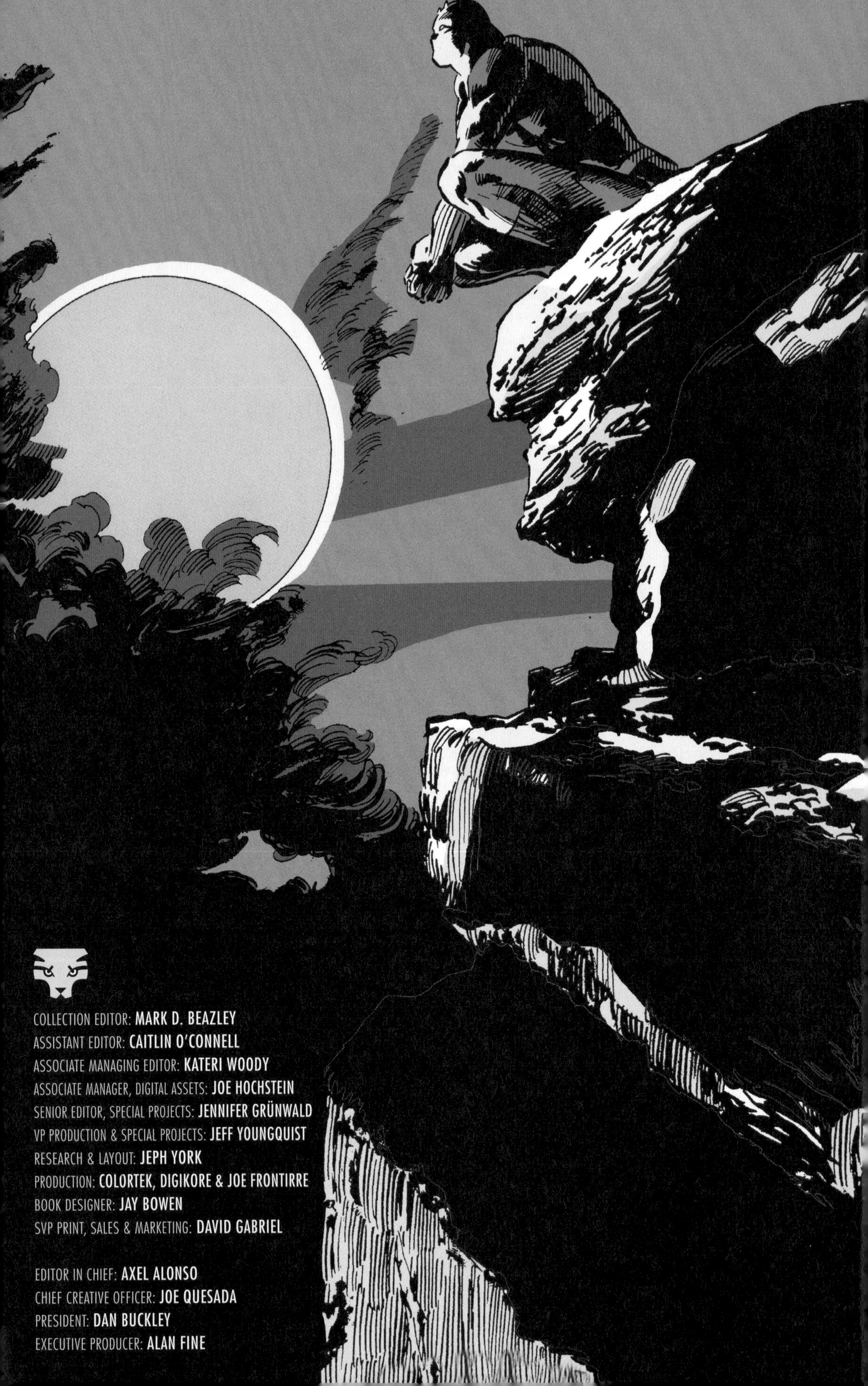

COLLECTION EDITOR: **MARK D. BEAZLEY**
ASSISTANT EDITOR: **CAITLIN O'CONNELL**
ASSOCIATE MANAGING EDITOR: **KATERI WOODY**
ASSOCIATE MANAGER, DIGITAL ASSETS: **JOE HOCHSTEIN**
SENIOR EDITOR, SPECIAL PROJECTS: **JENNIFER GRÜNWALD**
VP PRODUCTION & SPECIAL PROJECTS: **JEFF YOUNGQUIST**
RESEARCH & LAYOUT: **JEPH YORK**
PRODUCTION: **COLORTEK, DIGIKORE & JOE FRONTIRRE**
BOOK DESIGNER: **JAY BOWEN**
SVP PRINT, SALES & MARKETING: **DAVID GABRIEL**

EDITOR IN CHIEF: **AXEL ALONSO**
CHIEF CREATIVE OFFICER: **JOE QUESADA**
PRESIDENT: **DAN BUCKLEY**
EXECUTIVE PRODUCER: **ALAN FINE**

BLACK PANTHER
PANTHER'S QUEST

WRITER: **DON McGREGOR**

PENCILER: **GENE COLAN**

INKER: **TOM PALMER**

COLORISTS: **GLYNIS OLIVER** (#13-20 & #23)
AND **MIKE ROCKWITZ** (#21 & #24-37)
WITH **GREGORY WRIGHT** (#22)

LETTERERS: **JOE ROSEN** (#13-30 & #32-37) WITH **JADE MOEDE** (#31)

ASSISTANT EDITORS: **MIKE ROCKWITZ** (#13-30) & **KELLY CORVESE** (#31-37)

EDITOR: **TERRY KAVANAGH**

FRONT COVER ARTISTS: **BILL REINHOLD & VERONICA GANDINI**

BACK COVER ARTISTS: **JON BOGDANOVE & HILARY BARTA**

BLACK PANTHER CREATED BY **STAN LEE & JACK KIRBY**

BLACK PANTHER: PANTHER'S QUEST. Contains material originally published in magazine form as MARVEL COMICS PRESENTS (1988) #13-37. First printing 2017. ISBN# 978-1-302-90803-4. Published by MARVEL WORLDWIDE, INC., a subsidiary of MARVEL ENTERTAINMENT, LLC. OFFICE OF PUBLICATION: 135 West 50th Street, New York, NY 10020. Copyright © 2017 MARVEL No similarity between any of the names, characters, persons, and/or institutions in this magazine with those of any living or dead person or institution is intended, and any such similarity which may exist is purely coincidental. **Printed in the U.S.A.** DAN BUCKLEY, President, Marvel Entertainment; JOE QUESADA, Chief Creative Officer; TOM BREVOORT, SVP of Publishing; DAVID BOGART, SVP of Business Affairs & Operations, Publishing & Partnership; C.B. CEBULSKI, VP of Brand Management & Development, Asia; DAVID GABRIEL, SVP of Sales & Marketing, Publishing; JEFF YOUNGQUIST, VP of Production & Special Projects; DAN CARR, Executive Director of Publishing Technology; ALEX MORALES, Director of Publishing Operations; SUSAN CRESPI, Production Manager; STAN LEE, Chairman Emeritus. For information regarding advertising in Marvel Comics or on Marvel.com, please contact Jonathan Parkhideh, VP of Digital Media & Marketing Solutions, at jparkhideh@marvel.com. For Marvel subscription inquiries, please call 888-511-5480. **Manufactured between 11/3/2017 and 12/5/2017 by LSC COMMUNICATIONS INC., KENDALLVILLE, IN, USA.**

10 9 8 7 6 5 4 3 2 1

TO FOLLOW THE TRACK OF THE GREAT CAT WITH RENEWED WONDER ON HIS PANTHER'S QUEST

(FROM "PANTHER'S RAGE" TO "PANTHER'S PREY")

I had thought that T'Challa, the Black Panther, was gone from my life. I had missed him dearly when I'd stopped writing his adventures in 1976. You spend so much time with a character you write on a continuous basis that you live and breathe with them, sit staring at the blank sheet of paper, worrying if you are doing justice to them and your audience. You have to put aside the plans you had for the character, the one- or two-paragraph ideas that give you a direction for the series and the character. You find new characters and situations and themes that hold meaning for you, and you must concentrate on these new fictional lives and what that new book is about, else you never make your goodbyes and you can't get on with your work.

By 1988, I thought of T'Challa fondly whenever I was asked to sign old copies of *Jungle Action* at comic conventions. When some reader would recall a scene from "Panther's Rage" or "The Panther vs. The Klan" and ask about whatever happened to W'Kabi or Taku or Lloyd Lynne, or the Abbott & Costello duo of Tayete and Kazibe, it was the tone of voice someone speaks in about some television-series star whom they once felt they'd known intimately, and every once in a while wondered what happened to them. When asked those questions, I'd wonder about many of those characters also, but once the convention was over and the talk of ghosts passed, I'd be back in the present, facing the challenges of writing the lives of new characters I loved, seeing where their lives were headed. I never languished much new thought on these old friends, except for the futures I had sketched in while writing them, mostly because I never thought I'd be writing about any of the gang again, especially T'Challa.

T'Challa has always been one of the easiest characters for me to write. In somewhat the same manner that he is attuned to the Great Cat, I seemed to have a bond with him, not one that is easily describable nor an identification that is calculated; yet when I was writing about T'Challa's feelings, his way of seeing the world, this came spontaneously, a flow that was immediate and vital. He was essentially a decent, honest man trying to be the best leader he could be, something I think many of us wish for, and have often been disappointed by, in our hearts and minds.

Writing the rest of the strip was difficult. Creating Wakanda, delving into details about how such a society might work, where it might be located, etc., were stimulating questions. Since the book came out on a bimonthly schedule, I had two months to refine my initial concepts. There were other obligations to be met when a book appears only once every two months, and I made concessions to them. If I didn't include a scene with W'Kabi or Taku, let's say, in one issue, that would mean a four-month time span before readers would see them again. If one of them didn't appear for two issues in a row, you were talking about an absence of half a year. And yet, it was often an inescapable fact that there were times I only had 13 or 15 pages to chronicle each chapter of "Panther's Rage." By 1988, the goodbyes had been said a long time ago.

T'Challa was an old friend, but almost like one I'd known from another lifetime. I had just finished writing and directing the video version of *Detectives, Inc.*, and I was in the midst of tackling the postproduction phase of the movie. I was watching Alex Simmons as Ted Denning, Richard Douglass as Bob Rainier, and my wife, Marsha McGregor, as Deirdre Sevens, make these characters real, watching their movements for what seemed countless times to match movements between shots, when T'Challa came back into my life.

Michael Higgins called one night. He told me Marvel was going to start a new comic that would be published on a weekly or biweekly basis, and he was going to edit this yet-untitled comic. He wanted to know if I would be willing to work on the book.

"Doing what?" I asked.

Now, if the track of the Great Cat can sometimes be a tortuous trail to follow, so can many trails in the entertainment industry. And comics, like movies and television series, often start in one area and end somewhere completely different. Michael wasn't calling about the Black Panther, but rather Killraven, another character I had written for Marvel back in the 1970s, during the same time period I was studying Wakanda and the effects of revolution on the hidden nation. I alternated between the two books, *Jungle Action* and *Amazing Adventures*, in the 1970s.

If I did three pages of Killraven, I was behind three pages on the Black Panther, and vice versa. The rules of the game are unclear, but they seem to be, whatever you do, you are never ahead.

Michael and I had discussed the possibility of continuing the Killraven saga at length over the next couple of months. One afternoon he confided in me, with that look in his eye of secret amusement, a joke between just you and him, that he almost hadn't given me that initial phone call. "Why?" and "How come?" were the first questions that popped into my mind. He'd heard that I was doing movies and people told him I wasn't doing comics anymore.

Rumors. There is one thing there is never a dearth of: rumors. "Panther's Quest" and this book you're holding in your hands might not have happened because of rumors. Rumors spreading like wildfire, accepted as truth.

Even though I love writing the prose books and the screenplays, my love for comics was not diminished. I never had any plans to give up comics completely, no matter how successful, or unsuccessful, the other endeavors might be. I love them. Simple as that. I would not have devoted so much of my life to this medium if I did not believe in this wonderful combination of words and pictures that becomes its own irreplaceable realm for storytellers.

One night, Michael and I were sitting in a restaurant/neighborhood bar discussing what I felt I'd need to return to Killraven, and then confiding in him some of the general situations and themes the story would deal with. While we were talking, I was waiting to meet with a couple of people who wanted to discuss a film project based on a Succubae story I'd written years ago. Before "Killraven" or "Panther's Rage," even!

Michael and I had been talking for a couple of hours before I finally shrugged my shoulders and said, "So, okay, let's do it."

I'd ordered a Harveys Bristol Cream on the rocks when we first started talking. Every time I looked down, it seemed like a fresh drink was there. It could have been a magician's trick. I couldn't quite figure out how it had gotten there. Michael Higgins can do very good sleight of hand. Immediately upon my saying I'd do "Killraven," and now trying to clear my head so I would be able to focus on the next meeting, trying to shift from Wars between Worlds to the erotic arena of sexual warfare and a creature capable of draining the life from her sexual conquests, Michael seized the moment and said, with that spur-of-the-moment innocence that he has, as if this has just crossed his mind for the first time, "So, how about the Black Panther?"

I had been thinking about a seductress changing into a serpent. "What?" I asked, telling myself to be alert. Pay attention now. Everything is beginning to move rapidly.

"As long as you're coming back to Killraven, why not do a Panther also?"

I shook my head. No. Sorry, Michael, you're very persuasive, thanks, but no thanks. As much as I loved T'Challa, my parting on that series had not been an easy endeavor; it had caused me a lot of anguish and I had no desire to go back to having to spend half my energy and days on fighting behind the scenes, as had often been the case, to see the Panther through.

Who needed the grief? Not me.

Michael persevered. He does it in a gentle way. He has a conspiratorial twinkle in his eye that says, "Why the hell not? Come on!"

And somewhere along the way I said, because it was true, and never believing for a moment that I would end up writing that story, "I had wanted to do a story with the Panther searching for his mother in South Africa." I hadn't thought of that storyline in years, but if someone checks the letters page of *Jungle Action* or some fanzine interviews, I'll bet you'll find that idea mentioned. This was not a surefire topic to win the hearts and minds of many editors. They'd never go for it!

Michael laughed and slapped his hand down on the table. "Okay!" he said enthusiastically. "We'll do it!" Now, I knew I'd better pay attention and tell him all the reasons why he wouldn't want to do it, but to every reason Michael said, "I don't see a problem with that."

And right about then, as the two people arrived who wanted to discuss Succubae and film deals, T'Challa, the Black Panther, came back full force into my life. A few weeks later I'd start writing the final, absolute end to the "Killraven" / "The War of the Worlds," but "Panther's Quest" and "Panther's Prey" would be finished long before I would know when or if the Killraven project would come to completion.

The trail of the Great Cat and the comic-book biz had connected.

My mistake was that I thought Michael Higgins was kidding. After all our meetings discussing "Killraven" and "The Black Panther," with all the business talks out of the way, I settled down to do the work,

which is a totally separate endeavor from talking about what you are going to do. I had titled the penultimate war between the Martians and Earthlings "Final Battles, Final Lies, Final Truths."

I had just placed the blank sheet of paper for the final script for page two (*count 'em, two!*) when the phone rang and Michael Higgins began without preamble, "Don, I'm not going to be editing *Marvel Comics Presents*. I'm going to be a freelancer."

I laughed, because I knew he had to be kidding, and he thought I was going to fall for this gag because it was somewhere between 11 o'clock and midnight and he'd figured he would try to give me a little jolt for taking so long to decide whether to write the series.

"Get out of here, Michael," I said, letting him know he wasn't fooling me for a moment. Try to put one over on me, huh?

"I'm not kidding, Don."

Five minutes later, I was beginning to believe he wasn't kidding, and I told him, still with some disbelief, "What are you telling me, Michael — that after talking about this project for over two months, that on the day I actually start to write finished copy for this book, you're leaving?"

"I think you're finally getting it, Don," Michael said, laughing, and with that laugh I knew he wasn't kidding.

The next day, I called Tom DeFalco (who was Editor In Chief at the time) to ask him who would be editing the book. I believe this was the first time I had ever spoken with Tom, but hey, we're already going back to 1988 and I can forget things that happened yesterday. One of the reasons for writing a piece like this is so that there is some reasonable record for those who care about the history of how the book in their hands came to be. Even when many of the events are fairly recent, some details of who did what, when and where are already a bit vague, since the comic-book business, again, like the track of the Great Cat, not only can twist and stray off the main path but sometimes fade to faint prints that only the most skillful tracker can find.

Tom told me it didn't matter who the editor was; there was still going to be *Marvel Comics Presents* and to just keep doing the work. Part of the executive editor's freelance mantra: "Do the work. Do the work."

Terry Kavanagh took over the editorial position on the newly named, now biweekly *Marvel Comics Presents*. When he was given the assignment, Terry called me and asked to have lunch together.

I didn't know Terry. I didn't know if he was familiar with my work. I didn't know what he knew about these new projects that I had finally agreed to write.

I needn't have worried.

By the end of that first lunch, I was at ease with Terry; I instinctively liked him. I felt he understood how important it was to do an accurate story about apartheid that avoided the simplistic — that hopefully would bring alive human beings and not caricatures, as well as being a super hero story that would be exciting.

I enjoyed the exchange of personal adventures, and Terry's way of telling them — the acknowledgment of how absurd some situations can become. More important, though, was the fact that we both had a mutual love for the comics medium, and that he, like myself, shared an enthusiasm for the myriad possibilities of approach and style in comics.

Terry was, quite simply, a good editor. If he told you something one day, he didn't forget he said it the next. He didn't say one thing and then do another. He kept his word. He kept in touch with you when you were in the thick of the book, scared and exhilarated, sometimes at the same time. He was supportive, and he understood why I could not do a story where the hero whumps some bad guys and nasty old apartheid goes away. He took the heat when others questioned the wisdom of doing a 25-part story in *Marvel Comics Presents*.

I had always felt that the Black Panther worked better in a series of illustrated novels, ever since I first approached writing "Panther's Rage." It seemed to me that if the stories were to be set in Wakanda, and it was supposed to be a secret, magical place that no one outside its environs knew the whereabouts of (with the exception of the Fantastic Four), then it would be much more credible if the source of action revolved around one central protagonist, motivating others, to give conflict and cohesiveness to the series.

In March 1988, Terry, his then assistant editor, Mike Rockwitz, and I met with Gene Colan to discuss Gene's illustrating "Panther's Quest." Mike told me that the "Cactus Man" in the original "Panther's Rage" had given him nightmares when he was 11 years old. I figured out that the "Cactus Man" must have been Salamander K'Ruel. I told Mike I must have only been 14 when I wrote the stories. He was making me feel ancient.

During lunch, Terry and I talked with Gene to see what commitments he had to fulfill. We tried to calculate when Gene would be available to begin "Panther's Quest." At that time, I was writing the fourth or fifth chapter of "Killraven," which translated to somewhere around 40 pages of finished script, and the more time Gene needed to start would be a blessing for me—time for me to get way into the "Killraven" story, and more time to keep researching South Africa, talking with people, visiting museums, etc. Great!

I asked Gene to give me at least a week's notice as to when he'd want to start "Panther's Quest," and already in my mind I was upping the time span to a minimum of two months before Gene would be ready.

We had lunch on a Friday. Now, sometimes a writer hasn't a clue what sparks some ideas. Maybe, in this case, it was the fact that we'd been mulling over the Panther series that gave me a spark that weekend. I sure wasn't thinking consciously about the Panther, because I was in the thick of introducing all the old cast of "Killraven." Now, off and on I had been trying to come up with reasons as to why T'Challa's mother had never been heard of before, but for every reason I would tentatively come up with, there'd be lots of unanswered questions.

That weekend, all the questions were answered.

One moment I was in the apartment, the next I was transported into the Panther's world. It was suddenly clear to me what had happened to his mother and why. I rushed to the typewriter, because this is the type of thing you can lose, like something seen in a hole in thick mist for a brief glimpse before it is shrouded from sight. Sometimes you struggle for the ideas, and then there is that magical time when your fingers are conduits for translating ideas fed so quickly you can hardly keep up with them.

It was a damn good thing that happened, because before that point, I'll be honest, I hadn't had the faintest idea in the world what had happened to her or why she had never, ever been mentioned in any story involving the Panther.

It was a damn good thing because Gene Colan called me that Monday. Several of the projects he'd been doing were rescheduled, and rather than a month and a half or two months, he was ready to start "Panther's Quest" the next week.

I stammered. I stuttered. I was afraid to breathe. I had a deathly feeling of déjà vu, swept back to a time alternating between T'Challa and the Wakandans and Killraven and the Freemen, all of them demanding time.

I had gone back to waging battle with Killraven, M'Shulla, Old Skull, Carmilla Frost and the rest of the band after I typed down how "Panther's Quest" ended. I did not have a Patrick Slade or an Anton Pretorius created yet, but I knew the key part, the heart of the situation. I just didn't know how I was going to get there.

Gene said, in that soft, good-natured voice he has, "What's the matter, Don? You said to give you at least a week's notice. So, you've got a week."

"Uh, yes, Gene...I said that...I know I said that." I'm a writer—that's why I can come up with snappy one-liners like that.

"So you'll have the pages for me next Monday?" Gene asked.

"Sure," I said, in my squeakiest Mickey Mouse voice.

The day after I'd written the piece for the ending of "Panther's Quest," I'd come down with a virus, the kind that has you half in the Twilight Zone trying to remember what real life is like.

And now I'd hanged myself. I didn't have a week to write that first chapter of "Panther's Quest" but, really, two days. My friend Alex Simmons, who is also the actor who played Ted Denning, was getting married to Lorraine Walker up in the state of Maine. I was in the wedding party and due to drive up there on Thursday. That meant there was only Monday and Tuesday to write those eight pages if I were to keep my promise to Gene.

I called the doctor, told him I didn't have time to come into the office, and could he prescribe some antibiotics that would, if nothing else, temporarily take me out of the Twilight Zone? I sat behind the typewriter, tense. As much as I loved T'Challa, it was intimidating to come back under such pressurized circumstances. I was glad I had stuck with my decision not to feature all of the cast of "Panther's Rage" in that story, to save it for the next graphic novel. If I hadn't, I don't see how I'd have written those first eight pages in time.

I focused on T'Challa, and he was a pleasure to be with again, to glide through the high tree limbs, to follow the track of the Great Cat with renewed wonder and see his world with amber, penetrating eyes.

Starting with the second chapter of "Panther's Quest," I began the first of many treks of my own to the Schomburg museum up in Harlem, one of the major places I did research on South Africa. The people working there asked me if this was really going to appear in a Marvel comic. I said, "You got me. All I can assure you of right now is that I'm going to write it. If you see it in print, then, yes, Marvel did print it."

There was scant coverage of apartheid and South Africa as I began this. PBS had a half hour scheduled each Saturday focusing on life within such a fiercely segregated society.

As I started to write Chapter 5, *National Geographic* ran a big feature on South Africa. Two things occurred that affected the series directly. First, it turned out the name of the man responsible for Ramonda's disappearance in the story was also the name of a real-life political figure in South Africa's government. That meant I had to change the name before the first four chapters saw print. And whatever name I came up with had better have the same number of letters so it could fit over the old lettering.

The second fact in that *National Geographic* piece was that the South African government had just changed the pass laws. Everything I had written at the time was accurate, but now it would be wrong. Thus, this is one of the first times a Marvel comic was dated when a story was taking place, so that the sequence with passbooks would have been in effect the way they are described in the story.

Certain factors in comics are often set in cement. *Marvel Comics Presents* featured eight-page stories running, normally, eight chapters, sometimes ten. When I was writing Chapter 12, Terry Kavanagh asked me how long I thought the series would be. "I have to give them something, Don," Terry told me, referring to scheduled editorial meetings.

I had no idea how long. I was still researching the story and included as much factual material into the costumed hero aspects. I said, "25," off the top of my head. Thank God for Terry; his advocacy for "Panther's Quest" allowed me to focus on writing it and not having to fight for everything that might be different from the norm. One point could not be gotten around, and that was that every chapter in *Marvel Comics Presents* was eight pages. You will note that one chapter in "Panther's Quest" is ten pages! I needed the extra pages to include material that must appear in that sequence of the book. I also knew Terry had no six-page stories in his story inventory. I could only think of one way this could be accomplished. I told Terry I would sell my soul to the devil; I would write a six-page story for him on any character he wanted if I could have the ten pages for the Panther. And that's how the six-page Sub-Mariner story "Dying In Paradise," drawn by Jim Lee and colored by my wife, Marsha McGregor, came to be.

Another Gene Colan story: There are often times when a writer seems to only have few options to the way a story can go. I was writing about the neck-lacing ceremonies done at that time in black townships. In some instances, if a spy was caught, a car tire was placed around their neck, filled with gasoline and set afire. Now, I could have the Panther come in and rescue the guy, but I felt politically that made a statement. I could have the Panther come in and fail to rescue the guy, but that made another kind of statement, and I wanted to keep this a very human story, about how oppressive regimes make even the search of a son for his mother almost impossible, and the brutality that it creates in its inhumane treatments.

I struggled with it, and suddenly came up with the idea of bringing back two little boys, Theodore and Wally Olebogeng, whom I'd had no intention of using again, and that when the Panther goes to interfere with the neck-lacing, Theodore (think the Beav in a black township) is burned. There is a single chapter devoted just to the Panther trying to get this boy to a white hospital. The doctors truly try to save Theodore. But he dies.

The phone rings one night, around 11 o'clock, one of Gene's favorite times to call during those times.

"I can't do it," Gene tells me.

"Can't do what?" I have no clue what he is talking about.

His voice is really agitated. "I can't draw that, and don't ask me to, Don!"

"Can't draw what?

"You know. Don't pretend you don't know."

"I have no idea, Gene, what we are talking about."

"I tried to do it, and I can't."

"Can't do what, Gene?"

Finally he delivers the telling line. "The kid, Don. The kid."

"What about the kid?" I ask.

"The kid doesn't die."

"He doesn't what?" And my voice has risen.

Gene goes on to explain that it just tore his heart out, he cannot draw the scene that way. He has drawn it so Theodore lives.

I'm in a panic. I'm pleading with Gene. "No, Gene, this encapsulates for me what this entire series is about. If he lives we let everyone off the hook. And I don't want them off the hook. I want the reader to feel what this is!"

Gene continues that it is too tragic, I can't ask him to do such a thing. I plead my case ten ways from Sunday. This must last a good twenty minutes or more. I am near hysteria by now.

And then Gene laughs.

And says, "Get out of here, Don. I just wanted to see if you'd fall for it. I drew it exactly as you wanted!"

Man, I miss you, Gene!

When we were nearing the completion of "Panther's Quest," Terry asked me if I'd consider doing another Panther project. I knew there were readers from the "Panther's Rage" series who wanted to see what had happened to W'Kabi and Taku and the other supporting characters. Some readers still fondly mentioned Monica Lynne.

I had always wanted each Panther novel to be complete unto itself in theme and structure, while each would also take T'Challa forward. Each novel should show change in the characters' lives.

As with the Black-Panther-in-South-Africa storyline, I wasn't sure anyone would want to do this. I wanted T'Challa and Monica Lynne to get married.

And I had a title... "Panther's Prey."

— Don McGregor
FEBRUARY 1991–AUGUST 2017

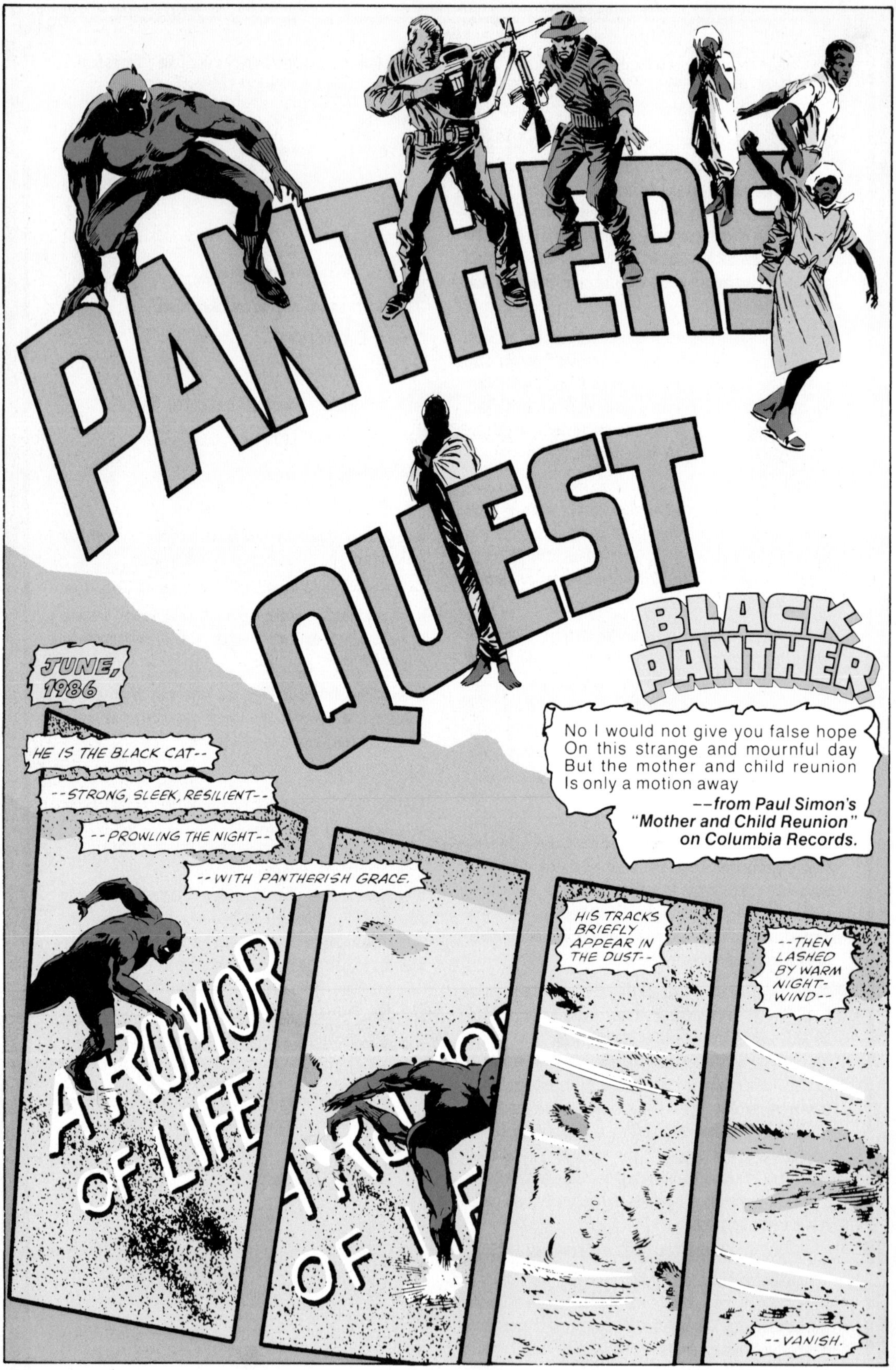
PANTHER'S QUEST
BLACK PANTHER
JUNE, 1986
No I would not give you false hope
On this strange and mournful day
But the mother and child reunion
Is only a motion away
--from Paul Simon's "Mother and Child Reunion" on Columbia Records.
HE IS THE BLACK CAT--
--STRONG, SLEEK, RESILIENT--
--PROWLING THE NIGHT--
--WITH PANTHERISH GRACE.
A RUMOR OF LIFE
HIS TRACKS BRIEFLY APPEAR IN THE DUST--
--THEN LASHED BY WARM NIGHT-WIND--
--VANISH.

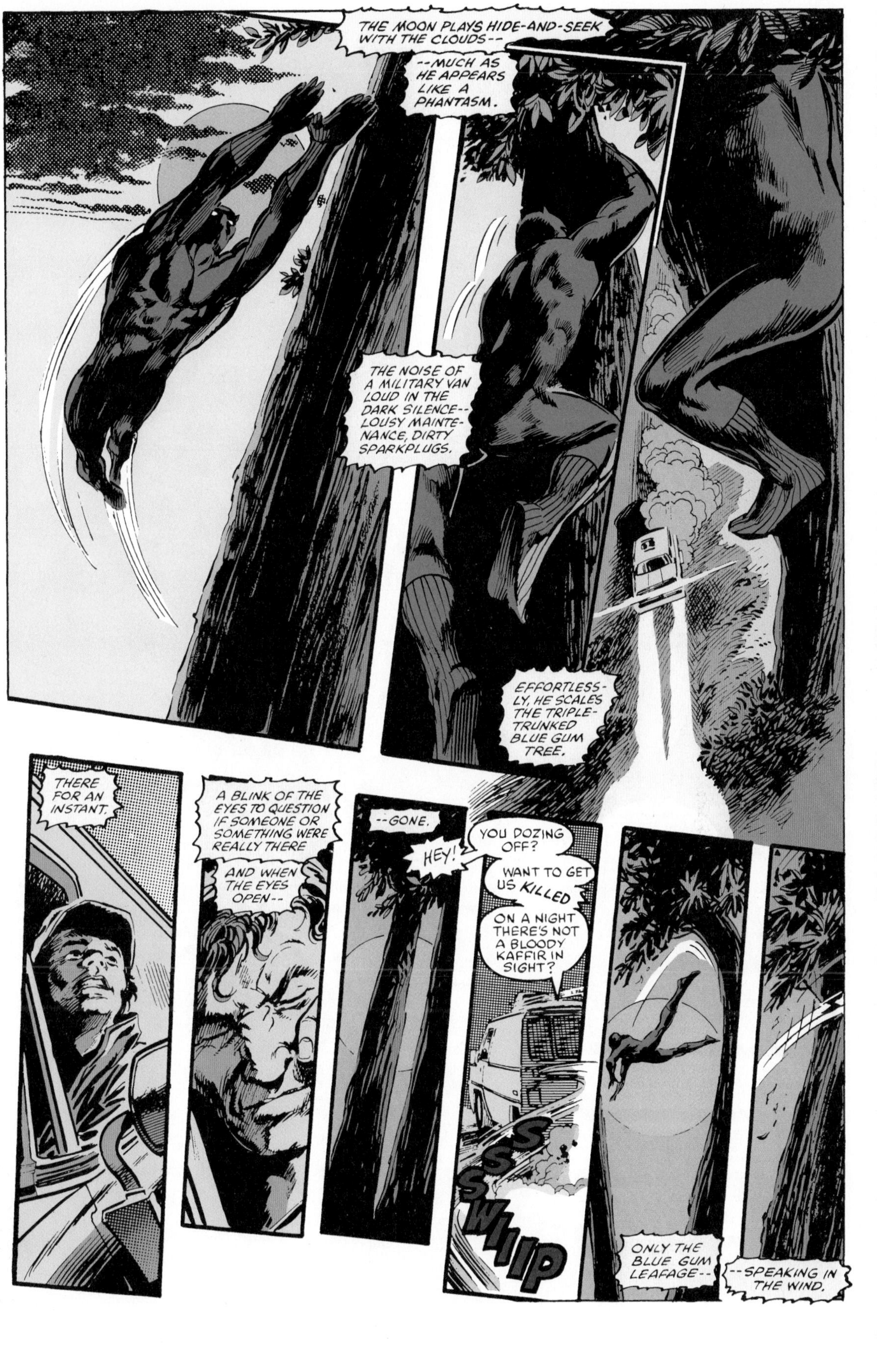
THE MOON PLAYS HIDE-AND-SEEK WITH THE CLOUDS--
--MUCH AS HE APPEARS LIKE A PHANTASM.
THE NOISE OF A MILITARY VAN LOUD IN THE DARK SILENCE--LOUSY MAINTENANCE, DIRTY SPARKPLUGS.
EFFORTLESSLY, HE SCALES THE TRIPLE-TRUNKED BLUE GUM TREE.
THERE FOR AN INSTANT.
A BLINK OF THE EYES TO QUESTION IF SOMEONE OR SOMETHING WERE REALLY THERE
AND WHEN THE EYES OPEN--
--GONE.
HEY!
YOU DOZING OFF?
WANT TO GET US KILLED
ON A NIGHT THERE'S NOT A BLOODY KAFFIR IN SIGHT?
SSSWIIIP
ONLY THE BLUE GUM LEAFAGE--
--SPEAKING IN THE WIND.

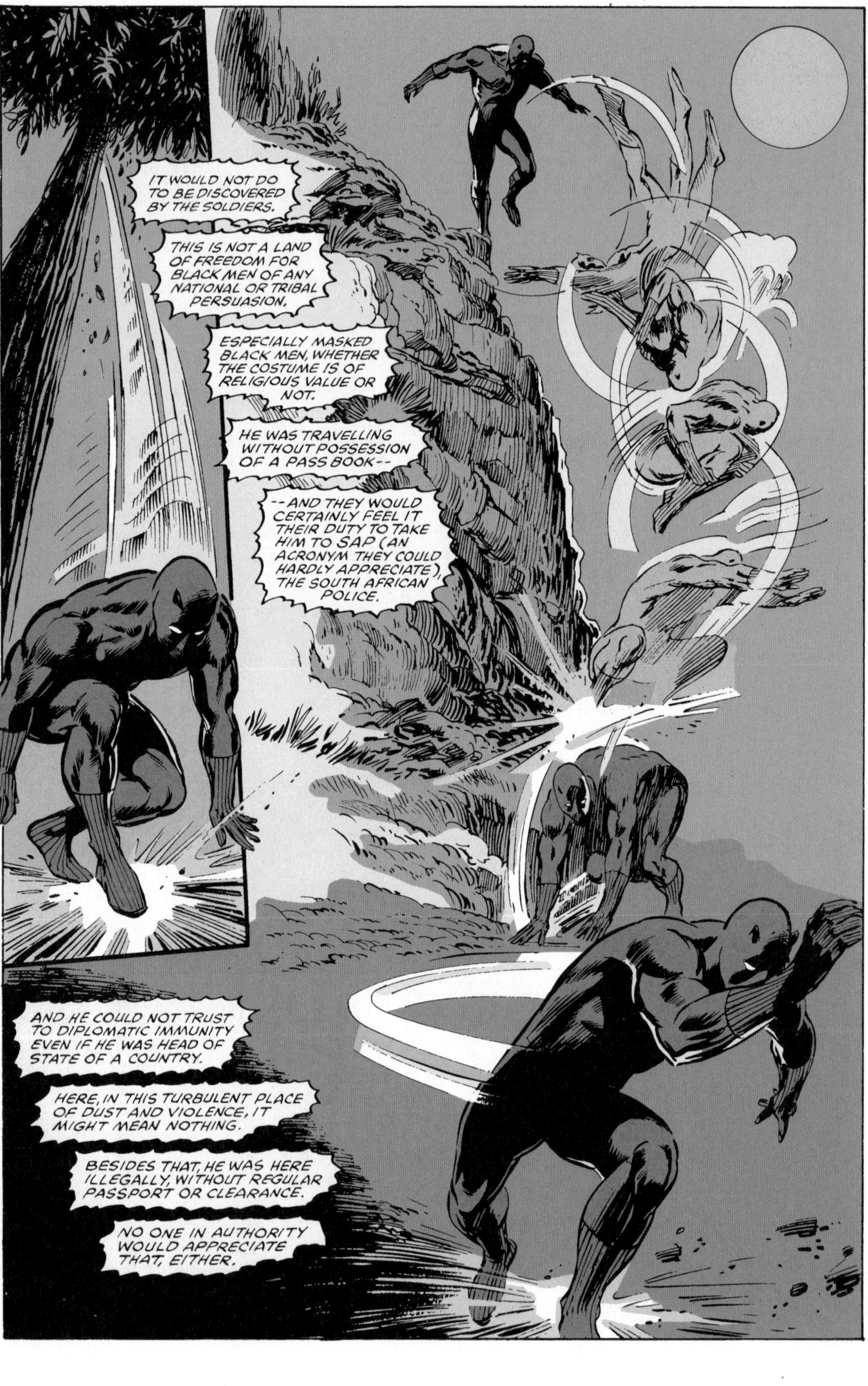
IT WOULD NOT DO TO BE DISCOVERED BY THE SOLDIERS.
THIS IS NOT A LAND OF FREEDOM FOR BLACK MEN OF ANY NATIONAL OR TRIBAL PERSUASION.
ESPECIALLY MASKED BLACK MEN, WHETHER THE COSTUME IS OF RELIGIOUS VALUE OR NOT.
HE WAS TRAVELLING WITHOUT POSSESSION OF A PASS BOOK--
--AND THEY WOULD CERTAINLY FEEL IT THEIR DUTY TO TAKE HIM TO SAP (AN ACRONYM THEY COULD HARDLY APPRECIATE), THE SOUTH AFRICAN POLICE.
AND HE COULD NOT TRUST TO DIPLOMATIC IMMUNITY EVEN IF HE WAS HEAD OF STATE OF A COUNTRY.
HERE, IN THIS TURBULENT PLACE OF DUST AND VIOLENCE, IT MIGHT MEAN NOTHING.
BESIDES THAT, HE WAS HERE ILLEGALLY, WITHOUT REGULAR PASSPORT OR CLEARANCE.
NO ONE IN AUTHORITY WOULD APPRECIATE THAT, EITHER.

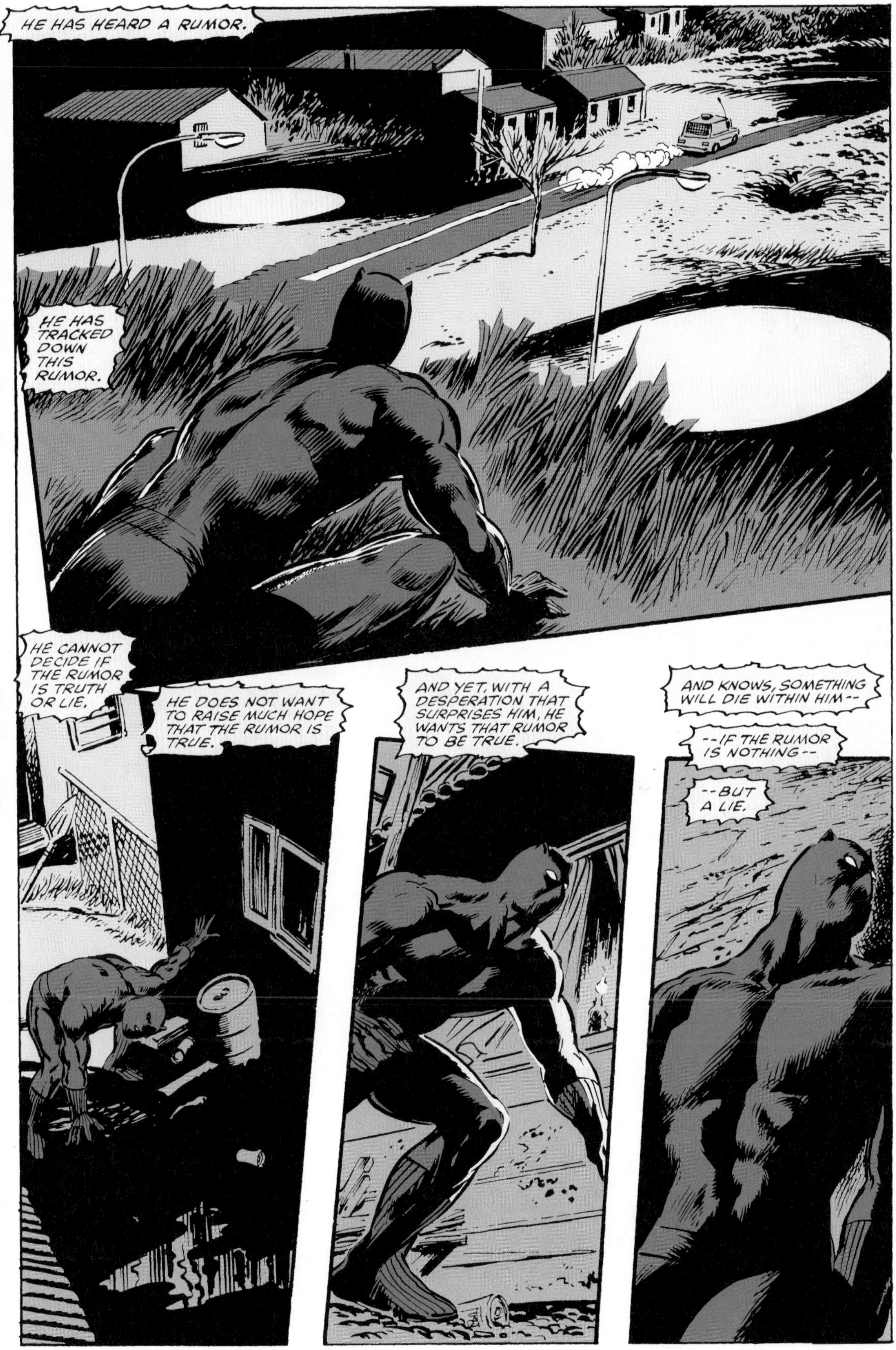
HE HAS HEARD A RUMOR.
HE HAS TRACKED DOWN THIS RUMOR.
HE CANNOT DECIDE IF THE RUMOR IS TRUTH OR LIE.
HE DOES NOT WANT TO RAISE MUCH HOPE THAT THE RUMOR IS TRUE.
AND YET, WITH A DESPERATION THAT SURPRISES HIM, HE WANTS THAT RUMOR TO BE TRUE.
AND KNOWS, SOMETHING WILL DIE WITHIN HIM--
--IF THE RUMOR IS NOTHING--
--BUT A LIE.

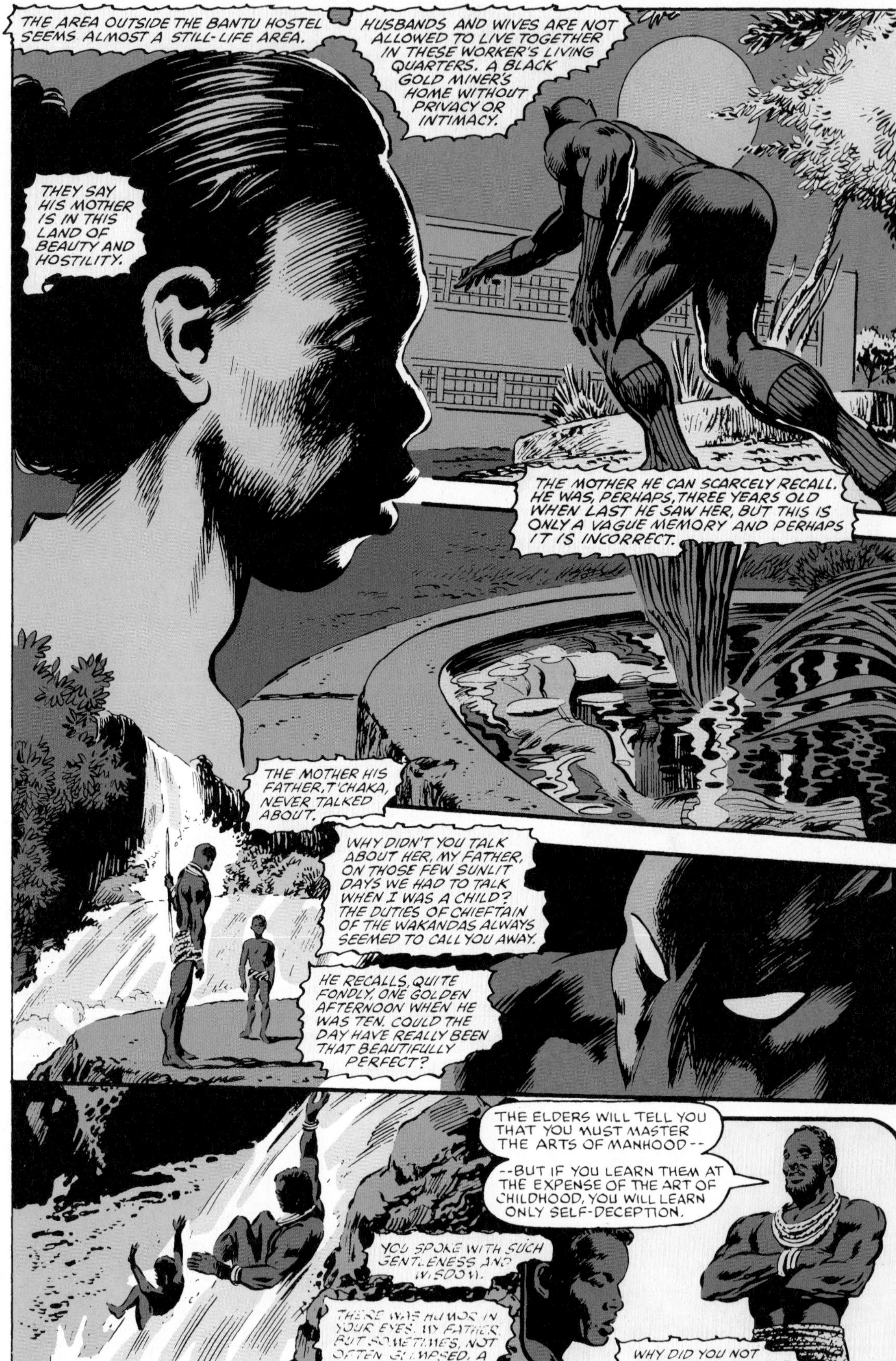
THE AREA OUTSIDE THE BANTU HOSTEL SEEMS ALMOST A STILL-LIFE AREA.
HUSBANDS AND WIVES ARE NOT ALLOWED TO LIVE TOGETHER IN THESE WORKER'S LIVING QUARTERS. A BLACK GOLD MINER'S HOME WITHOUT PRIVACY OR INTIMACY.
THEY SAY HIS MOTHER IS IN THIS LAND OF BEAUTY AND HOSTILITY.
THE MOTHER HE CAN SCARCELY RECALL. HE WAS, PERHAPS, THREE YEARS OLD WHEN LAST HE SAW HER, BUT THIS IS ONLY A VAGUE MEMORY AND PERHAPS IT IS INCORRECT.
THE MOTHER HIS FATHER, T'CHAKA, NEVER TALKED ABOUT.
WHY DIDN'T YOU TALK ABOUT HER, MY FATHER, ON THOSE FEW SUNLIT DAYS WE HAD TO TALK WHEN I WAS A CHILD? THE DUTIES OF CHIEFTAIN OF THE WAKANDAS ALWAYS SEEMED TO CALL YOU AWAY.
HE RECALLS, QUITE FONDLY, ONE GOLDEN AFTERNOON WHEN HE WAS TEN. COULD THE DAY HAVE REALLY BEEN THAT BEAUTIFULLY PERFECT?
THE ELDERS WILL TELL YOU THAT YOU MUST MASTER THE ARTS OF MANHOOD--
--BUT IF YOU LEARN THEM AT THE EXPENSE OF THE ART OF CHILDHOOD, YOU WILL LEARN ONLY SELF-DECEPTION.
YOU SPOKE WITH SUCH GENTLENESS AND WISDOM.
THERE WAS HUMOR IN YOUR EYES, MY FATHER. BUT SOMETIMES, NOT OFTEN GLIMPSED, A SECRET PAIN.
WHY DID YOU NOT SPEAK OF MY MOTHER?

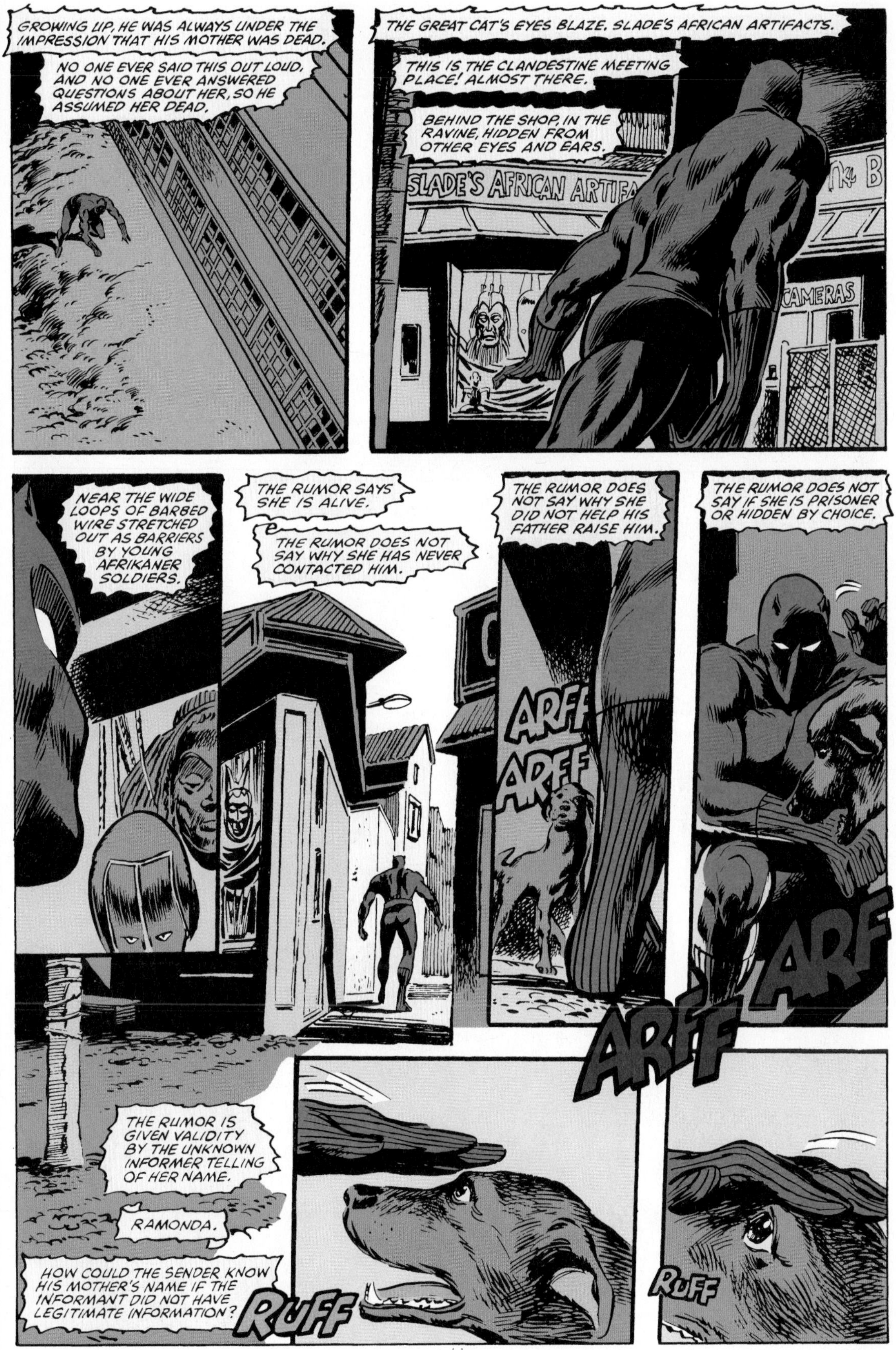
GROWING UP, HE WAS ALWAYS UNDER THE IMPRESSION THAT HIS MOTHER WAS DEAD.
NO ONE EVER SAID THIS OUT LOUD, AND NO ONE EVER ANSWERED QUESTIONS ABOUT HER, SO HE ASSUMED HER DEAD.
THE GREAT CAT'S EYES BLAZE. SLADE'S AFRICAN ARTIFACTS.
THIS IS THE CLANDESTINE MEETING PLACE! ALMOST THERE.
BEHIND THE SHOP, IN THE RAVINE, HIDDEN FROM OTHER EYES AND EARS.
SLADE'S AFRICAN ARTIFA
CAMERAS
NEAR THE WIDE LOOPS OF BARBED WIRE STRETCHED OUT AS BARRIERS BY YOUNG AFRIKANER SOLDIERS.
THE RUMOR SAYS SHE IS ALIVE.
THE RUMOR DOES NOT SAY WHY SHE HAS NEVER CONTACTED HIM.
THE RUMOR DOES NOT SAY WHY SHE DID NOT HELP HIS FATHER RAISE HIM.
ARFF
ARFF
THE RUMOR DOES NOT SAY IF SHE IS PRISONER OR HIDDEN BY CHOICE.
ARF
ARFF
THE RUMOR IS GIVEN VALIDITY BY THE UNKNOWN INFORMER TELLING OF HER NAME.
RAMONDA.
HOW COULD THE SENDER KNOW HIS MOTHER'S NAME IF THE INFORMANT DID NOT HAVE LEGITIMATE INFORMATION?
RUFF
RUFF

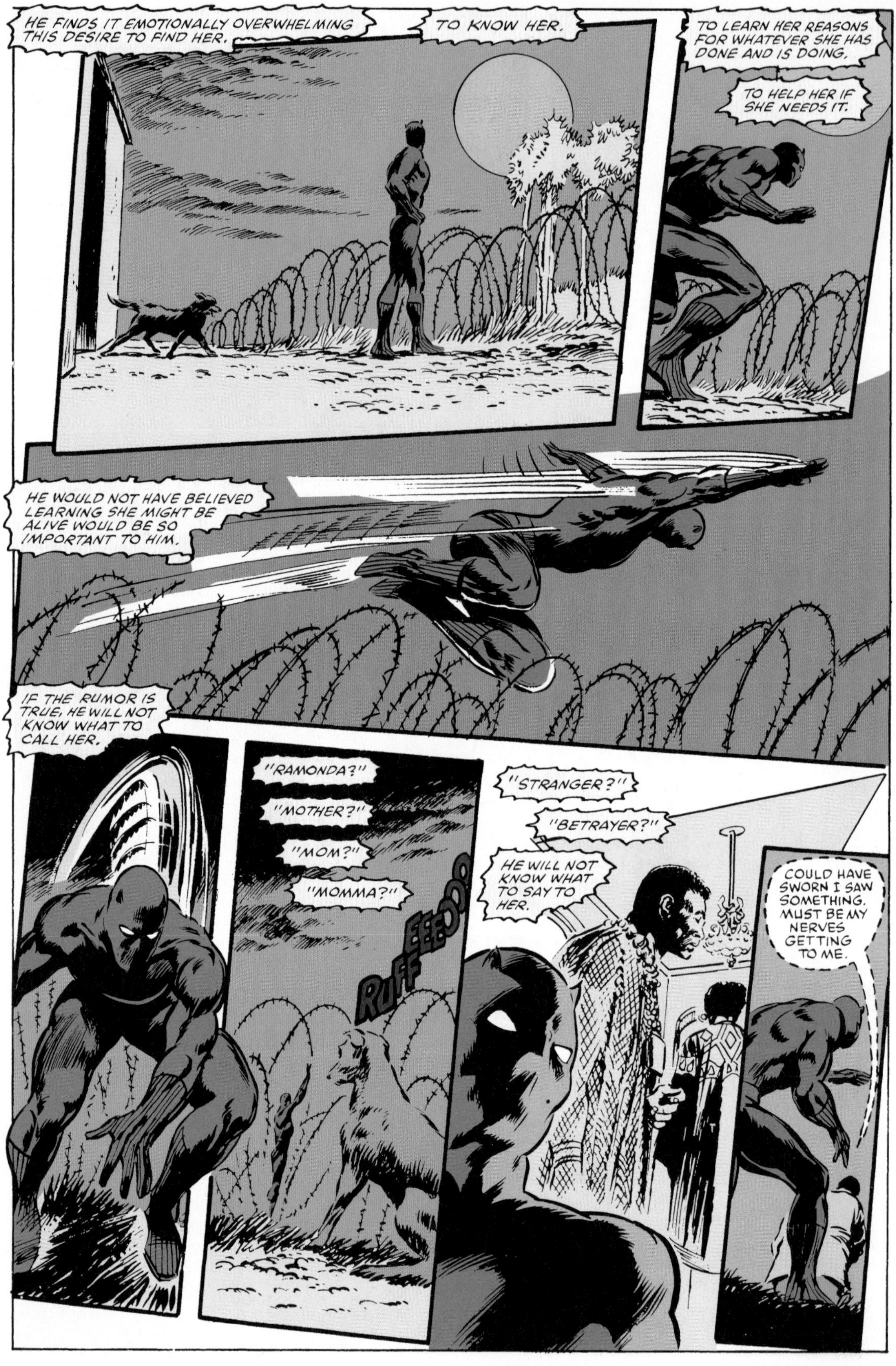

HE FINDS IT EMOTIONALLY OVERWHELMING THIS DESIRE TO FIND HER.
TO KNOW HER.
TO LEARN HER REASONS FOR WHATEVER SHE HAS DONE AND IS DOING.
TO HELP HER IF SHE NEEDS IT.
HE WOULD NOT HAVE BELIEVED LEARNING SHE MIGHT BE ALIVE WOULD BE SO IMPORTANT TO HIM.
IF THE RUMOR IS TRUE, HE WILL NOT KNOW WHAT TO CALL HER.
"RAMONDA?"
"MOTHER?"
"MOM?"
"MOMMA?"
RUFF
EEEOOO
"STRANGER?"
"BETRAYER?"
HE WILL NOT KNOW WHAT TO SAY TO HER.
COULD HAVE SWORN I SAW SOMETHING. MUST BE MY NERVES GETTING TO ME.

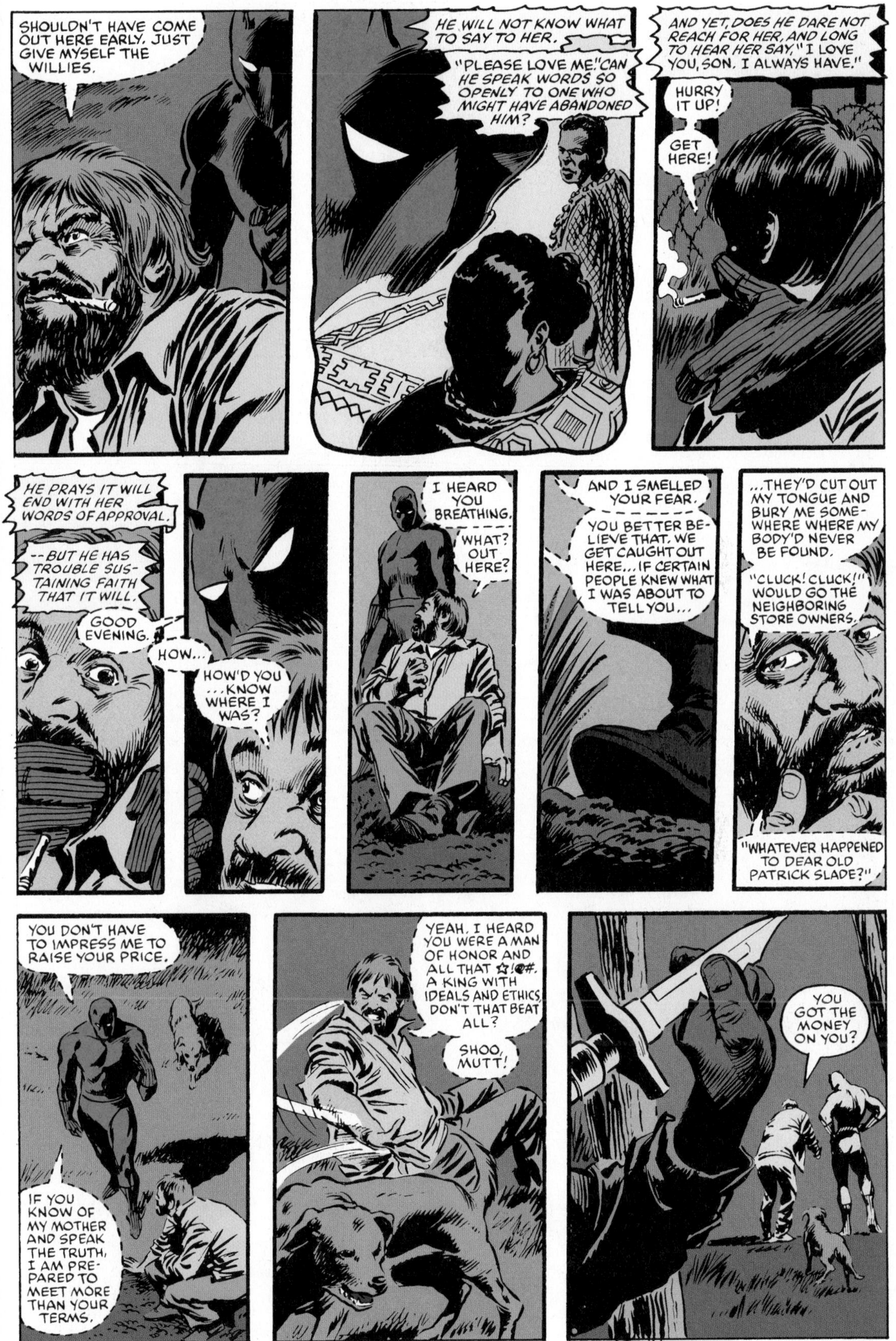
SHOULDN'T HAVE COME OUT HERE EARLY. JUST GIVE MYSELF THE WILLIES.
HE WILL NOT KNOW WHAT TO SAY TO HER.
"PLEASE LOVE ME." CAN HE SPEAK WORDS SO OPENLY TO ONE WHO MIGHT HAVE ABANDONED HIM?
AND YET, DOES HE DARE NOT REACH FOR HER, AND LONG TO HEAR HER SAY, "I LOVE YOU, SON. I ALWAYS HAVE."
HURRY IT UP!
GET HERE!
HE PRAYS IT WILL END WITH HER WORDS OF APPROVAL.
--BUT HE HAS TROUBLE SUSTAINING FAITH THAT IT WILL.
GOOD EVENING.
HOW...
HOW'D YOU ...KNOW WHERE I WAS?
I HEARD YOU BREATHING.
WHAT? OUT HERE?
AND I SMELLED YOUR FEAR.
YOU BETTER BELIEVE THAT. WE GET CAUGHT OUT HERE... IF CERTAIN PEOPLE KNEW WHAT I WAS ABOUT TO TELL YOU...
...THEY'D CUT OUT MY TONGUE AND BURY ME SOMEWHERE WHERE MY BODY'D NEVER BE FOUND.
"CLUCK! CLUCK!" WOULD GO THE NEIGHBORING STORE OWNERS.
"WHATEVER HAPPENED TO DEAR OLD PATRICK SLADE?"
YOU DON'T HAVE TO IMPRESS ME TO RAISE YOUR PRICE.
IF YOU KNOW OF MY MOTHER AND SPEAK THE TRUTH, I AM PREPARED TO MEET MORE THAN YOUR TERMS.
YEAH. I HEARD YOU WERE A MAN OF HONOR AND ALL THAT ☆!@#. A KING WITH IDEALS AND ETHICS. DON'T THAT BEAT ALL?
SHOO, MUTT!
YOU GOT THE MONEY ON YOU?
TO BE CONTINUED NEXT ISSUE...

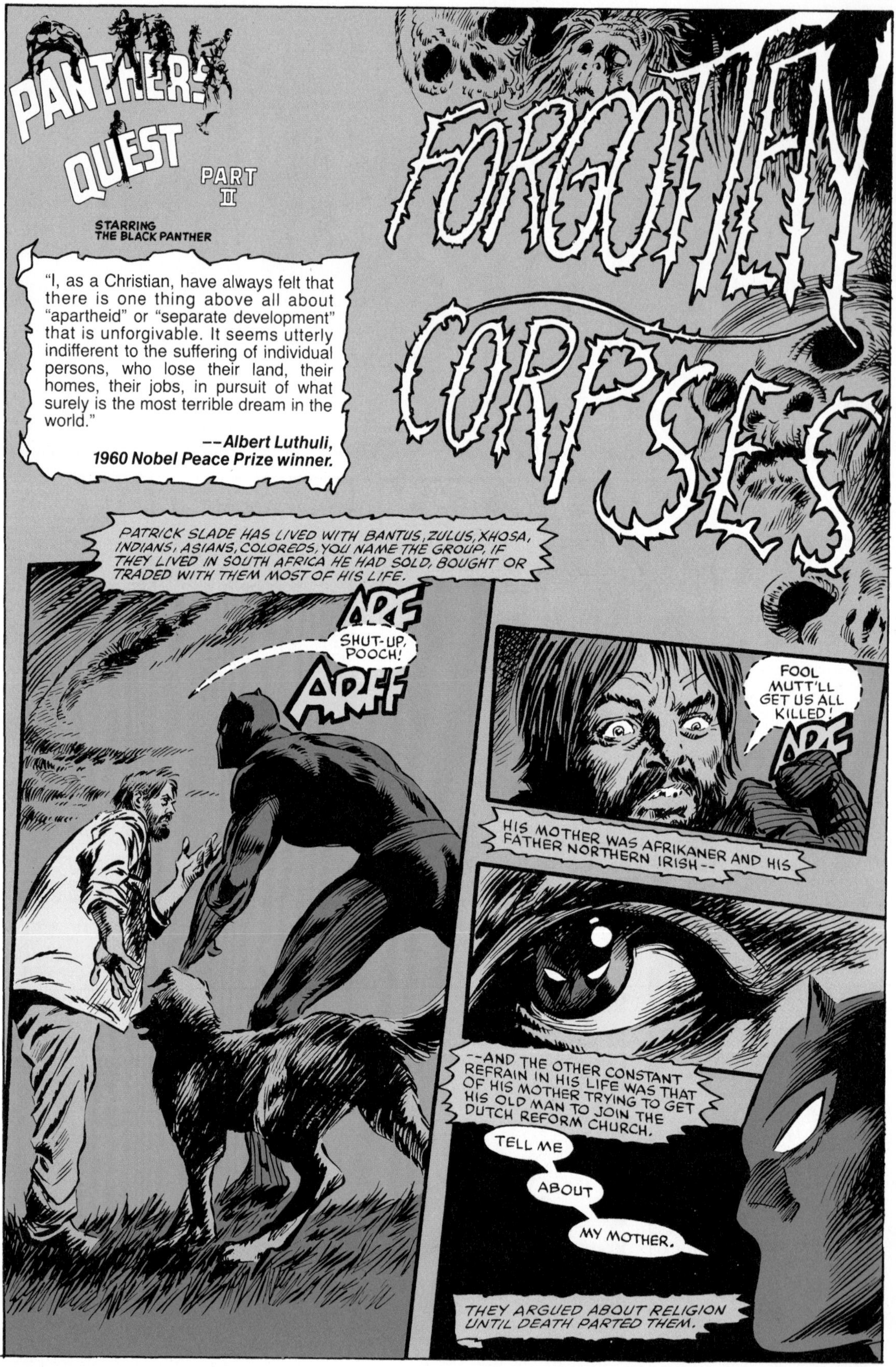
PANTHER'S QUEST
PART II
STARRING THE BLACK PANTHER
"I, as a Christian, have always felt that there is one thing above all about "apartheid" or "separate development" that is unforgivable. It seems utterly indifferent to the suffering of individual persons, who lose their land, their homes, their jobs, in pursuit of what surely is the most terrible dream in the world."
--Albert Luthuli, 1960 Nobel Peace Prize winner.
FORGOTTEN CORPSES
PATRICK SLADE HAS LIVED WITH BANTUS, ZULUS, XHOSA, INDIANS, ASIANS, COLOREDS, YOU NAME THE GROUP. IF THEY LIVED IN SOUTH AFRICA HE HAD SOLD, BOUGHT OR TRADED WITH THEM MOST OF HIS LIFE.
ARF
SHUT-UP, POOCH!
ARFF
FOOL MUTT'LL GET US ALL KILLED!
ARF
HIS MOTHER WAS AFRIKANER AND HIS FATHER NORTHERN IRISH--
--AND THE OTHER CONSTANT REFRAIN IN HIS LIFE WAS THAT OF HIS MOTHER TRYING TO GET HIS OLD MAN TO JOIN THE DUTCH REFORM CHURCH.
TELL ME
ABOUT
MY MOTHER.
THEY ARGUED ABOUT RELIGION UNTIL DEATH PARTED THEM.

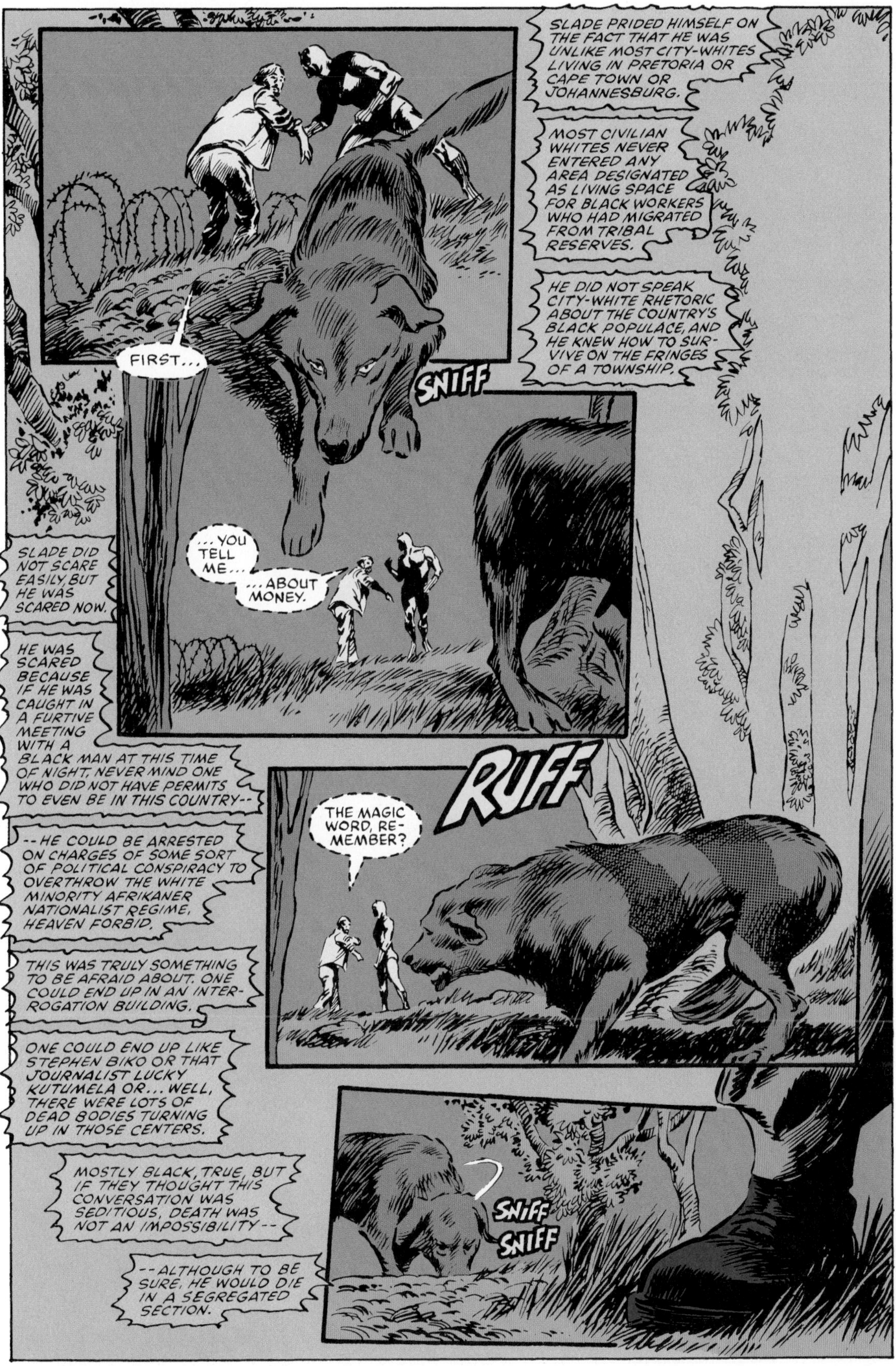
SLADE PRIDED HIMSELF ON THE FACT THAT HE WAS UNLIKE MOST CITY-WHITES LIVING IN PRETORIA OR CAPE TOWN OR JOHANNESBURG.
MOST CIVILIAN WHITES NEVER ENTERED ANY AREA DESIGNATED AS LIVING SPACE FOR BLACK WORKERS WHO HAD MIGRATED FROM TRIBAL RESERVES.
HE DID NOT SPEAK CITY-WHITE RHETORIC ABOUT THE COUNTRY'S BLACK POPULACE, AND HE KNEW HOW TO SURVIVE ON THE FRINGES OF A TOWNSHIP.
FIRST...
SNIFF
...YOU TELL ME...
...ABOUT MONEY.
SLADE DID NOT SCARE EASILY, BUT HE WAS SCARED NOW.
HE WAS SCARED BECAUSE IF HE WAS CAUGHT IN A FURTIVE MEETING WITH A BLACK MAN AT THIS TIME OF NIGHT, NEVER MIND ONE WHO DID NOT HAVE PERMITS TO EVEN BE IN THIS COUNTRY--
RUFF
THE MAGIC WORD, REMEMBER?
--HE COULD BE ARRESTED ON CHARGES OF SOME SORT OF POLITICAL CONSPIRACY TO OVERTHROW THE WHITE MINORITY AFRIKANER NATIONALIST REGIME, HEAVEN FORBID.
THIS WAS TRULY SOMETHING TO BE AFRAID ABOUT. ONE COULD END UP IN AN INTERROGATION BUILDING.
ONE COULD END UP LIKE STEPHEN BIKO OR THAT JOURNALIST LUCKY KUTUMELA OR... WELL, THERE WERE LOTS OF DEAD BODIES TURNING UP IN THOSE CENTERS.
MOSTLY BLACK, TRUE, BUT IF THEY THOUGHT THIS CONVERSATION WAS SEDITIOUS, DEATH WAS NOT AN IMPOSSIBILITY--
SNIFF SNIFF
--ALTHOUGH TO BE SURE, HE WOULD DIE IN A SEGREGATED SECTION.

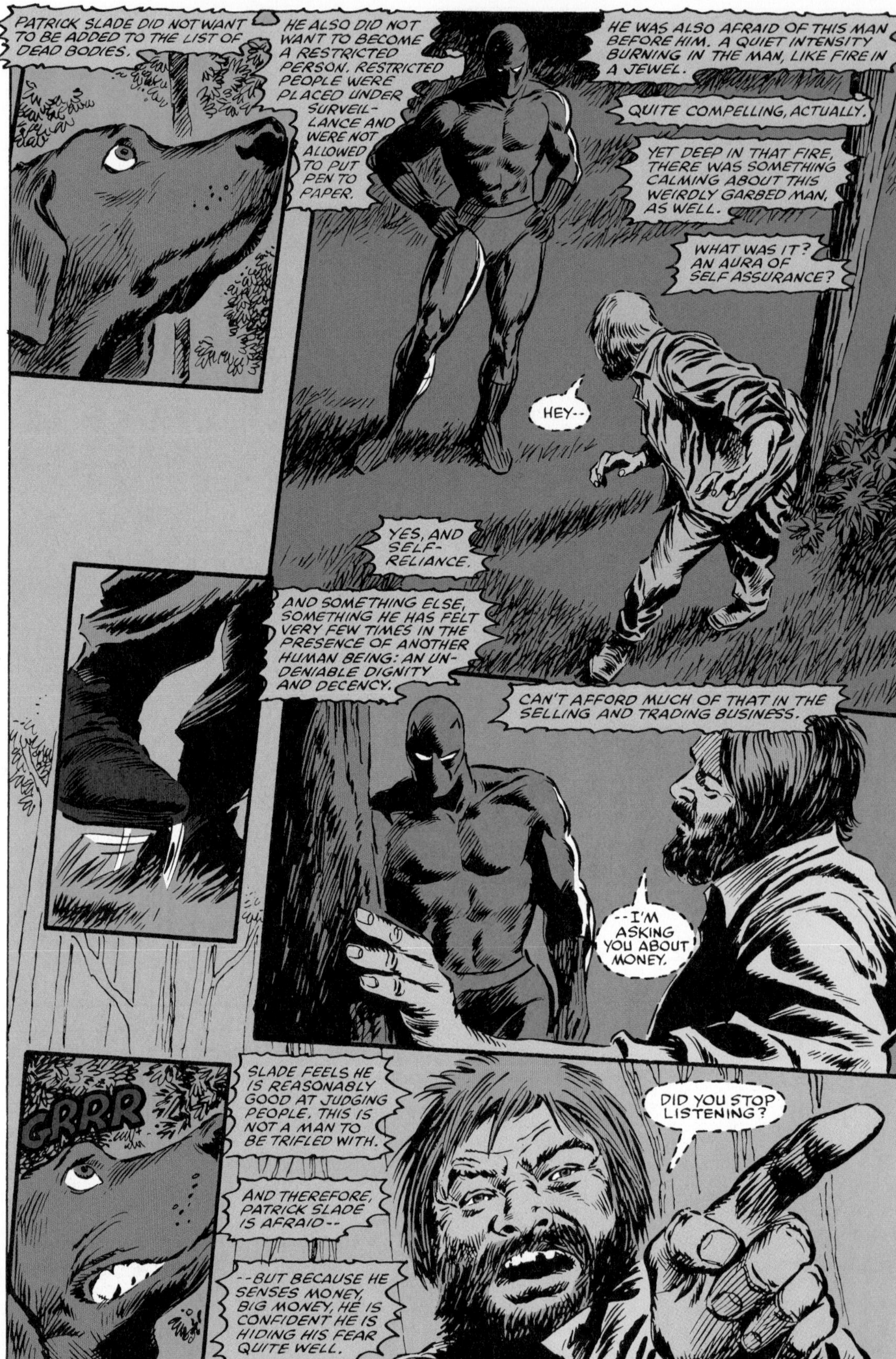
PATRICK SLADE DID NOT WANT TO BE ADDED TO THE LIST OF DEAD BODIES.
HE ALSO DID NOT WANT TO BECOME A RESTRICTED PERSON. RESTRICTED PEOPLE WERE PLACED UNDER SURVEIL-LANCE AND WERE NOT ALLOWED TO PUT PEN TO PAPER.
HE WAS ALSO AFRAID OF THIS MAN BEFORE HIM. A QUIET INTENSITY BURNING IN THE MAN, LIKE FIRE IN A JEWEL.
QUITE COMPELLING, ACTUALLY.
YET DEEP IN THAT FIRE, THERE WAS SOMETHING CALMING ABOUT THIS WEIRDLY GARBED MAN, AS WELL.
WHAT WAS IT? AN AURA OF SELF ASSURANCE?
HEY--
YES, AND SELF-RELIANCE.
AND SOMETHING ELSE, SOMETHING HE HAS FELT VERY FEW TIMES IN THE PRESENCE OF ANOTHER HUMAN BEING: AN UN-DENIABLE DIGNITY AND DECENCY.
CAN'T AFFORD MUCH OF THAT IN THE SELLING AND TRADING BUSINESS.
--I'M ASKING YOU ABOUT MONEY.
GRRR
SLADE FEELS HE IS REASONABLY GOOD AT JUDGING PEOPLE. THIS IS NOT A MAN TO BE TRIFLED WITH.
AND THEREFORE, PATRICK SLADE IS AFRAID--
--BUT BECAUSE HE SENSES MONEY, BIG MONEY, HE IS CONFIDENT HE IS HIDING HIS FEAR QUITE WELL.
DID YOU STOP LISTENING?

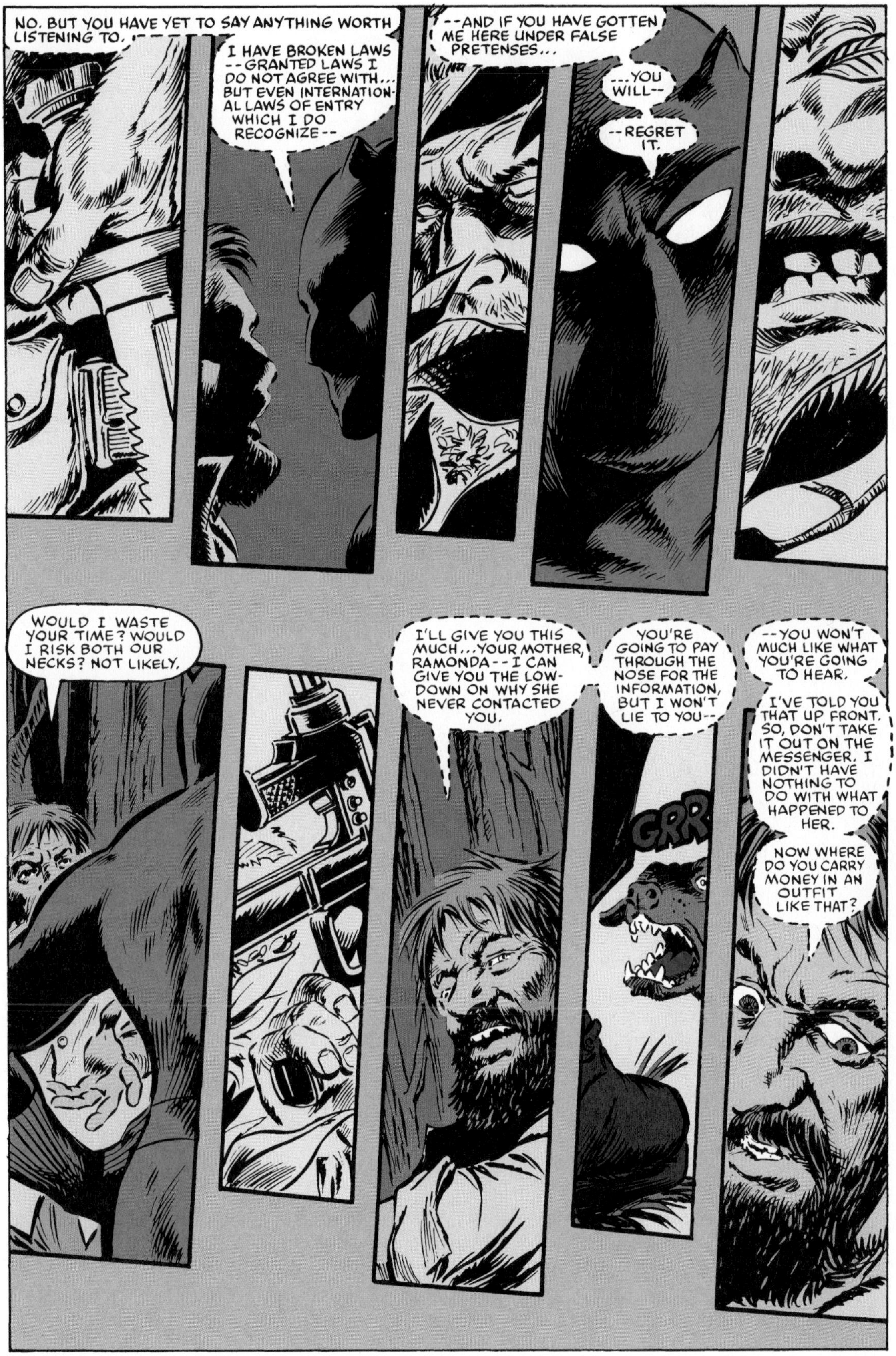
NO. BUT YOU HAVE YET TO SAY ANYTHING WORTH LISTENING TO.
I HAVE BROKEN LAWS --GRANTED LAWS I DO NOT AGREE WITH... BUT EVEN INTERNATIONAL LAWS OF ENTRY WHICH I DO RECOGNIZE--
--AND IF YOU HAVE GOTTEN ME HERE UNDER FALSE PRETENSES...
...YOU WILL--
--REGRET IT.
WOULD I WASTE YOUR TIME? WOULD I RISK BOTH OUR NECKS? NOT LIKELY.
I'LL GIVE YOU THIS MUCH...YOUR MOTHER, RAMONDA--I CAN GIVE YOU THE LOW-DOWN ON WHY SHE NEVER CONTACTED YOU.
YOU'RE GOING TO PAY THROUGH THE NOSE FOR THE INFORMATION, BUT I WON'T LIE TO YOU--
GRR
--YOU WON'T MUCH LIKE WHAT YOU'RE GOING TO HEAR.
I'VE TOLD YOU THAT UP FRONT. SO, DON'T TAKE IT OUT ON THE MESSENGER. I DIDN'T HAVE NOTHING TO DO WITH WHAT HAPPENED TO HER.
NOW WHERE DO YOU CARRY MONEY IN AN OUTFIT LIKE THAT?

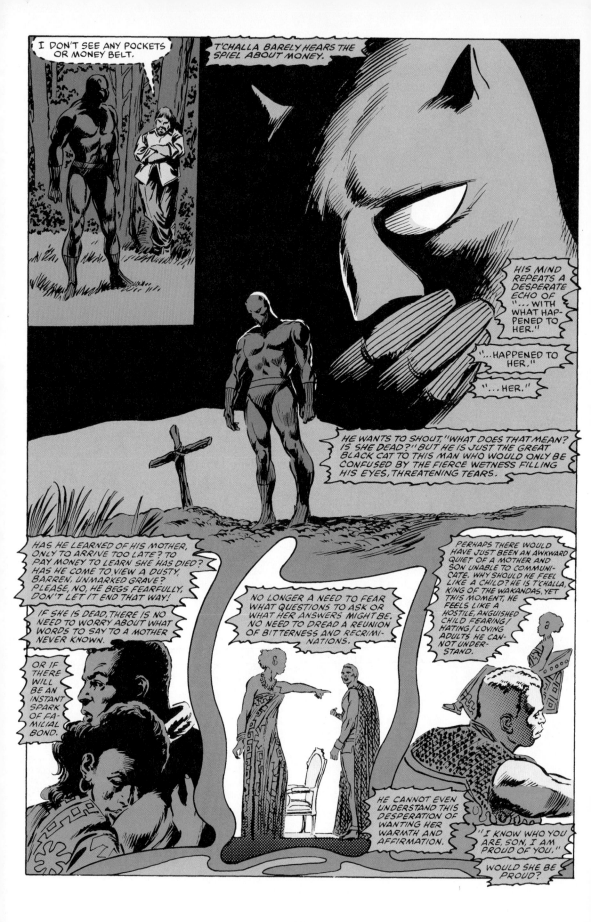

I DON'T SEE ANY POCKETS OR MONEY BELT.

T'CHALLA BARELY HEARS THE SPIEL ABOUT MONEY.

HIS MIND REPEATS A DESPERATE ECHO OF "...WITH WHAT HAPPENED TO HER."

"...HAPPENED TO HER."

"...HER."

HE WANTS TO SHOUT, "WHAT DOES THAT MEAN? IS SHE DEAD?" BUT HE IS JUST THE GREAT BLACK CAT TO THIS MAN WHO WOULD ONLY BE CONFUSED BY THE FIERCE WETNESS FILLING HIS EYES, THREATENING TEARS.

HAS HE LEARNED OF HIS MOTHER, ONLY TO ARRIVE TOO LATE? TO PAY MONEY TO LEARN SHE HAS DIED? HAS HE COME TO VIEW A DUSTY, BARREN, UNMARKED GRAVE? PLEASE, NO, HE BEGS FEARFULLY, DON'T LET IT END THAT WAY!

IF SHE IS DEAD, THERE IS NO NEED TO WORRY ABOUT WHAT WORDS TO SAY TO A MOTHER NEVER KNOWN.

OR IF THERE WILL BE AN INSTANT SPARK OF FA- MILIAL BOND.

NO LONGER A NEED TO FEAR WHAT QUESTIONS TO ASK OR WHAT HER ANSWERS MIGHT BE. NO NEED TO DREAD A REUNION OF BITTERNESS AND RECRIMI- NATIONS.

PERHAPS THERE WOULD HAVE JUST BEEN AN AWKWARD QUIET OF A MOTHER AND SON UNABLE TO COMMUNI- CATE. WHY SHOULD HE FEEL LIKE A CHILD? HE IS T'CHALLA, KING OF THE WAKANDAS, YET THIS MOMENT, HE FEELS LIKE A HOSTILE, ANGUISHED CHILD FEARING / HATING / LOVING ADULTS HE CAN- NOT UNDER- STAND.

HE CANNOT EVEN UNDERSTAND THIS DESPERATION OF WANTING HER WARMTH AND AFFIRMATION.

"I KNOW WHO YOU ARE, SON, I AM PROUD OF YOU."

WOULD SHE BE PROUD?

20

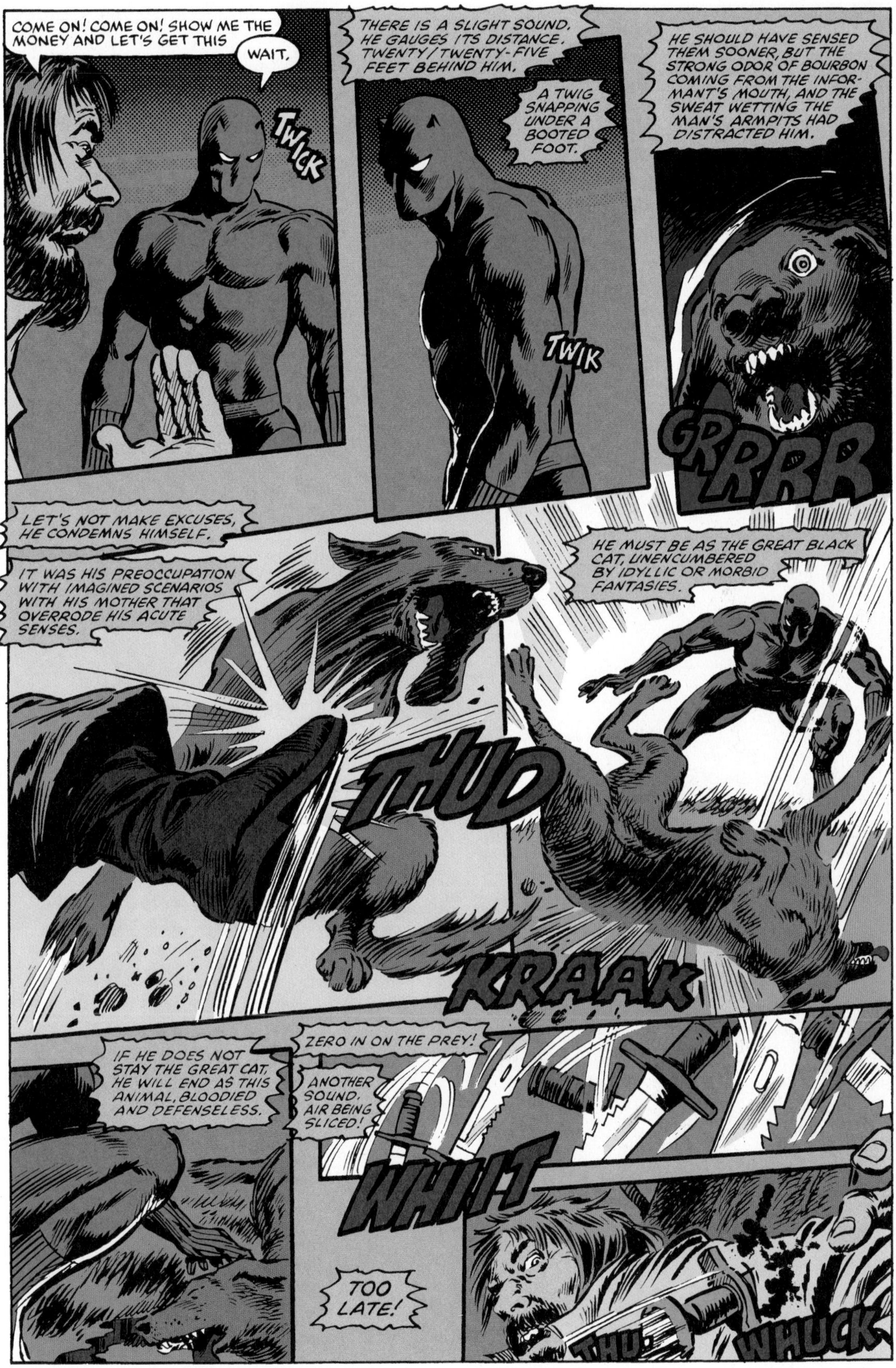
COME ON! COME ON! SHOW ME THE MONEY AND LET'S GET THIS
WAIT.
TWICK
THERE IS A SLIGHT SOUND. HE GAUGES ITS DISTANCE. TWENTY/TWENTY-FIVE FEET BEHIND HIM.
A TWIG SNAPPING UNDER A BOOTED FOOT.
TWIK
HE SHOULD HAVE SENSED THEM SOONER, BUT THE STRONG ODOR OF BOURBON COMING FROM THE INFORMANT'S MOUTH, AND THE SWEAT WETTING THE MAN'S ARMPITS HAD DISTRACTED HIM.
GRRRRR
LET'S NOT MAKE EXCUSES, HE CONDEMNS HIMSELF.
IT WAS HIS PREOCCUPATION WITH IMAGINED SCENARIOS WITH HIS MOTHER THAT OVERRODE HIS ACUTE SENSES.
THUD
HE MUST BE AS THE GREAT BLACK CAT, UNENCUMBERED BY IDYLLIC OR MORBID FANTASIES.
KRAAK
IF HE DOES NOT STAY THE GREAT CAT, HE WILL END AS THIS ANIMAL, BLOODIED AND DEFENSELESS.
ZERO IN ON THE PREY!
ANOTHER SOUND. AIR BEING SLICED!
WHIIT
TOO LATE!
THU
WHUCK

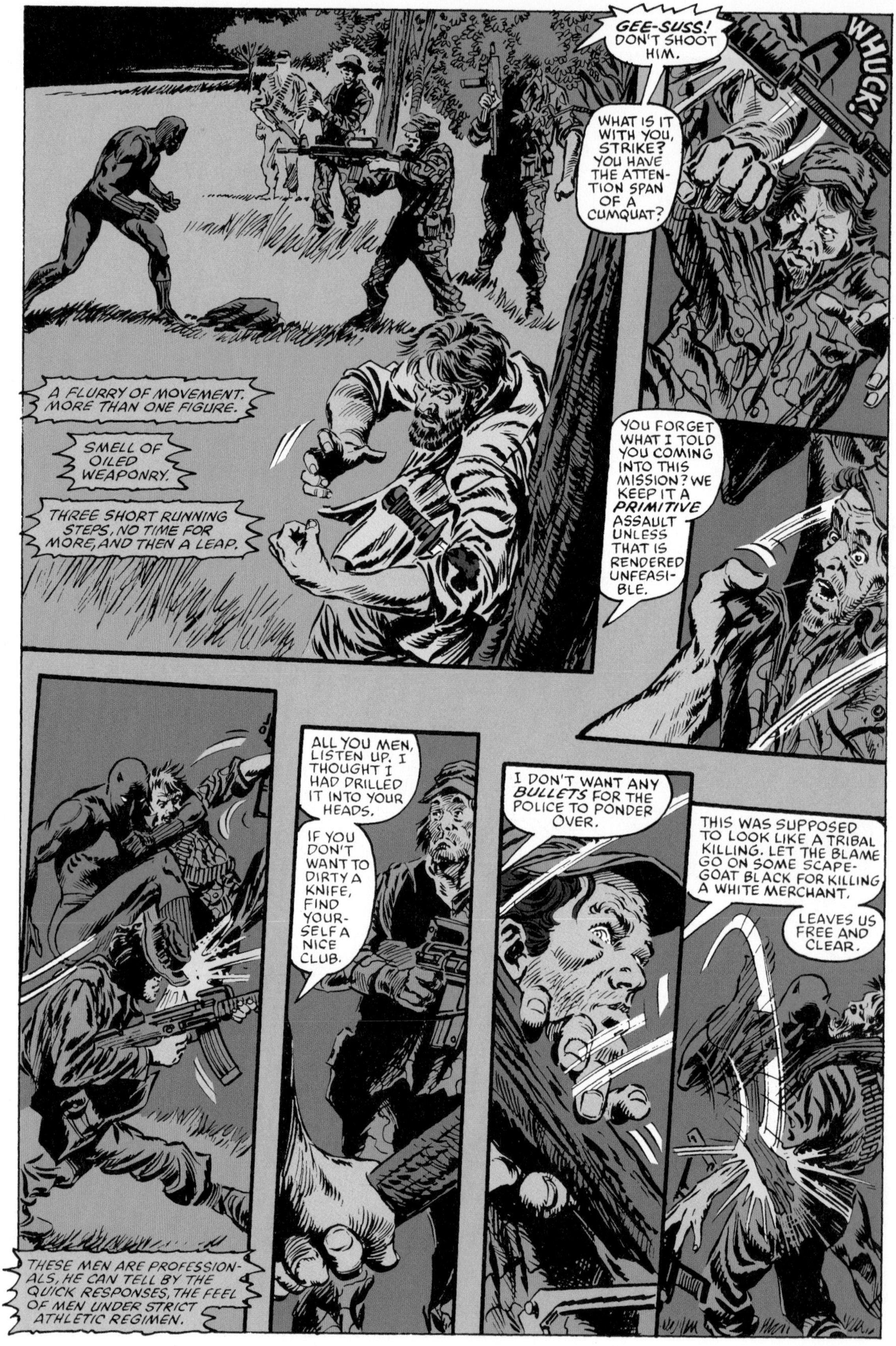
GEE-SUSS! DON'T SHOOT HIM.
WHUCK!
WHAT IS IT WITH YOU, STRIKE? YOU HAVE THE ATTENTION SPAN OF A CUMQUAT?
A FLURRY OF MOVEMENT. MORE THAN ONE FIGURE.
SMELL OF OILED WEAPONRY.
THREE SHORT RUNNING STEPS, NO TIME FOR MORE, AND THEN A LEAP.
YOU FORGET WHAT I TOLD YOU COMING INTO THIS MISSION? WE KEEP IT A PRIMITIVE ASSAULT UNLESS THAT IS RENDERED UNFEASIBLE.
THESE MEN ARE PROFESSIONALS, HE CAN TELL BY THE QUICK RESPONSES, THE FEEL OF MEN UNDER STRICT ATHLETIC REGIMEN.
ALL YOU MEN, LISTEN UP. I THOUGHT I HAD DRILLED IT INTO YOUR HEADS.
IF YOU DON'T WANT TO DIRTY A KNIFE, FIND YOURSELF A NICE CLUB.
I DON'T WANT ANY BULLETS FOR THE POLICE TO PONDER OVER.
THIS WAS SUPPOSED TO LOOK LIKE A TRIBAL KILLING. LET THE BLAME GO ON SOME SCAPEGOAT BLACK FOR KILLING A WHITE MERCHANT.
LEAVES US FREE AND CLEAR.

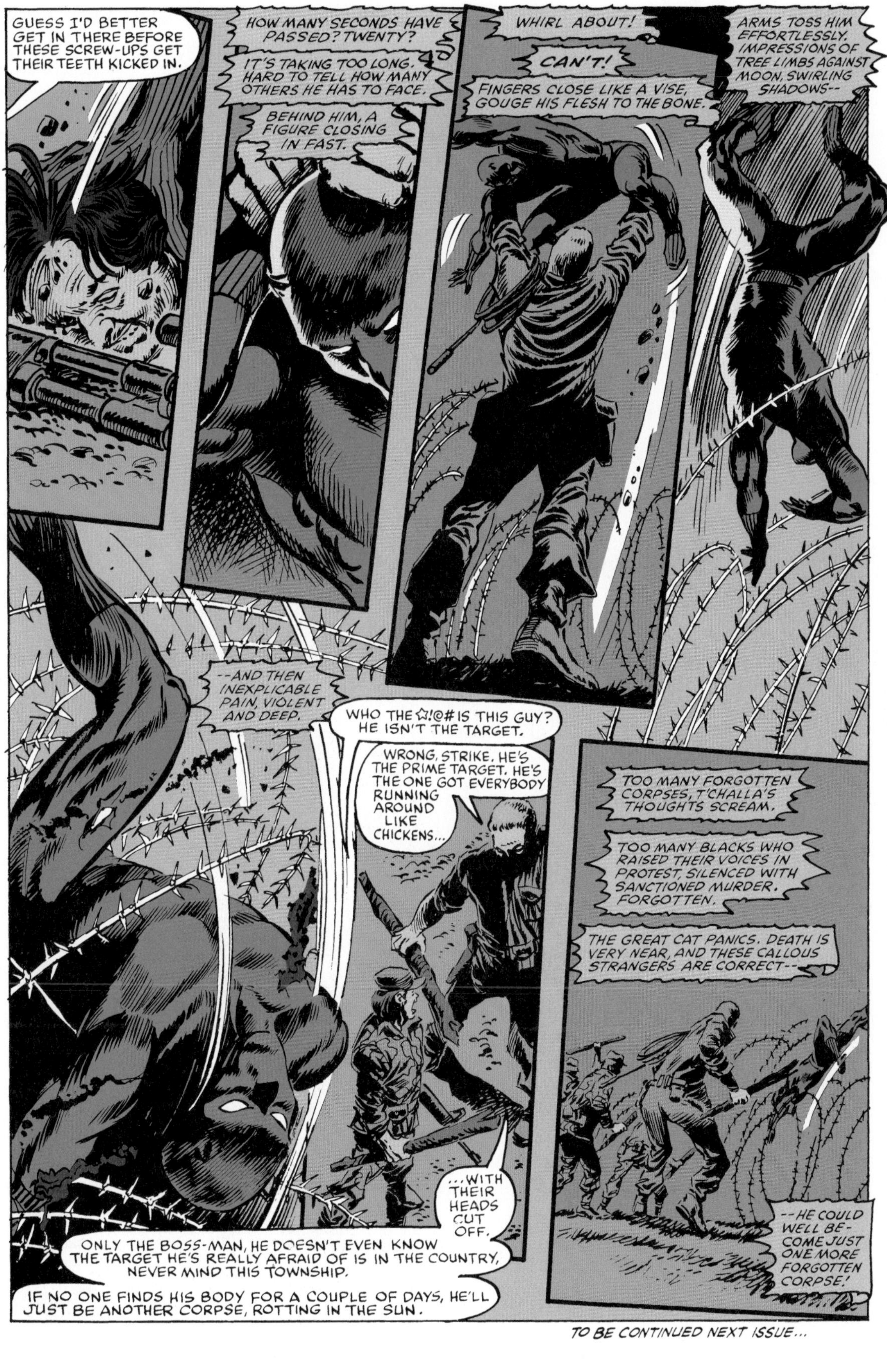
GUESS I'D BETTER GET IN THERE BEFORE THESE SCREW-UPS GET THEIR TEETH KICKED IN.
HOW MANY SECONDS HAVE PASSED? TWENTY?
IT'S TAKING TOO LONG. HARD TO TELL HOW MANY OTHERS HE HAS TO FACE.
BEHIND HIM, A FIGURE CLOSING IN FAST.
WHIRL ABOUT!
CAN'T!
FINGERS CLOSE LIKE A VISE, GOUGE HIS FLESH TO THE BONE.
ARMS TOSS HIM EFFORTLESSLY. IMPRESSIONS OF TREE LIMBS AGAINST MOON, SWIRLING SHADOWS--
--AND THEN INEXPLICABLE PAIN, VIOLENT AND DEEP.
WHO THE ☆!@# IS THIS GUY? HE ISN'T THE TARGET.
WRONG, STRIKE. HE'S THE PRIME TARGET. HE'S THE ONE GOT EVERYBODY RUNNING AROUND LIKE CHICKENS...
...WITH THEIR HEADS CUT OFF.
ONLY THE BOSS-MAN, HE DOESN'T EVEN KNOW THE TARGET HE'S REALLY AFRAID OF IS IN THE COUNTRY, NEVER MIND THIS TOWNSHIP.
IF NO ONE FINDS HIS BODY FOR A COUPLE OF DAYS, HE'LL JUST BE ANOTHER CORPSE, ROTTING IN THE SUN.
TOO MANY FORGOTTEN CORPSES, T'CHALLA'S THOUGHTS SCREAM.
TOO MANY BLACKS WHO RAISED THEIR VOICES IN PROTEST, SILENCED WITH SANCTIONED MURDER. FORGOTTEN.
THE GREAT CAT PANICS. DEATH IS VERY NEAR, AND THESE CALLOUS STRANGERS ARE CORRECT--
--HE COULD WELL BECOME JUST ONE MORE FORGOTTEN CORPSE!

TO BE CONTINUED NEXT ISSUE...

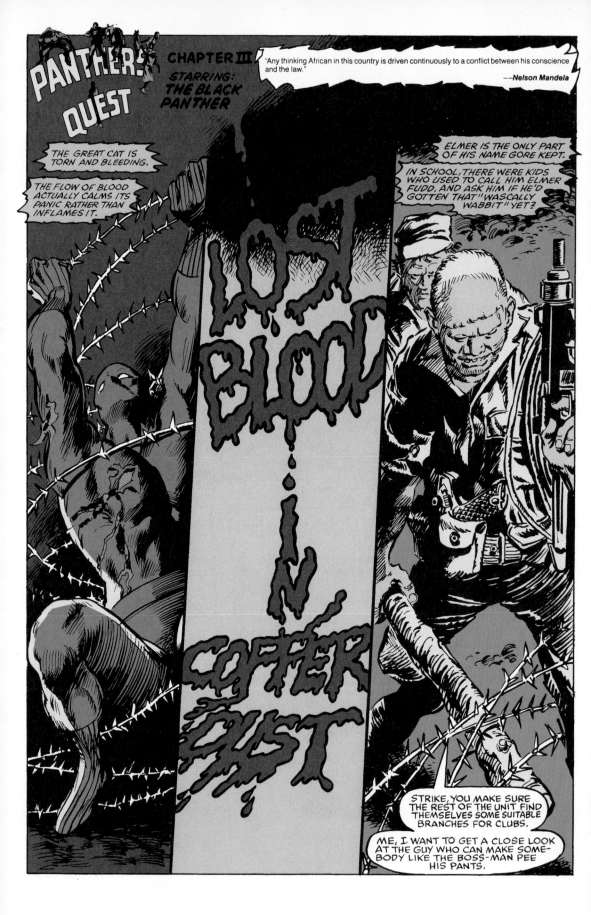

PANTHER'S QUEST

CHAPTER III

STARRING: THE BLACK PANTHER

"Any thinking African in this country is driven continuously to a conflict between his conscience and the law."

—Nelson Mandela

THE GREAT CAT IS TORN AND BLEEDING.

THE FLOW OF BLOOD ACTUALLY CALMS ITS PANIC RATHER THAN INFLAMES IT.

LOST BLOOD IN COPPER DUST

ELMER IS THE ONLY PART OF HIS NAME GORE KEPT.

IN SCHOOL, THERE WERE KIDS WHO USED TO CALL HIM ELMER FUDD, AND ASK HIM IF HE'D GOTTEN THAT "WASCALLY WABBIT" YET?

STRIKE, YOU MAKE SURE THE REST OF THE UNIT FIND THEMSELVES SOME SUITABLE BRANCHES FOR CLUBS.

ME, I WANT TO GET A CLOSE LOOK AT THE GUY WHO CAN MAKE SOME-BODY LIKE THE BOSS-MAN PEE HIS PANTS.

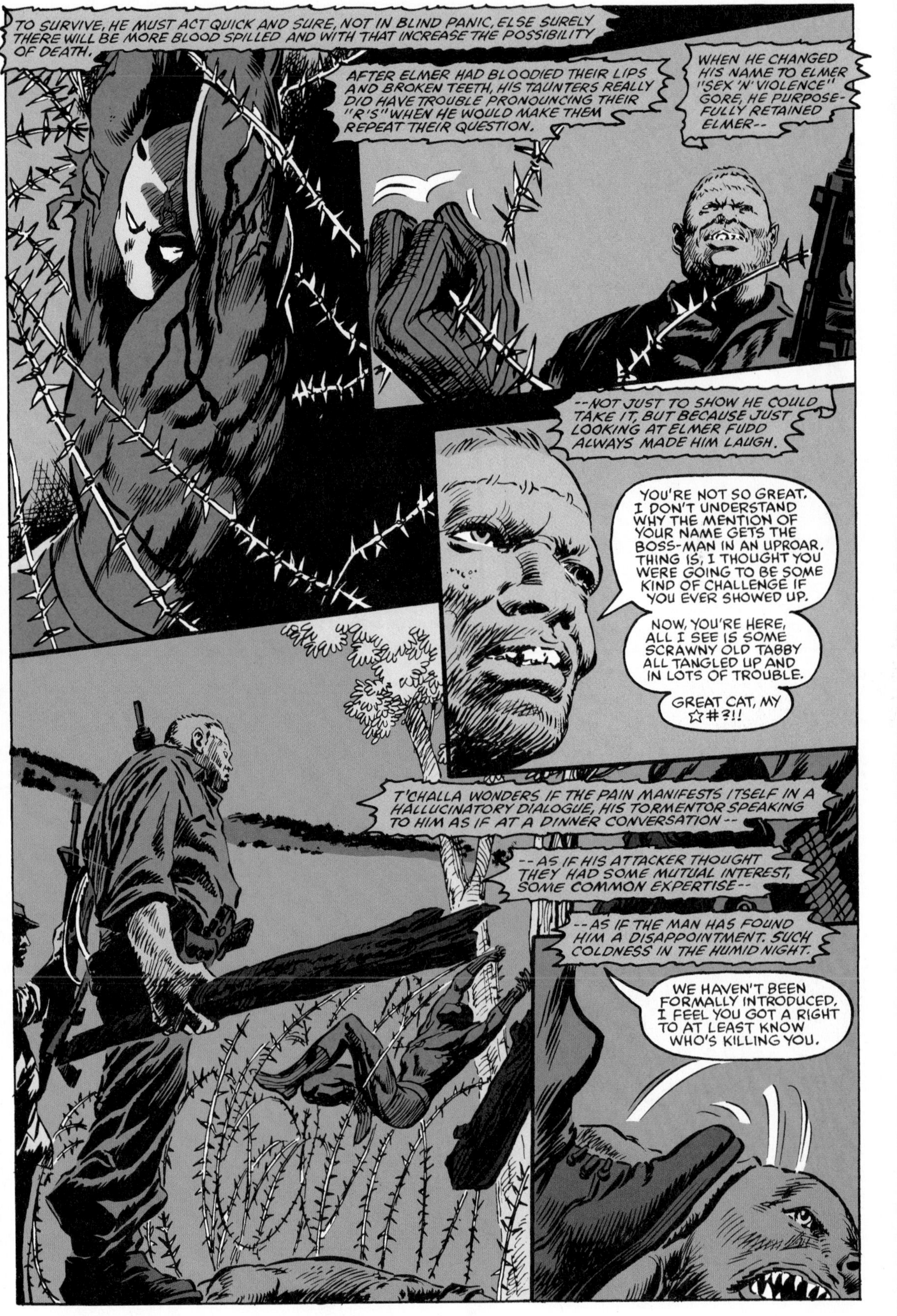
TO SURVIVE, HE MUST ACT QUICK AND SURE, NOT IN BLIND PANIC, ELSE SURELY THERE WILL BE MORE BLOOD SPILLED AND WITH THAT INCREASE THE POSSIBILITY OF DEATH.
AFTER ELMER HAD BLOODIED THEIR LIPS AND BROKEN TEETH, HIS TAUNTERS REALLY DID HAVE TROUBLE PRONOUNCING THEIR "R'S" WHEN HE WOULD MAKE THEM REPEAT THEIR QUESTION.
WHEN HE CHANGED HIS NAME TO ELMER "SEX 'N' VIOLENCE" GORE, HE PURPOSE-FULLY RETAINED ELMER--
--NOT JUST TO SHOW HE COULD TAKE IT, BUT BECAUSE JUST LOOKING AT ELMER FUDD ALWAYS MADE HIM LAUGH.
YOU'RE NOT SO GREAT. I DON'T UNDERSTAND WHY THE MENTION OF YOUR NAME GETS THE BOSS-MAN IN AN UPROAR. THING IS, I THOUGHT YOU WERE GOING TO BE SOME KIND OF CHALLENGE IF YOU EVER SHOWED UP.
NOW, YOU'RE HERE, ALL I SEE IS SOME SCRAWNY OLD TABBY ALL TANGLED UP AND IN LOTS OF TROUBLE.
GREAT CAT, MY ☆#?!!
T'CHALLA WONDERS IF THE PAIN MANIFESTS ITSELF IN A HALLUCINATORY DIALOGUE, HIS TORMENTOR SPEAKING TO HIM AS IF AT A DINNER CONVERSATION--
--AS IF HIS ATTACKER THOUGHT THEY HAD SOME MUTUAL INTEREST, SOME COMMON EXPERTISE--
--AS IF THE MAN HAS FOUND HIM A DISAPPOINTMENT. SUCH COLDNESS IN THE HUMID NIGHT.
WE HAVEN'T BEEN FORMALLY INTRODUCED. I FEEL YOU GOT A RIGHT TO AT LEAST KNOW WHO'S KILLING YOU.

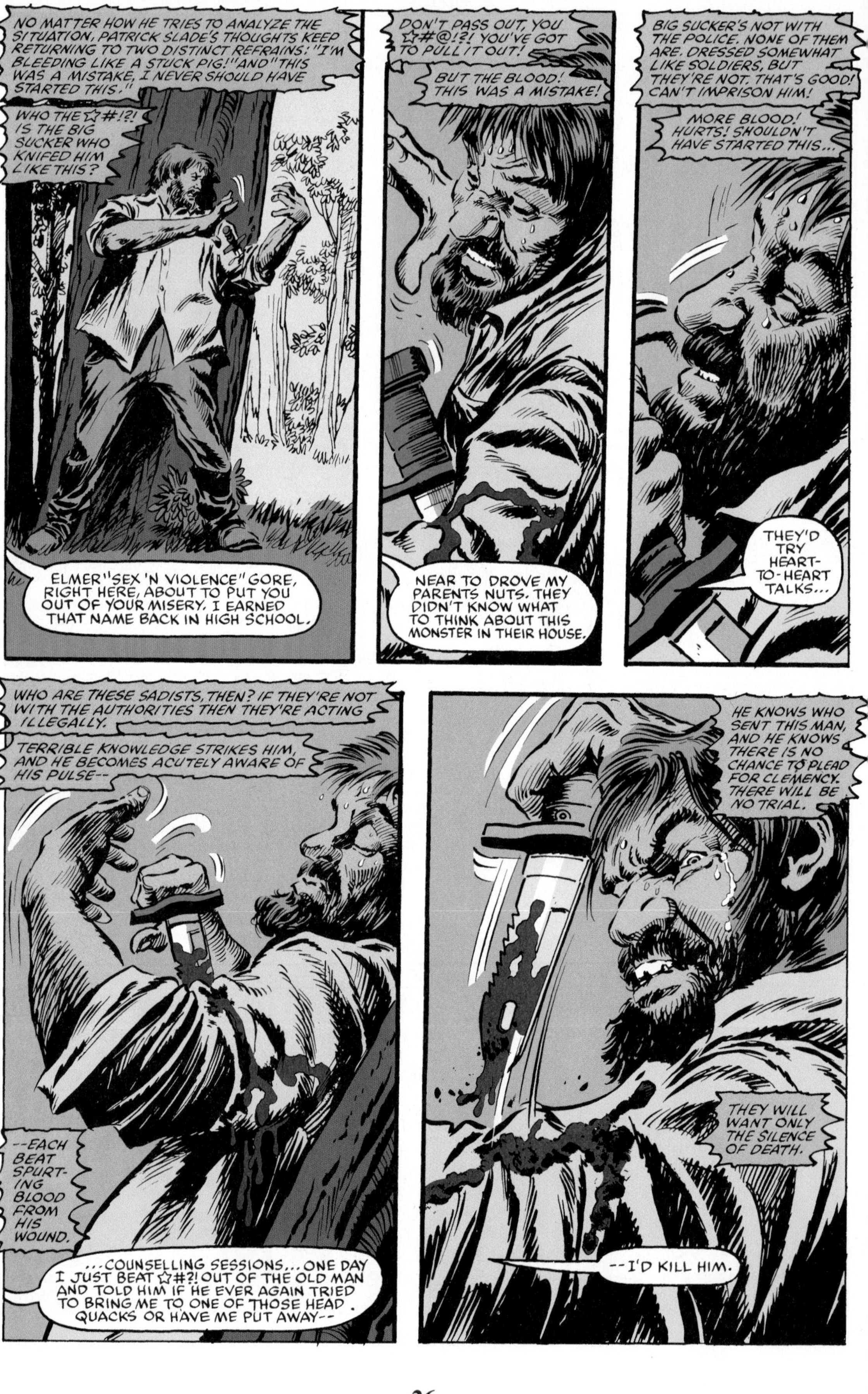
NO MATTER HOW HE TRIES TO ANALYZE THE SITUATION, PATRICK SLADE'S THOUGHTS KEEP RETURNING TO TWO DISTINCT REFRAINS: "I'M BLEEDING LIKE A STUCK PIG!" AND "THIS WAS A MISTAKE, I NEVER SHOULD HAVE STARTED THIS."
WHO THE ☆#!?! IS THE BIG SUCKER WHO KNIFED HIM LIKE THIS?
ELMER "SEX 'N VIOLENCE" GORE, RIGHT HERE, ABOUT TO PUT YOU OUT OF YOUR MISERY. I EARNED THAT NAME BACK IN HIGH SCHOOL.
DON'T PASS OUT, YOU ☆#@!?! YOU'VE GOT TO PULL IT OUT!
BUT THE BLOOD! THIS WAS A MISTAKE!
NEAR TO DROVE MY PARENTS NUTS. THEY DIDN'T KNOW WHAT TO THINK ABOUT THIS MONSTER IN THEIR HOUSE.
BIG SUCKER'S NOT WITH THE POLICE. NONE OF THEM ARE. DRESSED SOMEWHAT LIKE SOLDIERS, BUT THEY'RE NOT. THAT'S GOOD! CAN'T IMPRISON HIM!
MORE BLOOD! HURTS! SHOULDN'T HAVE STARTED THIS...
THEY'D TRY HEART-TO-HEART TALKS...
WHO ARE THESE SADISTS, THEN? IF THEY'RE NOT WITH THE AUTHORITIES THEN THEY'RE ACTING ILLEGALLY.
TERRIBLE KNOWLEDGE STRIKES HIM, AND HE BECOMES ACUTELY AWARE OF HIS PULSE--
--EACH BEAT SPURTING BLOOD FROM HIS WOUND.
...COUNSELLING SESSIONS... ONE DAY I JUST BEAT ☆#?! OUT OF THE OLD MAN AND TOLD HIM IF HE EVER AGAIN TRIED TO BRING ME TO ONE OF THOSE HEAD QUACKS OR HAVE ME PUT AWAY--
HE KNOWS WHO SENT THIS MAN, AND HE KNOWS THERE IS NO CHANCE TO PLEAD FOR CLEMENCY. THERE WILL BE NO TRIAL.
THEY WILL WANT ONLY THE SILENCE OF DEATH.
--I'D KILL HIM.

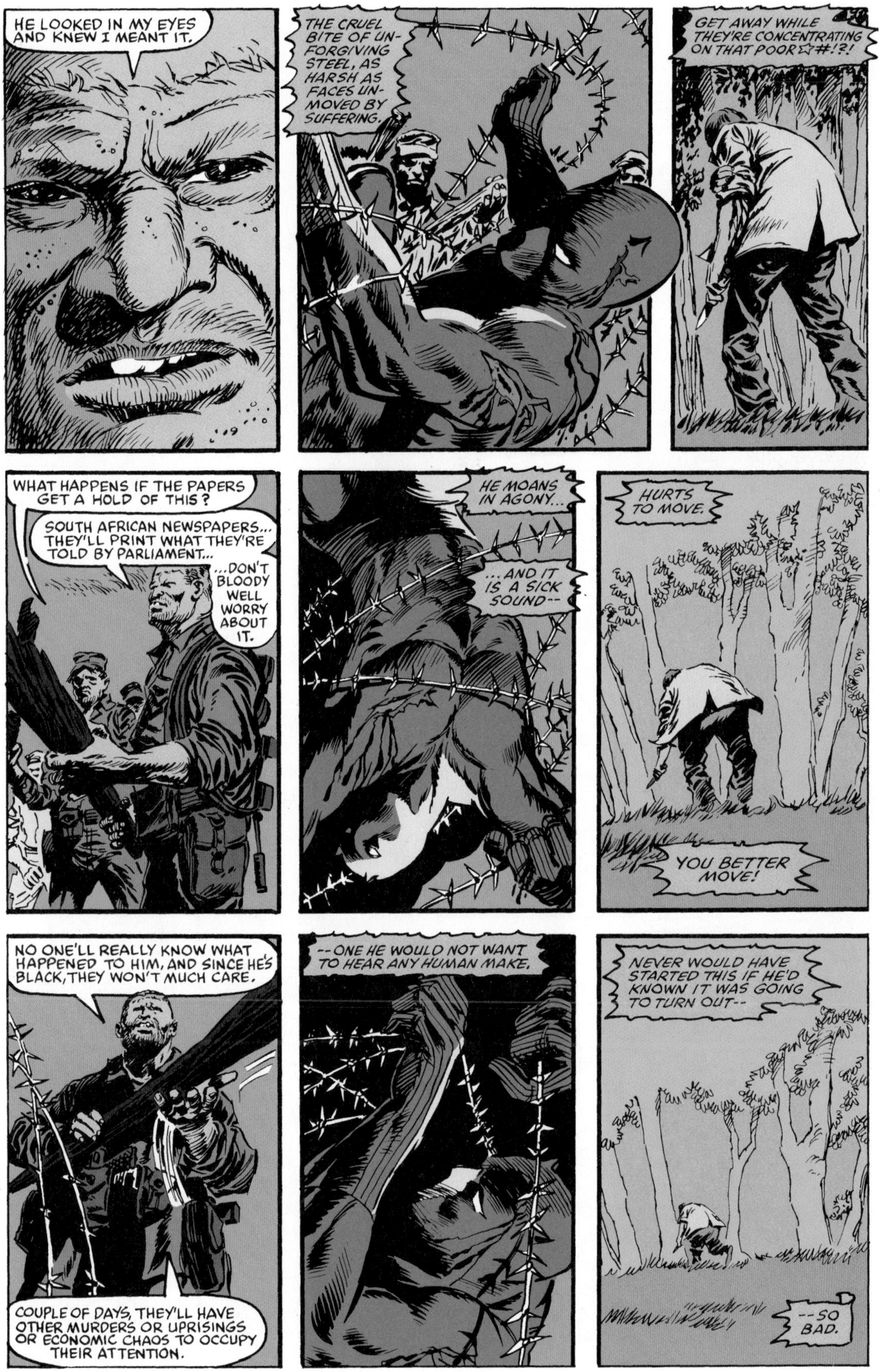
HE LOOKED IN MY EYES AND KNEW I MEANT IT.
THE CRUEL BITE OF UN-FORGIVING STEEL, AS HARSH AS FACES UN-MOVED BY SUFFERING.
GET AWAY WHILE THEY'RE CONCENTRATING ON THAT POOR☆#!?!
WHAT HAPPENS IF THE PAPERS GET A HOLD OF THIS?
SOUTH AFRICAN NEWSPAPERS... THEY'LL PRINT WHAT THEY'RE TOLD BY PARLIAMENT...
...DON'T BLOODY WELL WORRY ABOUT IT.
HE MOANS IN AGONY...
...AND IT IS A SICK SOUND--
HURTS TO MOVE.
YOU BETTER MOVE!
NO ONE'LL REALLY KNOW WHAT HAPPENED TO HIM, AND SINCE HE'S BLACK, THEY WON'T MUCH CARE.
COUPLE OF DAYS, THEY'LL HAVE OTHER MURDERS OR UPRISINGS OR ECONOMIC CHAOS TO OCCUPY THEIR ATTENTION.
--ONE HE WOULD NOT WANT TO HEAR ANY HUMAN MAKE.
NEVER WOULD HAVE STARTED THIS IF HE'D KNOWN IT WAS GOING TO TURN OUT--
--SO BAD.

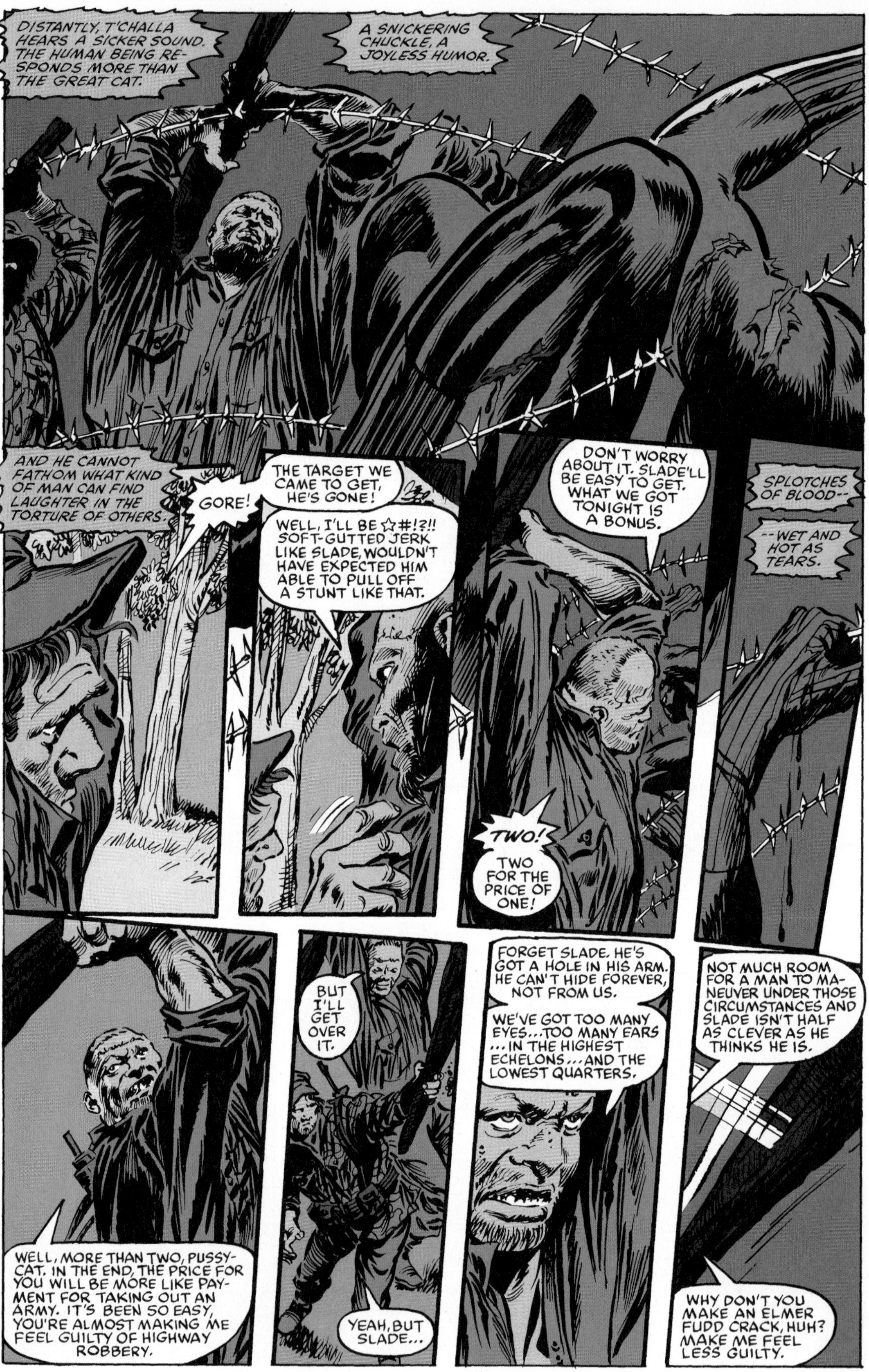
DISTANTLY, T'CHALLA HEARS A SICKER SOUND. THE HUMAN BEING RESPONDS MORE THAN THE GREAT CAT.
A SNICKERING CHUCKLE, A JOYLESS HUMOR.
AND HE CANNOT FATHOM WHAT KIND OF MAN CAN FIND LAUGHTER IN THE TORTURE OF OTHERS.
GORE!
THE TARGET WE CAME TO GET, HE'S GONE!
WELL, I'LL BE ☆#!?!! SOFT-GUTTED JERK LIKE SLADE, WOULDN'T HAVE EXPECTED HIM ABLE TO PULL OFF A STUNT LIKE THAT.
DON'T WORRY ABOUT IT. SLADE'LL BE EASY TO GET. WHAT WE GOT TONIGHT IS A BONUS.
TWO!
TWO FOR THE PRICE OF ONE!
SPLOTCHES OF BLOOD--
--WET AND HOT AS TEARS.
WELL, MORE THAN TWO, PUSSY-CAT. IN THE END, THE PRICE FOR YOU WILL BE MORE LIKE PAYMENT FOR TAKING OUT AN ARMY. IT'S BEEN SO EASY, YOU'RE ALMOST MAKING ME FEEL GUILTY OF HIGHWAY ROBBERY.
BUT I'LL GET OVER IT.
YEAH, BUT SLADE...
FORGET SLADE. HE'S GOT A HOLE IN HIS ARM. HE CAN'T HIDE FOREVER, NOT FROM US.
WE'VE GOT TOO MANY EYES... TOO MANY EARS ... IN THE HIGHEST ECHELONS... AND THE LOWEST QUARTERS.
NOT MUCH ROOM FOR A MAN TO MANEUVER UNDER THOSE CIRCUMSTANCES AND SLADE ISN'T HALF AS CLEVER AS HE THINKS HE IS.
WHY DON'T YOU MAKE AN ELMER FUDD CRACK, HUH? MAKE ME FEEL LESS GUILTY.

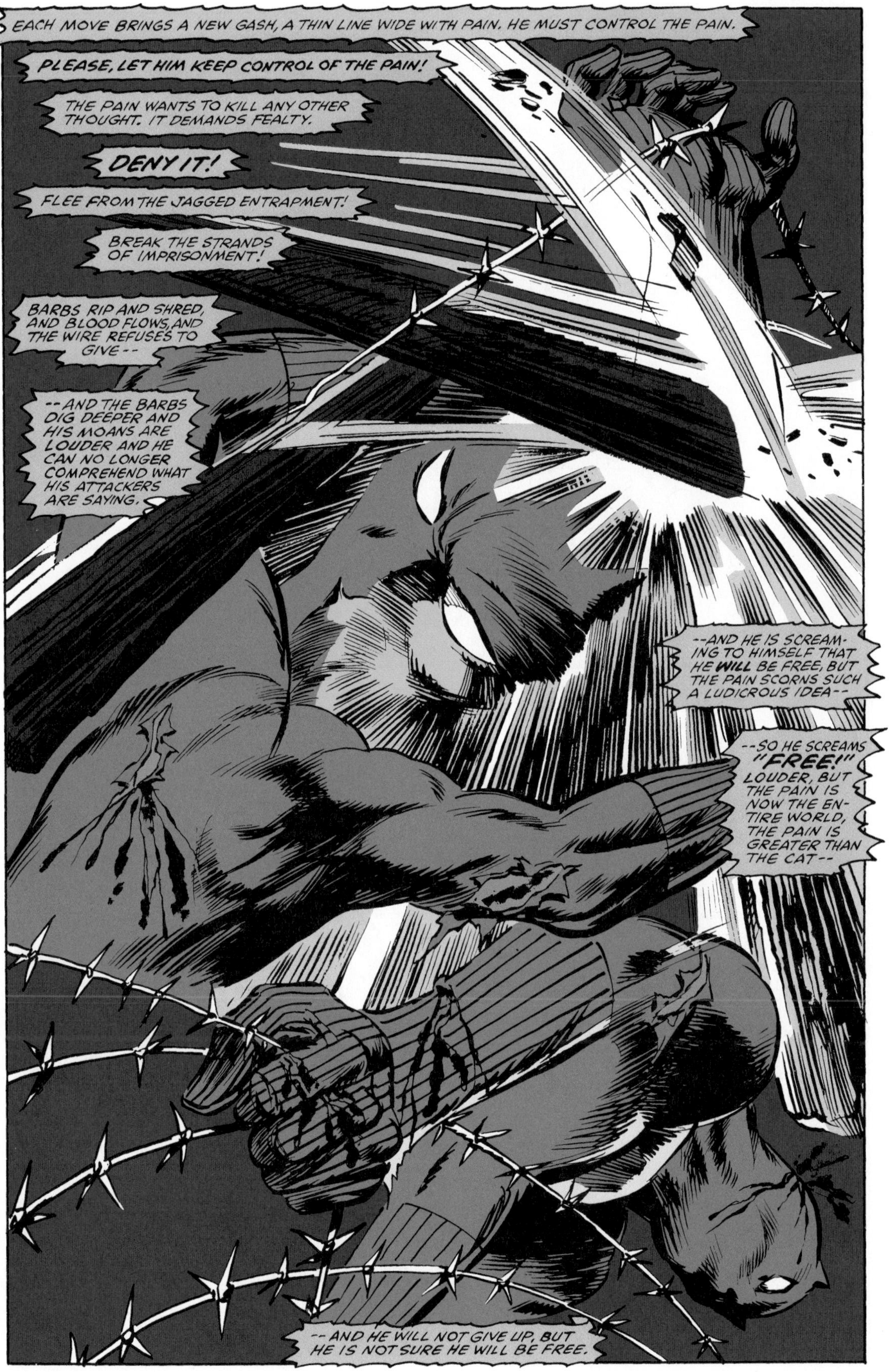
EACH MOVE BRINGS A NEW GASH, A THIN LINE WIDE WITH PAIN. HE MUST CONTROL THE PAIN.
PLEASE, LET HIM KEEP CONTROL OF THE PAIN!
THE PAIN WANTS TO KILL ANY OTHER THOUGHT. IT DEMANDS FEALTY.
DENY IT!
FLEE FROM THE JAGGED ENTRAPMENT!
BREAK THE STRANDS OF IMPRISONMENT!
BARBS RIP AND SHRED, AND BLOOD FLOWS, AND THE WIRE REFUSES TO GIVE--
--AND THE BARBS DIG DEEPER AND HIS MOANS ARE LOUDER AND HE CAN NO LONGER COMPREHEND WHAT HIS ATTACKERS ARE SAYING.
--AND HE IS SCREAMING TO HIMSELF THAT HE WILL BE FREE, BUT THE PAIN SCORNS SUCH A LUDICROUS IDEA--
--SO HE SCREAMS "FREE!" LOUDER, BUT THE PAIN IS NOW THE ENTIRE WORLD, THE PAIN IS GREATER THAN THE CAT--
--AND HE WILL NOT GIVE UP, BUT HE IS NOT SURE HE WILL BE FREE.

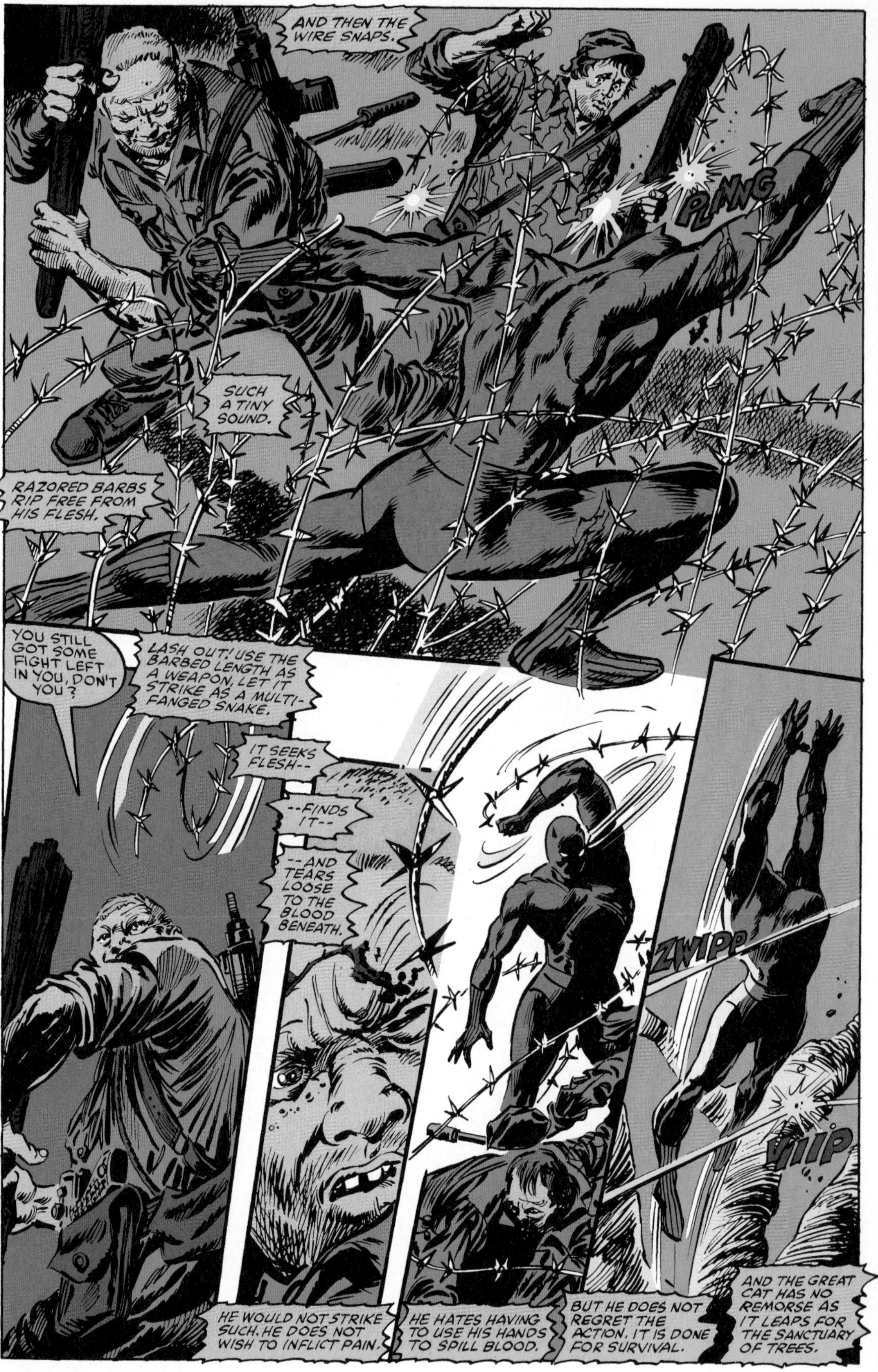
AND THEN THE WIRE SNAPS.
PLINNG
SUCH A TINY SOUND.
RAZORED BARBS RIP FREE FROM HIS FLESH.
YOU STILL GOT SOME FIGHT LEFT IN YOU, DON'T YOU?
LASH OUT! USE THE BARBED LENGTH AS A WEAPON, LET IT STRIKE AS A MULTI-FANGED SNAKE.
IT SEEKS FLESH--
--FINDS IT--
--AND TEARS LOOSE TO THE BLOOD BENEATH.
ZWIPP
VIIIP
HE WOULD NOT STRIKE SUCH. HE DOES NOT WISH TO INFLICT PAIN.
HE HATES HAVING TO USE HIS HANDS TO SPILL BLOOD.
BUT HE DOES NOT REGRET THE ACTION. IT IS DONE FOR SURVIVAL.
AND THE GREAT CAT HAS NO REMORSE AS IT LEAPS FOR THE SANCTUARY OF TREES.

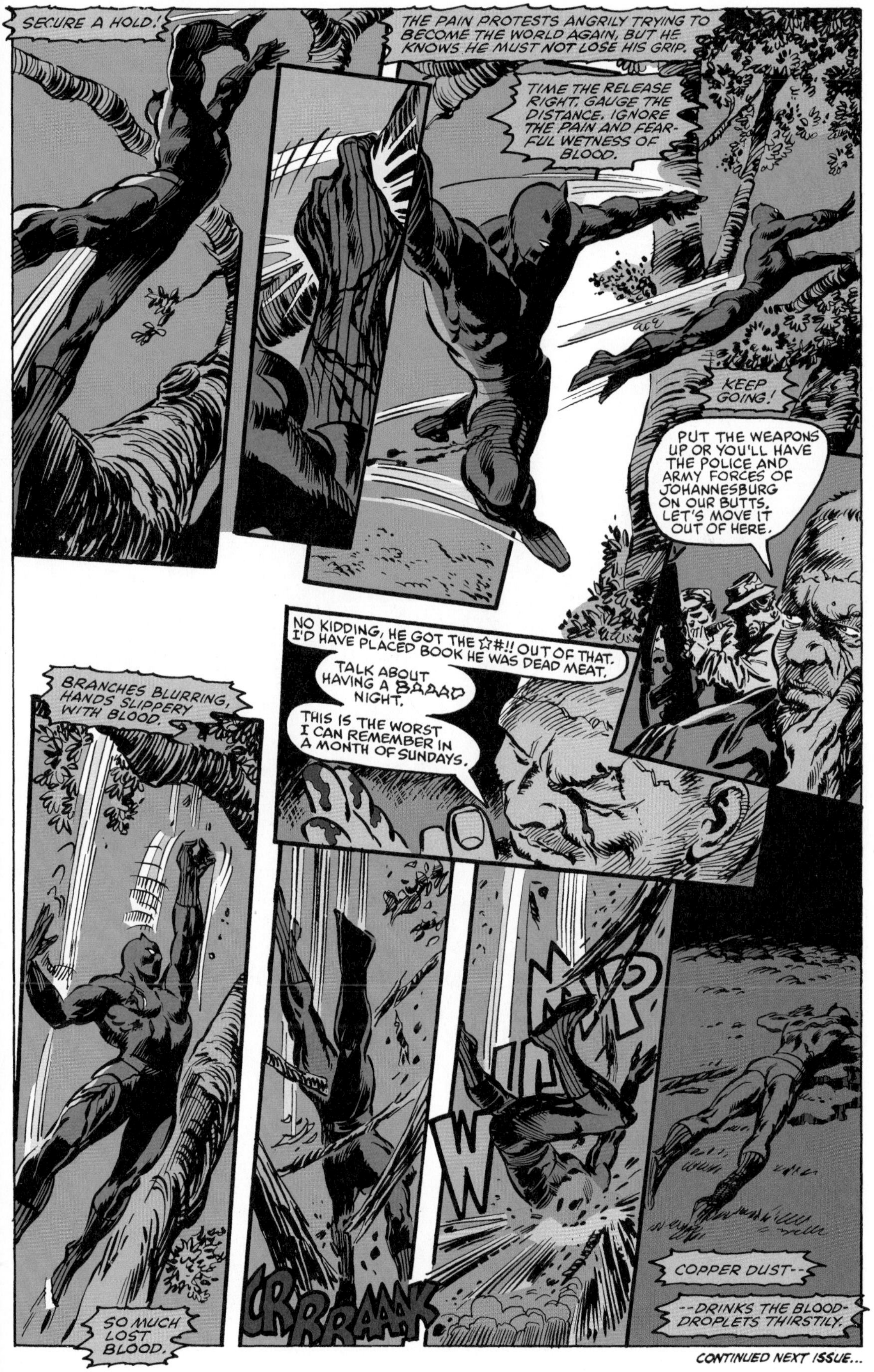

SECURE A HOLD!
THE PAIN PROTESTS ANGRILY TRYING TO BECOME THE WORLD AGAIN, BUT HE KNOWS HE MUST NOT LOSE HIS GRIP.
TIME THE RELEASE RIGHT. GAUGE THE DISTANCE. IGNORE THE PAIN AND FEARFUL WETNESS OF BLOOD.
KEEP GOING!
PUT THE WEAPONS UP OR YOU'LL HAVE THE POLICE AND ARMY FORCES OF JOHANNESBURG ON OUR BUTTS. LET'S MOVE IT OUT OF HERE.
NO KIDDING, HE GOT THE ☆#!! OUT OF THAT. I'D HAVE PLACED BOOK HE WAS DEAD MEAT.
TALK ABOUT HAVING A BAAAD NIGHT.
THIS IS THE WORST I CAN REMEMBER IN A MONTH OF SUNDAYS.
BRANCHES BLURRING, HANDS SLIPPERY WITH BLOOD.
SO MUCH LOST BLOOD.
CRRRAAAK
WHAP
COPPER DUST--
--DRINKS THE BLOOD-DROPLETS THIRSTILY.

CONTINUED NEXT ISSUE...

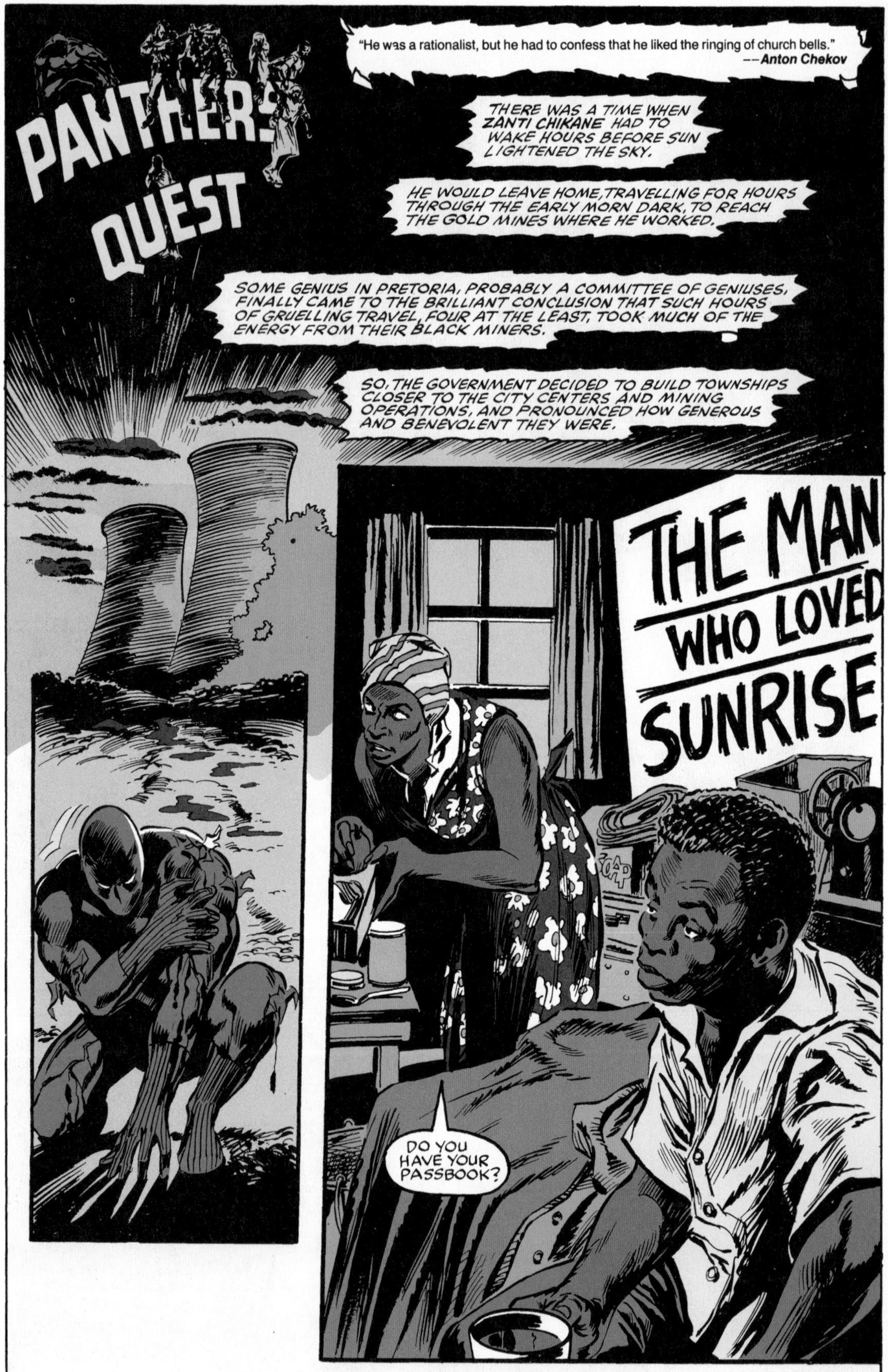

PANTHER'S QUEST
"He was a rationalist, but he had to confess that he liked the ringing of church bells."
--Anton Chekov
THERE WAS A TIME WHEN ZANTI CHIKANE HAD TO WAKE HOURS BEFORE SUN LIGHTENED THE SKY.
HE WOULD LEAVE HOME, TRAVELLING FOR HOURS THROUGH THE EARLY MORN DARK, TO REACH THE GOLD MINES WHERE HE WORKED.
SOME GENIUS IN PRETORIA, PROBABLY A COMMITTEE OF GENIUSES, FINALLY CAME TO THE BRILLIANT CONCLUSION THAT SUCH HOURS OF GRUELLING TRAVEL, FOUR AT THE LEAST, TOOK MUCH OF THE ENERGY FROM THEIR BLACK MINERS.
SO, THE GOVERNMENT DECIDED TO BUILD TOWNSHIPS CLOSER TO THE CITY CENTERS AND MINING OPERATIONS, AND PRONOUNCED HOW GENEROUS AND BENEVOLENT THEY WERE.
THE MAN WHO LOVED SUNRISE
DO YOU HAVE YOUR PASSBOOK?

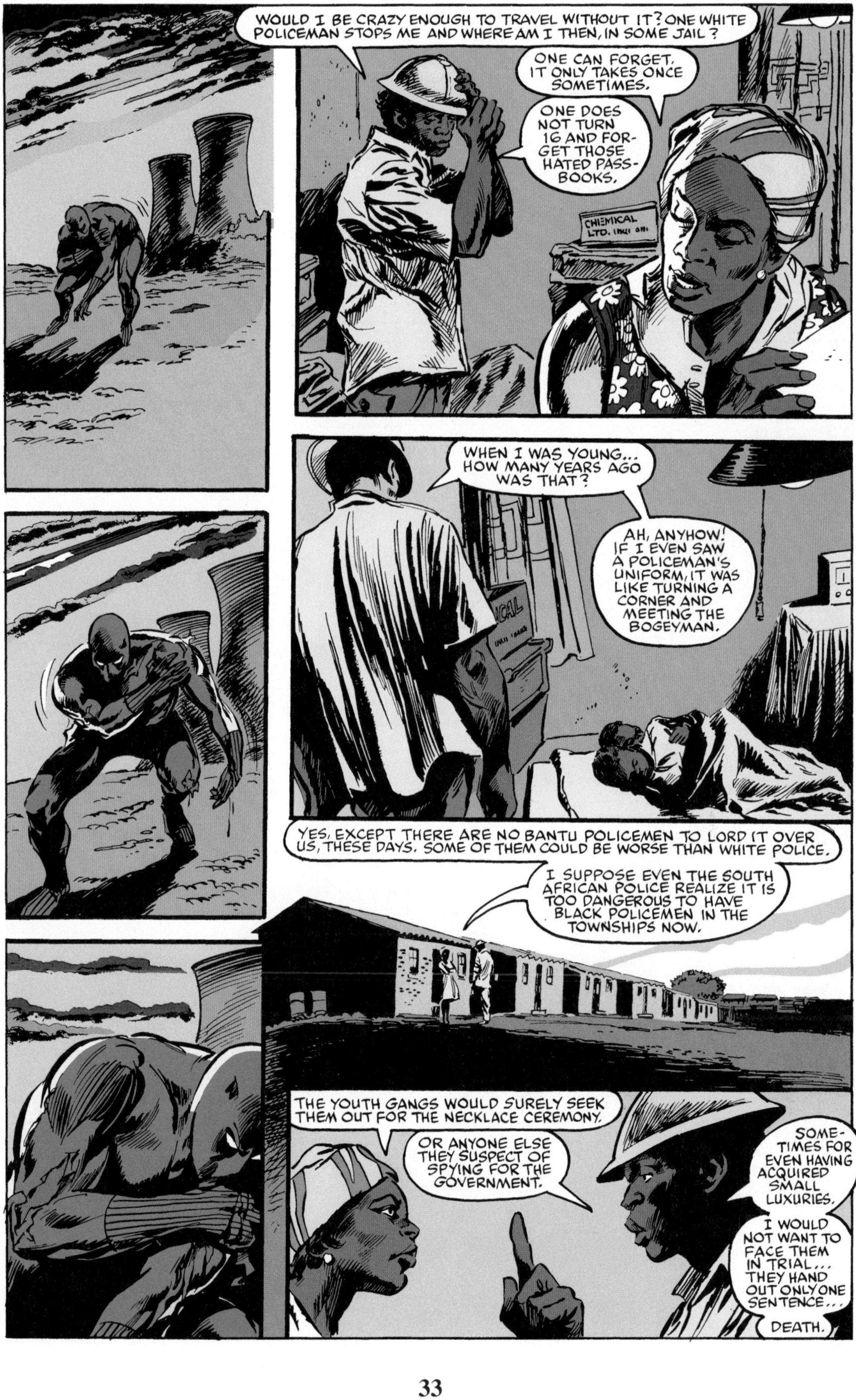
WOULD I BE CRAZY ENOUGH TO TRAVEL WITHOUT IT? ONE WHITE POLICEMAN STOPS ME AND WHERE AM I THEN, IN SOME JAIL?
ONE CAN FORGET. IT ONLY TAKES ONCE SOMETIMES.
ONE DOES NOT TURN 16 AND FORGET THOSE HATED PASSBOOKS.
CHEMICAL LTD.
WHEN I WAS YOUNG... HOW MANY YEARS AGO WAS THAT?
AH, ANYHOW! IF I EVEN SAW A POLICEMAN'S UNIFORM, IT WAS LIKE TURNING A CORNER AND MEETING THE BOGEYMAN.
YES, EXCEPT THERE ARE NO BANTU POLICEMEN TO LORD IT OVER US, THESE DAYS. SOME OF THEM COULD BE WORSE THAN WHITE POLICE.
I SUPPOSE EVEN THE SOUTH AFRICAN POLICE REALIZE IT IS TOO DANGEROUS TO HAVE BLACK POLICEMEN IN THE TOWNSHIPS NOW.
THE YOUTH GANGS WOULD SURELY SEEK THEM OUT FOR THE NECKLACE CEREMONY.
OR ANYONE ELSE THEY SUSPECT OF SPYING FOR THE GOVERNMENT.
SOMETIMES FOR EVEN HAVING ACQUIRED SMALL LUXURIES.
I WOULD NOT WANT TO FACE THEM IN TRIAL... THEY HAND OUT ONLY ONE SENTENCE...
DEATH.

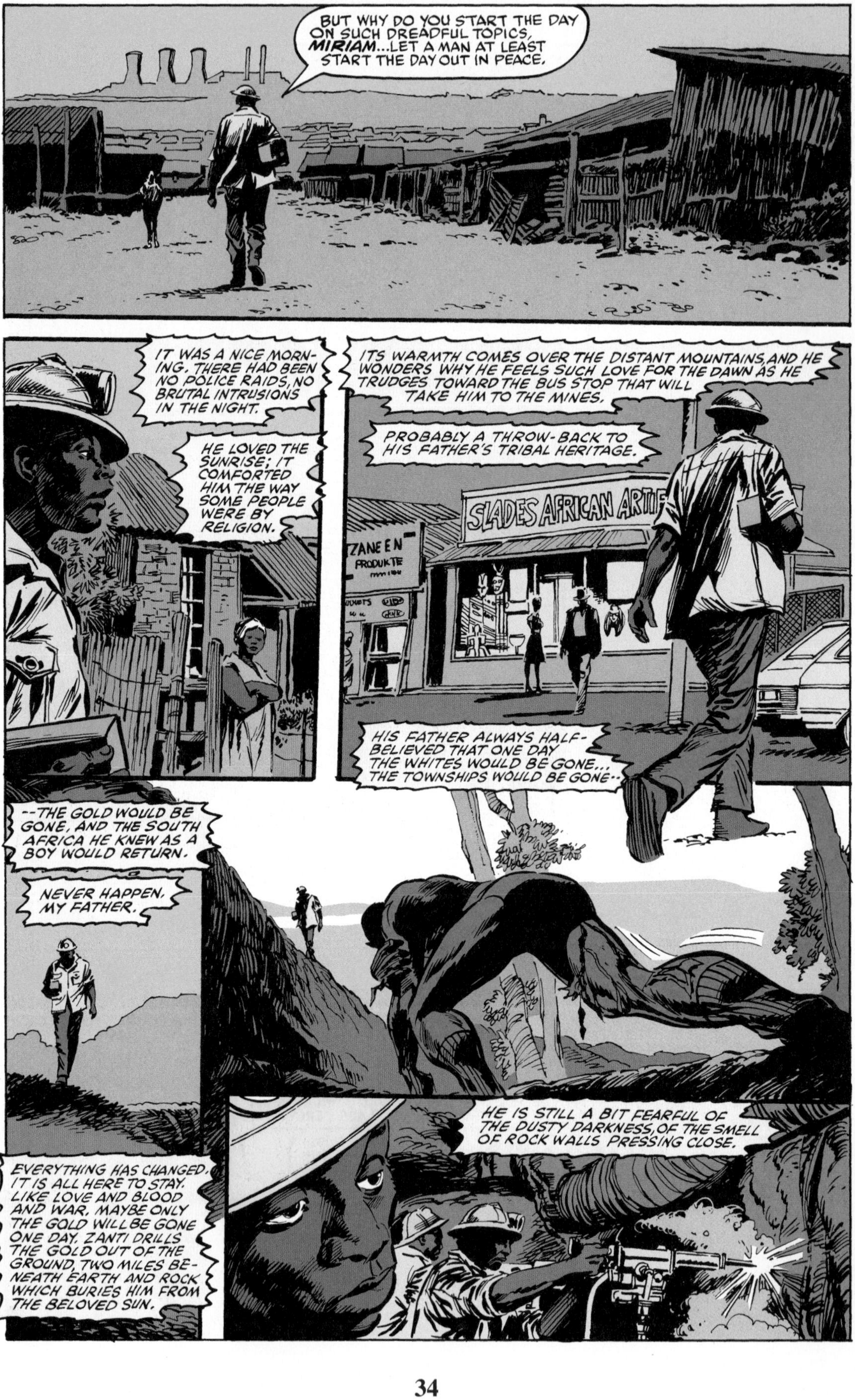
BUT WHY DO YOU START THE DAY ON SUCH DREADFUL TOPICS, MIRIAM...LET A MAN AT LEAST START THE DAY OUT IN PEACE.
IT WAS A NICE MORNING. THERE HAD BEEN NO POLICE RAIDS, NO BRUTAL INTRUSIONS IN THE NIGHT.
HE LOVED THE SUNRISE; IT COMFORTED HIM THE WAY SOME PEOPLE WERE BY RELIGION.
ITS WARMTH COMES OVER THE DISTANT MOUNTAINS, AND HE WONDERS WHY HE FEELS SUCH LOVE FOR THE DAWN AS HE TRUDGES TOWARD THE BUS STOP THAT WILL TAKE HIM TO THE MINES.
PROBABLY A THROW-BACK TO HIS FATHER'S TRIBAL HERITAGE.
SLADES AFRICAN ARTIF
ZANEEN
PRODUKTE
HIS FATHER ALWAYS HALF-BELIEVED THAT ONE DAY THE WHITES WOULD BE GONE... THE TOWNSHIPS WOULD BE GONE--
--THE GOLD WOULD BE GONE, AND THE SOUTH AFRICA HE KNEW AS A BOY WOULD RETURN.
NEVER HAPPEN, MY FATHER.
HE IS STILL A BIT FEARFUL OF THE DUSTY DARKNESS, OF THE SMELL OF ROCK WALLS PRESSING CLOSE.
EVERYTHING HAS CHANGED. IT IS ALL HERE TO STAY. LIKE LOVE AND BLOOD AND WAR, MAYBE ONLY THE GOLD WILL BE GONE ONE DAY. ZANTI DRILLS THE GOLD OUT OF THE GROUND, TWO MILES BENEATH EARTH AND ROCK WHICH BURIES HIM FROM THE BELOVED SUN.

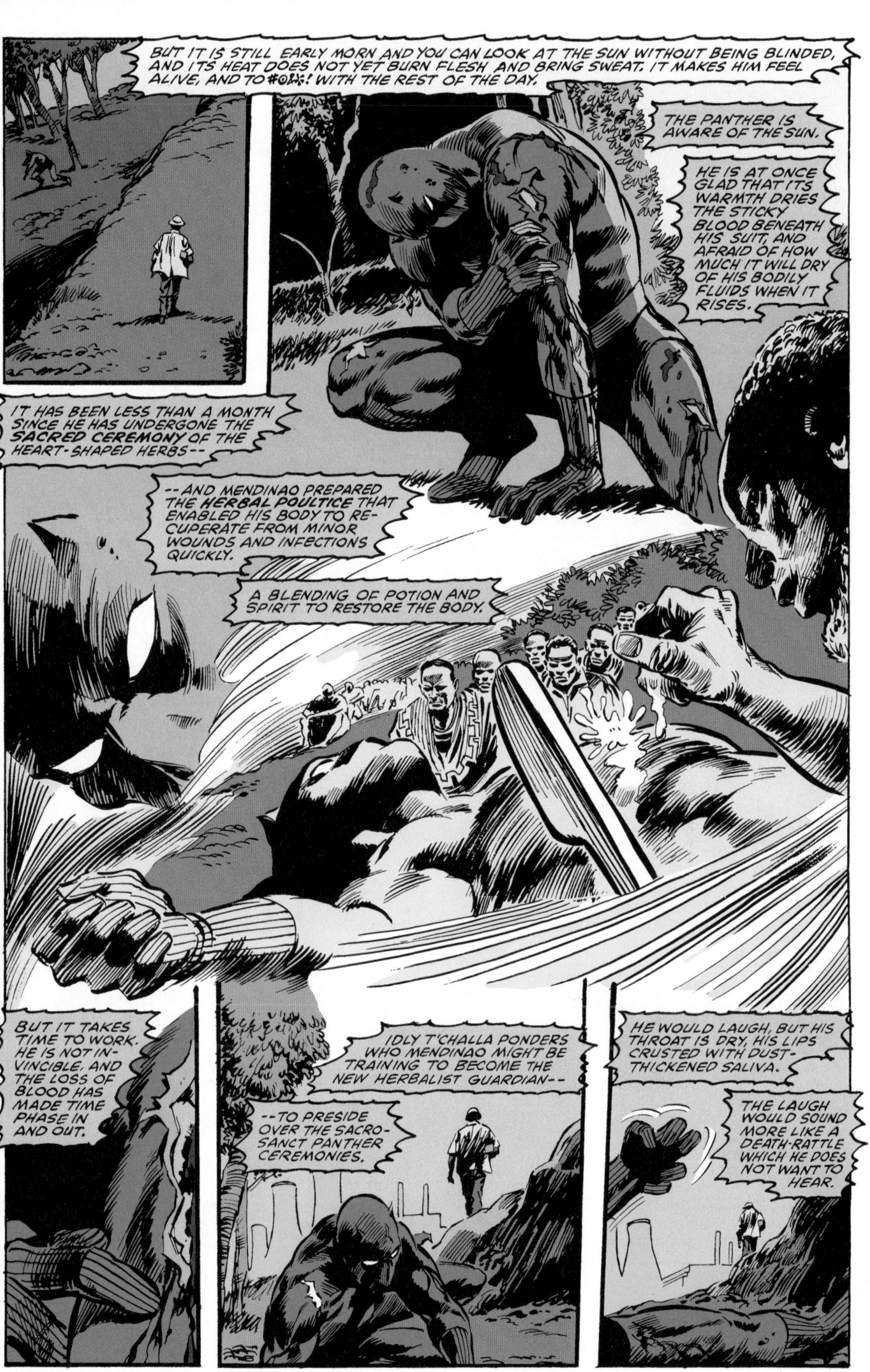
BUT IT IS STILL EARLY MORN AND YOU CAN LOOK AT THE SUN WITHOUT BEING BLINDED, AND ITS HEAT DOES NOT YET BURN FLESH AND BRING SWEAT. IT MAKES HIM FEEL ALIVE, AND TO #@!*! WITH THE REST OF THE DAY.
THE PANTHER IS AWARE OF THE SUN.
HE IS AT ONCE GLAD THAT ITS WARMTH DRIES THE STICKY BLOOD BENEATH HIS SUIT, AND AFRAID OF HOW MUCH IT WILL DRY OF HIS BODILY FLUIDS WHEN IT RISES.
IT HAS BEEN LESS THAN A MONTH SINCE HE HAS UNDERGONE THE SACRED CEREMONY OF THE HEART-SHAPED HERBS--
--AND MENDINAO PREPARED THE HERBAL POULTICE THAT ENABLED HIS BODY TO RECUPERATE FROM MINOR WOUNDS AND INFECTIONS QUICKLY.
A BLENDING OF POTION AND SPIRIT TO RESTORE THE BODY.
BUT IT TAKES TIME TO WORK. HE IS NOT INVINCIBLE, AND THE LOSS OF BLOOD HAS MADE TIME PHASE IN AND OUT.
IDLY T'CHALLA PONDERS WHO MENDINAO MIGHT BE TRAINING TO BECOME THE NEW HERBALIST GUARDIAN--
--TO PRESIDE OVER THE SACROSANCT PANTHER CEREMONIES.
HE WOULD LAUGH, BUT HIS THROAT IS DRY, HIS LIPS CRUSTED WITH DUST-THICKENED SALIVA.
THE LAUGH WOULD SOUND MORE LIKE A DEATH-RATTLE WHICH HE DOES NOT WANT TO HEAR.

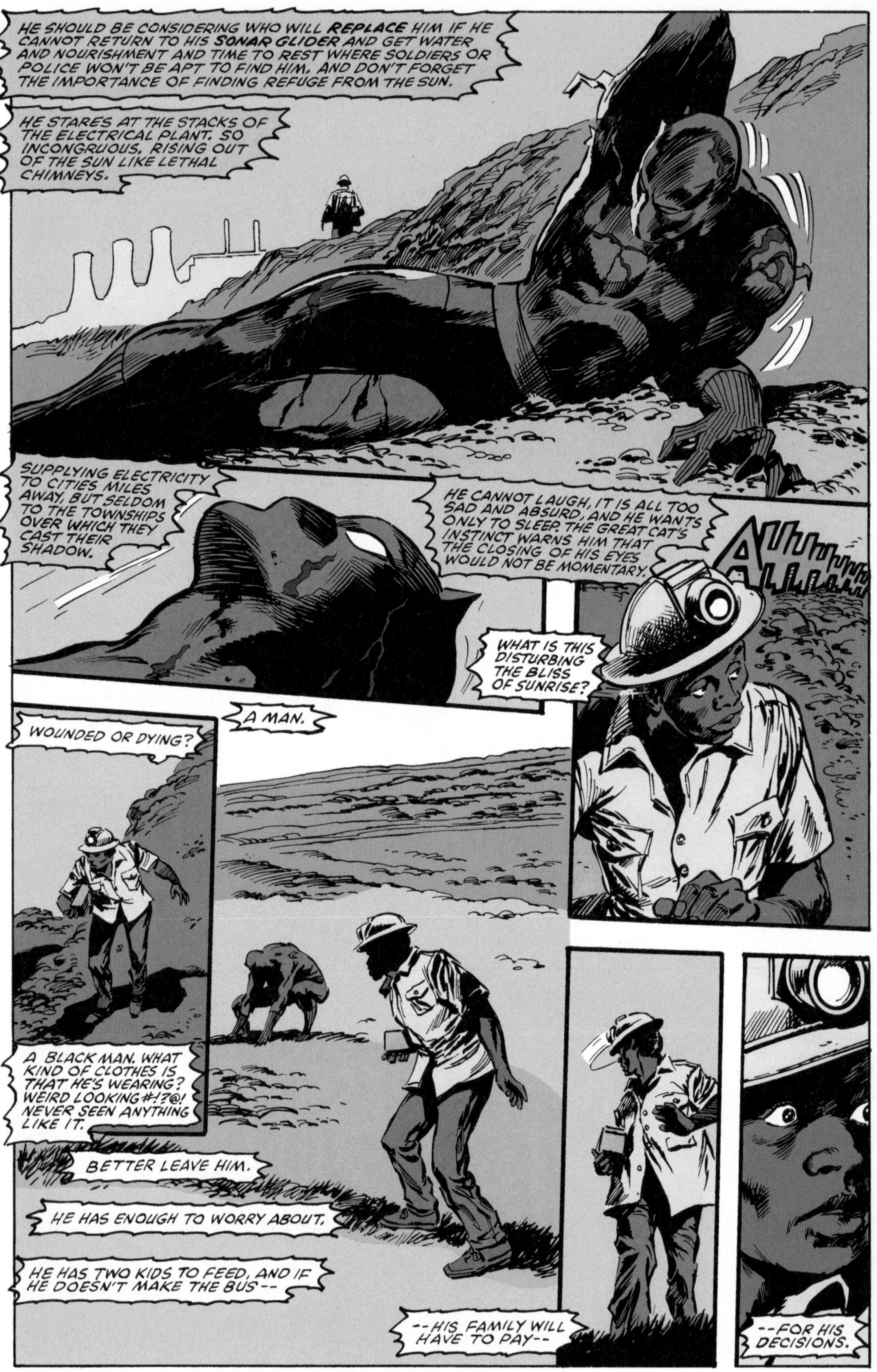
HE SHOULD BE CONSIDERING WHO WILL REPLACE HIM IF HE CANNOT RETURN TO HIS SONAR GLIDER AND GET WATER AND NOURISHMENT AND TIME TO REST WHERE SOLDIERS OR POLICE WON'T BE APT TO FIND HIM. AND DON'T FORGET THE IMPORTANCE OF FINDING REFUGE FROM THE SUN.
HE STARES AT THE STACKS OF THE ELECTRICAL PLANT. SO INCONGRUOUS, RISING OUT OF THE SUN LIKE LETHAL CHIMNEYS.
SUPPLYING ELECTRICITY TO CITIES MILES AWAY, BUT SELDOM TO THE TOWNSHIPS OVER WHICH THEY CAST THEIR SHADOW.
HE CANNOT LAUGH, IT IS ALL TOO SAD AND ABSURD, AND HE WANTS ONLY TO SLEEP. THE GREAT CAT'S INSTINCT WARNS HIM THAT THE CLOSING OF HIS EYES WOULD NOT BE MOMENTARY.
AUHHHH
WHAT IS THIS DISTURBING THE BLISS OF SUNRISE?
WOUNDED OR DYING?
A MAN.
A BLACK MAN. WHAT KIND OF CLOTHES IS THAT HE'S WEARING? WEIRD LOOKING #!?@! NEVER SEEN ANYTHING LIKE IT.
BETTER LEAVE HIM.
HE HAS ENOUGH TO WORRY ABOUT.
HE HAS TWO KIDS TO FEED, AND IF HE DOESN'T MAKE THE BUS--
--HIS FAMILY WILL HAVE TO PAY--
--FOR HIS DECISIONS.

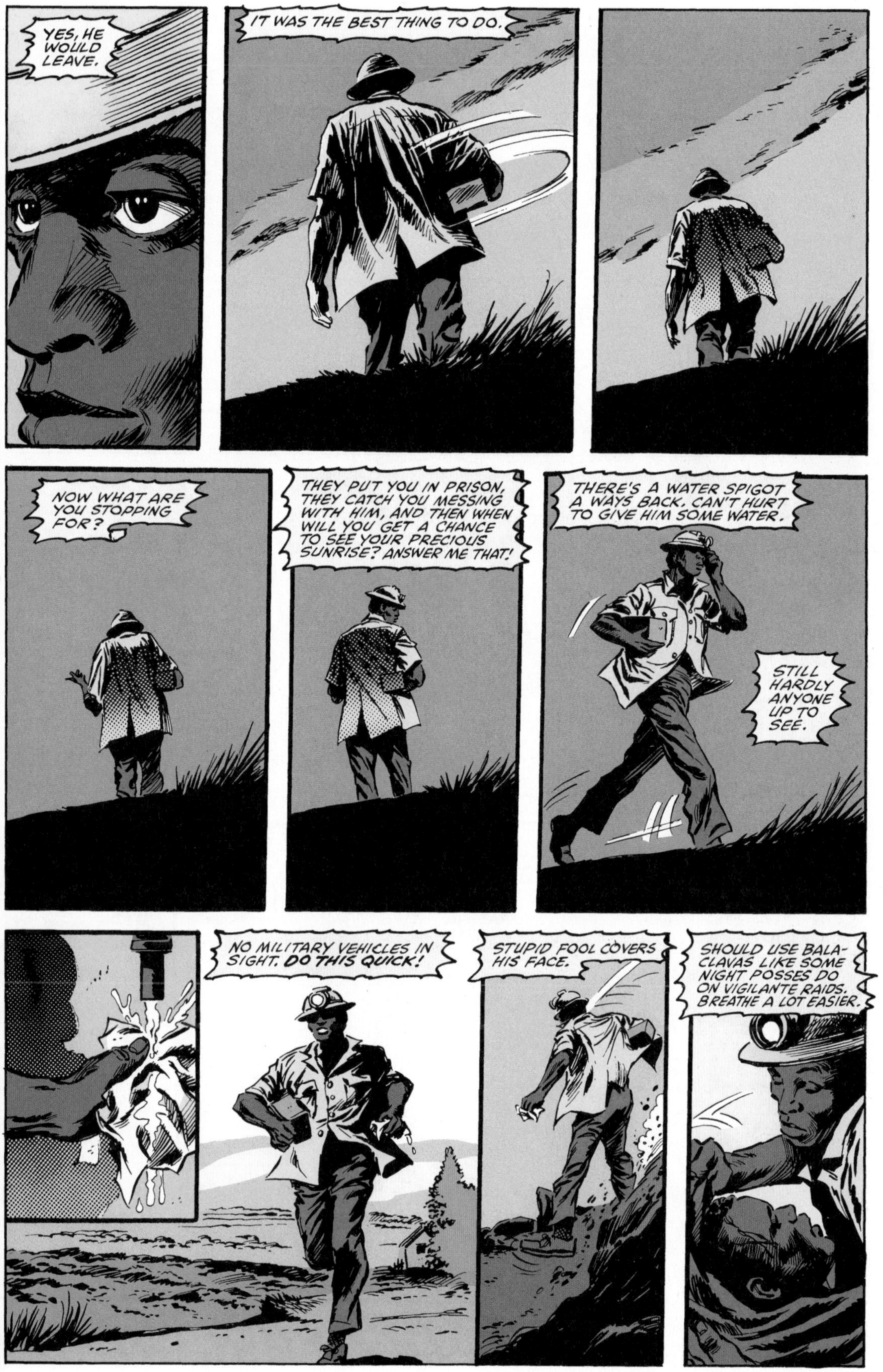
YES, HE WOULD LEAVE.
IT WAS THE BEST THING TO DO.
NOW WHAT ARE YOU STOPPING FOR?
THEY PUT YOU IN PRISON, THEY CATCH YOU MESSING WITH HIM, AND THEN WHEN WILL YOU GET A CHANCE TO SEE YOUR PRECIOUS SUNRISE? ANSWER ME THAT!
THERE'S A WATER SPIGOT A WAYS BACK. CAN'T HURT TO GIVE HIM SOME WATER.
STILL HARDLY ANYONE UP TO SEE.
NO MILITARY VEHICLES IN SIGHT. DO THIS QUICK!
STUPID FOOL COVERS HIS FACE.
SHOULD USE BALA-CLAVAS LIKE SOME NIGHT POSSES DO ON VIGILANTE RAIDS. BREATHE A LOT EASIER.

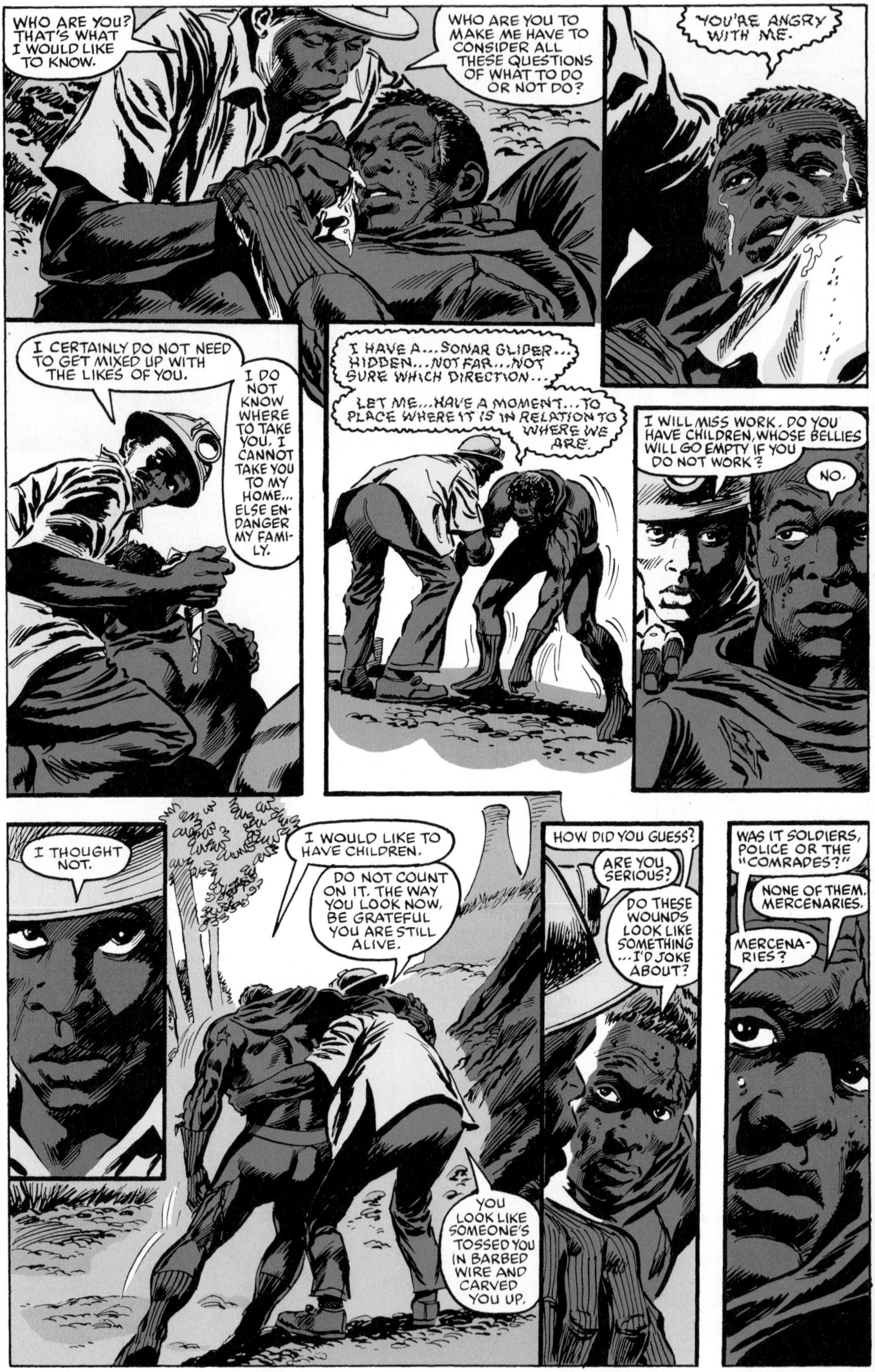
WHO ARE YOU? THAT'S WHAT I WOULD LIKE TO KNOW.
WHO ARE YOU TO MAKE ME HAVE TO CONSIDER ALL THESE QUESTIONS OF WHAT TO DO OR NOT DO?
YOU'RE ANGRY WITH ME.
I CERTAINLY DO NOT NEED TO GET MIXED UP WITH THE LIKES OF YOU.
I DO NOT KNOW WHERE TO TAKE YOU. I CANNOT TAKE YOU TO MY HOME... ELSE ENDANGER MY FAMILY.
I HAVE A... SONAR GLIDER... HIDDEN... NOT FAR... NOT SURE WHICH DIRECTION...
LET ME... HAVE A MOMENT... TO PLACE WHERE IT IS IN RELATION TO WHERE WE ARE.
I WILL MISS WORK. DO YOU HAVE CHILDREN, WHOSE BELLIES WILL GO EMPTY IF YOU DO NOT WORK?
NO.
I THOUGHT NOT.
I WOULD LIKE TO HAVE CHILDREN.
DO NOT COUNT ON IT. THE WAY YOU LOOK NOW, BE GRATEFUL YOU ARE STILL ALIVE.
YOU LOOK LIKE SOMEONE'S TOSSED YOU IN BARBED WIRE AND CARVED YOU UP.
HOW DID YOU GUESS?
ARE YOU SERIOUS?
DO THESE WOUNDS LOOK LIKE SOMETHING ...I'D JOKE ABOUT?
WAS IT SOLDIERS, POLICE OR THE "COMRADES?"
NONE OF THEM. MERCENARIES.
MERCENARIES?

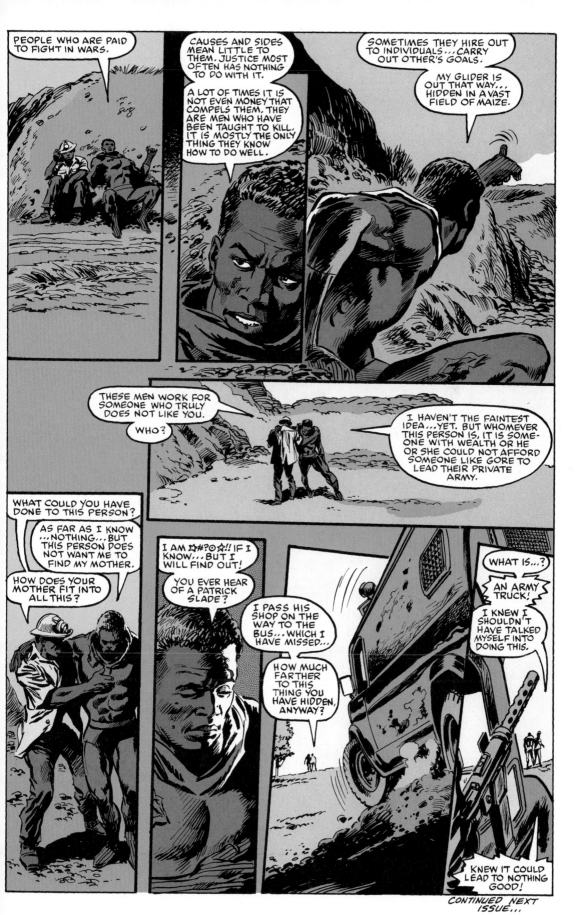

PEOPLE WHO ARE PAID TO FIGHT IN WARS.

CAUSES AND SIDES MEAN LITTLE TO THEM. JUSTICE MOST OFTEN HAS NOTHING TO DO WITH IT.

A LOT OF TIMES IT IS NOT EVEN MONEY THAT COMPELS THEM, THEY ARE MEN WHO HAVE BEEN TAUGHT TO KILL. IT IS MOSTLY THE ONLY THING THEY KNOW HOW TO DO WELL.

SOMETIMES THEY HIRE OUT TO INDIVIDUALS...CARRY OUT OTHER'S GOALS.

MY GLIDER IS OUT THAT WAY... HIDDEN IN A VAST FIELD OF MAIZE.

THESE MEN WORK FOR SOMEONE WHO TRULY DOES NOT LIKE YOU.

WHO?

I HAVEN'T THE FAINTEST IDEA...YET. BUT WHOMEVER THIS PERSON IS, IT IS SOME-ONE WITH WEALTH OR HE OR SHE COULD NOT AFFORD SOMEONE LIKE GORE TO LEAD THEIR PRIVATE ARMY.

WHAT COULD YOU HAVE DONE TO THIS PERSON?

AS FAR AS I KNOW ...NOTHING...BUT THIS PERSON DOES NOT WANT ME TO FIND MY MOTHER.

HOW DOES YOUR MOTHER FIT INTO ALL THIS?

I AM ✪#?○✪!! IF I KNOW,...BUT I WILL FIND OUT!

YOU EVER HEAR OF A PATRICK SLADE?

I PASS HIS SHOP ON THE WAY TO THE BUS...WHICH I HAVE MISSED...

HOW MUCH FARTHER TO THIS THING YOU HAVE HIDDEN, ANYWAY?

WHAT IS...?

AN ARMY TRUCK!

I KNEW I SHOULDN'T HAVE TALKED MYSELF INTO DOING THIS.

KNEW IT COULD LEAD TO NOTHING GOOD!

CONTINUED NEXT ISSUE...

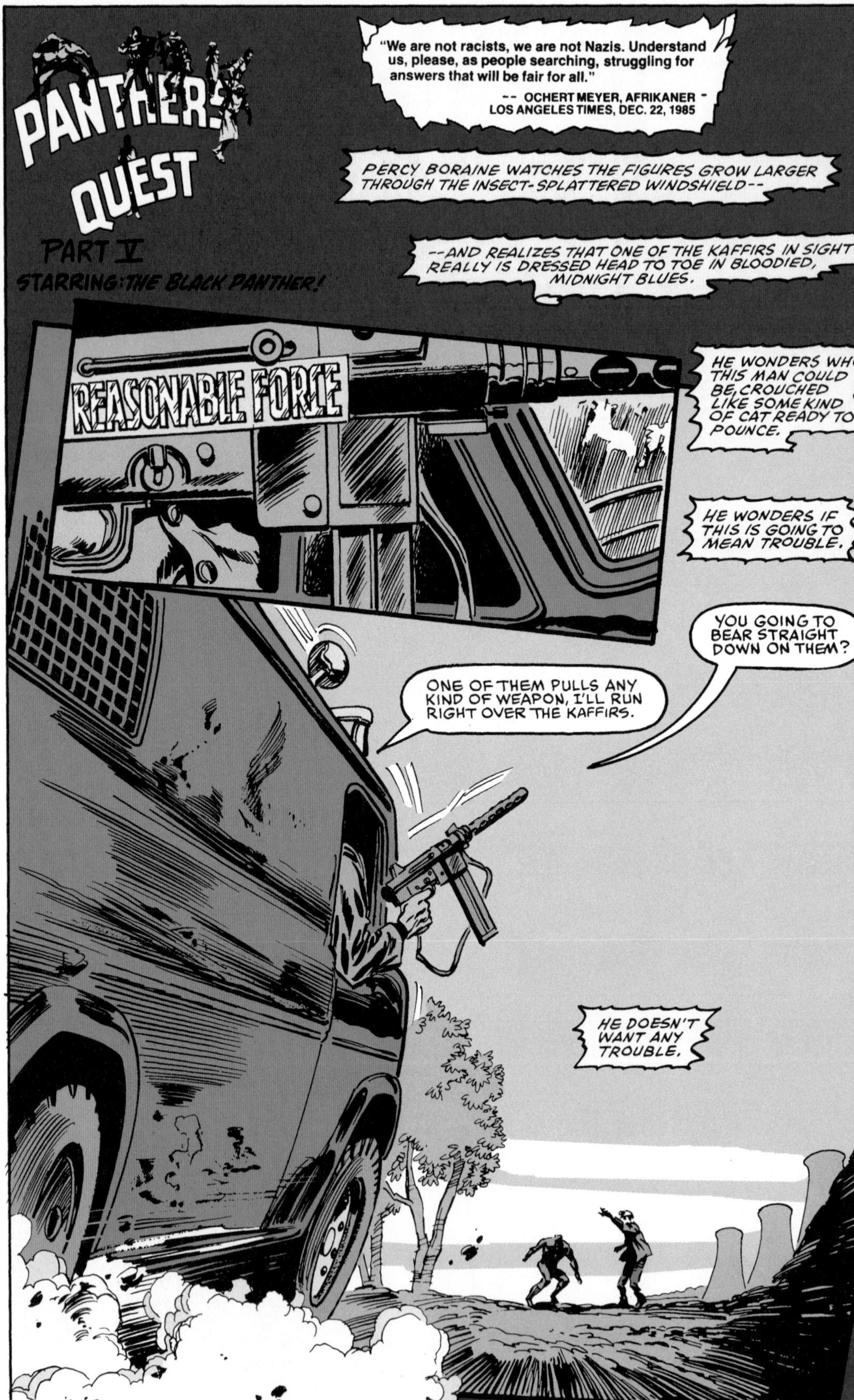
PANTHER'S QUEST
PART V
STARRING: THE BLACK PANTHER!
"We are not racists, we are not Nazis. Understand us, please, as people searching, struggling for answers that will be fair for all."
-- OCHERT MEYER, AFRIKANER - LOS ANGELES TIMES, DEC. 22, 1985
PERCY BORAINE WATCHES THE FIGURES GROW LARGER THROUGH THE INSECT-SPLATTERED WINDSHIELD--
--AND REALIZES THAT ONE OF THE KAFFIRS IN SIGHT REALLY IS DRESSED HEAD TO TOE IN BLOODIED, MIDNIGHT BLUES.
REASONABLE FORCE
HE WONDERS WHO THIS MAN COULD BE, CROUCHED LIKE SOME KIND OF CAT READY TO POUNCE.
HE WONDERS IF THIS IS GOING TO MEAN TROUBLE.
YOU GOING TO BEAR STRAIGHT DOWN ON THEM?
ONE OF THEM PULLS ANY KIND OF WEAPON, I'LL RUN RIGHT OVER THE KAFFIRS.
HE DOESN'T WANT ANY TROUBLE.

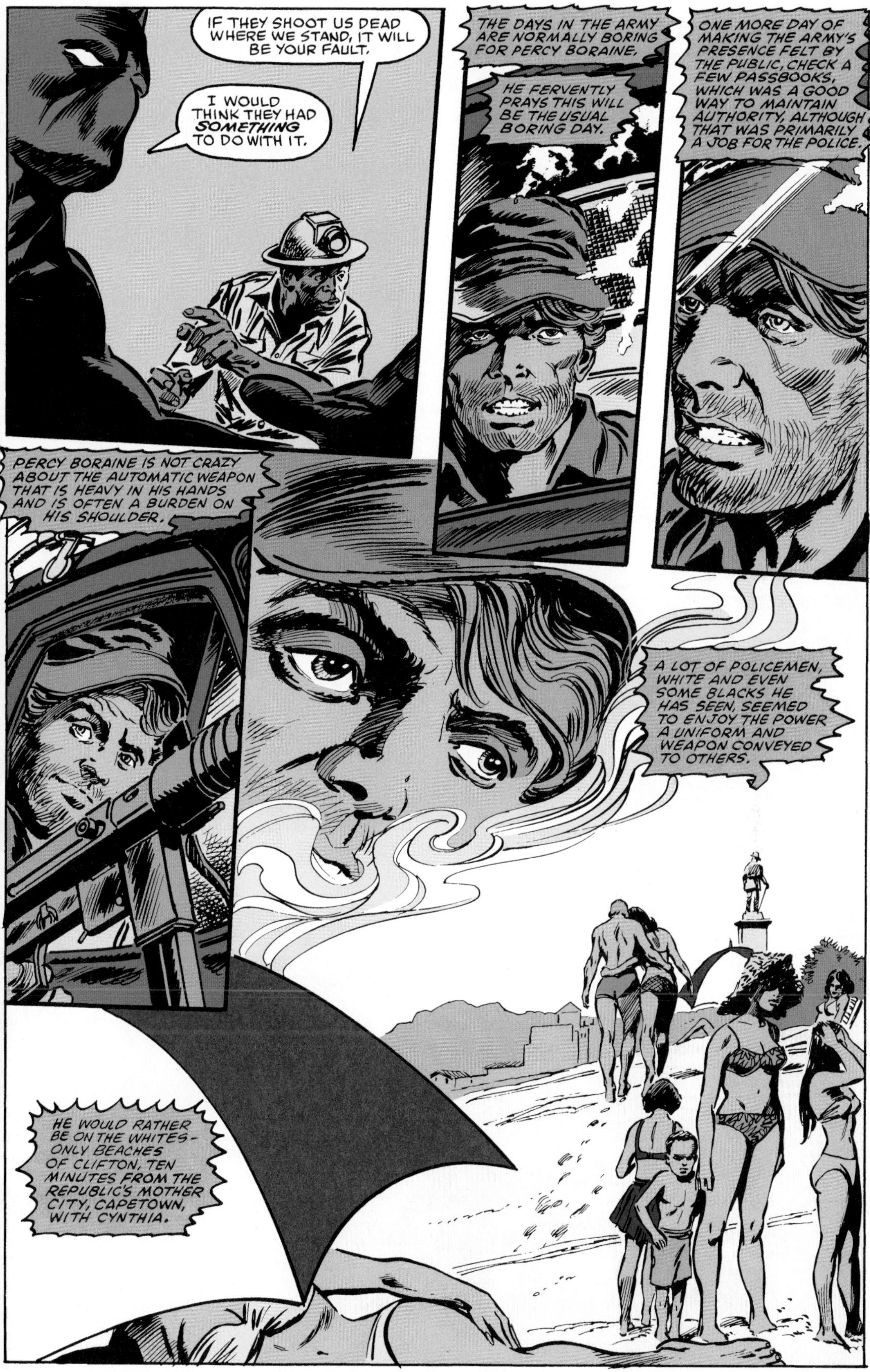
IF THEY SHOOT US DEAD WHERE WE STAND, IT WILL BE YOUR FAULT.
I WOULD THINK THEY HAD SOMETHING TO DO WITH IT.
THE DAYS IN THE ARMY ARE NORMALLY BORING FOR PERCY BORAINE.
HE FERVENTLY PRAYS THIS WILL BE THE USUAL BORING DAY.
ONE MORE DAY OF MAKING THE ARMY'S PRESENCE FELT BY THE PUBLIC, CHECK A FEW PASSBOOKS, WHICH WAS A GOOD WAY TO MAINTAIN AUTHORITY, ALTHOUGH THAT WAS PRIMARILY A JOB FOR THE POLICE.
PERCY BORAINE IS NOT CRAZY ABOUT THE AUTOMATIC WEAPON THAT IS HEAVY IN HIS HANDS AND IS OFTEN A BURDEN ON HIS SHOULDER.
A LOT OF POLICEMEN, WHITE AND EVEN SOME BLACKS HE HAS SEEN, SEEMED TO ENJOY THE POWER A UNIFORM AND WEAPON CONVEYED TO OTHERS.
HE WOULD RATHER BE ON THE WHITES-ONLY BEACHES OF CLIFTON, TEN MINUTES FROM THE REPUBLIC'S MOTHER CITY, CAPETOWN, WITH CYNTHIA.

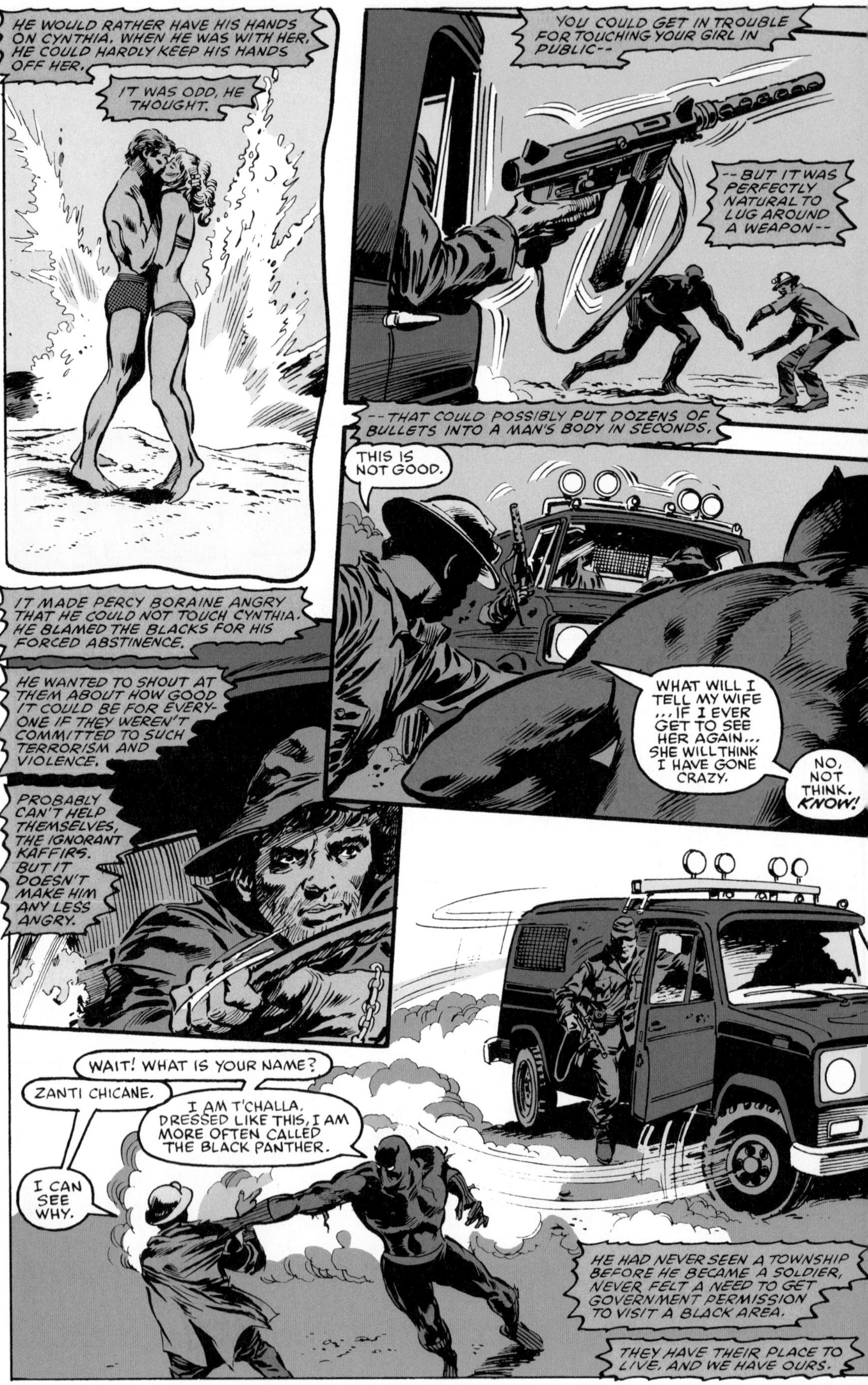
HE WOULD RATHER HAVE HIS HANDS ON CYNTHIA. WHEN HE WAS WITH HER, HE COULD HARDLY KEEP HIS HANDS OFF HER.
IT WAS ODD, HE THOUGHT.
YOU COULD GET IN TROUBLE FOR TOUCHING YOUR GIRL IN PUBLIC--
--BUT IT WAS PERFECTLY NATURAL TO LUG AROUND A WEAPON--
--THAT COULD POSSIBLY PUT DOZENS OF BULLETS INTO A MAN'S BODY IN SECONDS.
THIS IS NOT GOOD.
WHAT WILL I TELL MY WIFE ...IF I EVER GET TO SEE HER AGAIN... SHE WILL THINK I HAVE GONE CRAZY.
NO, NOT THINK. KNOW!
IT MADE PERCY BORAINE ANGRY THAT HE COULD NOT TOUCH CYNTHIA. HE BLAMED THE BLACKS FOR HIS FORCED ABSTINENCE.
HE WANTED TO SHOUT AT THEM ABOUT HOW GOOD IT COULD BE FOR EVERYONE IF THEY WEREN'T COMMITTED TO SUCH TERRORISM AND VIOLENCE.
PROBABLY CAN'T HELP THEMSELVES, THE IGNORANT KAFFIRS. BUT IT DOESN'T MAKE HIM ANY LESS ANGRY.
WAIT! WHAT IS YOUR NAME?
ZANTI CHICANE.
I AM T'CHALLA. DRESSED LIKE THIS, I AM MORE OFTEN CALLED THE BLACK PANTHER.
I CAN SEE WHY.
HE HAD NEVER SEEN A TOWNSHIP BEFORE HE BECAME A SOLDIER, NEVER FELT A NEED TO GET GOVERNMENT PERMISSION TO VISIT A BLACK AREA.
THEY HAVE THEIR PLACE TO LIVE, AND WE HAVE OURS.

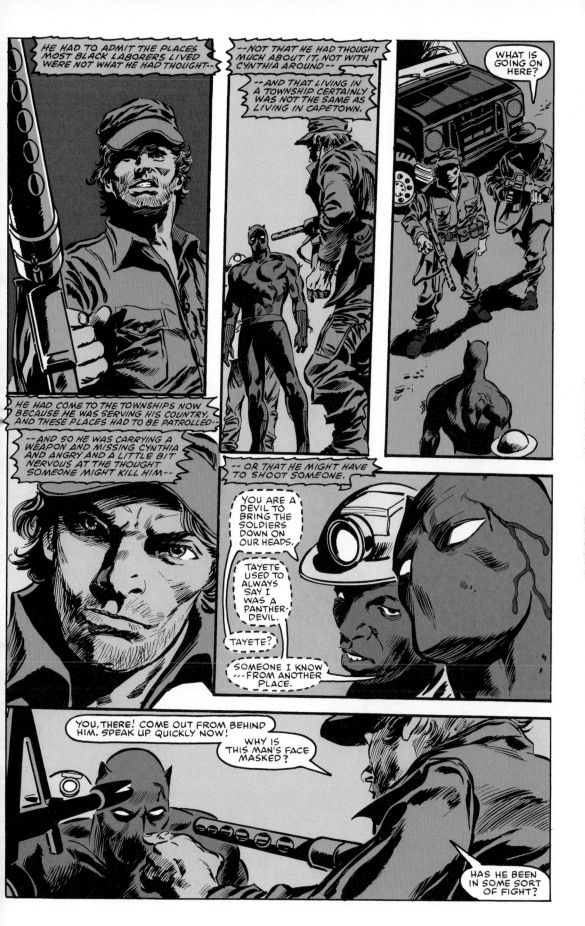

HE HAD TO ADMIT THE PLACES MOST BLACK LABORERS LIVED WERE NOT WHAT HE HAD THOUGHT--

--NOT THAT HE HAD THOUGHT MUCH ABOUT IT, NOT WITH CYNTHIA AROUND --

--AND THAT LIVING IN A TOWNSHIP CERTAINLY WAS NOT THE SAME AS LIVING IN CAPETOWN.

WHAT IS GOING ON HERE?

HE HAD COME TO THE TOWNSHIPS NOW BECAUSE HE WAS SERVING HIS COUNTRY, AND THESE PLACES HAD TO BE PATROLLED--

--AND SO HE WAS CARRYING A WEAPON AND MISSING CYNTHIA AND ANGRY AND A LITTLE BIT NERVOUS AT THE THOUGHT SOMEONE MIGHT KILL HIM--

-- OR THAT HE MIGHT HAVE TO SHOOT SOMEONE.

YOU ARE A DEVIL TO BRING THE SOLDIERS DOWN ON OUR HEADS.

TAYETE USED TO ALWAYS SAY I WAS A PANTHER-DEVIL.

TAYETE?

SOMEONE I KNOW ...FROM ANOTHER PLACE.

YOU, THERE! COME OUT FROM BEHIND HIM. SPEAK UP QUICKLY NOW!

WHY IS THIS MAN'S FACE MASKED?

HAS HE BEEN IN SOME SORT OF FIGHT?

43

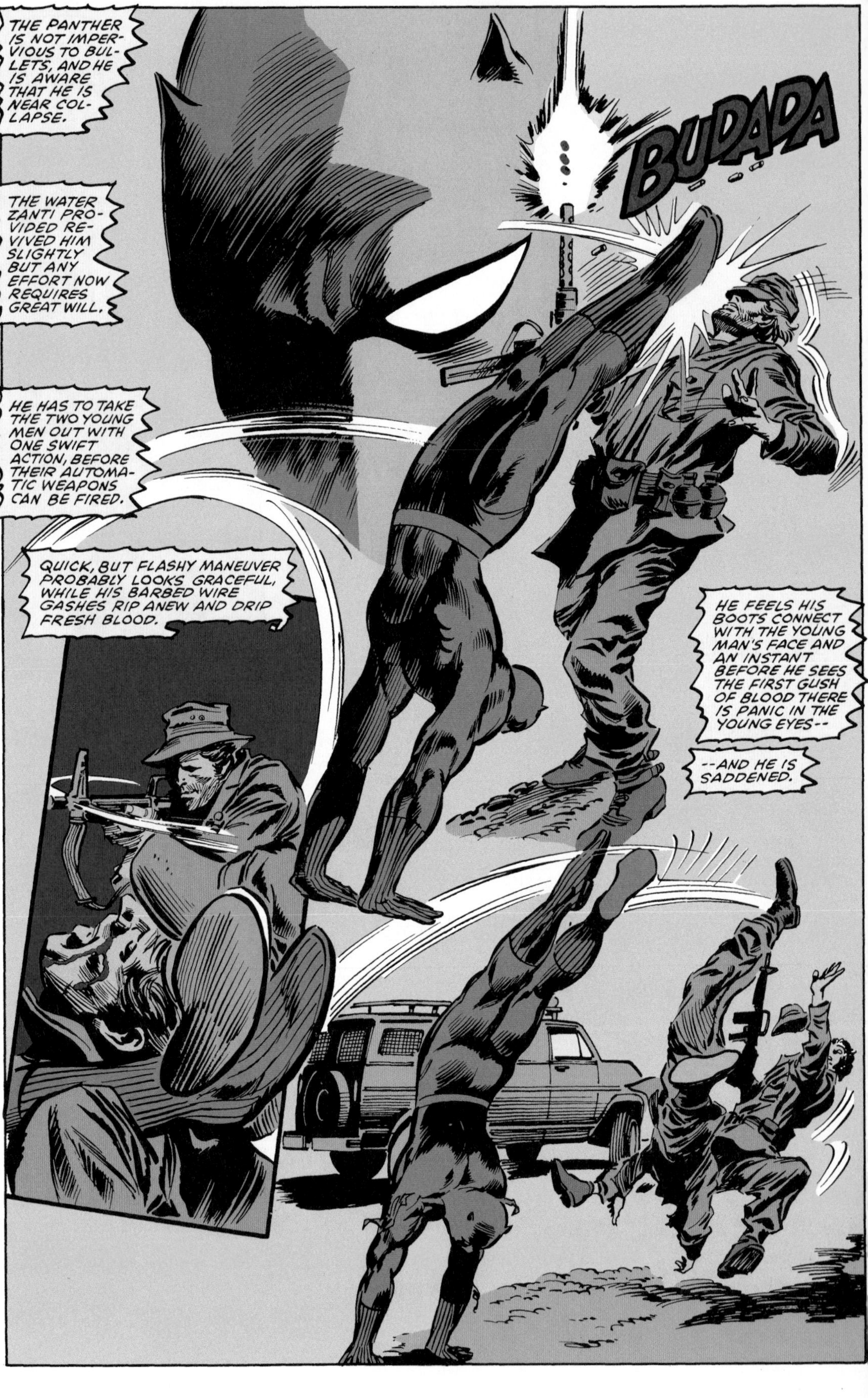
THE PANTHER IS NOT IMPERVIOUS TO BULLETS, AND HE IS AWARE THAT HE IS NEAR COLLAPSE.
BUDADA
THE WATER ZANTI PROVIDED REVIVED HIM SLIGHTLY BUT ANY EFFORT NOW REQUIRES GREAT WILL.
HE HAS TO TAKE THE TWO YOUNG MEN OUT WITH ONE SWIFT ACTION, BEFORE THEIR AUTOMATIC WEAPONS CAN BE FIRED.
QUICK, BUT FLASHY MANEUVER PROBABLY LOOKS GRACEFUL, WHILE HIS BARBED WIRE GASHES RIP ANEW AND DRIP FRESH BLOOD.
HE FEELS HIS BOOTS CONNECT WITH THE YOUNG MAN'S FACE AND AN INSTANT BEFORE HE SEES THE FIRST GUSH OF BLOOD THERE IS PANIC IN THE YOUNG EYES--
--AND HE IS SADDENED.

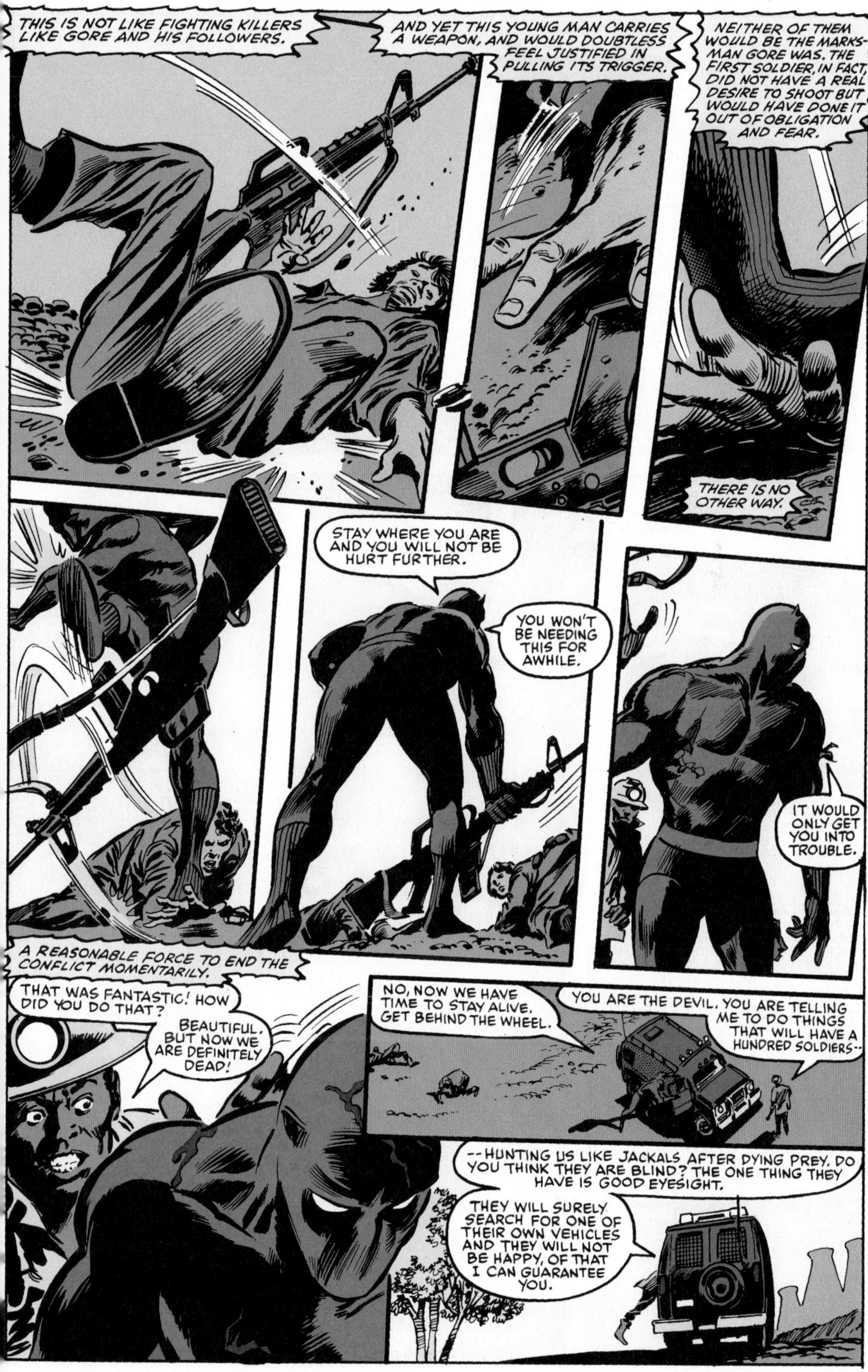
THIS IS NOT LIKE FIGHTING KILLERS LIKE GORE AND HIS FOLLOWERS.
AND YET THIS YOUNG MAN CARRIES A WEAPON, AND WOULD DOUBTLESS FEEL JUSTIFIED IN PULLING ITS TRIGGER.
NEITHER OF THEM WOULD BE THE MARKSMAN GORE WAS. THE FIRST SOLDIER, IN FACT, DID NOT HAVE A REAL DESIRE TO SHOOT BUT WOULD HAVE DONE IT OUT OF OBLIGATION AND FEAR.
THERE IS NO OTHER WAY.
STAY WHERE YOU ARE AND YOU WILL NOT BE HURT FURTHER.
YOU WON'T BE NEEDING THIS FOR AWHILE.
IT WOULD ONLY GET YOU INTO TROUBLE.
A REASONABLE FORCE TO END THE CONFLICT MOMENTARILY.
THAT WAS FANTASTIC! HOW DID YOU DO THAT?
BEAUTIFUL. BUT NOW WE ARE DEFINITELY DEAD!
NO, NOW WE HAVE TIME TO STAY ALIVE. GET BEHIND THE WHEEL.
YOU ARE THE DEVIL. YOU ARE TELLING ME TO DO THINGS THAT WILL HAVE A HUNDRED SOLDIERS--
--HUNTING US LIKE JACKALS AFTER DYING PREY. DO YOU THINK THEY ARE BLIND? THE ONE THING THEY HAVE IS GOOD EYESIGHT.
THEY WILL SURELY SEARCH FOR ONE OF THEIR OWN VEHICLES AND THEY WILL NOT BE HAPPY, OF THAT I CAN GUARANTEE YOU.

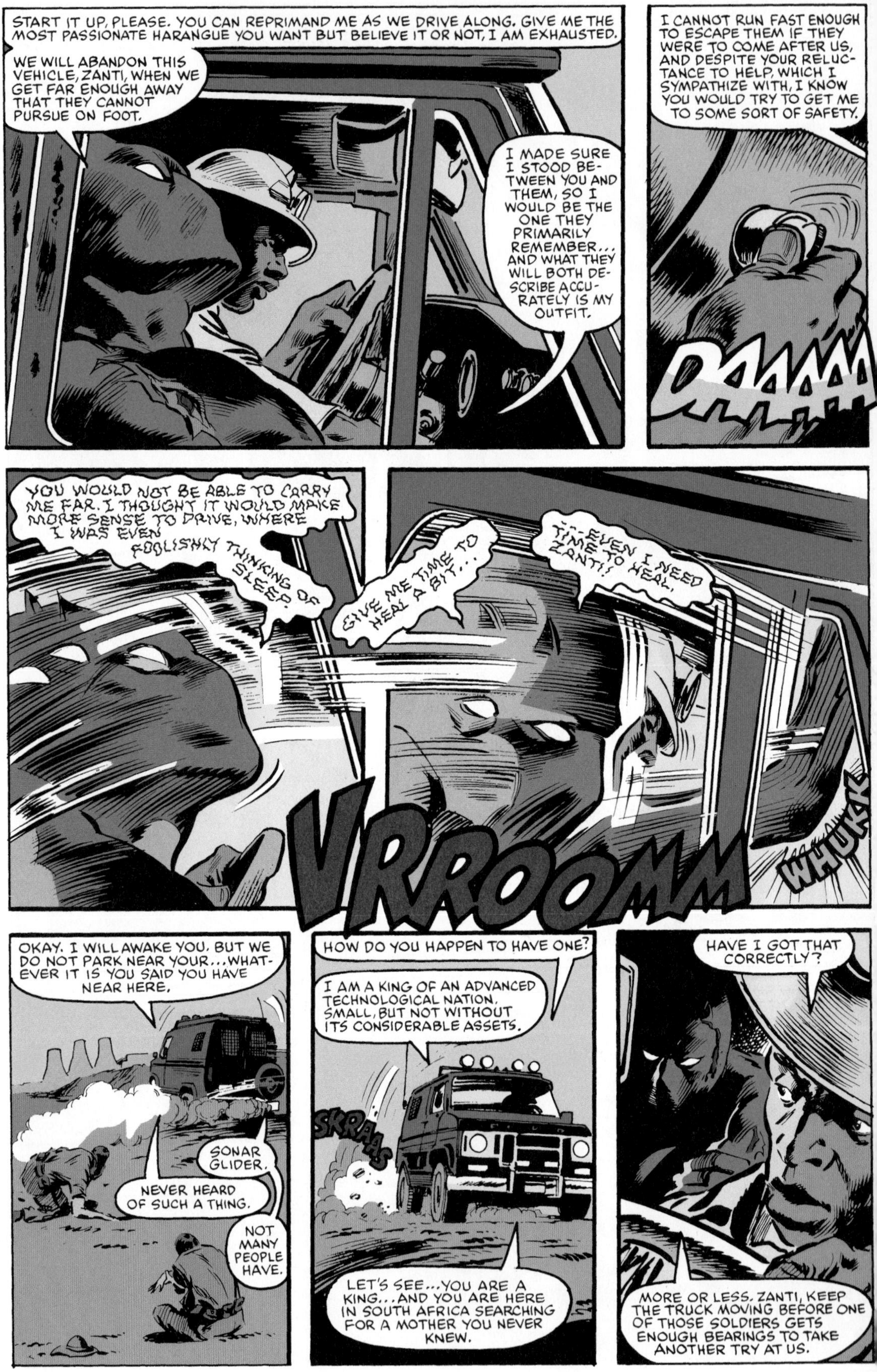
START IT UP, PLEASE. YOU CAN REPRIMAND ME AS WE DRIVE ALONG. GIVE ME THE MOST PASSIONATE HARANGUE YOU WANT BUT BELIEVE IT OR NOT, I AM EXHAUSTED.
WE WILL ABANDON THIS VEHICLE, ZANTI, WHEN WE GET FAR ENOUGH AWAY THAT THEY CANNOT PURSUE ON FOOT.
I MADE SURE I STOOD BETWEEN YOU AND THEM, SO I WOULD BE THE ONE THEY PRIMARILY REMEMBER... AND WHAT THEY WILL BOTH DESCRIBE ACCURATELY IS MY OUTFIT.
I CANNOT RUN FAST ENOUGH TO ESCAPE THEM IF THEY WERE TO COME AFTER US, AND DESPITE YOUR RELUCTANCE TO HELP, WHICH I SYMPATHIZE WITH, I KNOW YOU WOULD TRY TO GET ME TO SOME SORT OF SAFETY.
DAAAAA
YOU WOULD NOT BE ABLE TO CARRY ME FAR. I THOUGHT IT WOULD MAKE MORE SENSE TO DRIVE, WHERE I WAS EVEN FOOLISHLY THINKING OF SLEEP.
GIVE ME TIME TO HEAL A BIT...
...EVEN I NEED TIME TO HEAL, ZANTI!
VRROOMM
WHUKK
OKAY. I WILL AWAKE YOU. BUT WE DO NOT PARK NEAR YOUR... WHATEVER IT IS YOU SAID YOU HAVE NEAR HERE.
SONAR GLIDER.
NEVER HEARD OF SUCH A THING.
NOT MANY PEOPLE HAVE.
HOW DO YOU HAPPEN TO HAVE ONE?
I AM A KING OF AN ADVANCED TECHNOLOGICAL NATION. SMALL, BUT NOT WITHOUT ITS CONSIDERABLE ASSETS.
SKRAAS
LET'S SEE... YOU ARE A KING... AND YOU ARE HERE IN SOUTH AFRICA SEARCHING FOR A MOTHER YOU NEVER KNEW.
HAVE I GOT THAT CORRECTLY?
MORE OR LESS. ZANTI, KEEP THE TRUCK MOVING BEFORE ONE OF THOSE SOLDIERS GETS ENOUGH BEARINGS TO TAKE ANOTHER TRY AT US.

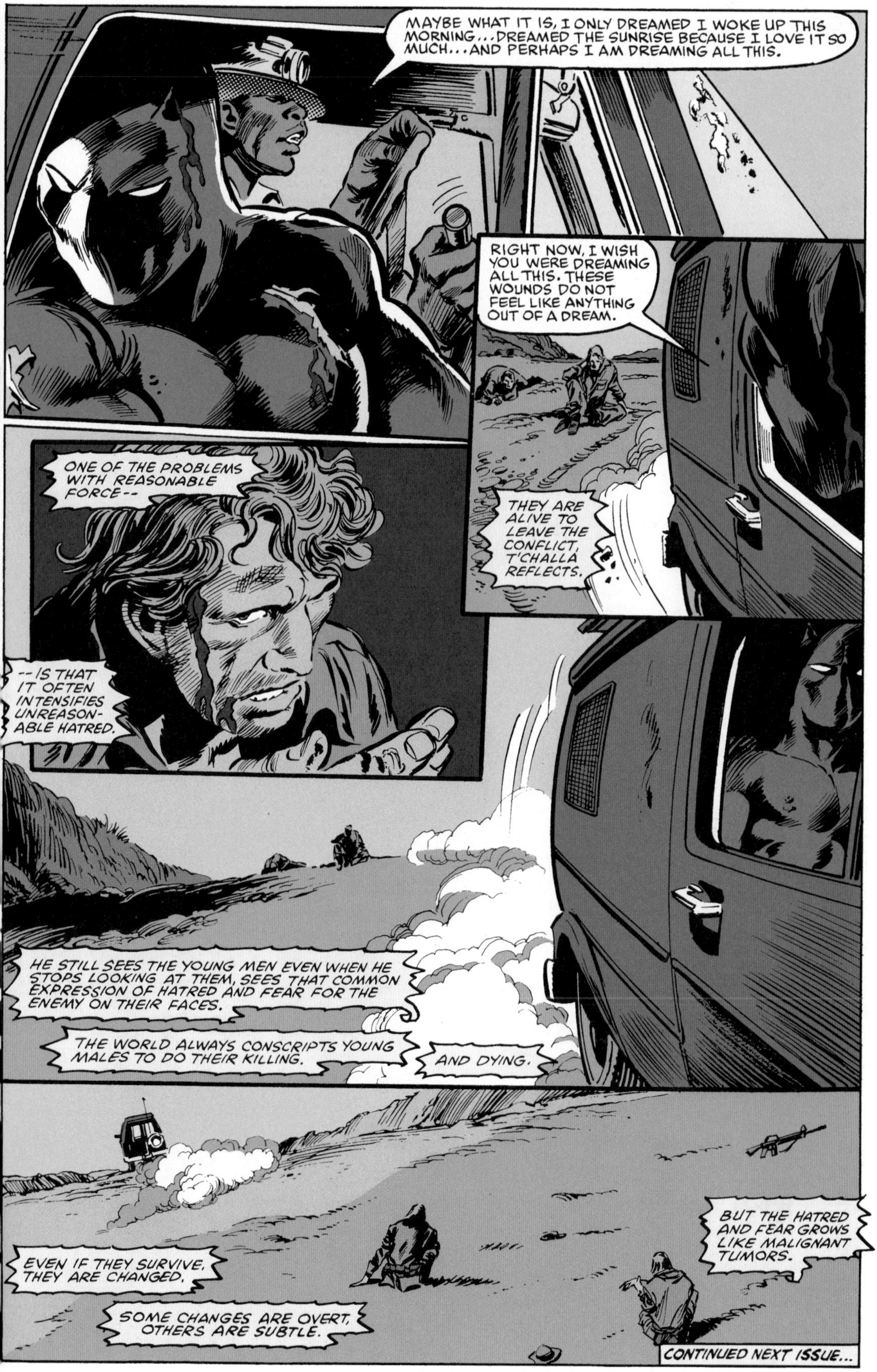
MAYBE WHAT IT IS, I ONLY DREAMED I WOKE UP THIS MORNING... DREAMED THE SUNRISE BECAUSE I LOVE IT SO MUCH... AND PERHAPS I AM DREAMING ALL THIS.
RIGHT NOW, I WISH YOU WERE DREAMING ALL THIS. THESE WOUNDS DO NOT FEEL LIKE ANYTHING OUT OF A DREAM.
THEY ARE ALIVE TO LEAVE THE CONFLICT, T'CHALLA REFLECTS.
ONE OF THE PROBLEMS WITH REASONABLE FORCE--
--IS THAT IT OFTEN INTENSIFIES UNREASON-ABLE HATRED.
HE STILL SEES THE YOUNG MEN EVEN WHEN HE STOPS LOOKING AT THEM, SEES THAT COMMON EXPRESSION OF HATRED AND FEAR FOR THE ENEMY ON THEIR FACES.
THE WORLD ALWAYS CONSCRIPTS YOUNG MALES TO DO THEIR KILLING.
AND DYING.
EVEN IF THEY SURVIVE, THEY ARE CHANGED.
SOME CHANGES ARE OVERT, OTHERS ARE SUBTLE.
BUT THE HATRED AND FEAR GROWS LIKE MALIGNANT TUMORS.
CONTINUED NEXT ISSUE...

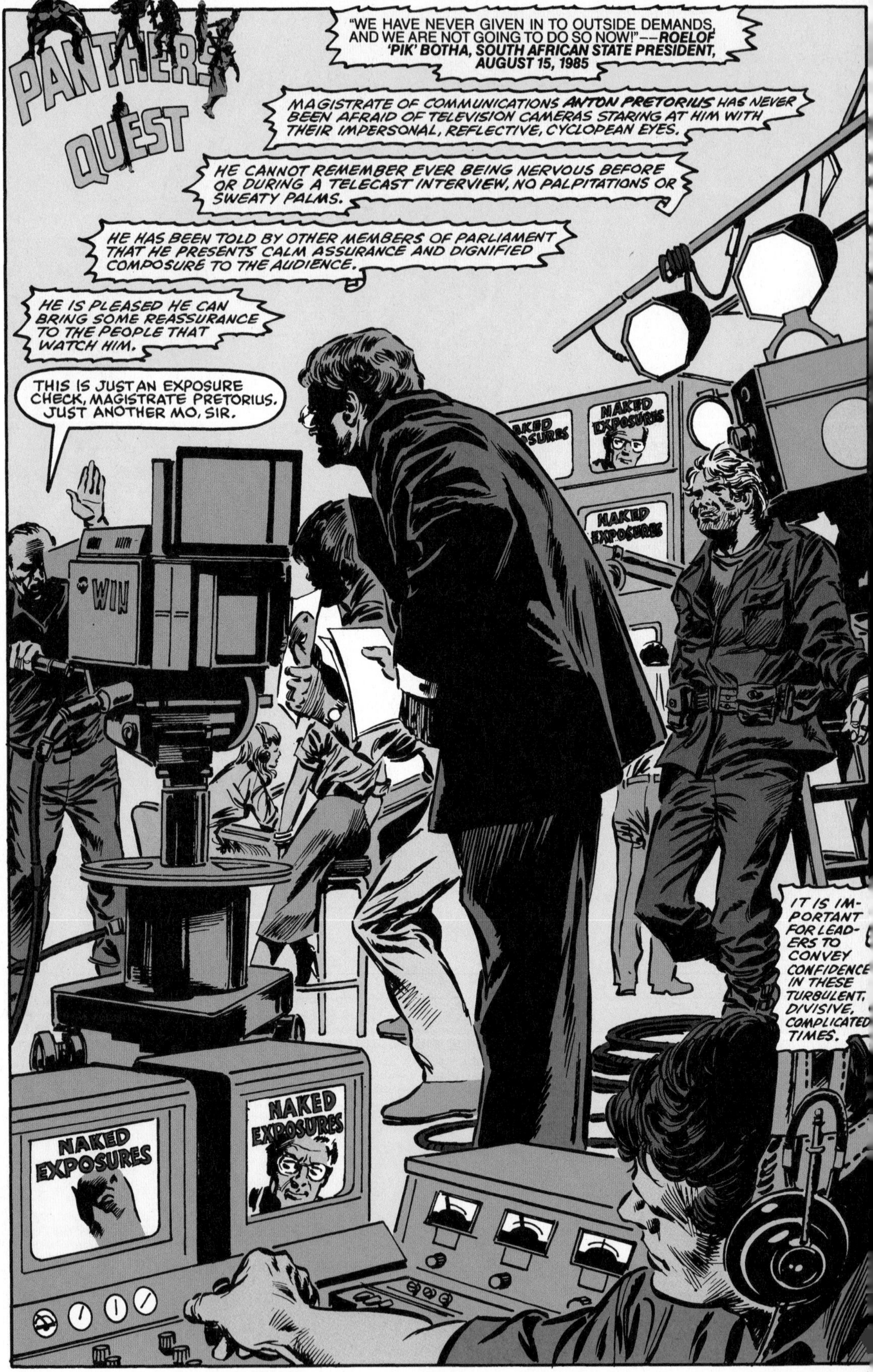
PANTHER'S QUEST
"WE HAVE NEVER GIVEN IN TO OUTSIDE DEMANDS, AND WE ARE NOT GOING TO DO SO NOW!"--ROELOF 'PIK' BOTHA, SOUTH AFRICAN STATE PRESIDENT, AUGUST 15, 1985
MAGISTRATE OF COMMUNICATIONS ANTON PRETORIUS HAS NEVER BEEN AFRAID OF TELEVISION CAMERAS STARING AT HIM WITH THEIR IMPERSONAL, REFLECTIVE, CYCLOPEAN EYES.
HE CANNOT REMEMBER EVER BEING NERVOUS BEFORE OR DURING A TELECAST INTERVIEW, NO PALPITATIONS OR SWEATY PALMS.
HE HAS BEEN TOLD BY OTHER MEMBERS OF PARLIAMENT THAT HE PRESENTS CALM ASSURANCE AND DIGNIFIED COMPOSURE TO THE AUDIENCE.
HE IS PLEASED HE CAN BRING SOME REASSURANCE TO THE PEOPLE THAT WATCH HIM.
THIS IS JUST AN EXPOSURE CHECK, MAGISTRATE PRETORIUS. JUST ANOTHER MO, SIR.
NAKED EXPOSURES
WIN
IT IS IMPORTANT FOR LEADERS TO CONVEY CONFIDENCE IN THESE TURBULENT, DIVISIVE, COMPLICATED TIMES.
NAKED EXPOSURES
NAKED EXPOSURES

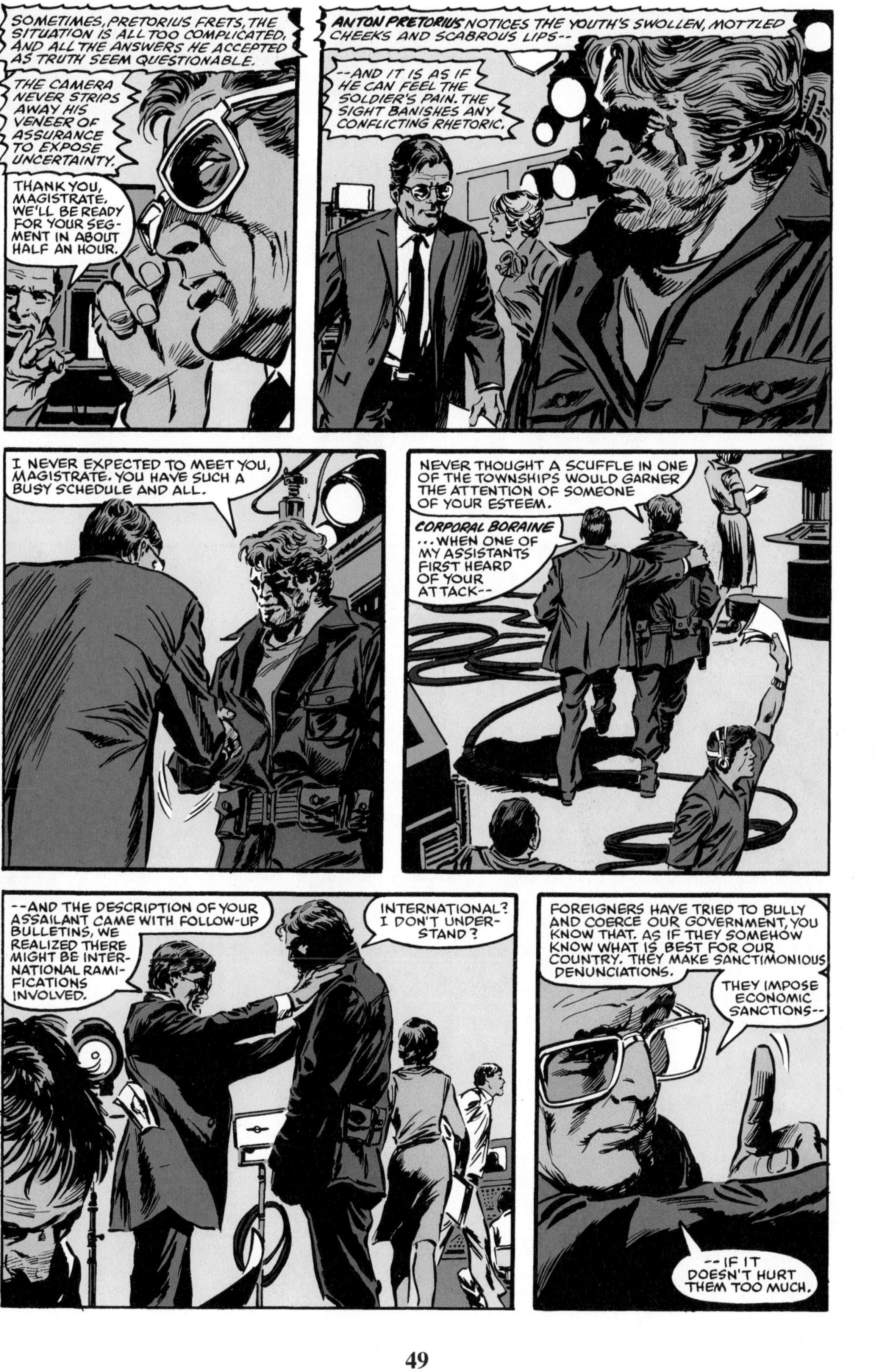
SOMETIMES, PRETORIUS FRETS, THE SITUATION IS ALL TOO COMPLICATED, AND ALL THE ANSWERS HE ACCEPTED AS TRUTH SEEM QUESTIONABLE.
THE CAMERA NEVER STRIPS AWAY HIS VENEER OF ASSURANCE TO EXPOSE UNCERTAINTY.
THANK YOU, MAGISTRATE. WE'LL BE READY FOR YOUR SEGMENT IN ABOUT HALF AN HOUR.
ANTON PRETORIUS NOTICES THE YOUTH'S SWOLLEN, MOTTLED CHEEKS AND SCABROUS LIPS--
--AND IT IS AS IF HE CAN FEEL THE SOLDIER'S PAIN. THE SIGHT BANISHES ANY CONFLICTING RHETORIC.
I NEVER EXPECTED TO MEET YOU, MAGISTRATE. YOU HAVE SUCH A BUSY SCHEDULE AND ALL.
NEVER THOUGHT A SCUFFLE IN ONE OF THE TOWNSHIPS WOULD GARNER THE ATTENTION OF SOMEONE OF YOUR ESTEEM.
CORPORAL BORAINE ... WHEN ONE OF MY ASSISTANTS FIRST HEARD OF YOUR ATTACK--
--AND THE DESCRIPTION OF YOUR ASSAILANT CAME WITH FOLLOW-UP BULLETINS, WE REALIZED THERE MIGHT BE INTERNATIONAL RAMIFICATIONS INVOLVED.
INTERNATIONAL? I DON'T UNDERSTAND?
FOREIGNERS HAVE TRIED TO BULLY AND COERCE OUR GOVERNMENT, YOU KNOW THAT. AS IF THEY SOMEHOW KNOW WHAT IS BEST FOR OUR COUNTRY. THEY MAKE SANCTIMONIOUS DENUNCIATIONS.
THEY IMPOSE ECONOMIC SANCTIONS--
--IF IT DOESN'T HURT THEM TOO MUCH.

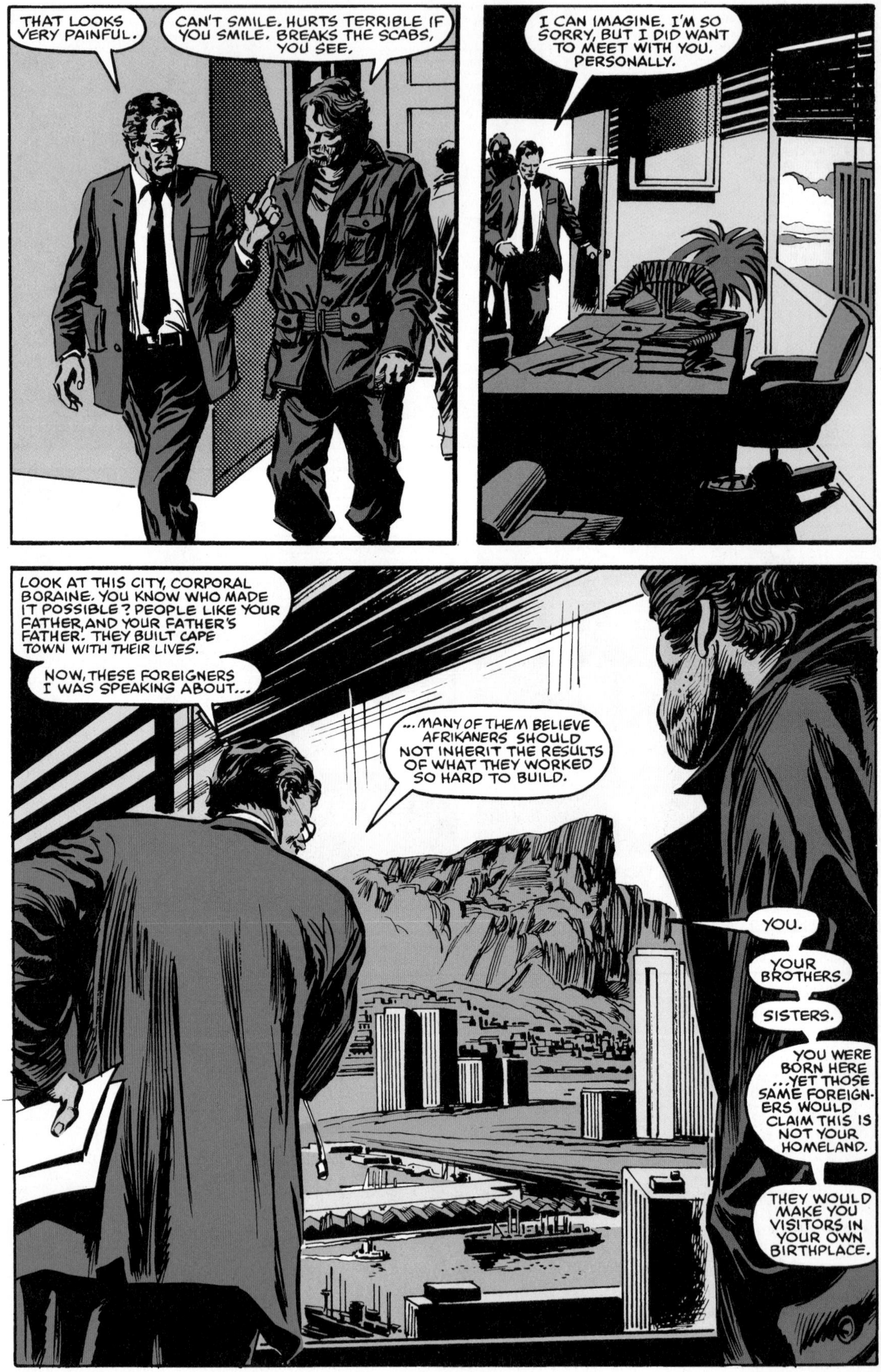
THAT LOOKS VERY PAINFUL.
CAN'T SMILE. HURTS TERRIBLE IF YOU SMILE. BREAKS THE SCABS, YOU SEE.
I CAN IMAGINE. I'M SO SORRY, BUT I DID WANT TO MEET WITH YOU, PERSONALLY.
LOOK AT THIS CITY, CORPORAL BORAINE. YOU KNOW WHO MADE IT POSSIBLE? PEOPLE LIKE YOUR FATHER, AND YOUR FATHER'S FATHER. THEY BUILT CAPE TOWN WITH THEIR LIVES.
NOW, THESE FOREIGNERS I WAS SPEAKING ABOUT...
...MANY OF THEM BELIEVE AFRIKANERS SHOULD NOT INHERIT THE RESULTS OF WHAT THEY WORKED SO HARD TO BUILD.
YOU.
YOUR BROTHERS.
SISTERS.
YOU WERE BORN HERE ...YET THOSE SAME FOREIGN-ERS WOULD CLAIM THIS IS NOT YOUR HOMELAND.
THEY WOULD MAKE YOU VISITORS IN YOUR OWN BIRTHPLACE.

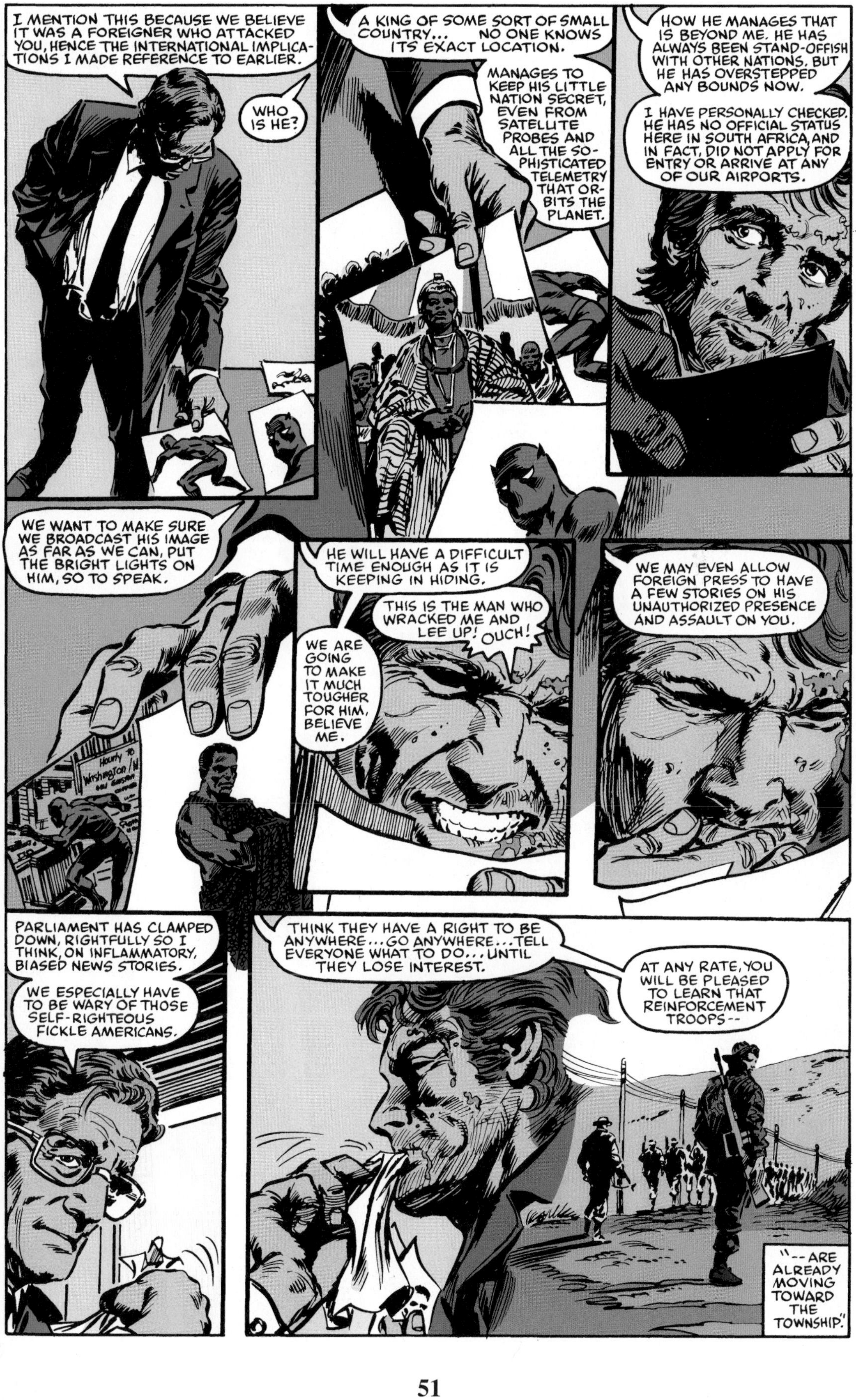
I MENTION THIS BECAUSE WE BELIEVE IT WAS A FOREIGNER WHO ATTACKED YOU, HENCE THE INTERNATIONAL IMPLICATIONS I MADE REFERENCE TO EARLIER.
WHO IS HE?
A KING OF SOME SORT OF SMALL COUNTRY... NO ONE KNOWS ITS EXACT LOCATION.
MANAGES TO KEEP HIS LITTLE NATION SECRET, EVEN FROM SATELLITE PROBES AND ALL THE SOPHISTICATED TELEMETRY THAT ORBITS THE PLANET.
HOW HE MANAGES THAT IS BEYOND ME. HE HAS ALWAYS BEEN STAND-OFFISH WITH OTHER NATIONS. BUT HE HAS OVERSTEPPED ANY BOUNDS NOW.
I HAVE PERSONALLY CHECKED. HE HAS NO OFFICIAL STATUS HERE IN SOUTH AFRICA, AND IN FACT, DID NOT APPLY FOR ENTRY OR ARRIVE AT ANY OF OUR AIRPORTS.
WE WANT TO MAKE SURE WE BROADCAST HIS IMAGE AS FAR AS WE CAN, PUT THE BRIGHT LIGHTS ON HIM, SO TO SPEAK.
HE WILL HAVE A DIFFICULT TIME ENOUGH AS IT IS KEEPING IN HIDING.
THIS IS THE MAN WHO WRACKED ME AND LEE UP!
OUCH!
WE ARE GOING TO MAKE IT MUCH TOUGHER FOR HIM, BELIEVE ME.
WE MAY EVEN ALLOW FOREIGN PRESS TO HAVE A FEW STORIES ON HIS UNAUTHORIZED PRESENCE AND ASSAULT ON YOU.
PARLIAMENT HAS CLAMPED DOWN, RIGHTFULLY SO I THINK, ON INFLAMMATORY, BIASED NEWS STORIES.
WE ESPECIALLY HAVE TO BE WARY OF THOSE SELF-RIGHTEOUS FICKLE AMERICANS.
THINK THEY HAVE A RIGHT TO BE ANYWHERE...GO ANYWHERE...TELL EVERYONE WHAT TO DO... UNTIL THEY LOSE INTEREST.
AT ANY RATE, YOU WILL BE PLEASED TO LEARN THAT REINFORCEMENT TROOPS--
"--ARE ALREADY MOVING TOWARD THE TOWNSHIP."

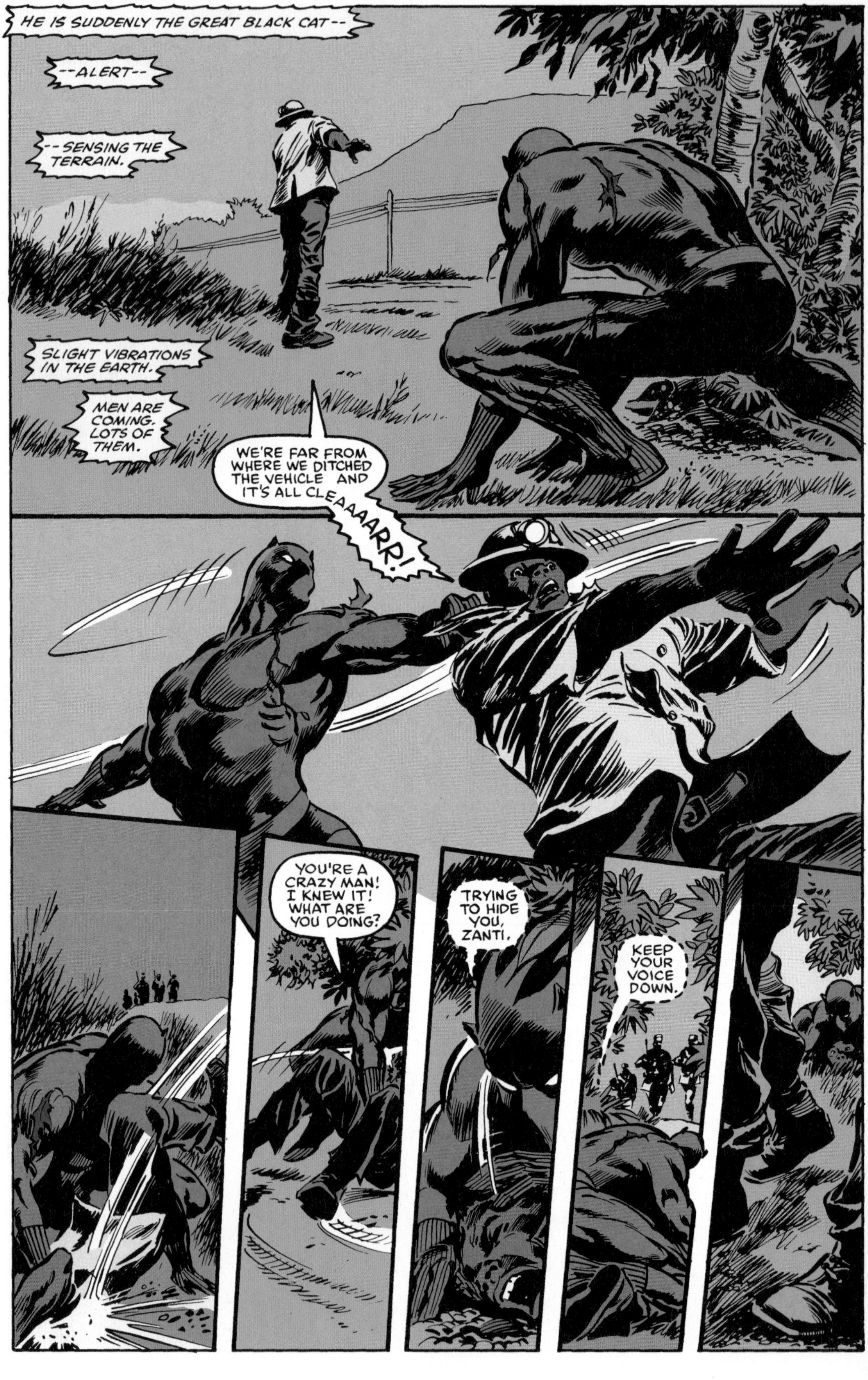
HE IS SUDDENLY THE GREAT BLACK CAT--
--ALERT--
--SENSING THE TERRAIN.
SLIGHT VIBRATIONS IN THE EARTH.
MEN ARE COMING. LOTS OF THEM.
WE'RE FAR FROM WHERE WE DITCHED THE VEHICLE AND IT'S ALL CLEAAAAARR!
YOU'RE A CRAZY MAN! I KNEW IT! WHAT ARE YOU DOING?
TRYING TO HIDE YOU, ZANTI.
KEEP YOUR VOICE DOWN.

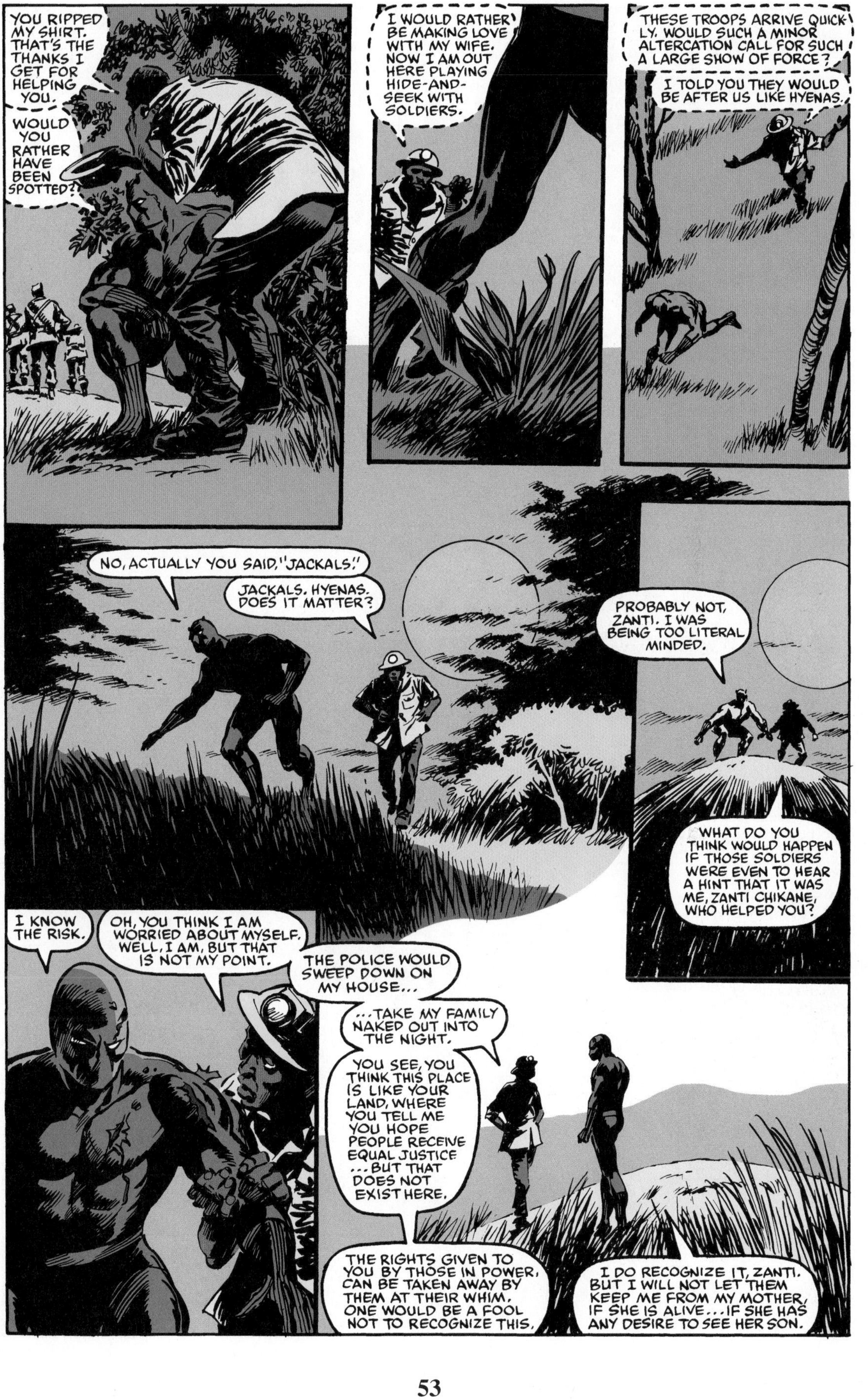
YOU RIPPED MY SHIRT. THAT'S THE THANKS I GET FOR HELPING YOU.
WOULD YOU RATHER HAVE BEEN SPOTTED?
I WOULD RATHER BE MAKING LOVE WITH MY WIFE. NOW I AM OUT HERE PLAYING HIDE-AND-SEEK WITH SOLDIERS.
THESE TROOPS ARRIVE QUICKLY. WOULD SUCH A MINOR ALTERCATION CALL FOR SUCH A LARGE SHOW OF FORCE?
I TOLD YOU THEY WOULD BE AFTER US LIKE HYENAS.
NO, ACTUALLY YOU SAID, "JACKALS."
JACKALS. HYENAS. DOES IT MATTER?
PROBABLY NOT, ZANTI. I WAS BEING TOO LITERAL MINDED.
WHAT DO YOU THINK WOULD HAPPEN IF THOSE SOLDIERS WERE EVEN TO HEAR A HINT THAT IT WAS ME, ZANTI CHIKANE, WHO HELPED YOU?
I KNOW THE RISK.
OH, YOU THINK I AM WORRIED ABOUT MYSELF. WELL, I AM, BUT THAT IS NOT MY POINT.
THE POLICE WOULD SWEEP DOWN ON MY HOUSE...
...TAKE MY FAMILY NAKED OUT INTO THE NIGHT.
YOU SEE, YOU THINK THIS PLACE IS LIKE YOUR LAND, WHERE YOU TELL ME YOU HOPE PEOPLE RECEIVE EQUAL JUSTICE ...BUT THAT DOES NOT EXIST HERE.
THE RIGHTS GIVEN TO YOU BY THOSE IN POWER, CAN BE TAKEN AWAY BY THEM AT THEIR WHIM. ONE WOULD BE A FOOL NOT TO RECOGNIZE THIS.
I DO RECOGNIZE IT, ZANTI. BUT I WILL NOT LET THEM KEEP ME FROM MY MOTHER, IF SHE IS ALIVE... IF SHE HAS ANY DESIRE TO SEE HER SON.

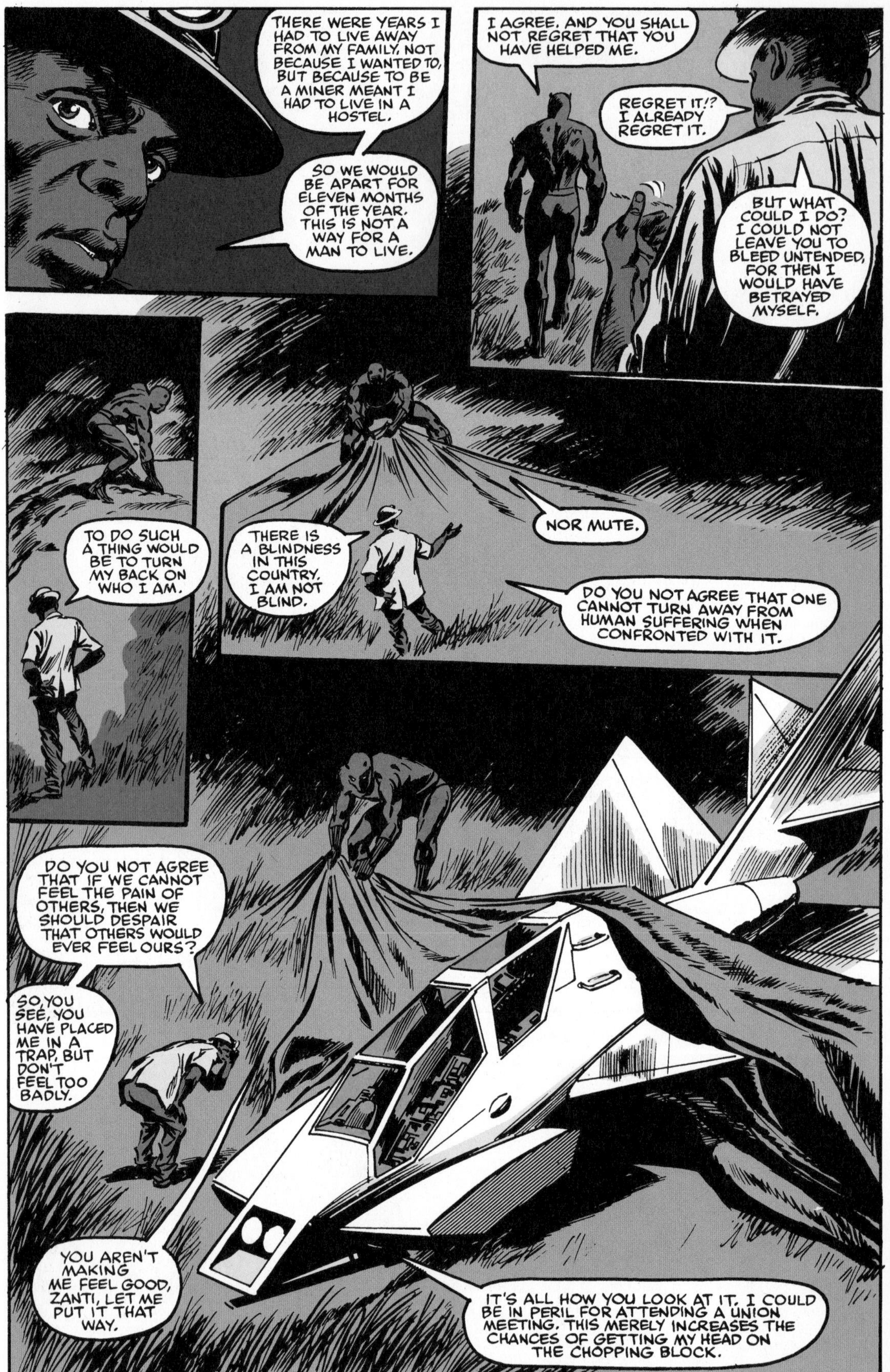
THERE WERE YEARS I HAD TO LIVE AWAY FROM MY FAMILY, NOT BECAUSE I WANTED TO, BUT BECAUSE TO BE A MINER MEANT I HAD TO LIVE IN A HOSTEL.
SO WE WOULD BE APART FOR ELEVEN MONTHS OF THE YEAR. THIS IS NOT A WAY FOR A MAN TO LIVE.
I AGREE. AND YOU SHALL NOT REGRET THAT YOU HAVE HELPED ME.
REGRET IT!? I ALREADY REGRET IT.
BUT WHAT COULD I DO? I COULD NOT LEAVE YOU TO BLEED UNTENDED, FOR THEN I WOULD HAVE BETRAYED MYSELF.
TO DO SUCH A THING WOULD BE TO TURN MY BACK ON WHO I AM.
THERE IS A BLINDNESS IN THIS COUNTRY. I AM NOT BLIND.
NOR MUTE.
DO YOU NOT AGREE THAT ONE CANNOT TURN AWAY FROM HUMAN SUFFERING WHEN CONFRONTED WITH IT.
DO YOU NOT AGREE THAT IF WE CANNOT FEEL THE PAIN OF OTHERS, THEN WE SHOULD DESPAIR THAT OTHERS WOULD EVER FEEL OURS?
SO, YOU SEE, YOU HAVE PLACED ME IN A TRAP, BUT DON'T FEEL TOO BADLY.
YOU AREN'T MAKING ME FEEL GOOD, ZANTI, LET ME PUT IT THAT WAY.
IT'S ALL HOW YOU LOOK AT IT. I COULD BE IN PERIL FOR ATTENDING A UNION MEETING. THIS MERELY INCREASES THE CHANCES OF GETTING MY HEAD ON THE CHOPPING BLOCK.

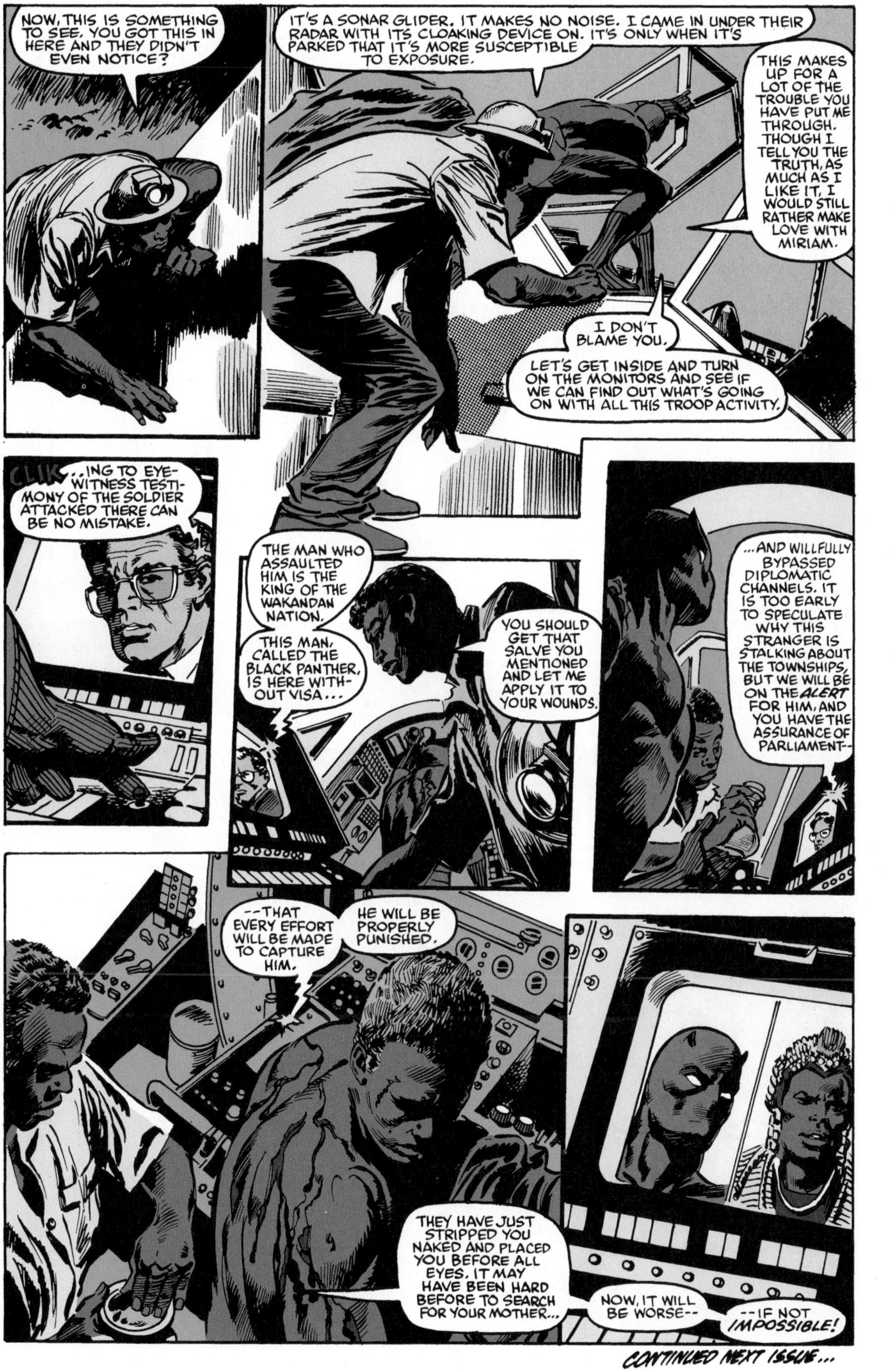
NOW, THIS IS SOMETHING TO SEE. YOU GOT THIS IN HERE AND THEY DIDN'T EVEN NOTICE?
IT'S A SONAR GLIDER. IT MAKES NO NOISE. I CAME IN UNDER THEIR RADAR WITH ITS CLOAKING DEVICE ON. IT'S ONLY WHEN IT'S PARKED THAT IT'S MORE SUSCEPTIBLE TO EXPOSURE.
THIS MAKES UP FOR A LOT OF THE TROUBLE YOU HAVE PUT ME THROUGH. THOUGH I TELL YOU THE TRUTH, AS MUCH AS I LIKE IT, I WOULD STILL RATHER MAKE LOVE WITH MIRIAM.
I DON'T BLAME YOU.
LET'S GET INSIDE AND TURN ON THE MONITORS AND SEE IF WE CAN FIND OUT WHAT'S GOING ON WITH ALL THIS TROOP ACTIVITY.
CLIK
..ING TO EYE-WITNESS TESTI-MONY OF THE SOLDIER ATTACKED THERE CAN BE NO MISTAKE.
THE MAN WHO ASSAULTED HIM IS THE KING OF THE WAKANDAN NATION.
THIS MAN, CALLED THE BLACK PANTHER, IS HERE WITH-OUT VISA...
YOU SHOULD GET THAT SALVE YOU MENTIONED AND LET ME APPLY IT TO YOUR WOUNDS.
...AND WILLFULLY BYPASSED DIPLOMATIC CHANNELS. IT IS TOO EARLY TO SPECULATE WHY THIS STRANGER IS STALKING ABOUT THE TOWNSHIPS, BUT WE WILL BE ON THE ALERT FOR HIM, AND YOU HAVE THE ASSURANCE OF PARLIAMENT--
--THAT EVERY EFFORT WILL BE MADE TO CAPTURE HIM.
HE WILL BE PROPERLY PUNISHED.
THEY HAVE JUST STRIPPED YOU NAKED AND PLACED YOU BEFORE ALL EYES. IT MAY HAVE BEEN HARD BEFORE TO SEARCH FOR YOUR MOTHER...
NOW, IT WILL BE WORSE--
--IF NOT IMPOSSIBLE!
CONTINUED NEXT ISSUE...

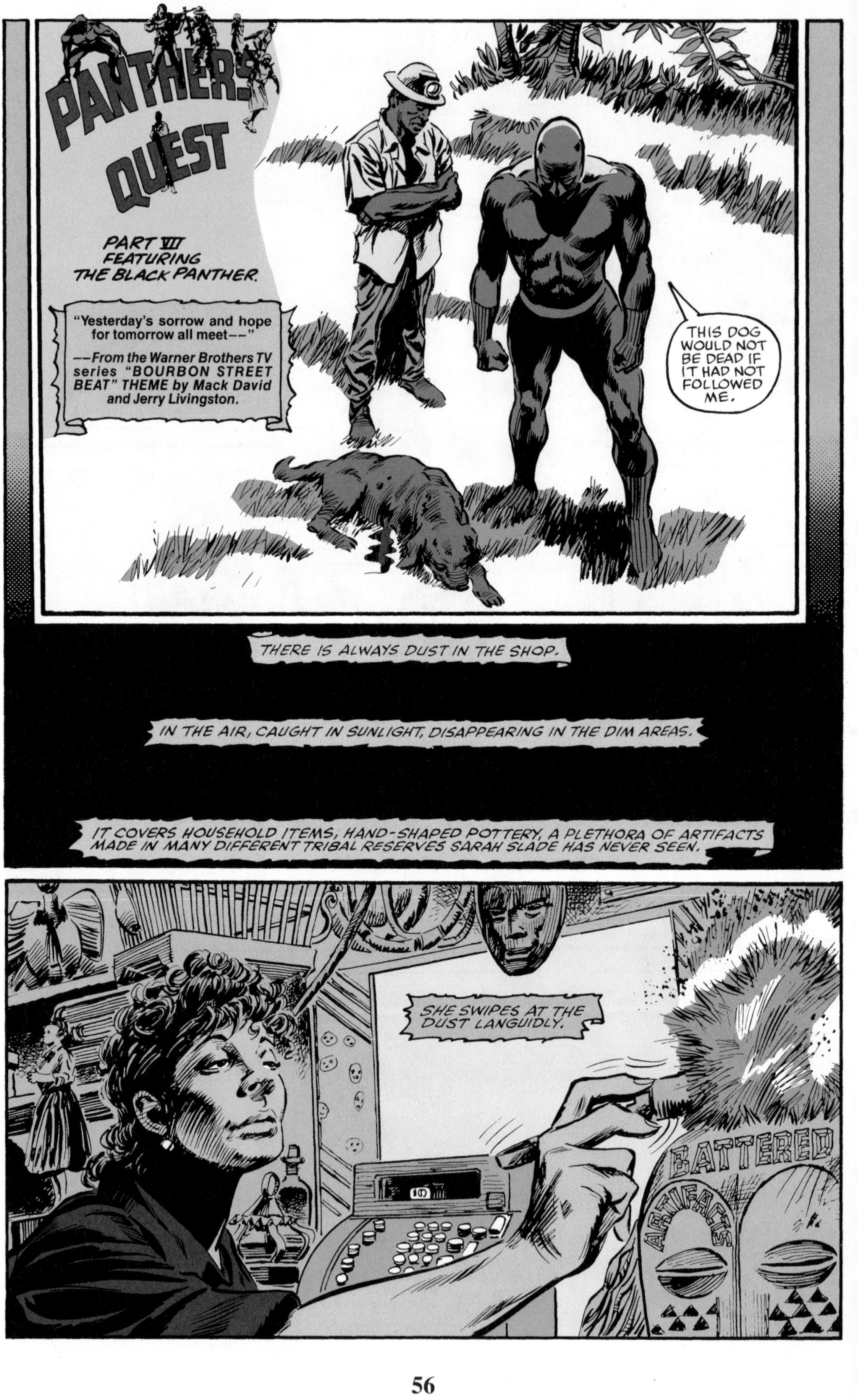
PANTHER'S QUEST
PART VII
FEATURING
THE BLACK PANTHER.
"Yesterday's sorrow and hope for tomorrow all meet--"
--From the Warner Brothers TV series "BOURBON STREET BEAT" THEME by Mack David and Jerry Livingston.
THIS DOG WOULD NOT BE DEAD IF IT HAD NOT FOLLOWED ME.
THERE IS ALWAYS DUST IN THE SHOP.
IN THE AIR, CAUGHT IN SUNLIGHT, DISAPPEARING IN THE DIM AREAS.
IT COVERS HOUSEHOLD ITEMS, HAND-SHAPED POTTERY, A PLETHORA OF ARTIFACTS MADE IN MANY DIFFERENT TRIBAL RESERVES SARAH SLADE HAS NEVER SEEN.
SHE SWIPES AT THE DUST LANGUIDLY.
BATTERED
ARTIFACTS

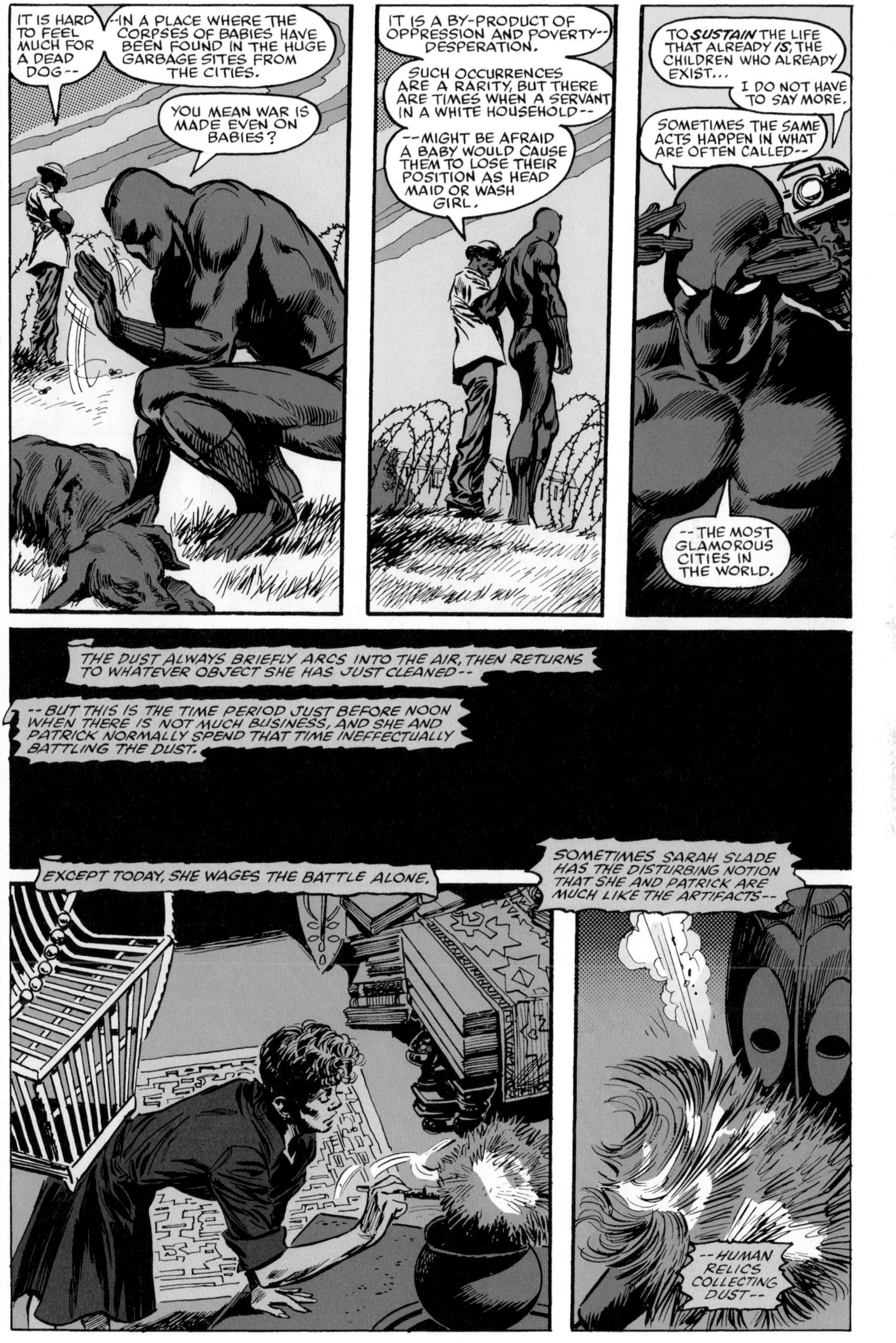
IT IS HARD TO FEEL MUCH FOR A DEAD DOG--
--IN A PLACE WHERE THE CORPSES OF BABIES HAVE BEEN FOUND IN THE HUGE GARBAGE SITES FROM THE CITIES.
YOU MEAN WAR IS MADE EVEN ON BABIES?
IT IS A BY-PRODUCT OF OPPRESSION AND POVERTY-- DESPERATION.
SUCH OCCURRENCES ARE A RARITY, BUT THERE ARE TIMES WHEN A SERVANT IN A WHITE HOUSEHOLD--
--MIGHT BE AFRAID A BABY WOULD CAUSE THEM TO LOSE THEIR POSITION AS HEAD MAID OR WASH GIRL.
TO SUSTAIN THE LIFE THAT ALREADY IS, THE CHILDREN WHO ALREADY EXIST...
I DO NOT HAVE TO SAY MORE.
SOMETIMES THE SAME ACTS HAPPEN IN WHAT ARE OFTEN CALLED--
--THE MOST GLAMOROUS CITIES IN THE WORLD.
THE DUST ALWAYS BRIEFLY ARCS INTO THE AIR, THEN RETURNS TO WHATEVER OBJECT SHE HAS JUST CLEANED--
--BUT THIS IS THE TIME PERIOD JUST BEFORE NOON WHEN THERE IS NOT MUCH BUSINESS, AND SHE AND PATRICK NORMALLY SPEND THAT TIME INEFFECTUALLY BATTLING THE DUST.
EXCEPT TODAY, SHE WAGES THE BATTLE ALONE.
SOMETIMES SARAH SLADE HAS THE DISTURBING NOTION THAT SHE AND PATRICK ARE MUCH LIKE THE ARTIFACTS--
--HUMAN RELICS COLLECTING DUST--

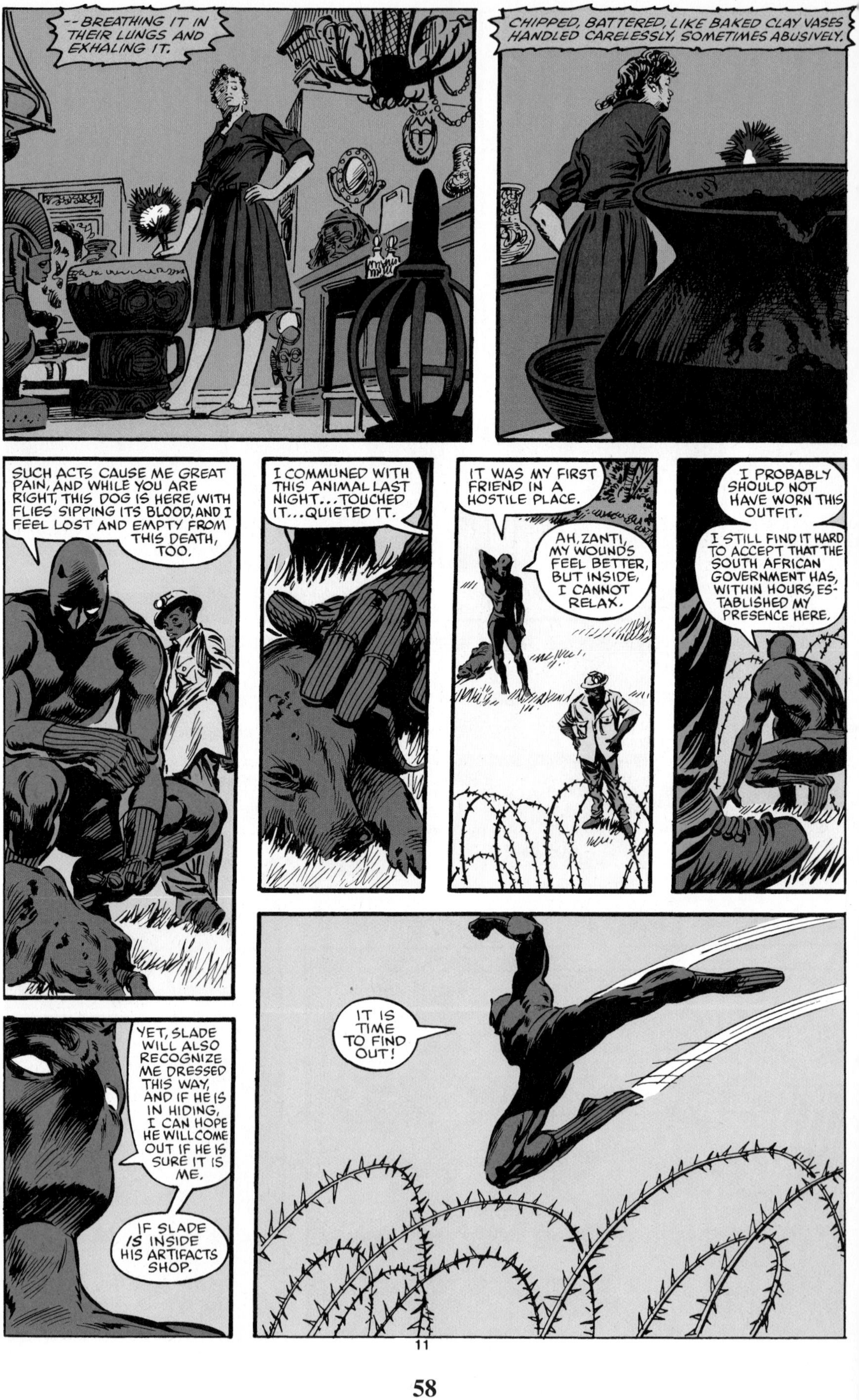
--BREATHING IT IN THEIR LUNGS AND EXHALING IT.
CHIPPED, BATTERED, LIKE BAKED CLAY VASES HANDLED CARELESSLY, SOMETIMES ABUSIVELY.
SUCH ACTS CAUSE ME GREAT PAIN, AND WHILE YOU ARE RIGHT, THIS DOG IS HERE, WITH FLIES SIPPING ITS BLOOD, AND I FEEL LOST AND EMPTY FROM THIS DEATH, TOO.
I COMMUNED WITH THIS ANIMAL LAST NIGHT... TOUCHED IT... QUIETED IT.
IT WAS MY FIRST FRIEND IN A HOSTILE PLACE.
AH, ZANTI, MY WOUNDS FEEL BETTER, BUT INSIDE, I CANNOT RELAX.
I PROBABLY SHOULD NOT HAVE WORN THIS OUTFIT.
I STILL FIND IT HARD TO ACCEPT THAT THE SOUTH AFRICAN GOVERNMENT HAS, WITHIN HOURS, ESTABLISHED MY PRESENCE HERE.
YET, SLADE WILL ALSO RECOGNIZE ME DRESSED THIS WAY, AND IF HE IS IN HIDING, I CAN HOPE HE WILL COME OUT IF HE IS SURE IT IS ME.
IF SLADE *IS* INSIDE HIS ARTIFACTS SHOP.
IT IS TIME TO FIND OUT!

11

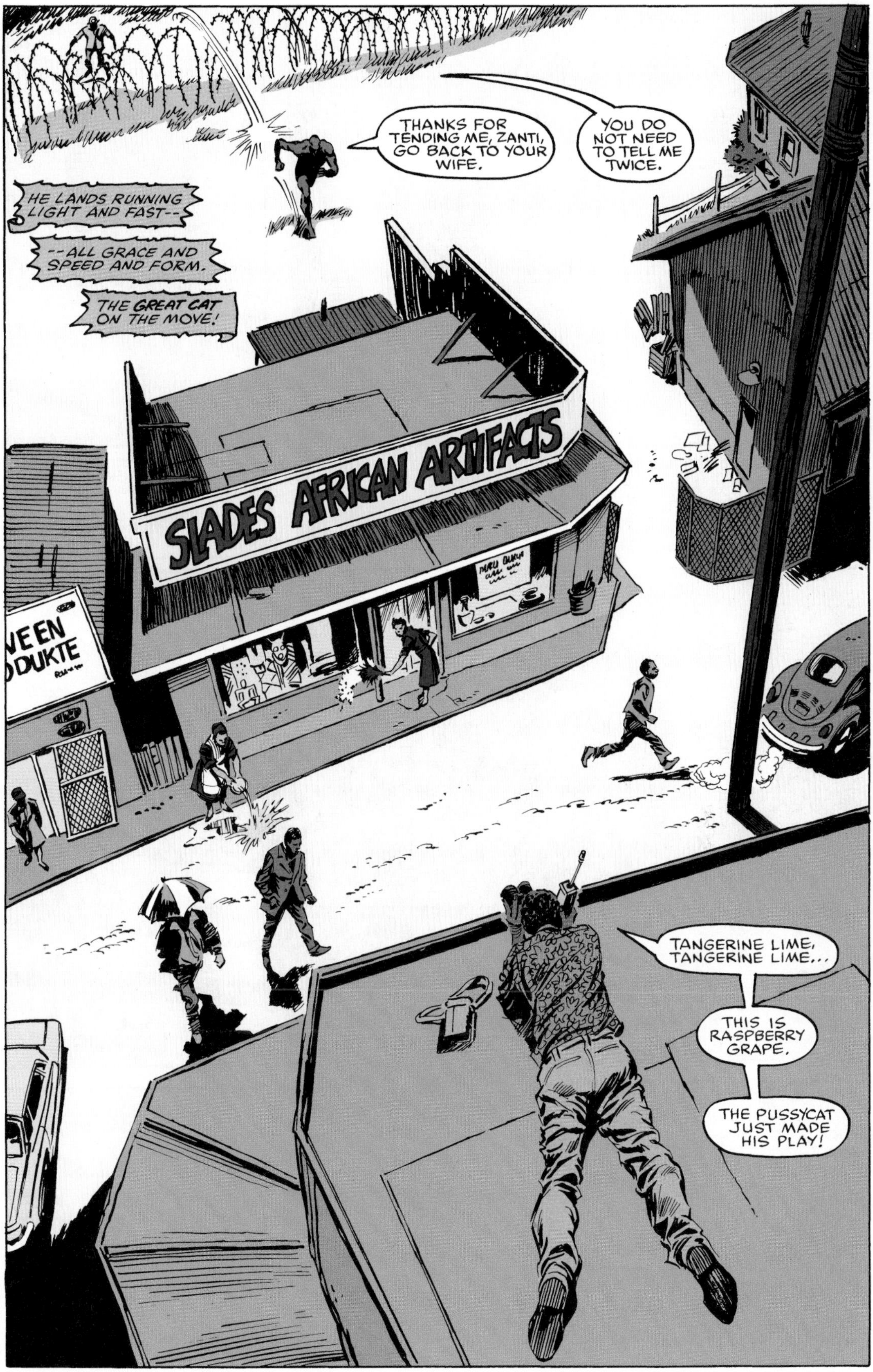
THANKS FOR TENDING ME, ZANTI, GO BACK TO YOUR WIFE.
YOU DO NOT NEED TO TELL ME TWICE.
HE LANDS RUNNING LIGHT AND FAST--
--ALL GRACE AND SPEED AND FORM.
THE GREAT CAT ON THE MOVE!
SLADES AFRICAN ARTIFACTS
TANGERINE LIME, TANGERINE LIME...
THIS IS RASPBERRY GRAPE.
THE PUSSYCAT JUST MADE HIS PLAY!

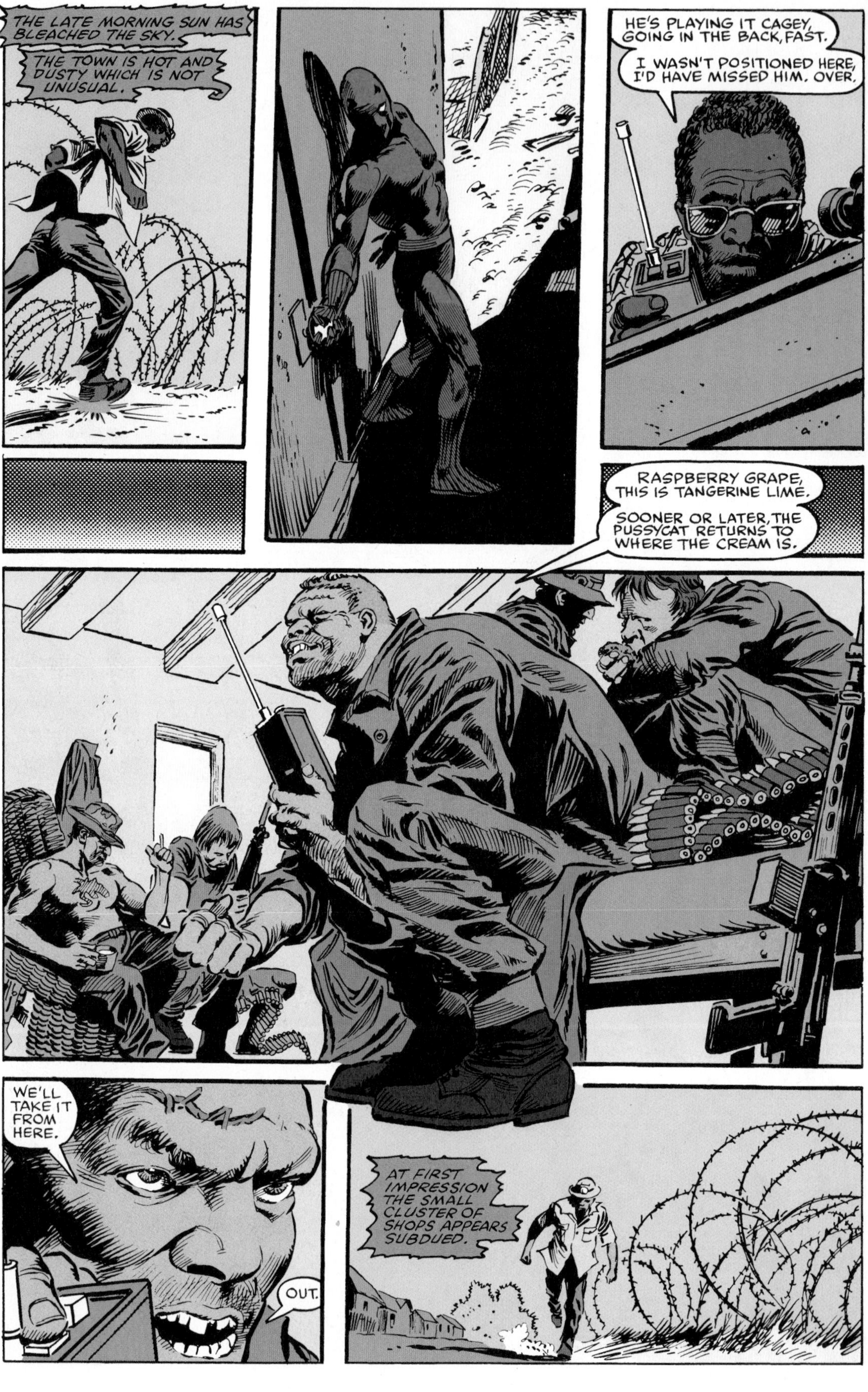
THE LATE MORNING SUN HAS BLEACHED THE SKY.
THE TOWN IS HOT AND DUSTY WHICH IS NOT UNUSUAL.
HE'S PLAYING IT CAGEY, GOING IN THE BACK, FAST.
I WASN'T POSITIONED HERE, I'D HAVE MISSED HIM. OVER.
RASPBERRY GRAPE, THIS IS TANGERINE LIME.
SOONER OR LATER, THE PUSSYCAT RETURNS TO WHERE THE CREAM IS.
WE'LL TAKE IT FROM HERE.
OUT.
AT FIRST IMPRESSION THE SMALL CLUSTER OF SHOPS APPEARS SUBDUED.

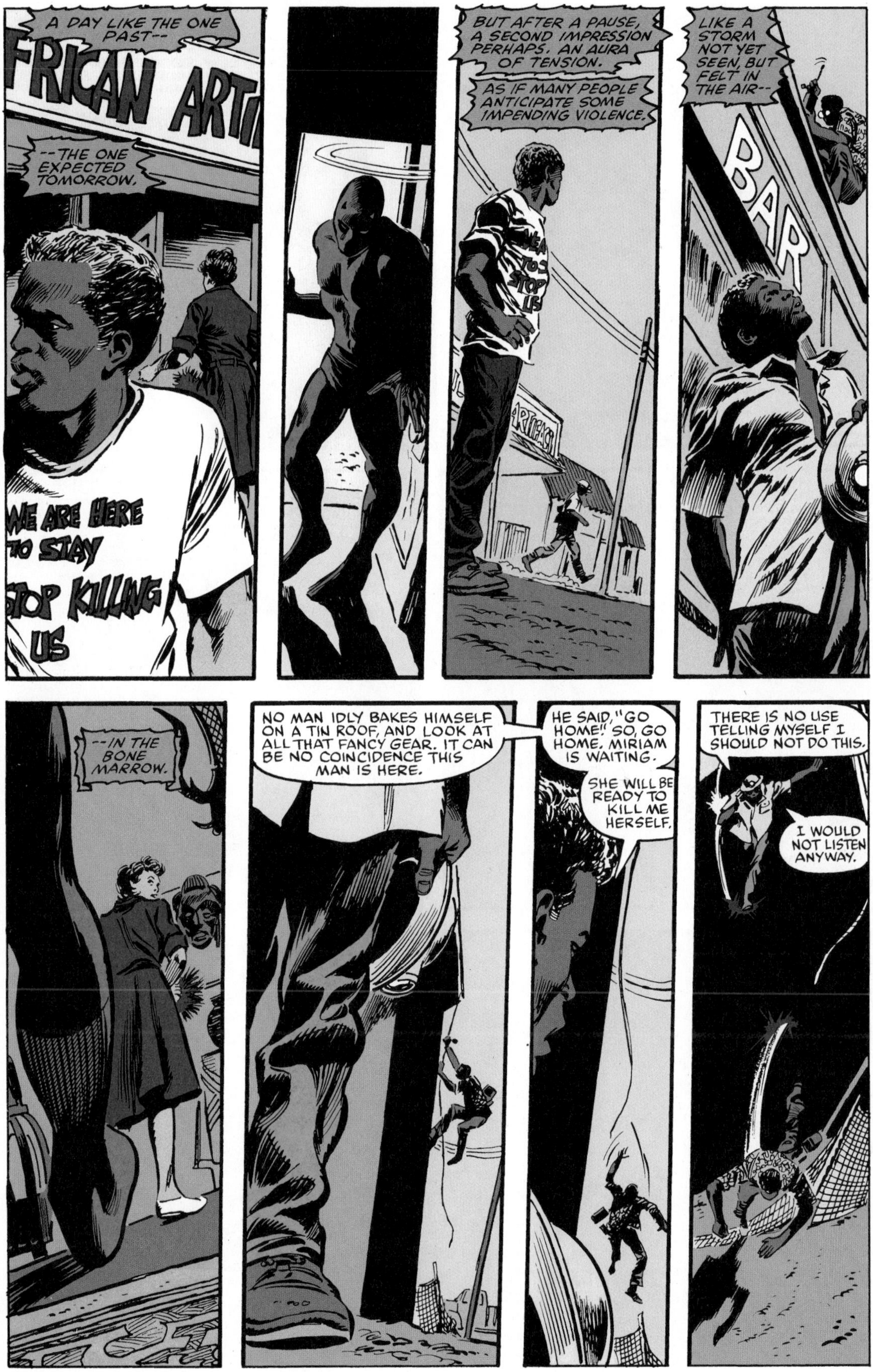

A DAY LIKE THE ONE PAST--
FRICAN ARTI
--THE ONE EXPECTED TOMORROW.
WE ARE HERE TO STAY STOP KILLING US
BUT AFTER A PAUSE, A SECOND IMPRESSION PERHAPS. AN AURA OF TENSION.
AS IF MANY PEOPLE ANTICIPATE SOME IMPENDING VIOLENCE.
LIKE A STORM NOT YET SEEN, BUT FELT IN THE AIR--
BAR
--IN THE BONE MARROW.
NO MAN IDLY BAKES HIMSELF ON A TIN ROOF, AND LOOK AT ALL THAT FANCY GEAR. IT CAN BE NO COINCIDENCE THIS MAN IS HERE.
HE SAID, "GO HOME!" SO, GO HOME. MIRIAM IS WAITING.
SHE WILL BE READY TO KILL ME HERSELF.
THERE IS NO USE TELLING MYSELF I SHOULD NOT DO THIS.
I WOULD NOT LISTEN ANYWAY.

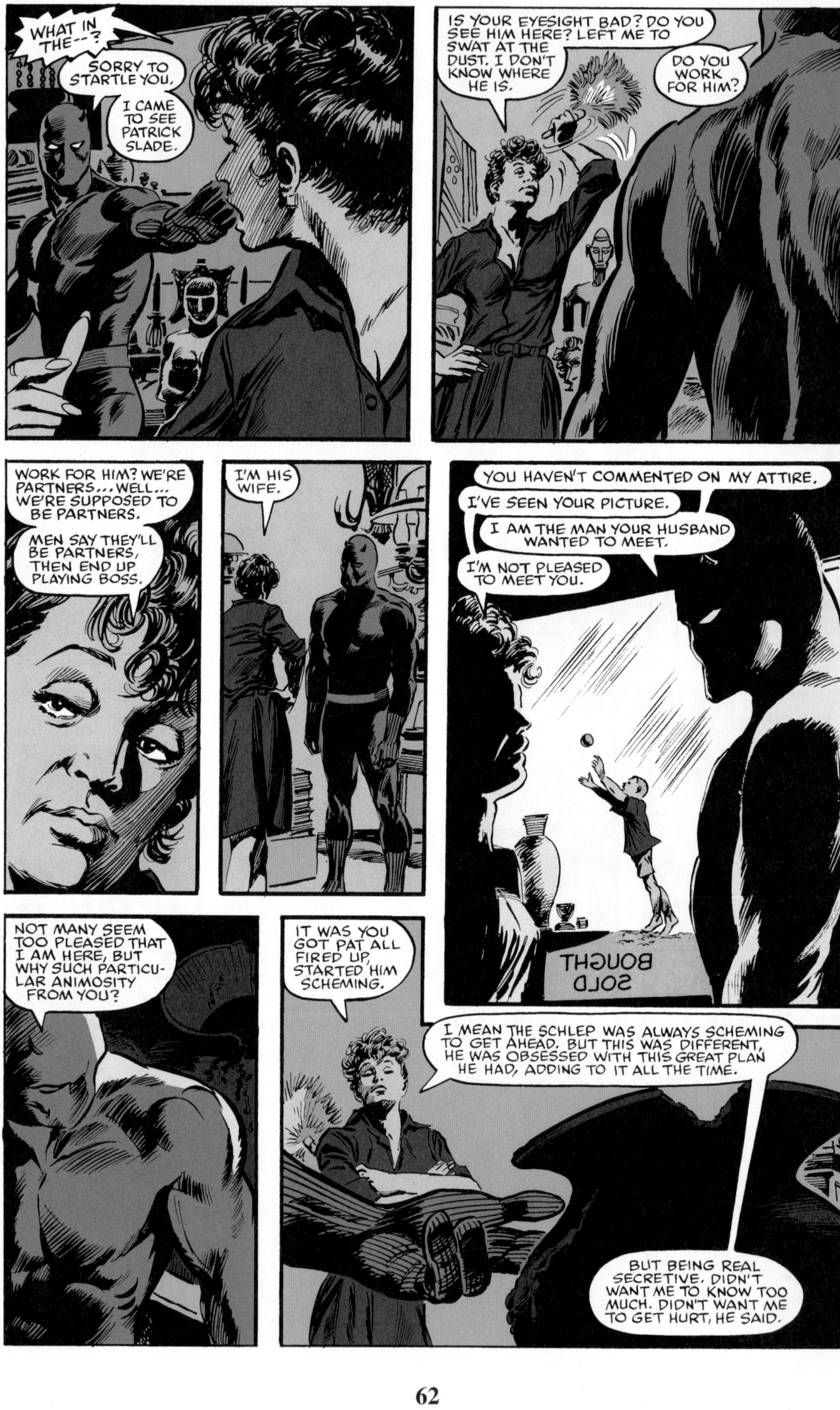
WHAT IN THE--?
SORRY TO STARTLE YOU.
I CAME TO SEE PATRICK SLADE.
IS YOUR EYESIGHT BAD? DO YOU SEE HIM HERE? LEFT ME TO SWAT AT THE DUST. I DON'T KNOW WHERE HE IS.
DO YOU WORK FOR HIM?
WORK FOR HIM? WE'RE PARTNERS... WELL... WE'RE SUPPOSED TO BE PARTNERS.
MEN SAY THEY'LL BE PARTNERS, THEN END UP PLAYING BOSS.
I'M HIS WIFE.
YOU HAVEN'T COMMENTED ON MY ATTIRE.
I'VE SEEN YOUR PICTURE.
I AM THE MAN YOUR HUSBAND WANTED TO MEET.
I'M NOT PLEASED TO MEET YOU.
NOT MANY SEEM TOO PLEASED THAT I AM HERE, BUT WHY SUCH PARTICULAR ANIMOSITY FROM YOU?
IT WAS YOU GOT PAT ALL FIRED UP, STARTED HIM SCHEMING.
I MEAN THE SCHLEP WAS ALWAYS SCHEMING TO GET AHEAD. BUT THIS WAS DIFFERENT, HE WAS OBSESSED WITH THIS GREAT PLAN HE HAD, ADDING TO IT ALL THE TIME.
BUT BEING REAL SECRETIVE. DIDN'T WANT ME TO KNOW TOO MUCH. DIDN'T WANT ME TO GET HURT, HE SAID.

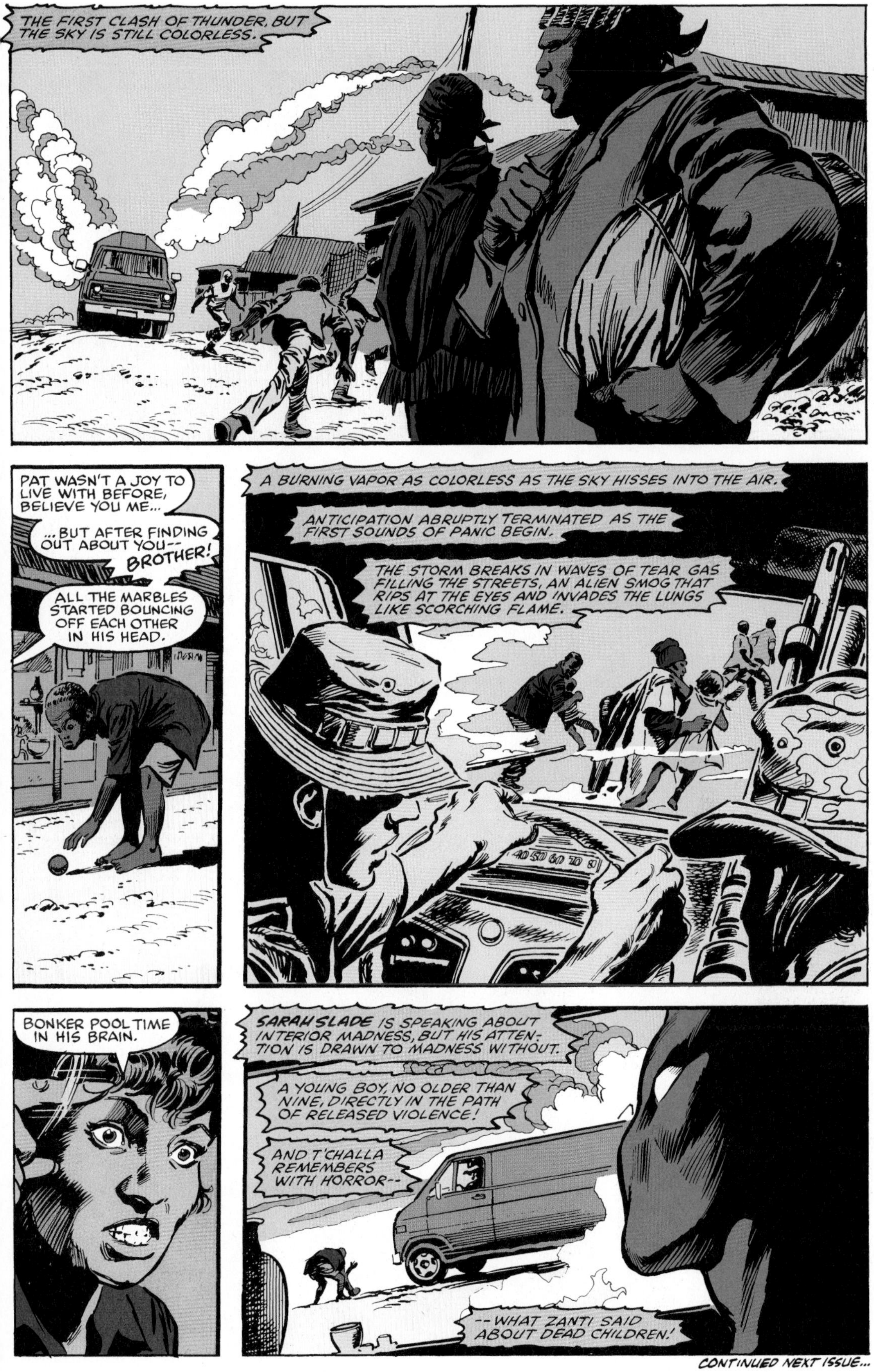
THE FIRST CLASH OF THUNDER, BUT THE SKY IS STILL COLORLESS.
PAT WASN'T A JOY TO LIVE WITH BEFORE, BELIEVE YOU ME...
...BUT AFTER FINDING OUT ABOUT YOU-- BROTHER!
ALL THE MARBLES STARTED BOUNCING OFF EACH OTHER IN HIS HEAD.
A BURNING VAPOR AS COLORLESS AS THE SKY HISSES INTO THE AIR.
ANTICIPATION ABRUPTLY TERMINATED AS THE FIRST SOUNDS OF PANIC BEGIN.
THE STORM BREAKS IN WAVES OF TEAR GAS FILLING THE STREETS, AN ALIEN SMOG THAT RIPS AT THE EYES AND INVADES THE LUNGS LIKE SCORCHING FLAME.
BONKER POOL TIME IN HIS BRAIN.
SARAH SLADE IS SPEAKING ABOUT INTERIOR MADNESS, BUT HIS ATTENTION IS DRAWN TO MADNESS WITHOUT.
A YOUNG BOY, NO OLDER THAN NINE, DIRECTLY IN THE PATH OF RELEASED VIOLENCE!
AND T'CHALLA REMEMBERS WITH HORROR--
--WHAT ZANTI SAID ABOUT DEAD CHILDREN!

CONTINUED NEXT ISSUE...

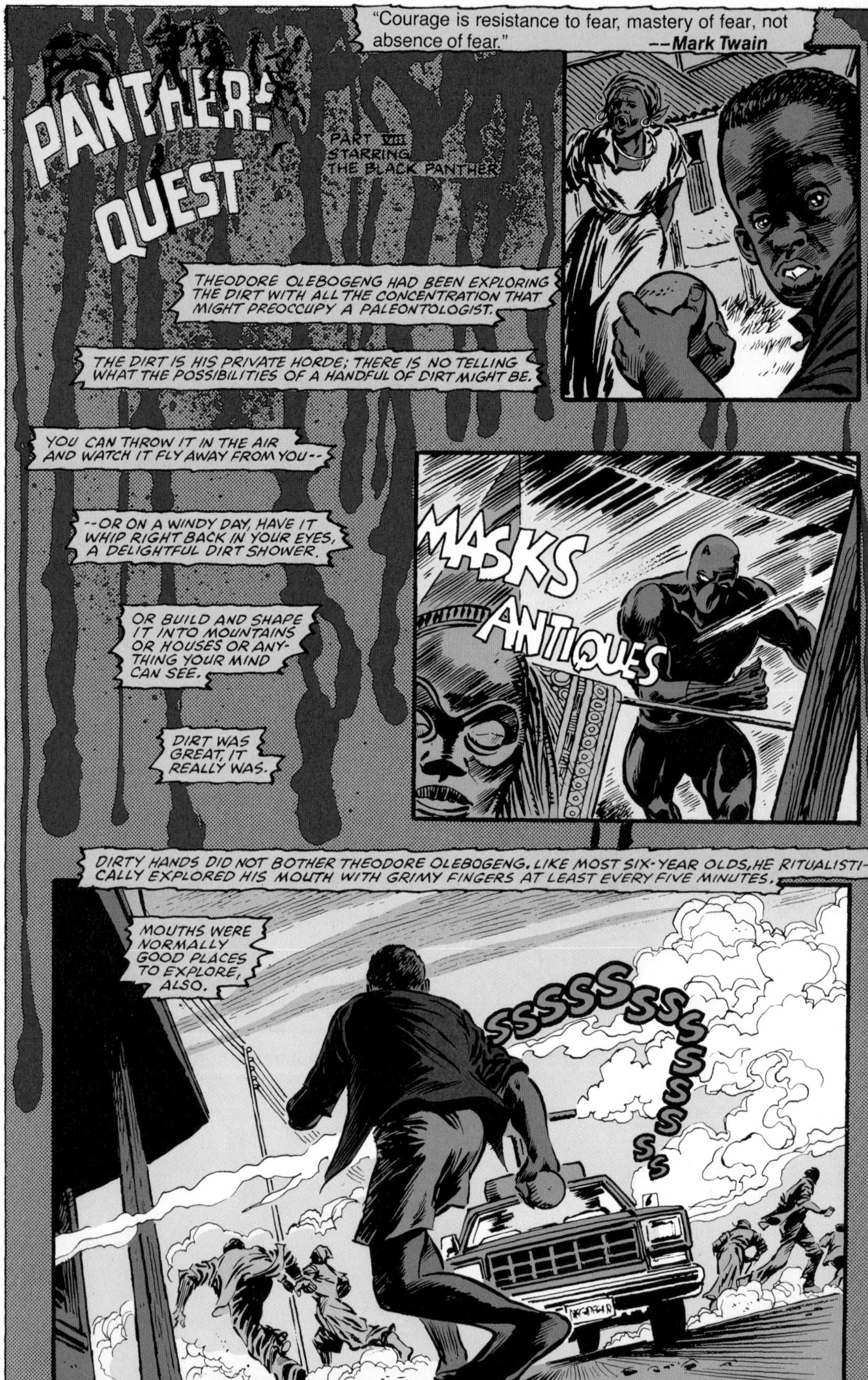
"Courage is resistance to fear, mastery of fear, not absence of fear." --Mark Twain
PANTHER'S QUEST
PART VIII STARRING THE BLACK PANTHER
THEODORE OLEBOGENG HAD BEEN EXPLORING THE DIRT WITH ALL THE CONCENTRATION THAT MIGHT PREOCCUPY A PALEONTOLOGIST.
THE DIRT IS HIS PRIVATE HORDE; THERE IS NO TELLING WHAT THE POSSIBILITIES OF A HANDFUL OF DIRT MIGHT BE.
YOU CAN THROW IT IN THE AIR AND WATCH IT FLY AWAY FROM YOU--
--OR ON A WINDY DAY, HAVE IT WHIP RIGHT BACK IN YOUR EYES, A DELIGHTFUL DIRT SHOWER.
OR BUILD AND SHAPE IT INTO MOUNTAINS OR HOUSES OR ANYTHING YOUR MIND CAN SEE.
DIRT WAS GREAT, IT REALLY WAS.
MASKS
ANTIQUES
DIRTY HANDS DID NOT BOTHER THEODORE OLEBOGENG. LIKE MOST SIX-YEAR OLDS, HE RITUALISTICALLY EXPLORED HIS MOUTH WITH GRIMY FINGERS AT LEAST EVERY FIVE MINUTES.
MOUTHS WERE NORMALLY GOOD PLACES TO EXPLORE, ALSO.
SSSSSSSSSSSSSSSS

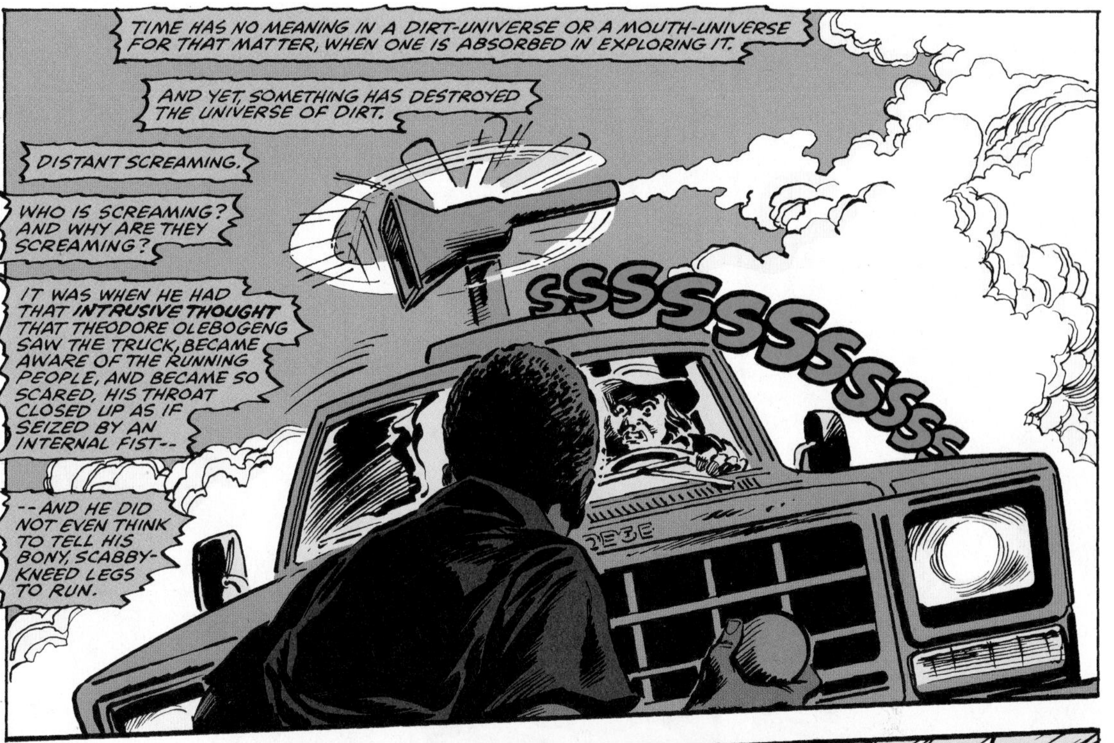
TIME HAS NO MEANING IN A DIRT-UNIVERSE OR A MOUTH-UNIVERSE FOR THAT MATTER, WHEN ONE IS ABSORBED IN EXPLORING IT.
AND YET, SOMETHING HAS DESTROYED THE UNIVERSE OF DIRT.
DISTANT SCREAMING.
WHO IS SCREAMING? AND WHY ARE THEY SCREAMING?
IT WAS WHEN HE HAD THAT INTRUSIVE THOUGHT THAT THEODORE OLEBOGENG SAW THE TRUCK, BECAME AWARE OF THE RUNNING PEOPLE, AND BECAME SO SCARED, HIS THROAT CLOSED UP AS IF SEIZED BY AN INTERNAL FIST--
--AND HE DID NOT EVEN THINK TO TELL HIS BONY, SCABBY-KNEED LEGS TO RUN.
SSSSSSSSSSSSSSS

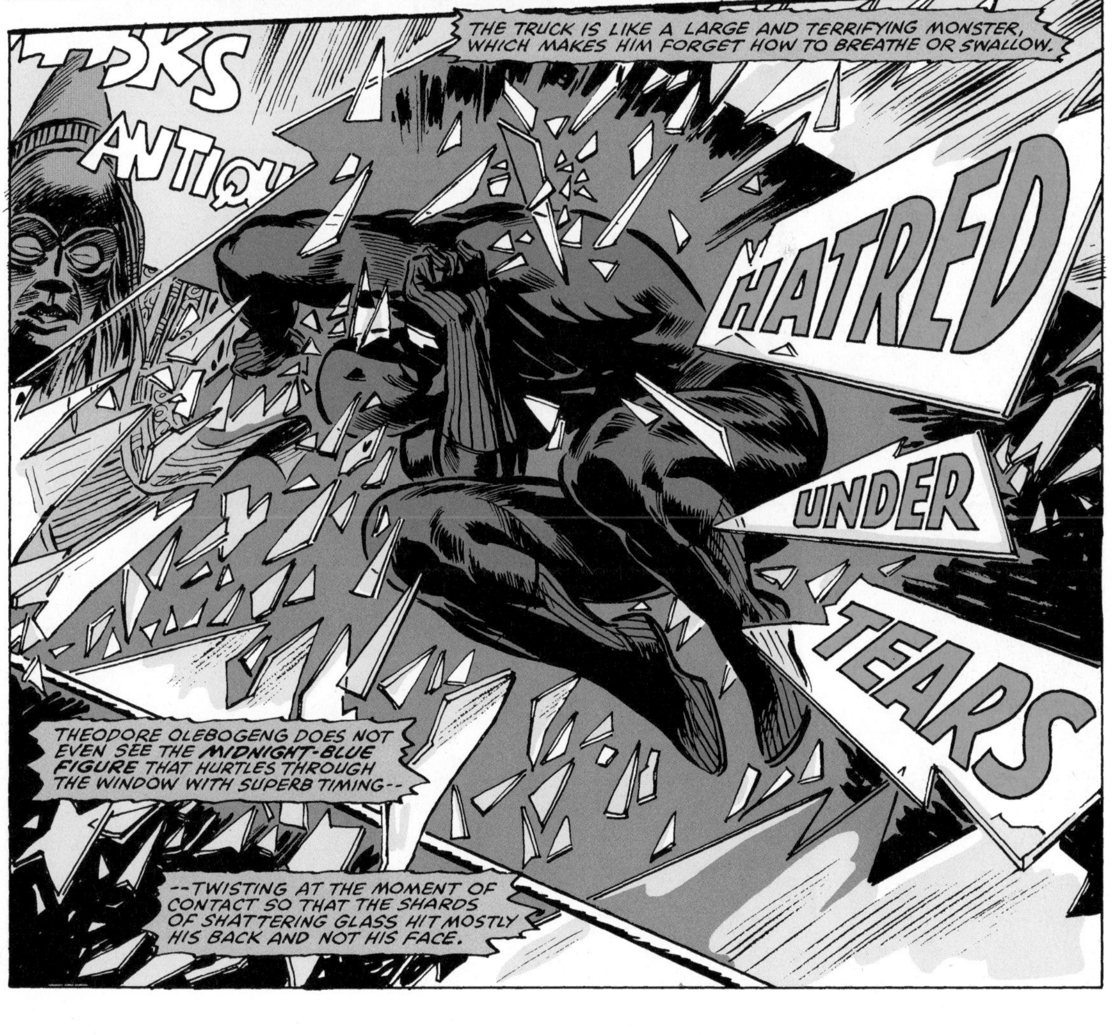
THE TRUCK IS LIKE A LARGE AND TERRIFYING MONSTER, WHICH MAKES HIM FORGET HOW TO BREATHE OR SWALLOW.
TSKS
ANTIQU
HATRED
UNDER
TEARS
THEODORE OLEBOGENG DOES NOT EVEN SEE THE MIDNIGHT-BLUE FIGURE THAT HURTLES THROUGH THE WINDOW WITH SUPERB TIMING--
--TWISTING AT THE MOMENT OF CONTACT SO THAT THE SHARDS OF SHATTERING GLASS HIT MOSTLY HIS BACK AND NOT HIS FACE.

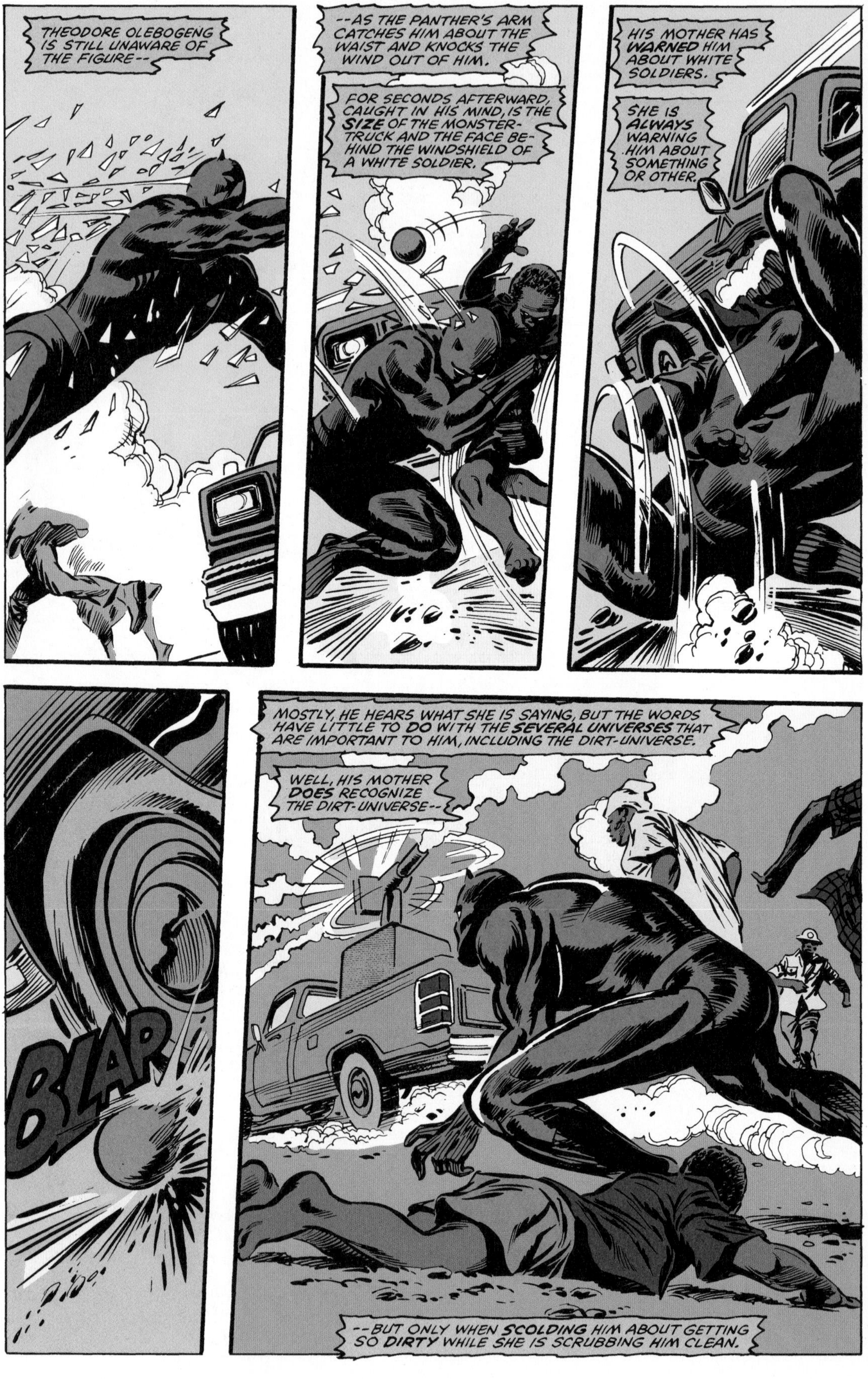
THEODORE OLEBOGENG IS STILL UNAWARE OF THE FIGURE--
--AS THE PANTHER'S ARM CATCHES HIM ABOUT THE WAIST AND KNOCKS THE WIND OUT OF HIM.
FOR SECONDS AFTERWARD, CAUGHT IN HIS MIND, IS THE SIZE OF THE MONSTER-TRUCK AND THE FACE BEHIND THE WINDSHIELD OF A WHITE SOLDIER.
HIS MOTHER HAS WARNED HIM ABOUT WHITE SOLDIERS.
SHE IS ALWAYS WARNING HIM ABOUT SOMETHING OR OTHER.
BLAP
MOSTLY, HE HEARS WHAT SHE IS SAYING, BUT THE WORDS HAVE LITTLE TO DO WITH THE SEVERAL UNIVERSES THAT ARE IMPORTANT TO HIM, INCLUDING THE DIRT-UNIVERSE.
WELL, HIS MOTHER DOES RECOGNIZE THE DIRT-UNIVERSE--
--BUT ONLY WHEN SCOLDING HIM ABOUT GETTING SO DIRTY WHILE SHE IS SCRUBBING HIM CLEAN.

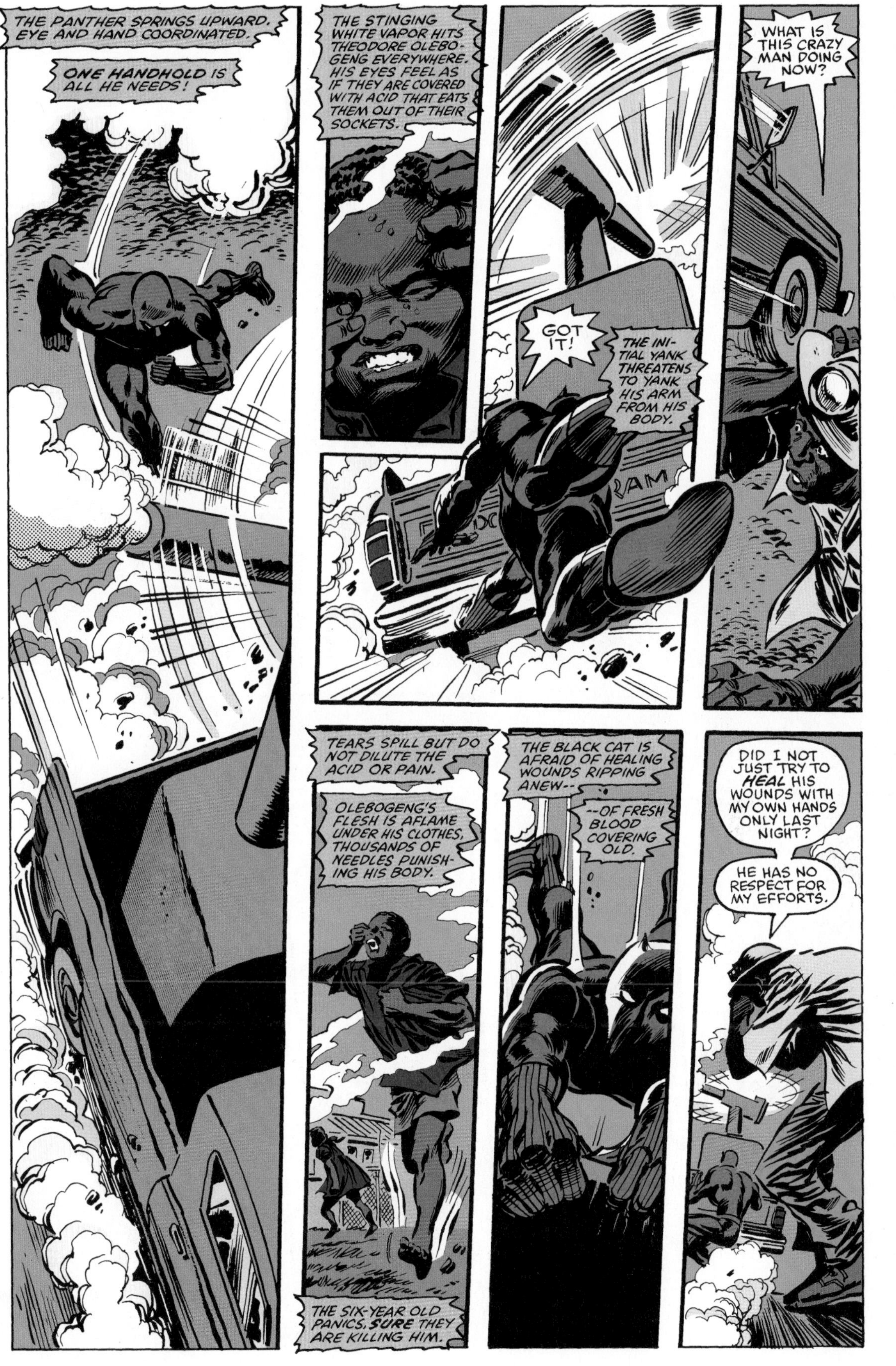
THE PANTHER SPRINGS UPWARD, EYE AND HAND COORDINATED.
ONE HANDHOLD IS ALL HE NEEDS!
THE STINGING WHITE VAPOR HITS THEODORE OLEBOGENG EVERYWHERE. HIS EYES FEEL AS IF THEY ARE COVERED WITH ACID THAT EATS THEM OUT OF THEIR SOCKETS.
GOT IT!
THE INITIAL YANK THREATENS TO YANK HIS ARM FROM HIS BODY.
WHAT IS THIS CRAZY MAN DOING NOW?
TEARS SPILL BUT DO NOT DILUTE THE ACID OR PAIN.
OLEBOGENG'S FLESH IS AFLAME UNDER HIS CLOTHES, THOUSANDS OF NEEDLES PUNISHING HIS BODY.
THE SIX-YEAR OLD PANICS, SURE THEY ARE KILLING HIM.
THE BLACK CAT IS AFRAID OF HEALING WOUNDS RIPPING ANEW--
--OF FRESH BLOOD COVERING OLD.
DID I NOT JUST TRY TO HEAL HIS WOUNDS WITH MY OWN HANDS ONLY LAST NIGHT?
HE HAS NO RESPECT FOR MY EFFORTS.

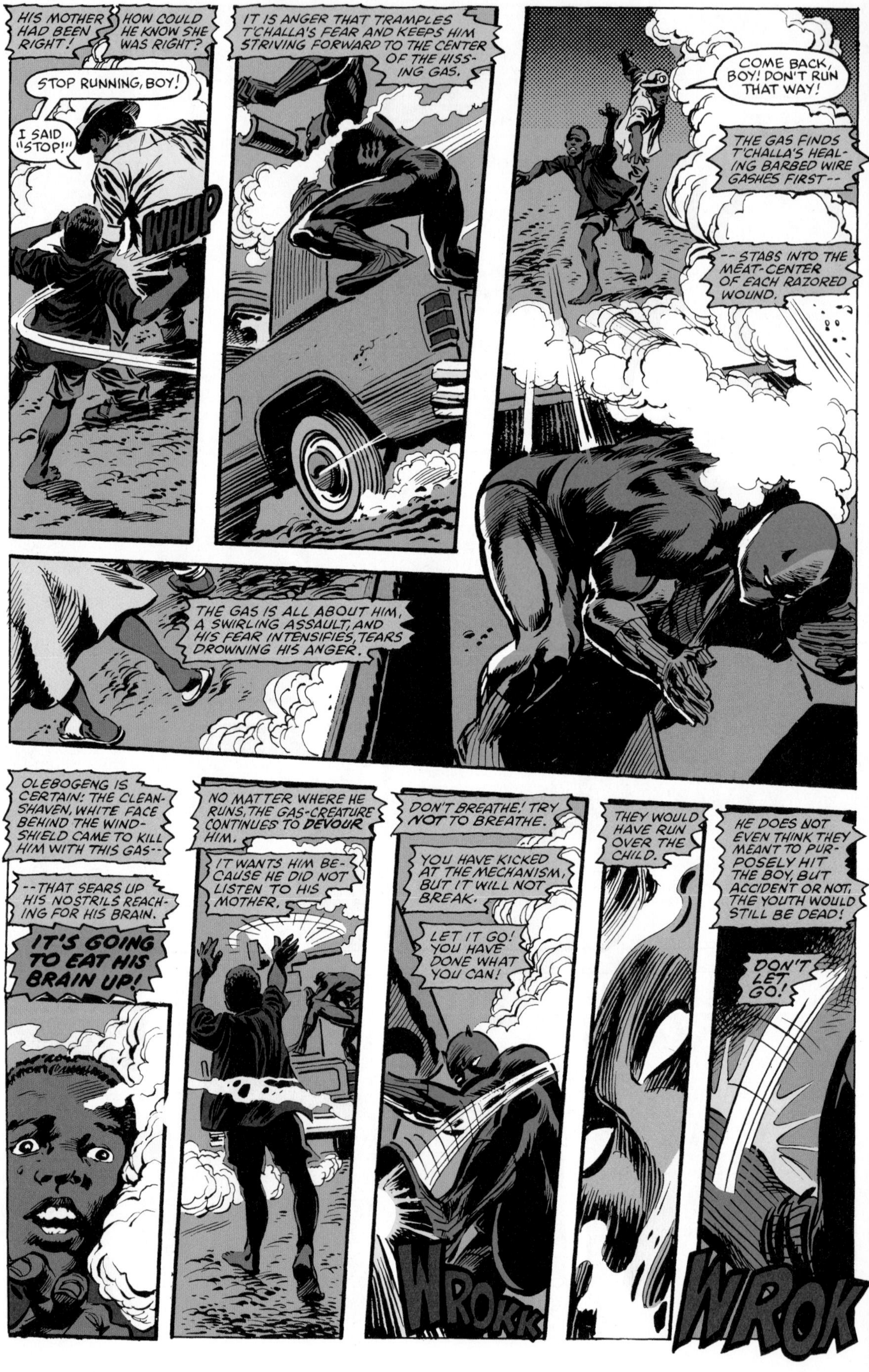
HIS MOTHER HAD BEEN RIGHT!
HOW COULD HE KNOW SHE WAS RIGHT?
STOP RUNNING, BOY!
I SAID "STOP!"
WHUP
IT IS ANGER THAT TRAMPLES T'CHALLA'S FEAR AND KEEPS HIM STRIVING FORWARD TO THE CENTER OF THE HISSING GAS.
COME BACK, BOY! DON'T RUN THAT WAY!
THE GAS FINDS T'CHALLA'S HEALING BARBED WIRE GASHES FIRST--
--STABS INTO THE MEAT-CENTER OF EACH RAZORED WOUND.
THE GAS IS ALL ABOUT HIM, A SWIRLING ASSAULT, AND HIS FEAR INTENSIFIES, TEARS DROWNING HIS ANGER.
OLEBOGENG IS CERTAIN: THE CLEAN-SHAVEN, WHITE FACE BEHIND THE WINDSHIELD CAME TO KILL HIM WITH THIS GAS--
--THAT SEARS UP HIS NOSTRILS REACHING FOR HIS BRAIN.
IT'S GOING TO EAT HIS BRAIN UP!
NO MATTER WHERE HE RUNS, THE GAS-CREATURE CONTINUES TO DEVOUR HIM.
IT WANTS HIM BECAUSE HE DID NOT LISTEN TO HIS MOTHER.
DON'T BREATHE! TRY NOT TO BREATHE.
YOU HAVE KICKED AT THE MECHANISM, BUT IT WILL NOT BREAK.
LET IT GO! YOU HAVE DONE WHAT YOU CAN!
WROKK
THEY WOULD HAVE RUN OVER THE CHILD.
HE DOES NOT EVEN THINK THEY MEANT TO PURPOSELY HIT THE BOY, BUT ACCIDENT OR NOT, THE YOUTH WOULD STILL BE DEAD!
DON'T LET GO!
WROK

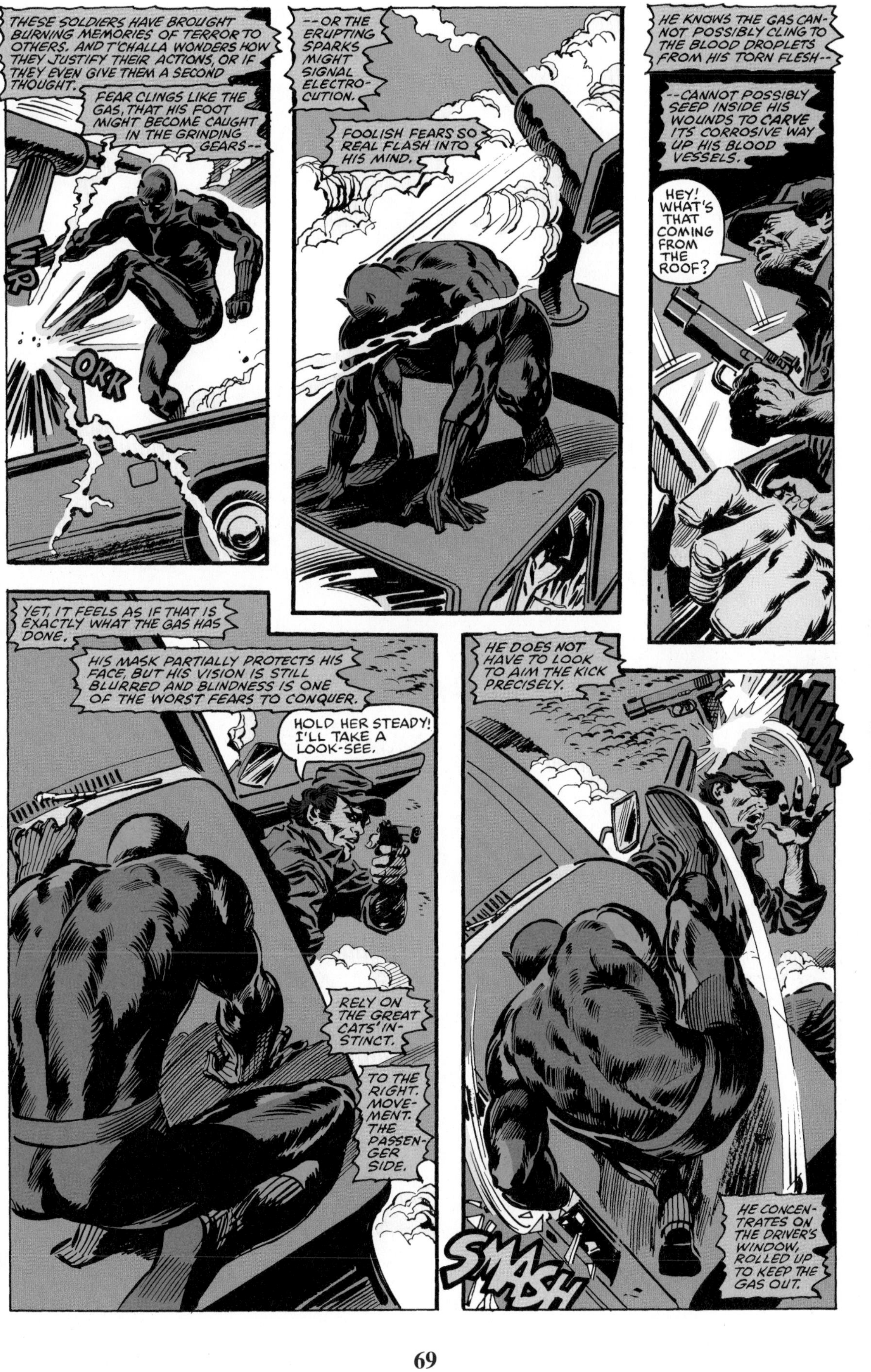

THESE SOLDIERS HAVE BROUGHT BURNING MEMORIES OF TERROR TO OTHERS. AND T'CHALLA WONDERS HOW THEY JUSTIFY THEIR ACTIONS, OR IF THEY EVEN GIVE THEM A SECOND THOUGHT.
FEAR CLINGS LIKE THE GAS, THAT HIS FOOT MIGHT BECOME CAUGHT IN THE GRINDING GEARS--
WR
OKK
--OR THE ERUPTING SPARKS MIGHT SIGNAL ELECTRO-CUTION.
FOOLISH FEARS SO REAL FLASH INTO HIS MIND.
HE KNOWS THE GAS CAN-NOT POSSIBLY CLING TO THE BLOOD DROPLETS FROM HIS TORN FLESH--
--CANNOT POSSIBLY SEEP INSIDE HIS WOUNDS TO CARVE ITS CORROSIVE WAY UP HIS BLOOD VESSELS.
HEY! WHAT'S THAT COMING FROM THE ROOF?
YET, IT FEELS AS IF THAT IS EXACTLY WHAT THE GAS HAS DONE.
HIS MASK PARTIALLY PROTECTS HIS FACE, BUT HIS VISION IS STILL BLURRED AND BLINDNESS IS ONE OF THE WORST FEARS TO CONQUER.
HOLD HER STEADY! I'LL TAKE A LOOK-SEE.
RELY ON THE GREAT CATS' IN-STINCT.
TO THE RIGHT. MOVE-MENT. THE PASSEN-GER SIDE.
HE DOES NOT HAVE TO LOOK TO AIM THE KICK PRECISELY.
WHAK
HE CONCEN-TRATES ON THE DRIVER'S WINDOW, ROLLED UP TO KEEP THE GAS OUT.
SMASH

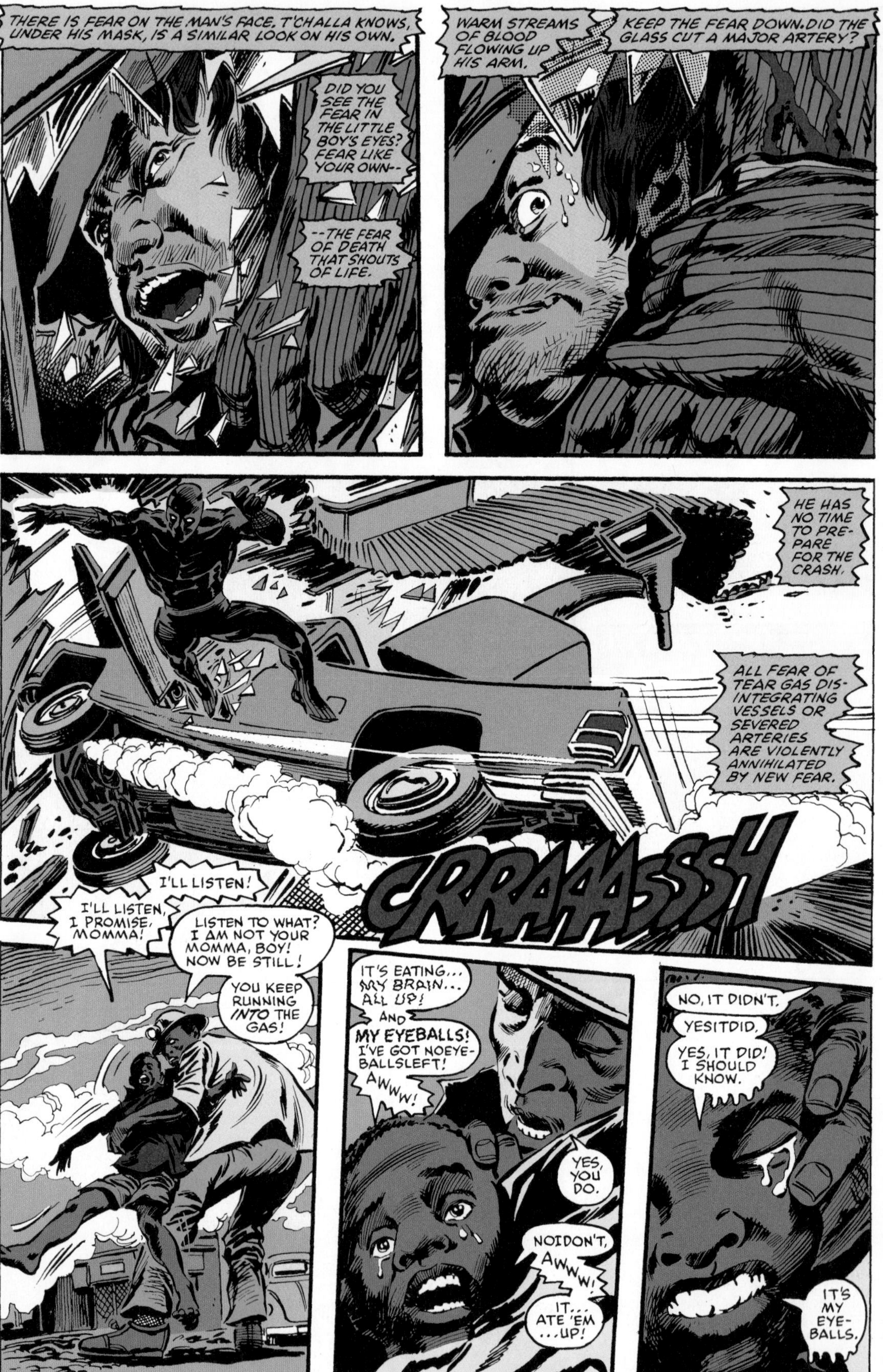
THERE IS FEAR ON THE MAN'S FACE. T'CHALLA KNOWS, UNDER HIS MASK, IS A SIMILAR LOOK ON HIS OWN.
DID YOU SEE THE FEAR IN THE LITTLE BOY'S EYES? FEAR LIKE YOUR OWN--
--THE FEAR OF DEATH THAT SHOUTS OF LIFE.
WARM STREAMS OF BLOOD FLOWING UP HIS ARM.
KEEP THE FEAR DOWN. DID THE GLASS CUT A MAJOR ARTERY?
HE HAS NO TIME TO PREPARE FOR THE CRASH.
ALL FEAR OF TEAR GAS DISINTEGRATING VESSELS OR SEVERED ARTERIES ARE VIOLENTLY ANNIHILATED BY NEW FEAR.
CRRAAAASSSH
I'LL LISTEN!
I'LL LISTEN, I PROMISE, MOMMA!
LISTEN TO WHAT? I AM NOT YOUR MOMMA, BOY! NOW BE STILL!
YOU KEEP RUNNING INTO THE GAS!
IT'S EATING... MY BRAIN... ALL UP!
AND MY EYEBALLS! I'VE GOT NOEYEBALLSLEFT!
AWWW!
YES, YOU DO.
NOIDON'T.
AWWW!
IT... ATE 'EM ...UP!
NO, IT DIDN'T.
YESITDID.
YES, IT DID! I SHOULD KNOW.
IT'S MY EYEBALLS.

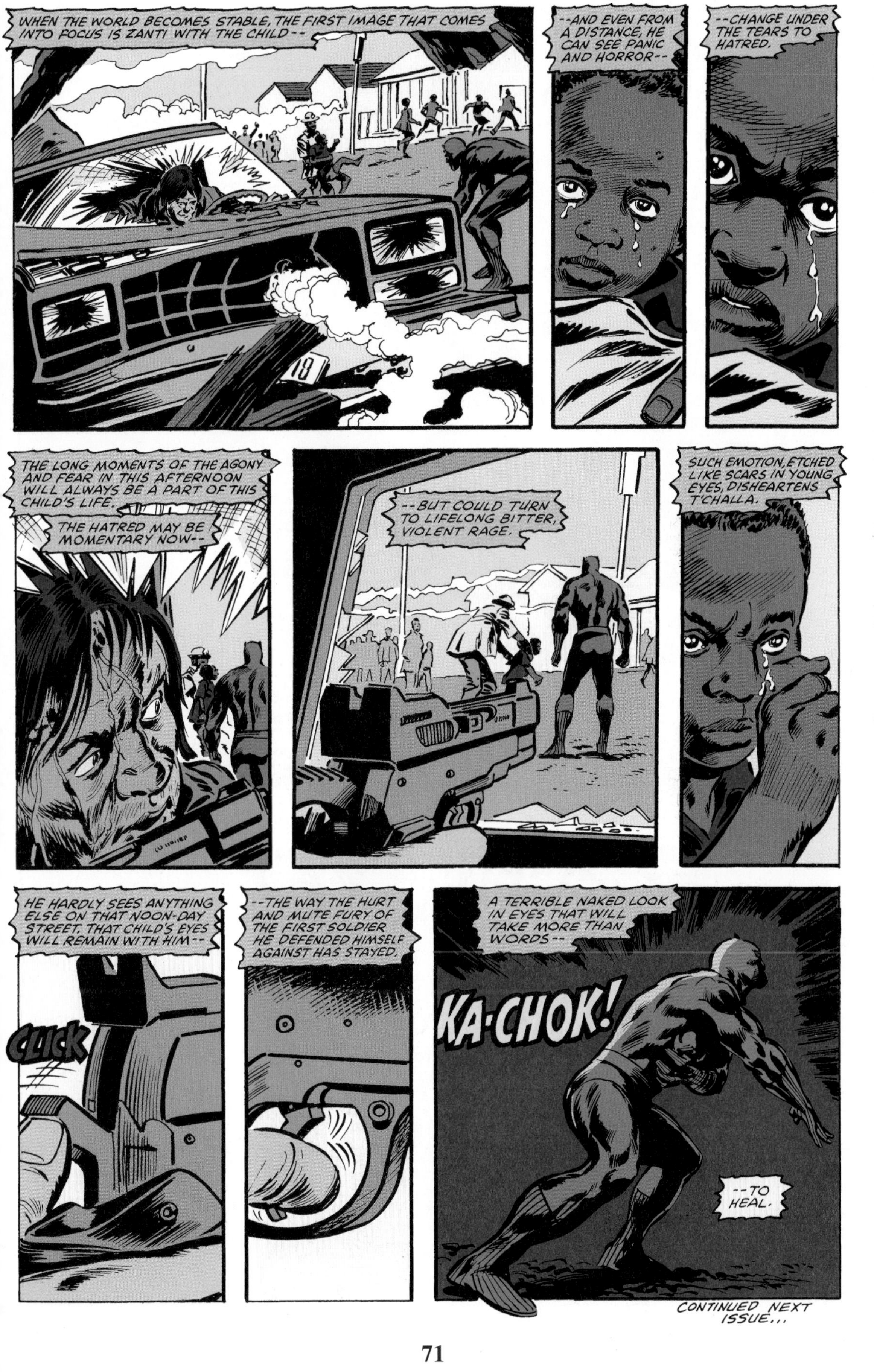
WHEN THE WORLD BECOMES STABLE, THE FIRST IMAGE THAT COMES INTO FOCUS IS ZANTI WITH THE CHILD--
--AND EVEN FROM A DISTANCE, HE CAN SEE PANIC AND HORROR--
--CHANGE UNDER THE TEARS TO HATRED.
THE LONG MOMENTS OF THE AGONY AND FEAR IN THIS AFTERNOON WILL ALWAYS BE A PART OF THIS CHILD'S LIFE.
THE HATRED MAY BE MOMENTARY NOW--
--BUT COULD TURN TO LIFELONG BITTER, VIOLENT RAGE.
SUCH EMOTION, ETCHED LIKE SCARS IN YOUNG EYES, DISHEARTENS T'CHALLA.
HE HARDLY SEES ANYTHING ELSE ON THAT NOON-DAY STREET. THAT CHILD'S EYES WILL REMAIN WITH HIM--
CLICK
--THE WAY THE HURT AND MUTE FURY OF THE FIRST SOLDIER HE DEFENDED HIMSELF AGAINST HAS STAYED.
A TERRIBLE NAKED LOOK IN EYES THAT WILL TAKE MORE THAN WORDS--
KA-CHOK!
--TO HEAL.
CONTINUED NEXT ISSUE...

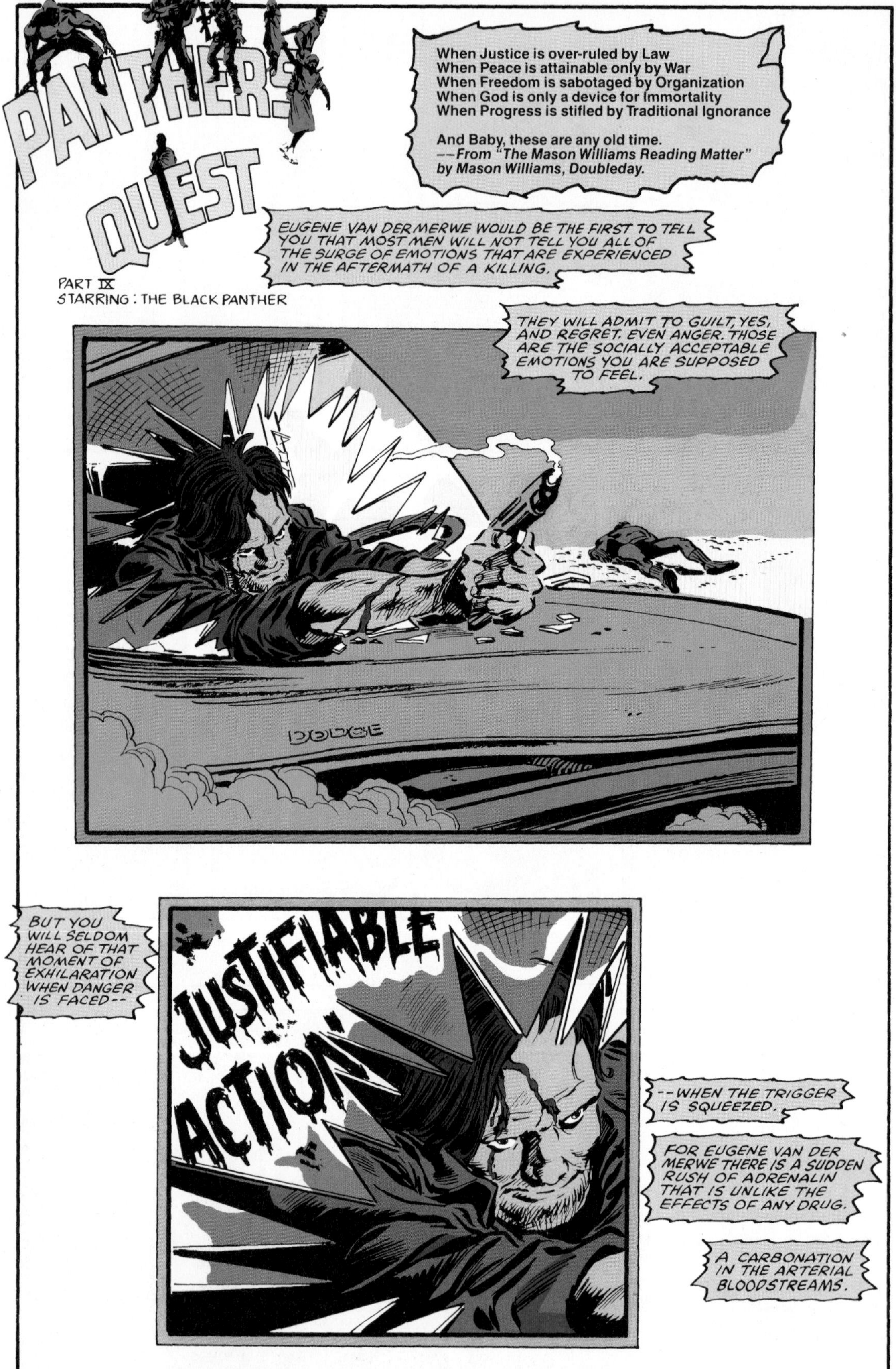
PANTHER'S QUEST
When Justice is over-ruled by Law
When Peace is attainable only by War
When Freedom is sabotaged by Organization
When God is only a device for Immortality
When Progress is stifled by Traditional Ignorance
And Baby, these are any old time.
--From "The Mason Williams Reading Matter" by Mason Williams, Doubleday.
EUGENE VAN DER MERWE WOULD BE THE FIRST TO TELL YOU THAT MOST MEN WILL NOT TELL YOU ALL OF THE SURGE OF EMOTIONS THAT ARE EXPERIENCED IN THE AFTERMATH OF A KILLING.
PART IX
STARRING: THE BLACK PANTHER
THEY WILL ADMIT TO GUILT, YES, AND REGRET. EVEN ANGER. THOSE ARE THE SOCIALLY ACCEPTABLE EMOTIONS YOU ARE SUPPOSED TO FEEL.
DODGE
BUT YOU WILL SELDOM HEAR OF THAT MOMENT OF EXHILARATION WHEN DANGER IS FACED--
JUSTIFIABLE ACTION
--WHEN THE TRIGGER IS SQUEEZED.
FOR EUGENE VAN DER MERWE THERE IS A SUDDEN RUSH OF ADRENALIN THAT IS UNLIKE THE EFFECTS OF ANY DRUG.
A CARBONATION IN THE ARTERIAL BLOODSTREAMS.

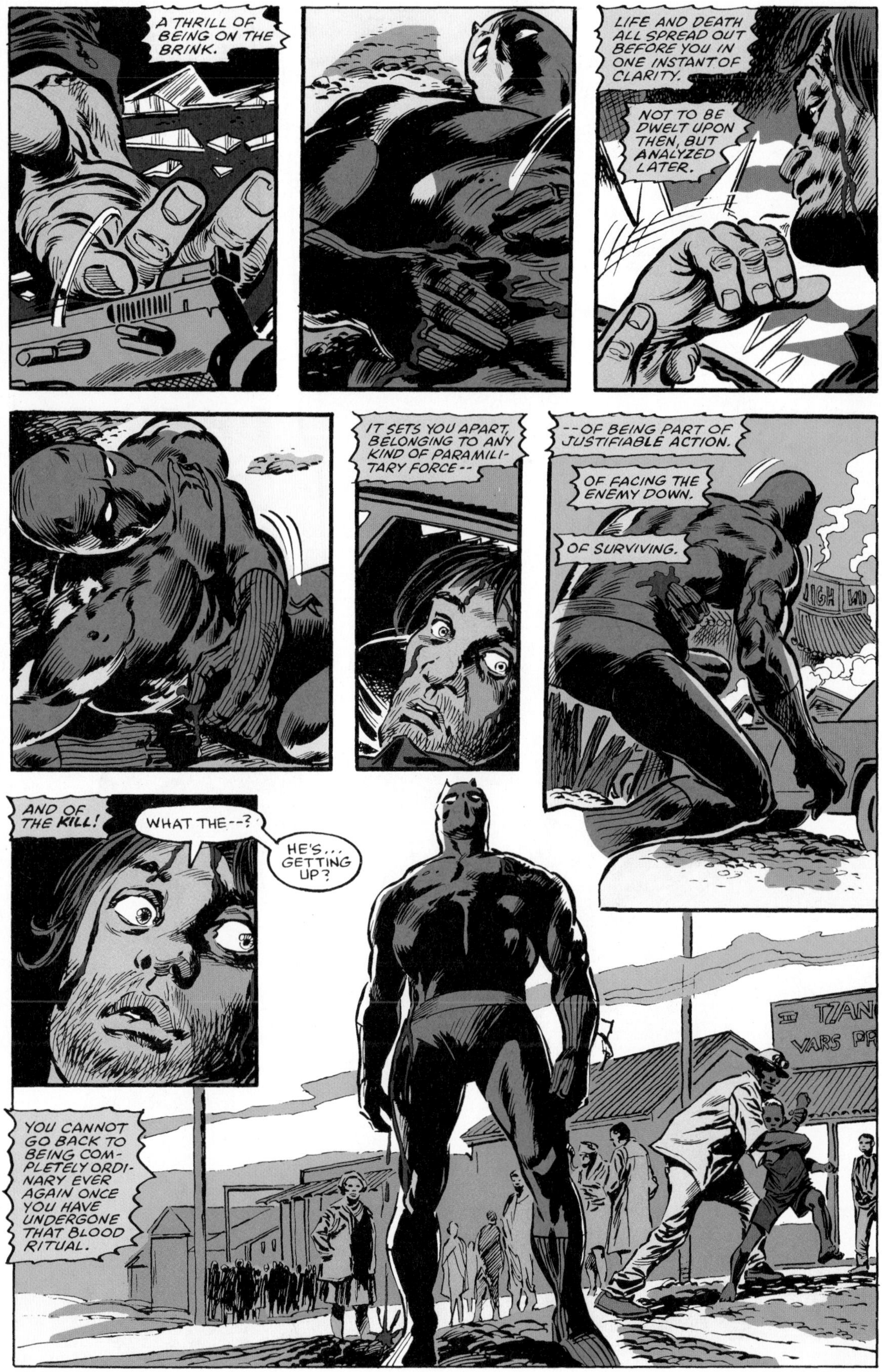

A THRILL OF BEING ON THE BRINK.
LIFE AND DEATH ALL SPREAD OUT BEFORE YOU IN ONE INSTANT OF CLARITY.
NOT TO BE DWELT UPON THEN, BUT ANALYZED LATER.
IT SETS YOU APART, BELONGING TO ANY KIND OF PARAMILITARY FORCE--
--OF BEING PART OF JUSTIFIABLE ACTION.
OF FACING THE ENEMY DOWN.
OF SURVIVING.
AND OF THE KILL!
WHAT THE--?
HE'S... GETTING UP?
YOU CANNOT GO BACK TO BEING COMPLETELY ORDINARY EVER AGAIN ONCE YOU HAVE UNDERGONE THAT BLOOD RITUAL.

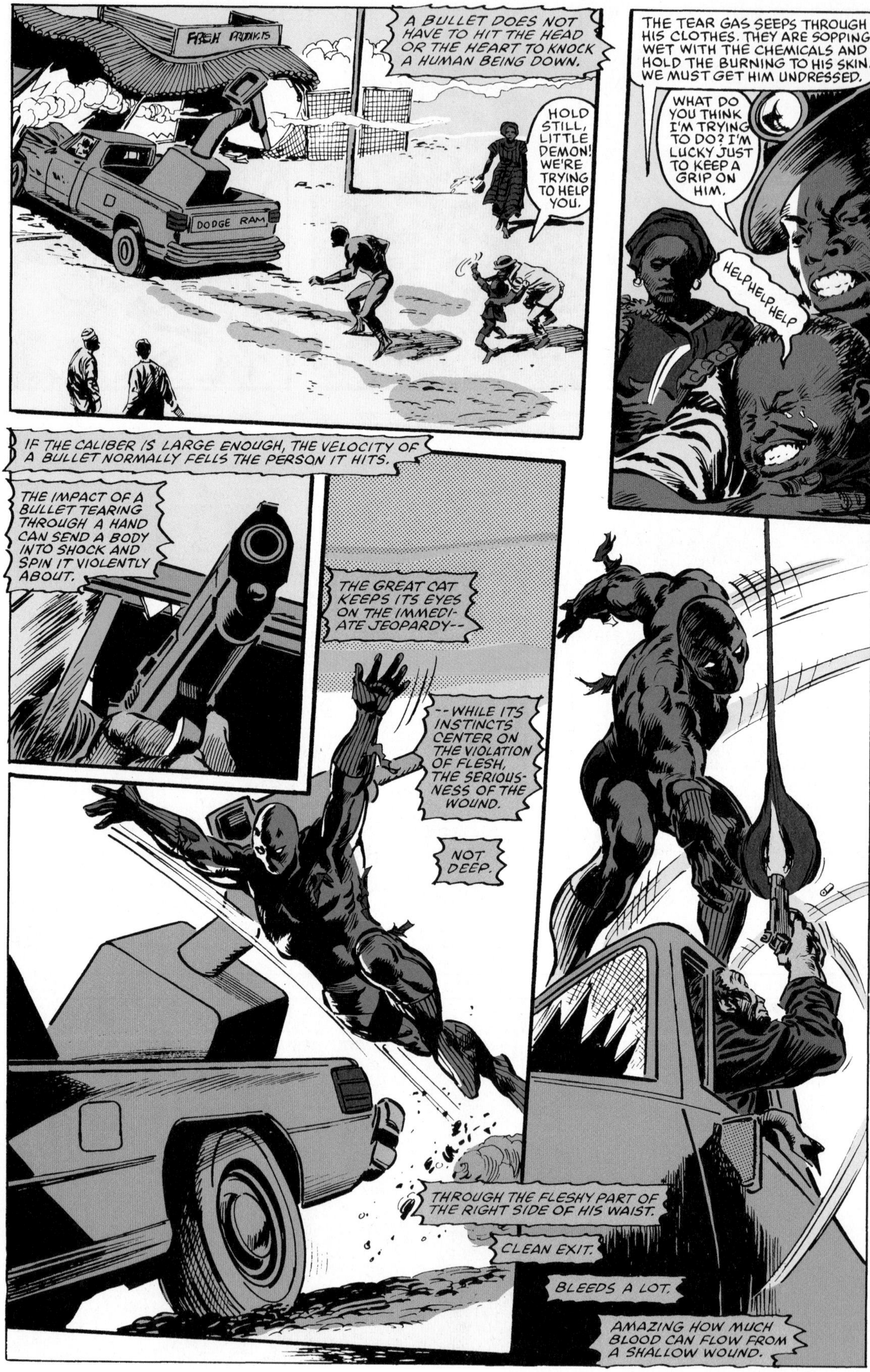
FRESH PRODUCTS
A BULLET DOES NOT HAVE TO HIT THE HEAD OR THE HEART TO KNOCK A HUMAN BEING DOWN.
HOLD STILL, LITTLE DEMON! WE'RE TRYING TO HELP YOU.
DODGE RAM
THE TEAR GAS SEEPS THROUGH HIS CLOTHES. THEY ARE SOPPING WET WITH THE CHEMICALS AND HOLD THE BURNING TO HIS SKIN. WE MUST GET HIM UNDRESSED.
WHAT DO YOU THINK I'M TRYING TO DO? I'M LUCKY JUST TO KEEP A GRIP ON HIM.
HELP HELP HELP
IF THE CALIBER IS LARGE ENOUGH, THE VELOCITY OF A BULLET NORMALLY FELLS THE PERSON IT HITS.
THE IMPACT OF A BULLET TEARING THROUGH A HAND CAN SEND A BODY INTO SHOCK AND SPIN IT VIOLENTLY ABOUT.
THE GREAT CAT KEEPS ITS EYES ON THE IMMEDIATE JEOPARDY--
--WHILE ITS INSTINCTS CENTER ON THE VIOLATION OF FLESH, THE SERIOUSNESS OF THE WOUND.
NOT DEEP.
THROUGH THE FLESHY PART OF THE RIGHT SIDE OF HIS WAIST.
CLEAN EXIT.
BLEEDS A LOT.
AMAZING HOW MUCH BLOOD CAN FLOW FROM A SHALLOW WOUND.

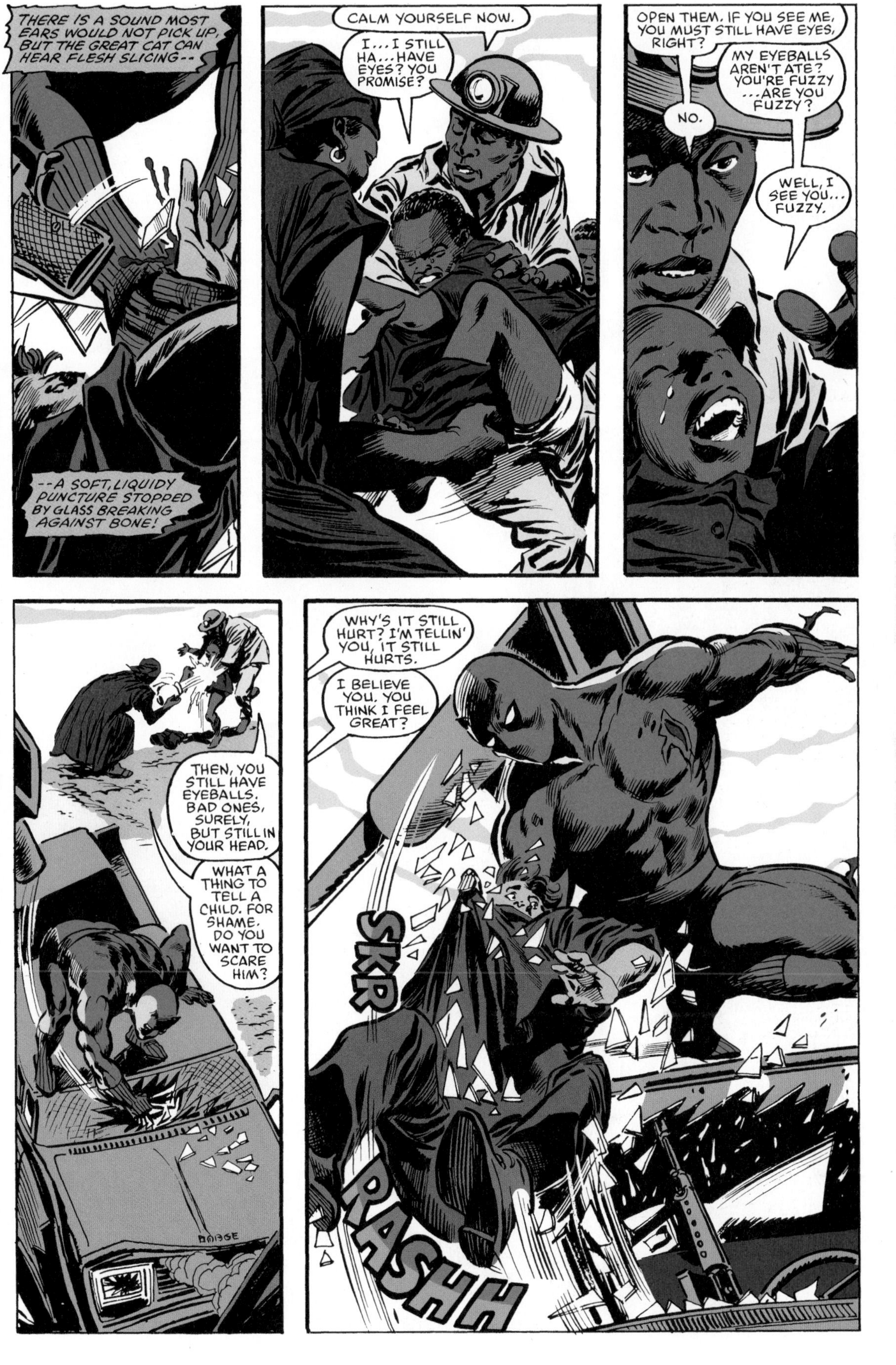

THERE IS A SOUND MOST EARS WOULD NOT PICK UP, BUT THE GREAT CAT CAN HEAR FLESH SLICING--
--A SOFT, LIQUIDY PUNCTURE STOPPED BY GLASS BREAKING AGAINST BONE!
CALM YOURSELF NOW.
I...I STILL HA...HAVE EYES? YOU PROMISE?
OPEN THEM. IF YOU SEE ME, YOU MUST STILL HAVE EYES, RIGHT?
NO.
MY EYEBALLS AREN'T ATE? YOU'RE FUZZY ...ARE YOU FUZZY?
WELL, I SEE YOU... FUZZY.
THEN, YOU STILL HAVE EYEBALLS. BAD ONES, SURELY, BUT STILL IN YOUR HEAD.
WHAT A THING TO TELL A CHILD. FOR SHAME. DO YOU WANT TO SCARE HIM?
WHY'S IT STILL HURT? I'M TELLIN' YOU, IT STILL HURTS.
I BELIEVE YOU. YOU THINK I FEEL GREAT?
SKR
RASHH

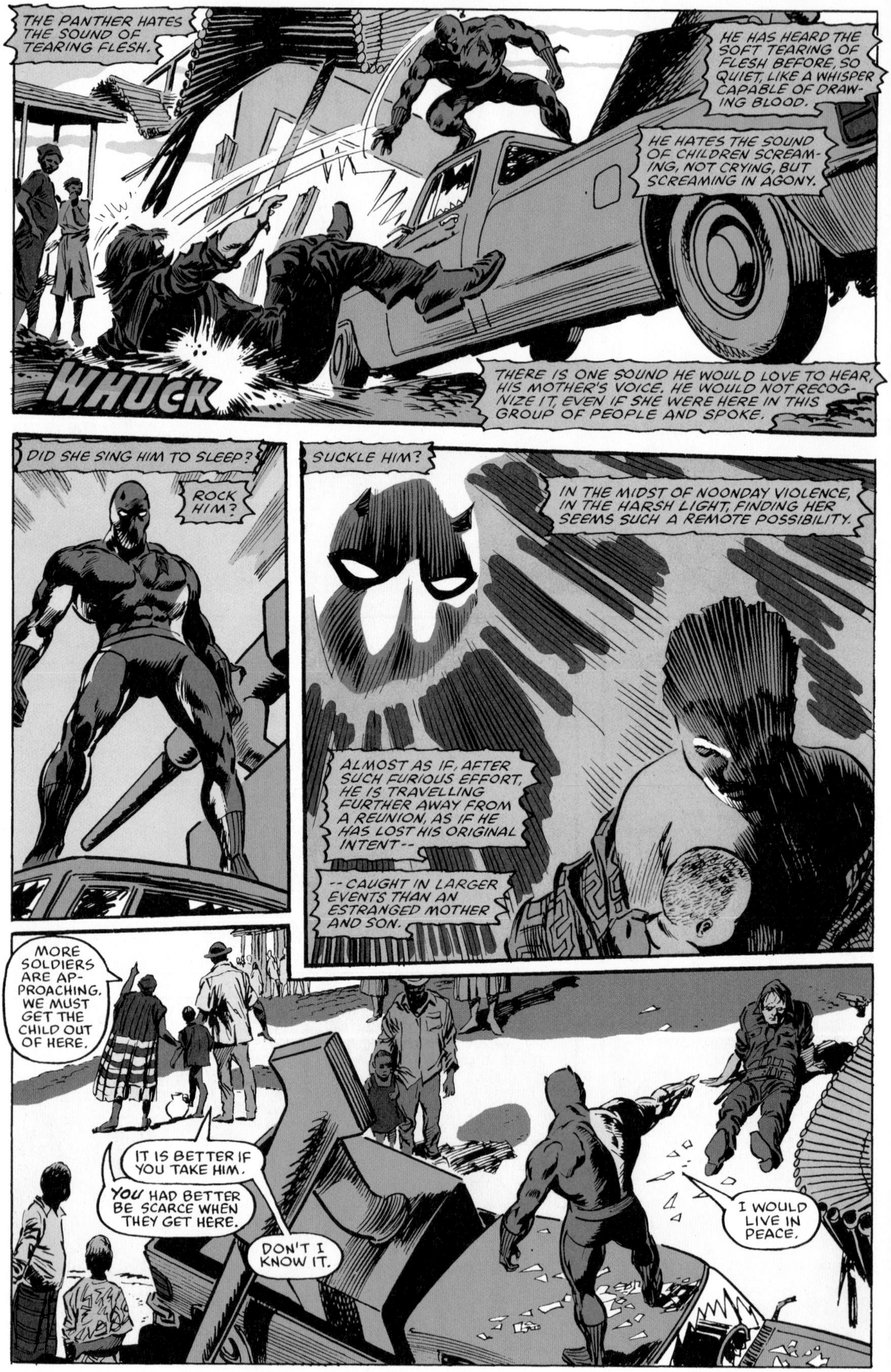
THE PANTHER HATES THE SOUND OF TEARING FLESH.
HE HAS HEARD THE SOFT TEARING OF FLESH BEFORE, SO QUIET, LIKE A WHISPER CAPABLE OF DRAWING BLOOD.
HE HATES THE SOUND OF CHILDREN SCREAMING, NOT CRYING, BUT SCREAMING IN AGONY.
WHUCK
THERE IS ONE SOUND HE WOULD LOVE TO HEAR, HIS MOTHER'S VOICE. HE WOULD NOT RECOGNIZE IT, EVEN IF SHE WERE HERE IN THIS GROUP OF PEOPLE AND SPOKE.
DID SHE SING HIM TO SLEEP?
ROCK HIM?
SUCKLE HIM?
IN THE MIDST OF NOONDAY VIOLENCE, IN THE HARSH LIGHT, FINDING HER SEEMS SUCH A REMOTE POSSIBILITY.
ALMOST AS IF, AFTER SUCH FURIOUS EFFORT, HE IS TRAVELLING FURTHER AWAY FROM A REUNION, AS IF HE HAS LOST HIS ORIGINAL INTENT--
--CAUGHT IN LARGER EVENTS THAN AN ESTRANGED MOTHER AND SON.
MORE SOLDIERS ARE APPROACHING. WE MUST GET THE CHILD OUT OF HERE.
IT IS BETTER IF YOU TAKE HIM.
YOU HAD BETTER BE SCARCE WHEN THEY GET HERE.
DON'T I KNOW IT.
I WOULD LIVE IN PEACE.

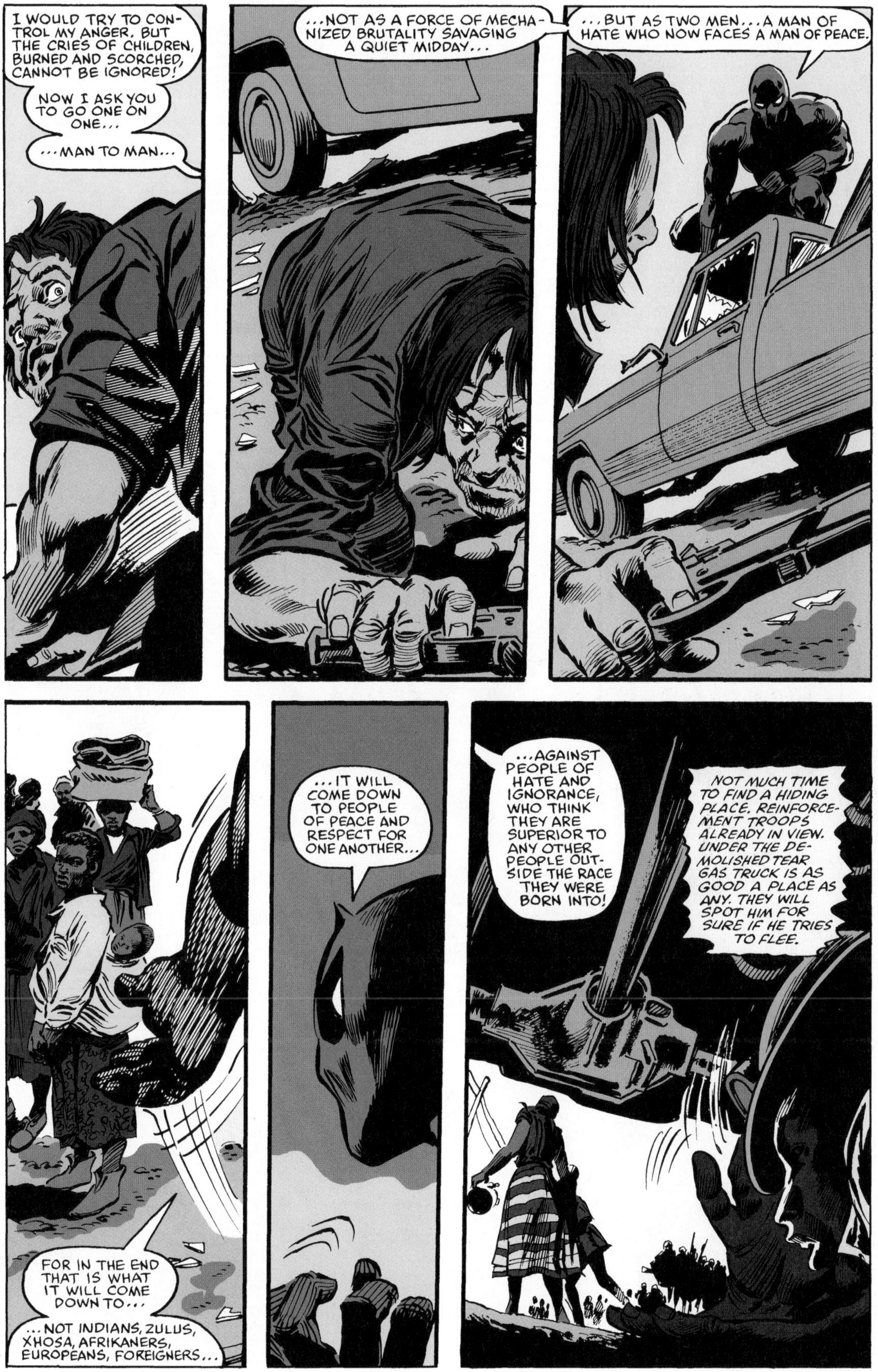
I WOULD TRY TO CONTROL MY ANGER. BUT THE CRIES OF CHILDREN, BURNED AND SCORCHED, CANNOT BE IGNORED!
NOW I ASK YOU TO GO ONE ON ONE...
...MAN TO MAN...
...NOT AS A FORCE OF MECHANIZED BRUTALITY SAVAGING A QUIET MIDDAY...
...BUT AS TWO MEN...A MAN OF HATE WHO NOW FACES A MAN OF PEACE.
FOR IN THE END THAT IS WHAT IT WILL COME DOWN TO...
...NOT INDIANS, ZULUS, XHOSA, AFRIKANERS, EUROPEANS, FOREIGNERS...
...IT WILL COME DOWN TO PEOPLE OF PEACE AND RESPECT FOR ONE ANOTHER...
...AGAINST PEOPLE OF HATE AND IGNORANCE, WHO THINK THEY ARE SUPERIOR TO ANY OTHER PEOPLE OUTSIDE THE RACE THEY WERE BORN INTO!
NOT MUCH TIME TO FIND A HIDING PLACE. REINFORCEMENT TROOPS ALREADY IN VIEW. UNDER THE DEMOLISHED TEAR GAS TRUCK IS AS GOOD A PLACE AS ANY. THEY WILL SPOT HIM FOR SURE IF HE TRIES TO FLEE.

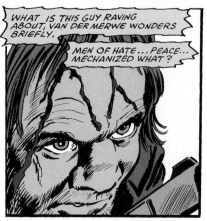

WHAT IS THIS GUY RAVING ABOUT, VAN DER MERWE WONDERS BRIEFLY.

MEN OF HATE... PEACE... MECHANIZED WHAT?

MAN DOESN'T MAKE ANY SENSE.

PROBABLY SOME WEIRD COMMUNIST INSPIRED GUERRILLA FIGHTER JUSTIFYING AN ASSAULT ON CIVILIZED AUTHORITY.

THE TENSION BETWEEN THE TWO MEN IS PALPABLE, AND VAN DER MERWE IS VERY ALIVE WITH THAT AWARENESS.

INDISPUTABLY, THE POWER OF THE MAN RADIATES OUTWARD, AND VAN DER MERWE KNOWS HE MUST NOT WAVER.

HE MUST HAVE TOTAL CONVICTION HE CAN AIM HIS WEAPON BEFORE THE TERRORIST STRIKES.

INDECISIVENESS IN SUCH A SITUATION CAN GET YOU KILLED!

GET UP!

WHUCT

NOW, LET US SEE IF YOU CAN DO WHAT LITTLE CHILDREN HAD TO DO BECAUSE OF YOU!

YOU WATCHED LITTLE CHILDREN FALL--

--AND THEY MANAGED TO GET UP.

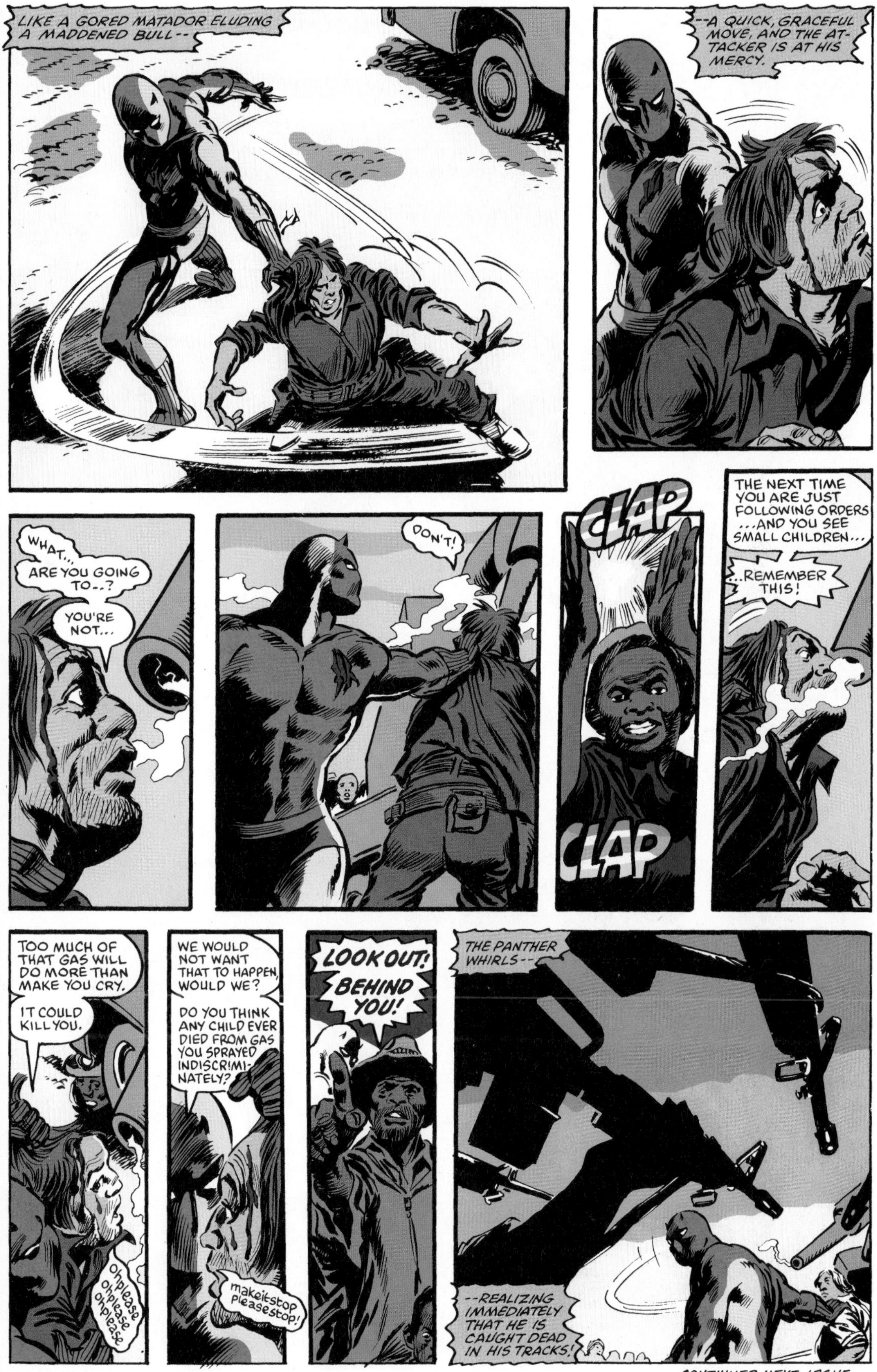
LIKE A GORED MATADOR ELUDING A MADDENED BULL--
--A QUICK, GRACEFUL MOVE, AND THE AT-TACKER IS AT HIS MERCY.
WHAT... ARE YOU GOING TO--?
YOU'RE NOT...
DON'T!
CLAP
CLAP
THE NEXT TIME YOU ARE JUST FOLLOWING ORDERS ...AND YOU SEE SMALL CHILDREN...
...REMEMBER THIS!
TOO MUCH OF THAT GAS WILL DO MORE THAN MAKE YOU CRY.
IT COULD KILL YOU.
ohplease ohplease ohplease
WE WOULD NOT WANT THAT TO HAPPEN, WOULD WE?
DO YOU THINK ANY CHILD EVER DIED FROM GAS YOU SPRAYED INDISCRIMI-NATELY?
makeitstop pleasestop!
LOOK OUT! BEHIND YOU!
THE PANTHER WHIRLS--
--REALIZING IMMEDIATELY THAT HE IS CAUGHT DEAD IN HIS TRACKS!

CONTINUED NEXT ISSUE...

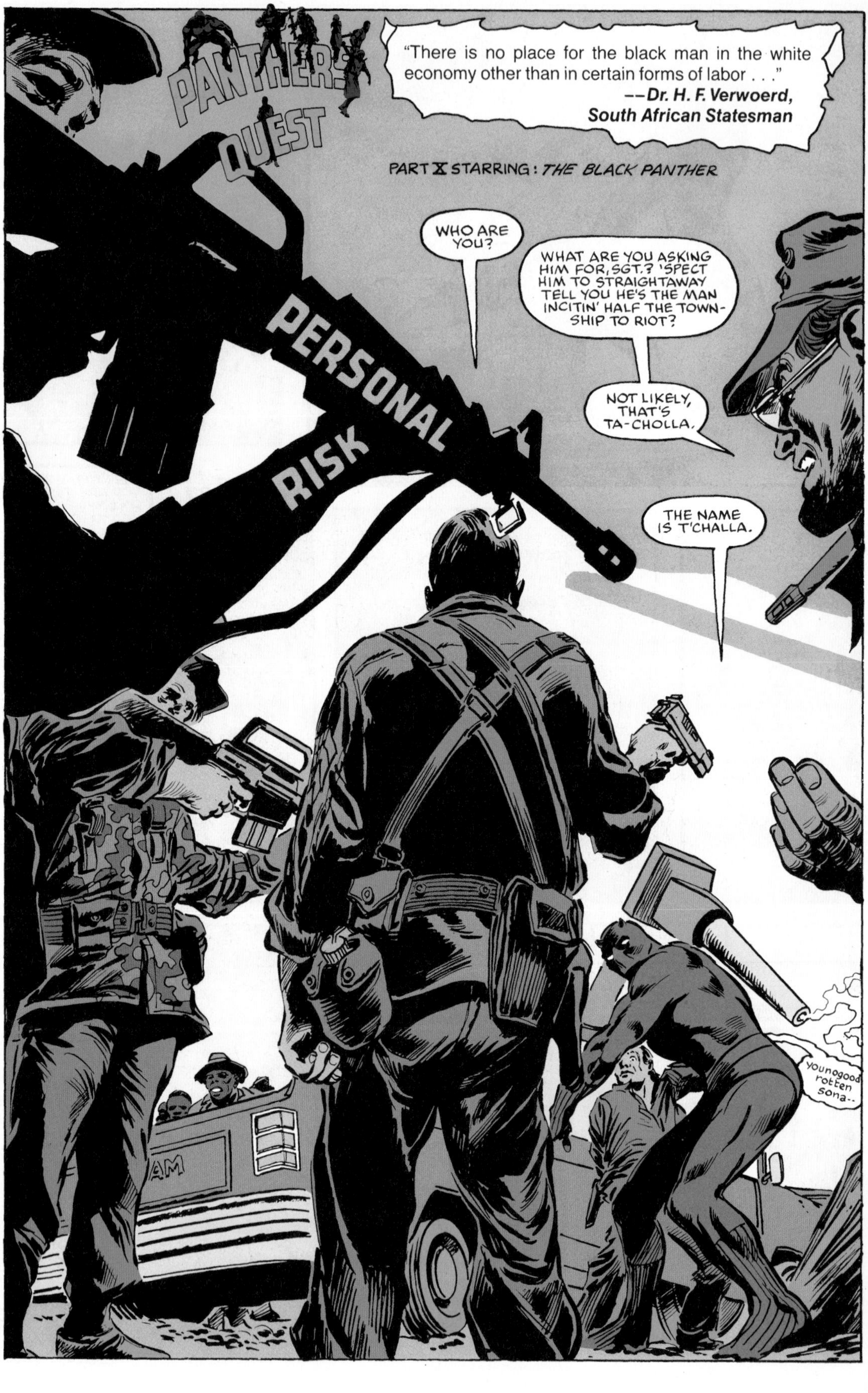
PANTHER'S QUEST
"There is no place for the black man in the white economy other than in certain forms of labor . . ."
--Dr. H. F. Verwoerd, South African Statesman
PART X STARRING: THE BLACK PANTHER
PERSONAL RISK
WHO ARE YOU?
WHAT ARE YOU ASKING HIM FOR, SGT.? 'SPECT HIM TO STRAIGHTAWAY TELL YOU HE'S THE MAN INCITIN' HALF THE TOWNSHIP TO RIOT?
NOT LIKELY, THAT'S TA-CHOLLA.
THE NAME IS T'CHALLA.
younogood rotten sona--

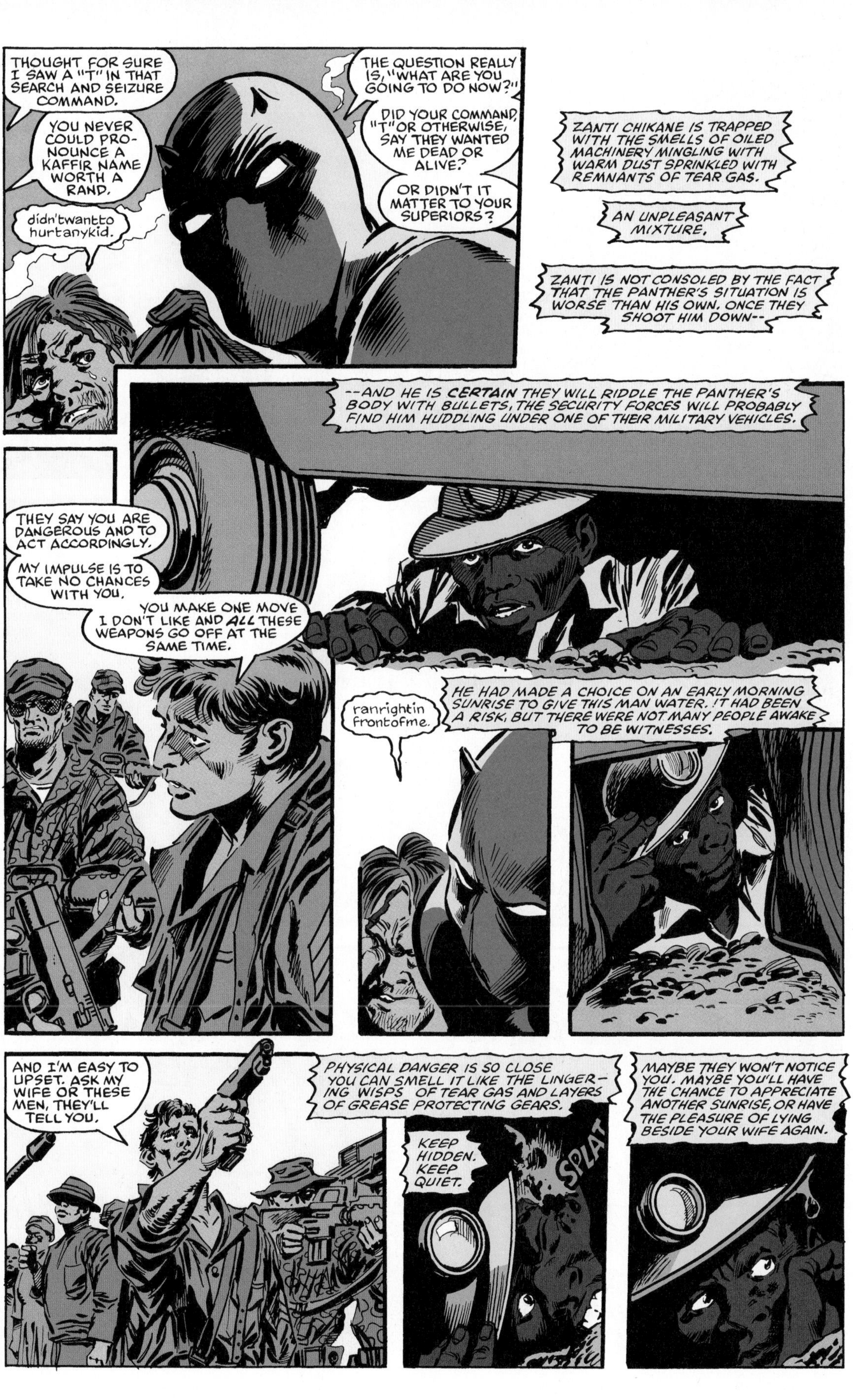
THOUGHT FOR SURE I SAW A "T" IN THAT SEARCH AND SEIZURE COMMAND.
YOU NEVER COULD PRONOUNCE A KAFFIR NAME WORTH A RAND.
didn'twantto hurtanykid.
THE QUESTION REALLY IS, "WHAT ARE YOU GOING TO DO NOW?"
DID YOUR COMMAND, "T" OR OTHERWISE, SAY THEY WANTED ME DEAD OR ALIVE?
OR DIDN'T IT MATTER TO YOUR SUPERIORS?
ZANTI CHIKANE IS TRAPPED WITH THE SMELLS OF OILED MACHINERY MINGLING WITH WARM DUST SPRINKLED WITH REMNANTS OF TEAR GAS.
AN UNPLEASANT MIXTURE.
ZANTI IS NOT CONSOLED BY THE FACT THAT THE PANTHER'S SITUATION IS WORSE THAN HIS OWN. ONCE THEY SHOOT HIM DOWN--
--AND HE IS CERTAIN THEY WILL RIDDLE THE PANTHER'S BODY WITH BULLETS, THE SECURITY FORCES WILL PROBABLY FIND HIM HUDDLING UNDER ONE OF THEIR MILITARY VEHICLES.
THEY SAY YOU ARE DANGEROUS AND TO ACT ACCORDINGLY.
MY IMPULSE IS TO TAKE NO CHANCES WITH YOU.
YOU MAKE ONE MOVE I DON'T LIKE AND ALL THESE WEAPONS GO OFF AT THE SAME TIME.
ranrightin frontofme.
HE HAD MADE A CHOICE ON AN EARLY MORNING SUNRISE TO GIVE THIS MAN WATER. IT HAD BEEN A RISK, BUT THERE WERE NOT MANY PEOPLE AWAKE TO BE WITNESSES.
AND I'M EASY TO UPSET. ASK MY WIFE OR THESE MEN, THEY'LL TELL YOU.
PHYSICAL DANGER IS SO CLOSE YOU CAN SMELL IT LIKE THE LINGERING WISPS OF TEAR GAS AND LAYERS OF GREASE PROTECTING GEARS.
KEEP HIDDEN. KEEP QUIET.
SPLAT
MAYBE THEY WON'T NOTICE YOU. MAYBE YOU'LL HAVE THE CHANCE TO APPRECIATE ANOTHER SUNRISE, OR HAVE THE PLEASURE OF LYING BESIDE YOUR WIFE AGAIN.

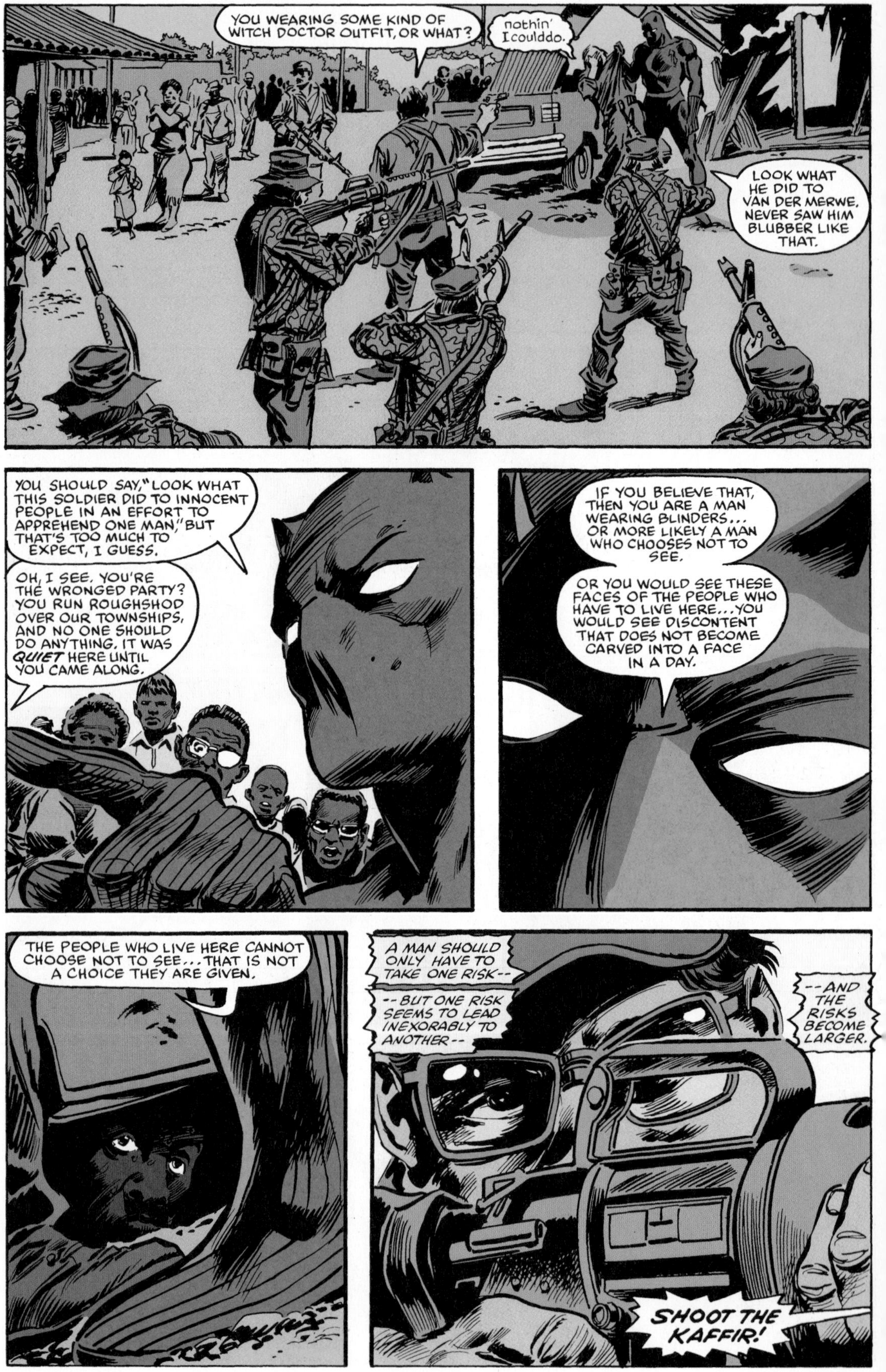
YOU WEARING SOME KIND OF WITCH DOCTOR OUTFIT, OR WHAT?
nothin' Icoulddo.
LOOK WHAT HE DID TO VAN DER MERWE. NEVER SAW HIM BLUBBER LIKE THAT.
YOU SHOULD SAY, "LOOK WHAT THIS SOLDIER DID TO INNOCENT PEOPLE IN AN EFFORT TO APPREHEND ONE MAN," BUT THAT'S TOO MUCH TO EXPECT, I GUESS.
OH, I SEE. YOU'RE THE WRONGED PARTY? YOU RUN ROUGHSHOD OVER OUR TOWNSHIPS, AND NO ONE SHOULD DO ANYTHING. IT WAS QUIET HERE UNTIL YOU CAME ALONG.
IF YOU BELIEVE THAT, THEN YOU ARE A MAN WEARING BLINDERS... OR MORE LIKELY A MAN WHO CHOOSES NOT TO SEE.
OR YOU WOULD SEE THESE FACES OF THE PEOPLE WHO HAVE TO LIVE HERE... YOU WOULD SEE DISCONTENT THAT DOES NOT BECOME CARVED INTO A FACE IN A DAY.
THE PEOPLE WHO LIVE HERE CANNOT CHOOSE NOT TO SEE... THAT IS NOT A CHOICE THEY ARE GIVEN.
A MAN SHOULD ONLY HAVE TO TAKE ONE RISK--
--BUT ONE RISK SEEMS TO LEAD INEXORABLY TO ANOTHER--
--AND THE RISKS BECOME LARGER.
SHOOT THE KAFFIR!

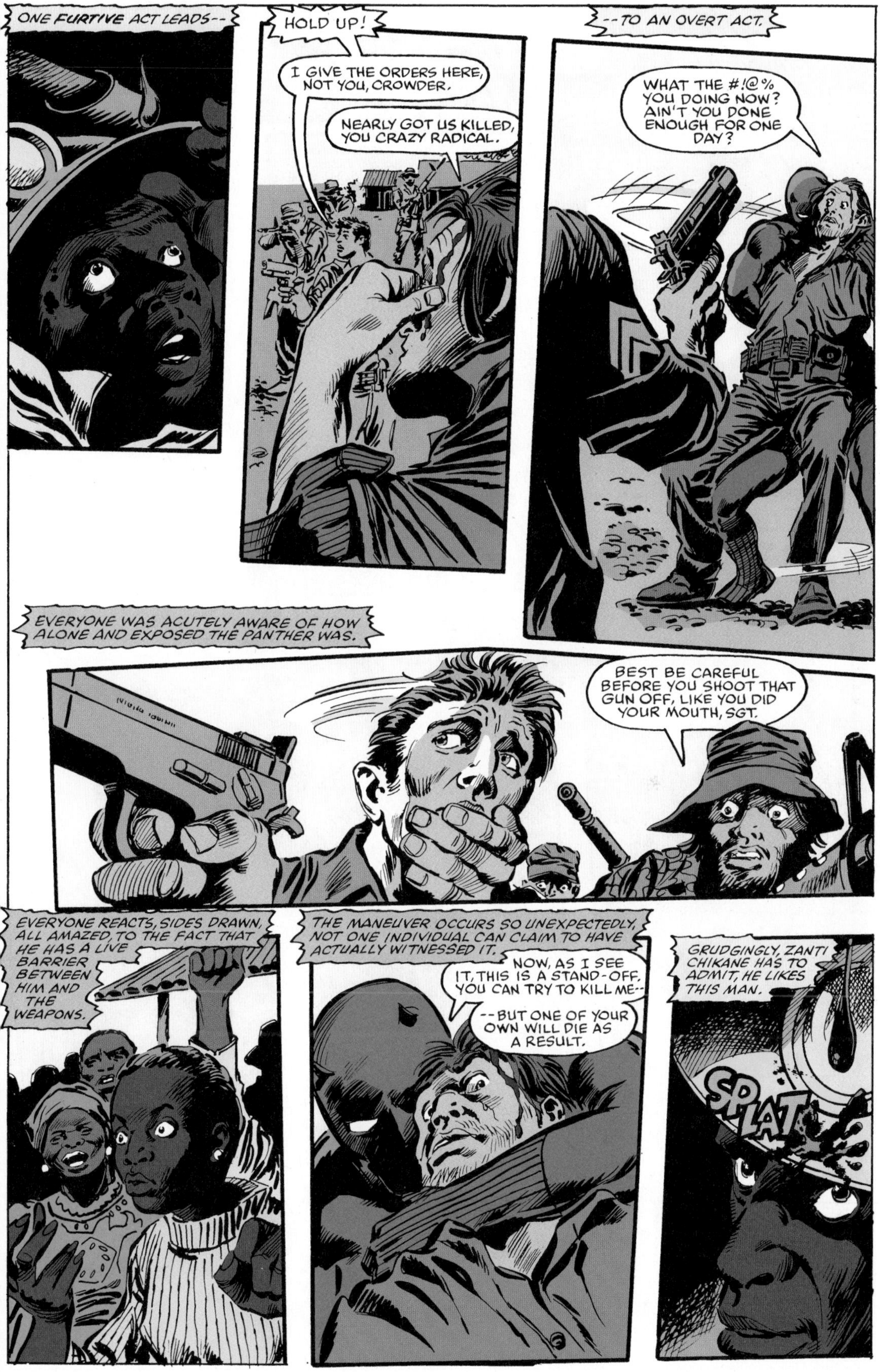
ONE FURTIVE ACT LEADS--
HOLD UP!
I GIVE THE ORDERS HERE, NOT YOU, CROWDER.
NEARLY GOT US KILLED, YOU CRAZY RADICAL.
--TO AN OVERT ACT.
WHAT THE #!@% YOU DOING NOW? AIN'T YOU DONE ENOUGH FOR ONE DAY?
EVERYONE WAS ACUTELY AWARE OF HOW ALONE AND EXPOSED THE PANTHER WAS.
BEST BE CAREFUL BEFORE YOU SHOOT THAT GUN OFF, LIKE YOU DID YOUR MOUTH, SGT.
EVERYONE REACTS, SIDES DRAWN, ALL AMAZED, TO THE FACT THAT HE HAS A LIVE BARRIER BETWEEN HIM AND THE WEAPONS.
THE MANEUVER OCCURS SO UNEXPECTEDLY, NOT ONE INDIVIDUAL CAN CLAIM TO HAVE ACTUALLY WITNESSED IT.
NOW, AS I SEE IT, THIS IS A STAND-OFF. YOU CAN TRY TO KILL ME--
--BUT ONE OF YOUR OWN WILL DIE AS A RESULT.
GRUDGINGLY, ZANTI CHIKANE HAS TO ADMIT, HE LIKES THIS MAN.
SPLAT

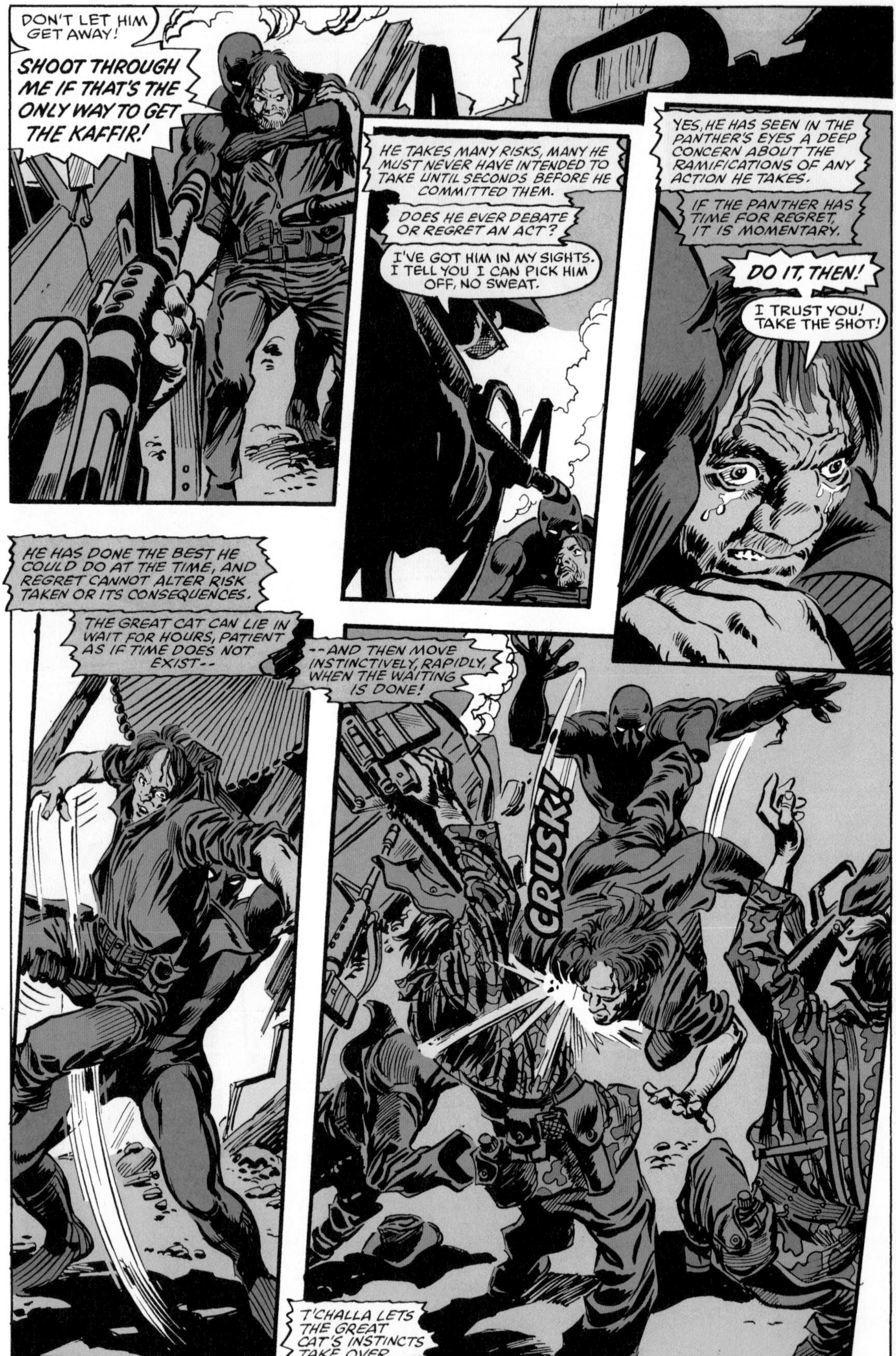
DON'T LET HIM GET AWAY!
SHOOT THROUGH ME IF THAT'S THE ONLY WAY TO GET THE KAFFIR!
HE TAKES MANY RISKS, MANY HE MUST NEVER HAVE INTENDED TO TAKE UNTIL SECONDS BEFORE HE COMMITTED THEM.
DOES HE EVER DEBATE OR REGRET AN ACT?
I'VE GOT HIM IN MY SIGHTS. I TELL YOU I CAN PICK HIM OFF, NO SWEAT.
YES, HE HAS SEEN IN THE PANTHER'S EYES A DEEP CONCERN ABOUT THE RAMIFICATIONS OF ANY ACTION HE TAKES.
IF THE PANTHER HAS TIME FOR REGRET, IT IS MOMENTARY.
DO IT, THEN!
I TRUST YOU! TAKE THE SHOT!
HE HAS DONE THE BEST HE COULD DO AT THE TIME, AND REGRET CANNOT ALTER RISK TAKEN OR ITS CONSEQUENCES.
THE GREAT CAT CAN LIE IN WAIT FOR HOURS, PATIENT AS IF TIME DOES NOT EXIST--
--AND THEN MOVE INSTINCTIVELY, RAPIDLY, WHEN THE WAITING IS DONE!
CRUSK!
T'CHALLA LETS THE GREAT CAT'S INSTINCTS TAKE OVER.

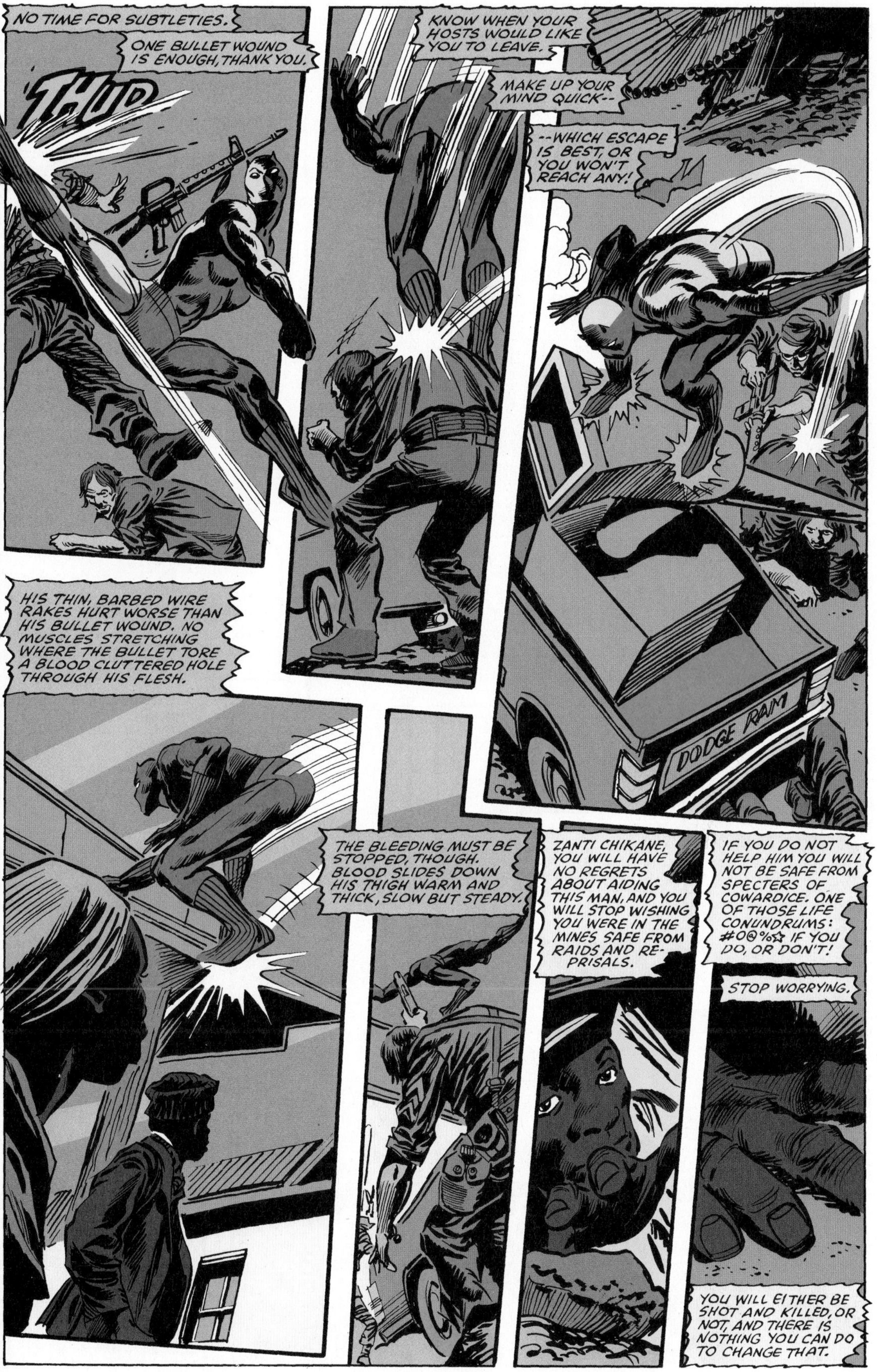
NO TIME FOR SUBTLETIES.
ONE BULLET WOUND IS ENOUGH, THANK YOU.
THUD
KNOW WHEN YOUR HOSTS WOULD LIKE YOU TO LEAVE.
MAKE UP YOUR MIND QUICK--
--WHICH ESCAPE IS BEST, OR YOU WON'T REACH ANY!
HIS THIN, BARBED WIRE RAKES HURT WORSE THAN HIS BULLET WOUND. NO MUSCLES STRETCHING WHERE THE BULLET TORE A BLOOD CLUTTERED HOLE THROUGH HIS FLESH.
DODGE RAM
THE BLEEDING MUST BE STOPPED, THOUGH. BLOOD SLIDES DOWN HIS THIGH WARM AND THICK, SLOW BUT STEADY.
ZANTI CHIKANE, YOU WILL HAVE NO REGRETS ABOUT AIDING THIS MAN, AND YOU WILL STOP WISHING YOU WERE IN THE MINES SAFE FROM RAIDS AND RE-PRISALS.
IF YOU DO NOT HELP HIM YOU WILL NOT BE SAFE FROM SPECTERS OF COWARDICE. ONE OF THOSE LIFE CONUNDRUMS: #0@%☆ IF YOU DO, OR DON'T!
STOP WORRYING.
YOU WILL EITHER BE SHOT AND KILLED, OR NOT, AND THERE IS NOTHING YOU CAN DO TO CHANGE THAT.

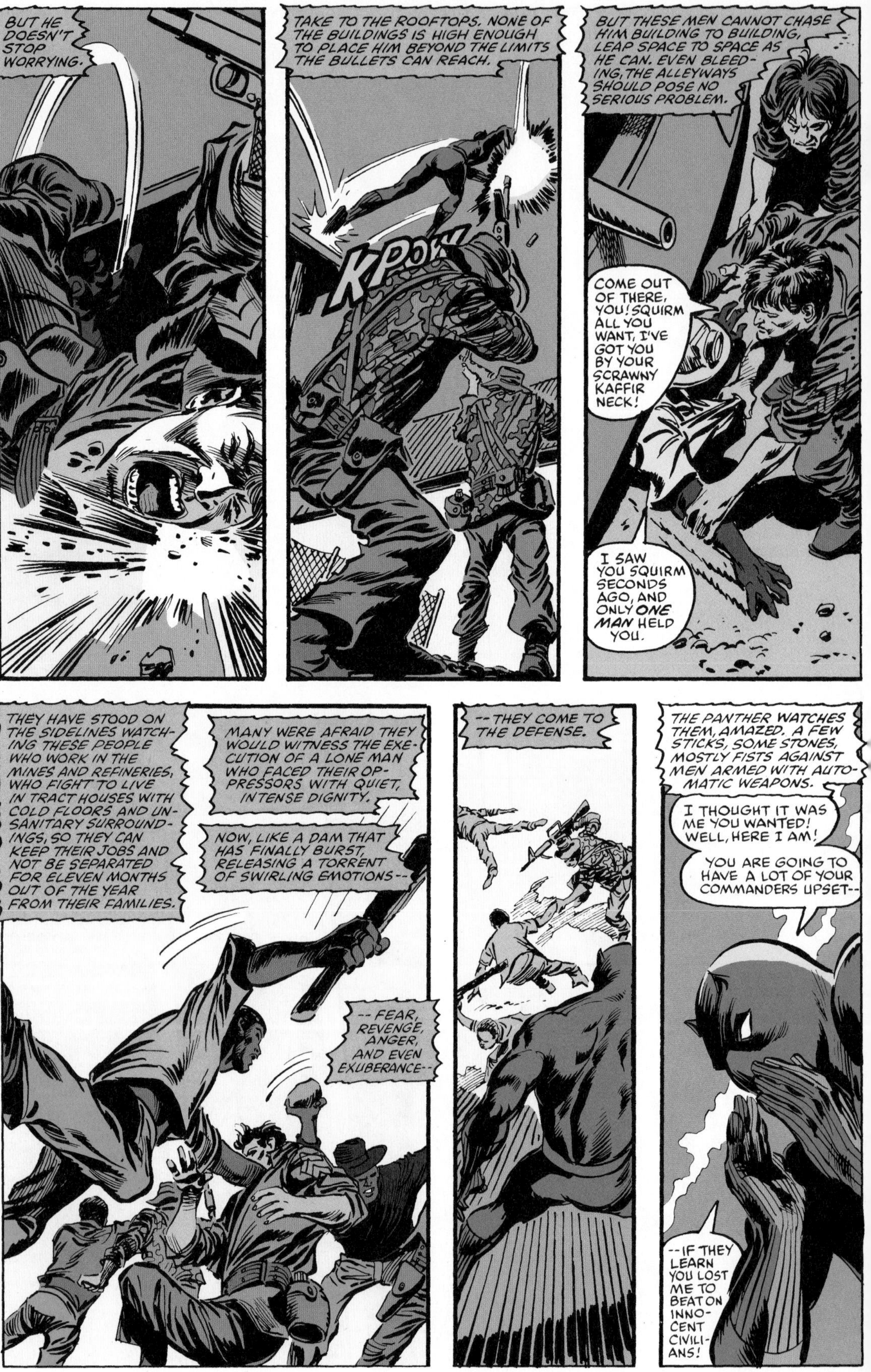
BUT HE DOESN'T STOP WORRYING.
TAKE TO THE ROOFTOPS. NONE OF THE BUILDINGS IS HIGH ENOUGH TO PLACE HIM BEYOND THE LIMITS THE BULLETS CAN REACH.
KPOW
BUT THESE MEN CANNOT CHASE HIM BUILDING TO BUILDING, LEAP SPACE TO SPACE AS HE CAN. EVEN BLEEDING, THE ALLEYWAYS SHOULD POSE NO SERIOUS PROBLEM.
COME OUT OF THERE, YOU! SQUIRM ALL YOU WANT, I'VE GOT YOU BY YOUR SCRAWNY KAFFIR NECK!
I SAW YOU SQUIRM SECONDS AGO, AND ONLY ONE MAN HELD YOU.
THEY HAVE STOOD ON THE SIDELINES WATCHING THESE PEOPLE WHO WORK IN THE MINES AND REFINERIES, WHO FIGHT TO LIVE IN TRACT HOUSES WITH COLD FLOORS AND UNSANITARY SURROUNDINGS, SO THEY CAN KEEP THEIR JOBS AND NOT BE SEPARATED FOR ELEVEN MONTHS OUT OF THE YEAR FROM THEIR FAMILIES.
MANY WERE AFRAID THEY WOULD WITNESS THE EXECUTION OF A LONE MAN WHO FACED THEIR OPPRESSORS WITH QUIET, INTENSE DIGNITY.
NOW, LIKE A DAM THAT HAS FINALLY BURST, RELEASING A TORRENT OF SWIRLING EMOTIONS--
--FEAR, REVENGE, ANGER, AND EVEN EXUBERANCE--
--THEY COME TO THE DEFENSE.
THE PANTHER WATCHES THEM, AMAZED. A FEW STICKS, SOME STONES, MOSTLY FISTS AGAINST MEN ARMED WITH AUTOMATIC WEAPONS.
I THOUGHT IT WAS ME YOU WANTED! WELL, HERE I AM!
YOU ARE GOING TO HAVE A LOT OF YOUR COMMANDERS UPSET--
--IF THEY LEARN YOU LOST ME TO BEAT ON INNOCENT CIVILIANS!

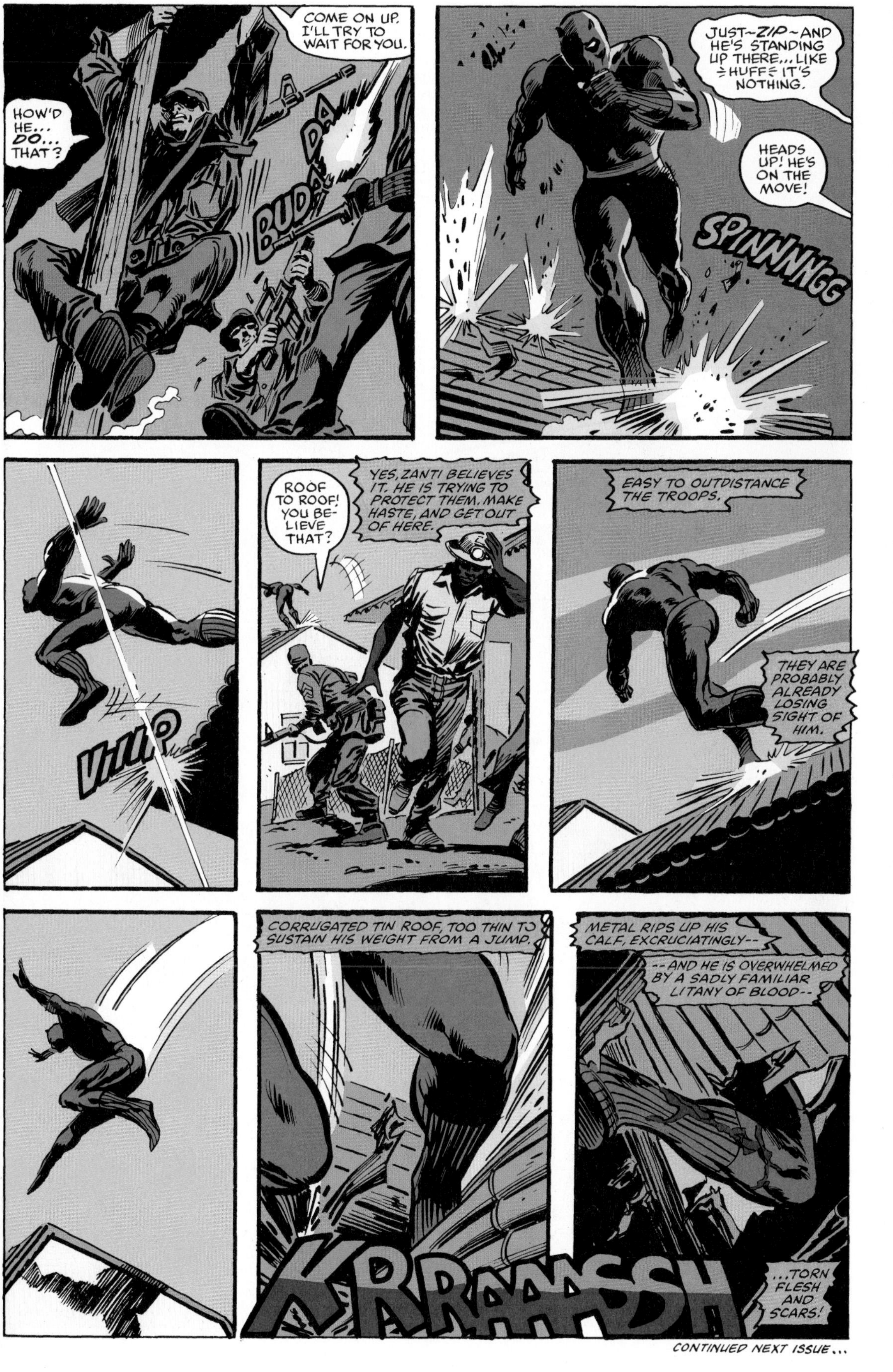

COME ON UP. I'LL TRY TO WAIT FOR YOU.
HOW'D HE... DO... THAT?
DA
BUD
JUST~ZIP~AND HE'S STANDING UP THERE... LIKE =HUFF= IT'S NOTHING.
HEADS UP! HE'S ON THE MOVE!
SPINNNNGG
VHIP
ROOF TO ROOF! YOU BELIEVE THAT?
YES, ZANTI BELIEVES IT. HE IS TRYING TO PROTECT THEM. MAKE HASTE, AND GET OUT OF HERE.
EASY TO OUTDISTANCE THE TROOPS.
THEY ARE PROBABLY ALREADY LOSING SIGHT OF HIM.
CORRUGATED TIN ROOF, TOO THIN TO SUSTAIN HIS WEIGHT FROM A JUMP.
METAL RIPS UP HIS CALF, EXCRUCIATINGLY--
--AND HE IS OVERWHELMED BY A SADLY FAMILIAR LITANY OF BLOOD--
KRAAASSH
...TORN FLESH AND SCARS!

CONTINUED NEXT ISSUE...

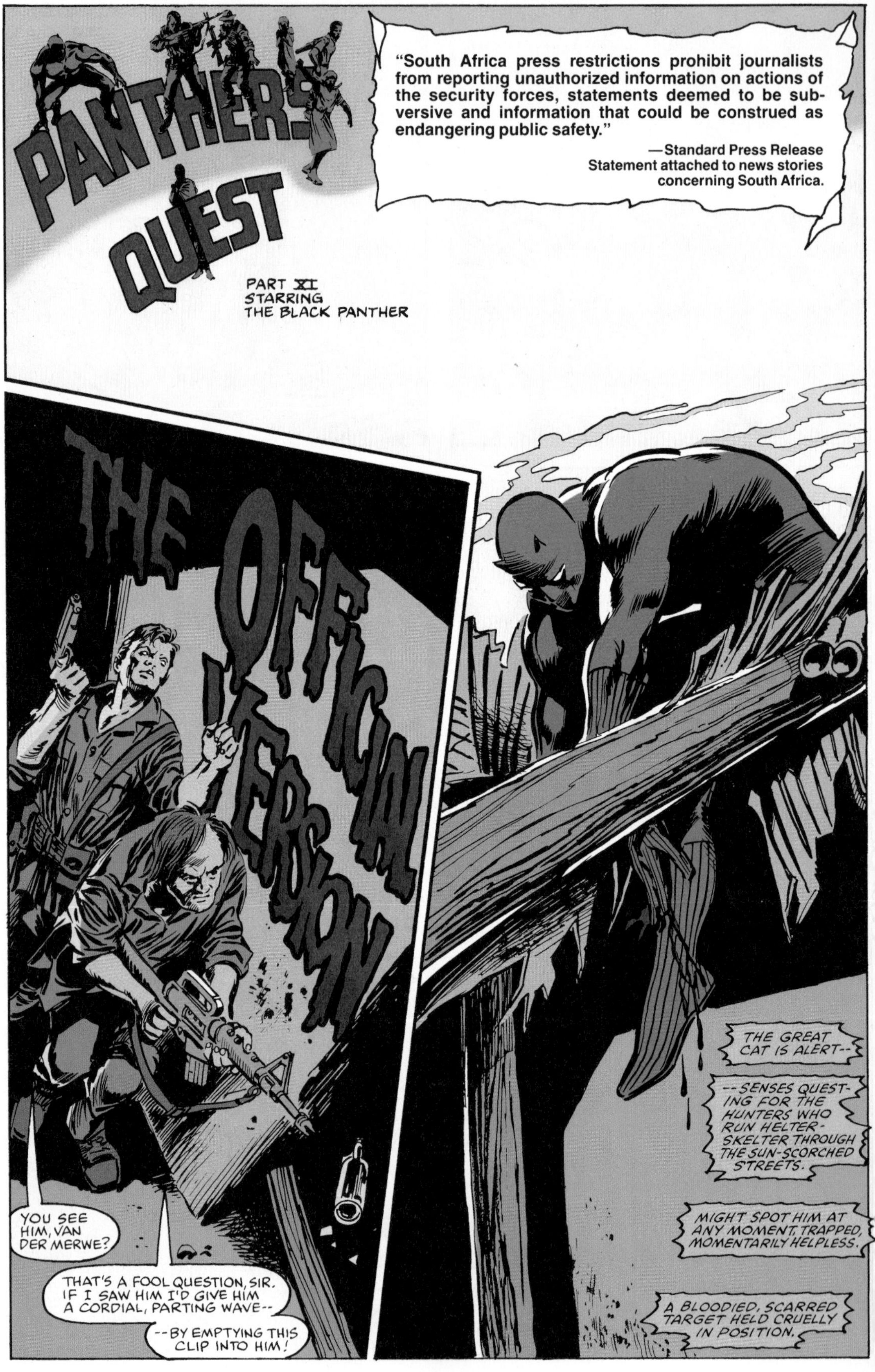
PANTHER'S QUEST
"South Africa press restrictions prohibit journalists from reporting unauthorized information on actions of the security forces, statements deemed to be subversive and information that could be construed as endangering public safety."
—Standard Press Release Statement attached to news stories concerning South Africa.
PART XI
STARRING
THE BLACK PANTHER
THE OFFICIAL VERSION
THE GREAT CAT IS ALERT--
--SENSES QUESTING FOR THE HUNTERS WHO RUN HELTER-SKELTER THROUGH THE SUN-SCORCHED STREETS.
MIGHT SPOT HIM AT ANY MOMENT, TRAPPED, MOMENTARILY HELPLESS.
A BLOODIED, SCARRED TARGET HELD CRUELLY IN POSITION.
YOU SEE HIM, VAN DER MERWE?
THAT'S A FOOL QUESTION, SIR. IF I SAW HIM I'D GIVE HIM A CORDIAL, PARTING WAVE--
--BY EMPTYING THIS CLIP INTO HIM!

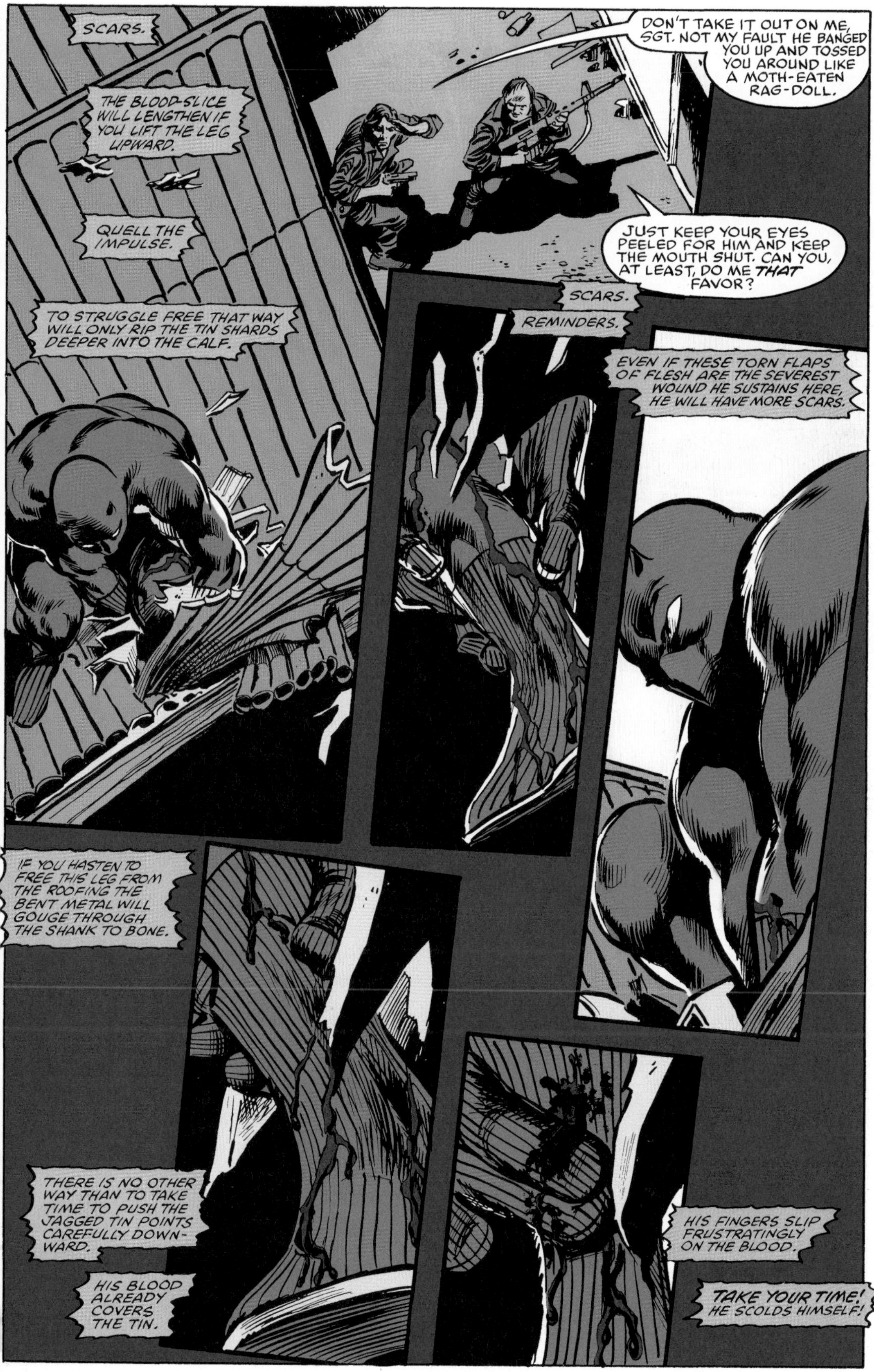

SCARS.
THE BLOOD-SLICE WILL LENGTHEN IF YOU LIFT THE LEG UPWARD.
QUELL THE IMPULSE.
TO STRUGGLE FREE THAT WAY WILL ONLY RIP THE TIN SHARDS DEEPER INTO THE CALF.
DON'T TAKE IT OUT ON ME, SGT. NOT MY FAULT HE BANGED YOU UP AND TOSSED YOU AROUND LIKE A MOTH-EATEN RAG-DOLL.
JUST KEEP YOUR EYES PEELED FOR HIM AND KEEP THE MOUTH SHUT. CAN YOU, AT LEAST, DO ME THAT FAVOR?
SCARS.
REMINDERS.
EVEN IF THESE TORN FLAPS OF FLESH ARE THE SEVEREST WOUND HE SUSTAINS HERE, HE WILL HAVE MORE SCARS.
IF YOU HASTEN TO FREE THIS LEG FROM THE ROOFING THE BENT METAL WILL GOUGE THROUGH THE SHANK TO BONE.
THERE IS NO OTHER WAY THAN TO TAKE TIME TO PUSH THE JAGGED TIN POINTS CAREFULLY DOWNWARD.
HIS BLOOD ALREADY COVERS THE TIN.
HIS FINGERS SLIP FRUSTRATINGLY ON THE BLOOD.
TAKE YOUR TIME! HE SCOLDS HIMSELF!

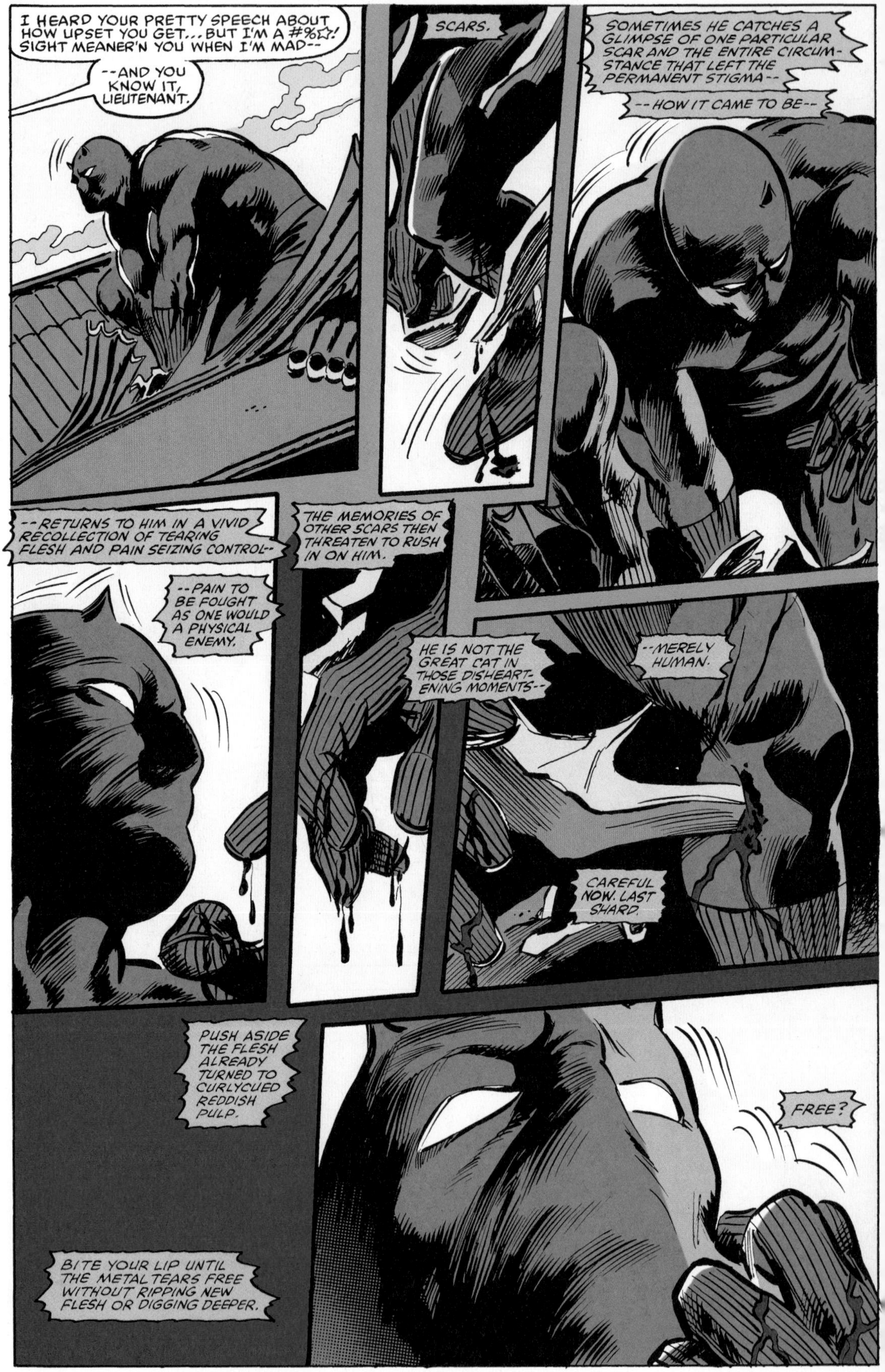

I HEARD YOUR PRETTY SPEECH ABOUT HOW UPSET YOU GET... BUT I'M A #%☆! SIGHT MEANER'N YOU WHEN I'M MAD--
--AND YOU KNOW IT, LIEUTENANT.
SCARS.
SOMETIMES HE CATCHES A GLIMPSE OF ONE PARTICULAR SCAR AND THE ENTIRE CIRCUMSTANCE THAT LEFT THE PERMANENT STIGMA--
--HOW IT CAME TO BE--
--RETURNS TO HIM IN A VIVID RECOLLECTION OF TEARING FLESH AND PAIN SEIZING CONTROL--
--PAIN TO BE FOUGHT AS ONE WOULD A PHYSICAL ENEMY.
THE MEMORIES OF OTHER SCARS THEN THREATEN TO RUSH IN ON HIM.
HE IS NOT THE GREAT CAT IN THOSE DISHEARTENING MOMENTS--
--MERELY HUMAN.
CAREFUL NOW. LAST SHARD.
PUSH ASIDE THE FLESH ALREADY TURNED TO CURLYCUED REDDISH PULP.
BITE YOUR LIP UNTIL THE METAL TEARS FREE WITHOUT RIPPING NEW FLESH OR DIGGING DEEPER.
FREE?

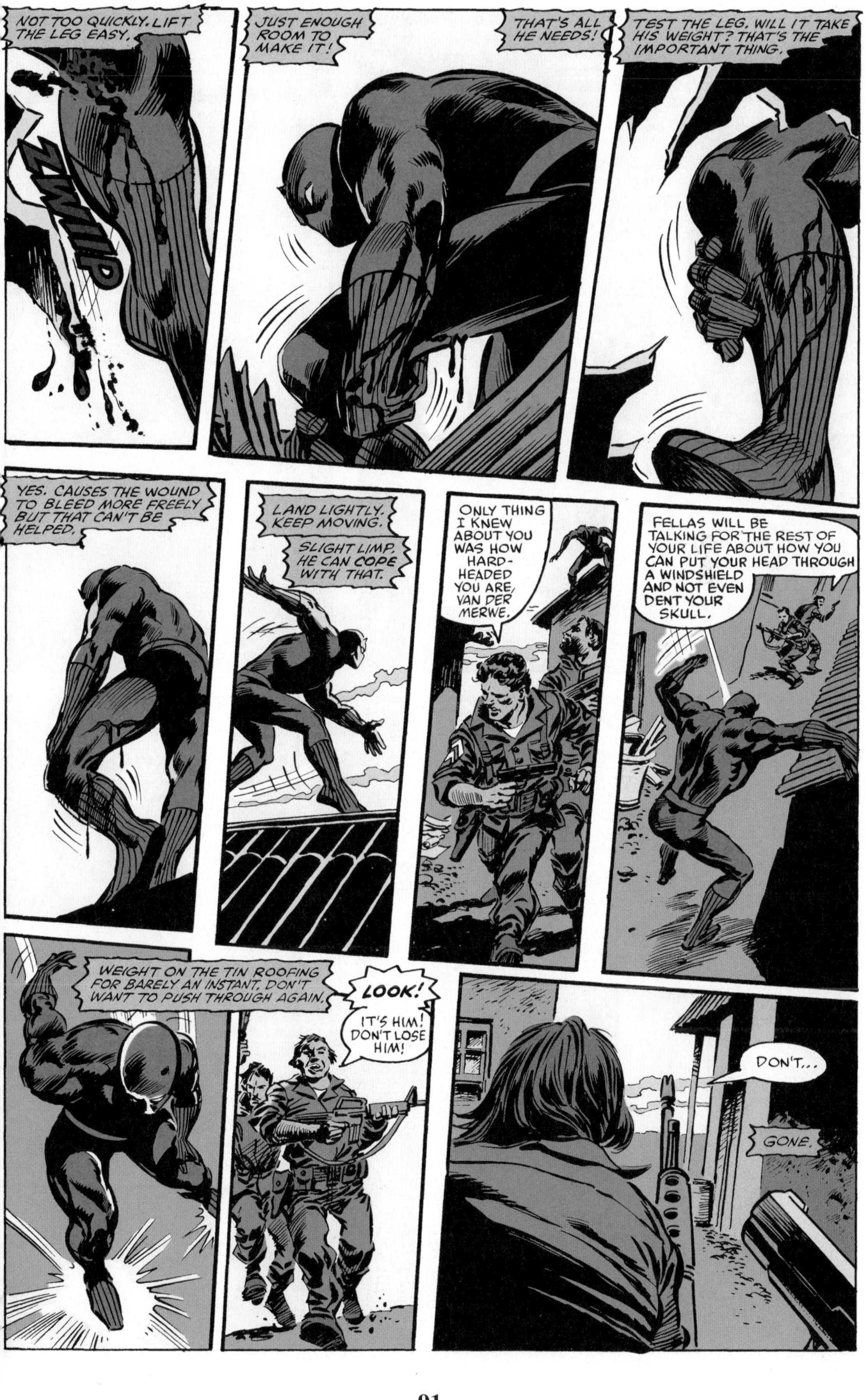

NOT TOO QUICKLY. LIFT THE LEG EASY.
ZWIIIP
JUST ENOUGH ROOM TO MAKE IT!
THAT'S ALL HE NEEDS!
TEST THE LEG. WILL IT TAKE HIS WEIGHT? THAT'S THE IMPORTANT THING.
YES. CAUSES THE WOUND TO BLEED MORE FREELY BUT THAT CAN'T BE HELPED.
LAND LIGHTLY. KEEP MOVING.
SLIGHT LIMP. HE CAN COPE WITH THAT.
ONLY THING I KNEW ABOUT YOU WAS HOW HARD-HEADED YOU ARE, VAN DER MERWE.
FELLAS WILL BE TALKING FOR THE REST OF YOUR LIFE ABOUT HOW YOU CAN PUT YOUR HEAD THROUGH A WINDSHIELD AND NOT EVEN DENT YOUR SKULL.
WEIGHT ON THE TIN ROOFING FOR BARELY AN INSTANT. DON'T WANT TO PUSH THROUGH AGAIN.
LOOK!
IT'S HIM! DON'T LOSE HIM!
DON'T...
GONE.

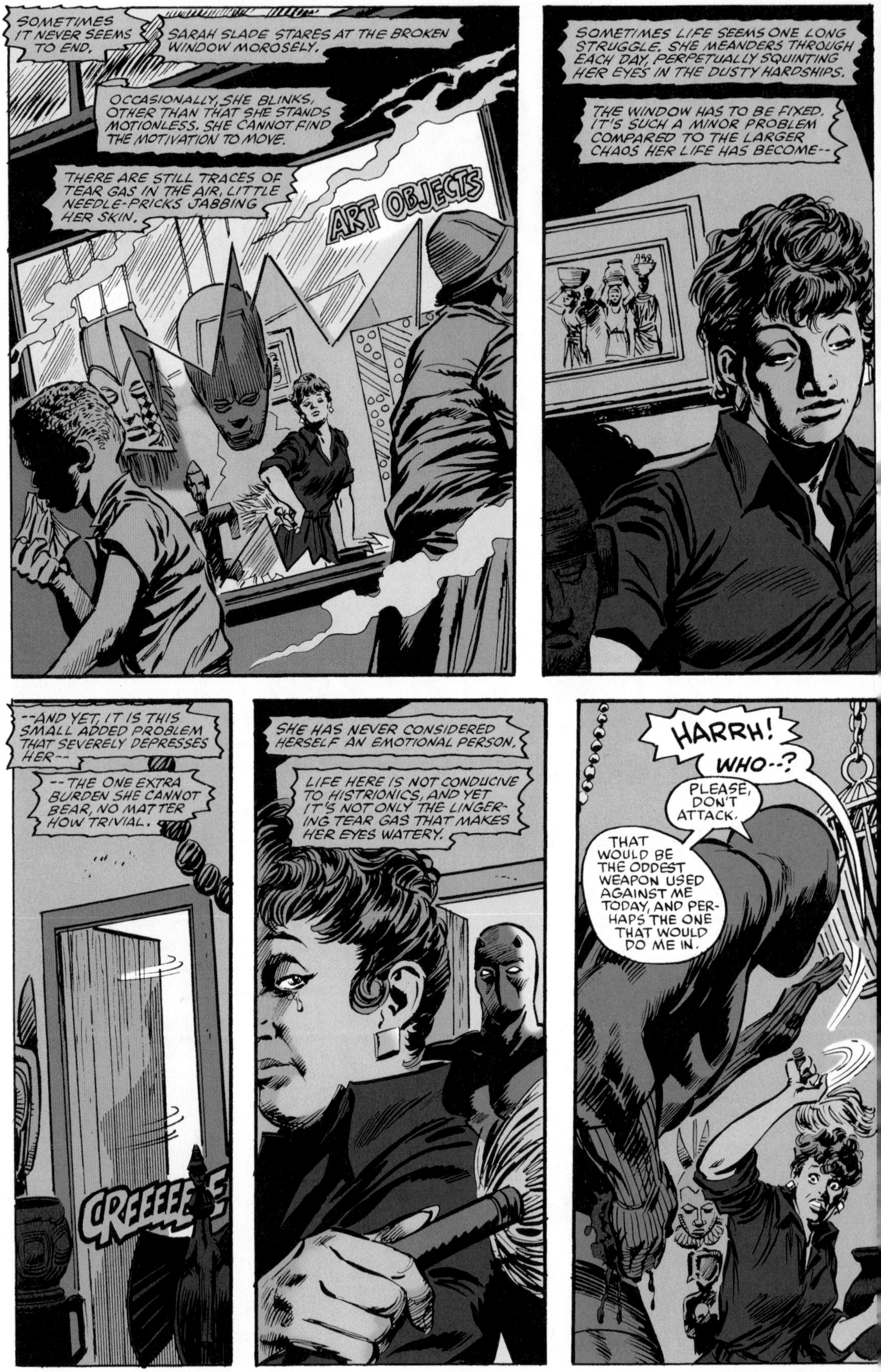
SOMETIMES IT NEVER SEEMS TO END.
SARAH SLADE STARES AT THE BROKEN WINDOW MOROSELY.
OCCASIONALLY, SHE BLINKS, OTHER THAN THAT SHE STANDS MOTIONLESS. SHE CANNOT FIND THE MOTIVATION TO MOVE.
THERE ARE STILL TRACES OF TEAR GAS IN THE AIR, LITTLE NEEDLE-PRICKS JABBING HER SKIN.
ART OBJECTS
SOMETIMES LIFE SEEMS ONE LONG STRUGGLE. SHE MEANDERS THROUGH EACH DAY, PERPETUALLY SQUINTING HER EYES IN THE DUSTY HARDSHIPS.
THE WINDOW HAS TO BE FIXED. IT'S SUCH A MINOR PROBLEM COMPARED TO THE LARGER CHAOS HER LIFE HAS BECOME--
--AND YET, IT IS THIS SMALL ADDED PROBLEM THAT SEVERELY DEPRESSES HER--
--THE ONE EXTRA BURDEN SHE CANNOT BEAR, NO MATTER HOW TRIVIAL.
CREEEEEE
SHE HAS NEVER CONSIDERED HERSELF AN EMOTIONAL PERSON.
LIFE HERE IS NOT CONDUCIVE TO HISTRIONICS, AND YET IT'S NOT ONLY THE LINGERING TEAR GAS THAT MAKES HER EYES WATERY.
HARRH!
WHO--?
PLEASE, DON'T ATTACK.
THAT WOULD BE THE ODDEST WEAPON USED AGAINST ME TODAY, AND PERHAPS THE ONE THAT WOULD DO ME IN.

LOOK AT THAT WINDOW SMASHED TO KINGDOM COME.

YOU KNOW WHAT IT'LL TAKE TO FIX THAT?

I'LL HAVE TO WHINE AND THREATEN, IT'LL TAKE ME A WEEK TO GET SOMEONE TO FIND A REPLACEMENT! NOT TO MENTION THE COST!

WHY'D YOU BREAK MY WINDOW?

I THOUGHT A WINDOW WAS WORTH A BOY'S LIFE.

WHAT BOY?

I DIDN'T SEE NO BOY!

ONE MINUTE I'M TALKING TO YOU AND THE NEXT YOU'RE LEAPING THROUGH MY WINDOW.

YOU AND THOSE SOLDIERS, YOU'VE ALL GOT YOUR NERVE.

THIS SHOULD MORE THAN COVER THE COST.

I CANNOT DO ANYTHING ABOUT THE WHINING AND THREATENING REQUIRED.

THERE'S BLOOD ON THIS.

IT'S HONEST BLOOD. IT'S MY OWN.

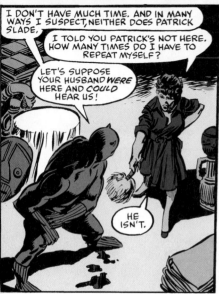

I DON'T HAVE MUCH TIME. AND IN MANY WAYS I SUSPECT, NEITHER DOES PATRICK SLADE.

I TOLD YOU PATRICK'S NOT HERE. HOW MANY TIMES DO I HAVE TO REPEAT MYSELF?

LET'S SUPPOSE YOUR HUSBAND *WERE* HERE AND *COULD* HEAR US!

HE ISN'T.

THEN LET'S TAKE ANOTHER SUPPOSITION... IF HE *SHOULD* RETURN, TELL HIM I WILL COME TOMORROW NIGHT, WHEN THE SITUATION SHOULD QUIET A BIT.

TELL HIM, I HAVE THE MONEY HE WANTS, AND I WILL TRY TO HELP HIM. I WILL RELY ON YOUR DISCRETION.

WE'LL ALL RELY...

...ON EACH OTHER'S DISCRETION.

SLAM

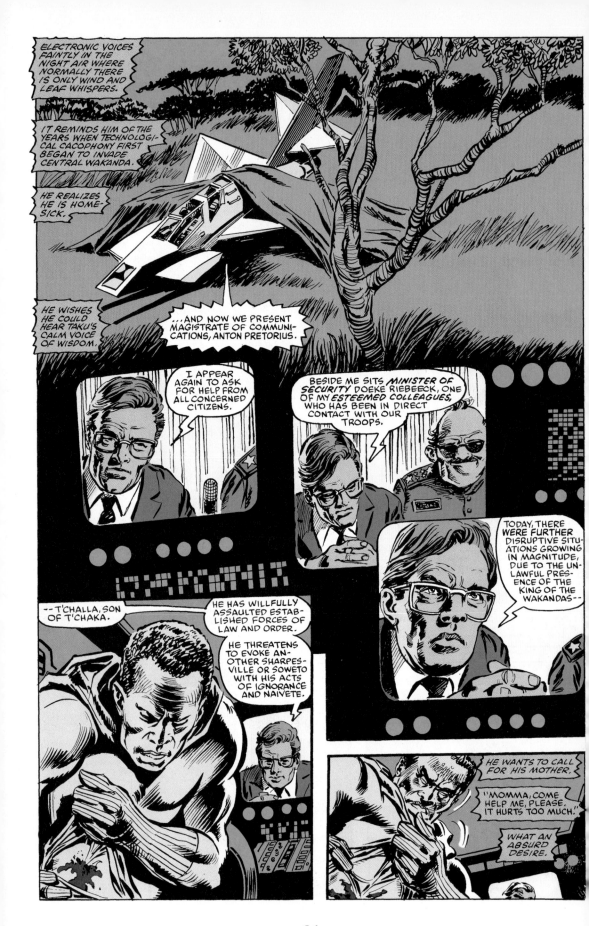

ELECTRONIC VOICES FAINTLY IN THE NIGHT AIR WHERE NORMALLY THERE IS ONLY WIND AND LEAF WHISPERS.

IT REMINDS HIM OF THE YEARS WHEN TECHNOLOGICAL CACOPHONY FIRST BEGAN TO INVADE CENTRAL WAKANDA.

HE REALIZES HE IS HOMESICK.

HE WISHES HE COULD HEAR TAKU'S CALM VOICE OF WISDOM.

...AND NOW WE PRESENT MAGISTRATE OF COMMUNICATIONS, ANTON PRETORIUS.

I APPEAR AGAIN TO ASK FOR HELP FROM ALL CONCERNED CITIZENS.

BESIDE ME SITS *MINISTER OF SECURITY* DOEKE RIEBEECK, ONE OF MY *ESTEEMED COLLEAGUES*, WHO HAS BEEN IN DIRECT CONTACT WITH OUR TROOPS.

TODAY, THERE WERE FURTHER DISRUPTIVE SITUATIONS GROWING IN MAGNITUDE, DUE TO THE UNLAWFUL PRESENCE OF THE KING OF THE WAKANDAS--

--T'CHALLA, SON OF T'CHAKA.

HE HAS WILLFULLY ASSAULTED ESTABLISHED FORCES OF LAW AND ORDER.

HE THREATENS TO EVOKE ANOTHER SHARPESVILLE OR SOWETO WITH HIS ACTS OF IGNORANCE AND NAIVETE.

HE WANTS TO CALL FOR HIS MOTHER.

"MOMMA, COME HELP ME, PLEASE, IT HURTS TOO MUCH."

WHAT AN ABSURD DESIRE.

94

"MINISTER RIEBEECK, WOULD YOU CARE TO COMMENT?"

"THANK YOU, MAGISTRATE PRETORIUS, I AM COMPELLED TO INFORM YOU THAT THE BLACK PANTHER IS TOO DANGEROUS AN INTERLOPER TO BE ALLOWED TO RUN RAMPANT."

HOW RIDICULOUS.

HE CAME HERE TO FIND HER...HELP HER IF SHE NEEDED IT.

FROM ITS INCEPTION, HE HAS KNOWN THERE IS A DUALITY IN THIS QUEST--

--FOR HE HAS WANTED HER TO FIND HIM.

IN THE BEGINNING HE HAD HOPED IT WOULD END WITH HER WORDS OF APPROVAL AND FEARED IT WOULD NOT.

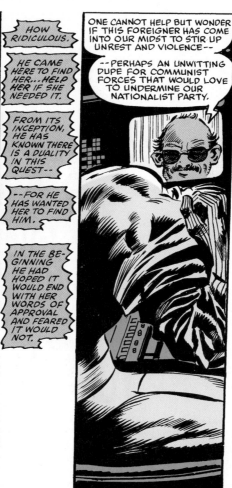

"ONE CANNOT HELP BUT WONDER IF THIS FOREIGNER HAS COME INTO OUR MIDST TO STIR UP UNREST AND VIOLENCE--"

"--PERHAPS AN UNWITTING DUPE FOR COMMUNIST FORCES THAT WOULD LOVE TO UNDERMINE OUR NATIONALIST PARTY."

"THE COMMUNISTS WISH TO ENFLAME ANIMOSITY TOWARD AFRIKANERS. THE PANTHER HELPS THEM VOLUNTARILY OR INVOLUNTARILY, BUT EITHER WAY, HE MUST BE STOPPED."

"ALL OF YOU WHO CAN HEAR MY VOICE CAN HELP PUT AN END TO THE BLACK PANTHER'S ACTS OF BARBARISM."

"IN CONCLUSION, REPORT ANY SIGHTINGS TO YOUR LOCAL POLICE OR NEAREST SECURITY FORCES."

LISTEN TO THEM REPORTING FALLACIES AS TRUTH. THE TURBULENT EVENTS IN THIS OPPRESSED TOWNSHIP--

--THE POLITICAL REPERCUSSIONS HAVE OFTEN MADE HIM FORGET HIS MOTHER. THE PURITY OF THE SINGULAR, INDIVIDUAL QUEST SCATTERED AND OBSCURED BY SOCIETAL CONDITIONS AND DEMANDS.

"WITH YOUR CONCERTED EFFORTS, WE WILL STOP HIS CAMPAIGN OF BLOODSHED BEFORE IT SPREADS FURTHER."

"THANK YOU ALL. I KNOW WE WILL WORK TOGETHER ON THIS, AND AS WE ALWAYS HAVE--"

"--PREVAIL."

MORNING IS A LONG TIME AWAY.

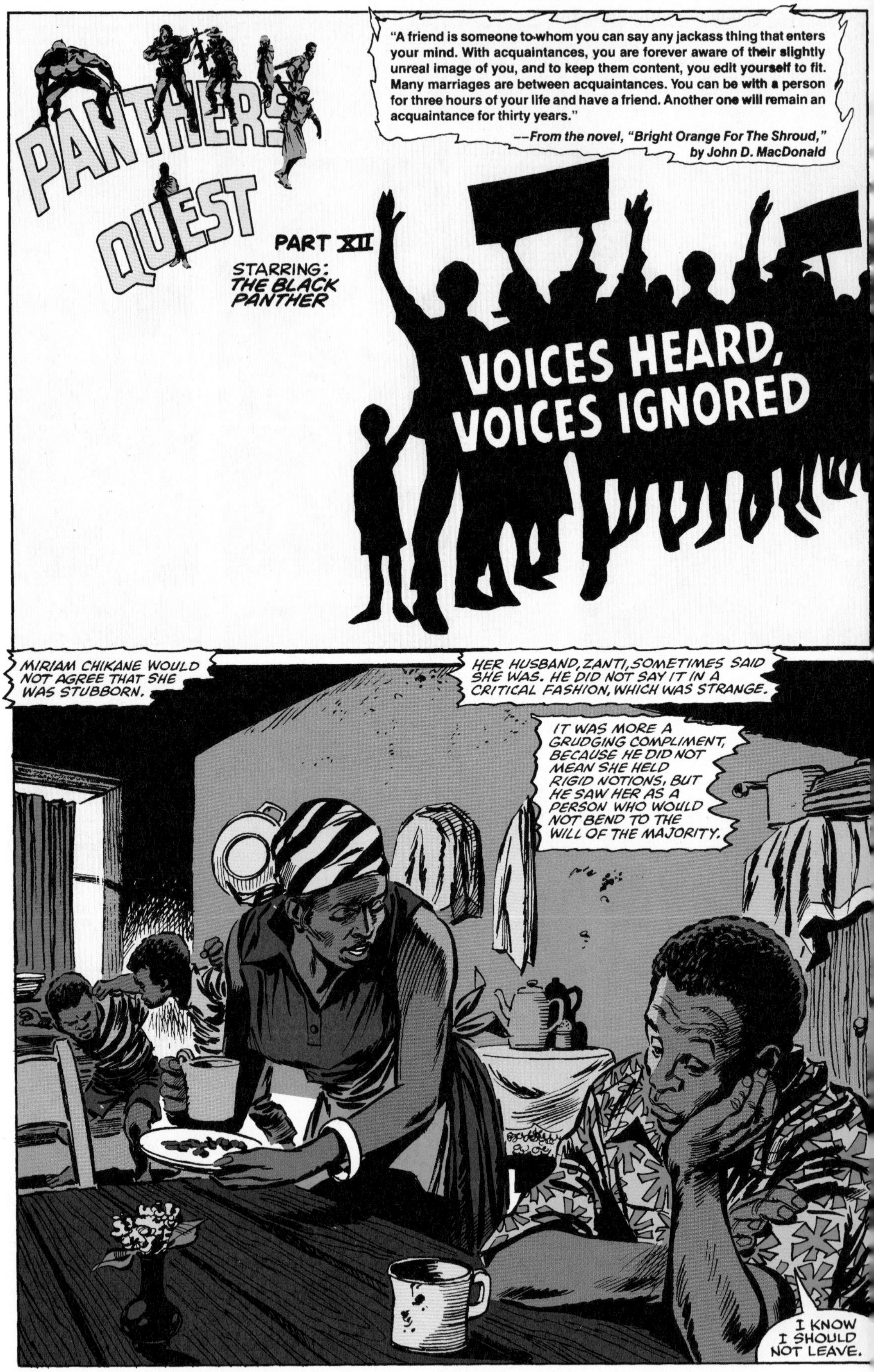
"A friend is someone to whom you can say any jackass thing that enters your mind. With acquaintances, you are forever aware of their slightly unreal image of you, and to keep them content, you edit yourself to fit. Many marriages are between acquaintances. You can be with a person for three hours of your life and have a friend. Another one will remain an acquaintance for thirty years."
--From the novel, "Bright Orange For The Shroud," by John D. MacDonald
PANTHER'S QUEST
PART XII
STARRING: THE BLACK PANTHER
VOICES HEARD, VOICES IGNORED
MIRIAM CHIKANE WOULD NOT AGREE THAT SHE WAS STUBBORN.
HER HUSBAND, ZANTI, SOMETIMES SAID SHE WAS. HE DID NOT SAY IT IN A CRITICAL FASHION, WHICH WAS STRANGE.
IT WAS MORE A GRUDGING COMPLIMENT, BECAUSE HE DID NOT MEAN SHE HELD RIGID NOTIONS, BUT HE SAW HER AS A PERSON WHO WOULD NOT BEND TO THE WILL OF THE MAJORITY.
I KNOW I SHOULD NOT LEAVE.

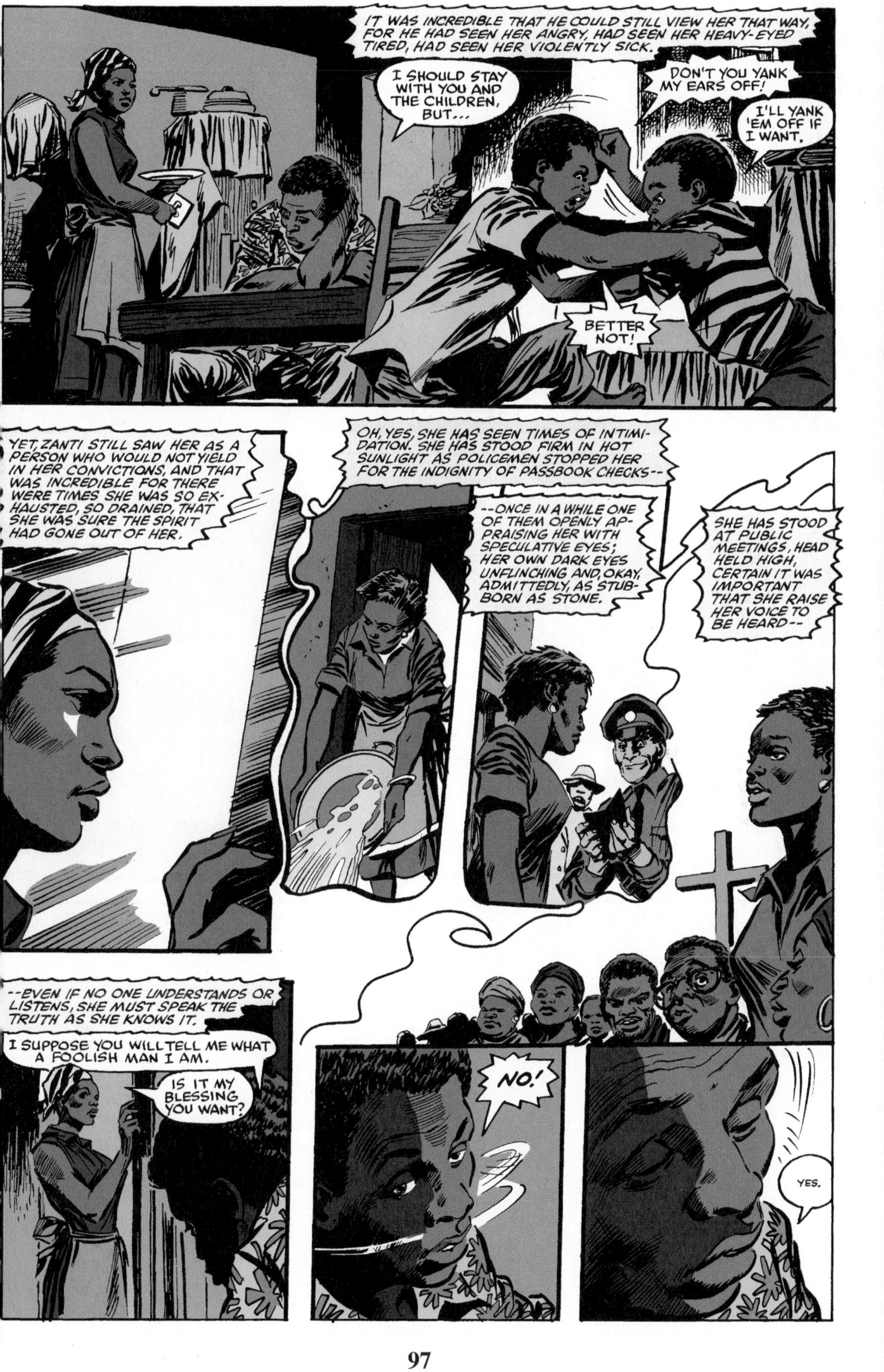
IT WAS INCREDIBLE THAT HE COULD STILL VIEW HER THAT WAY, FOR HE HAD SEEN HER ANGRY, HAD SEEN HER HEAVY-EYED TIRED, HAD SEEN HER VIOLENTLY SICK.
I SHOULD STAY WITH YOU AND THE CHILDREN, BUT...
DON'T YOU YANK MY EARS OFF!
I'LL YANK 'EM OFF IF I WANT.
BETTER NOT!
YET, ZANTI STILL SAW HER AS A PERSON WHO WOULD NOT YIELD IN HER CONVICTIONS, AND THAT WAS INCREDIBLE FOR THERE WERE TIMES SHE WAS SO EXHAUSTED, SO DRAINED, THAT SHE WAS SURE THE SPIRIT HAD GONE OUT OF HER.
OH, YES, SHE HAS SEEN TIMES OF INTIMIDATION. SHE HAS STOOD FIRM IN HOT SUNLIGHT AS POLICEMEN STOPPED HER FOR THE INDIGNITY OF PASSBOOK CHECKS--
--ONCE IN A WHILE ONE OF THEM OPENLY APPRAISING HER WITH SPECULATIVE EYES; HER OWN DARK EYES UNFLINCHING AND, OKAY, ADMITTEDLY, AS STUBBORN AS STONE.
SHE HAS STOOD AT PUBLIC MEETINGS, HEAD HELD HIGH, CERTAIN IT WAS IMPORTANT THAT SHE RAISE HER VOICE TO BE HEARD--
--EVEN IF NO ONE UNDERSTANDS OR LISTENS, SHE MUST SPEAK THE TRUTH AS SHE KNOWS IT.
I SUPPOSE YOU WILL TELL ME WHAT A FOOLISH MAN I AM.
IS IT MY BLESSING YOU WANT?
NO!
YES.

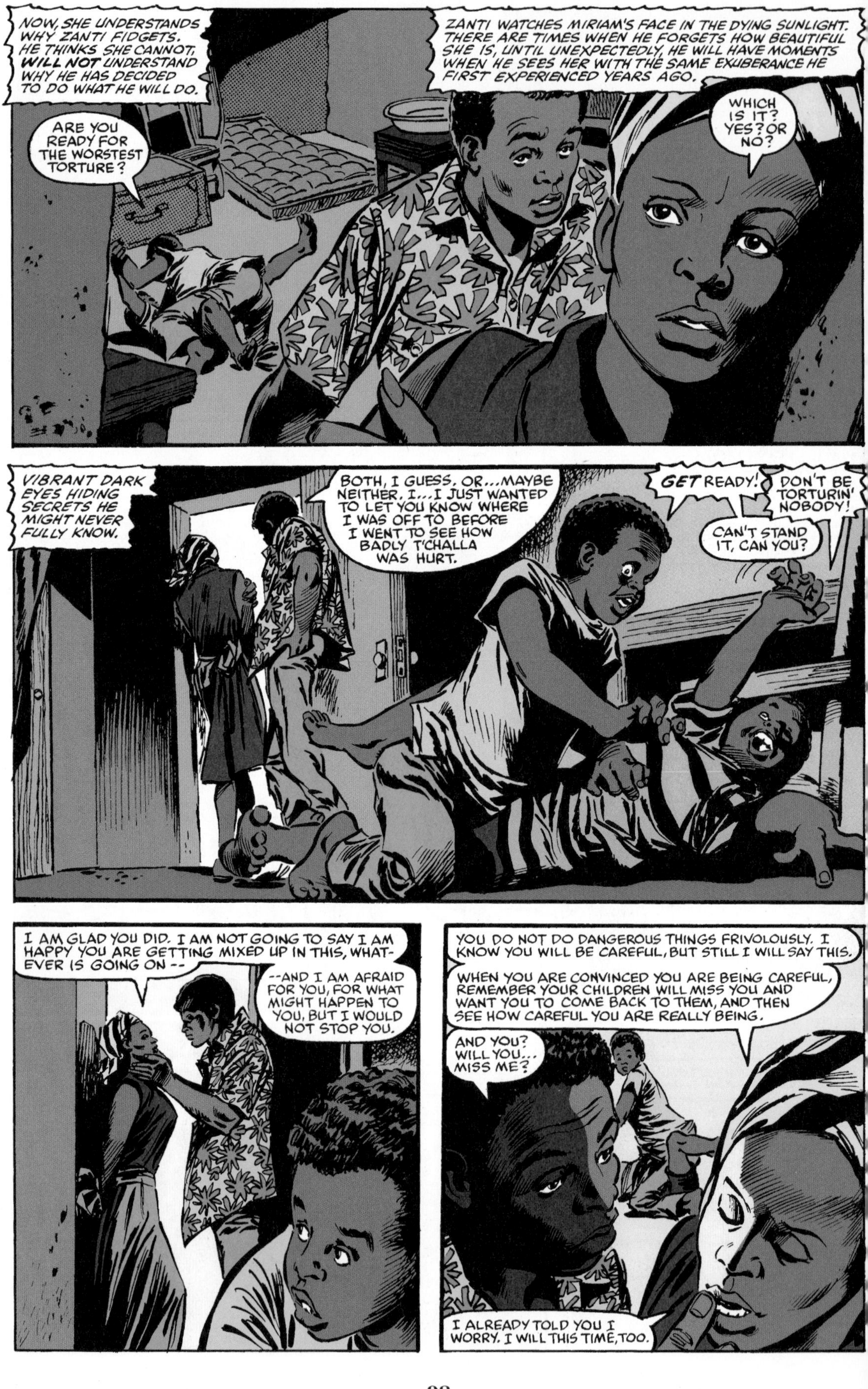

NOW, SHE UNDERSTANDS WHY ZANTI FIDGETS. HE THINKS SHE CANNOT, **WILL NOT** UNDERSTAND WHY HE HAS DECIDED TO DO WHAT HE WILL DO.
ZANTI WATCHES MIRIAM'S FACE IN THE DYING SUNLIGHT. THERE ARE TIMES WHEN HE FORGETS HOW BEAUTIFUL SHE IS, UNTIL UNEXPECTEDLY, HE WILL HAVE MOMENTS WHEN HE SEES HER WITH THE SAME EXUBERANCE HE FIRST EXPERIENCED YEARS AGO.
ARE YOU READY FOR THE WORSTEST TORTURE?
WHICH IS IT? YES? OR NO?
VIBRANT DARK EYES HIDING SECRETS HE MIGHT NEVER FULLY KNOW.
BOTH, I GUESS. OR... MAYBE NEITHER. I... I JUST WANTED TO LET YOU KNOW WHERE I WAS OFF TO BEFORE I WENT TO SEE HOW BADLY T'CHALLA WAS HURT.
GET READY!
DON'T BE TORTURIN' NOBODY!
CAN'T STAND IT, CAN YOU?
I AM GLAD YOU DID. I AM NOT GOING TO SAY I AM HAPPY YOU ARE GETTING MIXED UP IN THIS, WHAT-EVER IS GOING ON --
--AND I AM AFRAID FOR YOU, FOR WHAT MIGHT HAPPEN TO YOU, BUT I WOULD NOT STOP YOU.
YOU DO NOT DO DANGEROUS THINGS FRIVOLOUSLY. I KNOW YOU WILL BE CAREFUL, BUT STILL I WILL SAY THIS.
WHEN YOU ARE CONVINCED YOU ARE BEING CAREFUL, REMEMBER YOUR CHILDREN WILL MISS YOU AND WANT YOU TO COME BACK TO THEM, AND THEN SEE HOW CAREFUL YOU ARE REALLY BEING.
AND YOU? WILL YOU... MISS ME?
I ALREADY TOLD YOU I WORRY. I WILL THIS TIME, TOO.

HE TASTES HER LIPS, WARM AND HUNGRY--

--AND HE DOES NOT WANT TO LEAVE.

FATHER, I WANT TO GO WITH YOU.

NO, NOT THIS TIME.

WHERE YOU GOING?

TO TRY TO HELP A MAN.

I CAN HELP. I CAN BE A BIG HELP.

YES, I KNOW THAT. YOU HELP ME, MY SON, DID YOU KNOW THAT?

YOU MEAN LIKE WHEN WE PATCHED UP THE CEILING AND I HANDED YOU THE BOARDS?

YES, THAT.

I DID THAT GOOD, DIDN'T I?

VERY GOOD.

BUT YOU HELP ME IN OTHER WAYS YOU WILL NOT UNDERSTAND UNTIL YOU ARE OLDER. YOU HELP ME TRY TO DO THE RIGHT THING WHEN PERHAPS I WOULD TRY TO LOOK AWAY FROM IT.

YOU WILL NOT BE GONE LONG?

I WILL TRY NOT TO BE. ON THAT, I PROMISE.

'BYE, FATHER.

DID YOU HEAR ME, FATHER?

I HEAR YOU. GOOD-BYE NOW.

I'M GOING!

ARE YOU DEAF? WE JUST SAID, "GOOD-BYE."

BUT...

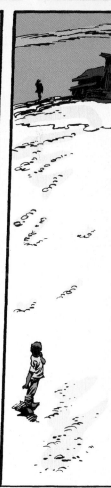

99

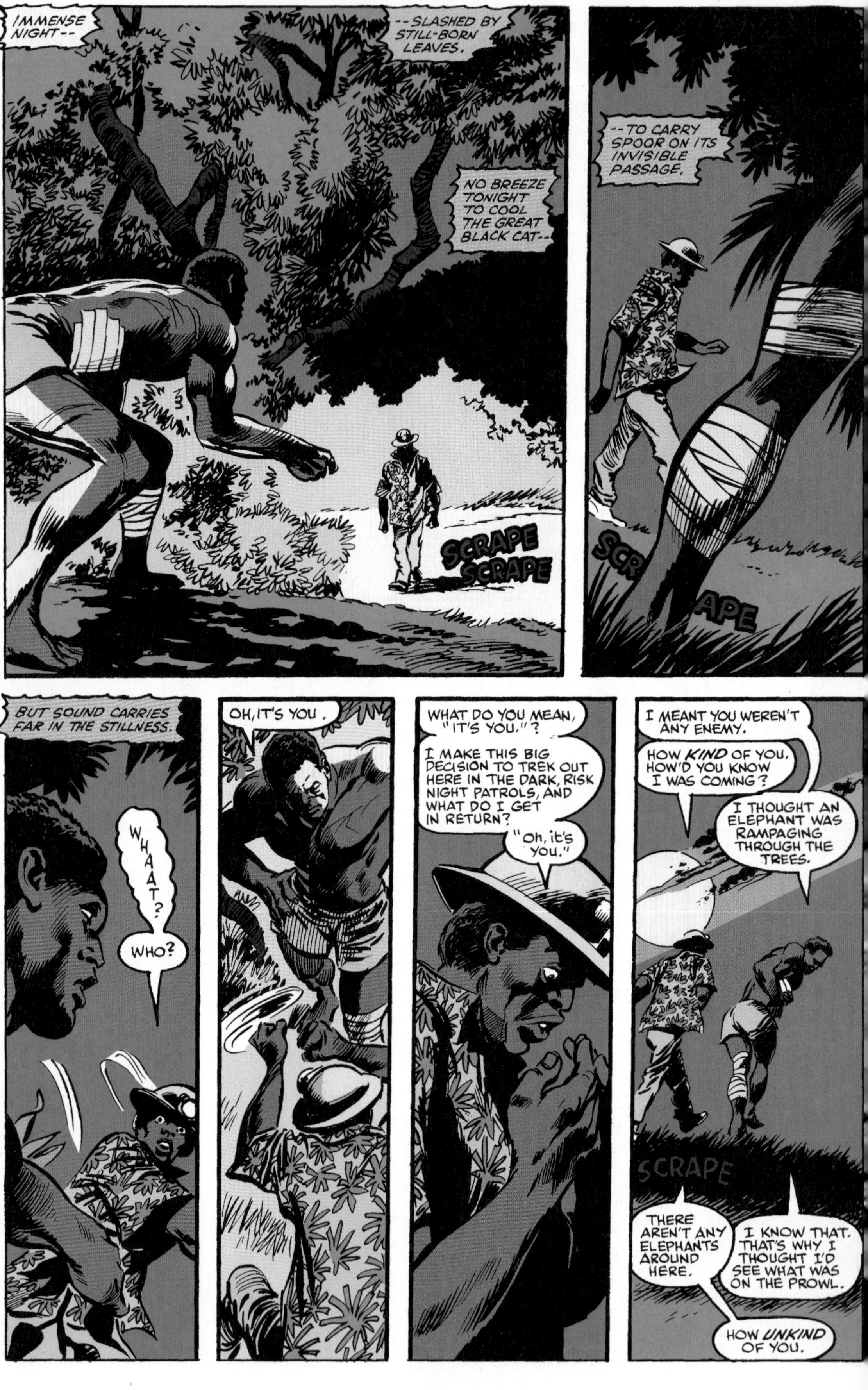
IMMENSE NIGHT--
--SLASHED BY STILL-BORN LEAVES.
NO BREEZE TONIGHT TO COOL THE GREAT BLACK CAT--
SCRAPE SCRAPE
--TO CARRY SPOOR ON ITS INVISIBLE PASSAGE.
SCR APE
BUT SOUND CARRIES FAR IN THE STILLNESS.
WHAAAT?
WHO?
OH, IT'S YOU.
WHAT DO YOU MEAN, "IT'S YOU."?
I MAKE THIS BIG DECISION TO TREK OUT HERE IN THE DARK, RISK NIGHT PATROLS, AND WHAT DO I GET IN RETURN?
"Oh, it's you."
I MEANT YOU WEREN'T ANY ENEMY.
HOW KIND OF YOU. HOW'D YOU KNOW I WAS COMING?
I THOUGHT AN ELEPHANT WAS RAMPAGING THROUGH THE TREES.
SCRAPE
THERE AREN'T ANY ELEPHANTS AROUND HERE.
I KNOW THAT. THAT'S WHY I THOUGHT I'D SEE WHAT WAS ON THE PROWL.
HOW UNKIND OF YOU.

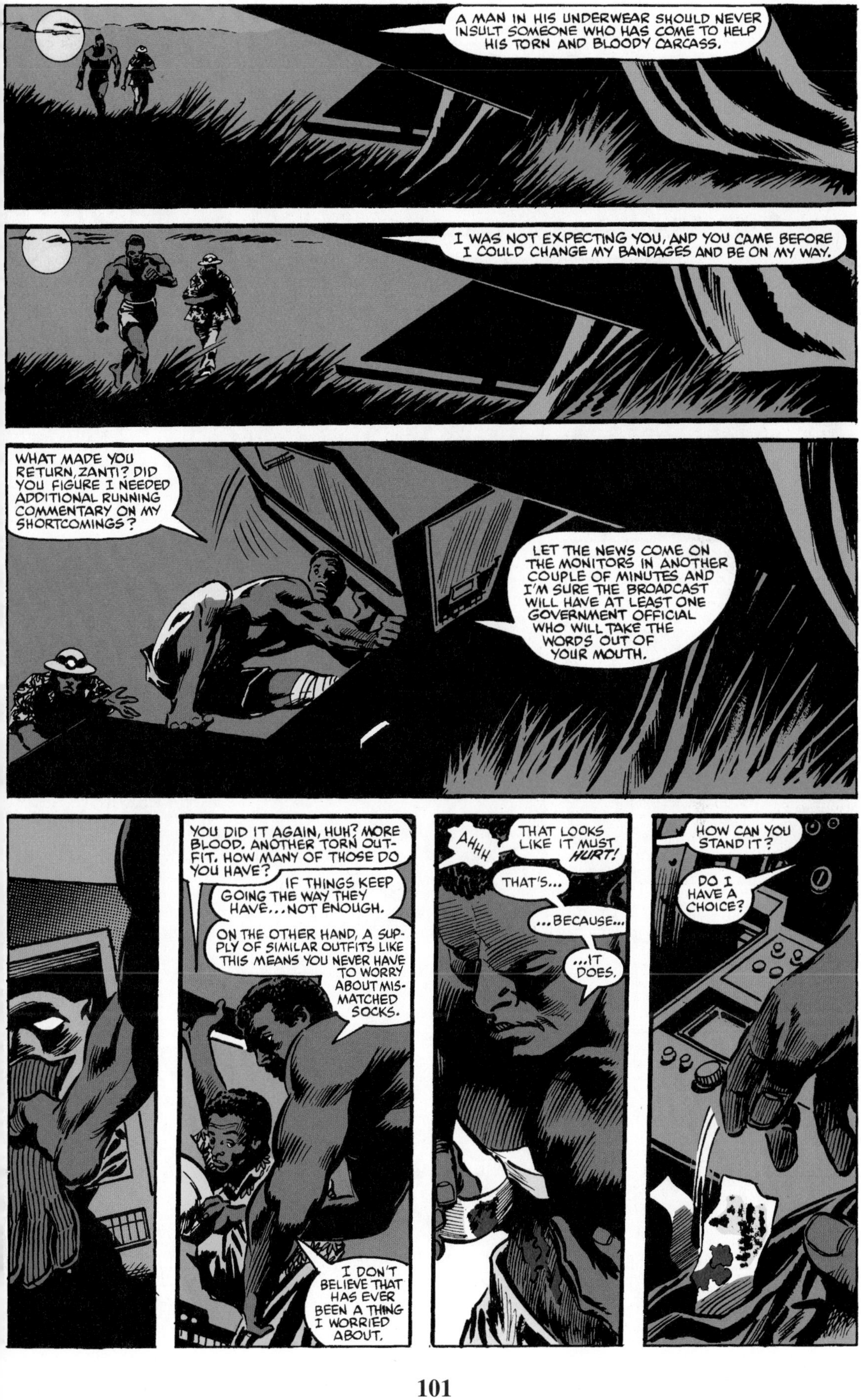
A MAN IN HIS UNDERWEAR SHOULD NEVER INSULT SOMEONE WHO HAS COME TO HELP HIS TORN AND BLOODY CARCASS.
I WAS NOT EXPECTING YOU, AND YOU CAME BEFORE I COULD CHANGE MY BANDAGES AND BE ON MY WAY.
WHAT MADE YOU RETURN, ZANTI? DID YOU FIGURE I NEEDED ADDITIONAL RUNNING COMMENTARY ON MY SHORTCOMINGS?
LET THE NEWS COME ON THE MONITORS IN ANOTHER COUPLE OF MINUTES AND I'M SURE THE BROADCAST WILL HAVE AT LEAST ONE GOVERNMENT OFFICIAL WHO WILL TAKE THE WORDS OUT OF YOUR MOUTH.
YOU DID IT AGAIN, HUH? MORE BLOOD. ANOTHER TORN OUTFIT. HOW MANY OF THOSE DO YOU HAVE?
IF THINGS KEEP GOING THE WAY THEY HAVE... NOT ENOUGH.
ON THE OTHER HAND, A SUPPLY OF SIMILAR OUTFITS LIKE THIS MEANS YOU NEVER HAVE TO WORRY ABOUT MISMATCHED SOCKS.
I DON'T BELIEVE THAT HAS EVER BEEN A THING I WORRIED ABOUT.
AHHH
THAT LOOKS LIKE IT MUST HURT!
THAT'S...
...BECAUSE...
...IT DOES.
HOW CAN YOU STAND IT?
DO I HAVE A CHOICE?

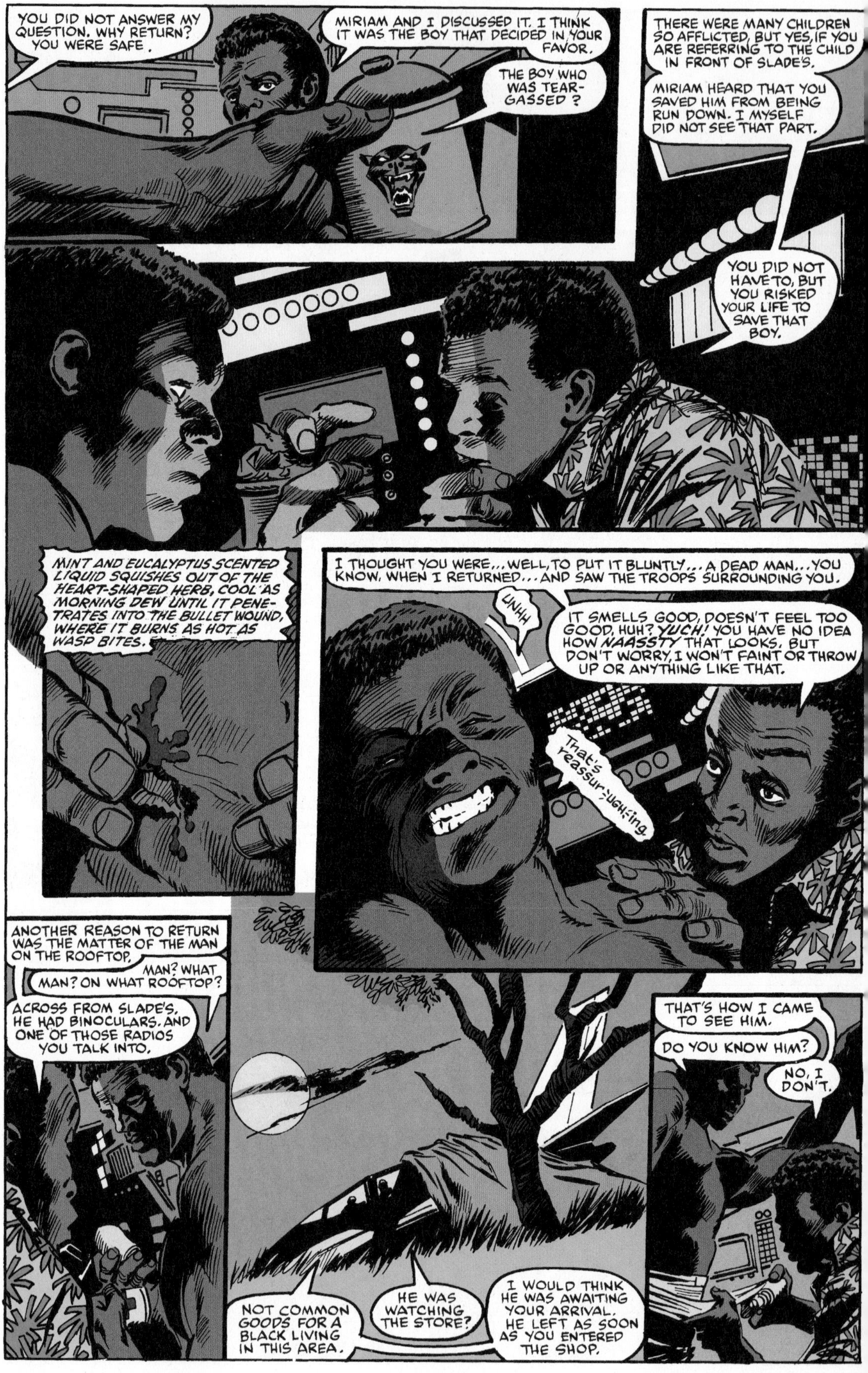
YOU DID NOT ANSWER MY QUESTION. WHY RETURN? YOU WERE SAFE.
MIRIAM AND I DISCUSSED IT. I THINK IT WAS THE BOY THAT DECIDED IN YOUR FAVOR.
THE BOY WHO WAS TEAR-GASSED?
THERE WERE MANY CHILDREN SO AFFLICTED, BUT YES, IF YOU ARE REFERRING TO THE CHILD IN FRONT OF SLADE'S.
MIRIAM HEARD THAT YOU SAVED HIM FROM BEING RUN DOWN. I MYSELF DID NOT SEE THAT PART.
YOU DID NOT HAVE TO, BUT YOU RISKED YOUR LIFE TO SAVE THAT BOY.
MINT AND EUCALYPTUS SCENTED LIQUID SQUISHES OUT OF THE HEART-SHAPED HERB, COOL AS MORNING DEW UNTIL IT PENETRATES INTO THE BULLET WOUND, WHERE IT BURNS AS HOT AS WASP BITES.
I THOUGHT YOU WERE... WELL, TO PUT IT BLUNTLY... A DEAD MAN... YOU KNOW, WHEN I RETURNED... AND SAW THE TROOPS SURROUNDING YOU.
UNHH
IT SMELLS GOOD, DOESN'T FEEL TOO GOOD, HUH? YUCH! YOU HAVE NO IDEA HOW NAASSTY THAT LOOKS. BUT DON'T WORRY, I WON'T FAINT OR THROW UP OR ANYTHING LIKE THAT.
That's reassur-ugh-ing.
ANOTHER REASON TO RETURN WAS THE MATTER OF THE MAN ON THE ROOFTOP.
MAN? WHAT MAN? ON WHAT ROOFTOP?
ACROSS FROM SLADE'S. HE HAD BINOCULARS. AND ONE OF THOSE RADIOS YOU TALK INTO.
NOT COMMON GOODS FOR A BLACK LIVING IN THIS AREA.
HE WAS WATCHING THE STORE?
I WOULD THINK HE WAS AWAITING YOUR ARRIVAL. HE LEFT AS SOON AS YOU ENTERED THE SHOP.
THAT'S HOW I CAME TO SEE HIM.
DO YOU KNOW HIM?
NO, I DON'T.

HE COULD HAVE BEEN A LEAD IF SLADE DOES NOT SHOW TONIGHT.

WELL... I DID FOLLOW HIM.

WHO? THE MAN?

WHO ELSE?

WHY DIDN'T YOU TELL ME?

I JUST DID.

YOU DON'T APPRECIATE WHAT I GO THROUGH FOR YOU. I *TRY* TO *PATCH* YOU UP AND YOU GO OUT AND GET *FRESH WOUNDS!* I REALLY SHOULD GIVE UP ON YOU.

WAIT UP, ZANTI! LET ME TURN OFF THE MUTING EFFECT.

MUTING

THAT'S A PICTURE OF W'KABI.

NEVER HEARD OF HIM. WHAT'S HE GOT, A METAL ARM?

OF A KIND, AND BEFORE YOU ASK, YES, IT HURT HIM WHEN HE LOST THE ARM.

I WASN'T GOING TO ASK THAT.

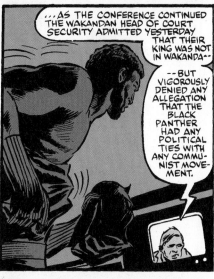

...AS THE CONFERENCE CONTINUED THE WAKANDAN HEAD OF COURT SECURITY ADMITTED YESTERDAY THAT THEIR KING WAS NOT IN WAKANDA--

--BUT VIGOROUSLY DENIED ANY ALLEGATION THAT THE BLACK PANTHER HAD ANY POLITICAL TIES WITH ANY COMMUNIST MOVEMENT.

THEY ALSO ARE EMPHATIC IN THEIR DENIALS THAT THEIR KING'S WHEREABOUTS IS ON SOUTH AFRICAN SOIL.

IN RESPONSE, MAGISTRATE OF COMMUNICATIONS ANTON PRETORIUS, VEHEMENTLY DENOUNCED THE WAKANDANS' LACK OF CANDOR.

MINISTER OF SECURITY DOEKE RIEBEECK STATED THERE ARE MANY RELIABLE WITNESSES AND VICTIMS IN SOUTH AFRICAN SECURITY FORCES, INCLUDING SPECIAL BRANCH AND NATIONAL INTELLIGENCE SERVICE PERSONNEL, TO ATTEST TO THE PANTHER'S ILLEGAL AND DANGEROUS PRESENCE IN SOUTH AFRICA.

VOICES THAT CANNOT BE IGNORED. HE CON

KLIK

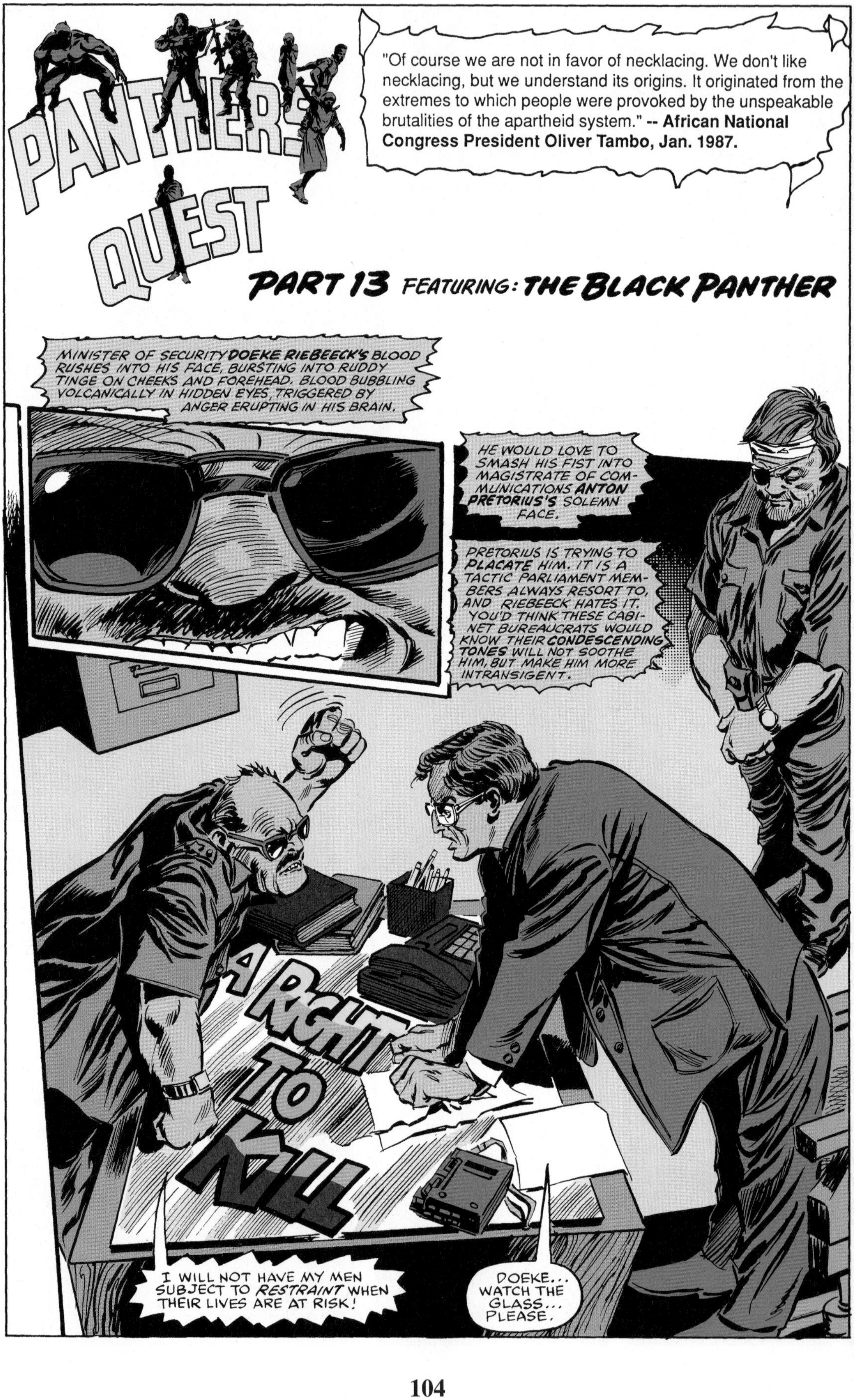
PANTHER'S QUEST
"Of course we are not in favor of necklacing. We don't like necklacing, but we understand its origins. It originated from the extremes to which people were provoked by the unspeakable brutalities of the apartheid system." -- African National Congress President Oliver Tambo, Jan. 1987.
PART 13 FEATURING: THE BLACK PANTHER
MINISTER OF SECURITY DOEKE RIEBEECK'S BLOOD RUSHES INTO HIS FACE, BURSTING INTO RUDDY TINGE ON CHEEKS AND FOREHEAD. BLOOD BUBBLING VOLCANICALLY IN HIDDEN EYES, TRIGGERED BY ANGER ERUPTING IN HIS BRAIN.
HE WOULD LOVE TO SMASH HIS FIST INTO MAGISTRATE OF COMMUNICATIONS ANTON PRETORIUS'S SOLEMN FACE.
PRETORIUS IS TRYING TO PLACATE HIM. IT IS A TACTIC PARLIAMENT MEMBERS ALWAYS RESORT TO, AND RIEBEECK HATES IT. YOU'D THINK THESE CABINET BUREAUCRATS WOULD KNOW THEIR CONDESCENDING TONES WILL NOT SOOTHE HIM, BUT MAKE HIM MORE INTRANSIGENT.
A RIGHT TO KILL
I WILL NOT HAVE MY MEN SUBJECT TO RESTRAINT WHEN THEIR LIVES ARE AT RISK!
DOEKE... WATCH THE GLASS... PLEASE.

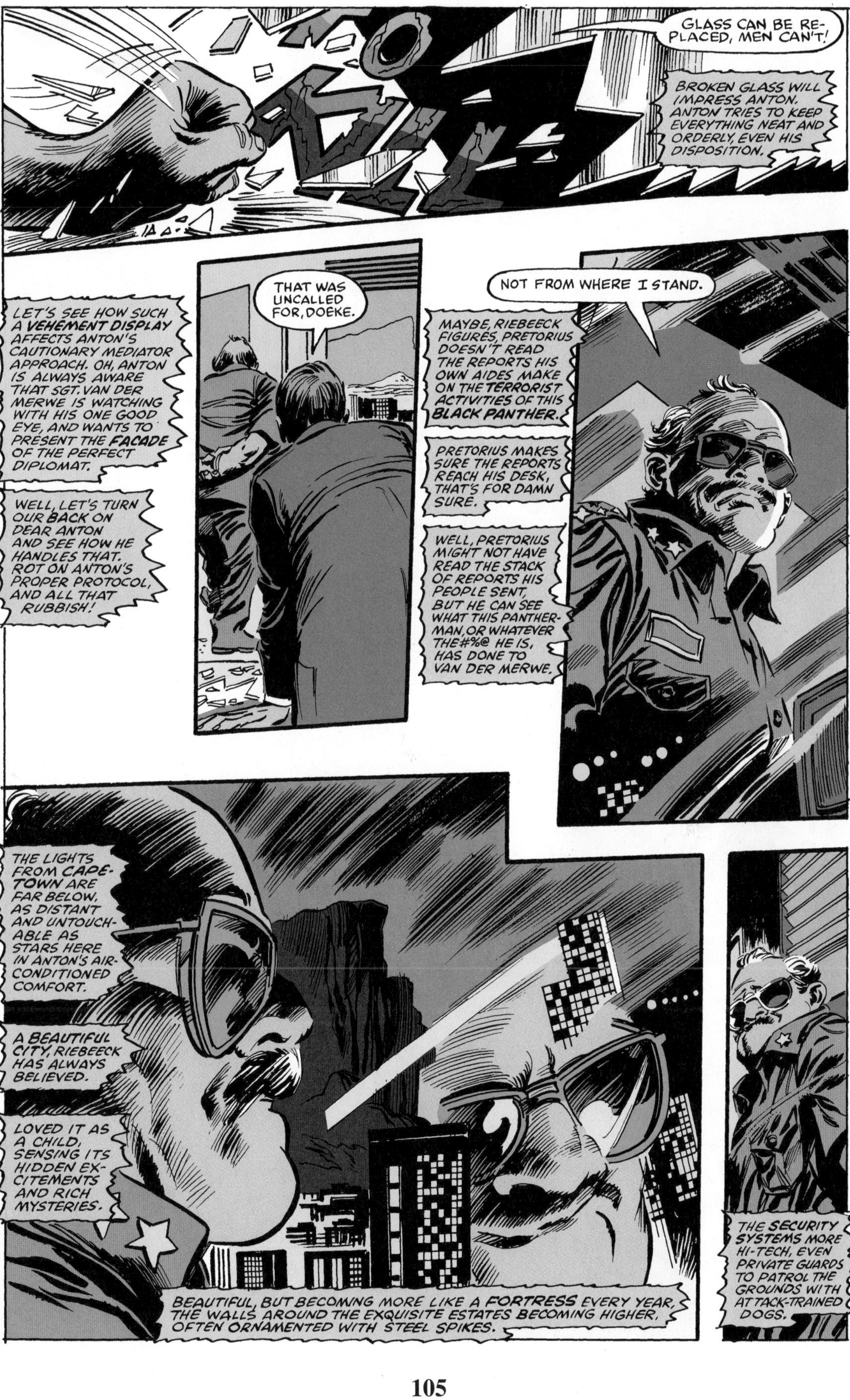
GLASS CAN BE RE-PLACED, MEN CAN'T!
BROKEN GLASS WILL IMPRESS ANTON. ANTON TRIES TO KEEP EVERYTHING NEAT AND ORDERLY, EVEN HIS DISPOSITION.
LET'S SEE HOW SUCH A VEHEMENT DISPLAY AFFECTS ANTON'S CAUTIONARY MEDIATOR APPROACH. OH, ANTON IS ALWAYS AWARE THAT SGT. VAN DER MERWE IS WATCHING WITH HIS ONE GOOD EYE, AND WANTS TO PRESENT THE FACADE OF THE PERFECT DIPLOMAT.
WELL, LET'S TURN OUR BACK ON DEAR ANTON AND SEE HOW HE HANDLES THAT. ROT ON ANTON'S PROPER PROTOCOL, AND ALL THAT RUBBISH!
THAT WAS UNCALLED FOR, DOEKE.
NOT FROM WHERE I STAND.
MAYBE, RIEBEECK FIGURES, PRETORIUS DOESN'T READ THE REPORTS HIS OWN AIDES MAKE ON THE TERRORIST ACTIVITIES OF THIS BLACK PANTHER.
PRETORIUS MAKES SURE THE REPORTS REACH HIS DESK, THAT'S FOR DAMN SURE.
WELL, PRETORIUS MIGHT NOT HAVE READ THE STACK OF REPORTS HIS PEOPLE SENT, BUT HE CAN SEE WHAT THIS PANTHER-MAN, OR WHATEVER THE#%@ HE IS, HAS DONE TO VAN DER MERWE.
THE LIGHTS FROM CAPE-TOWN ARE FAR BELOW, AS DISTANT AND UNTOUCH-ABLE AS STARS HERE IN ANTON'S AIR-CONDITIONED COMFORT.
A BEAUTIFUL CITY, RIEBEECK HAS ALWAYS BELIEVED.
LOVED IT AS A CHILD, SENSING ITS HIDDEN EX-CITEMENTS AND RICH MYSTERIES.
BEAUTIFUL, BUT BECOMING MORE LIKE A FORTRESS EVERY YEAR. THE WALLS AROUND THE EXQUISITE ESTATES BECOMING HIGHER, OFTEN ORNAMENTED WITH STEEL SPIKES.
THE SECURITY SYSTEMS MORE HI-TECH, EVEN PRIVATE GUARDS TO PATROL THE GROUNDS WITH ATTACK-TRAINED DOGS.

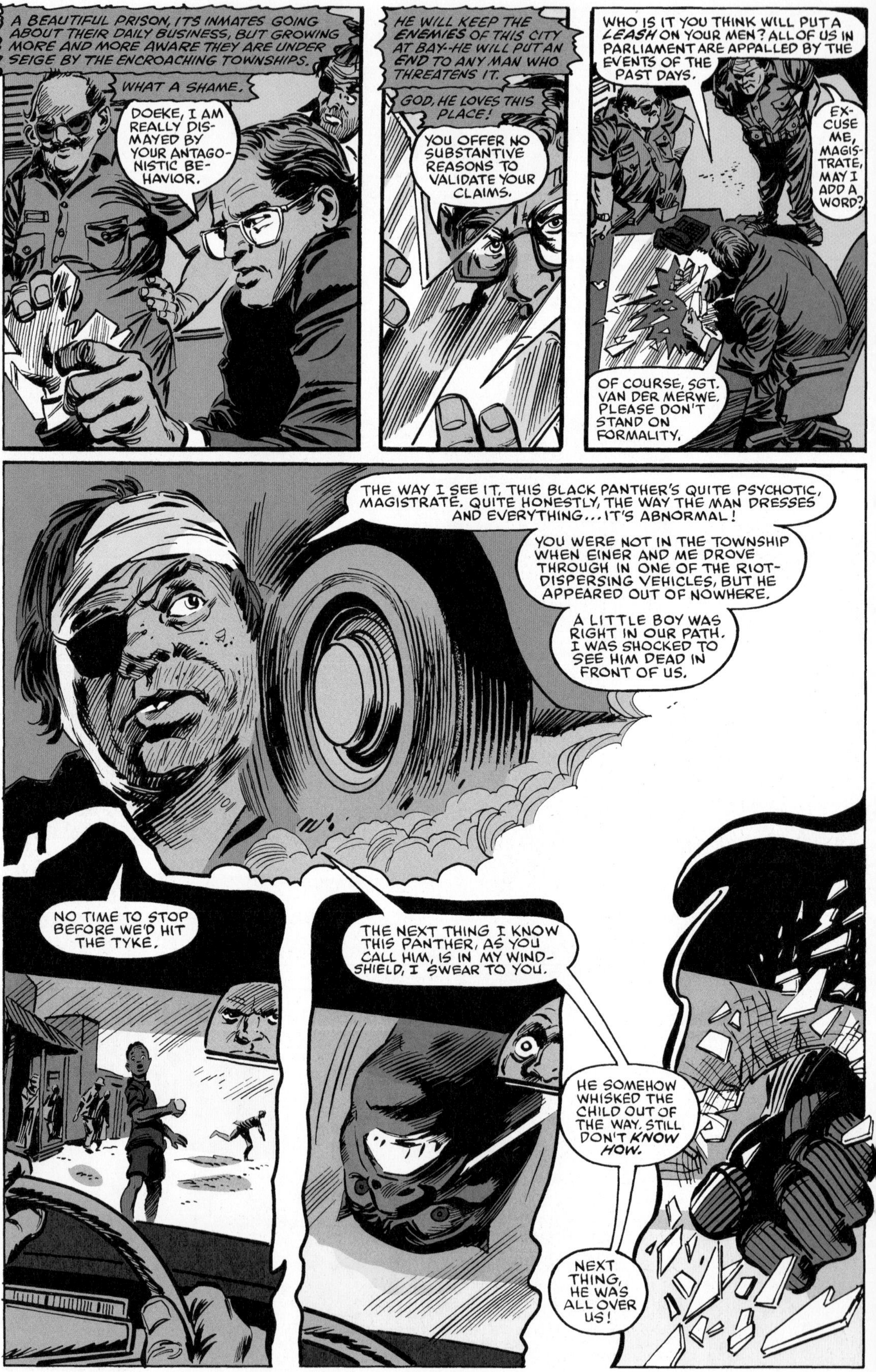
A BEAUTIFUL PRISON, ITS INMATES GOING ABOUT THEIR DAILY BUSINESS, BUT GROWING MORE AND MORE AWARE THEY ARE UNDER SEIGE BY THE ENCROACHING TOWNSHIPS.
WHAT A SHAME.
DOEKE, I AM REALLY DISMAYED BY YOUR ANTAGONISTIC BEHAVIOR.
HE WILL KEEP THE ENEMIES OF THIS CITY AT BAY--HE WILL PUT AN END TO ANY MAN WHO THREATENS IT.
GOD, HE LOVES THIS PLACE!
YOU OFFER NO SUBSTANTIVE REASONS TO VALIDATE YOUR CLAIMS.
WHO IS IT YOU THINK WILL PUT A LEASH ON YOUR MEN? ALL OF US IN PARLIAMENT ARE APPALLED BY THE EVENTS OF THE PAST DAYS.
EXCUSE ME, MAGISTRATE, MAY I ADD A WORD?
OF COURSE, SGT. VAN DER MERWE. PLEASE DON'T STAND ON FORMALITY.
THE WAY I SEE IT, THIS BLACK PANTHER'S QUITE PSYCHOTIC, MAGISTRATE. QUITE HONESTLY, THE WAY THE MAN DRESSES AND EVERYTHING... IT'S ABNORMAL!
YOU WERE NOT IN THE TOWNSHIP WHEN EINER AND ME DROVE THROUGH IN ONE OF THE RIOT-DISPERSING VEHICLES, BUT HE APPEARED OUT OF NOWHERE.
A LITTLE BOY WAS RIGHT IN OUR PATH. I WAS SHOCKED TO SEE HIM DEAD IN FRONT OF US.
NO TIME TO STOP BEFORE WE'D HIT THE TYKE.
THE NEXT THING I KNOW THIS PANTHER, AS YOU CALL HIM, IS IN MY WINDSHIELD, I SWEAR TO YOU.
HE SOMEHOW WHISKED THE CHILD OUT OF THE WAY. STILL DON'T KNOW HOW.
NEXT THING, HE WAS ALL OVER US!

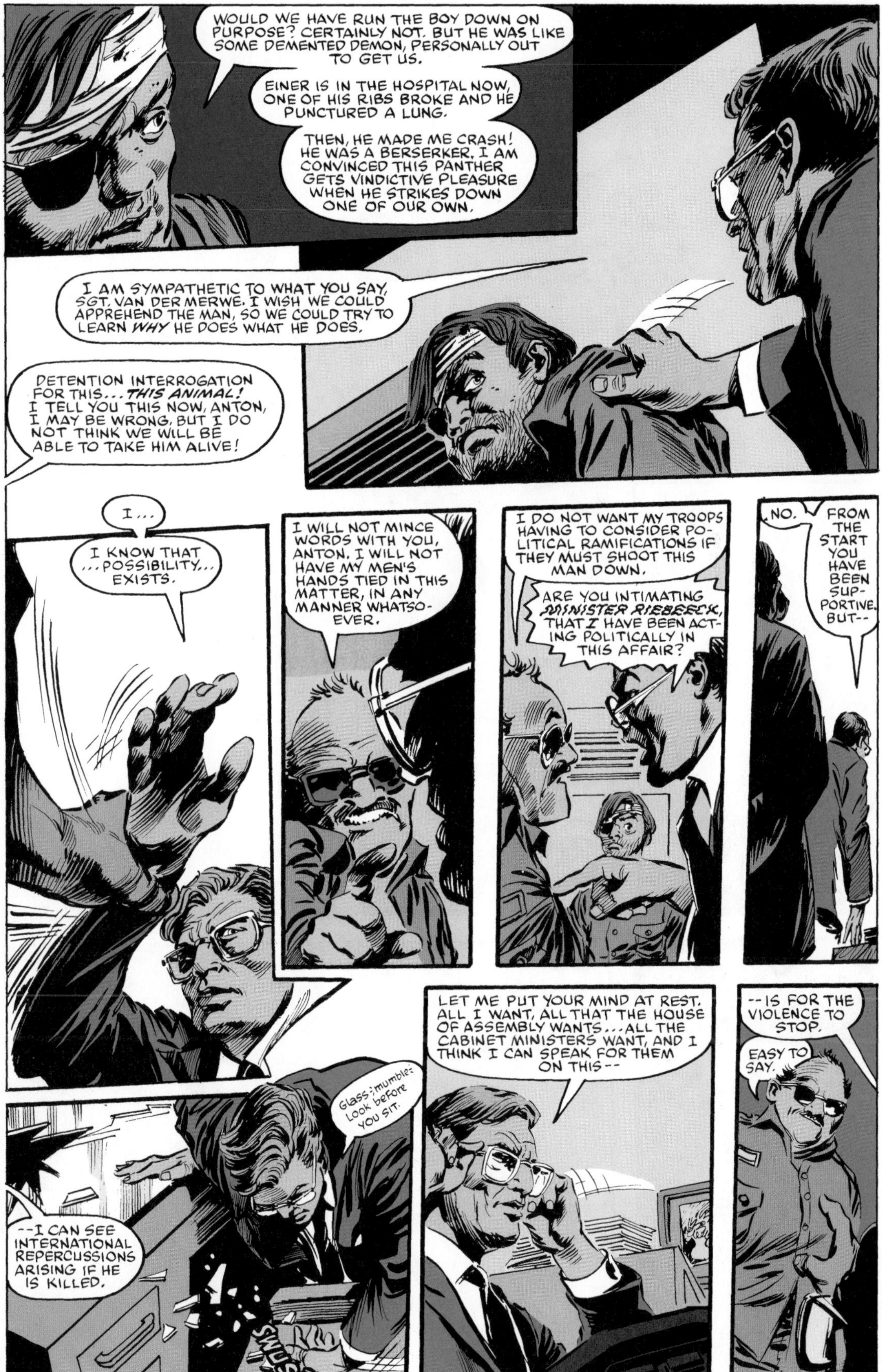
WOULD WE HAVE RUN THE BOY DOWN ON PURPOSE? CERTAINLY NOT. BUT HE WAS LIKE SOME DEMENTED DEMON, PERSONALLY OUT TO GET US.
EINER IS IN THE HOSPITAL NOW, ONE OF HIS RIBS BROKE AND HE PUNCTURED A LUNG.
THEN, HE MADE ME CRASH! HE WAS A BERSERKER. I AM CONVINCED THIS PANTHER GETS VINDICTIVE PLEASURE WHEN HE STRIKES DOWN ONE OF OUR OWN.
I AM SYMPATHETIC TO WHAT YOU SAY, SGT. VAN DER MERWE. I WISH WE COULD APPREHEND THE MAN, SO WE COULD TRY TO LEARN *WHY* HE DOES WHAT HE DOES.
DETENTION INTERROGATION FOR THIS... *THIS ANIMAL!* I TELL YOU THIS NOW, ANTON, I MAY BE WRONG, BUT I DO NOT THINK WE WILL BE ABLE TO TAKE HIM ALIVE!
I...
I KNOW THAT ...POSSIBILITY... EXISTS.
I WILL NOT MINCE WORDS WITH YOU, ANTON. I WILL NOT HAVE MY MEN'S HANDS TIED IN THIS MATTER, IN ANY MANNER WHATSOEVER.
I DO NOT WANT MY TROOPS HAVING TO CONSIDER POLITICAL RAMIFICATIONS IF THEY MUST SHOOT THIS MAN DOWN.
ARE YOU INTIMATING *MINISTER RIEBEECK,* THAT *I* HAVE BEEN ACTING POLITICALLY IN THIS AFFAIR?
NO.
FROM THE START YOU HAVE BEEN SUPPORTIVE. BUT--
--I CAN SEE INTERNATIONAL REPERCUSSIONS ARISING IF HE IS KILLED.
Glass; mumble: Look before you sit.
SWUSH
LET ME PUT YOUR MIND AT REST. ALL I WANT, ALL THAT THE HOUSE OF ASSEMBLY WANTS... ALL THE CABINET MINISTERS WANT, AND I THINK I CAN SPEAK FOR THEM ON THIS--
--IS FOR THE VIOLENCE TO STOP.
EASY TO SAY.

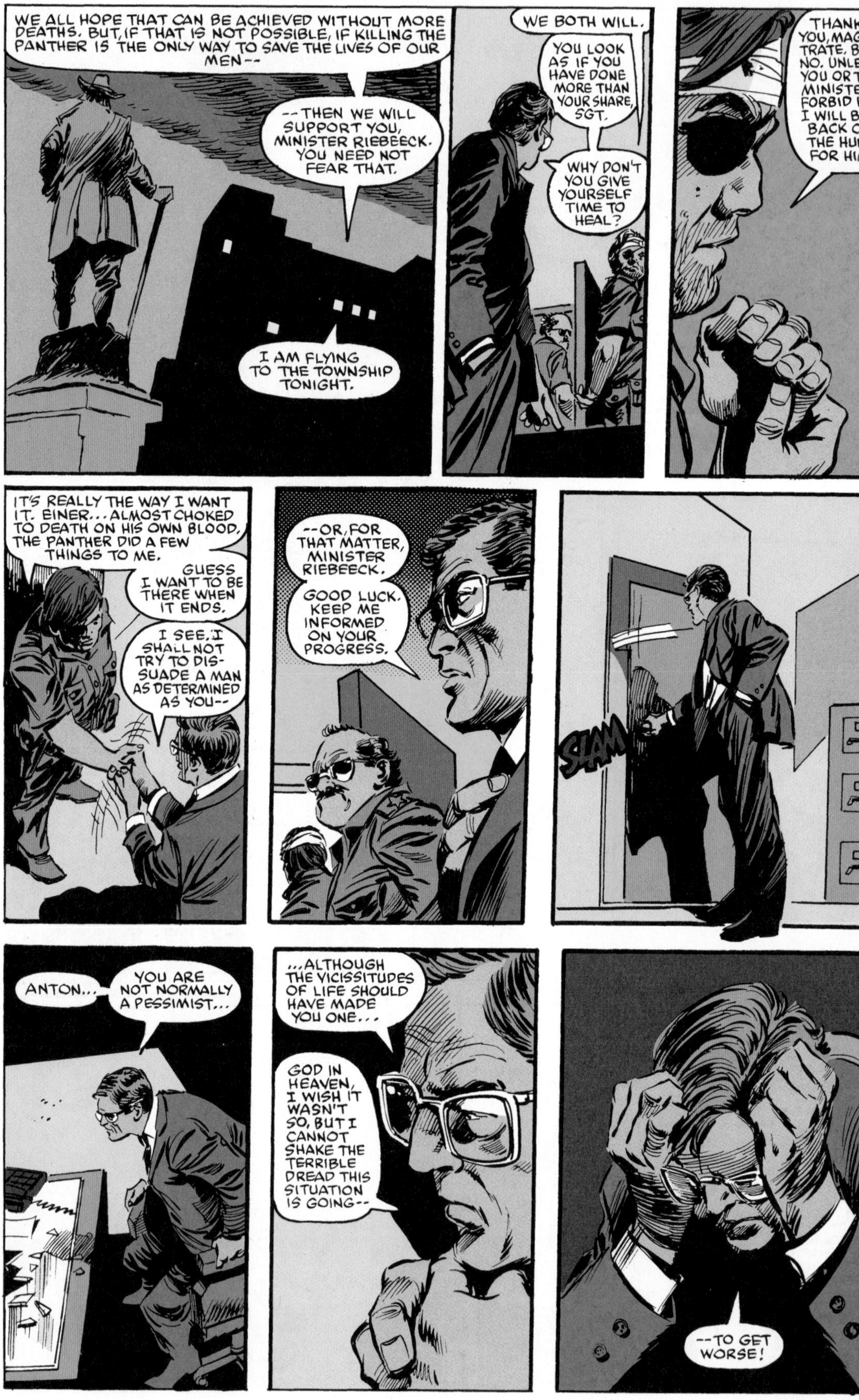

WE ALL HOPE THAT CAN BE ACHIEVED WITHOUT MORE DEATHS. BUT, IF THAT IS NOT POSSIBLE, IF KILLING THE PANTHER IS THE ONLY WAY TO SAVE THE LIVES OF OUR MEN--
--THEN WE WILL SUPPORT YOU, MINISTER RIEBEECK. YOU NEED NOT FEAR THAT.
I AM FLYING TO THE TOWNSHIP TONIGHT.
WE BOTH WILL.
YOU LOOK AS IF YOU HAVE DONE MORE THAN YOUR SHARE, SGT.
WHY DON'T YOU GIVE YOURSELF TIME TO HEAL?
THANK YOU, MAGISTRATE, BUT NO. UNLESS YOU OR THE MINISTER FORBID IT, I WILL BE BACK ON THE HUNT FOR HIM.
IT'S REALLY THE WAY I WANT IT. EINER... ALMOST CHOKED TO DEATH ON HIS OWN BLOOD. THE PANTHER DID A FEW THINGS TO ME.
GUESS I WANT TO BE THERE WHEN IT ENDS.
I SEE. I SHALL NOT TRY TO DISSUADE A MAN AS DETERMINED AS YOU--
--OR, FOR THAT MATTER, MINISTER RIEBEECK.
GOOD LUCK. KEEP ME INFORMED ON YOUR PROGRESS.
SLAM
ANTON...
YOU ARE NOT NORMALLY A PESSIMIST...
...ALTHOUGH THE VICISSITUDES OF LIFE SHOULD HAVE MADE YOU ONE...
GOD IN HEAVEN, I WISH IT WASN'T SO, BUT I CANNOT SHAKE THE TERRIBLE DREAD THIS SITUATION IS GOING--
--TO GET WORSE!

THE MAN REALLY DOES MOVE LIKE A CAT, ISN'T THAT SOMETHING?

ZANTI CHIKANE SHAKES HIS HEAD.

THE GREAT CAT SEEKS THE SOLACE AND SANCTUARY OF TREES, THE CARESS OF LEAF, THE REASSURANCE OF BARK.

THE HOUSE IS QUIET, BUT SOMEONE IS INSIDE. A BATTERY-POWERED RADIO PLAYING A GROUP ZANTI CALLED THE *ISOLINGO SOUL BROTHERS.*

WATCH OUT!

THE ARM DOESN'T BEND BACKWARDS!

I'M NOT SO GOOD AT THIS CLIMBING STUFF.

A FIGURE PASSES BY THE WINDOW, SIPPING LION BEER. THE MAN THEY ARE SEEKING, T'CHALLA SURMISES. WHO IS HE? A BLACK SPY FOR THE WHITE MINORITY RULE IN PRETORIA, SOUTH AFRICA'S ADMINISTRATIVE CAPITAL--

-- OR FOR THE CABINET MEMBERS IN CAPETOWN, WHERE LEGISLATIVE MEETINGS CONVENE?

BUT THEN HOW WOULD THIS SPY KNOW OF HIS INVOLVEMENT WITH PATRICK SLADE?

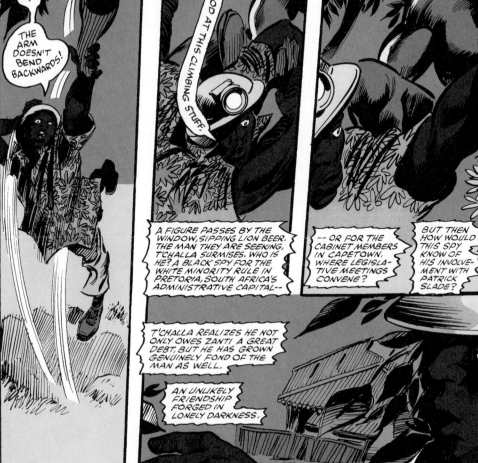

T'CHALLA REALIZES HE NOT ONLY OWES ZANTI A GREAT DEBT, BUT HE HAS GROWN GENUINELY FOND OF THE MAN AS WELL.

AN UNLIKELY FRIENDSHIP FORGED IN LONELY DARKNESS.

109

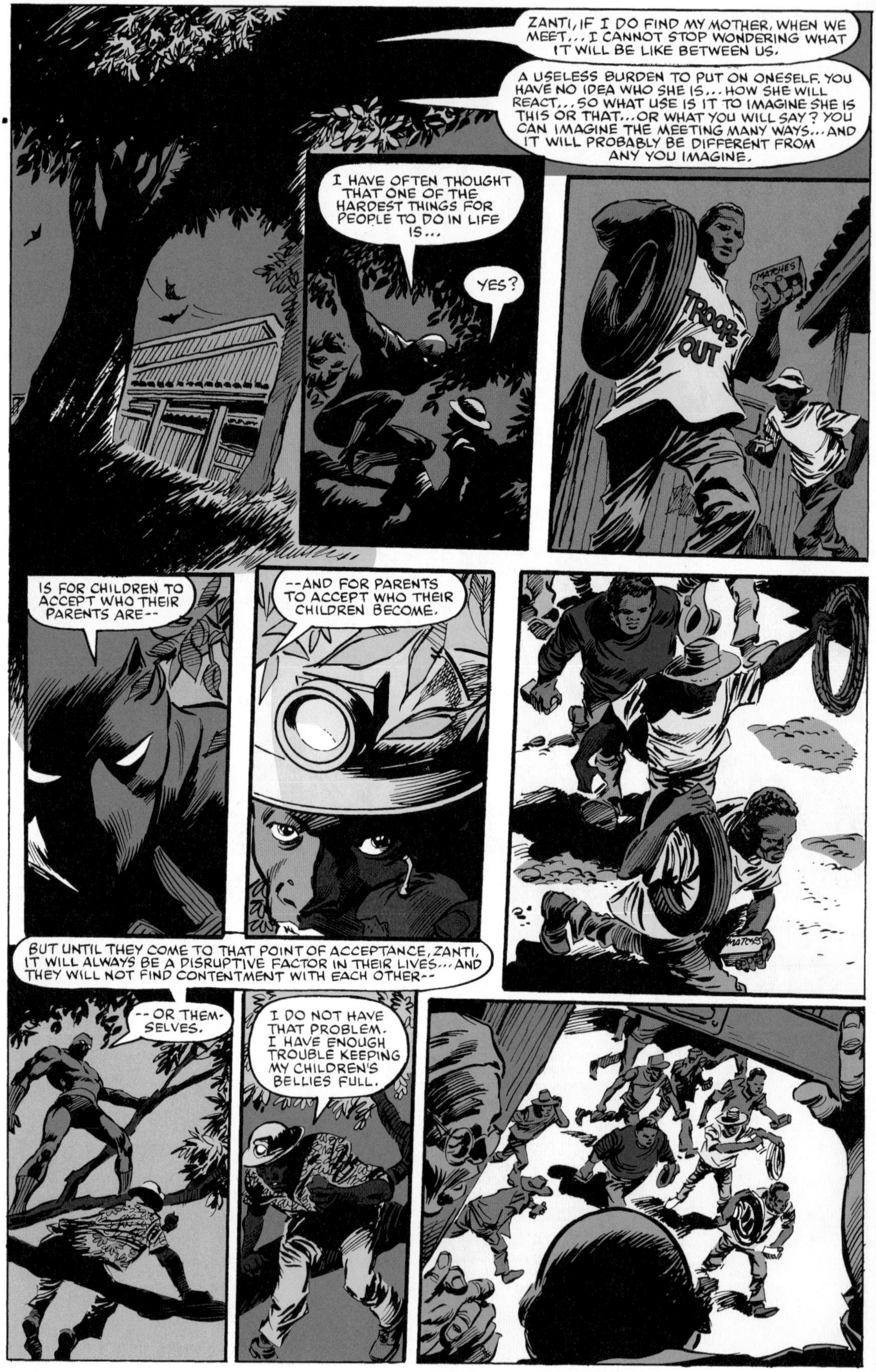
ZANTI, IF I DO FIND MY MOTHER, WHEN WE MEET... I CANNOT STOP WONDERING WHAT IT WILL BE LIKE BETWEEN US.
A USELESS BURDEN TO PUT ON ONESELF. YOU HAVE NO IDEA WHO SHE IS... HOW SHE WILL REACT... SO WHAT USE IS IT TO IMAGINE SHE IS THIS OR THAT... OR WHAT YOU WILL SAY? YOU CAN IMAGINE THE MEETING MANY WAYS... AND IT WILL PROBABLY BE DIFFERENT FROM ANY YOU IMAGINE.
I HAVE OFTEN THOUGHT THAT ONE OF THE HARDEST THINGS FOR PEOPLE TO DO IN LIFE IS...
YES?
MATCHES
TROOPS OUT
IS FOR CHILDREN TO ACCEPT WHO THEIR PARENTS ARE--
--AND FOR PARENTS TO ACCEPT WHO THEIR CHILDREN BECOME.
BUT UNTIL THEY COME TO THAT POINT OF ACCEPTANCE, ZANTI, IT WILL ALWAYS BE A DISRUPTIVE FACTOR IN THEIR LIVES... AND THEY WILL NOT FIND CONTENTMENT WITH EACH OTHER--
--OR THEMSELVES.
I DO NOT HAVE THAT PROBLEM. I HAVE ENOUGH TROUBLE KEEPING MY CHILDREN'S BELLIES FULL.

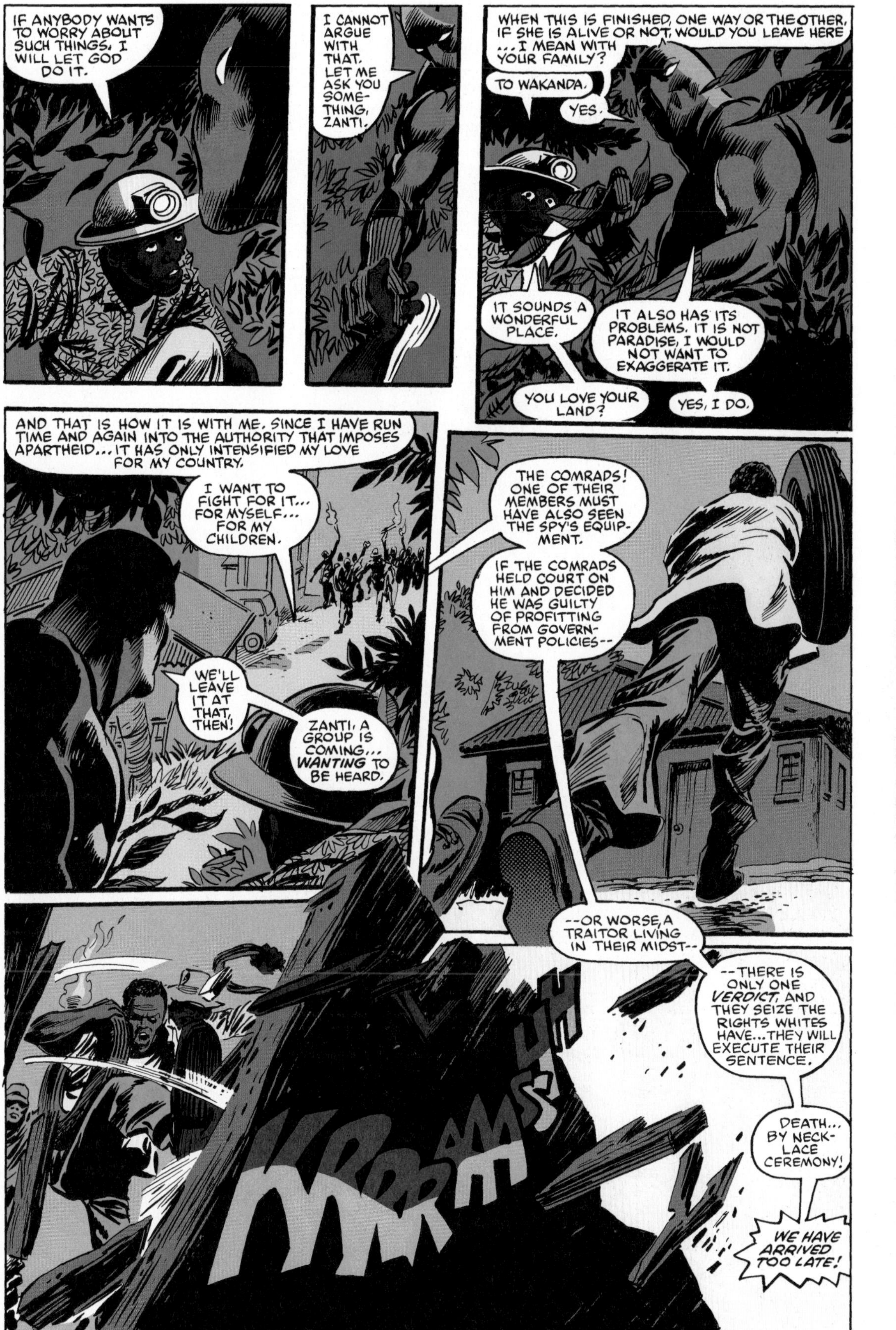
IF ANYBODY WANTS TO WORRY ABOUT SUCH THINGS, I WILL LET GOD DO IT.
I CANNOT ARGUE WITH THAT. LET ME ASK YOU SOMETHING, ZANTI.
WHEN THIS IS FINISHED, ONE WAY OR THE OTHER, IF SHE IS ALIVE OR NOT, WOULD YOU LEAVE HERE ...I MEAN WITH YOUR FAMILY?
TO WAKANDA.
YES.
IT SOUNDS A WONDERFUL PLACE.
IT ALSO HAS ITS PROBLEMS. IT IS NOT PARADISE. I WOULD NOT WANT TO EXAGGERATE IT.
YOU LOVE YOUR LAND?
YES, I DO.
AND THAT IS HOW IT IS WITH ME. SINCE I HAVE RUN TIME AND AGAIN INTO THE AUTHORITY THAT IMPOSES APARTHEID... IT HAS ONLY INTENSIFIED MY LOVE FOR MY COUNTRY.
I WANT TO FIGHT FOR IT... FOR MYSELF... FOR MY CHILDREN.
WE'LL LEAVE IT AT THAT, THEN!
ZANTI, A GROUP IS COMING... WANTING TO BE HEARD.
THE COMRADS! ONE OF THEIR MEMBERS MUST HAVE ALSO SEEN THE SPY'S EQUIPMENT.
IF THE COMRADS HELD COURT ON HIM AND DECIDED HE WAS GUILTY OF PROFITTING FROM GOVERNMENT POLICIES--
--OR WORSE, A TRAITOR LIVING IN THEIR MIDST--
--THERE IS ONLY ONE VERDICT, AND THEY SEIZE THE RIGHTS WHITES HAVE...THEY WILL EXECUTE THEIR SENTENCE.
DEATH... BY NECKLACE CEREMONY!
KRRBAMS
WE HAVE ARRIVED TOO LATE!

CONTINUED NEXT ISSUE...

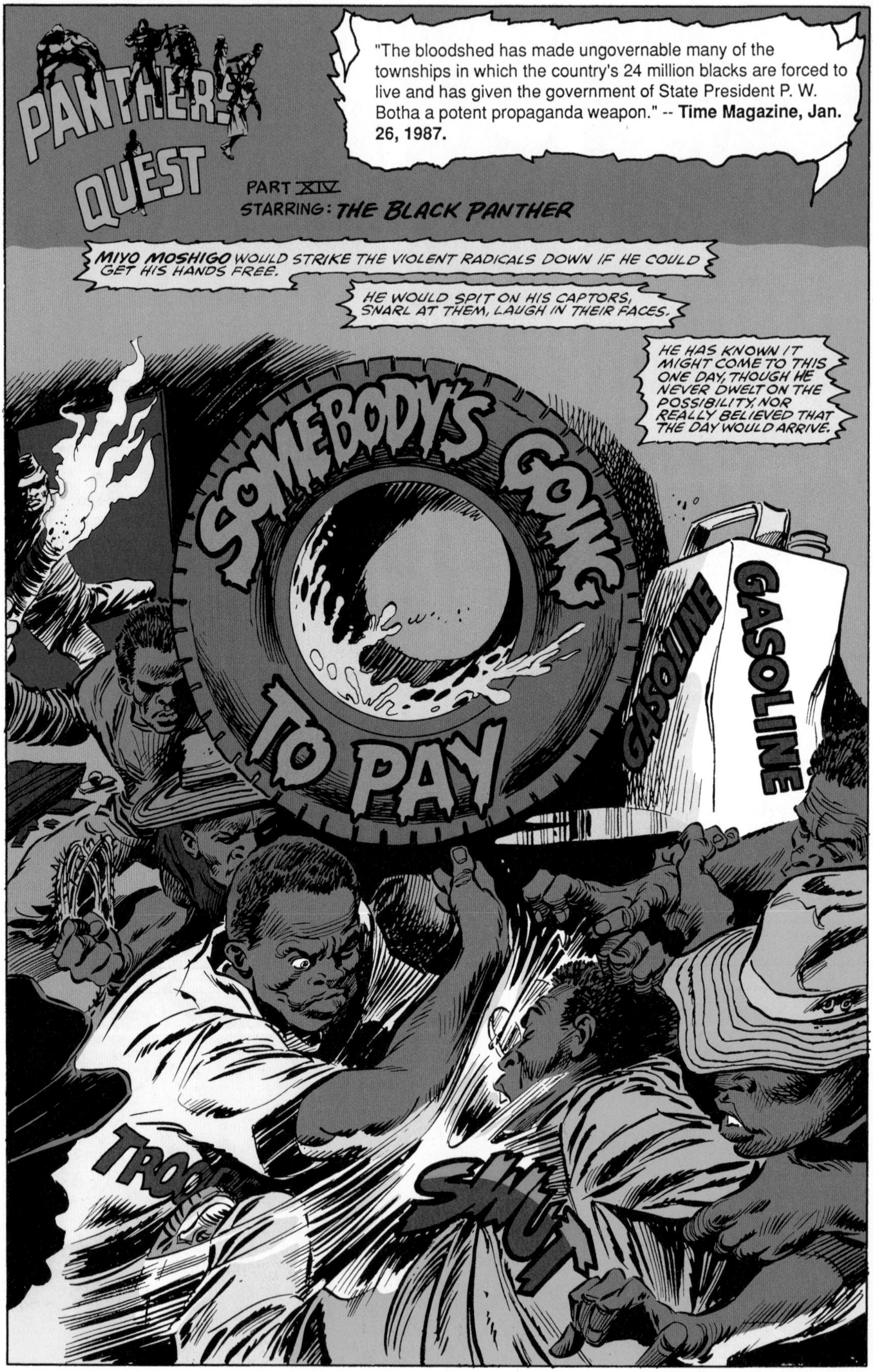
PANTHER'S QUEST
"The bloodshed has made ungovernable many of the townships in which the country's 24 million blacks are forced to live and has given the government of State President P. W. Botha a potent propaganda weapon." -- Time Magazine, Jan. 26, 1987.
PART XIV
STARRING: THE BLACK PANTHER
MIYO MOSHIGO WOULD STRIKE THE VIOLENT RADICALS DOWN IF HE COULD GET HIS HANDS FREE.
HE WOULD SPIT ON HIS CAPTORS, SNARL AT THEM, LAUGH IN THEIR FACES.
HE HAS KNOWN IT MIGHT COME TO THIS ONE DAY, THOUGH HE NEVER DWELT ON THE POSSIBILITY, NOR REALLY BELIEVED THAT THE DAY WOULD ARRIVE.
SOMEBODY'S GOING TO PAY
GASOLINE
GASOLINE

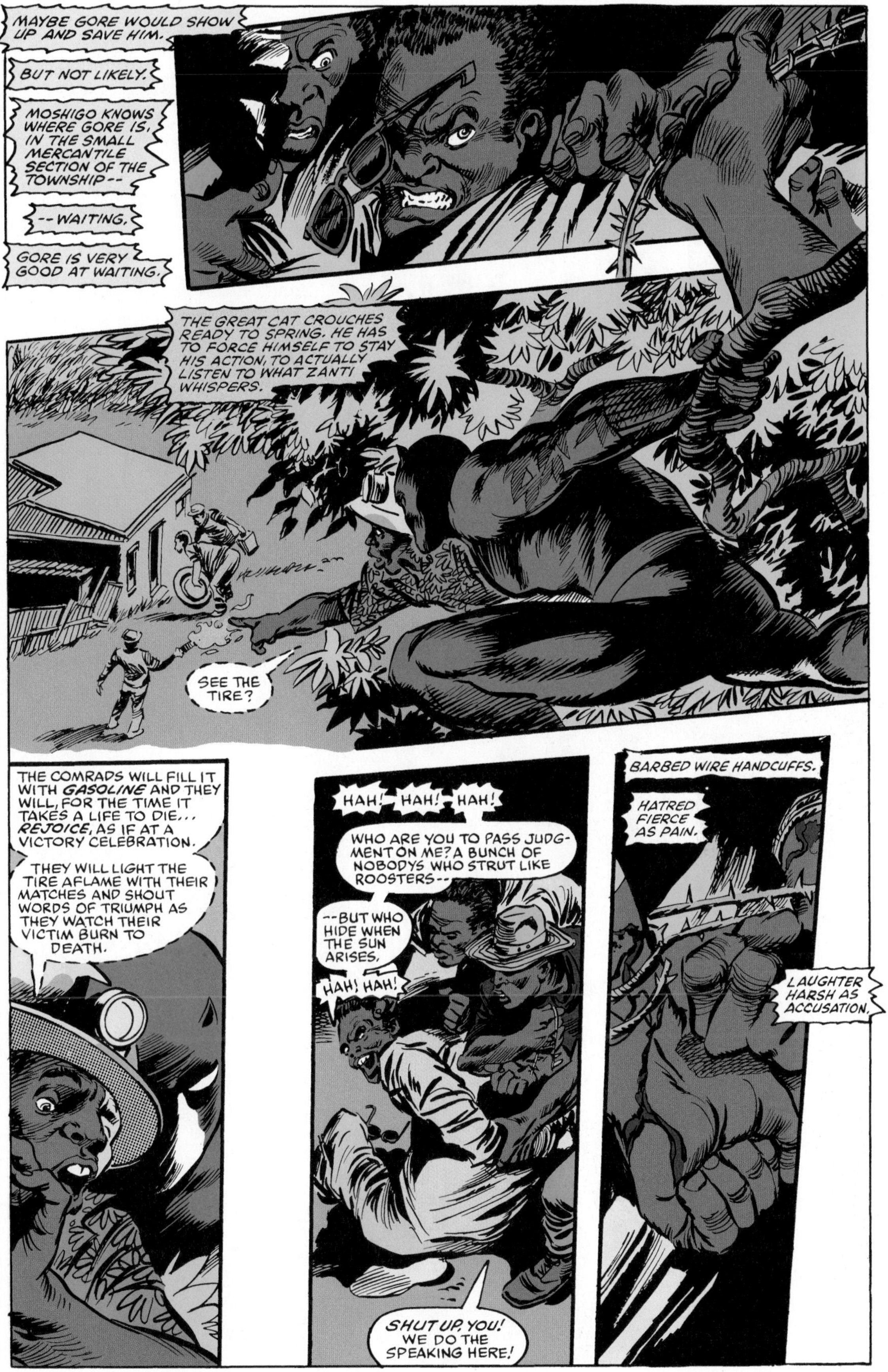
MAYBE GORE WOULD SHOW UP AND SAVE HIM.
BUT NOT LIKELY.
MOSHIGO KNOWS WHERE GORE IS, IN THE SMALL MERCANTILE SECTION OF THE TOWNSHIP--
--WAITING.
GORE IS VERY GOOD AT WAITING.
THE GREAT CAT CROUCHES READY TO SPRING. HE HAS TO FORCE HIMSELF TO STAY HIS ACTION, TO ACTUALLY LISTEN TO WHAT ZANTI WHISPERS.
SEE THE TIRE?
THE COMRADS WILL FILL IT WITH GASOLINE AND THEY WILL, FOR THE TIME IT TAKES A LIFE TO DIE... REJOICE, AS IF AT A VICTORY CELEBRATION.
THEY WILL LIGHT THE TIRE AFLAME WITH THEIR MATCHES AND SHOUT WORDS OF TRIUMPH AS THEY WATCH THEIR VICTIM BURN TO DEATH.
HAH! HAH! HAH!
WHO ARE YOU TO PASS JUDGMENT ON ME? A BUNCH OF NOBODYS WHO STRUT LIKE ROOSTERS--
--BUT WHO HIDE WHEN THE SUN ARISES.
HAH! HAH!
SHUT UP, YOU! WE DO THE SPEAKING HERE!
BARBED WIRE HANDCUFFS.
HATRED FIERCE AS PAIN.
LAUGHTER HARSH AS ACCUSATION.

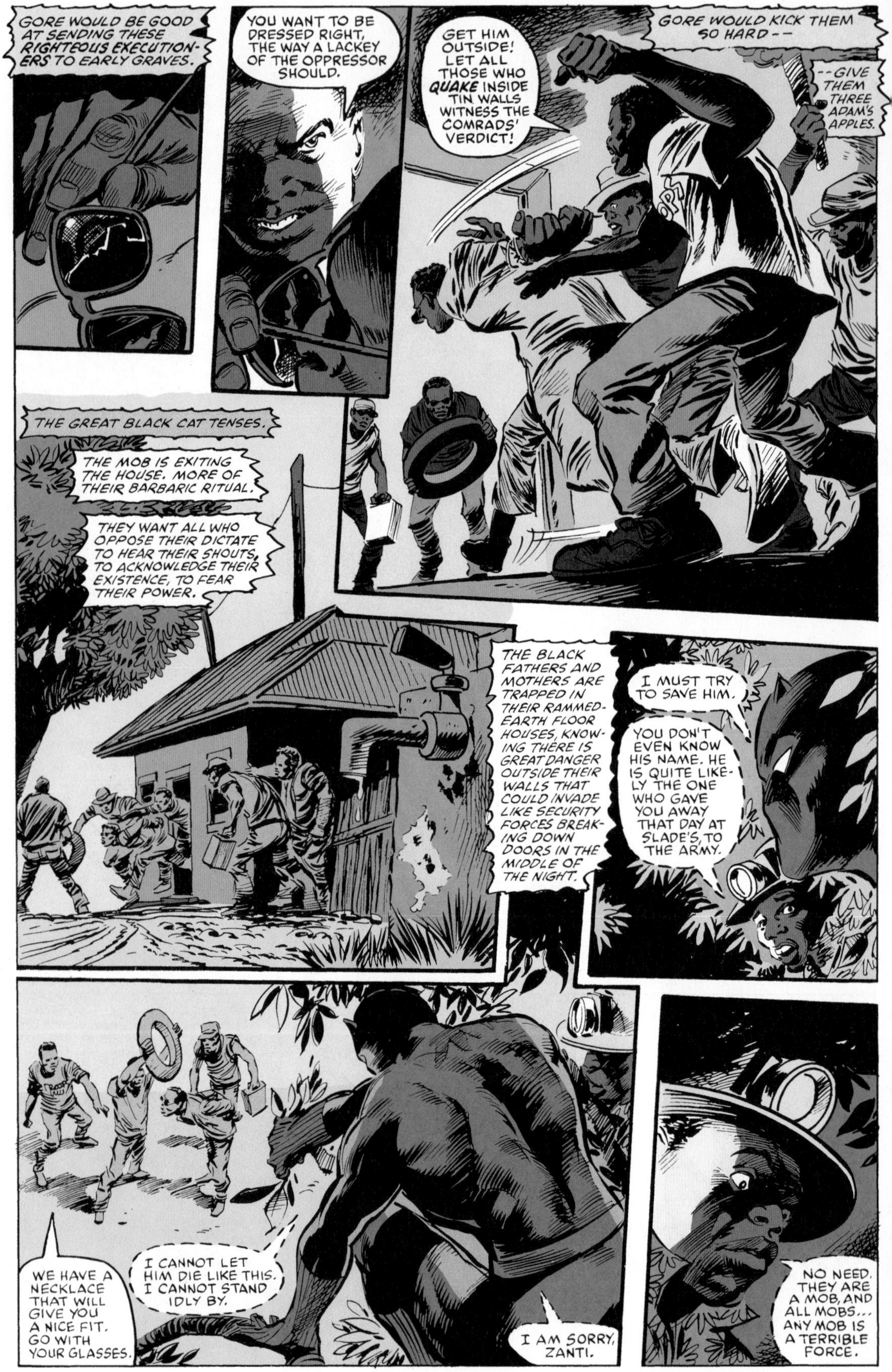
GORE WOULD BE GOOD AT SENDING THESE RIGHTEOUS EXECUTIONERS TO EARLY GRAVES.
YOU WANT TO BE DRESSED RIGHT, THE WAY A LACKEY OF THE OPPRESSOR SHOULD.
GET HIM OUTSIDE! LET ALL THOSE WHO QUAKE INSIDE TIN WALLS WITNESS THE COMRADS' VERDICT!
GORE WOULD KICK THEM SO HARD --
-- GIVE THEM THREE ADAM'S APPLES.
THE GREAT BLACK CAT TENSES.
THE MOB IS EXITING THE HOUSE. MORE OF THEIR BARBARIC RITUAL.
THEY WANT ALL WHO OPPOSE THEIR DICTATE TO HEAR THEIR SHOUTS, TO ACKNOWLEDGE THEIR EXISTENCE, TO FEAR THEIR POWER.
THE BLACK FATHERS AND MOTHERS ARE TRAPPED IN THEIR RAMMED-EARTH FLOOR HOUSES, KNOWING THERE IS GREAT DANGER OUTSIDE THEIR WALLS THAT COULD INVADE LIKE SECURITY FORCES BREAKING DOWN DOORS IN THE MIDDLE OF THE NIGHT.
I MUST TRY TO SAVE HIM.
YOU DON'T EVEN KNOW HIS NAME. HE IS QUITE LIKELY THE ONE WHO GAVE YOU AWAY THAT DAY AT SLADE'S, TO THE ARMY.
WE HAVE A NECKLACE THAT WILL GIVE YOU A NICE FIT. GO WITH YOUR GLASSES.
I CANNOT LET HIM DIE LIKE THIS. I CANNOT STAND IDLY BY.
I AM SORRY, ZANTI.
NO NEED. THEY ARE A MOB, AND ALL MOBS... ANY MOB IS A TERRIBLE FORCE.

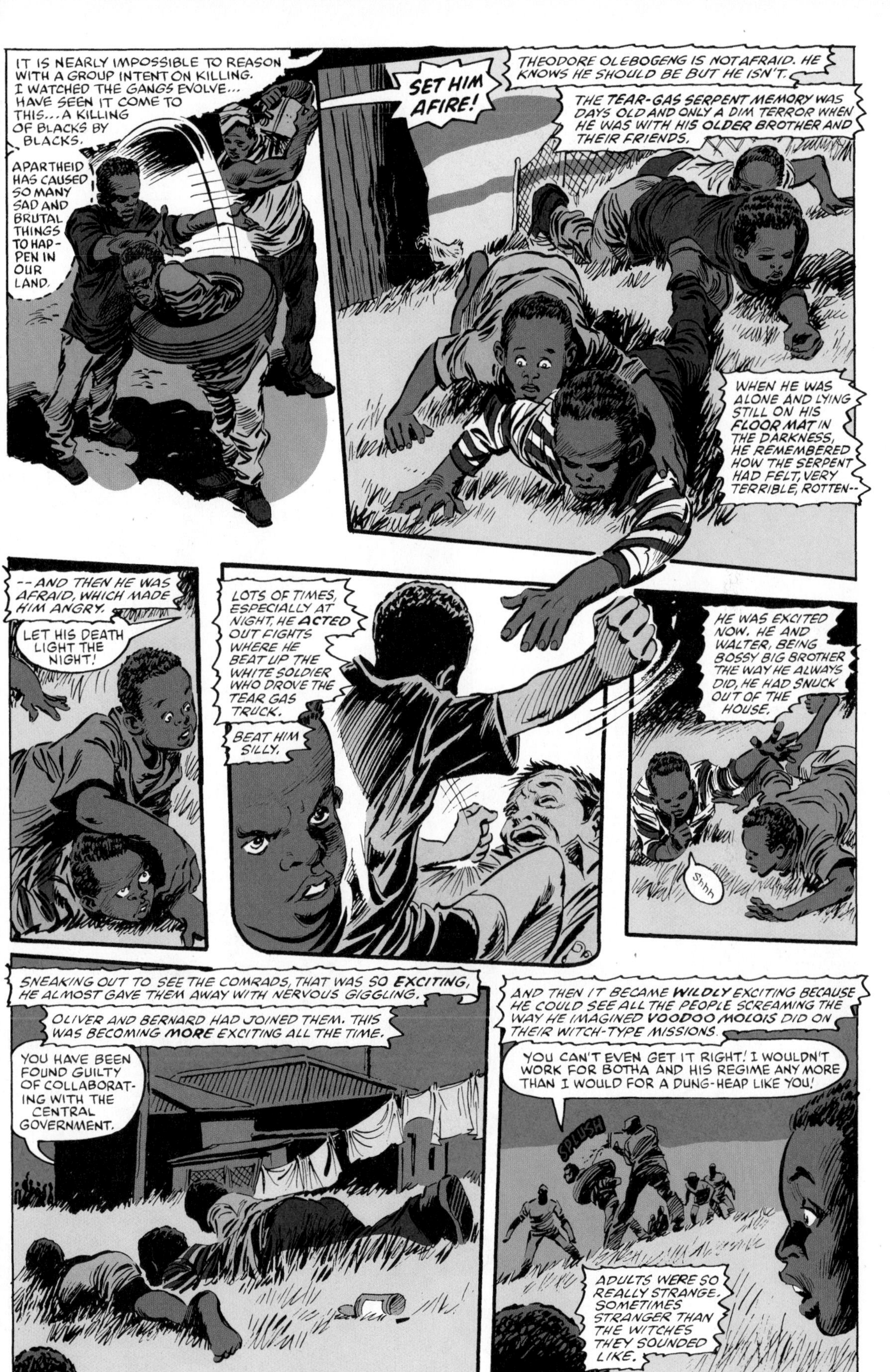

IT IS NEARLY IMPOSSIBLE TO REASON WITH A GROUP INTENT ON KILLING. I WATCHED THE GANGS EVOLVE... HAVE SEEN IT COME TO THIS... A KILLING OF BLACKS BY BLACKS.
APARTHEID HAS CAUSED SO MANY SAD AND BRUTAL THINGS TO HAPPEN IN OUR LAND.
SET HIM AFIRE!
THEODORE OLEBOGENG IS NOT AFRAID. HE KNOWS HE SHOULD BE BUT HE ISN'T.
THE TEAR-GAS SERPENT MEMORY WAS DAYS OLD AND ONLY A DIM TERROR WHEN HE WAS WITH HIS OLDER BROTHER AND THEIR FRIENDS.
WHEN HE WAS ALONE AND LYING STILL ON HIS FLOOR MAT IN THE DARKNESS, HE REMEMBERED HOW THE SERPENT HAD FELT, VERY TERRIBLE, ROTTEN--
--AND THEN HE WAS AFRAID, WHICH MADE HIM ANGRY.
LET HIS DEATH LIGHT THE NIGHT!
LOTS OF TIMES, ESPECIALLY AT NIGHT, HE ACTED OUT FIGHTS WHERE HE BEAT UP THE WHITE SOLDIER WHO DROVE THE TEAR GAS TRUCK.
BEAT HIM SILLY.
HE WAS EXCITED NOW. HE AND WALTER, BEING BOSSY BIG BROTHER THE WAY HE ALWAYS DID, HE HAD SNUCK OUT OF THE HOUSE.
Shhh
SNEAKING OUT TO SEE THE COMRADS, THAT WAS SO EXCITING, HE ALMOST GAVE THEM AWAY WITH NERVOUS GIGGLING.
OLIVER AND BERNARD HAD JOINED THEM. THIS WAS BECOMING MORE EXCITING ALL THE TIME.
YOU HAVE BEEN FOUND GUILTY OF COLLABORATING WITH THE CENTRAL GOVERNMENT.
AND THEN IT BECAME WILDLY EXCITING BECAUSE HE COULD SEE ALL THE PEOPLE SCREAMING THE WAY HE IMAGINED VOODOO MOLOIS DID ON THEIR WITCH-TYPE MISSIONS.
YOU CAN'T EVEN GET IT RIGHT! I WOULDN'T WORK FOR BOTHA AND HIS REGIME ANY MORE THAN I WOULD FOR A DUNG-HEAP LIKE YOU!
SPLUSH
ADULTS WERE SO REALLY STRANGE. SOMETIMES STRANGER THAN THE WITCHES THEY SOUNDED LIKE.

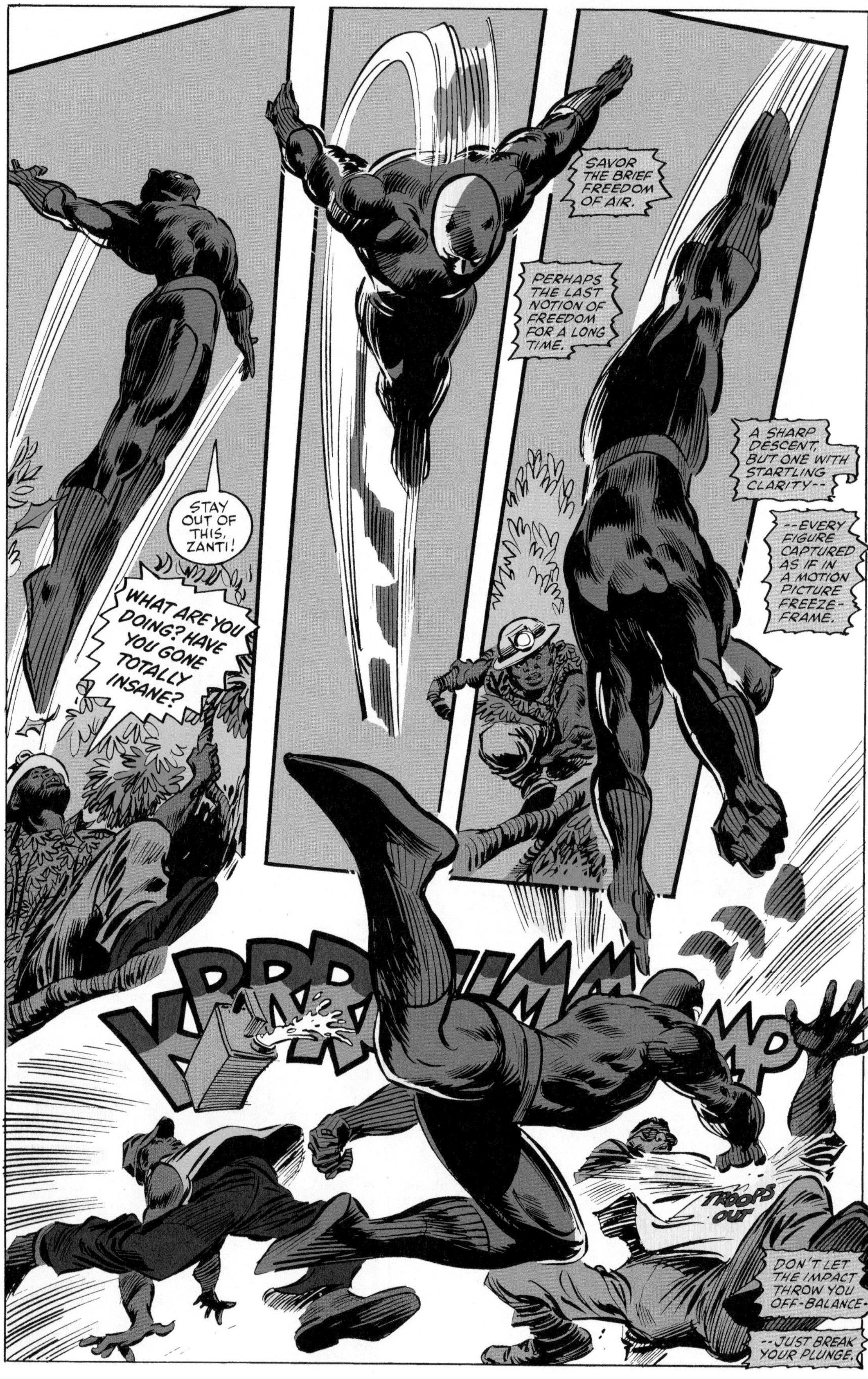
SAVOR THE BRIEF FREEDOM OF AIR.
PERHAPS THE LAST NOTION OF FREEDOM FOR A LONG TIME.
A SHARP DESCENT, BUT ONE WITH STARTLING CLARITY--
--EVERY FIGURE CAPTURED AS IF IN A MOTION PICTURE FREEZE-FRAME.
STAY OUT OF THIS, ZANTI!
WHAT ARE YOU DOING? HAVE YOU GONE TOTALLY INSANE?
KRRRUMMMMP
TROOPS OUT
DON'T LET THE IMPACT THROW YOU OFF-BALANCE--
--JUST BREAK YOUR PLUNGE.

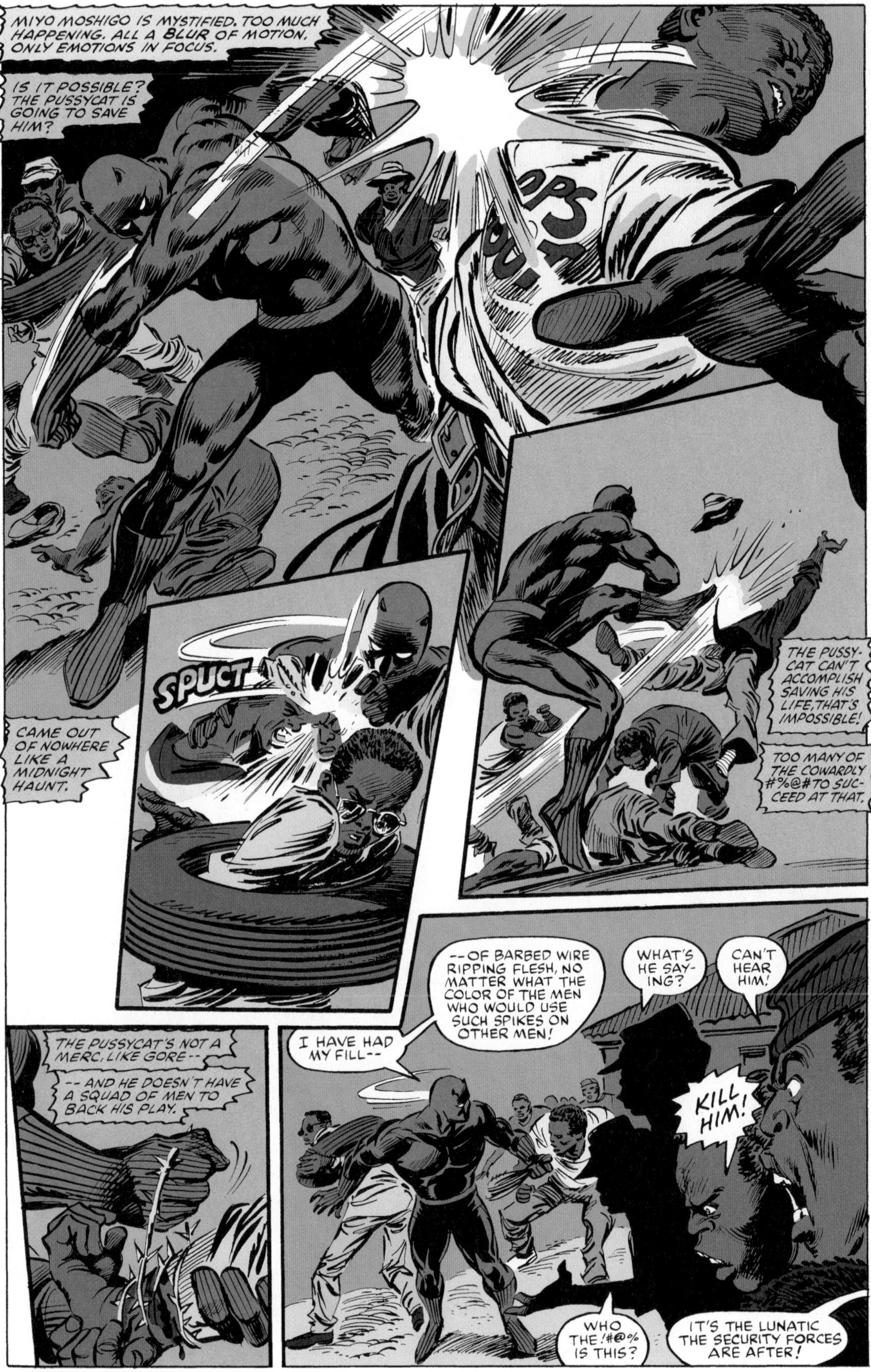

MIYO MOSHIGO IS MYSTIFIED. TOO MUCH HAPPENING. ALL A BLUR OF MOTION. ONLY EMOTIONS IN FOCUS.
IS IT POSSIBLE? THE PUSSYCAT IS GOING TO SAVE HIM?
OOPS
OUT
SPUCT
CAME OUT OF NOWHERE LIKE A MIDNIGHT HAUNT.
THE PUSSYCAT CAN'T ACCOMPLISH SAVING HIS LIFE, THAT'S IMPOSSIBLE!
TOO MANY OF THE COWARDLY #%@# TO SUCCEED AT THAT.
THE PUSSYCAT'S NOT A MERC, LIKE GORE--
--AND HE DOESN'T HAVE A SQUAD OF MEN TO BACK HIS PLAY.
I HAVE HAD MY FILL--
--OF BARBED WIRE RIPPING FLESH, NO MATTER WHAT THE COLOR OF THE MEN WHO WOULD USE SUCH SPIKES ON OTHER MEN!
WHAT'S HE SAYING?
CAN'T HEAR HIM!
KILL HIM!
WHO THE !#@% IS THIS?
IT'S THE LUNATIC THE SECURITY FORCES ARE AFTER!

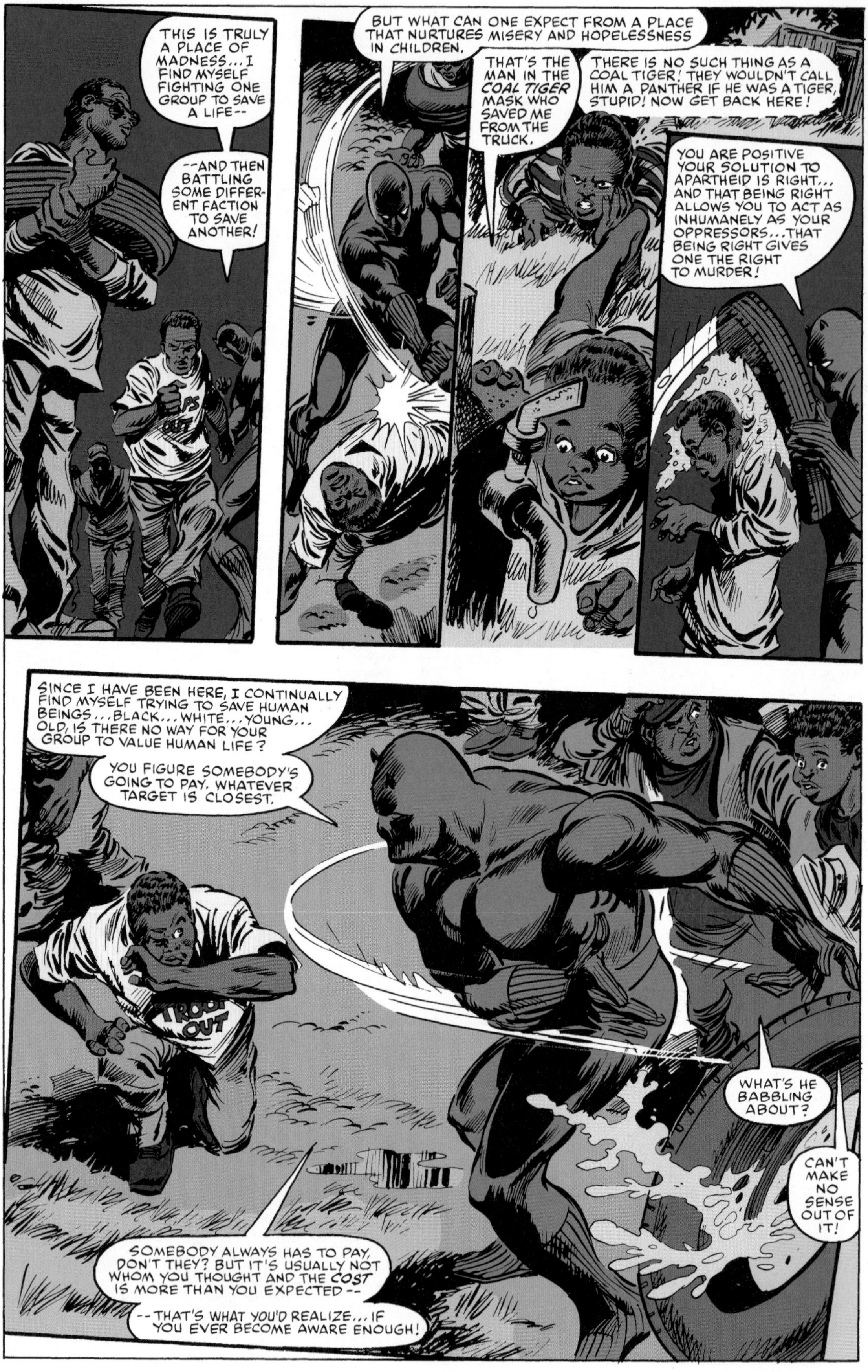

THIS IS TRULY A PLACE OF MADNESS... I FIND MYSELF FIGHTING ONE GROUP TO SAVE A LIFE--
--AND THEN BATTLING SOME DIFFERENT FACTION TO SAVE ANOTHER!
BUT WHAT CAN ONE EXPECT FROM A PLACE THAT NURTURES MISERY AND HOPELESSNESS IN CHILDREN.
THAT'S THE MAN IN THE COAL TIGER MASK WHO SAVED ME FROM THE TRUCK.
THERE IS NO SUCH THING AS A COAL TIGER! THEY WOULDN'T CALL HIM A PANTHER IF HE WAS A TIGER, STUPID! NOW GET BACK HERE!
YOU ARE POSITIVE YOUR SOLUTION TO APARTHEID IS RIGHT... AND THAT BEING RIGHT ALLOWS YOU TO ACT AS INHUMANELY AS YOUR OPPRESSORS... THAT BEING RIGHT GIVES ONE THE RIGHT TO MURDER!
SINCE I HAVE BEEN HERE, I CONTINUALLY FIND MYSELF TRYING TO SAVE HUMAN BEINGS... BLACK... WHITE... YOUNG... OLD, IS THERE NO WAY FOR YOUR GROUP TO VALUE HUMAN LIFE?
YOU FIGURE SOMEBODY'S GOING TO PAY. WHATEVER TARGET IS CLOSEST.
WHAT'S HE BABBLING ABOUT?
CAN'T MAKE NO SENSE OUT OF IT!
SOMEBODY ALWAYS HAS TO PAY, DON'T THEY? BUT IT'S USUALLY NOT WHOM YOU THOUGHT AND THE COST IS MORE THAN YOU EXPECTED--
--THAT'S WHAT YOU'D REALIZE... IF YOU EVER BECOME AWARE ENOUGH!

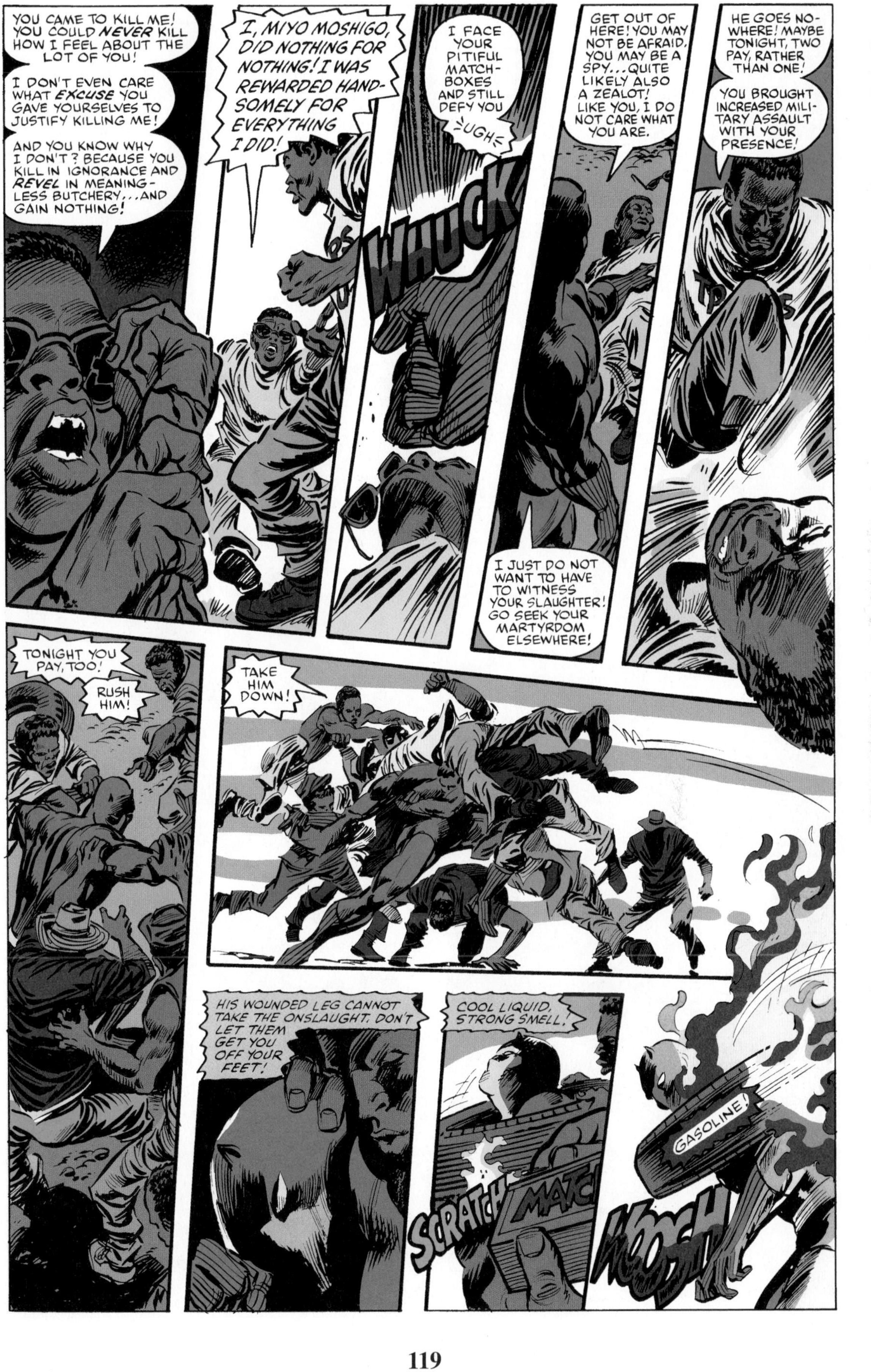
YOU CAME TO KILL ME! YOU COULD NEVER KILL HOW I FEEL ABOUT THE LOT OF YOU!
I DON'T EVEN CARE WHAT EXCUSE YOU GAVE YOURSELVES TO JUSTIFY KILLING ME!
AND YOU KNOW WHY I DON'T? BECAUSE YOU KILL IN IGNORANCE AND REVEL IN MEANINGLESS BUTCHERY... AND GAIN NOTHING!
I, MIYO MOSHIGO, DID NOTHING FOR NOTHING! I WAS REWARDED HANDSOMELY FOR EVERYTHING I DID!
I FACE YOUR PITIFUL MATCHBOXES AND STILL DEFY YOU
UGH
WHUCK
GET OUT OF HERE! YOU MAY NOT BE AFRAID. YOU MAY BE A SPY... QUITE LIKELY ALSO A ZEALOT! LIKE YOU, I DO NOT CARE WHAT YOU ARE.
I JUST DO NOT WANT TO HAVE TO WITNESS YOUR SLAUGHTER! GO SEEK YOUR MARTYRDOM ELSEWHERE!
HE GOES NOWHERE! MAYBE TONIGHT, TWO PAY, RATHER THAN ONE!
YOU BROUGHT INCREASED MILITARY ASSAULT WITH YOUR PRESENCE!
TONIGHT YOU PAY, TOO!
RUSH HIM!
TAKE HIM DOWN!
HIS WOUNDED LEG CANNOT TAKE THE ONSLAUGHT. DON'T LET THEM GET YOU OFF YOUR FEET!
COOL LIQUID, STRONG SMELL!
SCRATCH
MATCH
GASOLINE!
WOOSH

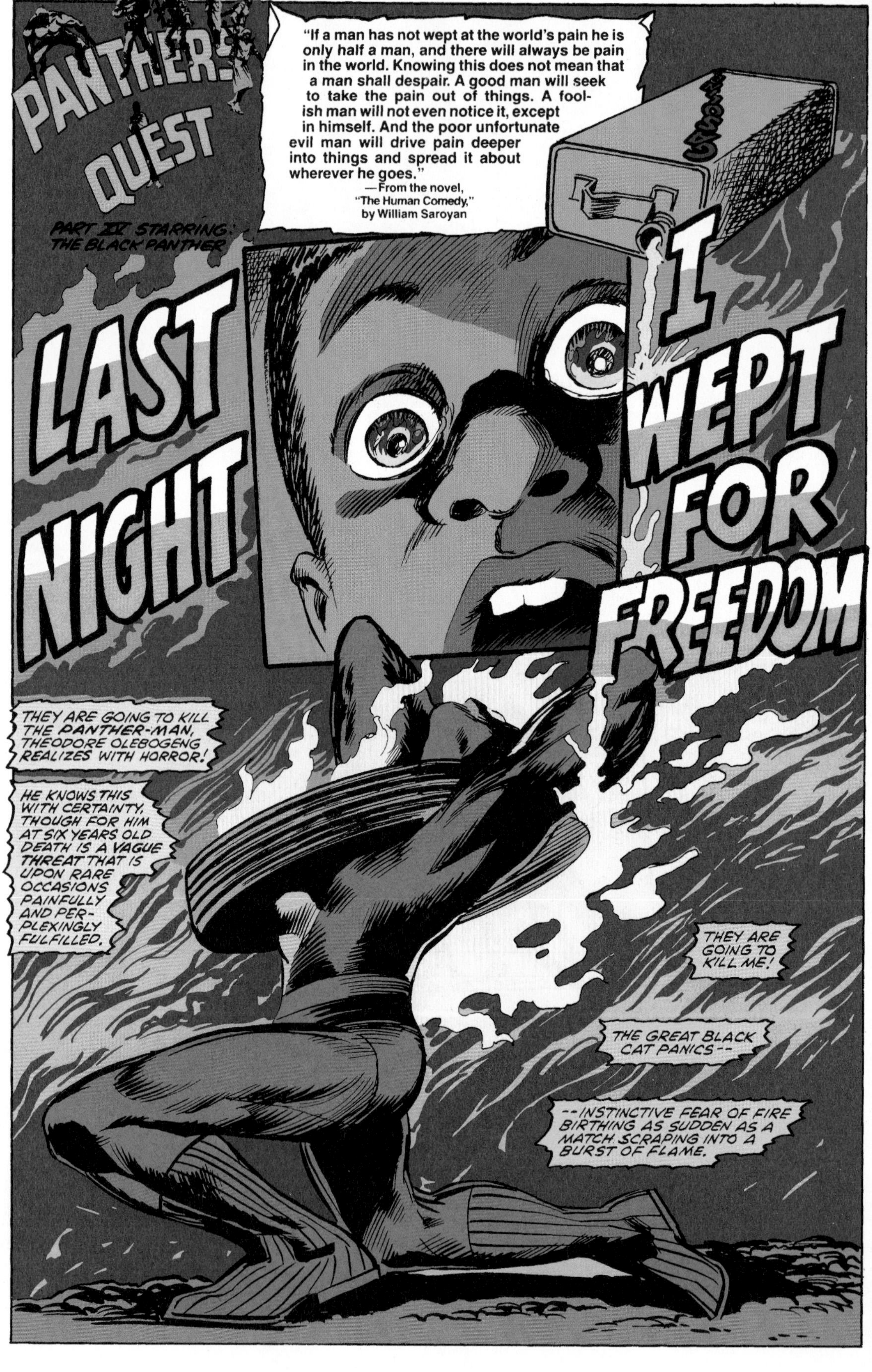
PANTHER'S QUEST
"If a man has not wept at the world's pain he is only half a man, and there will always be pain in the world. Knowing this does not mean that a man shall despair. A good man will seek to take the pain out of things. A foolish man will not even notice it, except in himself. And the poor unfortunate evil man will drive pain deeper into things and spread it about wherever he goes."
—From the novel, "The Human Comedy," by William Saroyan
PART IV STARRING: THE BLACK PANTHER
LAST NIGHT I WEPT FOR FREEDOM
THEY ARE GOING TO KILL THE PANTHER-MAN, THEODORE OLEBOGENG REALIZES WITH HORROR!
HE KNOWS THIS WITH CERTAINTY, THOUGH FOR HIM AT SIX YEARS OLD DEATH IS A VAGUE THREAT THAT IS UPON RARE OCCASIONS PAINFULLY AND PERPLEXINGLY FULFILLED.
THEY ARE GOING TO KILL ME!
THE GREAT BLACK CAT PANICS--
--INSTINCTIVE FEAR OF FIRE BIRTHING AS SUDDEN AS A MATCH SCRAPING INTO A BURST OF FLAME.

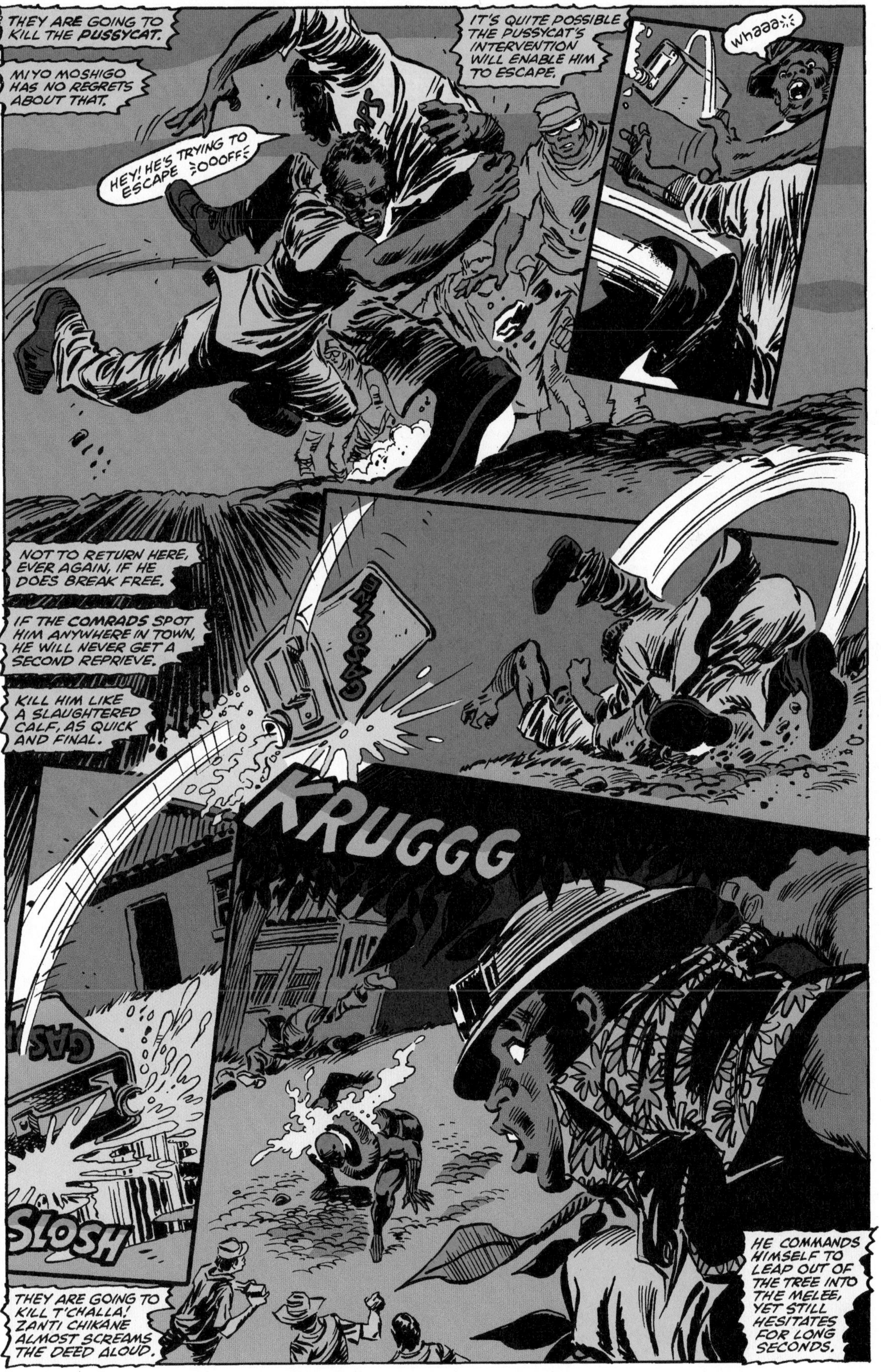
THEY ARE GOING TO KILL THE PUSSYCAT.
MIYO MOSHIGO HAS NO REGRETS ABOUT THAT.
HEY! HE'S TRYING TO ESCAPE OOOFF!
IT'S QUITE POSSIBLE THE PUSSYCAT'S INTERVENTION WILL ENABLE HIM TO ESCAPE.
WHAAA!
NOT TO RETURN HERE, EVER AGAIN, IF HE DOES BREAK FREE.
IF THE COMRADS SPOT HIM ANYWHERE IN TOWN, HE WILL NEVER GET A SECOND REPRIEVE.
KILL HIM LIKE A SLAUGHTERED CALF, AS QUICK AND FINAL.
GASOLINE
KRUGGG
SLOSH
THEY ARE GOING TO KILL T'CHALLA! ZANTI CHIKANE ALMOST SCREAMS THE DEED ALOUD.
HE COMMANDS HIMSELF TO LEAP OUT OF THE TREE INTO THE MELEE, YET STILL HESITATES FOR LONG SECONDS.

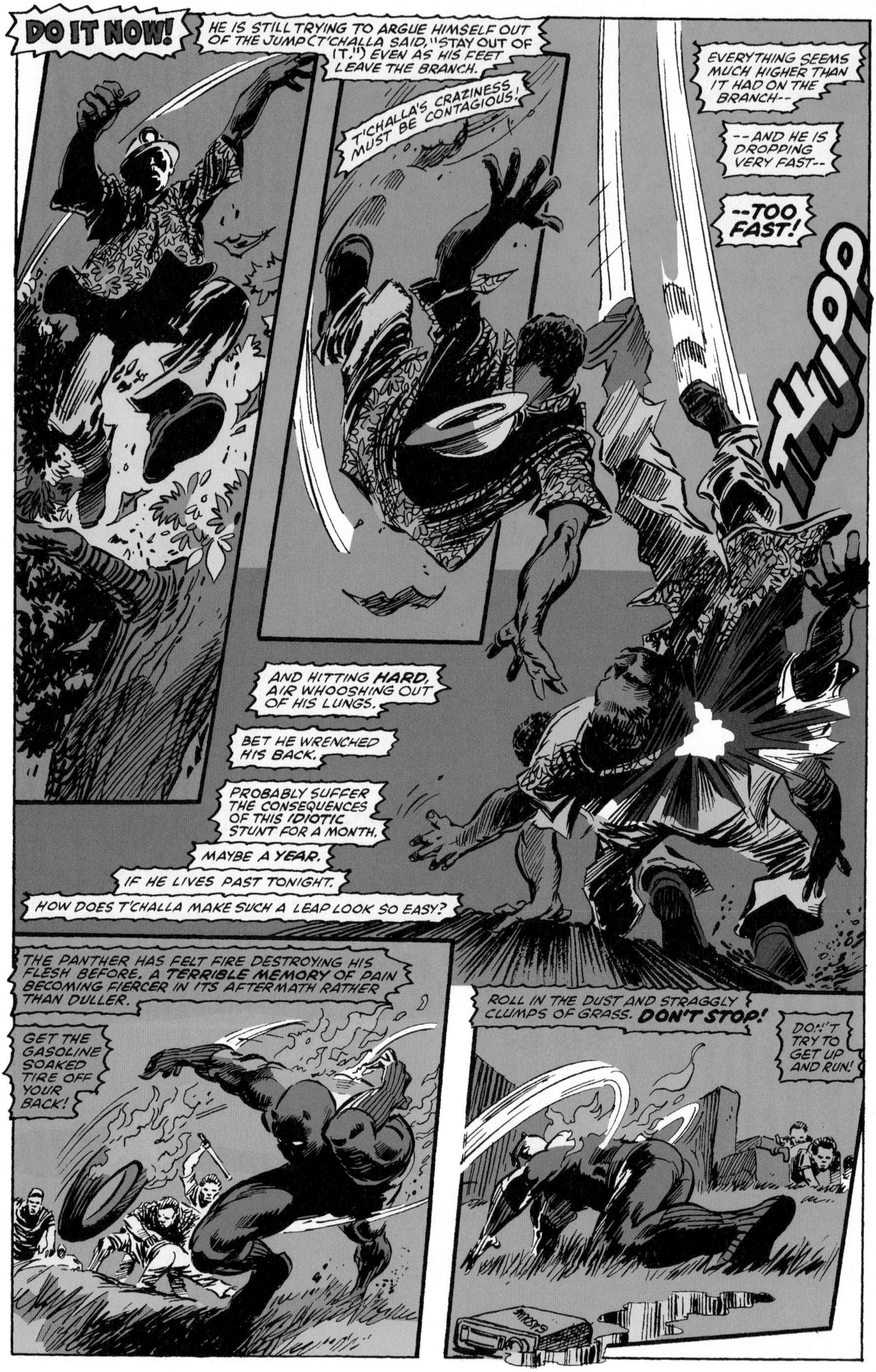
DO IT NOW!
HE IS STILL TRYING TO ARGUE HIMSELF OUT OF THE JUMP (T'CHALLA SAID, "STAY OUT OF IT.") EVEN AS HIS FEET LEAVE THE BRANCH.
T'CHALLA'S CRAZINESS MUST BE CONTAGIOUS!
EVERYTHING SEEMS MUCH HIGHER THAN IT HAD ON THE BRANCH--
--AND HE IS DROPPING VERY FAST--
--TOO FAST!
THUDD
AND HITTING HARD, AIR WHOOSHING OUT OF HIS LUNGS.
BET HE WRENCHED HIS BACK.
PROBABLY SUFFER THE CONSEQUENCES OF THIS IDIOTIC STUNT FOR A MONTH.
MAYBE A YEAR.
IF HE LIVES PAST TONIGHT.
HOW DOES T'CHALLA MAKE SUCH A LEAP LOOK SO EASY?
THE PANTHER HAS FELT FIRE DESTROYING HIS FLESH BEFORE. A TERRIBLE MEMORY OF PAIN BECOMING FIERCER IN ITS AFTERMATH RATHER THAN DULLER.
GET THE GASOLINE SOAKED TIRE OFF YOUR BACK!
ROLL IN THE DUST AND STRAGGLY CLUMPS OF GRASS. DON'T STOP!
DON'T TRY TO GET UP AND RUN!

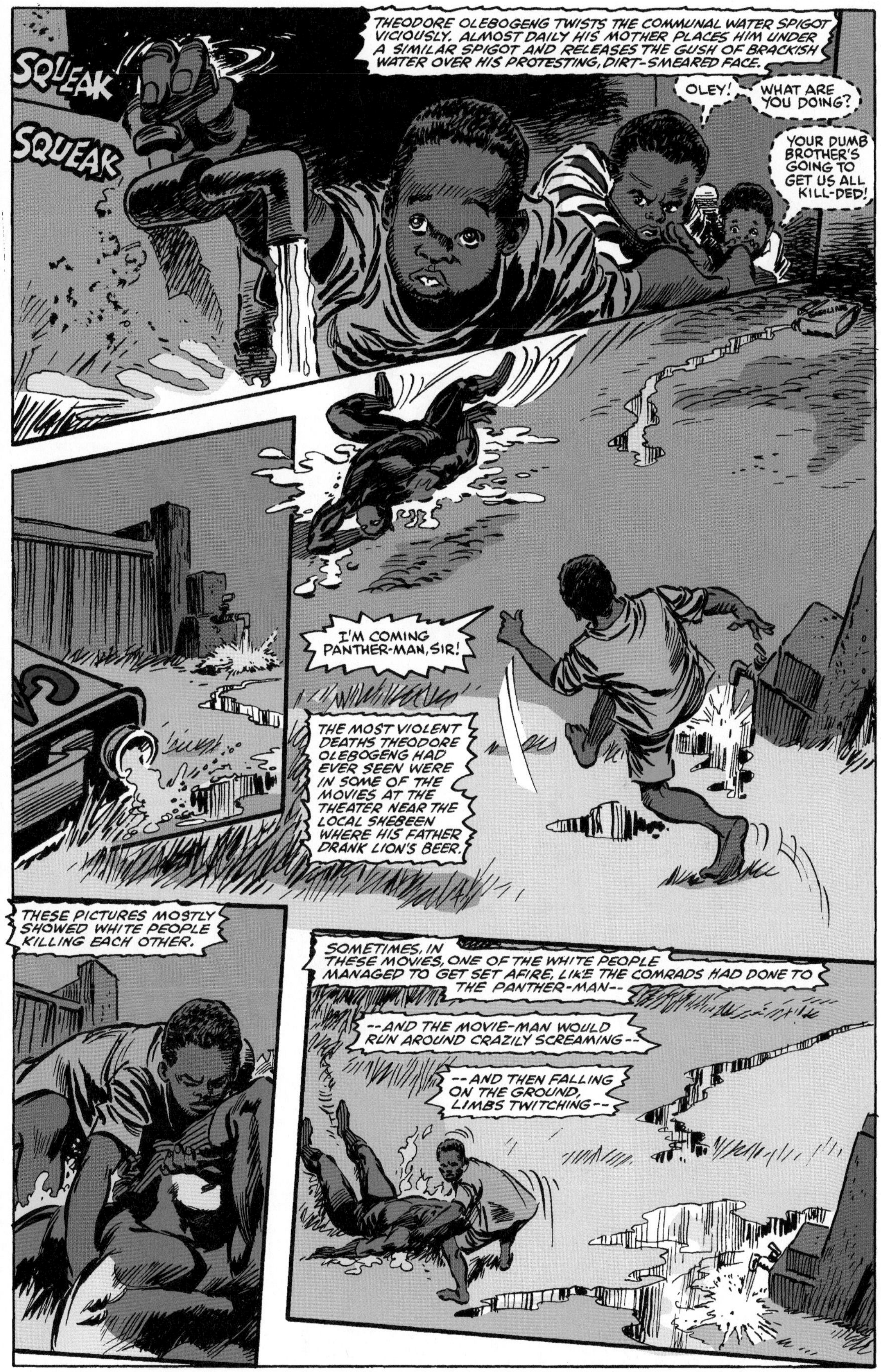
THEODORE OLEBOGENG TWISTS THE COMMUNAL WATER SPIGOT VICIOUSLY. ALMOST DAILY HIS MOTHER PLACES HIM UNDER A SIMILAR SPIGOT AND RELEASES THE GUSH OF BRACKISH WATER OVER HIS PROTESTING, DIRT-SMEARED FACE.
SQUEAK
SQUEAK
OLEY!
WHAT ARE YOU DOING?
YOUR DUMB BROTHER'S GOING TO GET US ALL KILL-DED!
I'M COMING PANTHER-MAN, SIR!
THE MOST VIOLENT DEATHS THEODORE OLEBOGENG HAD EVER SEEN WERE IN SOME OF THE MOVIES AT THE THEATER NEAR THE LOCAL SHEBEEN WHERE HIS FATHER DRANK LION'S BEER.
THESE PICTURES MOSTLY SHOWED WHITE PEOPLE KILLING EACH OTHER.
SOMETIMES, IN THESE MOVIES, ONE OF THE WHITE PEOPLE MANAGED TO GET SET AFIRE, LIKE THE COMRADS HAD DONE TO THE PANTHER-MAN--
--AND THE MOVIE-MAN WOULD RUN AROUND CRAZILY SCREAMING--
--AND THEN FALLING ON THE GROUND, LIMBS TWITCHING--

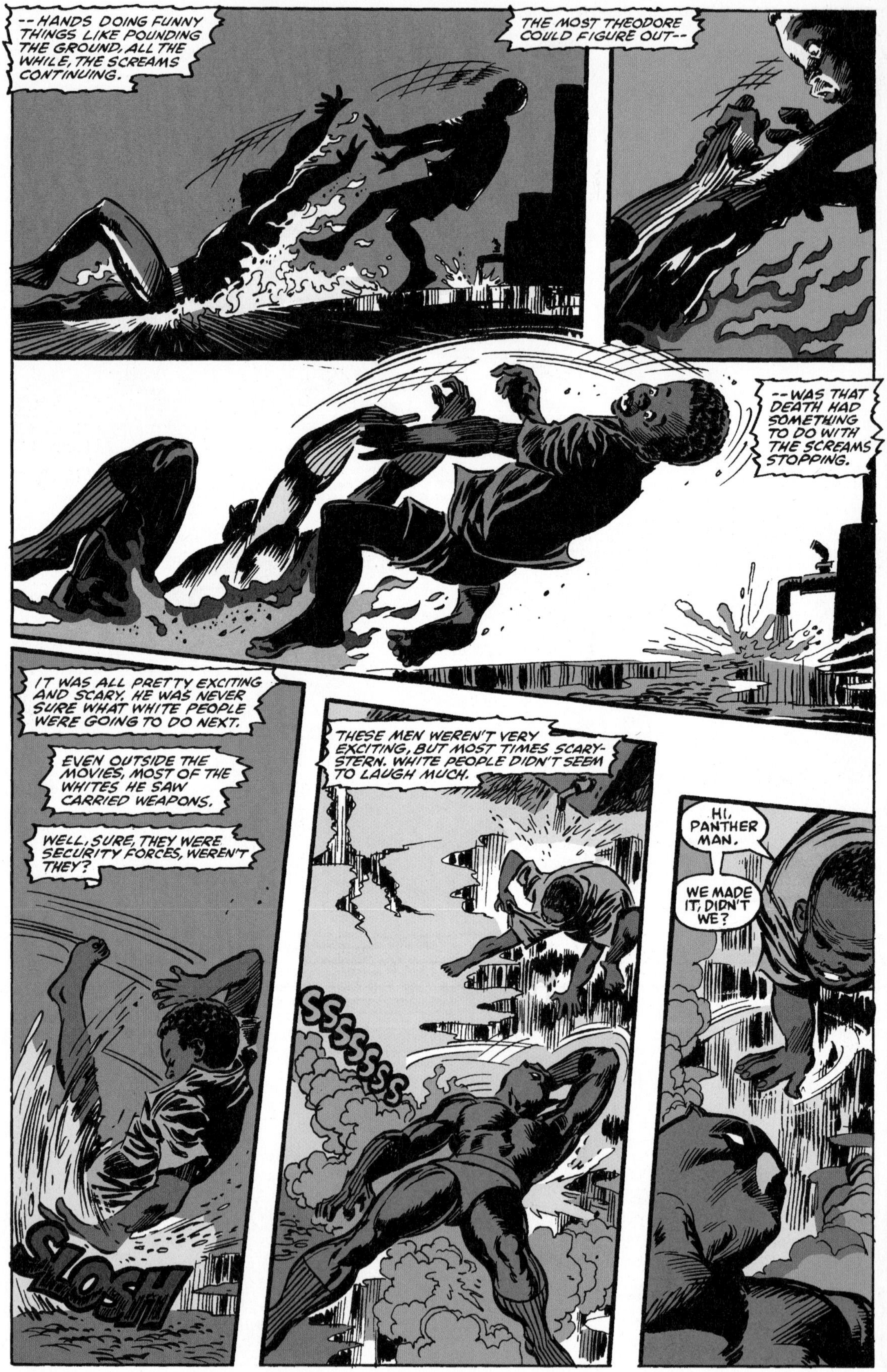
--HANDS DOING FUNNY THINGS LIKE POUNDING THE GROUND, ALL THE WHILE, THE SCREAMS CONTINUING.
THE MOST THEODORE COULD FIGURE OUT--
--WAS THAT DEATH HAD SOMETHING TO DO WITH THE SCREAMS STOPPING.
IT WAS ALL PRETTY EXCITING AND SCARY. HE WAS NEVER SURE WHAT WHITE PEOPLE WERE GOING TO DO NEXT.
EVEN OUTSIDE THE MOVIES, MOST OF THE WHITES HE SAW CARRIED WEAPONS.
WELL, SURE, THEY WERE SECURITY FORCES, WEREN'T THEY?
SLOSH
THESE MEN WEREN'T VERY EXCITING, BUT MOST TIMES SCARY-STERN. WHITE PEOPLE DIDN'T SEEM TO LAUGH MUCH.
SSSSSSS
HI, PANTHER MAN.
WE MADE IT, DIDN'T WE?

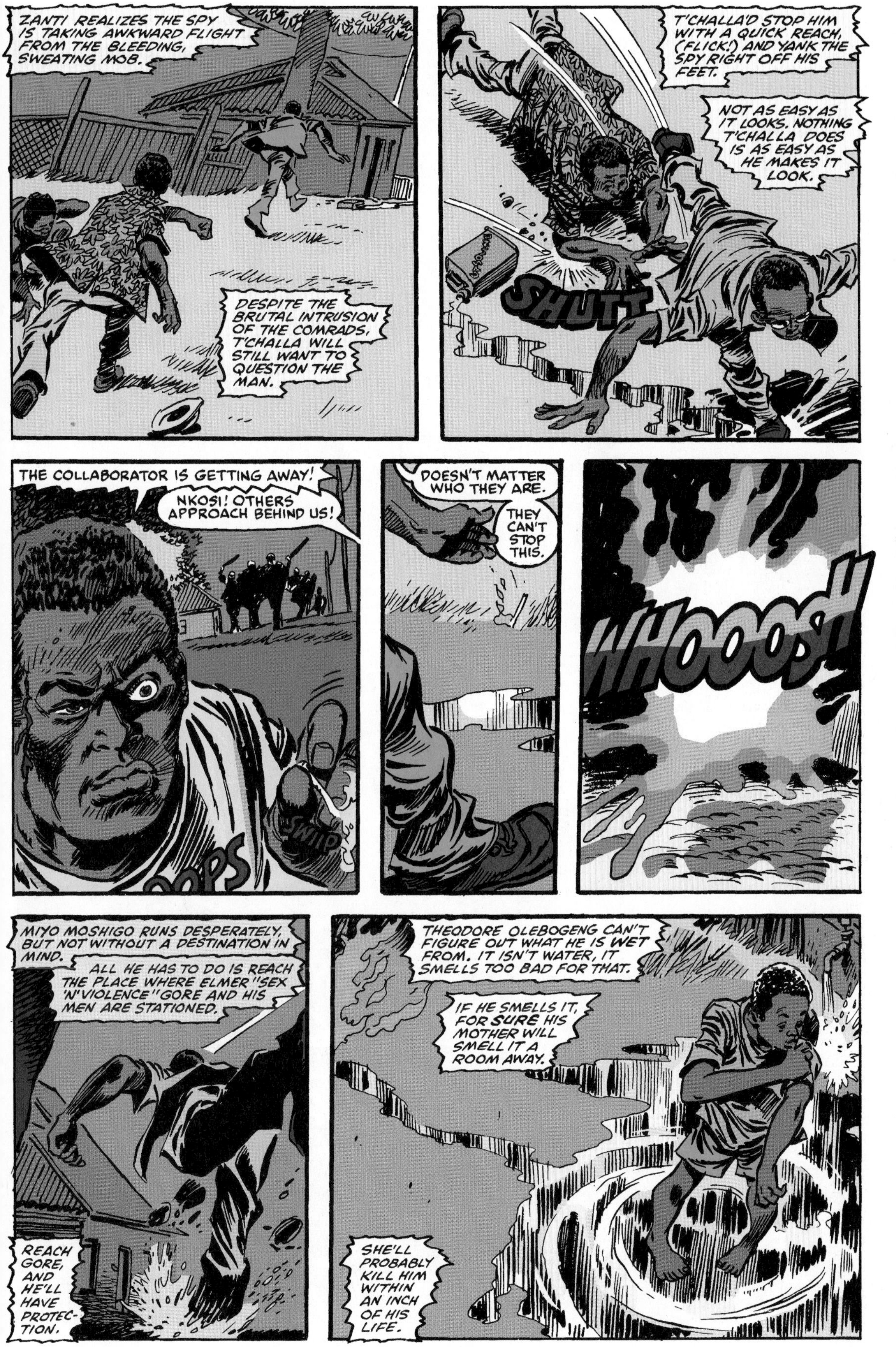
ZANTI REALIZES THE SPY IS TAKING AWKWARD FLIGHT FROM THE BLEEDING, SWEATING MOB.
DESPITE THE BRUTAL INTRUSION OF THE COMRADS, T'CHALLA WILL STILL WANT TO QUESTION THE MAN.
T'CHALLA'D STOP HIM WITH A QUICK REACH, (FLICK!) AND YANK THE SPY RIGHT OFF HIS FEET.
NOT AS EASY AS IT LOOKS. NOTHING T'CHALLA DOES IS AS EASY AS HE MAKES IT LOOK.
SHUTT
THE COLLABORATOR IS GETTING AWAY!
NKOSI! OTHERS APPROACH BEHIND US!
SWIP
DOESN'T MATTER WHO THEY ARE.
THEY CAN'T STOP THIS.
WHOOOSH!
MIYO MOSHIGO RUNS DESPERATELY, BUT NOT WITHOUT A DESTINATION IN MIND.
ALL HE HAS TO DO IS REACH THE PLACE WHERE ELMER "SEX 'N' VIOLENCE" GORE AND HIS MEN ARE STATIONED.
REACH GORE, AND HE'LL HAVE PROTECTION.
THEODORE OLEBOGENG CAN'T FIGURE OUT WHAT HE IS WET FROM. IT ISN'T WATER, IT SMELLS TOO BAD FOR THAT.
IF HE SMELLS IT, FOR SURE HIS MOTHER WILL SMELL IT A ROOM AWAY.
SHE'LL PROBABLY KILL HIM WITHIN AN INCH OF HIS LIFE.

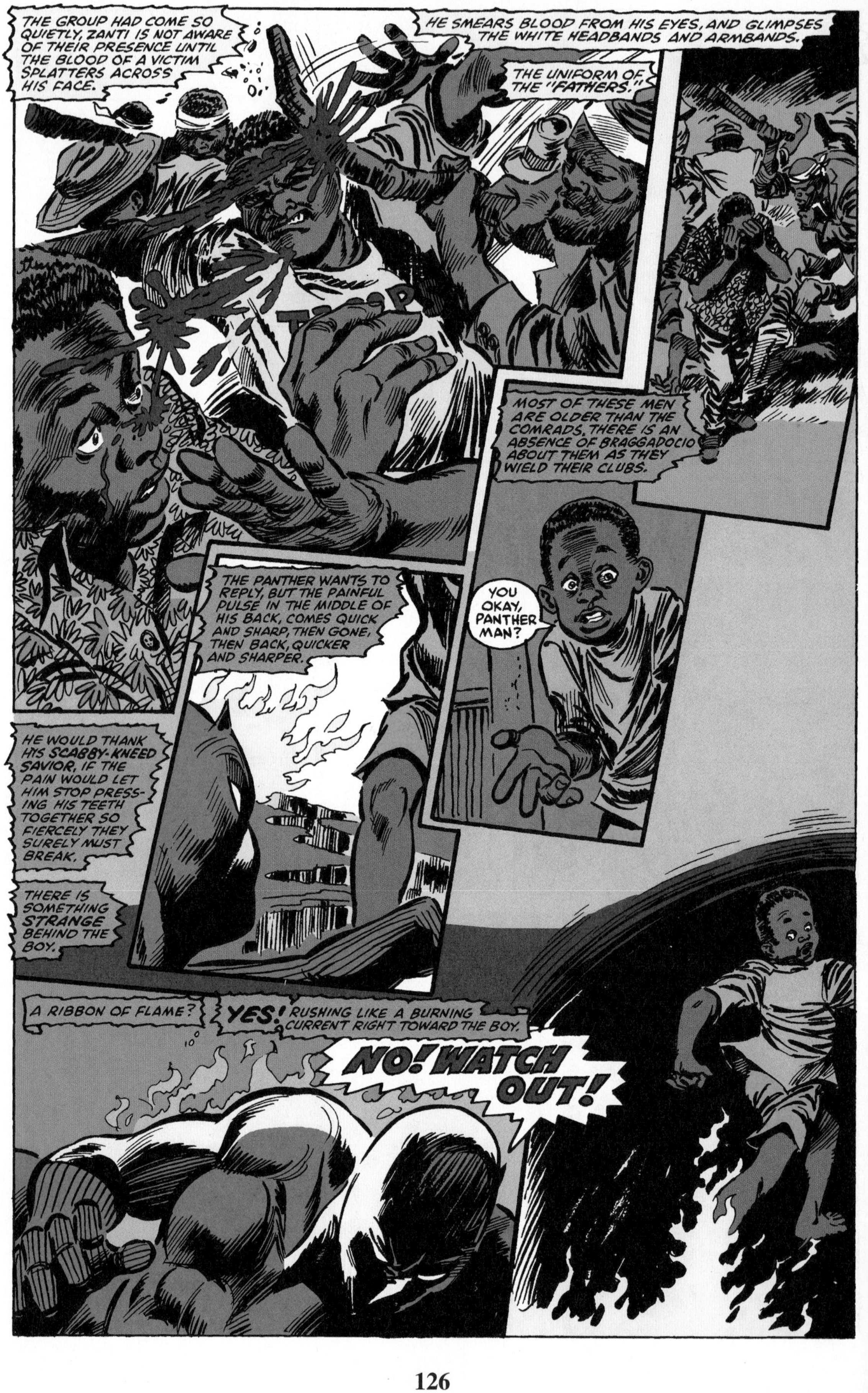

THE GROUP HAD COME SO QUIETLY, ZANTI IS NOT AWARE OF THEIR PRESENCE UNTIL THE BLOOD OF A VICTIM SPLATTERS ACROSS HIS FACE.
HE SMEARS BLOOD FROM HIS EYES, AND GLIMPSES THE WHITE HEADBANDS AND ARMBANDS.
THE UNIFORM OF THE "FATHERS."
MOST OF THESE MEN ARE OLDER THAN THE COMRADS. THERE IS AN ABSENCE OF BRAGGADOCIO ABOUT THEM AS THEY WIELD THEIR CLUBS.
THE PANTHER WANTS TO REPLY, BUT THE PAINFUL PULSE IN THE MIDDLE OF HIS BACK, COMES QUICK AND SHARP, THEN GONE, THEN BACK, QUICKER AND SHARPER.
YOU OKAY, PANTHER MAN?
HE WOULD THANK HIS SCABBY-KNEED SAVIOR, IF THE PAIN WOULD LET HIM STOP PRESSING HIS TEETH TOGETHER SO FIERCELY THEY SURELY MUST BREAK.
THERE IS SOMETHING STRANGE BEHIND THE BOY.
A RIBBON OF FLAME?
YES! RUSHING LIKE A BURNING CURRENT RIGHT TOWARD THE BOY.
NO! WATCH OUT!

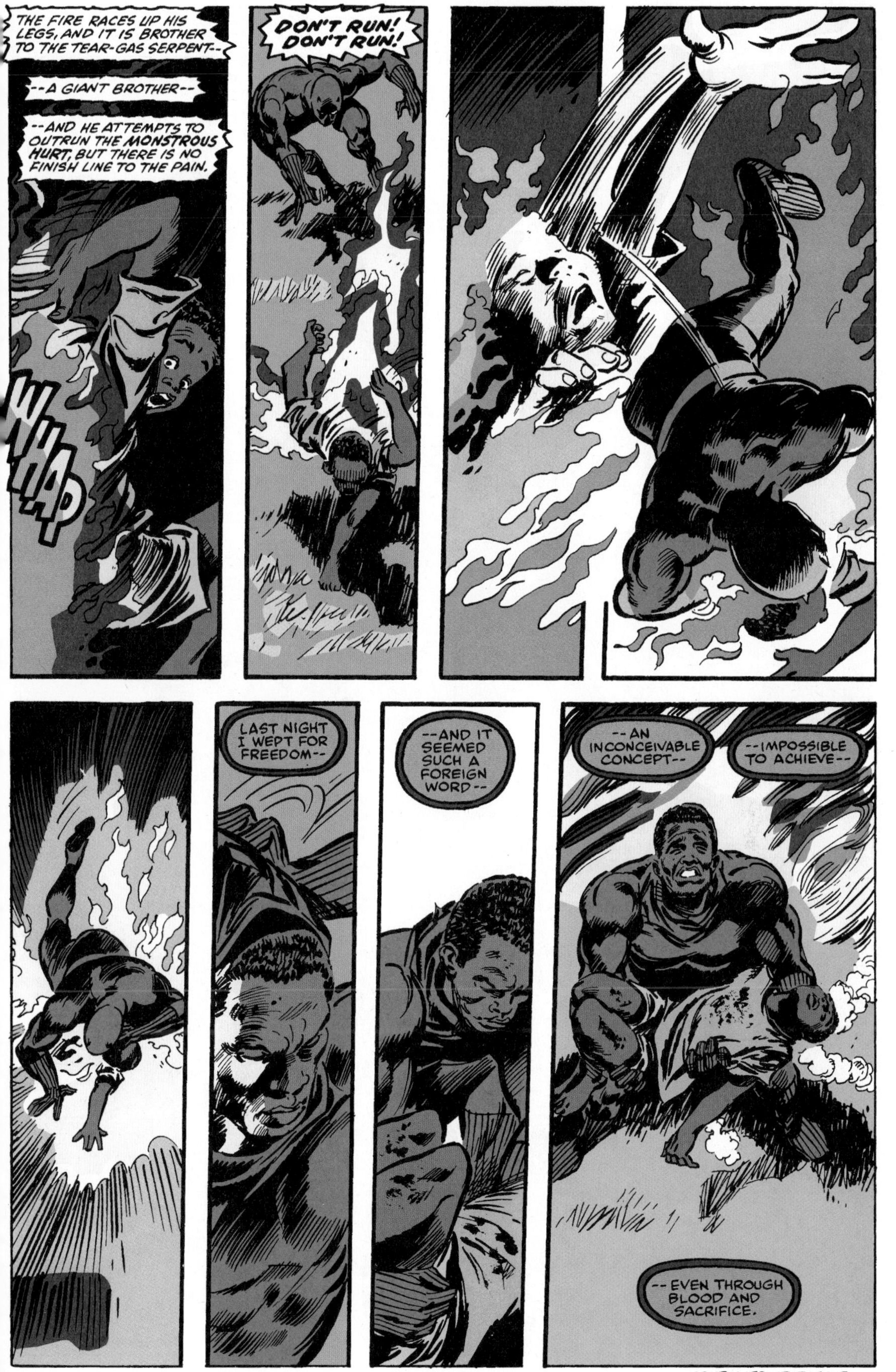
THE FIRE RACES UP HIS LEGS, AND IT IS BROTHER TO THE TEAR-GAS SERPENT--
--A GIANT BROTHER--
--AND HE ATTEMPTS TO OUTRUN THE **MONSTROUS HURT**, BUT THERE IS NO FINISH LINE TO THE PAIN.
WHAP
DON'T RUN! DON'T RUN!
LAST NIGHT I WEPT FOR FREEDOM--
--AND IT SEEMED SUCH A FOREIGN WORD--
--AN INCONCEIVABLE CONCEPT--
--IMPOSSIBLE TO ACHIEVE--
--EVEN THROUGH BLOOD AND SACRIFICE.

CONTINUED NEXT ISSUE...

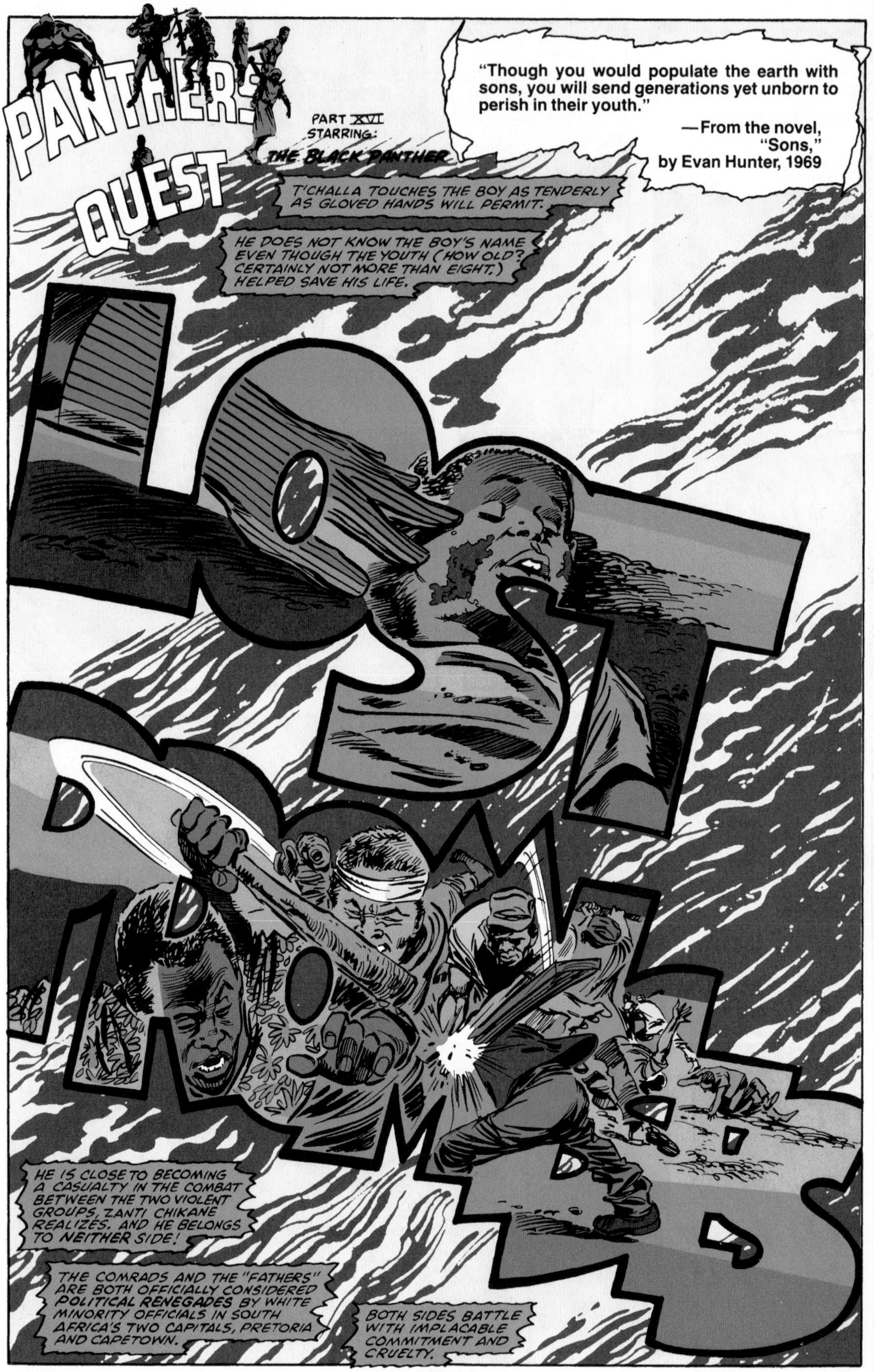
PANTHER'S QUEST
PART XVI
STARRING:
THE BLACK PANTHER
"Though you would populate the earth with sons, you will send generations yet unborn to perish in their youth."
—From the novel, "Sons," by Evan Hunter, 1969
T'CHALLA TOUCHES THE BOY AS TENDERLY AS GLOVED HANDS WILL PERMIT.
HE DOES NOT KNOW THE BOY'S NAME EVEN THOUGH THE YOUTH (HOW OLD? CERTAINLY NOT MORE THAN EIGHT.) HELPED SAVE HIS LIFE.
LOST MOM'S
HE IS CLOSE TO BECOMING A CASUALTY IN THE COMBAT BETWEEN THE TWO VIOLENT GROUPS, ZANTI CHIKANE REALIZES. AND HE BELONGS TO NEITHER SIDE!
THE COMRADS AND THE "FATHERS" ARE BOTH OFFICIALLY CONSIDERED POLITICAL RENEGADES BY WHITE MINORITY OFFICIALS IN SOUTH AFRICA'S TWO CAPITALS, PRETORIA AND CAPETOWN.
BOTH SIDES BATTLE WITH IMPLACABLE COMMITMENT AND CRUELTY.

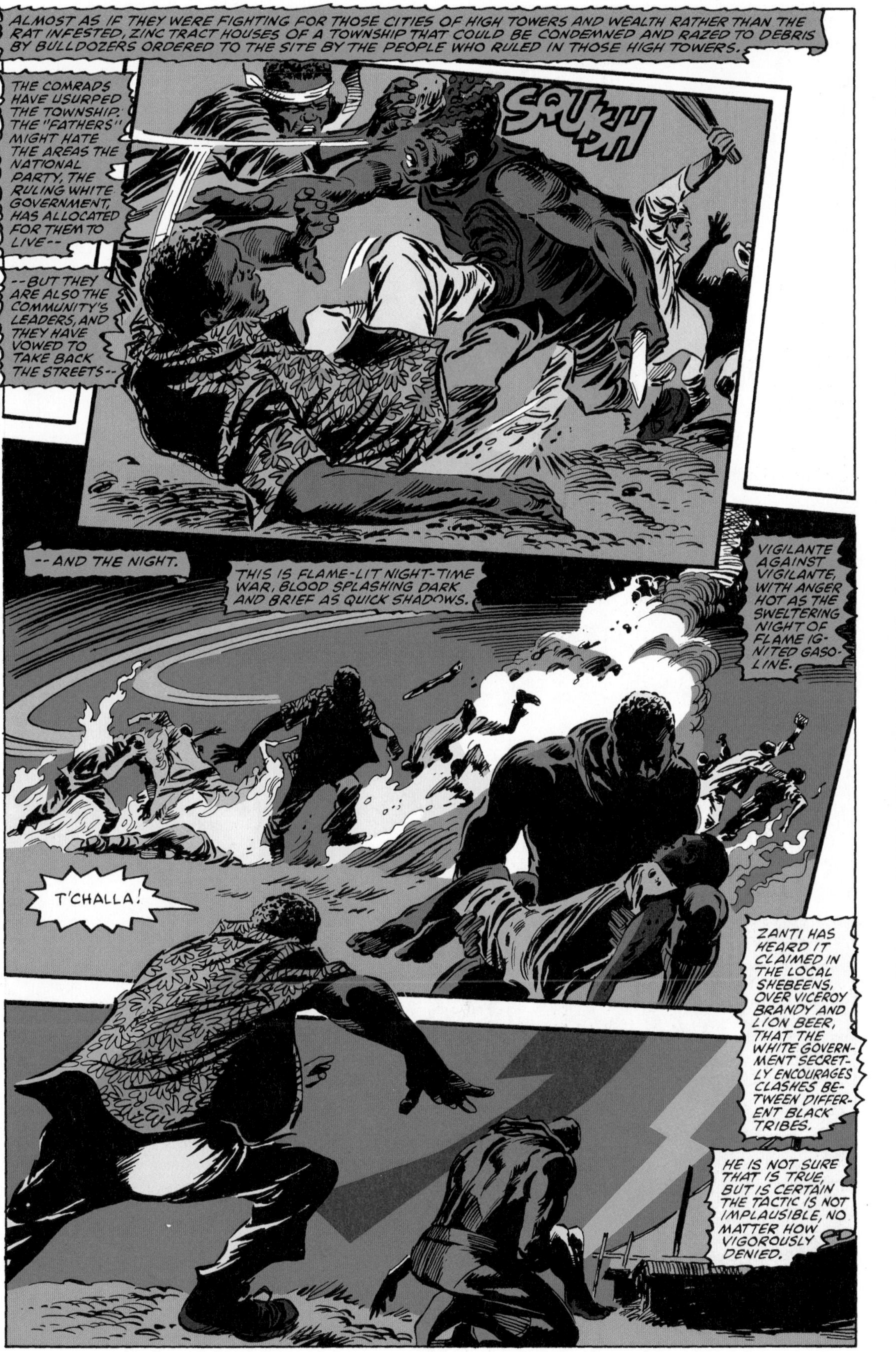
ALMOST AS IF THEY WERE FIGHTING FOR THOSE CITIES OF HIGH TOWERS AND WEALTH RATHER THAN THE RAT INFESTED, ZINC TRACT HOUSES OF A TOWNSHIP THAT COULD BE CONDEMNED AND RAZED TO DEBRIS BY BULLDOZERS ORDERED TO THE SITE BY THE PEOPLE WHO RULED IN THOSE HIGH TOWERS.
THE COMRADS HAVE USURPED THE TOWNSHIP. THE "FATHERS" MIGHT HATE THE AREAS THE NATIONAL PARTY, THE RULING WHITE GOVERNMENT, HAS ALLOCATED FOR THEM TO LIVE--
--BUT THEY ARE ALSO THE COMMUNITY'S LEADERS, AND THEY HAVE VOWED TO TAKE BACK THE STREETS--
SQUKH
--AND THE NIGHT.
THIS IS FLAME-LIT NIGHT-TIME WAR, BLOOD SPLASHING DARK AND BRIEF AS QUICK SHADOWS.
VIGILANTE AGAINST VIGILANTE, WITH ANGER HOT AS THE SWELTERING NIGHT OF FLAME IGNITED GASOLINE.
T'CHALLA!
ZANTI HAS HEARD IT CLAIMED IN THE LOCAL SHEBEENS, OVER VICEROY BRANDY AND LION BEER, THAT THE WHITE GOVERNMENT SECRETLY ENCOURAGES CLASHES BETWEEN DIFFERENT BLACK TRIBES.
HE IS NOT SURE THAT IS TRUE, BUT IS CERTAIN THE TACTIC IS NOT IMPLAUSIBLE, NO MATTER HOW VIGOROUSLY DENIED.

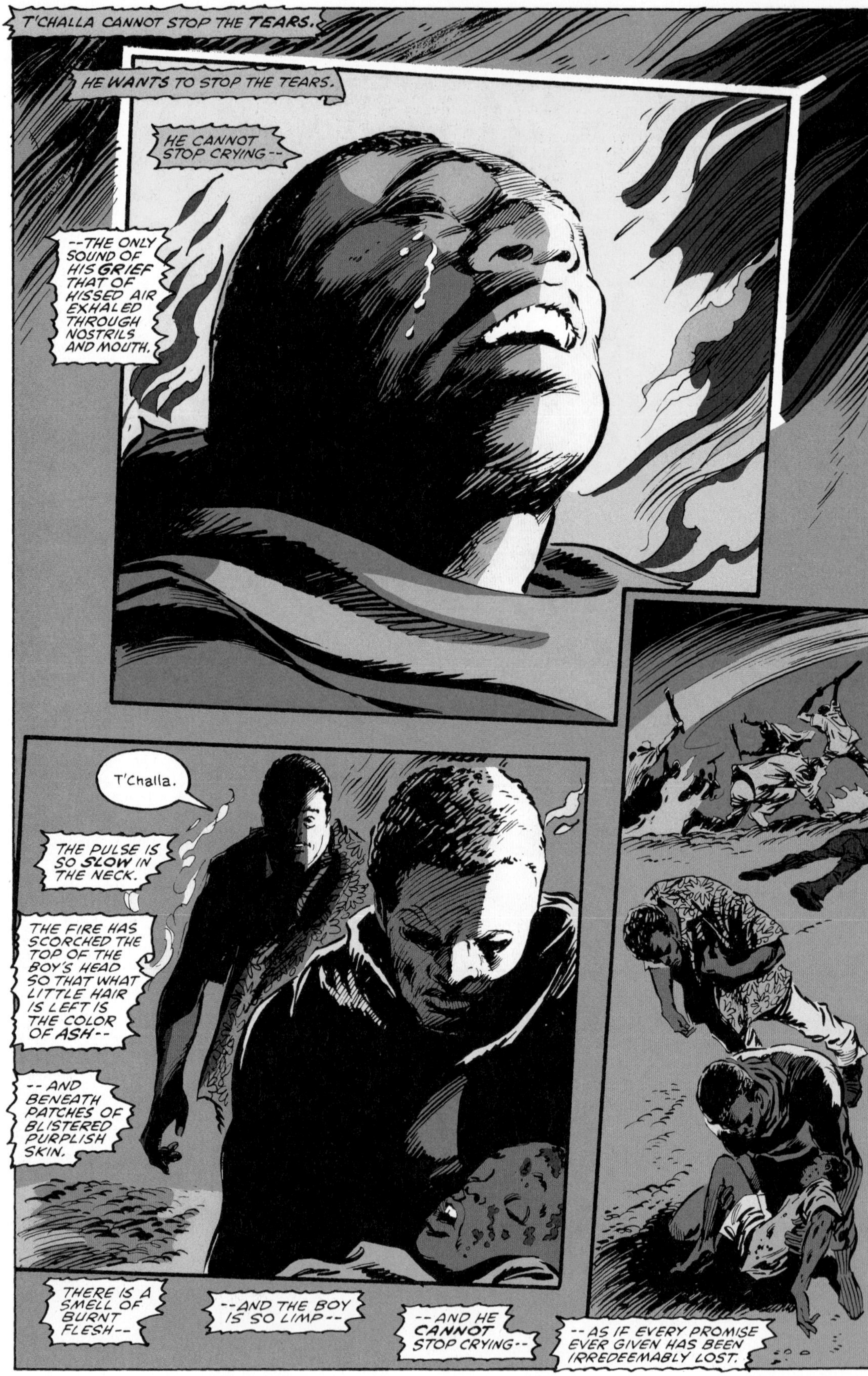
T'CHALLA CANNOT STOP THE TEARS.
HE WANTS TO STOP THE TEARS.
HE CANNOT STOP CRYING--
--THE ONLY SOUND OF HIS GRIEF THAT OF HISSED AIR EXHALED THROUGH NOSTRILS AND MOUTH.
T'Challa.
THE PULSE IS SO SLOW IN THE NECK.
THE FIRE HAS SCORCHED THE TOP OF THE BOY'S HEAD SO THAT WHAT LITTLE HAIR IS LEFT IS THE COLOR OF ASH--
--AND BENEATH PATCHES OF BLISTERED PURPLISH SKIN.
THERE IS A SMELL OF BURNT FLESH--
--AND THE BOY IS SO LIMP--
--AND HE CANNOT STOP CRYING--
--AS IF EVERY PROMISE EVER GIVEN HAS BEEN IRREDEEMABLY LOST.

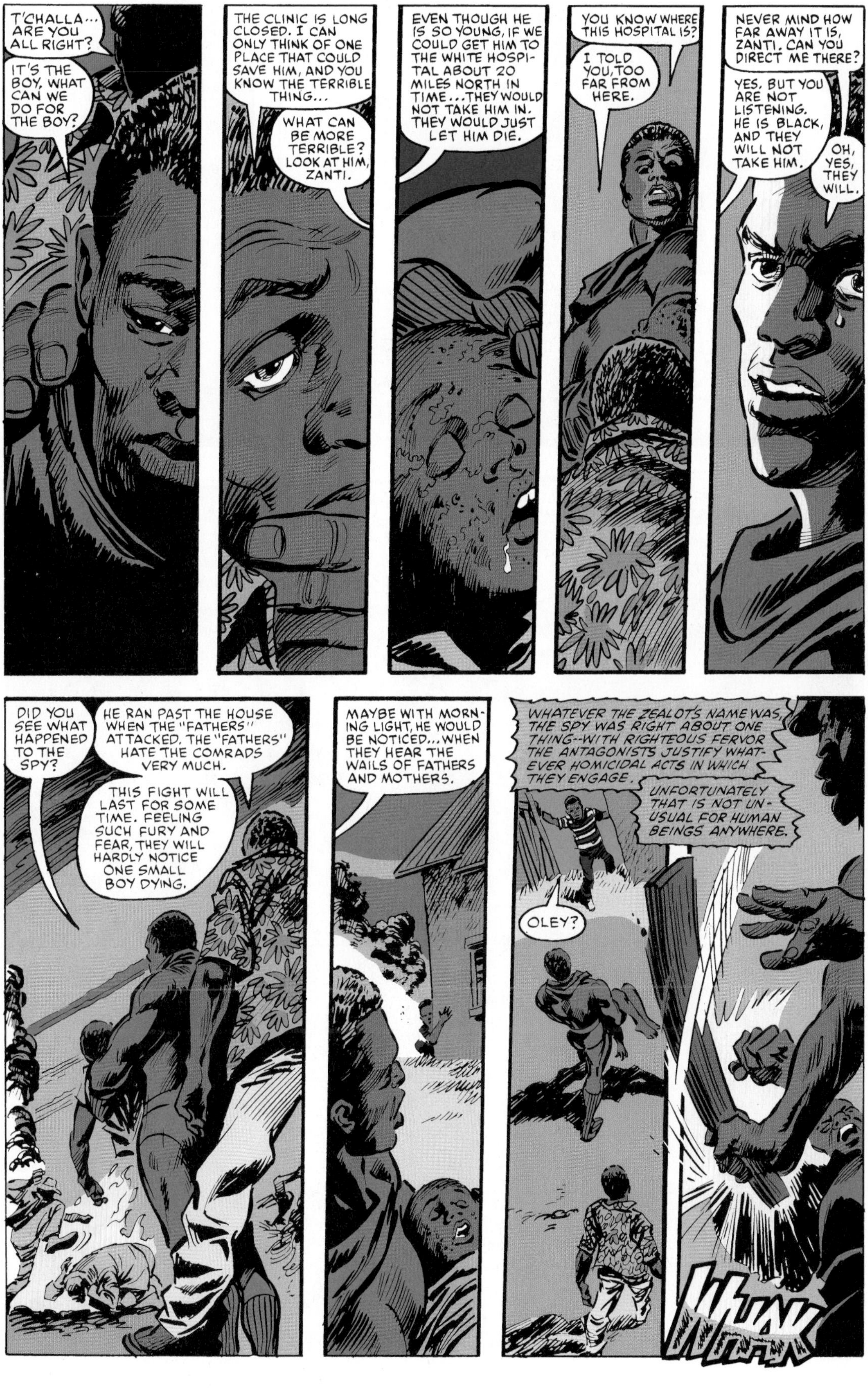
T'CHALLA... ARE YOU ALL RIGHT?
IT'S THE BOY. WHAT CAN WE DO FOR THE BOY?
THE CLINIC IS LONG CLOSED. I CAN ONLY THINK OF ONE PLACE THAT COULD SAVE HIM, AND YOU KNOW THE TERRIBLE THING...
WHAT CAN BE MORE TERRIBLE? LOOK AT HIM, ZANTI.
EVEN THOUGH HE IS SO YOUNG, IF WE COULD GET HIM TO THE WHITE HOSPITAL ABOUT 20 MILES NORTH IN TIME... THEY WOULD NOT TAKE HIM IN. THEY WOULD JUST LET HIM DIE.
YOU KNOW WHERE THIS HOSPITAL IS?
I TOLD YOU, TOO FAR FROM HERE.
NEVER MIND HOW FAR AWAY IT IS, ZANTI. CAN YOU DIRECT ME THERE?
YES. BUT YOU ARE NOT LISTENING. HE IS BLACK, AND THEY WILL NOT TAKE HIM.
OH, YES, THEY WILL.
DID YOU SEE WHAT HAPPENED TO THE SPY?
HE RAN PAST THE HOUSE WHEN THE "FATHERS" ATTACKED. THE "FATHERS" HATE THE COMRADS VERY MUCH.
THIS FIGHT WILL LAST FOR SOME TIME. FEELING SUCH FURY AND FEAR, THEY WILL HARDLY NOTICE ONE SMALL BOY DYING.
MAYBE WITH MORNING LIGHT, HE WOULD BE NOTICED... WHEN THEY HEAR THE WAILS OF FATHERS AND MOTHERS.
WHATEVER THE ZEALOT'S NAME WAS, THE SPY WAS RIGHT ABOUT ONE THING--WITH RIGHTEOUS FERVOR THE ANTAGONISTS JUSTIFY WHATEVER HOMICIDAL ACTS IN WHICH THEY ENGAGE.
UNFORTUNATELY THAT IS NOT UNUSUAL FOR HUMAN BEINGS ANYWHERE.
OLEY?
WHUNK

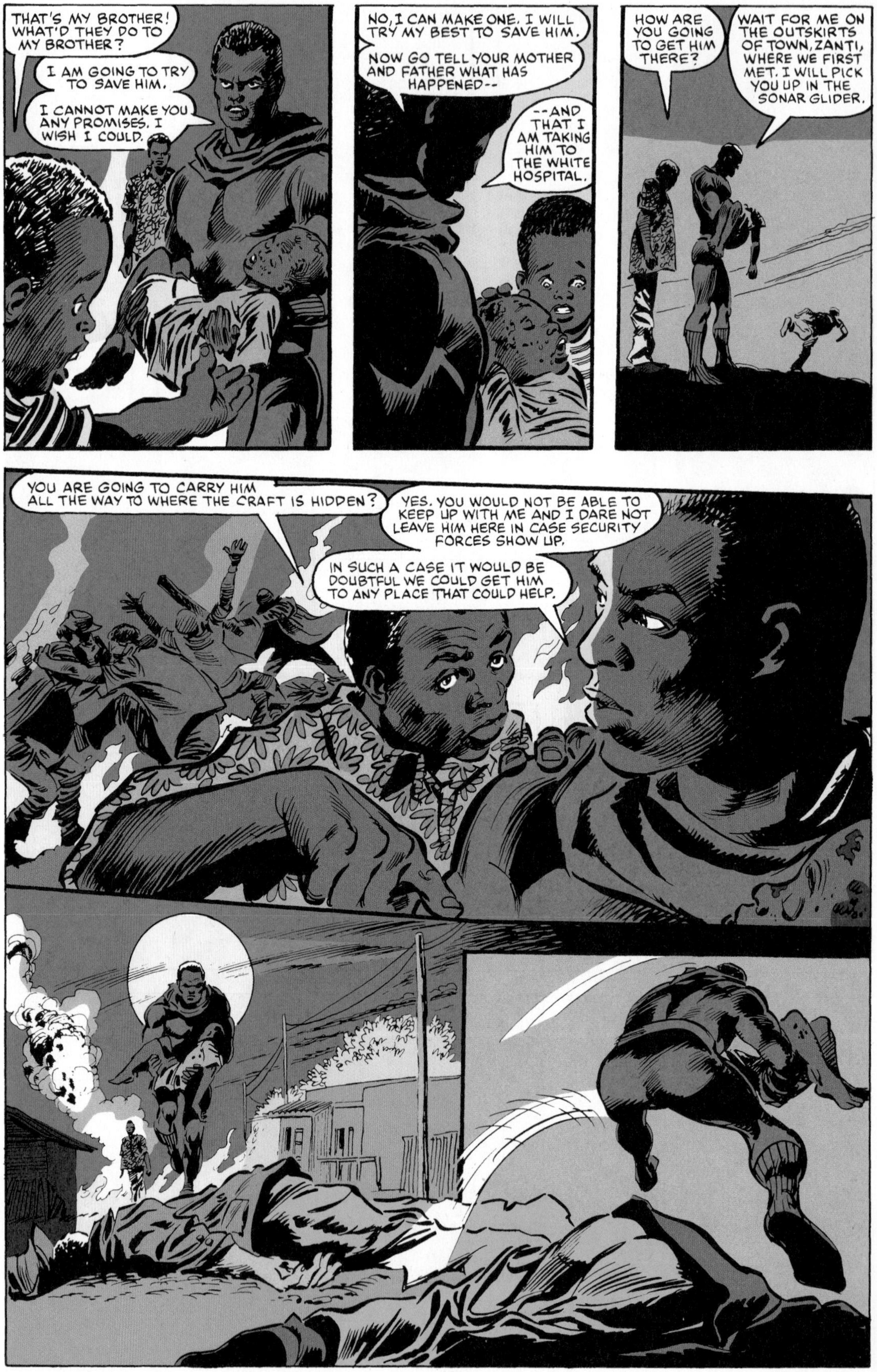

THAT'S MY BROTHER! WHAT'D THEY DO TO MY BROTHER?
I AM GOING TO TRY TO SAVE HIM.
I CANNOT MAKE YOU ANY PROMISES. I WISH I COULD.
NO, I CAN MAKE ONE. I WILL TRY MY BEST TO SAVE HIM.
NOW GO TELL YOUR MOTHER AND FATHER WHAT HAS HAPPENED--
--AND THAT I AM TAKING HIM TO THE WHITE HOSPITAL.
HOW ARE YOU GOING TO GET HIM THERE?
WAIT FOR ME ON THE OUTSKIRTS OF TOWN, ZANTI, WHERE WE FIRST MET. I WILL PICK YOU UP IN THE SONAR GLIDER.
YOU ARE GOING TO CARRY HIM ALL THE WAY TO WHERE THE CRAFT IS HIDDEN?
YES. YOU WOULD NOT BE ABLE TO KEEP UP WITH ME AND I DARE NOT LEAVE HIM HERE IN CASE SECURITY FORCES SHOW UP.
IN SUCH A CASE IT WOULD BE DOUBTFUL WE COULD GET HIM TO ANY PLACE THAT COULD HELP.

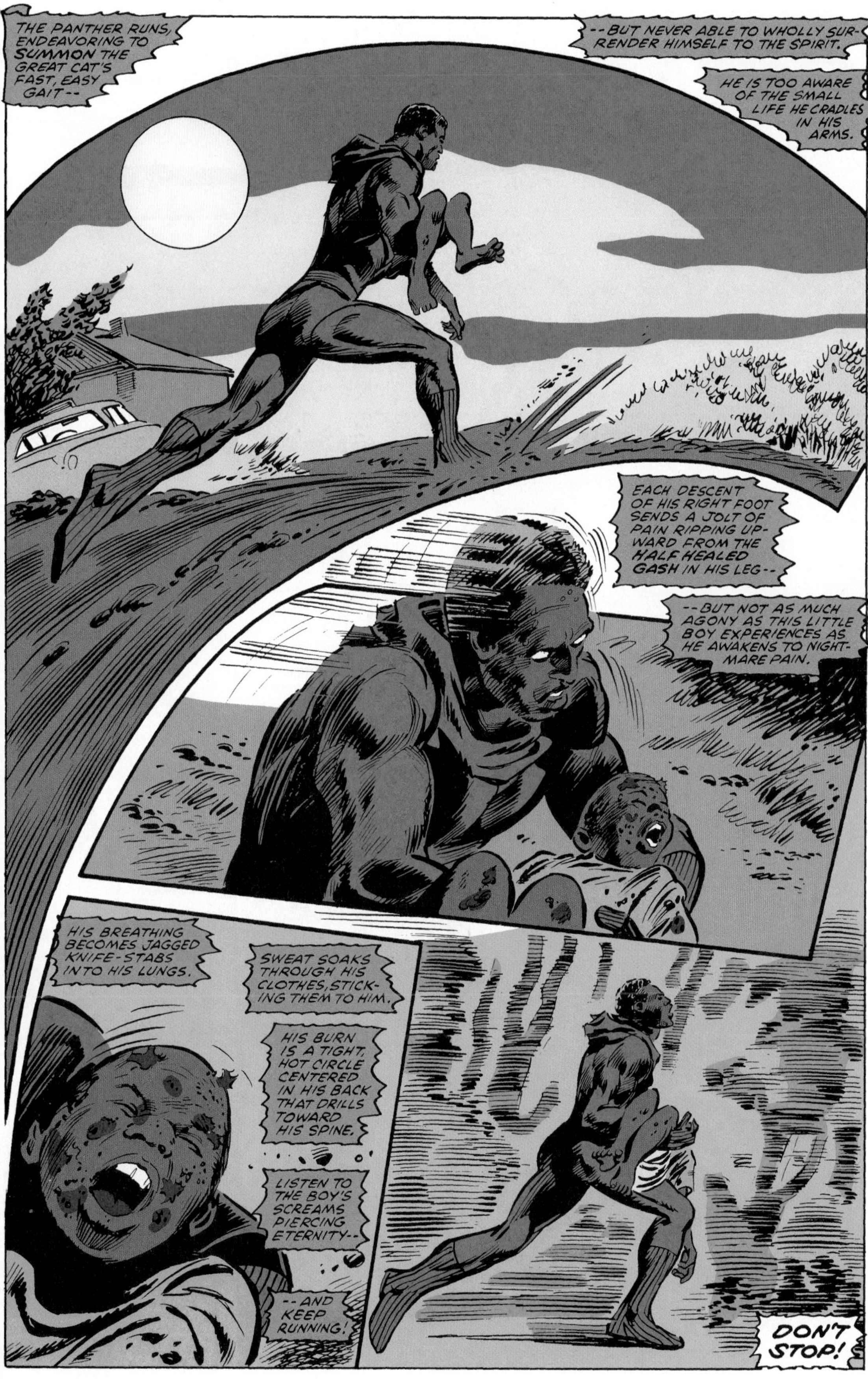
THE PANTHER RUNS, ENDEAVORING TO SUMMON THE GREAT CAT'S FAST, EASY GAIT--
--BUT NEVER ABLE TO WHOLLY SURRENDER HIMSELF TO THE SPIRIT.
HE IS TOO AWARE OF THE SMALL LIFE HE CRADLES IN HIS ARMS.
EACH DESCENT OF HIS RIGHT FOOT SENDS A JOLT OF PAIN RIPPING UPWARD FROM THE HALF HEALED GASH IN HIS LEG--
--BUT NOT AS MUCH AGONY AS THIS LITTLE BOY EXPERIENCES AS HE AWAKENS TO NIGHTMARE PAIN.
HIS BREATHING BECOMES JAGGED KNIFE-STABS INTO HIS LUNGS.
SWEAT SOAKS THROUGH HIS CLOTHES, STICKING THEM TO HIM.
HIS BURN IS A TIGHT, HOT CIRCLE CENTERED IN HIS BACK THAT DRILLS TOWARD HIS SPINE.
LISTEN TO THE BOY'S SCREAMS PIERCING ETERNITY--
--AND KEEP RUNNING!
DON'T STOP!

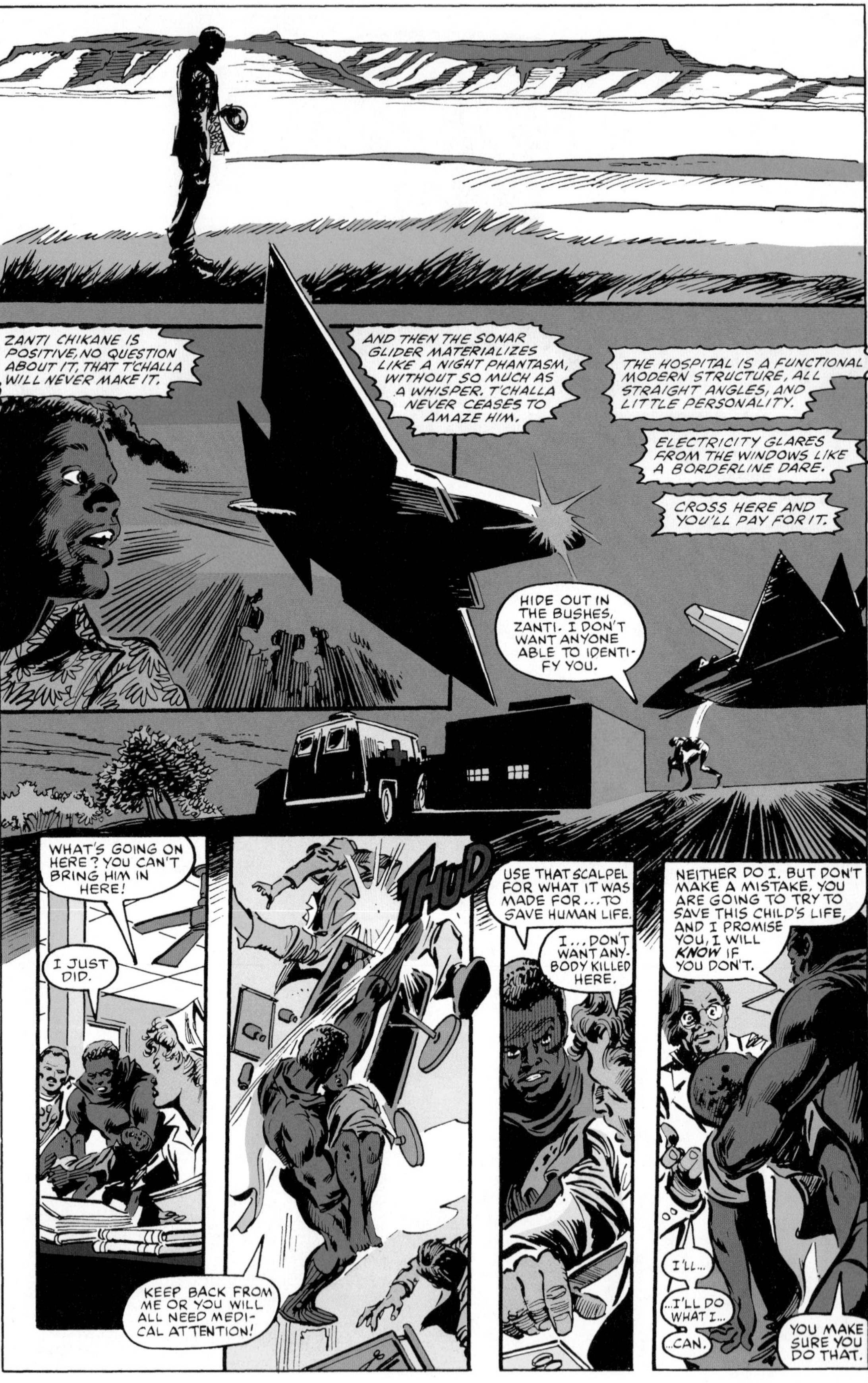
ZANTI CHIKANE IS POSITIVE, NO QUESTION ABOUT IT, THAT T'CHALLA WILL NEVER MAKE IT.
AND THEN THE SONAR GLIDER MATERIALIZES LIKE A NIGHT PHANTASM, WITHOUT SO MUCH AS A WHISPER. T'CHALLA NEVER CEASES TO AMAZE HIM.
THE HOSPITAL IS A FUNCTIONAL MODERN STRUCTURE, ALL STRAIGHT ANGLES, AND LITTLE PERSONALITY.
ELECTRICITY GLARES FROM THE WINDOWS LIKE A BORDERLINE DARE.
CROSS HERE AND YOU'LL PAY FOR IT.
HIDE OUT IN THE BUSHES, ZANTI. I DON'T WANT ANYONE ABLE TO IDENTIFY YOU.
WHAT'S GOING ON HERE? YOU CAN'T BRING HIM IN HERE!
I JUST DID.
THUD
KEEP BACK FROM ME OR YOU WILL ALL NEED MEDICAL ATTENTION!
USE THAT SCALPEL FOR WHAT IT WAS MADE FOR... TO SAVE HUMAN LIFE.
I... DON'T WANT ANYBODY KILLED HERE.
NEITHER DO I. BUT DON'T MAKE A MISTAKE, YOU ARE GOING TO TRY TO SAVE THIS CHILD'S LIFE, AND I PROMISE YOU, I WILL KNOW IF YOU DON'T.
I'LL...
...I'LL DO WHAT I...
...CAN.
YOU MAKE SURE YOU DO THAT.

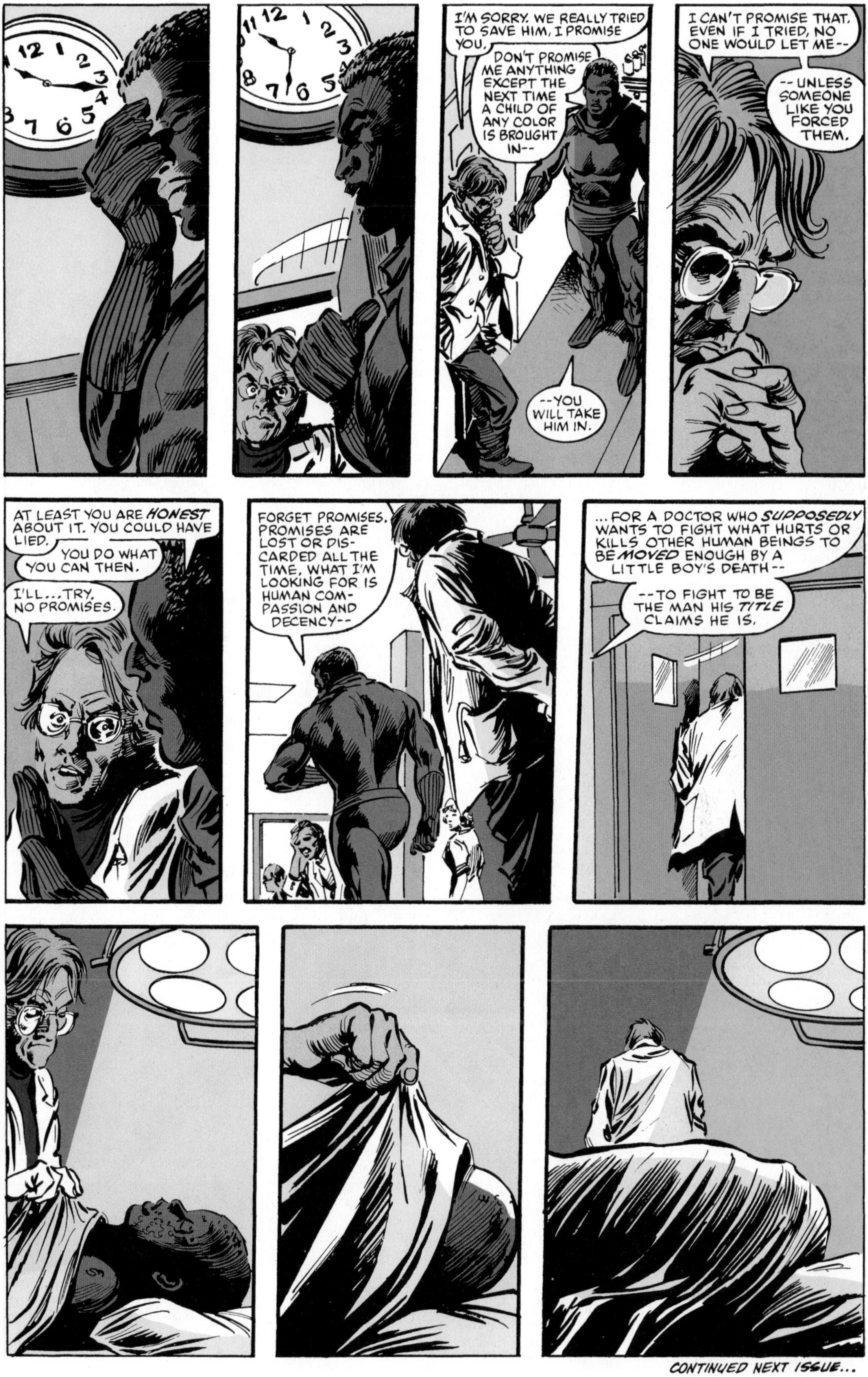
I'M SORRY. WE REALLY TRIED TO SAVE HIM, I PROMISE YOU.
DON'T PROMISE ME ANYTHING EXCEPT THE NEXT TIME A CHILD OF ANY COLOR IS BROUGHT IN--
--YOU WILL TAKE HIM IN.
I CAN'T PROMISE THAT. EVEN IF I TRIED, NO ONE WOULD LET ME--
--UNLESS SOMEONE LIKE YOU FORCED THEM.
AT LEAST YOU ARE HONEST ABOUT IT. YOU COULD HAVE LIED.
YOU DO WHAT YOU CAN THEN.
I'LL...TRY. NO PROMISES.
FORGET PROMISES. PROMISES ARE LOST OR DISCARDED ALL THE TIME. WHAT I'M LOOKING FOR IS HUMAN COMPASSION AND DECENCY--
...FOR A DOCTOR WHO SUPPOSEDLY WANTS TO FIGHT WHAT HURTS OR KILLS OTHER HUMAN BEINGS TO BE MOVED ENOUGH BY A LITTLE BOY'S DEATH--
--TO FIGHT TO BE THE MAN HIS TITLE CLAIMS HE IS.

CONTINUED NEXT ISSUE...

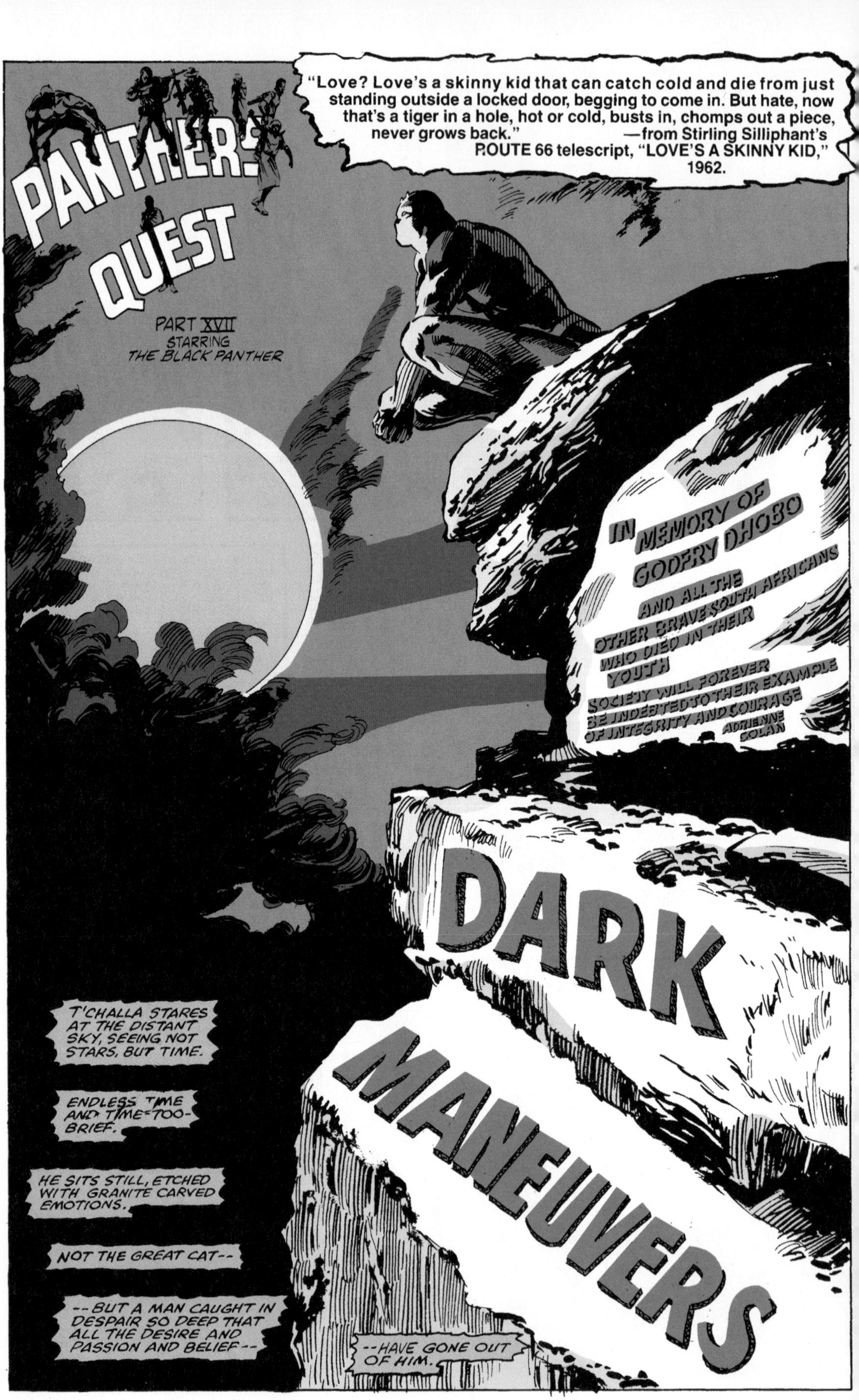

"Love? Love's a skinny kid that can catch cold and die from just standing outside a locked door, begging to come in. But hate, now that's a tiger in a hole, hot or cold, busts in, chomps out a piece, never grows back." —from Stirling Silliphant's ROUTE 66 telescript, "LOVE'S A SKINNY KID," 1962.
PANTHER'S QUEST
PART XVII STARRING THE BLACK PANTHER
IN MEMORY OF GODFRY DHOBO AND ALL THE OTHER BRAVE SOUTH AFRICANS WHO DIED IN THEIR YOUTH
SOCIETY WILL FOREVER BE INDEBTED TO THEIR EXAMPLE OF INTEGRITY AND COURAGE
ADRIENNE COLAN
DARK MANEUVERS
T'CHALLA STARES AT THE DISTANT SKY, SEEING NOT STARS, BUT TIME.
ENDLESS TIME AND TIME-TOO-BRIEF.
HE SITS STILL, ETCHED WITH GRANITE CARVED EMOTIONS.
NOT THE GREAT CAT--
--BUT A MAN CAUGHT IN DESPAIR SO DEEP THAT ALL THE DESIRE AND PASSION AND BELIEF--
--HAVE GONE OUT OF HIM.

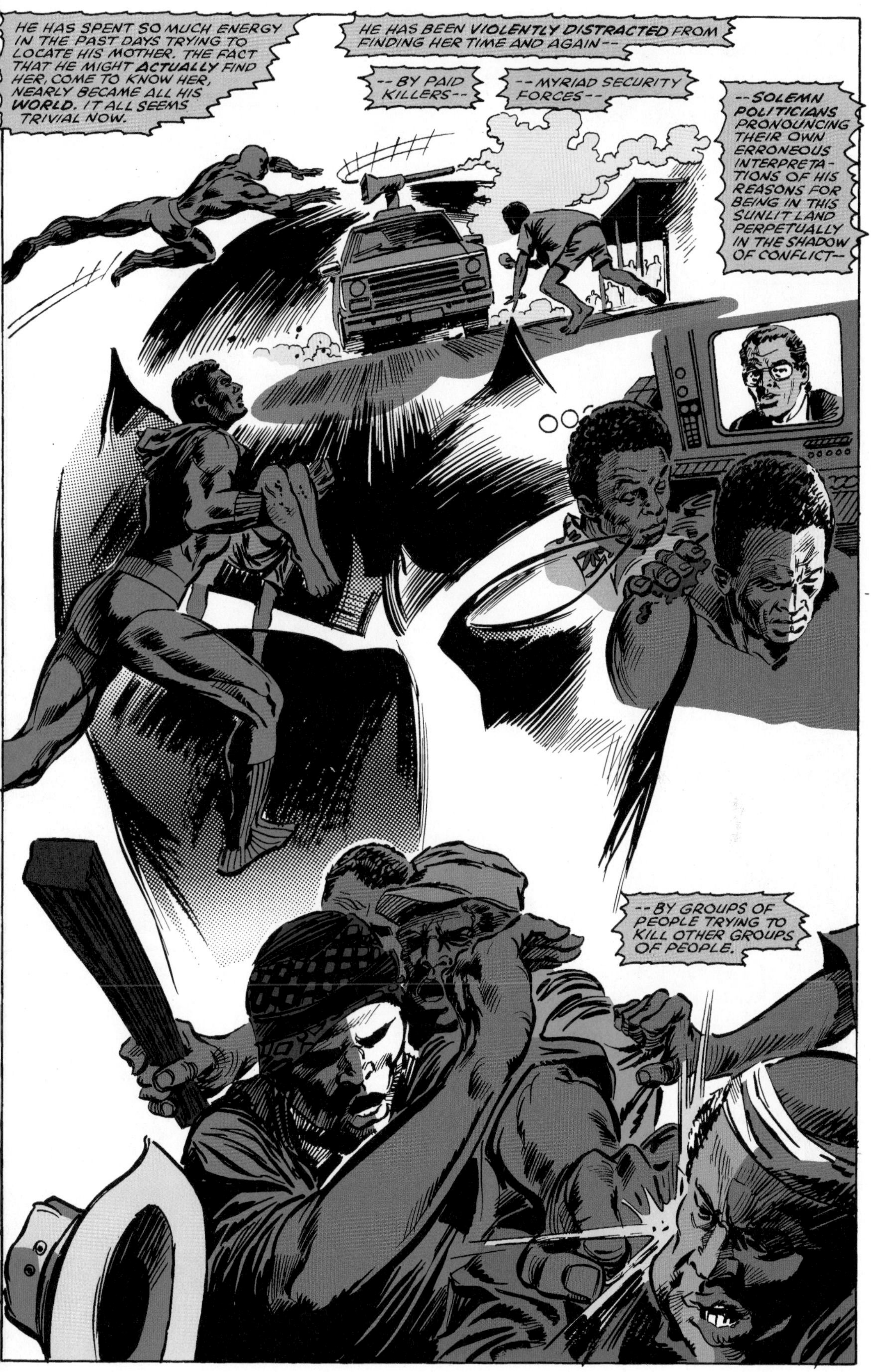
HE HAS SPENT SO MUCH ENERGY IN THE PAST DAYS TRYING TO LOCATE HIS MOTHER. THE FACT THAT HE MIGHT ACTUALLY FIND HER, COME TO KNOW HER, NEARLY BECAME ALL HIS WORLD. IT ALL SEEMS TRIVIAL NOW.
HE HAS BEEN VIOLENTLY DISTRACTED FROM FINDING HER TIME AND AGAIN--
--BY PAID KILLERS--
--MYRIAD SECURITY FORCES--
--SOLEMN POLITICIANS PRONOUNCING THEIR OWN ERRONEOUS INTERPRETATIONS OF HIS REASONS FOR BEING IN THIS SUNLIT LAND PERPETUALLY IN THE SHADOW OF CONFLICT--
--BY GROUPS OF PEOPLE TRYING TO KILL OTHER GROUPS OF PEOPLE.

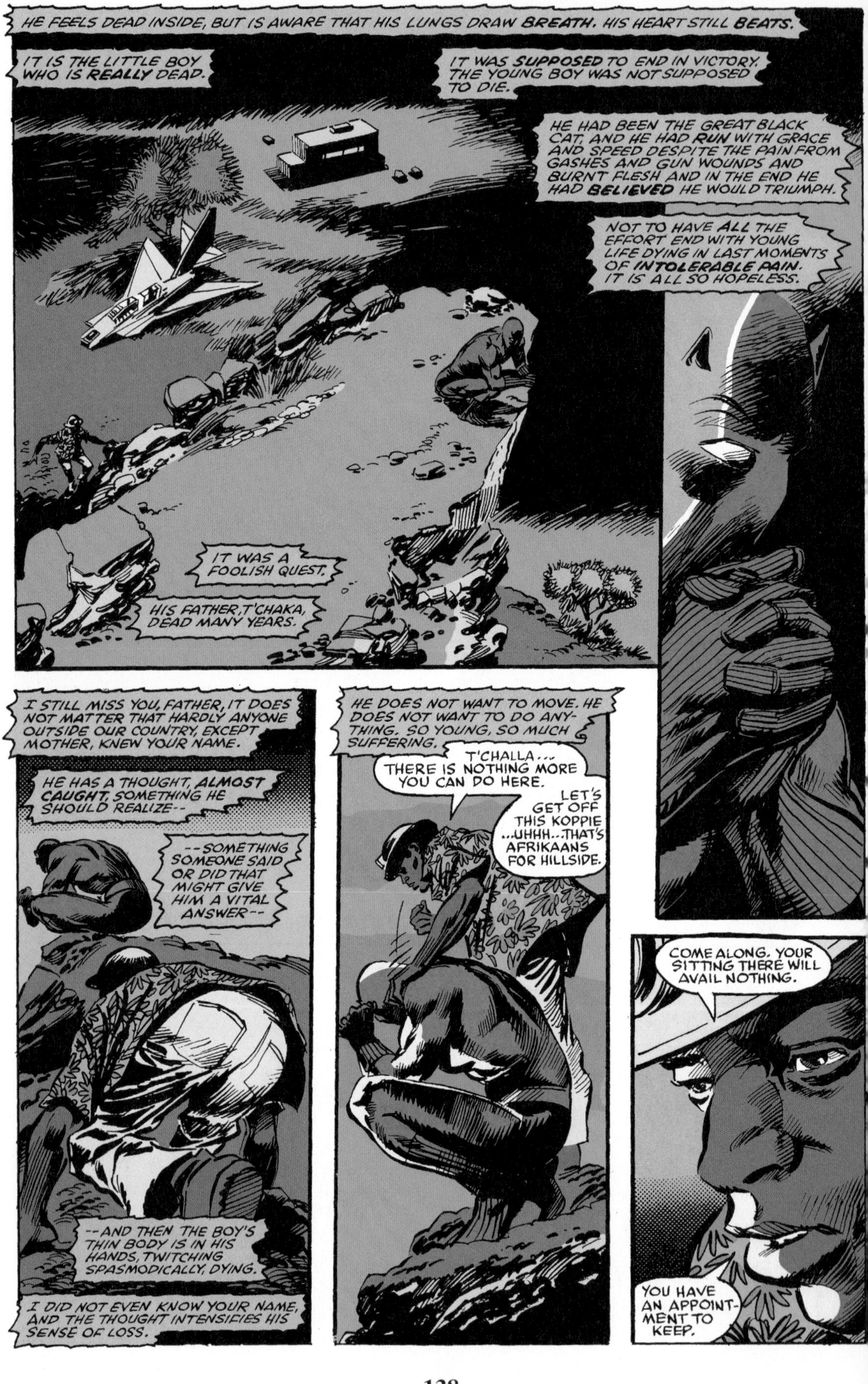
HE FEELS DEAD INSIDE, BUT IS AWARE THAT HIS LUNGS DRAW BREATH. HIS HEART STILL BEATS.
IT IS THE LITTLE BOY WHO IS REALLY DEAD.
IT WAS SUPPOSED TO END IN VICTORY. THE YOUNG BOY WAS NOT SUPPOSED TO DIE.
HE HAD BEEN THE GREAT BLACK CAT, AND HE HAD RUN WITH GRACE AND SPEED DESPITE THE PAIN FROM GASHES AND GUN WOUNDS AND BURNT FLESH AND IN THE END HE HAD BELIEVED HE WOULD TRIUMPH.
NOT TO HAVE ALL THE EFFORT END WITH YOUNG LIFE DYING IN LAST MOMENTS OF INTOLERABLE PAIN. IT IS ALL SO HOPELESS.
IT WAS A FOOLISH QUEST.
HIS FATHER, T'CHAKA, DEAD MANY YEARS.
I STILL MISS YOU, FATHER, IT DOES NOT MATTER THAT HARDLY ANYONE OUTSIDE OUR COUNTRY, EXCEPT MOTHER, KNEW YOUR NAME.
HE HAS A THOUGHT, ALMOST CAUGHT, SOMETHING HE SHOULD REALIZE--
--SOMETHING SOMEONE SAID OR DID THAT MIGHT GIVE HIM A VITAL ANSWER--
--AND THEN THE BOY'S THIN BODY IS IN HIS HANDS, TWITCHING SPASMODICALLY, DYING.
I DID NOT EVEN KNOW YOUR NAME, AND THE THOUGHT INTENSIFIES HIS SENSE OF LOSS.
HE DOES NOT WANT TO MOVE. HE DOES NOT WANT TO DO ANYTHING. SO YOUNG, SO MUCH SUFFERING.
T'CHALLA... THERE IS NOTHING MORE YOU CAN DO HERE.
LET'S GET OFF THIS KOPPIE ...UHHH...THAT'S AFRIKAANS FOR HILLSIDE.
COME ALONG. YOUR SITTING THERE WILL AVAIL NOTHING.
YOU HAVE AN APPOINTMENT TO KEEP.

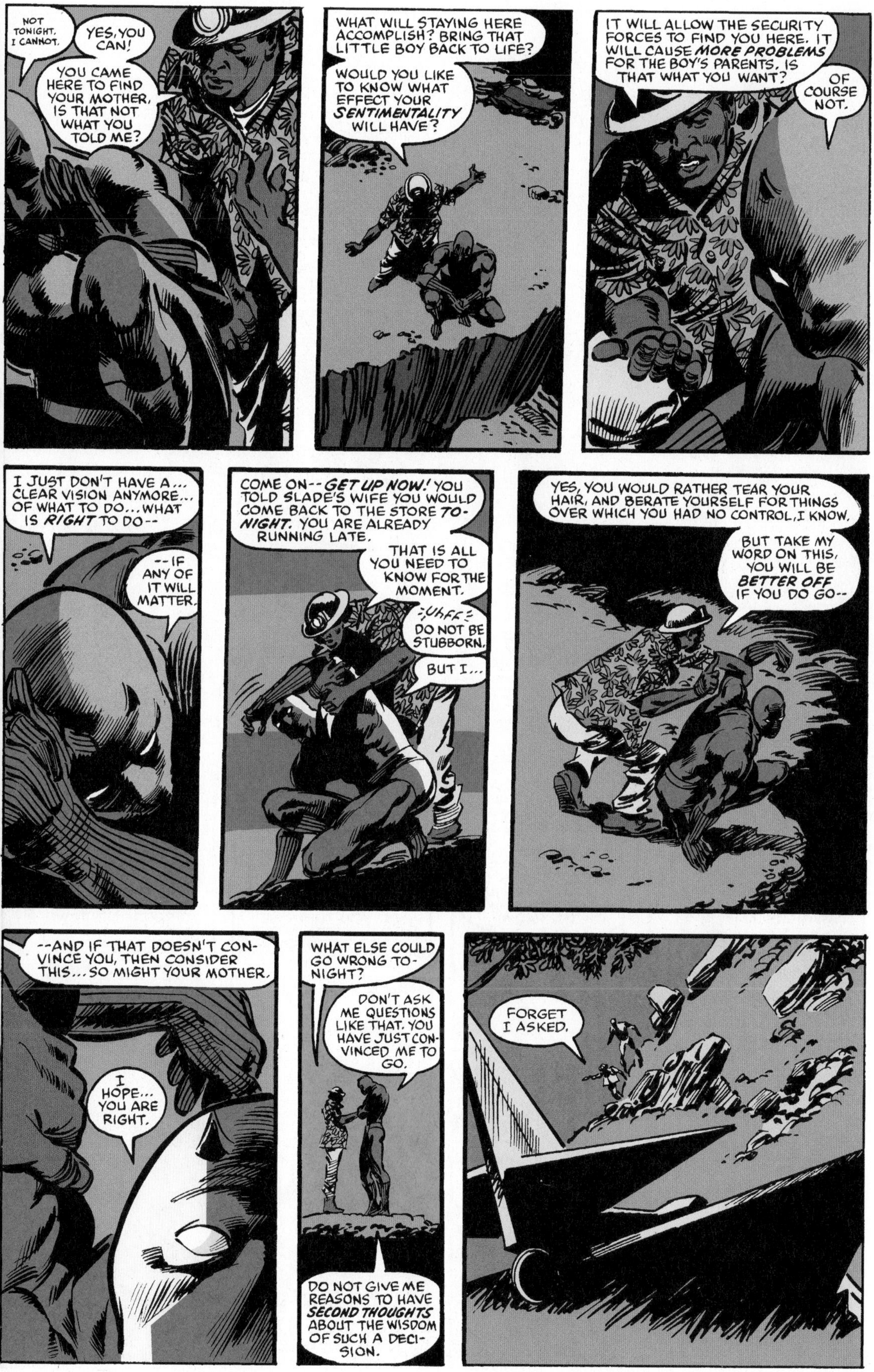
NOT TONIGHT. I CANNOT.
YES, YOU CAN!
YOU CAME HERE TO FIND YOUR MOTHER, IS THAT NOT WHAT YOU TOLD ME?
WHAT WILL STAYING HERE ACCOMPLISH? BRING THAT LITTLE BOY BACK TO LIFE?
WOULD YOU LIKE TO KNOW WHAT EFFECT YOUR SENTIMENTALITY WILL HAVE?
IT WILL ALLOW THE SECURITY FORCES TO FIND YOU HERE. IT WILL CAUSE MORE PROBLEMS FOR THE BOY'S PARENTS. IS THAT WHAT YOU WANT?
OF COURSE NOT.
I JUST DON'T HAVE A... CLEAR VISION ANYMORE... OF WHAT TO DO... WHAT IS RIGHT TO DO--
--IF ANY OF IT WILL MATTER.
COME ON--GET UP NOW! YOU TOLD SLADE'S WIFE YOU WOULD COME BACK TO THE STORE TO-NIGHT. YOU ARE ALREADY RUNNING LATE.
THAT IS ALL YOU NEED TO KNOW FOR THE MOMENT.
UHFF
DO NOT BE STUBBORN.
BUT I...
YES, YOU WOULD RATHER TEAR YOUR HAIR, AND BERATE YOURSELF FOR THINGS OVER WHICH YOU HAD NO CONTROL, I KNOW.
BUT TAKE MY WORD ON THIS, YOU WILL BE BETTER OFF IF YOU DO GO--
--AND IF THAT DOESN'T CONVINCE YOU, THEN CONSIDER THIS... SO MIGHT YOUR MOTHER.
I HOPE... YOU ARE RIGHT.
WHAT ELSE COULD GO WRONG TO-NIGHT?
DON'T ASK ME QUESTIONS LIKE THAT. YOU HAVE JUST CONVINCED ME TO GO.
DO NOT GIVE ME REASONS TO HAVE SECOND THOUGHTS ABOUT THE WISDOM OF SUCH A DECISION.
FORGET I ASKED.

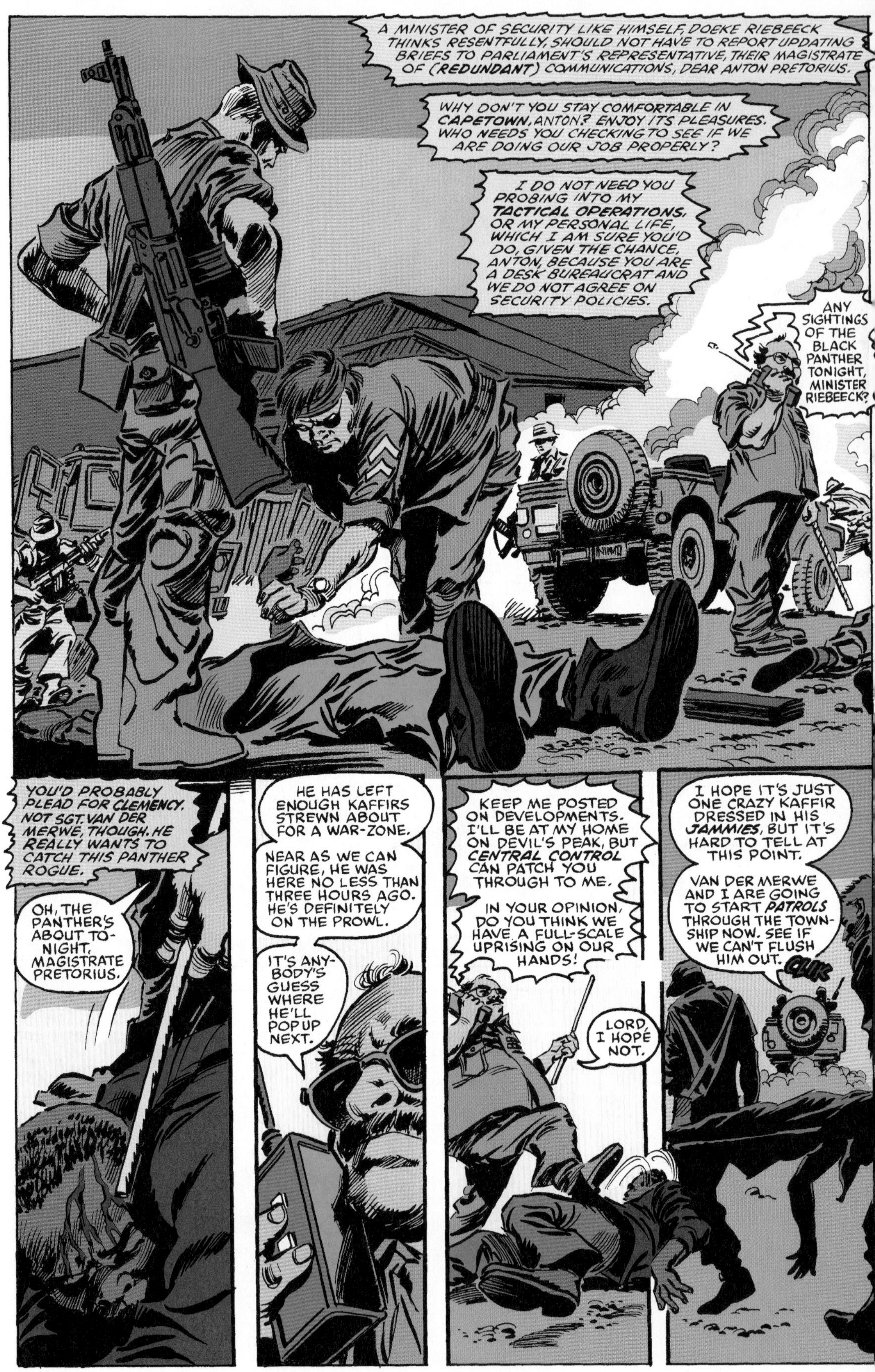
A MINISTER OF SECURITY LIKE HIMSELF, DOEKE RIEBEECK THINKS RESENTFULLY, SHOULD NOT HAVE TO REPORT UPDATING BRIEFS TO PARLIAMENT'S REPRESENTATIVE, THEIR MAGISTRATE OF (REDUNDANT) COMMUNICATIONS, DEAR ANTON PRETORIUS.
WHY DON'T YOU STAY COMFORTABLE IN CAPETOWN, ANTON? ENJOY ITS PLEASURES. WHO NEEDS YOU CHECKING TO SEE IF WE ARE DOING OUR JOB PROPERLY?
I DO NOT NEED YOU PROBING INTO MY TACTICAL OPERATIONS, OR MY PERSONAL LIFE, WHICH I AM SURE YOU'D DO, GIVEN THE CHANCE, ANTON, BECAUSE YOU ARE A DESK BUREAUCRAT AND WE DO NOT AGREE ON SECURITY POLICIES.
ANY SIGHTINGS OF THE BLACK PANTHER TONIGHT, MINISTER RIEBEECK?
YOU'D PROBABLY PLEAD FOR CLEMENCY. NOT SGT. VAN DER MERWE, THOUGH. HE REALLY WANTS TO CATCH THIS PANTHER ROGUE.
OH, THE PANTHER'S ABOUT TO-NIGHT, MAGISTRATE PRETORIUS.
HE HAS LEFT ENOUGH KAFFIRS STREWN ABOUT FOR A WAR-ZONE.
NEAR AS WE CAN FIGURE, HE WAS HERE NO LESS THAN THREE HOURS AGO. HE'S DEFINITELY ON THE PROWL.
IT'S ANY-BODY'S GUESS WHERE HE'LL POP UP NEXT.
KEEP ME POSTED ON DEVELOPMENTS. I'LL BE AT MY HOME ON DEVIL'S PEAK, BUT CENTRAL CONTROL CAN PATCH YOU THROUGH TO ME.
IN YOUR OPINION, DO YOU THINK WE HAVE A FULL-SCALE UPRISING ON OUR HANDS!
LORD, I HOPE NOT.
I HOPE IT'S JUST ONE CRAZY KAFFIR DRESSED IN HIS JAMMIES, BUT IT'S HARD TO TELL AT THIS POINT.
VAN DER MERWE AND I ARE GOING TO START PATROLS THROUGH THE TOWN-SHIP NOW. SEE IF WE CAN'T FLUSH HIM OUT.
CLIK

THE GREAT CAT STAYS CLOSE TO ALLEYWALL WALLS AND SHADOWS--

--GLIDING THROUGH THEM--

--UNTIL HE CAN CHECK THE BACK ENTRANCE TO SLADE'S AFRICAN ARTIFACTS.

THE STORE SMELLS MUSTY--

--ODORS HE RECALLS FROM HIS PREVIOUS VISIT.

THERE IS ANOTHER RECOGNIZABLE ESSENCE, THE SCENT OF--

--PATRICK SLADE.

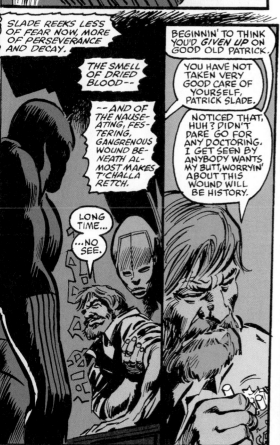

SLADE REEKS LESS OF FEAR NOW, MORE OF PERSEVERANCE AND DECAY.

THE SMELL OF DRIED BLOOD--

--AND OF THE NAUSEATING, FESTERING, GANGRENOUS WOUND BENEATH ALMOST MAKES T'CHALLA RETCH.

LONG TIME...

...NO SEE.

BEGINNIN' TO THINK YOU'D *GIVEN UP* ON GOOD OLD PATRICK.

YOU HAVE NOT TAKEN VERY GOOD CARE OF YOURSELF, PATRICK SLADE.

NOTICED THAT, HUH? DIDN'T DARE GO FOR ANY DOCTORING. I GET SEEN BY ANYBODY WANTS MY BUTT, WORRYIN' ABOUT THIS WOUND WILL BE HISTORY.

I'VE GOT TO COUNT ON YOU TO GET ME AND SARAH OUT OF THIS.

YOU ARE THE ONE WHO *STARTED* ALL THIS PAIN AND TRIBULATION, WITH A SCHEME TO MAKE MONEY OFF OF LOVE. WHY SHOULD I HELP YOU?

DRY, STALE SMOKE BURNS HIS NOSTRILS, COVERS SOME OF THE STENCH OF ROTTING FLESH. HE HAS TO QUELL A GAGGING REFLEX.

BECAUSE ≶COF≶ YOU'RE A DECENT MAN.

EVEN IF I DIDN'T KNOW THE TRUTH ABOUT YOUR MOTHER ≶KOFF≶ I THINK YOU'D STILL HELP ME ≶KOFF≶

141

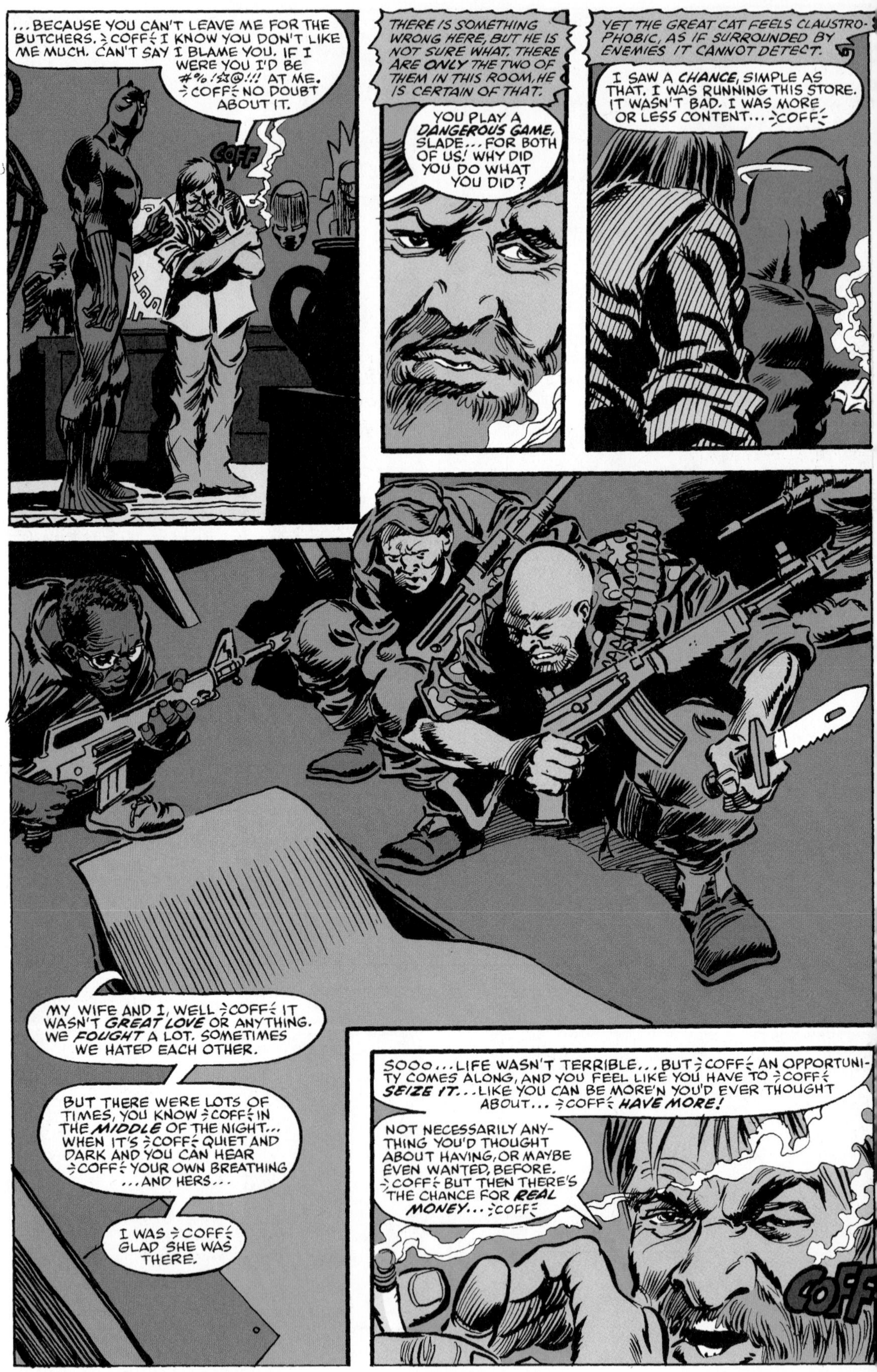
...BECAUSE YOU CAN'T LEAVE ME FOR THE BUTCHERS. ~COFF~ I KNOW YOU DON'T LIKE ME MUCH. CAN'T SAY I BLAME YOU. IF I WERE YOU I'D BE #%!☆@!!! AT ME. ~COFF~ NO DOUBT ABOUT IT.
COFF
THERE IS SOMETHING WRONG HERE, BUT HE IS NOT SURE WHAT. THERE ARE ONLY THE TWO OF THEM IN THIS ROOM, HE IS CERTAIN OF THAT.
YOU PLAY A DANGEROUS GAME, SLADE... FOR BOTH OF US! WHY DID YOU DO WHAT YOU DID?
YET THE GREAT CAT FEELS CLAUSTROPHOBIC, AS IF SURROUNDED BY ENEMIES IT CANNOT DETECT.
I SAW A CHANCE, SIMPLE AS THAT. I WAS RUNNING THIS STORE. IT WASN'T BAD. I WAS MORE OR LESS CONTENT... ~COFF~
MY WIFE AND I, WELL ~COFF~ IT WASN'T GREAT LOVE OR ANYTHING. WE FOUGHT A LOT. SOMETIMES WE HATED EACH OTHER.
BUT THERE WERE LOTS OF TIMES, YOU KNOW ~COFF~ IN THE MIDDLE OF THE NIGHT... WHEN IT'S ~COFF~ QUIET AND DARK AND YOU CAN HEAR ~COFF~ YOUR OWN BREATHING ...AND HERS...
I WAS ~COFF~ GLAD SHE WAS THERE.
SOOO... LIFE WASN'T TERRIBLE... BUT ~COFF~ AN OPPORTUNITY COMES ALONG, AND YOU FEEL LIKE YOU HAVE TO ~COFF~ SEIZE IT... LIKE YOU CAN BE MORE'N YOU'D EVER THOUGHT ABOUT... ~COFF~ HAVE MORE!
NOT NECESSARILY ANYTHING YOU'D THOUGHT ABOUT HAVING, OR MAYBE EVEN WANTED, BEFORE. ~COFF~ BUT THEN THERE'S THE CHANCE FOR REAL MONEY... ~COFF~
COFF

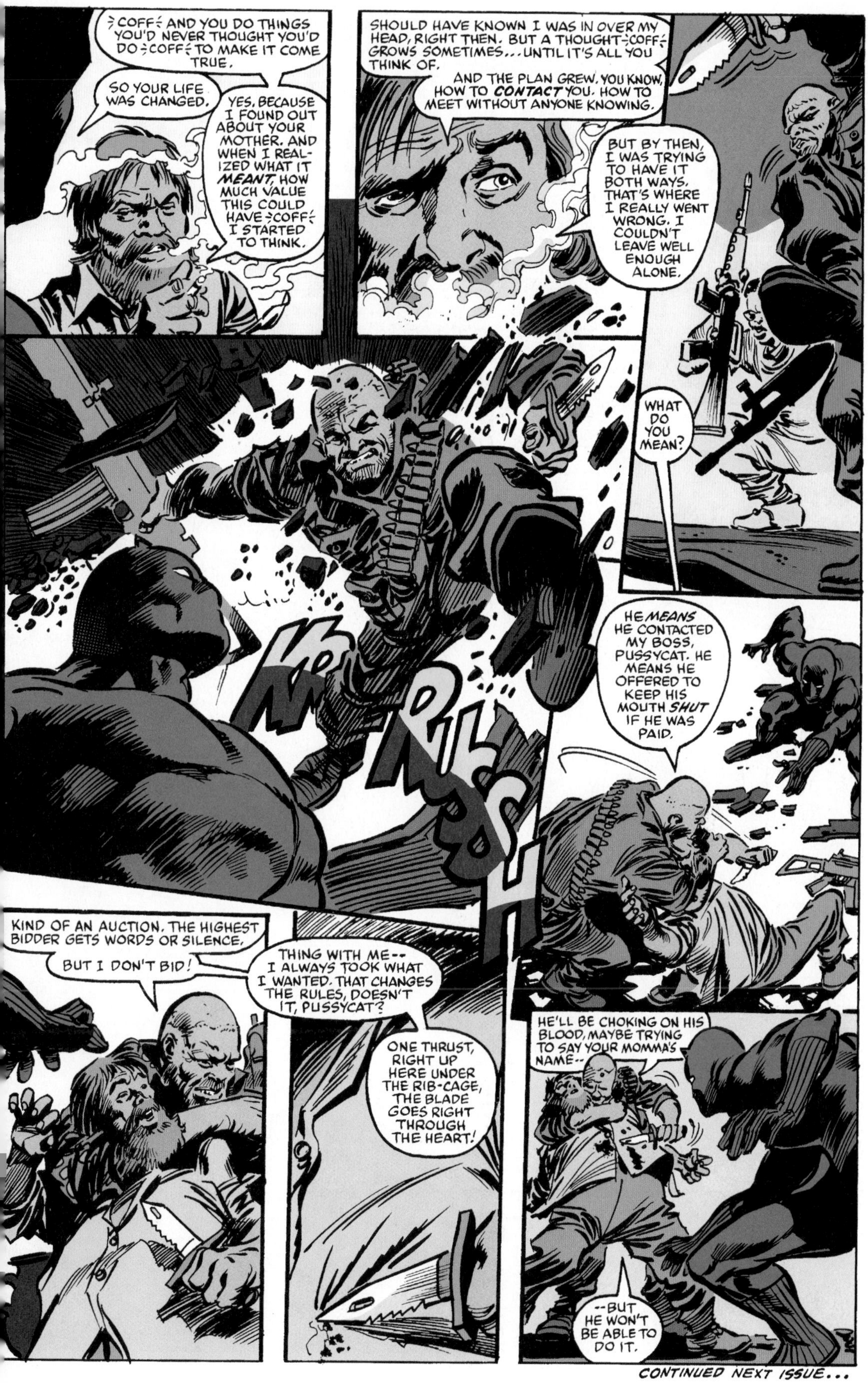

÷COFF÷ AND YOU DO THINGS YOU'D NEVER THOUGHT YOU'D DO ÷COFF÷ TO MAKE IT COME TRUE.
SO YOUR LIFE WAS CHANGED.
YES. BECAUSE I FOUND OUT ABOUT YOUR MOTHER. AND WHEN I REALIZED WHAT IT MEANT, HOW MUCH VALUE THIS COULD HAVE ÷COFF÷ I STARTED TO THINK.
SHOULD HAVE KNOWN I WAS IN OVER MY HEAD, RIGHT THEN. BUT A THOUGHT ÷COFF÷ GROWS SOMETIMES... UNTIL IT'S ALL YOU THINK OF.
AND THE PLAN GREW. YOU KNOW, HOW TO CONTACT YOU. HOW TO MEET WITHOUT ANYONE KNOWING.
BUT BY THEN, I WAS TRYING TO HAVE IT BOTH WAYS. THAT'S WHERE I REALLY WENT WRONG. I COULDN'T LEAVE WELL ENOUGH ALONE.
WHAT DO YOU MEAN?
HE MEANS HE CONTACTED MY BOSS, PUSSYCAT. HE MEANS HE OFFERED TO KEEP HIS MOUTH SHUT IF HE WAS PAID.
KIND OF AN AUCTION. THE HIGHEST BIDDER GETS WORDS OR SILENCE.
BUT I DON'T BID!
THING WITH ME-- I ALWAYS TOOK WHAT I WANTED. THAT CHANGES THE RULES, DOESN'T IT, PUSSYCAT?
ONE THRUST, RIGHT UP HERE UNDER THE RIB-CAGE, THE BLADE GOES RIGHT THROUGH THE HEART!
HE'LL BE CHOKING ON HIS BLOOD, MAYBE TRYING TO SAY YOUR MOMMA'S NAME--
--BUT HE WON'T BE ABLE TO DO IT.
CONTINUED NEXT ISSUE...

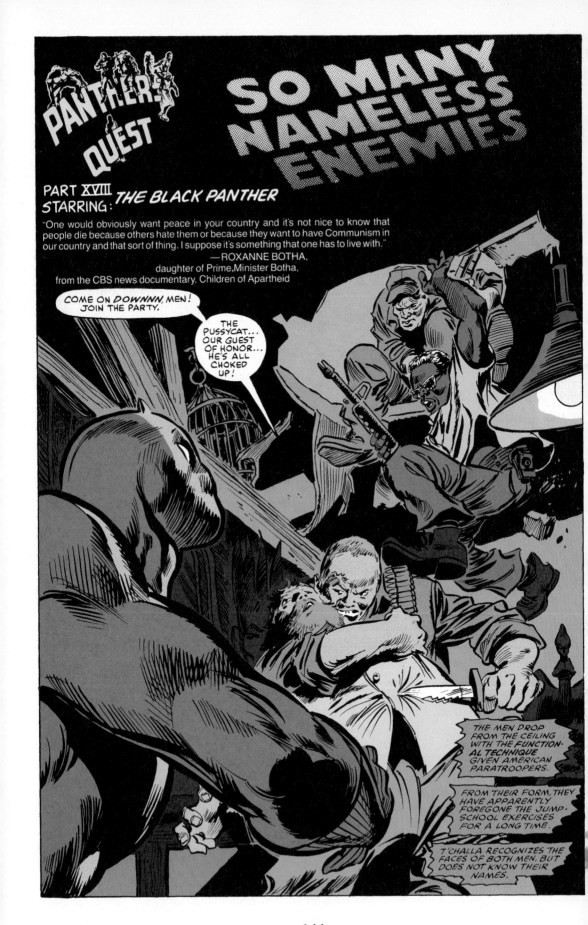

PANTHER'S QUEST

SO MANY NAMELESS ENEMIES

PART XVIII
STARRING: *THE BLACK PANTHER*

"One would obviously want peace in your country and it's not nice to know that people die because others hate them or because they want to have Communism in our country and that sort of thing. I suppose it's something that one has to live with."
—ROXANNE BOTHA,
daughter of Prime Minister Botha,
from the CBS news documentary, Children of Apartheid

COME ON *DOWNNN*, MEN!
JOIN THE PARTY.

THE *PUSSYCAT...*
OUR GUEST OF HONOR...
HE'S ALL *CHOKED* UP!

THE MEN DROP FROM THE CEILING WITH THE *FUNCTION-AL TECHNIQUE* GIVEN AMERICAN PARATROOPERS.

FROM THEIR FORM, THEY HAVE APPARENTLY FOREGONE THE JUMP-SCHOOL EXERCISES FOR A LONG TIME.

T'CHALLA RECOGNIZES THE FACES OF BOTH MEN, BUT DOES NOT KNOW THEIR NAMES.

SO MANY *STRANGERS* AFFECTING HIS LIFE LATELY... MANY OF THEM COMPLICATING OR COERCIVELY OBSTRUCTING HIS QUEST TO FIND HIS MOTHER.

A QUEST A PART OF HIM WISHES HE HAD *NEVER* BEGUN. IT HAS COST SO MUCH.

YET, IF OTHERS, SUCH AS THESE INTRUDERS, ARE COMPELLED TO TRY TO STOP HIM FROM LEARNING WHAT *HAPPENED* TO HER--

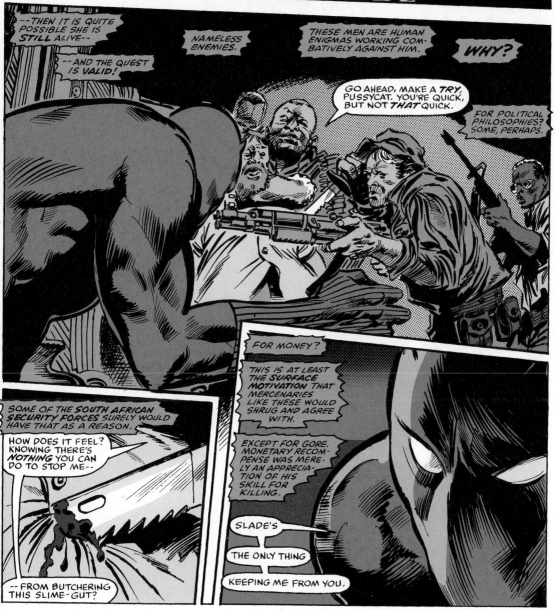

--THEN IT IS QUITE POSSIBLE SHE IS *STILL* ALIVE--

--AND THE QUEST IS *VALID!*

NAMELESS ENEMIES.

THESE MEN ARE HUMAN ENIGMAS WORKING COMBATIVELY AGAINST HIM.

WHY?

GO AHEAD, MAKE A *TRY*, PUSSYCAT. YOU'RE QUICK, BUT NOT *THAT* QUICK.

FOR POLITICAL PHILOSOPHIES? SOME, PERHAPS.

FOR MONEY?

THIS IS AT LEAST THE *SURFACE MOTIVATION* THAT MERCENARIES LIKE THESE WOULD SHRUG AND AGREE WITH.

EXCEPT FOR GORE. MONETARY RECOMPENSE WAS MERELY AN APPRECIATION OF HIS SKILL FOR KILLING.

SOME OF THE *SOUTH AFRICAN SECURITY FORCES* SURELY WOULD HAVE THAT AS A REASON.

HOW DOES IT FEEL? KNOWING THERE'S *NOTHING* YOU CAN DO TO STOP ME--

--FROM BUTCHERING THIS SLIME-GUT?

SLADE'S

THE ONLY THING

KEEPING ME FROM YOU.

145

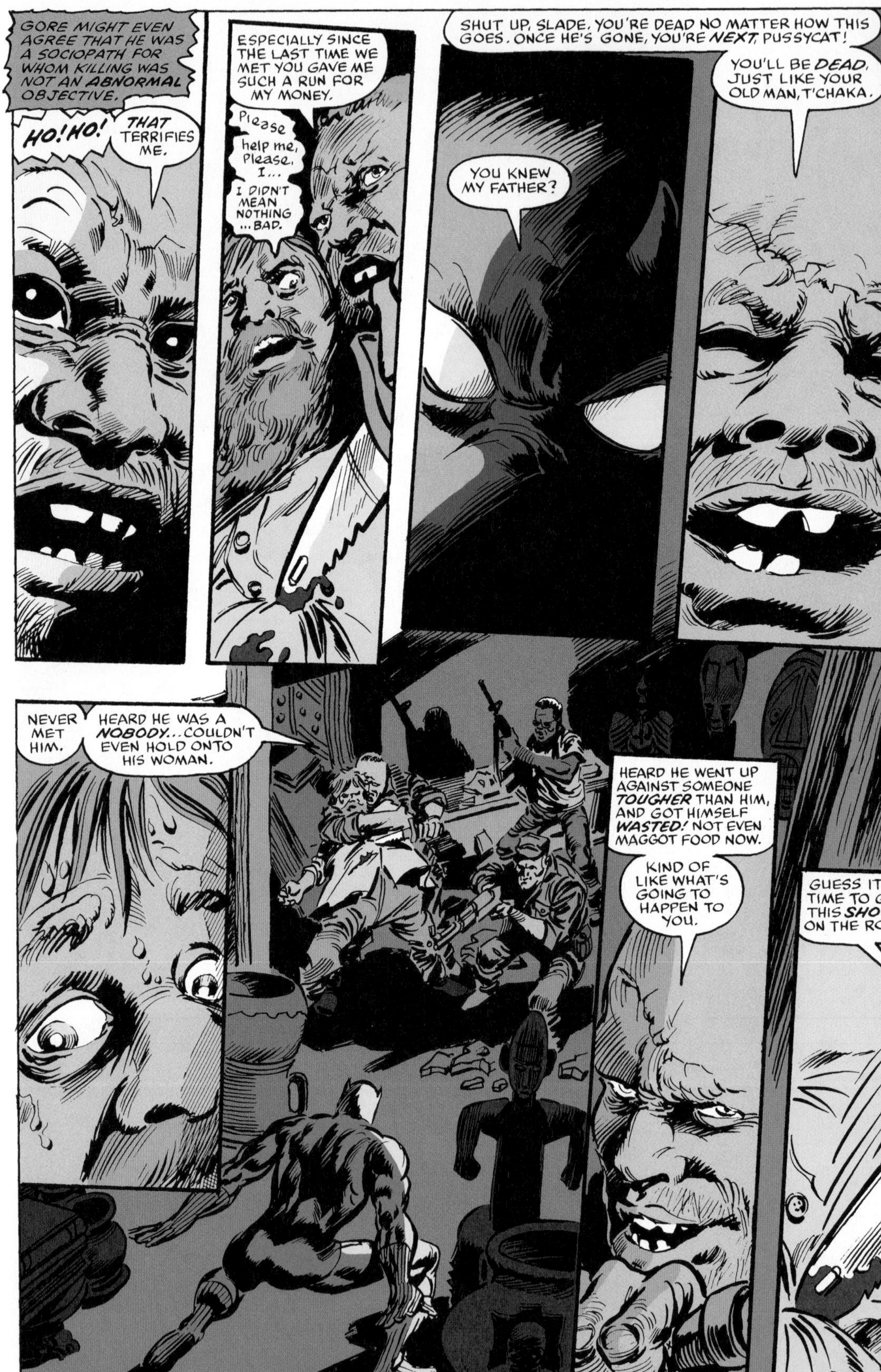
GORE MIGHT EVEN AGREE THAT HE WAS A SOCIOPATH FOR WHOM KILLING WAS NOT AN ABNORMAL OBJECTIVE.
HO! HO!
THAT TERRIFIES ME.
ESPECIALLY SINCE THE LAST TIME WE MET YOU GAVE ME SUCH A RUN FOR MY MONEY.
Please help me, Please, I...
I DIDN'T MEAN NOTHING ...BAD.
SHUT UP, SLADE. YOU'RE DEAD NO MATTER HOW THIS GOES. ONCE HE'S GONE, YOU'RE NEXT, PUSSYCAT!
YOU'LL BE DEAD, JUST LIKE YOUR OLD MAN, T'CHAKA.
YOU KNEW MY FATHER?
NEVER MET HIM.
HEARD HE WAS A NOBODY... COULDN'T EVEN HOLD ONTO HIS WOMAN.
HEARD HE WENT UP AGAINST SOMEONE TOUGHER THAN HIM, AND GOT HIMSELF WASTED! NOT EVEN MAGGOT FOOD NOW.
KIND OF LIKE WHAT'S GOING TO HAPPEN TO YOU.
GUESS IT'S TIME TO GET THIS SHOW ON THE ROAD.

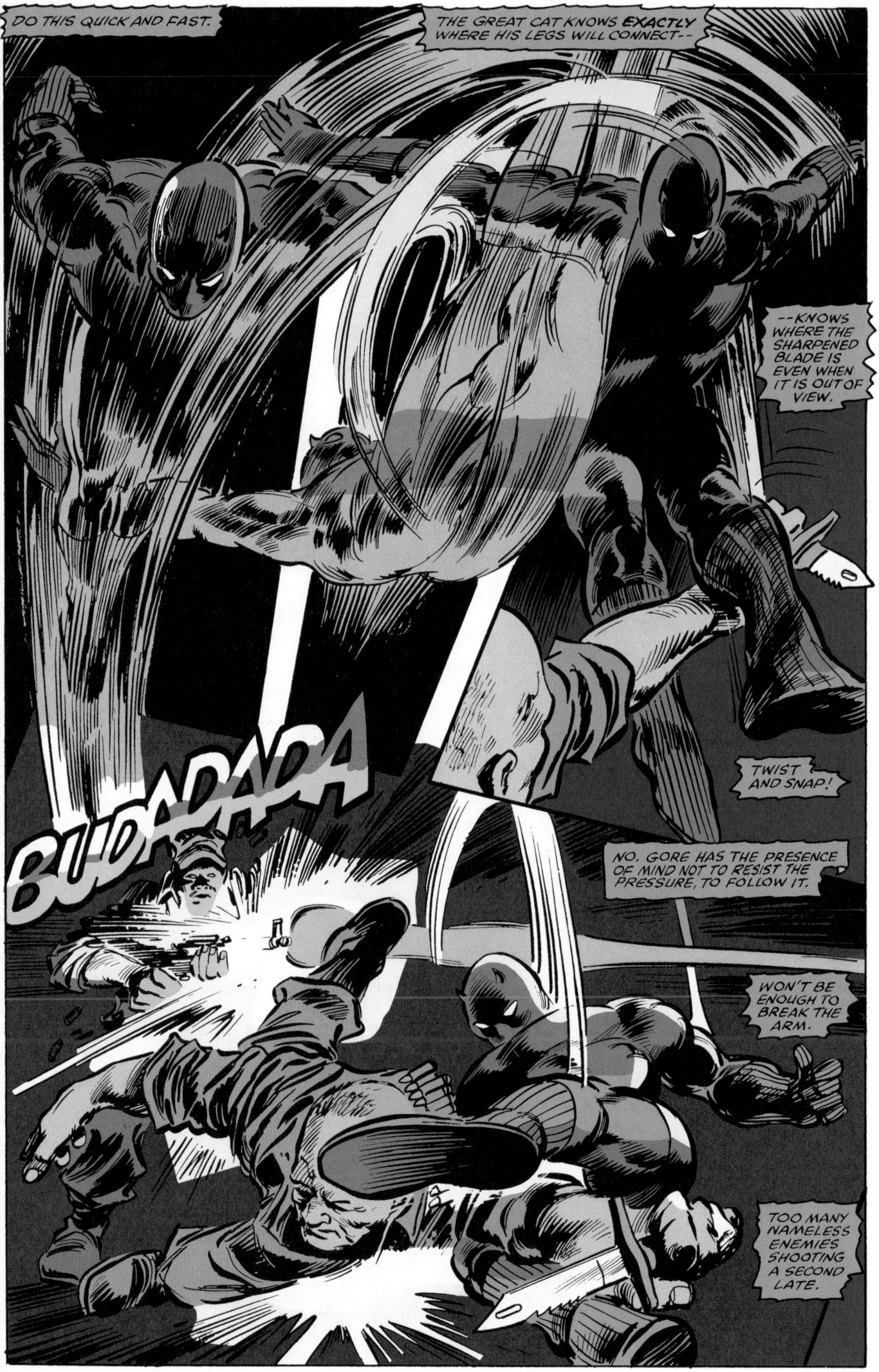
DO THIS QUICK AND FAST.
THE GREAT CAT KNOWS EXACTLY WHERE HIS LEGS WILL CONNECT--
--KNOWS WHERE THE SHARPENED BLADE IS EVEN WHEN IT IS OUT OF VIEW.
TWIST AND SNAP!
BUDADADA
NO. GORE HAS THE PRESENCE OF MIND NOT TO RESIST THE PRESSURE, TO FOLLOW IT.
WON'T BE ENOUGH TO BREAK THE ARM.
TOO MANY NAMELESS ENEMIES SHOOTING A SECOND LATE.

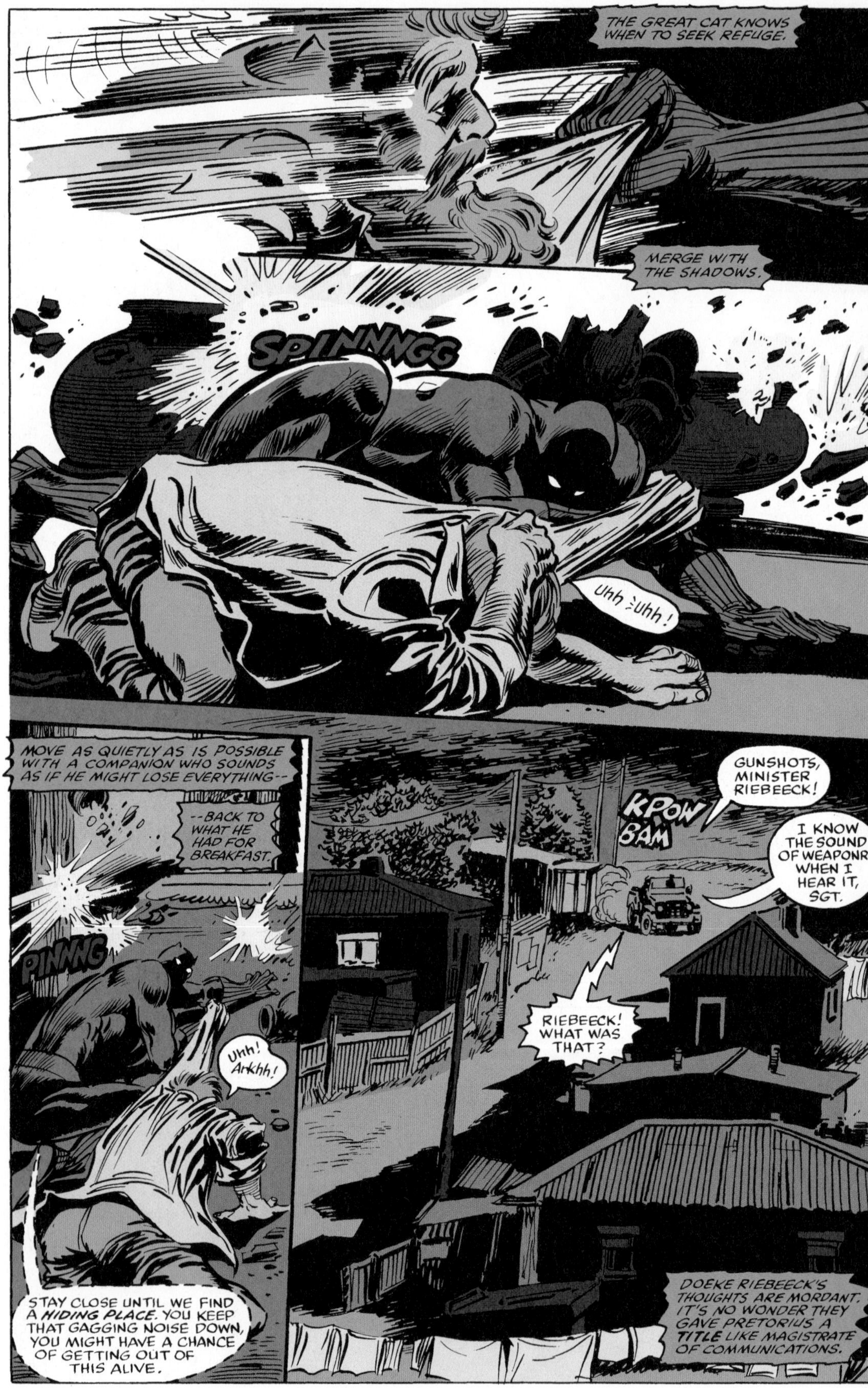
THE GREAT CAT KNOWS WHEN TO SEEK REFUGE.
MERGE WITH THE SHADOWS.
SPINNNGG
Uhh ≈Uhh!
MOVE AS QUIETLY AS IS POSSIBLE WITH A COMPANION WHO SOUNDS AS IF HE MIGHT LOSE EVERYTHING--
--BACK TO WHAT HE HAD FOR BREAKFAST.
PINNNG
Uhh! Arkhh!
STAY CLOSE UNTIL WE FIND A HIDING PLACE. YOU KEEP THAT GAGGING NOISE DOWN, YOU MIGHT HAVE A CHANCE OF GETTING OUT OF THIS ALIVE.
KPOW BAM
GUNSHOTS, MINISTER RIEBEECK!
I KNOW THE SOUND OF WEAPONRY WHEN I HEAR IT, SGT.
RIEBEECK! WHAT WAS THAT?
DOEKE RIEBEECK'S THOUGHTS ARE MORDANT. IT'S NO WONDER THEY GAVE PRETORIUS A TITLE LIKE MAGISTRATE OF COMMUNICATIONS.

THERE IS NO RESPITE FROM ANTON'S VOICE TONIGHT, ALWAYS WITH THE PROPER DIPLOMATIC CONCERN. DOES THE MAN NEVER LOSE HIS #@☆!?#!! TEMPER?
RIEBEECK IS ANGRY AT THE REASONABLE INQUIRIES FROM ANTON, ANGRIER THAT IT IS A REGULAR OCCURRENCE THAT HE AND SGT. VAN DER MERWE ARRIVE AT PLACES THEIR QUARRY HAS APPARENTLY TERRORIZED SHORTLY BEFORE THEIR ARRIVAL.
IT WOULD APPEAR OUR BELOVED MAGISTRATE DOESN'T KNOW A GUNSHOT WHEN HE HEARS ONE.
HE'S A VAST DISTANCE AWAY, SIR.
DON'T MAKE EXCUSES FOR HIM, SGT.! AND GET THIS VEHICLE WHERE THOSE SHOTS CAME FROM, NOW!
DOEKE, WHY AREN'T YOU REPORTING WHAT IS HAPPENING.
PRETORIUS, STOP BREATHING DOWN MY NECK AND JABBERING IN MY ACHING EAR!
I'LL HANDLE THE SITUATION AS I SEE FIT... AND YOU CAN HEAR ABOUT IT ALL IN THE MORNING. OUT!
CLIK
THE MAGISTRATE WON'T LIKE THAT.
IT WON'T BE THE FIRST THING ABOUT ME HE DOESN'T LIKE. HE'D REALLY GO ROUND THE BEND IF HE HAD A CLUE ABOUT HOW I ENJOY MYSELF ON MY OWN TIME.
ZANTI CHIKANE HAS NO DOUBT THE STARTLING GUNSHOTS ARE DIRECTED AT T'CHALLA.
IT IS HARD TO BELIEVE HOW MANY GUNS GO OFF WHEREVER THIS MAN TRAVELS.
ANOTHER REASON IT WAS DANGEROUS TO BE IN CLOSE PROXIMITY TO THIS MAN.
STILL, HE HAS TO WARN T'CHALLA. THE GUNFIRE IS ATTRACTING FURTHER UNWANTED COMPANY.
T'CHALLA! THERE'RE SOLDIERS COMING AND I THINK FROM MORE THAN ONE DIRECTION.
T'CHALLA? DO YOU HEAR ME?
YOU IN HERE?

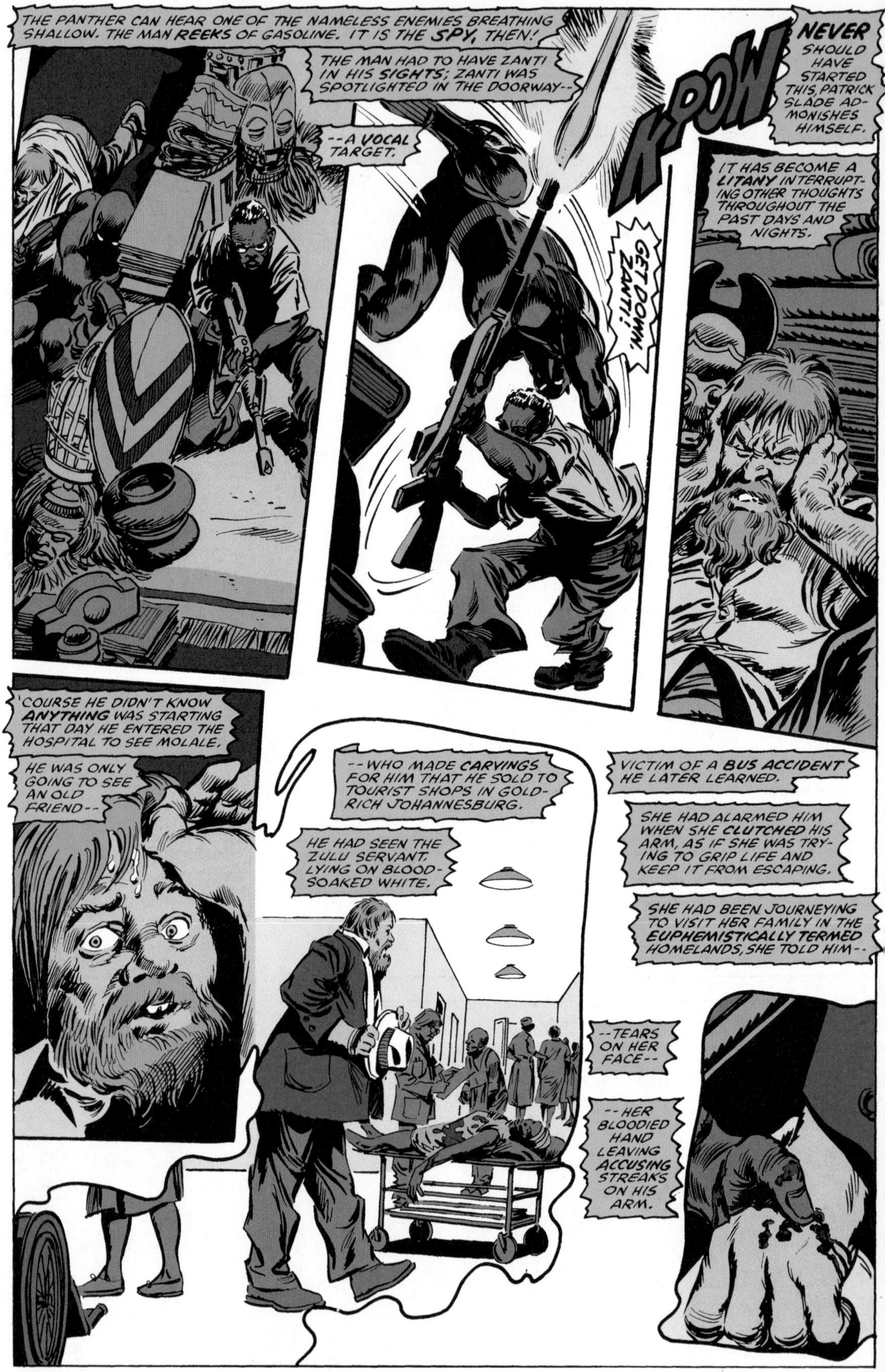
THE PANTHER CAN HEAR ONE OF THE NAMELESS ENEMIES BREATHING SHALLOW. THE MAN REEKS OF GASOLINE. IT IS THE SPY, THEN!
THE MAN HAD TO HAVE ZANTI IN HIS SIGHTS; ZANTI WAS SPOTLIGHTED IN THE DOORWAY--
--A VOCAL TARGET.
K-POW
GET DOWN, ZANTI!
NEVER SHOULD HAVE STARTED THIS, PATRICK SLADE ADMONISHES HIMSELF.
IT HAS BECOME A LITANY INTERRUPTING OTHER THOUGHTS THROUGHOUT THE PAST DAYS AND NIGHTS.
'COURSE HE DIDN'T KNOW ANYTHING WAS STARTING THAT DAY HE ENTERED THE HOSPITAL TO SEE MOLALE.
HE WAS ONLY GOING TO SEE AN OLD FRIEND--
--WHO MADE CARVINGS FOR HIM THAT HE SOLD TO TOURIST SHOPS IN GOLD-RICH JOHANNESBURG.
HE HAD SEEN THE ZULU SERVANT, LYING ON BLOOD-SOAKED WHITE.
VICTIM OF A BUS ACCIDENT HE LATER LEARNED.
SHE HAD ALARMED HIM WHEN SHE CLUTCHED HIS ARM, AS IF SHE WAS TRYING TO GRIP LIFE AND KEEP IT FROM ESCAPING.
SHE HAD BEEN JOURNEYING TO VISIT HER FAMILY IN THE EUPHEMISTICALLY TERMED HOMELANDS, SHE TOLD HIM--
--TEARS ON HER FACE--
--HER BLOODIED HAND LEAVING ACCUSING STREAKS ON HIS ARM.

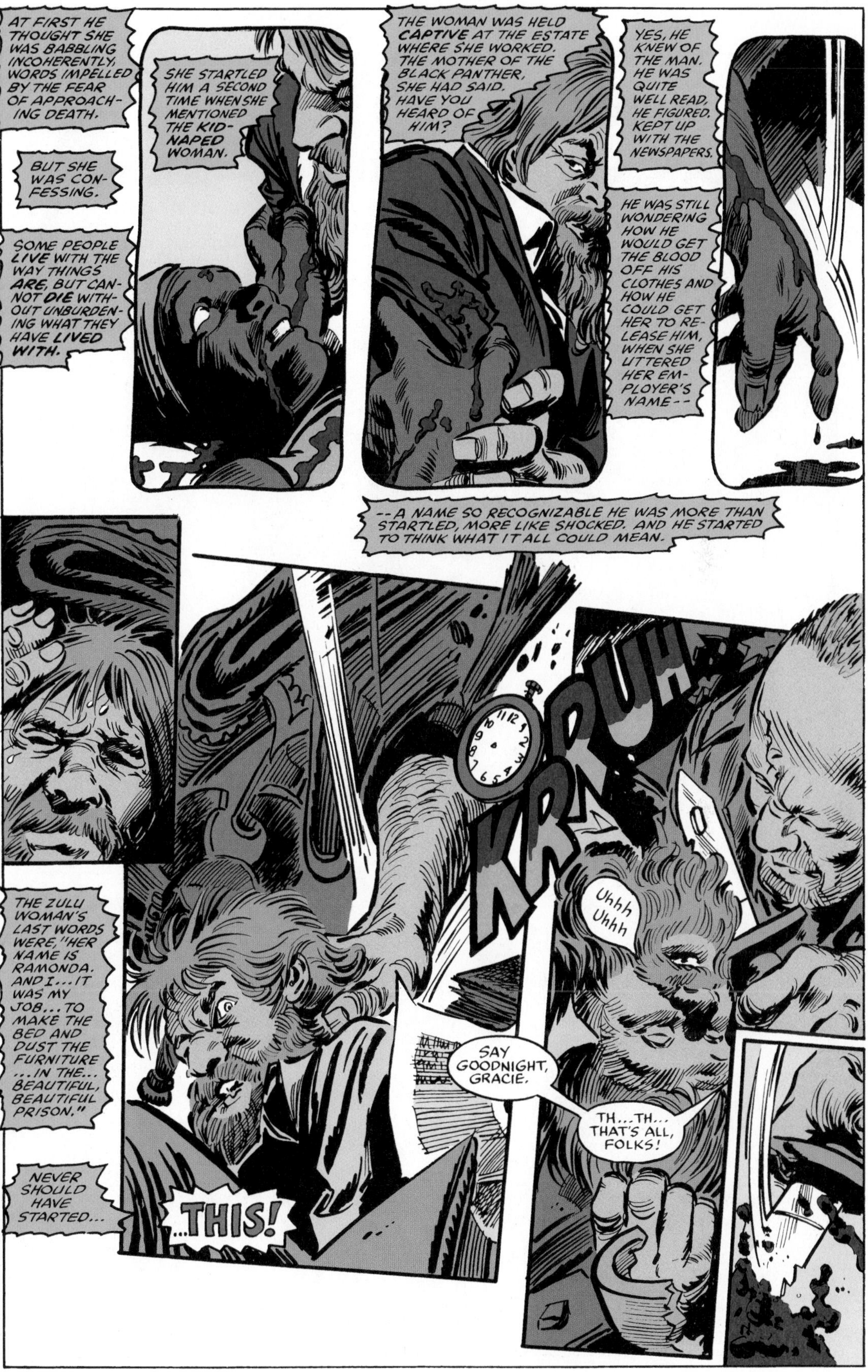
AT FIRST HE THOUGHT SHE WAS BABBLING INCOHERENTLY, WORDS IMPELLED BY THE FEAR OF APPROACHING DEATH.
BUT SHE WAS CONFESSING.
SOME PEOPLE LIVE WITH THE WAY THINGS ARE, BUT CANNOT DIE WITHOUT UNBURDENING WHAT THEY HAVE LIVED WITH.
SHE STARTLED HIM A SECOND TIME WHEN SHE MENTIONED THE KIDNAPED WOMAN.
THE WOMAN WAS HELD CAPTIVE AT THE ESTATE WHERE SHE WORKED. THE MOTHER OF THE BLACK PANTHER, SHE HAD SAID. HAVE YOU HEARD OF HIM?
YES, HE KNEW OF THE MAN. HE WAS QUITE WELL READ, HE FIGURED. KEPT UP WITH THE NEWSPAPERS.
HE WAS STILL WONDERING HOW HE WOULD GET THE BLOOD OFF HIS CLOTHES AND HOW HE COULD GET HER TO RELEASE HIM, WHEN SHE UTTERED HER EMPLOYER'S NAME--
--A NAME SO RECOGNIZABLE HE WAS MORE THAN STARTLED, MORE LIKE SHOCKED. AND HE STARTED TO THINK WHAT IT ALL COULD MEAN.
KRRUH
THE ZULU WOMAN'S LAST WORDS WERE, "HER NAME IS RAMONDA. AND I...IT WAS MY JOB...TO MAKE THE BED AND DUST THE FURNITURE ...IN THE... BEAUTIFUL, BEAUTIFUL PRISON."
Uhhh Uhhh
SAY GOODNIGHT, GRACIE.
TH...TH... THAT'S ALL, FOLKS!
NEVER SHOULD HAVE STARTED...
...THIS!

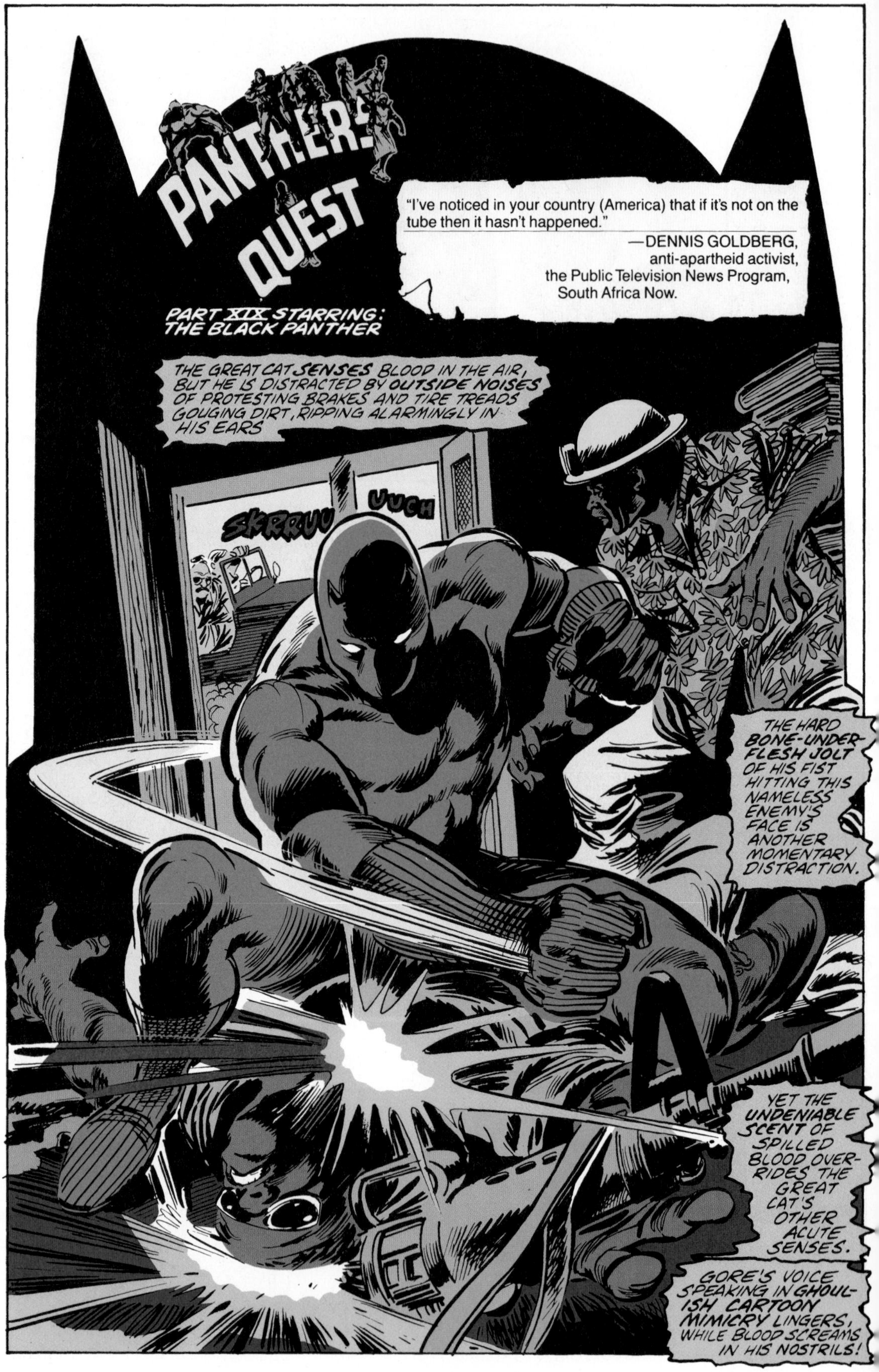
PANTHER'S QUEST
"I've noticed in your country (America) that if it's not on the tube then it hasn't happened."
—DENNIS GOLDBERG, anti-apartheid activist, the Public Television News Program, South Africa Now.
PART XIX STARRING: THE BLACK PANTHER
THE GREAT CAT SENSES BLOOD IN THE AIR, BUT HE IS DISTRACTED BY OUTSIDE NOISES OF PROTESTING BRAKES AND TIRE TREADS GOUGING DIRT, RIPPING ALARMINGLY IN HIS EARS
SKRRUU
UUCH
THE HARD BONE-UNDER-FLESH JOLT OF HIS FIST HITTING THIS NAMELESS ENEMY'S FACE IS ANOTHER MOMENTARY DISTRACTION.
YET THE UNDENIABLE SCENT OF SPILLED BLOOD OVER-RIDES THE GREAT CAT'S OTHER ACUTE SENSES.
GORE'S VOICE SPEAKING IN GHOULISH CARTOON MIMICRY LINGERS, WHILE BLOOD SCREAMS IN HIS NOSTRILS!

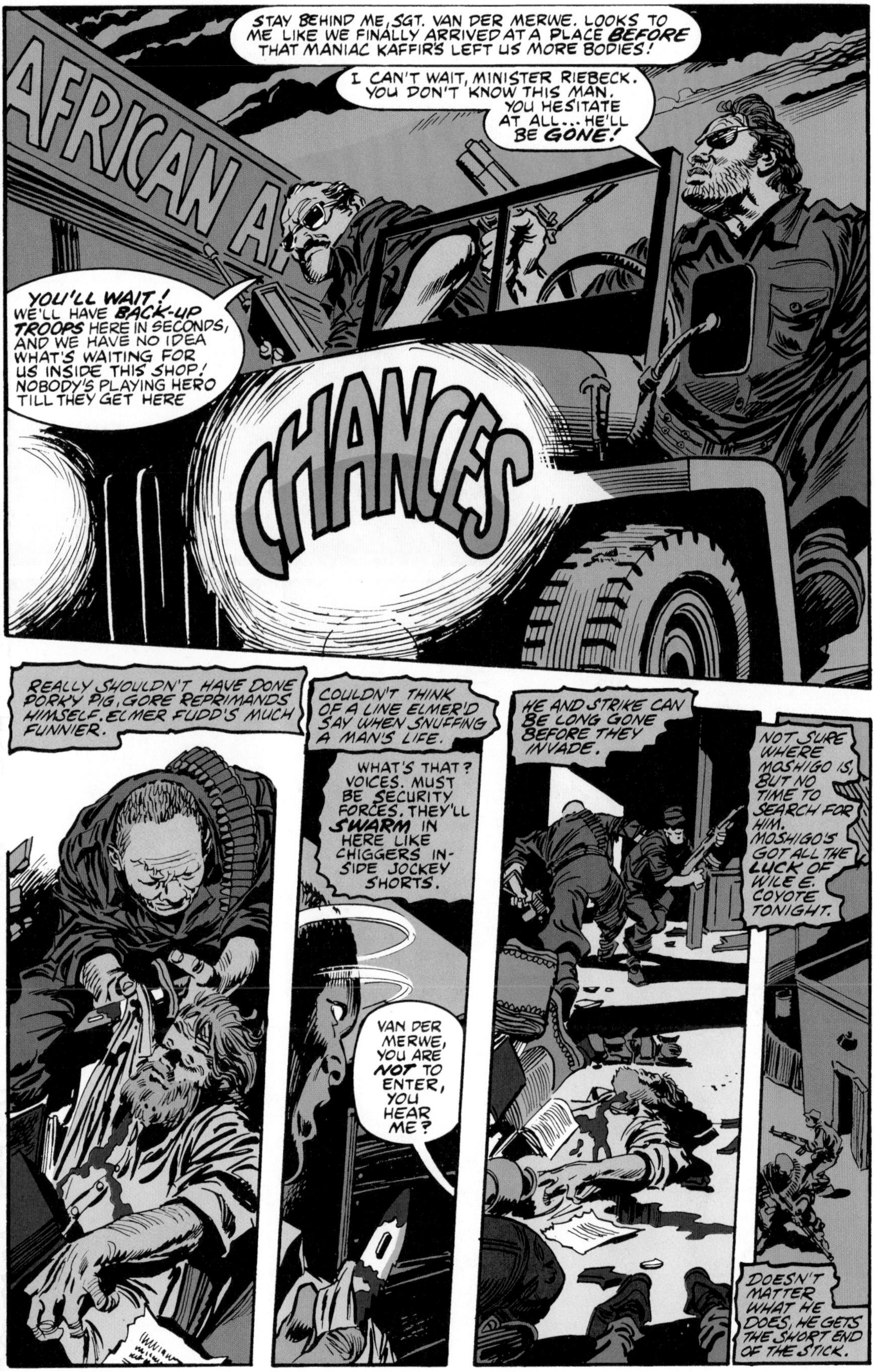

AFRICAN A
STAY BEHIND ME, SGT. VAN DER MERWE. LOOKS TO ME LIKE WE FINALLY ARRIVED AT A PLACE BEFORE THAT MANIAC KAFFIR'S LEFT US MORE BODIES!
I CAN'T WAIT, MINISTER RIEBECK. YOU DON'T KNOW THIS MAN. YOU HESITATE AT ALL... HE'LL BE GONE!
YOU'LL WAIT! WE'LL HAVE BACK-UP TROOPS HERE IN SECONDS, AND WE HAVE NO IDEA WHAT'S WAITING FOR US INSIDE THIS SHOP! NOBODY'S PLAYING HERO TILL THEY GET HERE
CHANCES
REALLY SHOULDN'T HAVE DONE PORKY PIG, GORE REPRIMANDS HIMSELF. ELMER FUDD'S MUCH FUNNIER.
COULDN'T THINK OF A LINE ELMER'D SAY WHEN SNUFFING A MAN'S LIFE.
WHAT'S THAT? VOICES. MUST BE SECURITY FORCES. THEY'LL SWARM IN HERE LIKE CHIGGERS INSIDE JOCKEY SHORTS.
VAN DER MERWE, YOU ARE NOT TO ENTER, YOU HEAR ME?
HE AND STRIKE CAN BE LONG GONE BEFORE THEY INVADE.
NOT SURE WHERE MOSHIGO IS, BUT NO TIME TO SEARCH FOR HIM. MOSHIGO'S GOT ALL THE LUCK OF WILE E. COYOTE TONIGHT.
DOESN'T MATTER WHAT HE DOES, HE GETS THE SHORT END OF THE STICK.

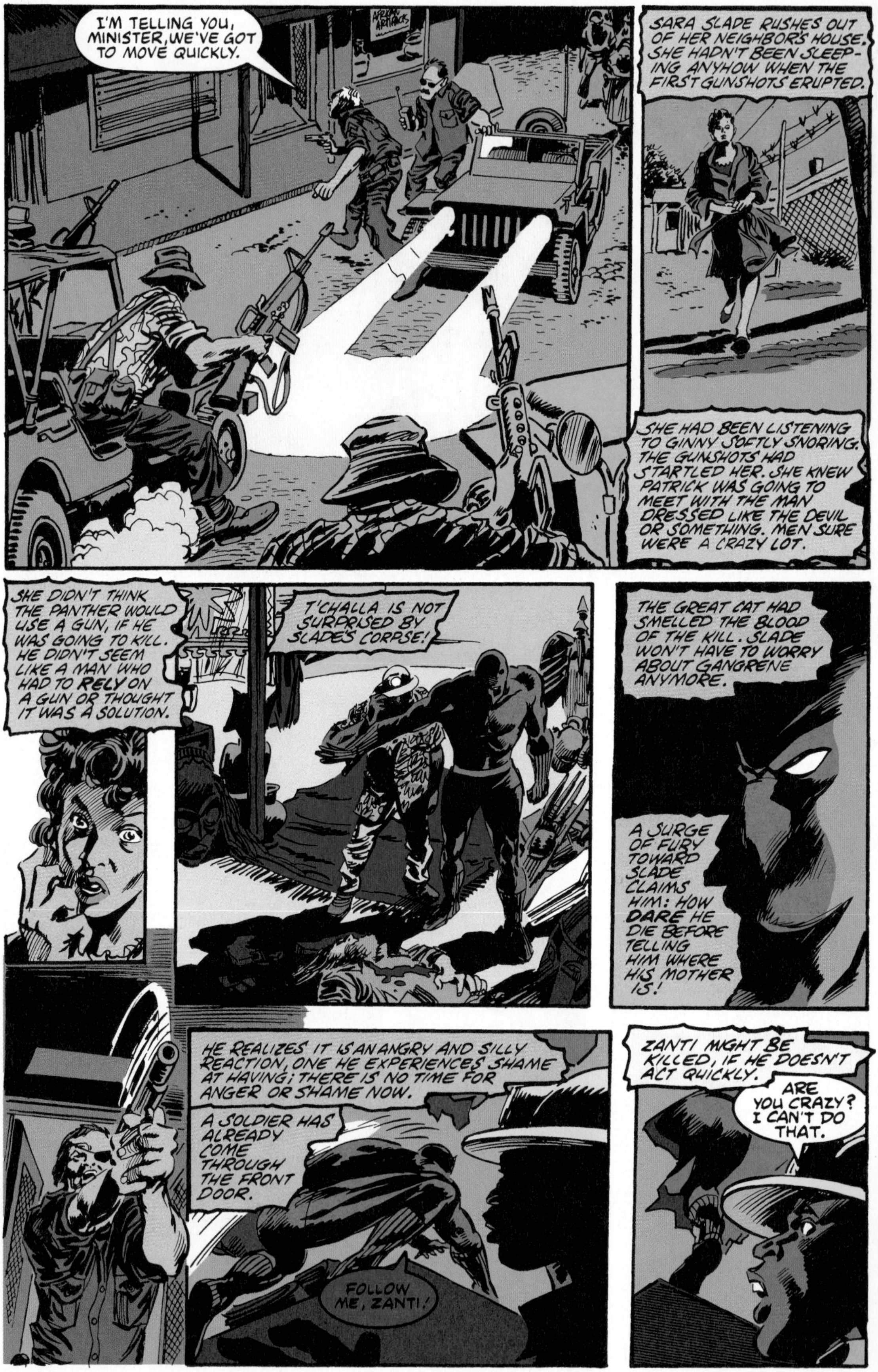

I'M TELLING YOU, MINISTER, WE'VE GOT TO MOVE QUICKLY.
SARA SLADE RUSHES OUT OF HER NEIGHBOR'S HOUSE. SHE HADN'T BEEN SLEEPING ANYHOW WHEN THE FIRST GUNSHOTS ERUPTED.
SHE HAD BEEN LISTENING TO GINNY SOFTLY SNORING. THE GUNSHOTS HAD STARTLED HER. SHE KNEW PATRICK WAS GOING TO MEET WITH THE MAN DRESSED LIKE THE DEVIL OR SOMETHING. MEN SURE WERE A CRAZY LOT.
SHE DIDN'T THINK THE PANTHER WOULD USE A GUN, IF HE WAS GOING TO KILL. HE DIDN'T SEEM LIKE A MAN WHO HAD TO RELY ON A GUN OR THOUGHT IT WAS A SOLUTION.
T'CHALLA IS NOT SURPRISED BY SLADE'S CORPSE!
THE GREAT CAT HAD SMELLED THE BLOOD OF THE KILL. SLADE WON'T HAVE TO WORRY ABOUT GANGRENE ANYMORE.
A SURGE OF FURY TOWARD SLADE CLAIMS HIM: HOW DARE HE DIE BEFORE TELLING HIM WHERE HIS MOTHER IS!
HE REALIZES IT IS AN ANGRY AND SILLY REACTION, ONE HE EXPERIENCES SHAME AT HAVING; THERE IS NO TIME FOR ANGER OR SHAME NOW.
A SOLDIER HAS ALREADY COME THROUGH THE FRONT DOOR.
FOLLOW ME, ZANTI!
ZANTI MIGHT BE KILLED, IF HE DOESN'T ACT QUICKLY.
ARE YOU CRAZY? I CAN'T DO THAT.

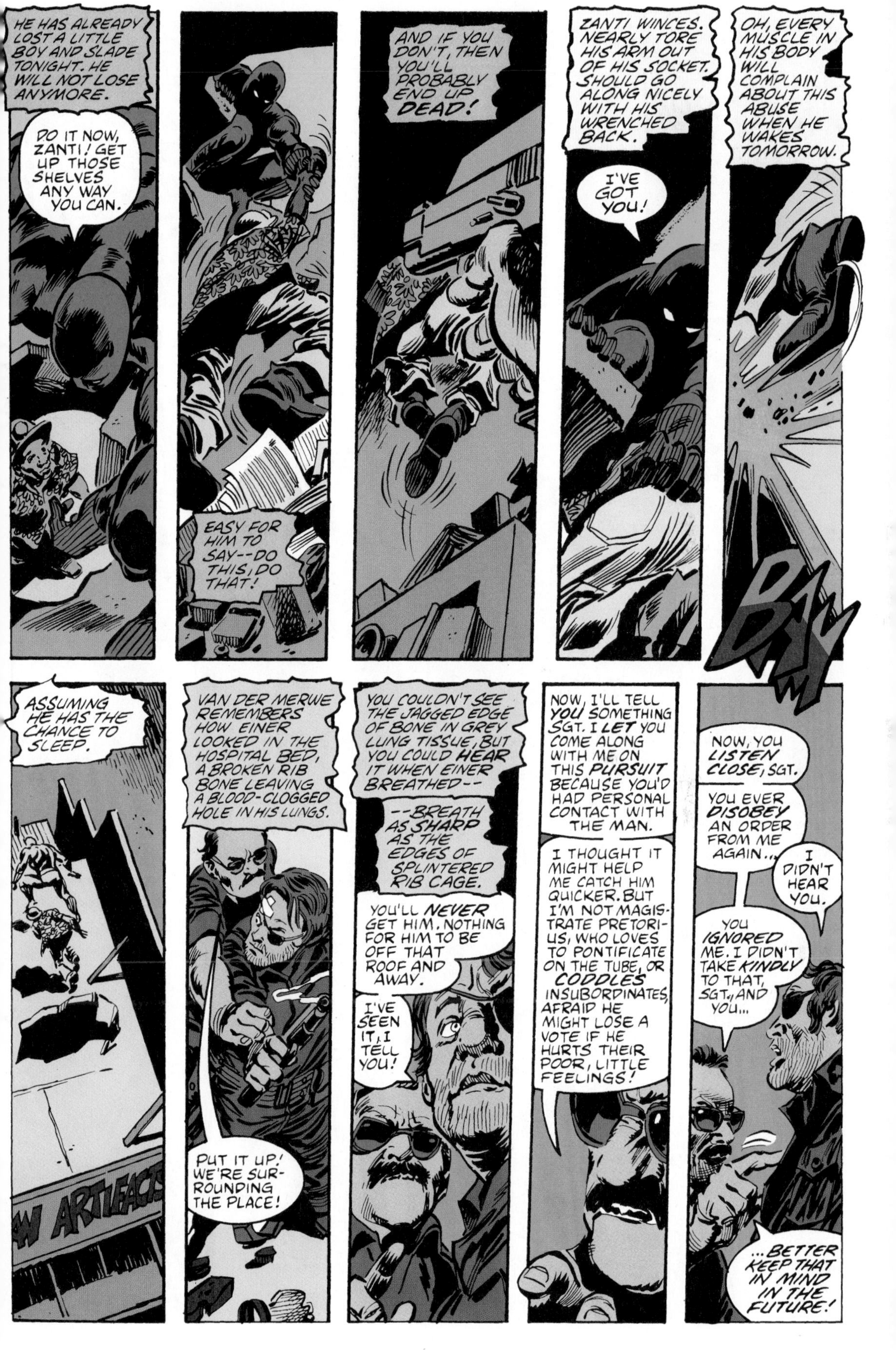
HE HAS ALREADY LOST A LITTLE BOY AND SLADE TONIGHT. HE WILL NOT LOSE ANYMORE.
DO IT NOW, ZANTI! GET UP THOSE SHELVES ANY WAY YOU CAN.
EASY FOR HIM TO SAY--DO THIS, DO THAT!
AND IF YOU DON'T, THEN YOU'LL PROBABLY END UP DEAD!
ZANTI WINCES. NEARLY TORE HIS ARM OUT OF HIS SOCKET. SHOULD GO ALONG NICELY WITH HIS WRENCHED BACK.
I'VE GOT YOU!
OH, EVERY MUSCLE IN HIS BODY WILL COMPLAIN ABOUT THIS ABUSE WHEN HE WAKES TOMORROW.
BAM
ASSUMING HE HAS THE CHANCE TO SLEEP.
W ARTIFACTS
VAN DER MERWE REMEMBERS HOW EINER LOOKED IN THE HOSPITAL BED, A BROKEN RIB BONE LEAVING A BLOOD-CLOGGED HOLE IN HIS LUNGS.
PUT IT UP! WE'RE SURROUNDING THE PLACE!
YOU COULDN'T SEE THE JAGGED EDGE OF BONE IN GREY LUNG TISSUE, BUT YOU COULD HEAR IT WHEN EINER BREATHED--
--BREATH AS SHARP AS THE EDGES OF SPLINTERED RIB CAGE.
YOU'LL NEVER GET HIM. NOTHING FOR HIM TO BE OFF THAT ROOF AND AWAY.
I'VE SEEN IT, I TELL YOU!
NOW, I'LL TELL YOU SOMETHING SGT. I LET YOU COME ALONG WITH ME ON THIS PURSUIT BECAUSE YOU'D HAD PERSONAL CONTACT WITH THE MAN.
I THOUGHT IT MIGHT HELP ME CATCH HIM QUICKER. BUT I'M NOT MAGISTRATE PRETORIUS, WHO LOVES TO PONTIFICATE ON THE TUBE, OR CODDLES INSUBORDINATES, AFRAID HE MIGHT LOSE A VOTE IF HE HURTS THEIR POOR, LITTLE FEELINGS!
NOW, YOU LISTEN CLOSE, SGT.
YOU EVER DISOBEY AN ORDER FROM ME AGAIN...
I DIDN'T HEAR YOU.
YOU IGNORED ME. I DIDN'T TAKE KINDLY TO THAT, SGT., AND YOU...
...BETTER KEEP THAT IN MIND IN THE FUTURE!

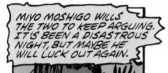

MIYO MOSHIGO WILLS THE TWO TO KEEP ARGUING. IT'S BEEN A DISASTROUS NIGHT, BUT MAYBE HE WILL LUCK OUT AGAIN.

AS SOON AS HE OPENS HIS EYES, ZANTI CHIKANE NODS HIS HEAD IN CONFIRMATION OF HIS ACHING PREDICTIONS. EVERY JOINT THROBS AND CREAKS AND CHASTISES HIM.

MAYBE HIS BODY WAS SO STIFF FROM SLEEPING MOST OF THE DAY IN THE CRAMPED QUARTERS OF THE SONAR GLIDER. IMAGINE--SLEEPING DURING THE DAY.

MORE LIKELY THOUGH, THE PAINS CAME FROM LEAPING OUT OF TREES--

--AND THROUGH ROOFTOPS.

THE MAGISTRATE OF COMMUNICATIONS IN PRETORIA IS ON THE MONITORS AGAIN. HE CAN NEVER REMEMBER THE MAN'S NAME. T'CHALLA MUST HAVE MANY OF THEM LOSING SLEEP, ALSO.

...AND SO, WHILE WE HAVE NOT *CAPTURED* THE BLACK PANTHER--

O°OOOOHHHHH

--I AM ASSURED OUR TROOPS ARE *CLOSING IN* ON HIM. INEVITABLY HE WILL BE BROUGHT IN TO JUSTICE, AND THE TERRIBLE COST OF HIS VIOLENCE... THE DEATHS LEFT IN HIS WAKE ...WHICH NOW INCLUDES A YOUNG BOY--

--WILL BE ACCOUNTED FOR. THIS IS ANTON PRETORIUS BIDDING YOU A GOOD NIGHT

THEY'RE BLAMING EVERY--

AHH!

--THING ON YOU!

WE NOW RETURN YOU TO OUR REGULAR SHOWING OF "HILL ST. BLUES."

THE COMRADS AND "FATHERS" AREN'T EVEN MENTIONED.

NOT THAT I THOUGHT WE WOULD HEAR ANYTHING BUT WHAT THE GOVERNMENT DECIDES THE PEOPLE SHOULD HEAR. DO YOU THINK THEY REALLY BELIEVE YOU KILLED THAT BOY?

I DON'T KNOW.

WHERE ARE YOU GOING?

I'M GOING TO TRY TO *LOCATE* SARAH SLADE.

IF THEY RECOGNIZE YOU...

I'VE GOT TO TAKE THE *CHANCE.*

THAT'S THE *SAME* AS RISK ISN'T IT?

NOT ALWAYS.

EXPLAIN THE DIFFER-ENCE TO ME SOMETIME.

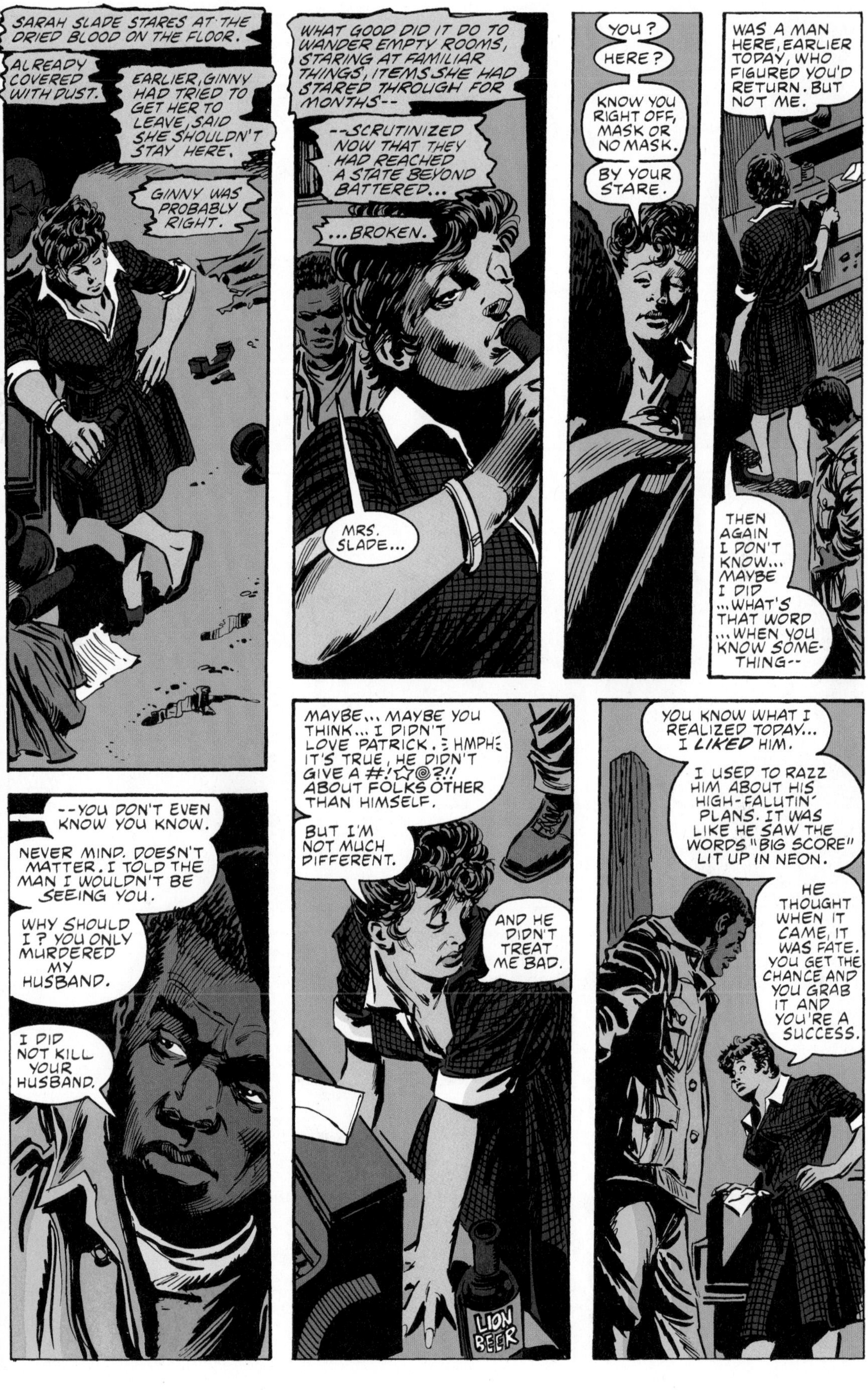

SARAH SLADE STARES AT THE DRIED BLOOD ON THE FLOOR.
ALREADY COVERED WITH DUST.
EARLIER, GINNY HAD TRIED TO GET HER TO LEAVE, SAID SHE SHOULDN'T STAY HERE.
GINNY WAS PROBABLY RIGHT.
WHAT GOOD DID IT DO TO WANDER EMPTY ROOMS, STARING AT FAMILIAR THINGS, ITEMS SHE HAD STARED THROUGH FOR MONTHS--
--SCRUTINIZED NOW THAT THEY HAD REACHED A STATE BEYOND BATTERED...
...BROKEN.
MRS. SLADE...
YOU?
HERE?
KNOW YOU RIGHT OFF, MASK OR NO MASK.
BY YOUR STARE.
WAS A MAN HERE, EARLIER TODAY, WHO FIGURED YOU'D RETURN. BUT NOT ME.
THEN AGAIN I DON'T KNOW... MAYBE I DID ...WHAT'S THAT WORD ...WHEN YOU KNOW SOMETHING--
--YOU DON'T EVEN KNOW YOU KNOW.
NEVER MIND. DOESN'T MATTER. I TOLD THE MAN I WOULDN'T BE SEEING YOU.
WHY SHOULD I? YOU ONLY MURDERED MY HUSBAND.
I DID NOT KILL YOUR HUSBAND.
MAYBE... MAYBE YOU THINK... I DIDN'T LOVE PATRICK. HMPH. IT'S TRUE, HE DIDN'T GIVE A #!☆◎?!! ABOUT FOLKS OTHER THAN HIMSELF.
BUT I'M NOT MUCH DIFFERENT.
AND HE DIDN'T TREAT ME BAD.
LION BEER
YOU KNOW WHAT I REALIZED TODAY... I LIKED HIM.
I USED TO RAZZ HIM ABOUT HIS HIGH-FALUTIN' PLANS. IT WAS LIKE HE SAW THE WORDS "BIG SCORE" LIT UP IN NEON.
HE THOUGHT WHEN IT CAME, IT WAS FATE. YOU GET THE CHANCE AND YOU GRAB IT AND YOU'RE A SUCCESS.

☆?!!, HE DIDN'T KNOW NOTHING ABOUT *SUCCESS* ...BUT HE WAS ALWAYS IN THERE *SLUGGIN'*. SO WHAT, WE WEREN'T PASSIONATE OR NOTHIN', YOU GET MY DRIFT. NO LOVEY-DOVEY KIND OF *STUFF*--

--BUT WE'D BOTH SETTLED ON EACH OTHER.

YEAH, SURE... HE'D LOOK AT THOSE LONG-LIMBED WOMEN ...BUT HE KNEW THEY WEREN'T FOR HIM ＝*SWALLOW*＝...

THIS--

--WAS LEFT FOR YOU... LIKE THE MAN SAID... "IN CASE YOU STOPPED BY."

WHO LEFT IT?

HEARD SOME BUDDY OF HIS CALL HIM *STRIKE*. DROVE OFF IN A RICKETY VOLKSWAGON TOWARD JOHANNESBURG.

BUT I GOT YOUR ATTENTION NOW, HUH? AT FIRST, I WAS GOING TO RIP THIS UP, I THOUGHT... TO #☆?! WITH YOU.

BUT THEN IT CAME TO ME...

...MAYBE THIS IS *MORE* PAINFUL... *HURT* YOU MORE IF YOU *DO* SEE IT.

I OPENED IT UP AND READ IT... AND IF YOU DID *SHOW*... DECIDED TO LET YOU HAVE IT.

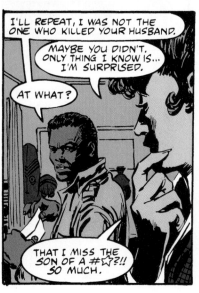

I'LL REPEAT, I WAS NOT THE ONE WHO KILLED YOUR HUSBAND.

MAYBE YOU DIDN'T. ONLY THING I KNOW IS... I'M SURPRISED.

AT WHAT?

THAT I MISS THE SON OF A #☆?!! SO MUCH.

NOW, GO...

READ YOUR LETTER.

AND IF YOU DIDN'T KILL PATRICK...

SLADES AFRICAN ARTIFACTS

I GUESS MAYBE I'M SORRY,... BUT NOT TOO MUCH... I'M TOO #☆?!! INVOLVED IN FEELING SORRY FOR MYSELF.

158

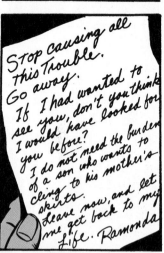

Stop causing all this Trouble. Go away. If I had wanted to see you, don't you think I would have looked for you before? I do not need the burden of a son who wants to cling to his mother's skirts. Leave now and let me get back to my Life. Ramonda

CONTINUED NEXT ISSUE...

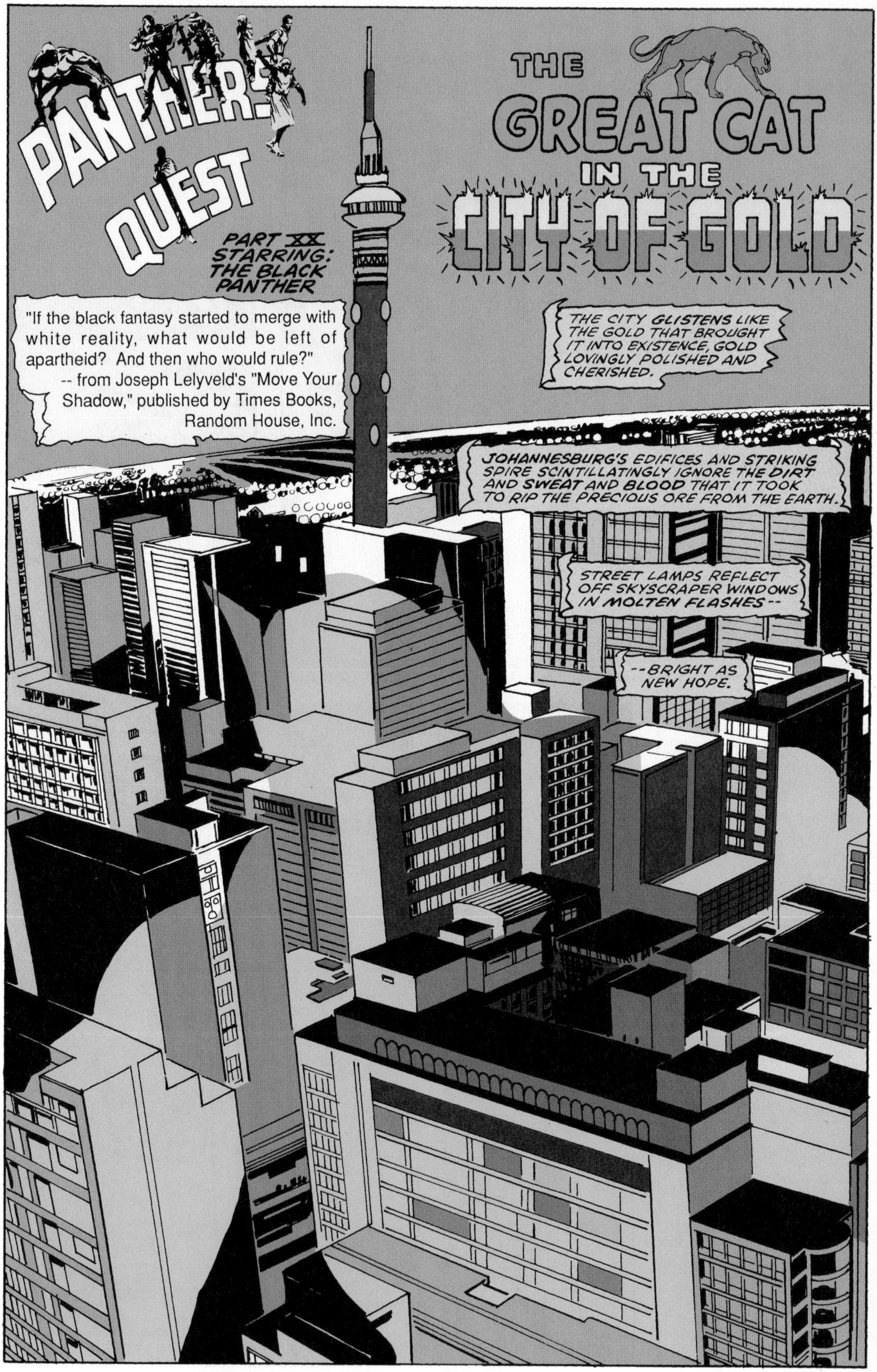
PANTHER'S QUEST
THE GREAT CAT IN THE CITY OF GOLD
PART XX STARRING: THE BLACK PANTHER
"If the black fantasy started to merge with white reality, what would be left of apartheid? And then who would rule?" -- from Joseph Lelyveld's "Move Your Shadow," published by Times Books, Random House, Inc.
THE CITY GLISTENS LIKE THE GOLD THAT BROUGHT IT INTO EXISTENCE, GOLD LOVINGLY POLISHED AND CHERISHED.
JOHANNESBURG'S EDIFICES AND STRIKING SPIRE SCINTILLATINGLY IGNORE THE DIRT AND SWEAT AND BLOOD THAT IT TOOK TO RIP THE PRECIOUS ORE FROM THE EARTH.
STREET LAMPS REFLECT OFF SKYSCRAPER WINDOWS IN MOLTEN FLASHES--
--BRIGHT AS NEW HOPE.

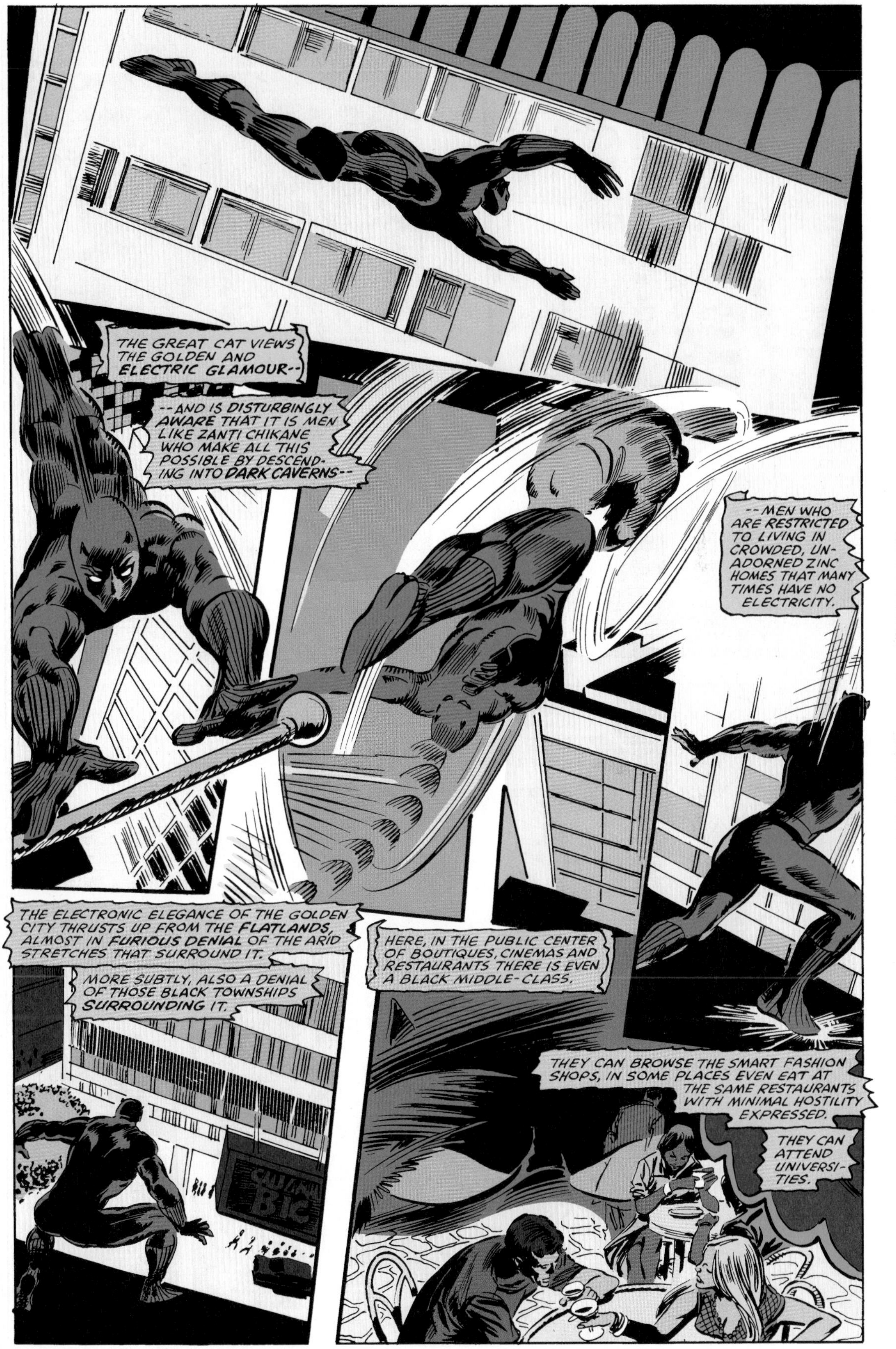
THE GREAT CAT VIEWS THE GOLDEN AND ELECTRIC GLAMOUR--
--AND IS DISTURBINGLY AWARE THAT IT IS MEN LIKE ZANTI CHIKANE WHO MAKE ALL THIS POSSIBLE BY DESCENDING INTO DARK CAVERNS--
--MEN WHO ARE RESTRICTED TO LIVING IN CROWDED, UNADORNED ZINC HOMES THAT MANY TIMES HAVE NO ELECTRICITY.
THE ELECTRONIC ELEGANCE OF THE GOLDEN CITY THRUSTS UP FROM THE FLATLANDS, ALMOST IN FURIOUS DENIAL OF THE ARID STRETCHES THAT SURROUND IT.
MORE SUBTLY, ALSO A DENIAL OF THOSE BLACK TOWNSHIPS SURROUNDING IT.
HERE, IN THE PUBLIC CENTER OF BOUTIQUES, CINEMAS AND RESTAURANTS THERE IS EVEN A BLACK MIDDLE-CLASS.
THEY CAN BROWSE THE SMART FASHION SHOPS, IN SOME PLACES EVEN EAT AT THE SAME RESTAURANTS WITH MINIMAL HOSTILITY EXPRESSED.
THEY CAN ATTEND UNIVERSITIES.

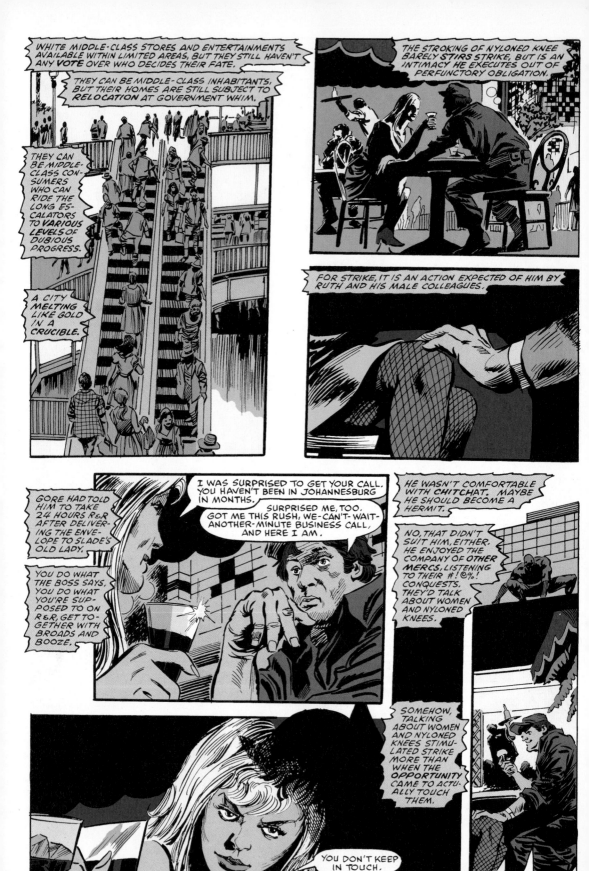

WHITE MIDDLE-CLASS STORES AND ENTERTAINMENTS AVAILABLE WITHIN LIMITED AREAS, BUT THEY STILL HAVEN'T ANY **VOTE** OVER WHO DECIDES THEIR FATE.

THEY CAN BE MIDDLE-CLASS INHABITANTS, BUT THEIR HOMES ARE STILL SUBJECT TO **RELOCATION** AT GOVERNMENT WHIM.

THEY CAN BE MIDDLE-CLASS CONSUMERS WHO CAN RIDE THE LONG ESCALATORS TO **VARIOUS LEVELS** OF DUBIOUS PROGRESS.

A CITY MELTING LIKE GOLD IN A CRUCIBLE.

THE STROKING OF NYLONED KNEE BARELY **STIRS** STRIKE, BUT IS AN INTIMACY HE EXECUTES OUT OF PERFUNCTORY OBLIGATION.

FOR STRIKE, IT IS AN ACTION EXPECTED OF HIM BY RUTH AND HIS MALE COLLEAGUES.

GORE HAD TOLD HIM TO TAKE 24 HOURS R&R AFTER DELIVERING THE ENVELOPE TO SLADE'S OLD LADY.

YOU DO WHAT THE BOSS SAYS. YOU DO WHAT YOU'RE SUPPOSED TO ON R&R, GET TOGETHER WITH BROADS AND BOOZE.

I WAS SURPRISED TO GET YOUR CALL. YOU HAVEN'T BEEN IN JOHANNESBURG IN MONTHS.

SURPRISED ME, TOO. GOT ME THIS RUSH, WE-CAN'T-WAIT-ANOTHER-MINUTE BUSINESS CALL, AND HERE I AM.

HE WASN'T COMFORTABLE WITH **CHITCHAT.** MAYBE HE SHOULD BECOME A HERMIT.

NO, THAT DIDN'T SUIT HIM, EITHER. HE ENJOYED THE COMPANY OF **OTHER** MERCS, LISTENING TO THEIR #!©%! CONQUESTS. THEY'D TALK ABOUT WOMEN AND NYLONED KNEES.

SOMEHOW, TALKING ABOUT WOMEN AND NYLONED KNEES STIMULATED STRIKE MORE THAN WHEN THE OPPORTUNITY CAME TO ACTUALLY TOUCH THEM.

YOU DON'T KEEP IN TOUCH.

NEITHER DO YOU, BABY. SO WHAT HAVE YOU BEEN UP TO WHILE THE BIG BAD WOLF'S AWAY?

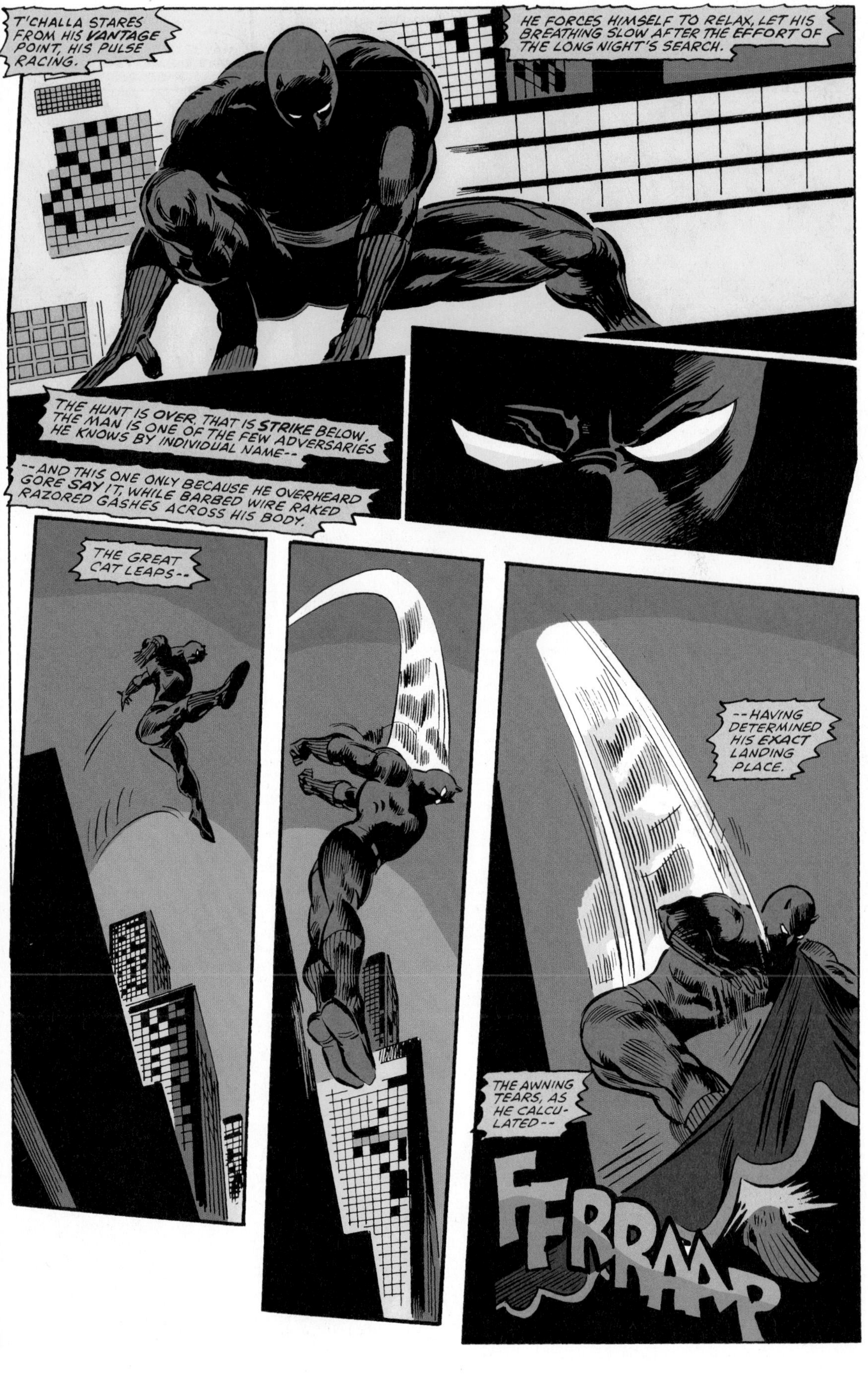

T'CHALLA STARES FROM HIS VANTAGE POINT, HIS PULSE RACING.
HE FORCES HIMSELF TO RELAX, LET HIS BREATHING SLOW AFTER THE EFFORT OF THE LONG NIGHT'S SEARCH.
THE HUNT IS OVER. THAT IS STRIKE BELOW. THE MAN IS ONE OF THE FEW ADVERSARIES HE KNOWS BY INDIVIDUAL NAME--
--AND THIS ONE ONLY BECAUSE HE OVERHEARD GORE SAY IT, WHILE BARBED WIRE RAKED RAZORED GASHES ACROSS HIS BODY.
THE GREAT CAT LEAPS--
--HAVING DETERMINED HIS EXACT LANDING PLACE.
THE AWNING TEARS, AS HE CALCU-LATED--
FFRRAAAP

--DEPOSITING HIM NEAR STRIKE, LIKE A WRATHFUL APPARITION.
WHAT THE--!?
YOU AREN'T SUPPOSED TO BE HERE!
YOU'RE SUPPOSED TO BE IN THE BOONIES GOIN' BANANAS OVER MOMMY!
WHUP
YOUR MISTAKE.
MAYBE GORE IS RIGHT, YOU DO HAVE THE ATTENTION SPAN OF A KUMQUAT.
WHOOOSH
RUTH WONDERS WHAT THE #!6% IS GOING ON, BUT SHE DOESN'T ASK THE QUESTION ALOUD.
YOU'RE VERY PANICKY, STRIKE!
WHATEVER HAPPENED TO GRACE UNDER PRES-SURE?
WAS THAT SOMETHING YOU NEVER HEARD OF--
--OR COULD NEVER LIVE UP TO?
LAST DATE WITH THIS CREEP. TOO COLD. EVEN HIS FINGERS ON HER KNEE, YOU'D THINK THAT'D BE WARM.
BUT EVEN IN INTIMATE TOUCH, STILL SUCH COLD DISTANCE. EYES HARD AS ICE.
RUTH STOPS WONDERING ABOUT WHAT THE !#% IS GOING ON--
--AND STARTS WONDER-ING ABOUT HER CHOICE IN MEN--
--BUT SHE DOES NOT VOICE THAT QUESTION OUT LOUD EITHER.

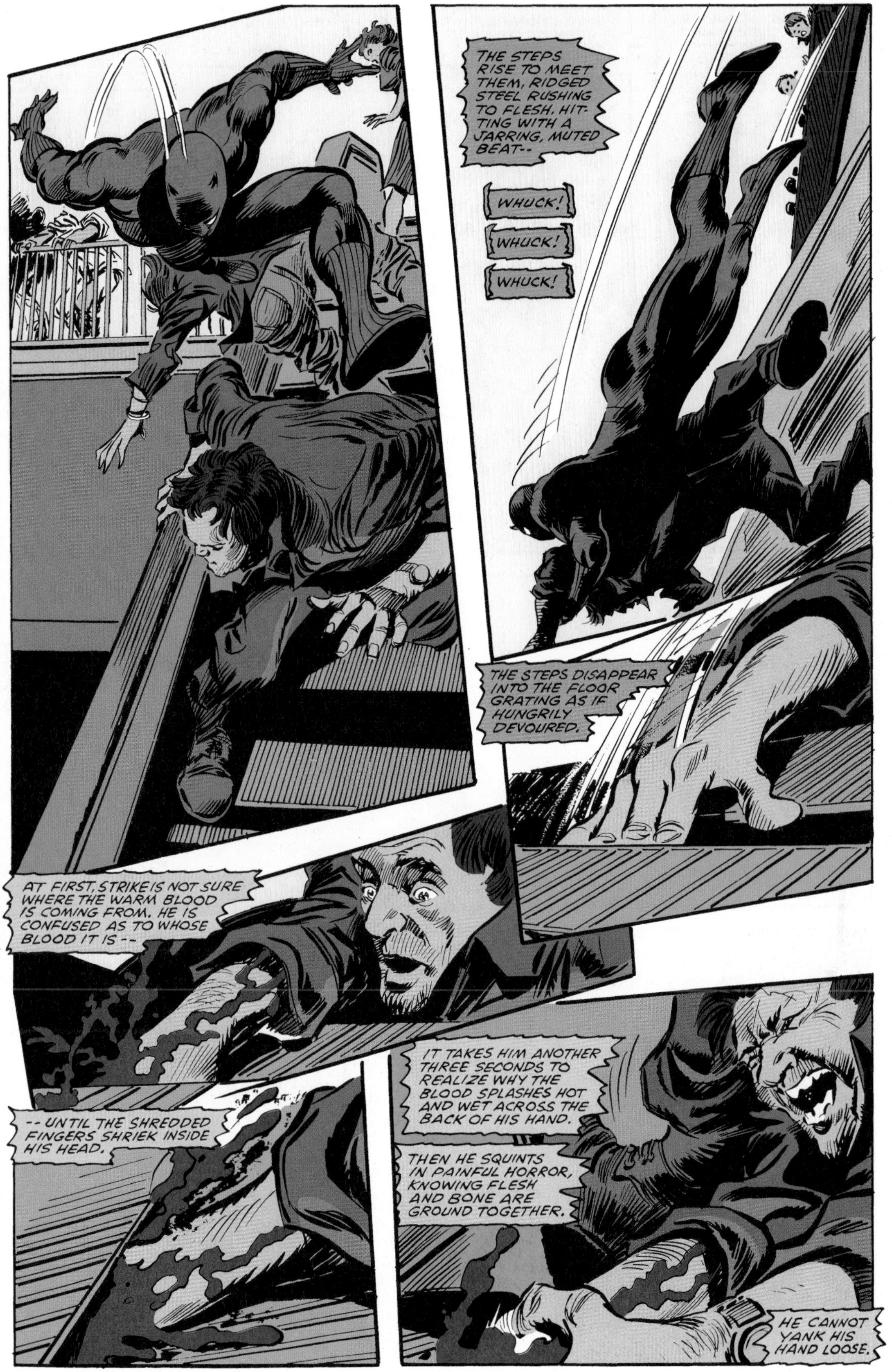
THE STEPS RISE TO MEET THEM, RIDGED STEEL RUSHING TO FLESH, HITTING WITH A JARRING, MUTED BEAT--
WHUCK!
WHUCK!
WHUCK!
THE STEPS DISAPPEAR INTO THE FLOOR GRATING AS IF HUNGRILY DEVOURED.
AT FIRST, STRIKE IS NOT SURE WHERE THE WARM BLOOD IS COMING FROM. HE IS CONFUSED AS TO WHOSE BLOOD IT IS --
-- UNTIL THE SHREDDED FINGERS SHRIEK INSIDE HIS HEAD.
IT TAKES HIM ANOTHER THREE SECONDS TO REALIZE WHY THE BLOOD SPLASHES HOT AND WET ACROSS THE BACK OF HIS HAND.
THEN HE SQUINTS IN PAINFUL HORROR, KNOWING FLESH AND BONE ARE GROUND TOGETHER.
HE CANNOT YANK HIS HAND LOOSE.

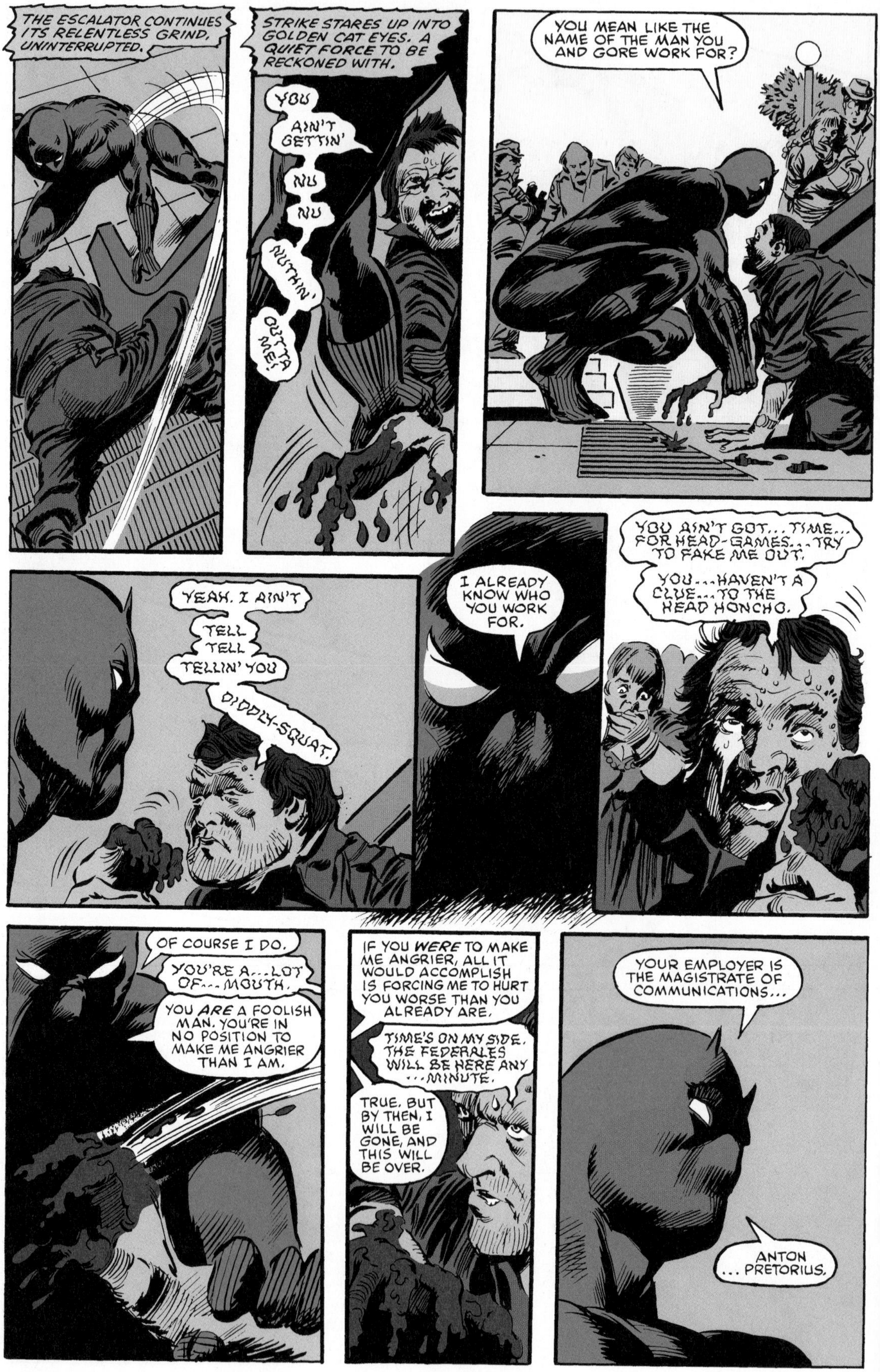

THE ESCALATOR CONTINUES ITS RELENTLESS GRIND, UNINTERRUPTED.
STRIKE STARES UP INTO GOLDEN CAT EYES. A QUIET FORCE TO BE RECKONED WITH.
YOU AIN'T GETTIN' NU NU NUTHIN' OUTTA ME!
YOU MEAN LIKE THE NAME OF THE MAN YOU AND GORE WORK FOR?
YEAH. I AIN'T TELL TELL TELLIN' YOU DIDDLY-SQUAT.
I ALREADY KNOW WHO YOU WORK FOR.
YOU AIN'T GOT... TIME... FOR HEAD-GAMES... TRY TO FAKE ME OUT.
YOU... HAVEN'T A CLUE... TO THE HEAD HONCHO.
OF COURSE I DO.
YOU'RE A... LOT OF... MOUTH.
YOU ARE A FOOLISH MAN. YOU'RE IN NO POSITION TO MAKE ME ANGRIER THAN I AM.
IF YOU WERE TO MAKE ME ANGRIER, ALL IT WOULD ACCOMPLISH IS FORCING ME TO HURT YOU WORSE THAN YOU ALREADY ARE.
TIME'S ON MY SIDE. THE FEDERALES WILL BE HERE ANY ... MINUTE.
TRUE. BUT BY THEN, I WILL BE GONE, AND THIS WILL BE OVER.
YOUR EMPLOYER IS THE MAGISTRATE OF COMMUNICATIONS...
ANTON ... PRETORIUS.

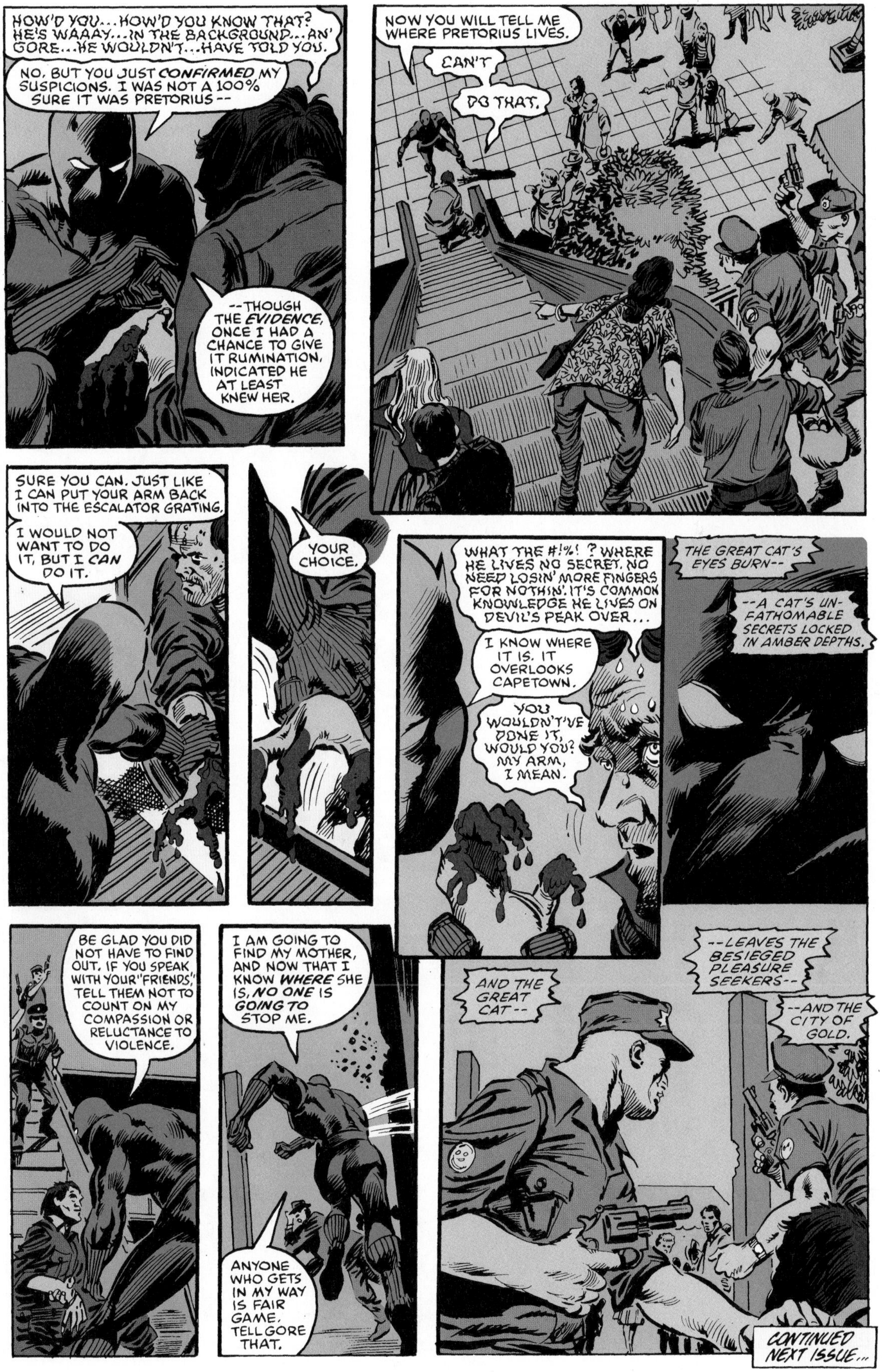

HOW'D YOU...HOW'D YOU KNOW THAT? HE'S WAAAY...IN THE BACKGROUND...AN' GORE...HE WOULDN'T...HAVE TOLD YOU.
NO. BUT YOU JUST CONFIRMED MY SUSPICIONS. I WAS NOT A 100% SURE IT WAS PRETORIUS --
--THOUGH THE EVIDENCE, ONCE I HAD A CHANCE TO GIVE IT RUMINATION, INDICATED HE AT LEAST KNEW HER.
NOW YOU WILL TELL ME WHERE PRETORIUS LIVES.
CAN'T
DO THAT.
SURE YOU CAN. JUST LIKE I CAN PUT YOUR ARM BACK INTO THE ESCALATOR GRATING.
I WOULD NOT WANT TO DO IT, BUT I CAN DO IT.
YOUR CHOICE.
WHAT THE #!%! ? WHERE HE LIVES NO SECRET. NO NEED LOSIN' MORE FINGERS FOR NOTHIN'. IT'S COMMON KNOWLEDGE HE LIVES ON DEVIL'S PEAK OVER...
I KNOW WHERE IT IS. IT OVERLOOKS CAPETOWN.
YOU WOULDN'T'VE DONE IT, WOULD YOU? MY ARM, I MEAN.
THE GREAT CAT'S EYES BURN--
--A CAT'S UN-FATHOMABLE SECRETS LOCKED IN AMBER DEPTHS.
BE GLAD YOU DID NOT HAVE TO FIND OUT. IF YOU SPEAK WITH YOUR "FRIENDS," TELL THEM NOT TO COUNT ON MY COMPASSION OR RELUCTANCE TO VIOLENCE.
I AM GOING TO FIND MY MOTHER, AND NOW THAT I KNOW WHERE SHE IS, NO ONE IS GOING TO STOP ME.
ANYONE WHO GETS IN MY WAY IS FAIR GAME. TELL GORE THAT.
AND THE GREAT CAT --
--LEAVES THE BESIEGED PLEASURE SEEKERS--
--AND THE CITY OF GOLD.
CONTINUED NEXT ISSUE...

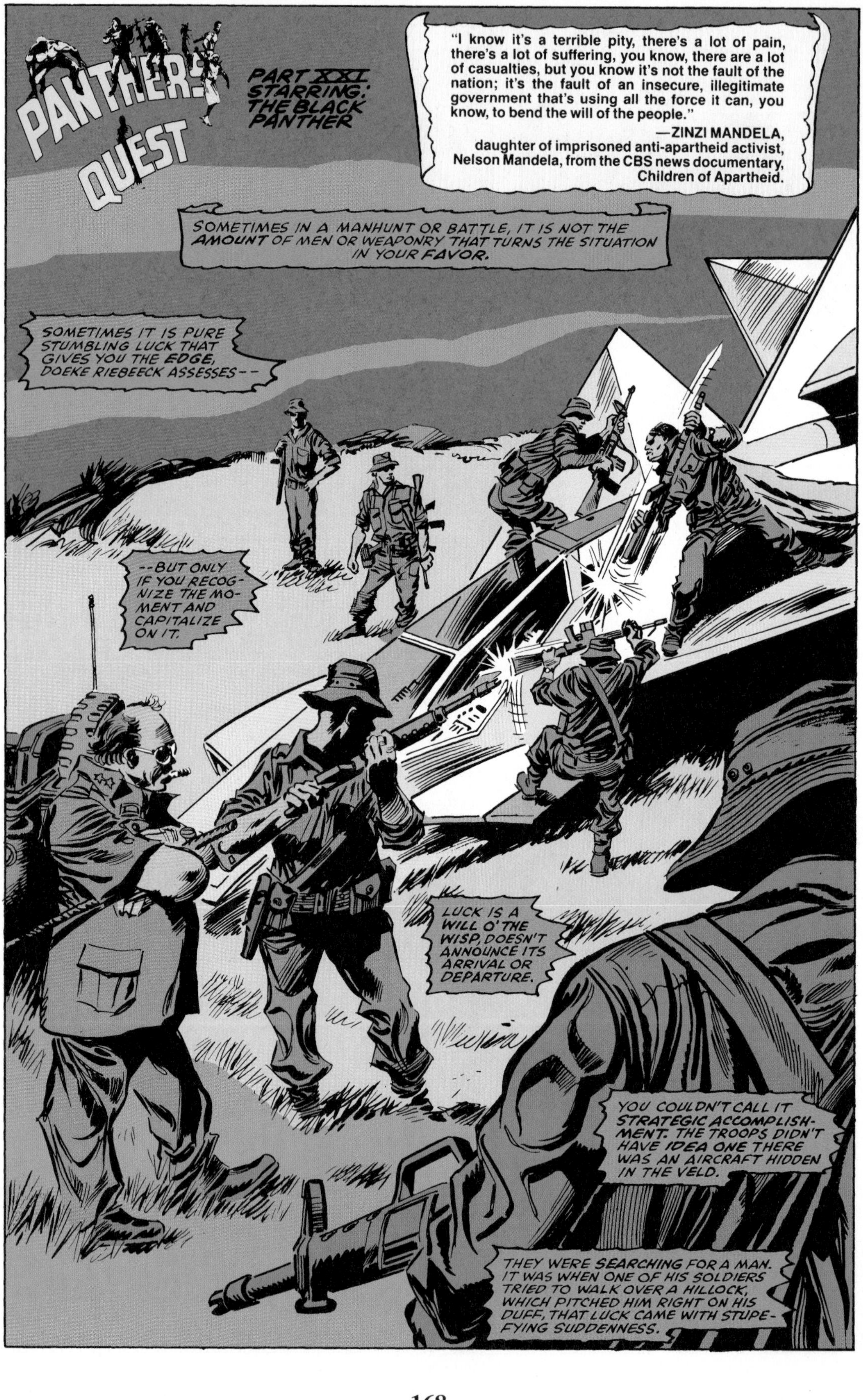
PANTHER'S QUEST
PART XXI STARRING: THE BLACK PANTHER
"I know it's a terrible pity, there's a lot of pain, there's a lot of suffering, you know, there are a lot of casualties, but you know it's not the fault of the nation; it's the fault of an insecure, illegitimate government that's using all the force it can, you know, to bend the will of the people."
—ZINZI MANDELA, daughter of imprisoned anti-apartheid activist, Nelson Mandela, from the CBS news documentary, Children of Apartheid.
SOMETIMES IN A MANHUNT OR BATTLE, IT IS NOT THE AMOUNT OF MEN OR WEAPONRY THAT TURNS THE SITUATION IN YOUR FAVOR.
SOMETIMES IT IS PURE STUMBLING LUCK THAT GIVES YOU THE EDGE, DOEKE RIEBEECK ASSESSES--
--BUT ONLY IF YOU RECOGNIZE THE MOMENT AND CAPITALIZE ON IT.
LUCK IS A WILL O' THE WISP, DOESN'T ANNOUNCE ITS ARRIVAL OR DEPARTURE.
YOU COULDN'T CALL IT STRATEGIC ACCOMPLISHMENT. THE TROOPS DIDN'T HAVE IDEA ONE THERE WAS AN AIRCRAFT HIDDEN IN THE VELD.
THEY WERE SEARCHING FOR A MAN. IT WAS WHEN ONE OF HIS SOLDIERS TRIED TO WALK OVER A HILLOCK, WHICH PITCHED HIM RIGHT ON HIS DUFF, THAT LUCK CAME WITH STUPEFYING SUDDENNESS.

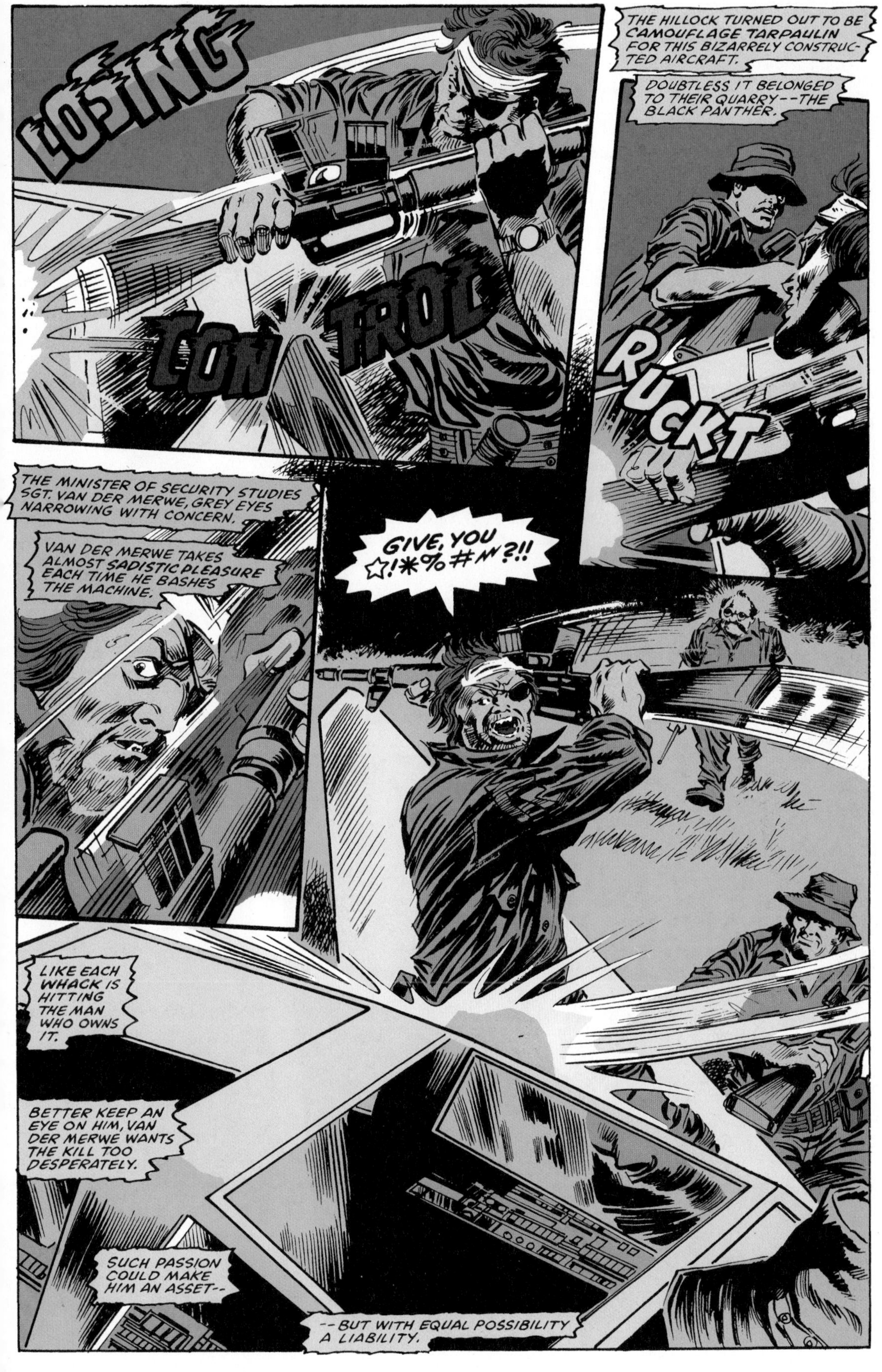
LOSING
CON TROL
THE HILLOCK TURNED OUT TO BE CAMOUFLAGE TARPAULIN FOR THIS BIZARRELY CONSTRUCTED AIRCRAFT.
DOUBTLESS IT BELONGED TO THEIR QUARRY--THE BLACK PANTHER.
RUCKT
THE MINISTER OF SECURITY STUDIES SGT. VAN DER MERWE, GREY EYES NARROWING WITH CONCERN.
VAN DER MERWE TAKES ALMOST SADISTIC PLEASURE EACH TIME HE BASHES THE MACHINE.
GIVE, YOU ☆!*%#≁?!!
LIKE EACH WHACK IS HITTING THE MAN WHO OWNS IT.
BETTER KEEP AN EYE ON HIM, VAN DER MERWE WANTS THE KILL TOO DESPERATELY.
SUCH PASSION COULD MAKE HIM AN ASSET--
--BUT WITH EQUAL POSSIBILITY A LIABILITY.

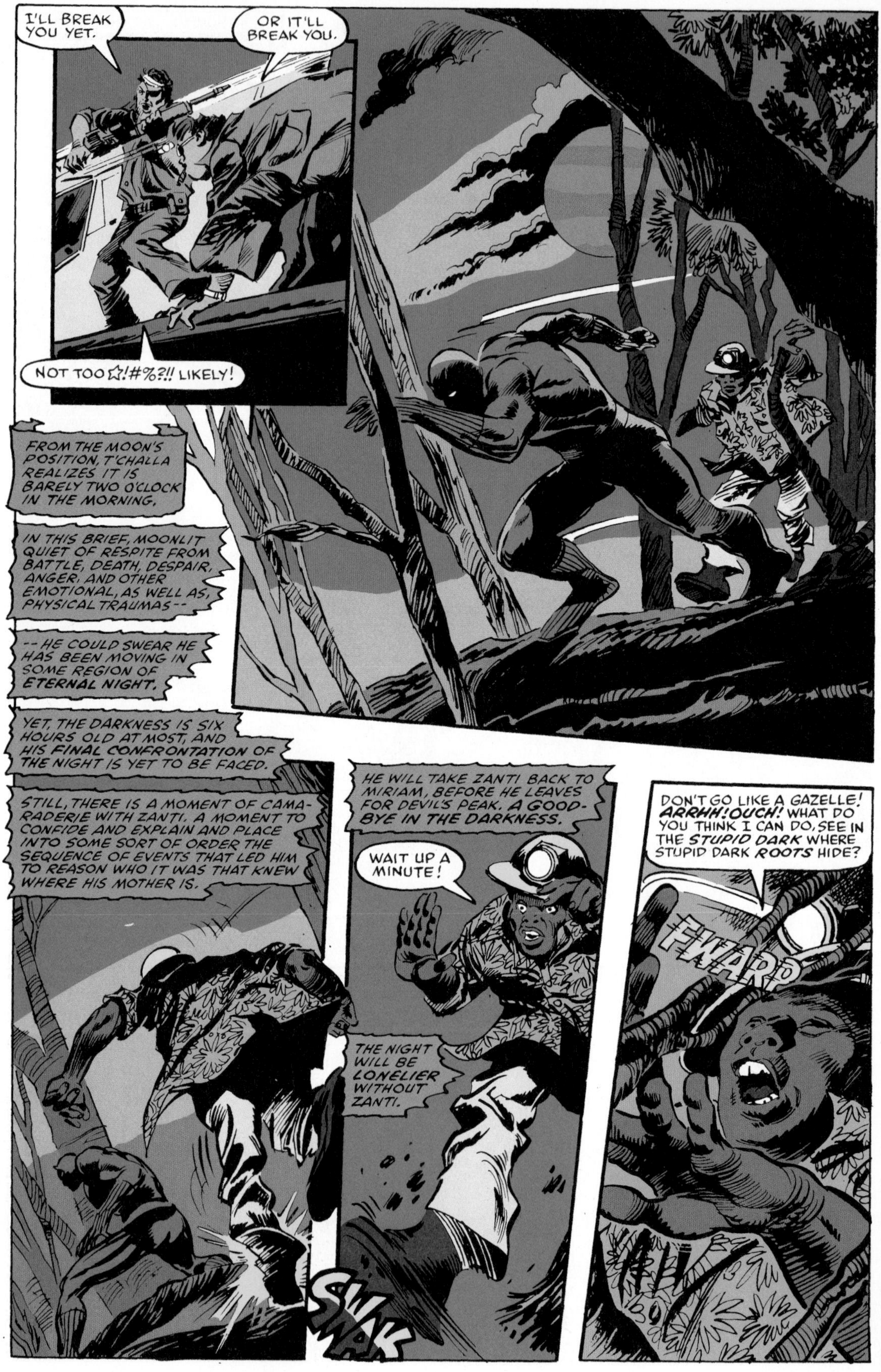

I'LL BREAK YOU YET.
OR IT'LL BREAK YOU.
NOT TOO ✩!#%?!! LIKELY!
FROM THE MOON'S POSITION, T'CHALLA REALIZES IT IS BARELY TWO O'CLOCK IN THE MORNING.
IN THIS BRIEF, MOONLIT QUIET OF RESPITE FROM BATTLE, DEATH, DESPAIR, ANGER, AND OTHER EMOTIONAL, AS WELL AS, PHYSICAL TRAUMAS--
--HE COULD SWEAR HE HAS BEEN MOVING IN SOME REGION OF ETERNAL NIGHT.
YET, THE DARKNESS IS SIX HOURS OLD AT MOST, AND HIS FINAL CONFRONTATION OF THE NIGHT IS YET TO BE FACED.
STILL, THERE IS A MOMENT OF CAMARADERIE WITH ZANTI. A MOMENT TO CONFIDE AND EXPLAIN AND PLACE INTO SOME SORT OF ORDER THE SEQUENCE OF EVENTS THAT LED HIM TO REASON WHO IT WAS THAT KNEW WHERE HIS MOTHER IS.
SWAK
HE WILL TAKE ZANTI BACK TO MIRIAM, BEFORE HE LEAVES FOR DEVIL'S PEAK. A GOOD-BYE IN THE DARKNESS.
WAIT UP A MINUTE!
THE NIGHT WILL BE LONELIER WITHOUT ZANTI.
DON'T GO LIKE A GAZELLE! ARRHH! OUCH! WHAT DO YOU THINK I CAN DO, SEE IN THE STUPID DARK WHERE STUPID DARK ROOTS HIDE?
FWARP

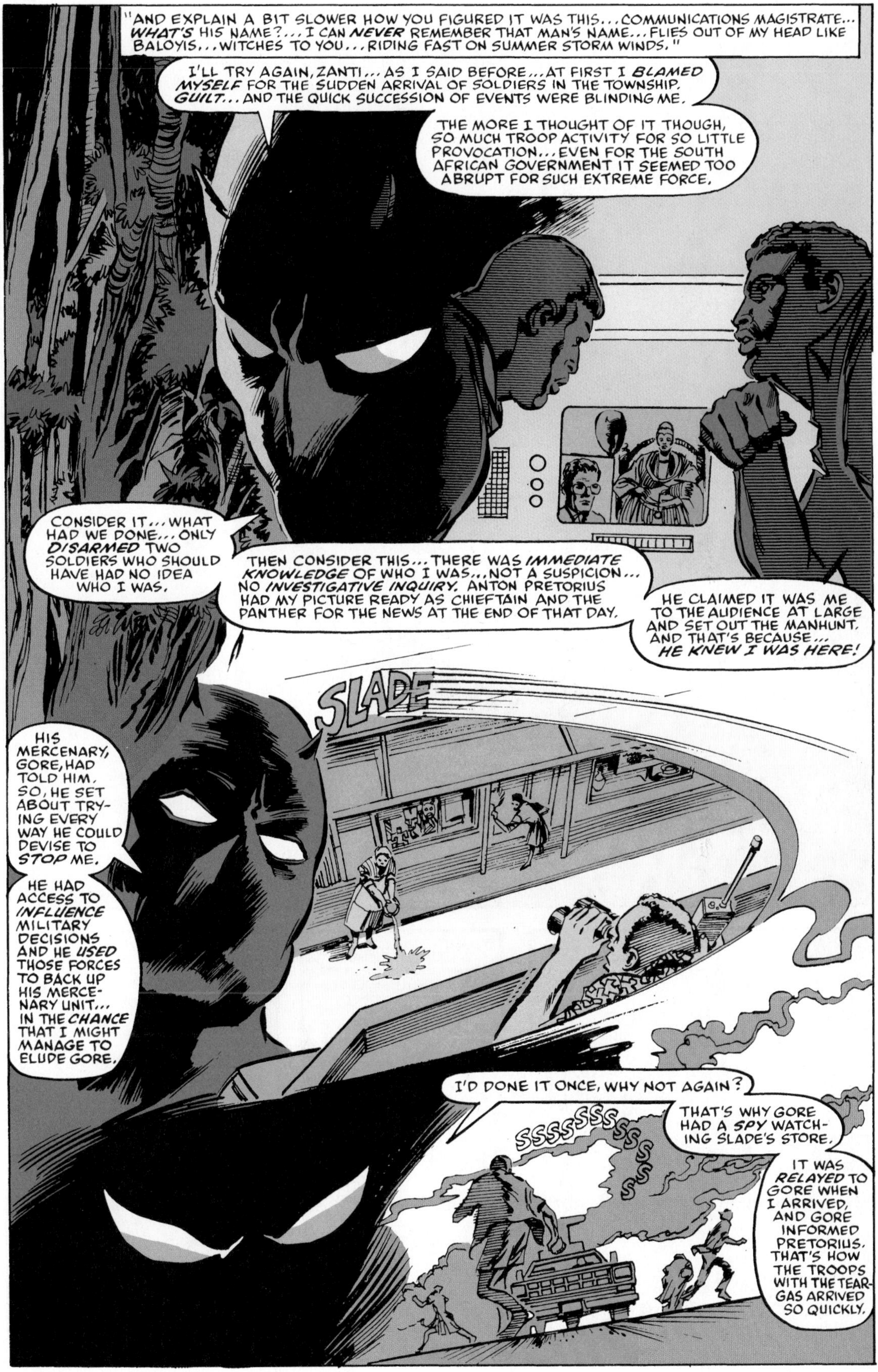
"AND EXPLAIN A BIT SLOWER HOW YOU FIGURED IT WAS THIS... COMMUNICATIONS MAGISTRATE... WHAT'S HIS NAME?... I CAN NEVER REMEMBER THAT MAN'S NAME... FLIES OUT OF MY HEAD LIKE BALOYIS... WITCHES TO YOU... RIDING FAST ON SUMMER STORM WINDS."
I'LL TRY AGAIN, ZANTI... AS I SAID BEFORE... AT FIRST I BLAMED MYSELF FOR THE SUDDEN ARRIVAL OF SOLDIERS IN THE TOWNSHIP. GUILT... AND THE QUICK SUCCESSION OF EVENTS WERE BLINDING ME.
THE MORE I THOUGHT OF IT THOUGH, SO MUCH TROOP ACTIVITY FOR SO LITTLE PROVOCATION... EVEN FOR THE SOUTH AFRICAN GOVERNMENT IT SEEMED TOO ABRUPT FOR SUCH EXTREME FORCE.
CONSIDER IT... WHAT HAD WE DONE... ONLY DISARMED TWO SOLDIERS WHO SHOULD HAVE HAD NO IDEA WHO I WAS.
THEN CONSIDER THIS... THERE WAS IMMEDIATE KNOWLEDGE OF WHO I WAS... NOT A SUSPICION... NO INVESTIGATIVE INQUIRY. ANTON PRETORIUS HAD MY PICTURE READY AS CHIEFTAIN AND THE PANTHER FOR THE NEWS AT THE END OF THAT DAY.
HE CLAIMED IT WAS ME TO THE AUDIENCE AT LARGE AND SET OUT THE MANHUNT. AND THAT'S BECAUSE... HE KNEW I WAS HERE!
SLADE
HIS MERCENARY, GORE, HAD TOLD HIM. SO, HE SET ABOUT TRYING EVERY WAY HE COULD DEVISE TO STOP ME.
HE HAD ACCESS TO INFLUENCE MILITARY DECISIONS AND HE USED THOSE FORCES TO BACK UP HIS MERCENARY UNIT... IN THE CHANCE THAT I MIGHT MANAGE TO ELUDE GORE.
I'D DONE IT ONCE, WHY NOT AGAIN?
THAT'S WHY GORE HAD A SPY WATCHING SLADE'S STORE.
SSSSSSSSSSSSS
IT WAS RELAYED TO GORE WHEN I ARRIVED, AND GORE INFORMED PRETORIUS. THAT'S HOW THE TROOPS WITH THE TEAR-GAS ARRIVED SO QUICKLY.

PRETORIUS'S NATURAL CAUTION WAS DYING TO DESPERATION.

BY NOW HE WAS *PRODDING* EVERYBODY...THE ARMY... HIS OWN PERSONAL SECURITY FORCES LED BY GORE.

WITH EACH *NEW INCIDENT* HE APPEARS TO HAVE BECOME MORE DETERMINED TO KEEP IT ALL *UNDER CONTROL* AND CURTAIL MY EFFORTS.

BUT HIS DESPERATION WAS MAKING HIM *CARELESS*. IN ONE OF HIS BROADCASTS, HE SAID SOMETHING HE SHOULD NOT HAVE READILY KNOWN...

...my father's name--

--T'Chaka.

AND OUTSIDE OF WAKANDA, WHO KNOWS MY FATHER'S NAME--

--BUT MY MOTHER.

WHHIP WHIP

ARE YOU OKAY?

YES, IF I DO NOT HAVE A CONCUSSION.

THIS...PREYTA... WHATEVER... CERTAINLY TRIED TO PERSUADE YOU TO GIVE UP.

ME, MYSELF...I WOULD PROBABLY HAVE SAID, "ENOUGH OF THIS" RIGHT AFTER THEY THREW ME IN BARBED WIRE--

--ALTHOUGH, IF I REALLY THINK ABOUT IT...I WOULD NOT HAVE BEEN ABLE TO GET *OUT* OF THE BARBED WIRE, SO EVERYTHING WOULD HAVE ENDED *RIGHT THEN.*

SNAP

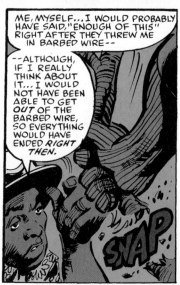

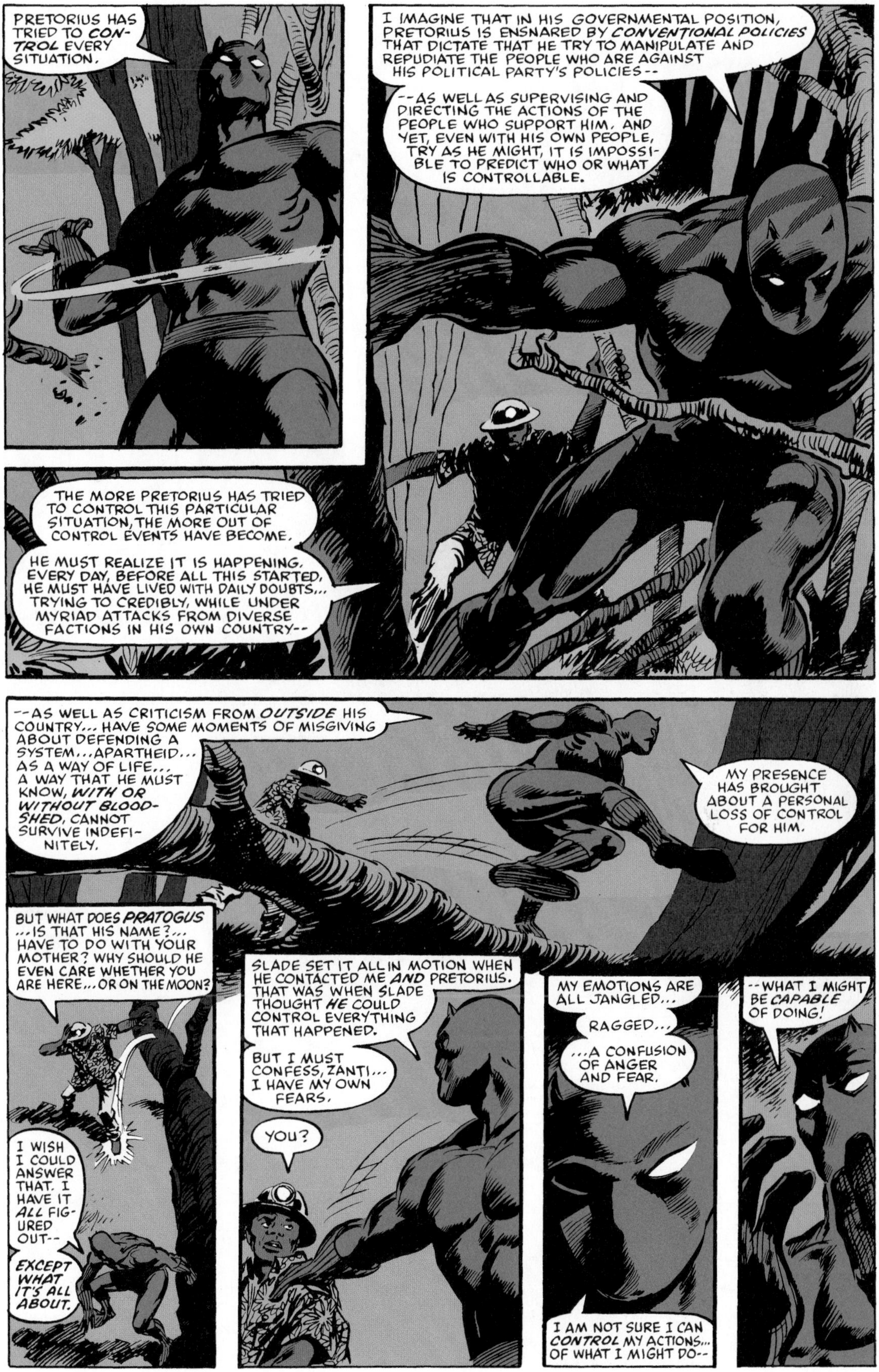

PRETORIUS HAS TRIED TO *CONTROL* EVERY SITUATION.
I IMAGINE THAT IN HIS GOVERNMENTAL POSITION, PRETORIUS IS ENSNARED BY *CONVENTIONAL POLICIES* THAT DICTATE THAT HE TRY TO MANIPULATE AND REPUDIATE THE PEOPLE WHO ARE AGAINST HIS POLITICAL PARTY'S POLICIES--
--AS WELL AS SUPERVISING AND DIRECTING THE ACTIONS OF THE PEOPLE WHO SUPPORT HIM. AND YET, EVEN WITH HIS OWN PEOPLE, TRY AS HE MIGHT, IT IS IMPOSSIBLE TO PREDICT WHO OR WHAT IS CONTROLLABLE.
THE MORE PRETORIUS HAS TRIED TO CONTROL THIS PARTICULAR SITUATION, THE MORE OUT OF CONTROL EVENTS HAVE BECOME.
HE MUST REALIZE IT IS HAPPENING. EVERY DAY, BEFORE ALL THIS STARTED, HE MUST HAVE LIVED WITH DAILY DOUBTS... TRYING TO CREDIBLY, WHILE UNDER MYRIAD ATTACKS FROM DIVERSE FACTIONS IN HIS OWN COUNTRY--
--AS WELL AS CRITICISM FROM *OUTSIDE* HIS COUNTRY... HAVE SOME MOMENTS OF MISGIVING ABOUT DEFENDING A SYSTEM...APARTHEID... AS A WAY OF LIFE... A WAY THAT HE MUST KNOW, *WITH OR WITHOUT BLOODSHED*, CANNOT SURVIVE INDEFINITELY.
MY PRESENCE HAS BROUGHT ABOUT A PERSONAL LOSS OF CONTROL FOR HIM.
BUT WHAT DOES *PRATOGUS* ...IS THAT HIS NAME?... HAVE TO DO WITH YOUR MOTHER? WHY SHOULD HE EVEN CARE WHETHER YOU ARE HERE...OR ON THE MOON?
I WISH I COULD ANSWER THAT. I HAVE IT *ALL* FIGURED OUT--
EXCEPT WHAT IT'S ALL ABOUT.
SLADE SET IT ALL IN MOTION WHEN HE CONTACTED ME *AND* PRETORIUS. THAT WAS WHEN SLADE THOUGHT *HE* COULD CONTROL EVERYTHING THAT HAPPENED.
BUT I MUST CONFESS, ZANTI... I HAVE MY OWN FEARS.
YOU?
MY EMOTIONS ARE ALL JANGLED...
RAGGED...
...A CONFUSION OF ANGER AND FEAR.
I AM NOT SURE I CAN *CONTROL* MY ACTIONS... OF WHAT I MIGHT DO--
--WHAT I MIGHT BE *CAPABLE* OF DOING!

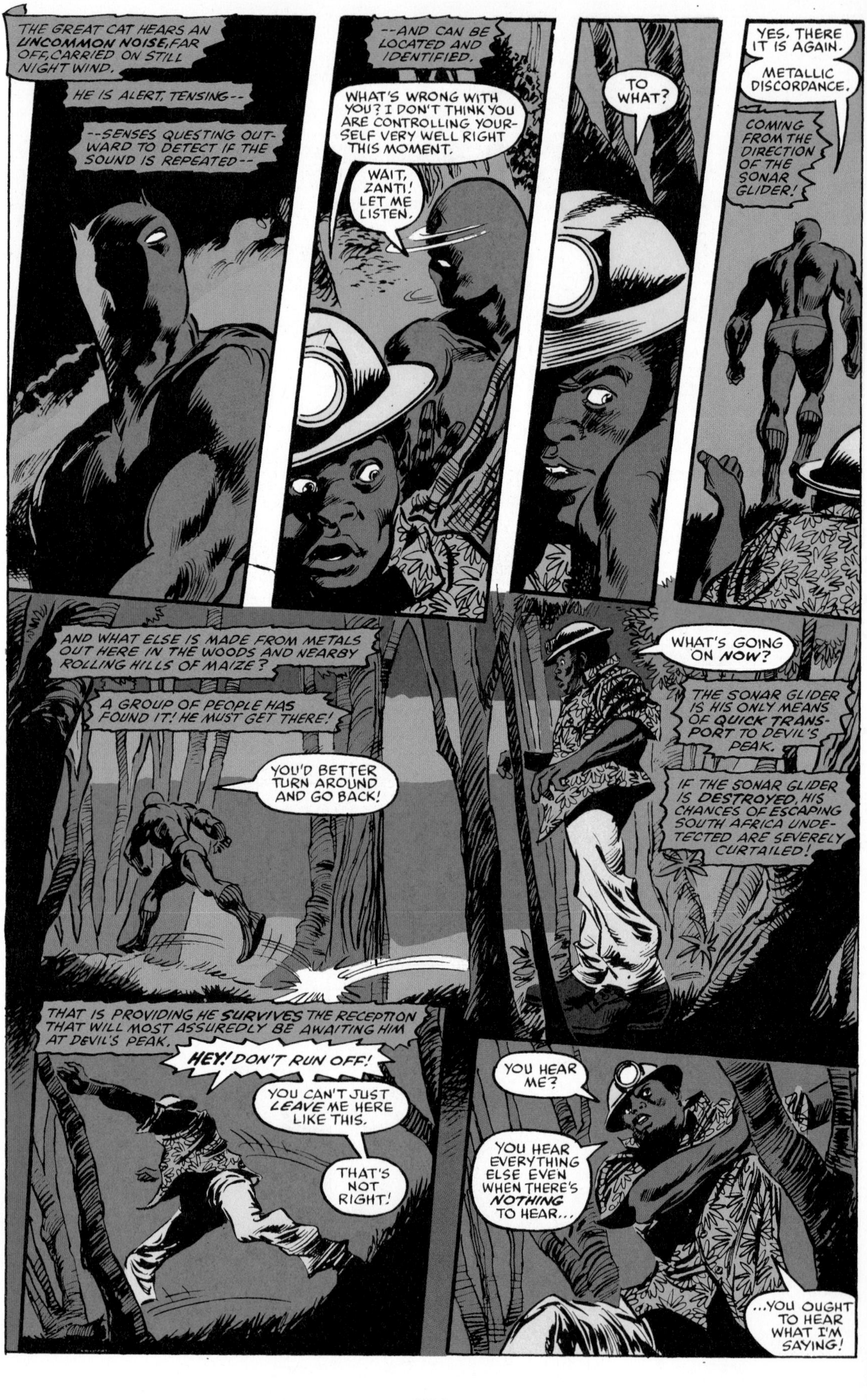
THE GREAT CAT HEARS AN UNCOMMON NOISE, FAR OFF, CARRIED ON STILL NIGHT WIND.
HE IS ALERT, TENSING--
--SENSES QUESTING OUTWARD TO DETECT IF THE SOUND IS REPEATED--
--AND CAN BE LOCATED AND IDENTIFIED.
WHAT'S WRONG WITH YOU? I DON'T THINK YOU ARE CONTROLLING YOURSELF VERY WELL RIGHT THIS MOMENT.
WAIT, ZANTI! LET ME LISTEN.
TO WHAT?
YES, THERE IT IS AGAIN.
METALLIC DISCORDANCE.
COMING FROM THE DIRECTION OF THE SONAR GLIDER!
AND WHAT ELSE IS MADE FROM METALS OUT HERE IN THE WOODS AND NEARBY ROLLING HILLS OF MAIZE?
A GROUP OF PEOPLE HAS FOUND IT! HE MUST GET THERE!
YOU'D BETTER TURN AROUND AND GO BACK!
WHAT'S GOING ON NOW?
THE SONAR GLIDER IS HIS ONLY MEANS OF QUICK TRANSPORT TO DEVIL'S PEAK.
IF THE SONAR GLIDER IS DESTROYED, HIS CHANCES OF ESCAPING SOUTH AFRICA UNDETECTED ARE SEVERELY CURTAILED!
THAT IS PROVIDING HE SURVIVES THE RECEPTION THAT WILL MOST ASSUREDLY BE AWAITING HIM AT DEVIL'S PEAK.
HEY! DON'T RUN OFF!
YOU CAN'T JUST LEAVE ME HERE LIKE THIS.
THAT'S NOT RIGHT!
YOU HEAR ME?
YOU HEAR EVERYTHING ELSE EVEN WHEN THERE'S NOTHING TO HEAR...
...YOU OUGHT TO HEAR WHAT I'M SAYING!

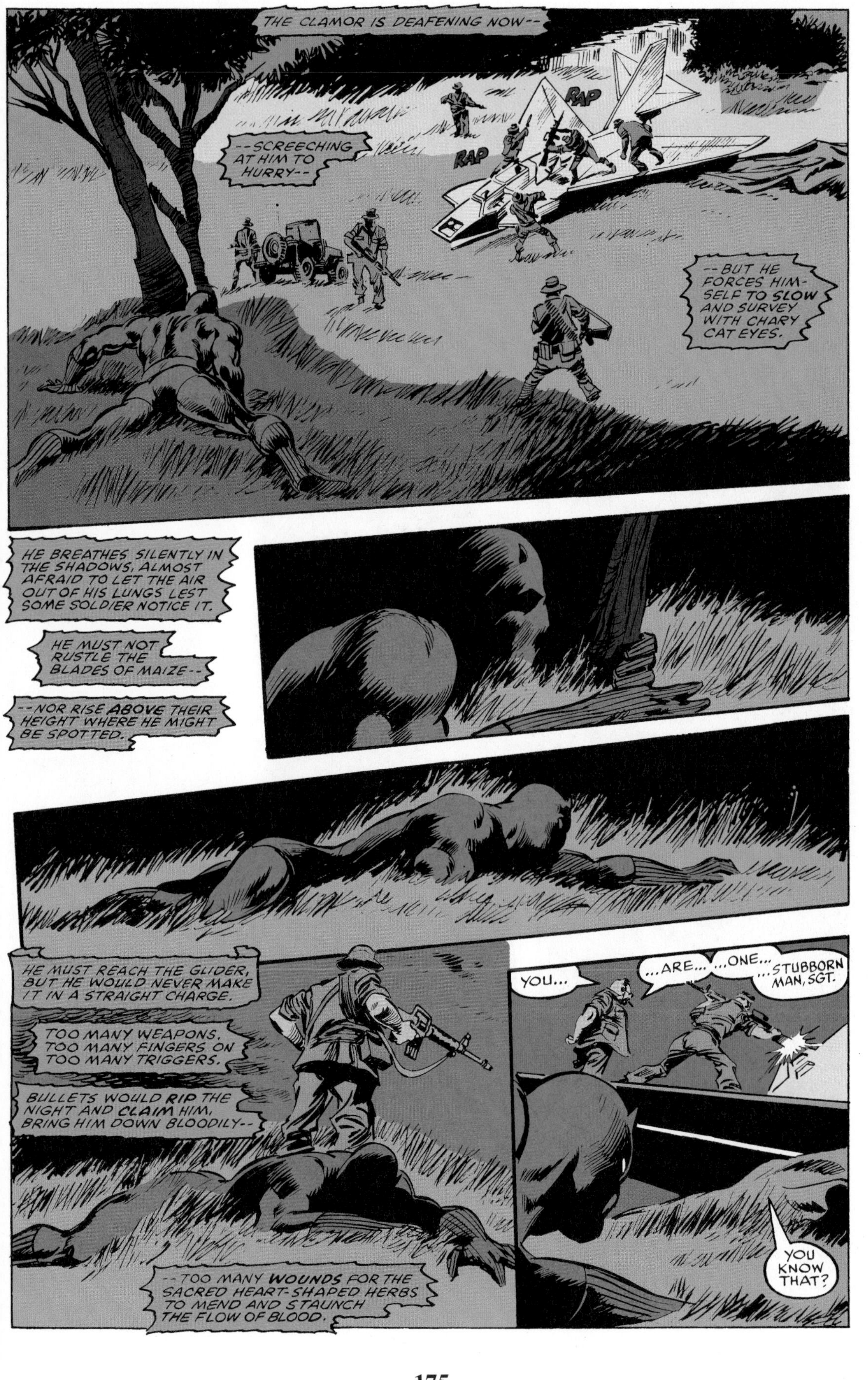
THE CLAMOR IS DEAFENING NOW--
RAP
--SCREECHING AT HIM TO HURRY--
RAP
--BUT HE FORCES HIMSELF TO SLOW AND SURVEY WITH CHARY CAT EYES.
HE BREATHES SILENTLY IN THE SHADOWS, ALMOST AFRAID TO LET THE AIR OUT OF HIS LUNGS LEST SOME SOLDIER NOTICE IT.
HE MUST NOT RUSTLE THE BLADES OF MAIZE--
--NOR RISE ABOVE THEIR HEIGHT WHERE HE MIGHT BE SPOTTED.
HE MUST REACH THE GLIDER, BUT HE WOULD NEVER MAKE IT IN A STRAIGHT CHARGE.
TOO MANY WEAPONS. TOO MANY FINGERS ON TOO MANY TRIGGERS.
BULLETS WOULD RIP THE NIGHT AND CLAIM HIM, BRING HIM DOWN BLOODILY--
--TOO MANY WOUNDS FOR THE SACRED HEART-SHAPED HERBS TO MEND AND STAUNCH THE FLOW OF BLOOD.
YOU...
...ARE... ...ONE... ...STUBBORN MAN, SGT.
YOU KNOW THAT?

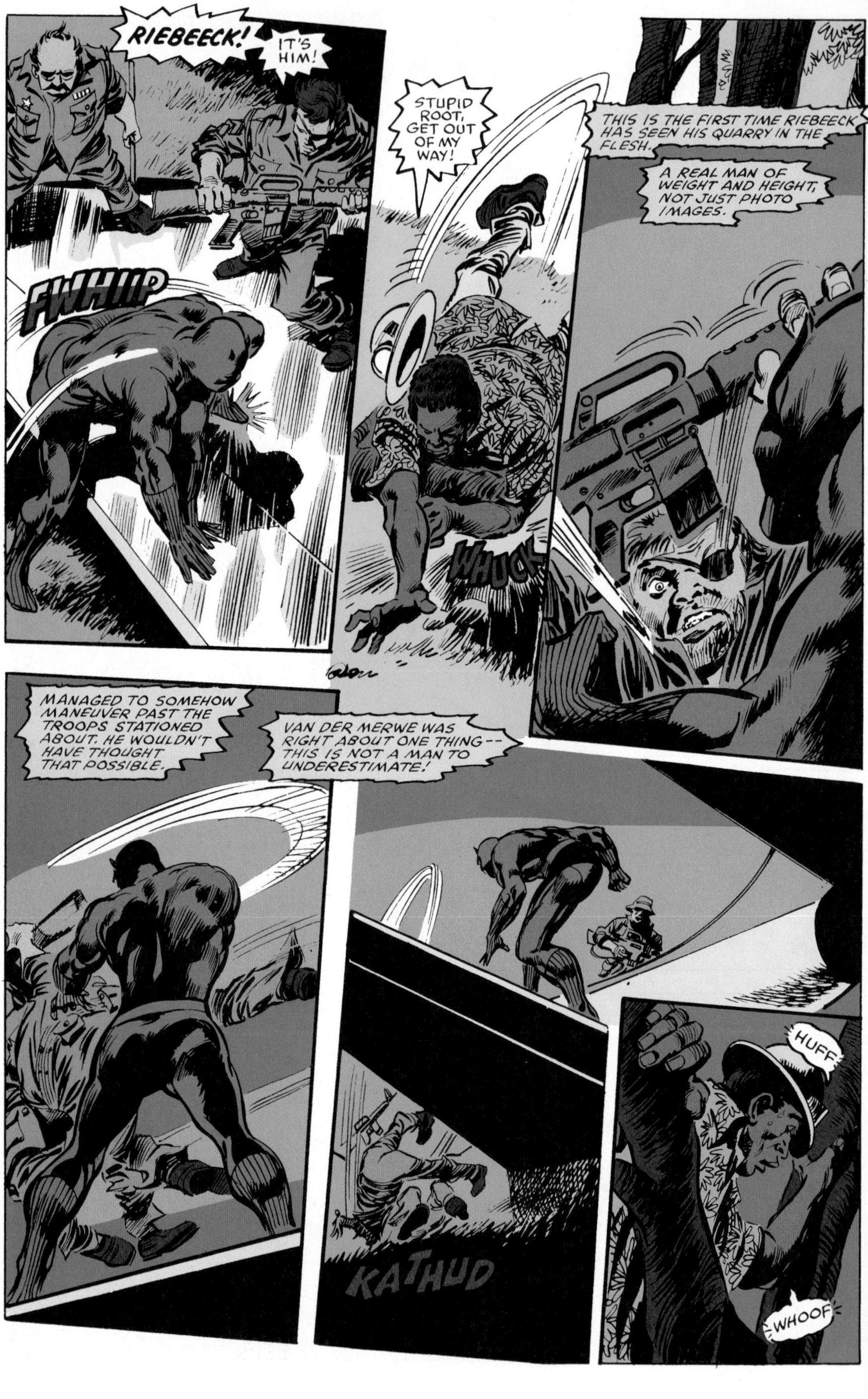

RIEBEECK!
IT'S HIM!
FWHUP
STUPID ROOT, GET OUT OF MY WAY!
WHUCK
THIS IS THE FIRST TIME RIEBEECK HAS SEEN HIS QUARRY IN THE FLESH.
A REAL MAN OF WEIGHT AND HEIGHT, NOT JUST PHOTO IMAGES.
MANAGED TO SOMEHOW MANEUVER PAST THE TROOPS STATIONED ABOUT. HE WOULDN'T HAVE THOUGHT THAT POSSIBLE.
VAN DER MERWE WAS RIGHT ABOUT ONE THING-- THIS IS NOT A MAN TO UNDERESTIMATE!
KATHUD
HUFF
WHOOF

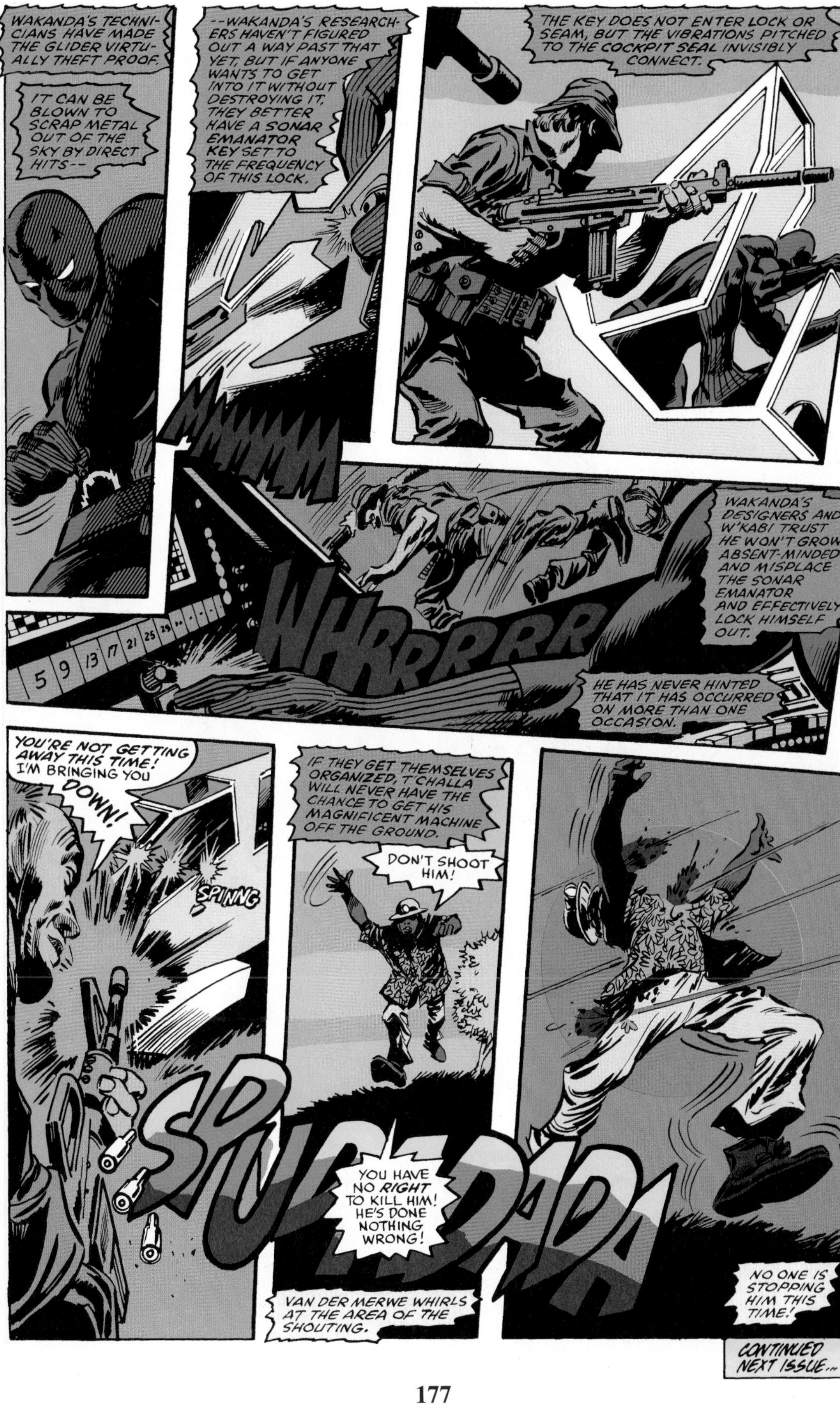
WAKANDA'S TECHNICIANS HAVE MADE THE GLIDER VIRTUALLY THEFT PROOF.
IT CAN BE BLOWN TO SCRAP METAL OUT OF THE SKY BY DIRECT HITS--
--WAKANDA'S RESEARCHERS HAVEN'T FIGURED OUT A WAY PAST THAT YET, BUT IF ANYONE WANTS TO GET INTO IT WITHOUT DESTROYING IT, THEY BETTER HAVE A SONAR EMANATOR KEY SET TO THE FREQUENCY OF THIS LOCK.
THE KEY DOES NOT ENTER LOCK OR SEAM, BUT THE VIBRATIONS PITCHED TO THE COCKPIT SEAL INVISIBLY CONNECT.
MMMMMM
WHRRRRR
5 9 13 17 21 25 29
WAKANDA'S DESIGNERS AND W'KABI TRUST HE WON'T GROW ABSENT-MINDED AND MISPLACE THE SONAR EMANATOR AND EFFECTIVELY LOCK HIMSELF OUT.
HE HAS NEVER HINTED THAT IT HAS OCCURRED ON MORE THAN ONE OCCASION.
YOU'RE NOT GETTING AWAY THIS TIME! I'M BRINGING YOU DOWN!
SPINNG
IF THEY GET THEMSELVES ORGANIZED, T'CHALLA WILL NEVER HAVE THE CHANCE TO GET HIS MAGNIFICENT MACHINE OFF THE GROUND.
DON'T SHOOT HIM!
SPUDDADA
YOU HAVE NO RIGHT TO KILL HIM! HE'S DONE NOTHING WRONG!
VAN DER MERWE WHIRLS AT THE AREA OF THE SHOUTING.
NO ONE IS STOPPING HIM THIS TIME!
CONTINUED NEXT ISSUE...

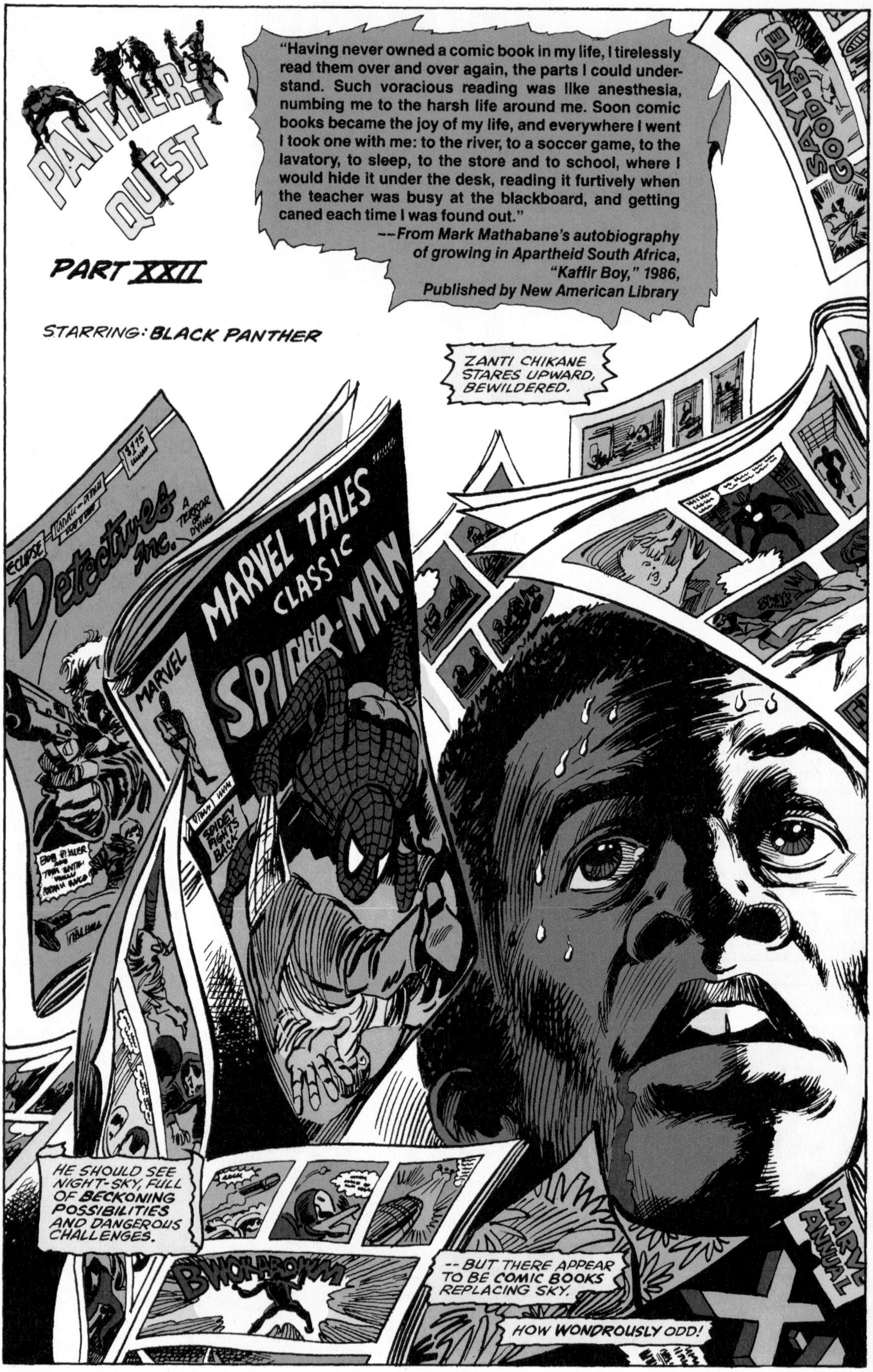
PANTHER'S QUEST
PART XXII
"Having never owned a comic book in my life, I tirelessly read them over and over again, the parts I could understand. Such voracious reading was like anesthesia, numbing me to the harsh life around me. Soon comic books became the joy of my life, and everywhere I went I took one with me: to the river, to a soccer game, to the lavatory, to sleep, to the store and to school, where I would hide it under the desk, reading it furtively when the teacher was busy at the blackboard, and getting caned each time I was found out."
--From Mark Mathabane's autobiography of growing in Apartheid South Africa, "Kaffir Boy," 1986, Published by New American Library
STARRING: BLACK PANTHER
ZANTI CHIKANE STARES UPWARD, BEWILDERED.
MARVEL TALES CLASSIC SPIDER-MAN
SPIDEY FIGHTS BACK
ECLIPSE Detectives Inc.
A TERROR OF DYING
GOOD-BYE
HE SHOULD SEE NIGHT-SKY, FULL OF BECKONING POSSIBILITIES AND DANGEROUS CHALLENGES.
-- BUT THERE APPEAR TO BE COMIC BOOKS REPLACING SKY.
HOW WONDROUSLY ODD!
MARVEL ANNUAL

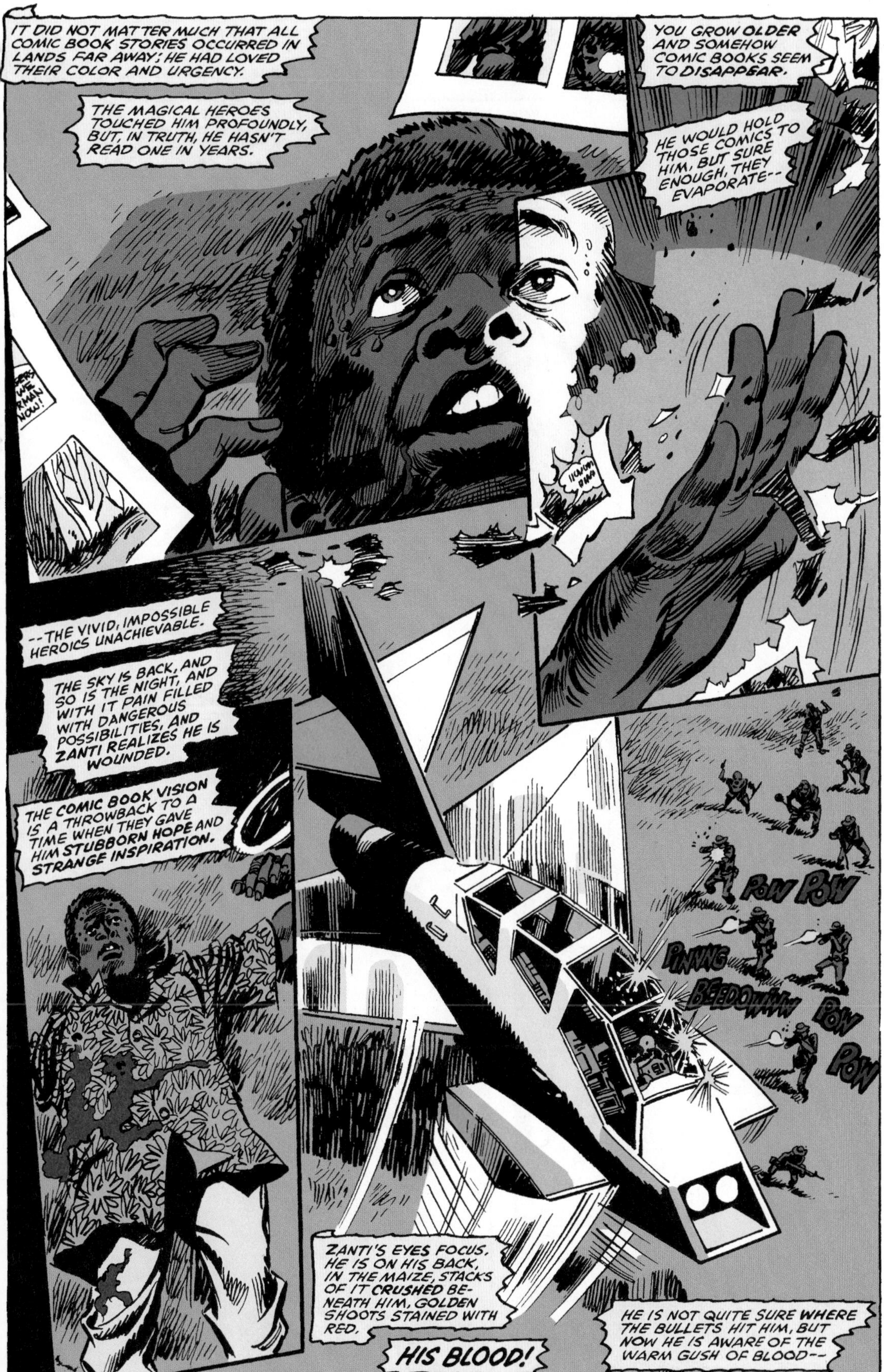
IT DID NOT MATTER MUCH THAT ALL COMIC BOOK STORIES OCCURRED IN LANDS FAR AWAY; HE HAD LOVED THEIR COLOR AND URGENCY.
THE MAGICAL HEROES TOUCHED HIM PROFOUNDLY, BUT, IN TRUTH, HE HASN'T READ ONE IN YEARS.
YOU GROW OLDER AND SOMEHOW COMIC BOOKS SEEM TO DISAPPEAR.
HE WOULD HOLD THOSE COMICS TO HIM, BUT SURE ENOUGH, THEY EVAPORATE--
--THE VIVID, IMPOSSIBLE HEROICS UNACHIEVABLE.
THE SKY IS BACK, AND SO IS THE NIGHT, AND WITH IT PAIN FILLED WITH DANGEROUS POSSIBILITIES, AND ZANTI REALIZES HE IS WOUNDED.
THE COMIC BOOK VISION IS A THROWBACK TO A TIME WHEN THEY GAVE HIM STUBBORN HOPE AND STRANGE INSPIRATION.
POW POW
PINNNG
BEEDOWWW
POW
POW
ZANTI'S EYES FOCUS. HE IS ON HIS BACK, IN THE MAIZE, STACKS OF IT CRUSHED BENEATH HIM, GOLDEN SHOOTS STAINED WITH RED.
HIS BLOOD!
HE IS NOT QUITE SURE WHERE THE BULLETS HIT HIM, BUT NOW HE IS AWARE OF THE WARM GUSH OF BLOOD--

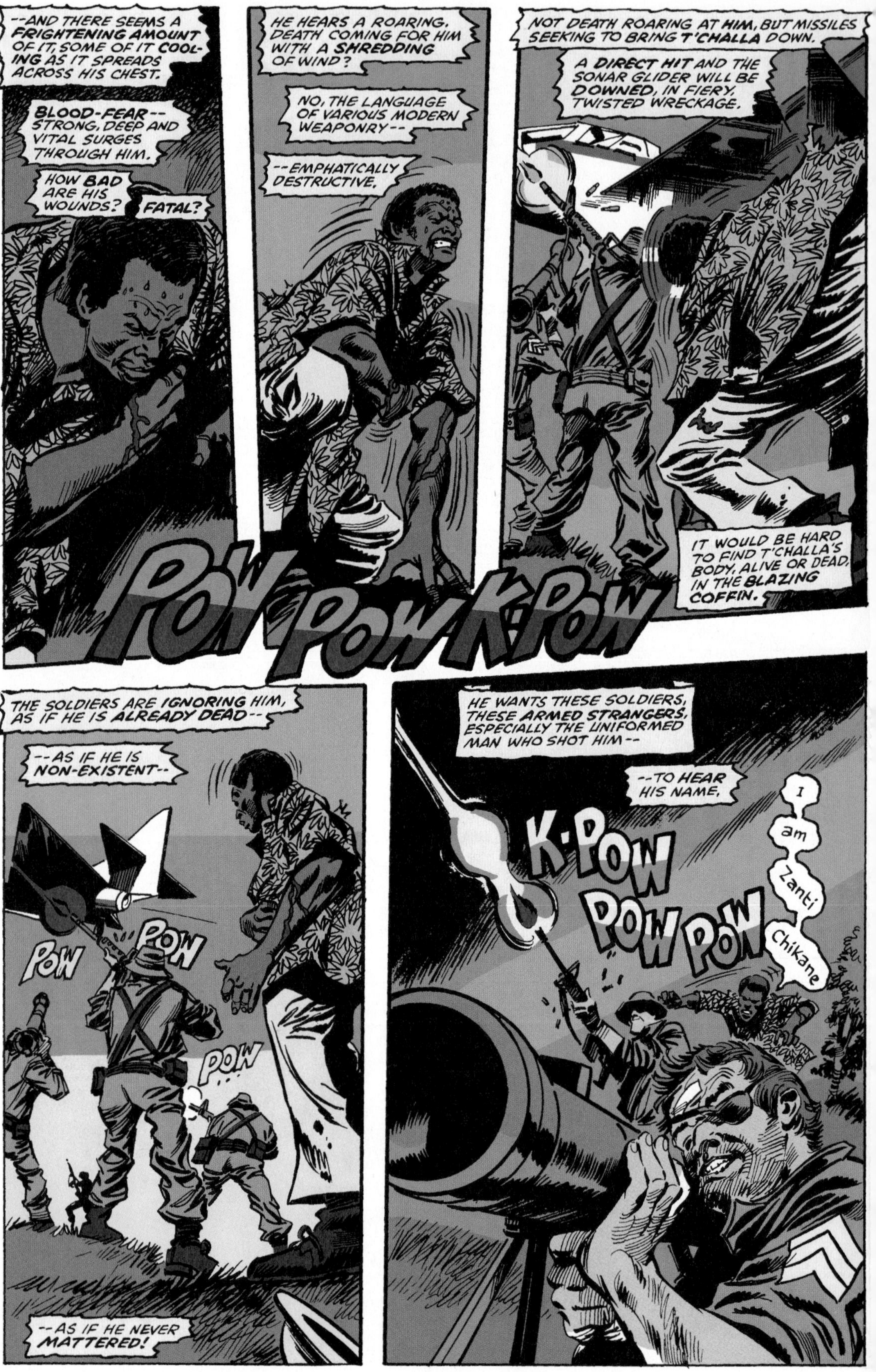
--AND THERE SEEMS A FRIGHTENING AMOUNT OF IT, SOME OF IT COOLING AS IT SPREADS ACROSS HIS CHEST.
BLOOD-FEAR--STRONG, DEEP AND VITAL SURGES THROUGH HIM.
HOW BAD ARE HIS WOUNDS?
FATAL?
HE HEARS A ROARING. DEATH COMING FOR HIM WITH A SHREDDING OF WIND?
NO, THE LANGUAGE OF VARIOUS MODERN WEAPONRY--
--EMPHATICALLY DESTRUCTIVE.
NOT DEATH ROARING AT HIM, BUT MISSILES SEEKING TO BRING T'CHALLA DOWN.
A DIRECT HIT AND THE SONAR GLIDER WILL BE DOWNED, IN FIERY, TWISTED WRECKAGE.
IT WOULD BE HARD TO FIND T'CHALLA'S BODY, ALIVE OR DEAD, IN THE BLAZING COFFIN.
POW POW K-POW
THE SOLDIERS ARE IGNORING HIM, AS IF HE IS ALREADY DEAD--
--AS IF HE IS NON-EXISTENT--
POW
POW
POW
--AS IF HE NEVER MATTERED!
HE WANTS THESE SOLDIERS, THESE ARMED STRANGERS, ESPECIALLY THE UNIFORMED MAN WHO SHOT HIM--
--TO HEAR HIS NAME.
K-POW
POW POW
I
am
Zanti
Chikane

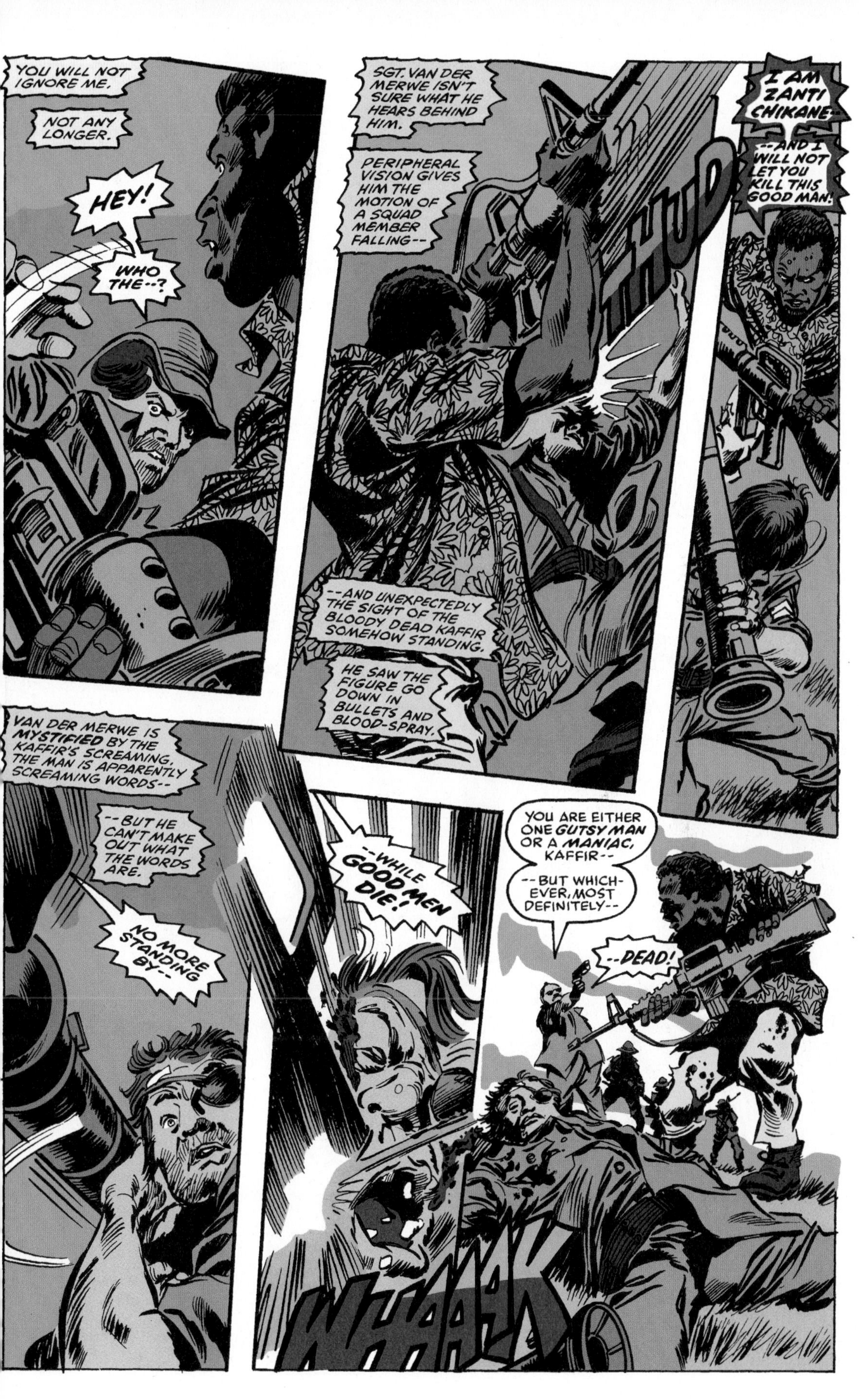

YOU WILL NOT IGNORE ME.
NOT ANY LONGER.
HEY!
WHO THE--?
SGT. VAN DER MERWE ISN'T SURE WHAT HE HEARS BEHIND HIM.
PERIPHERAL VISION GIVES HIM THE MOTION OF A SQUAD MEMBER FALLING--
THUD
--AND UNEXPECTEDLY THE SIGHT OF THE BLOODY DEAD KAFFIR SOMEHOW STANDING.
HE SAW THE FIGURE GO DOWN IN BULLETS AND BLOOD-SPRAY.
I AM ZANTI CHIKANE--
--AND I WILL NOT LET YOU KILL THIS GOOD MAN!
VAN DER MERWE IS MYSTIFIED BY THE KAFFIR'S SCREAMING. THE MAN IS APPARENTLY SCREAMING WORDS--
--BUT HE CAN'T MAKE OUT WHAT THE WORDS ARE.
NO MORE STANDING BY--
--WHILE GOOD MEN DIE!
YOU ARE EITHER ONE GUTSY MAN OR A MANIAC, KAFFIR--
--BUT WHICH-EVER, MOST DEFINITELY--
--DEAD!
WHAAA

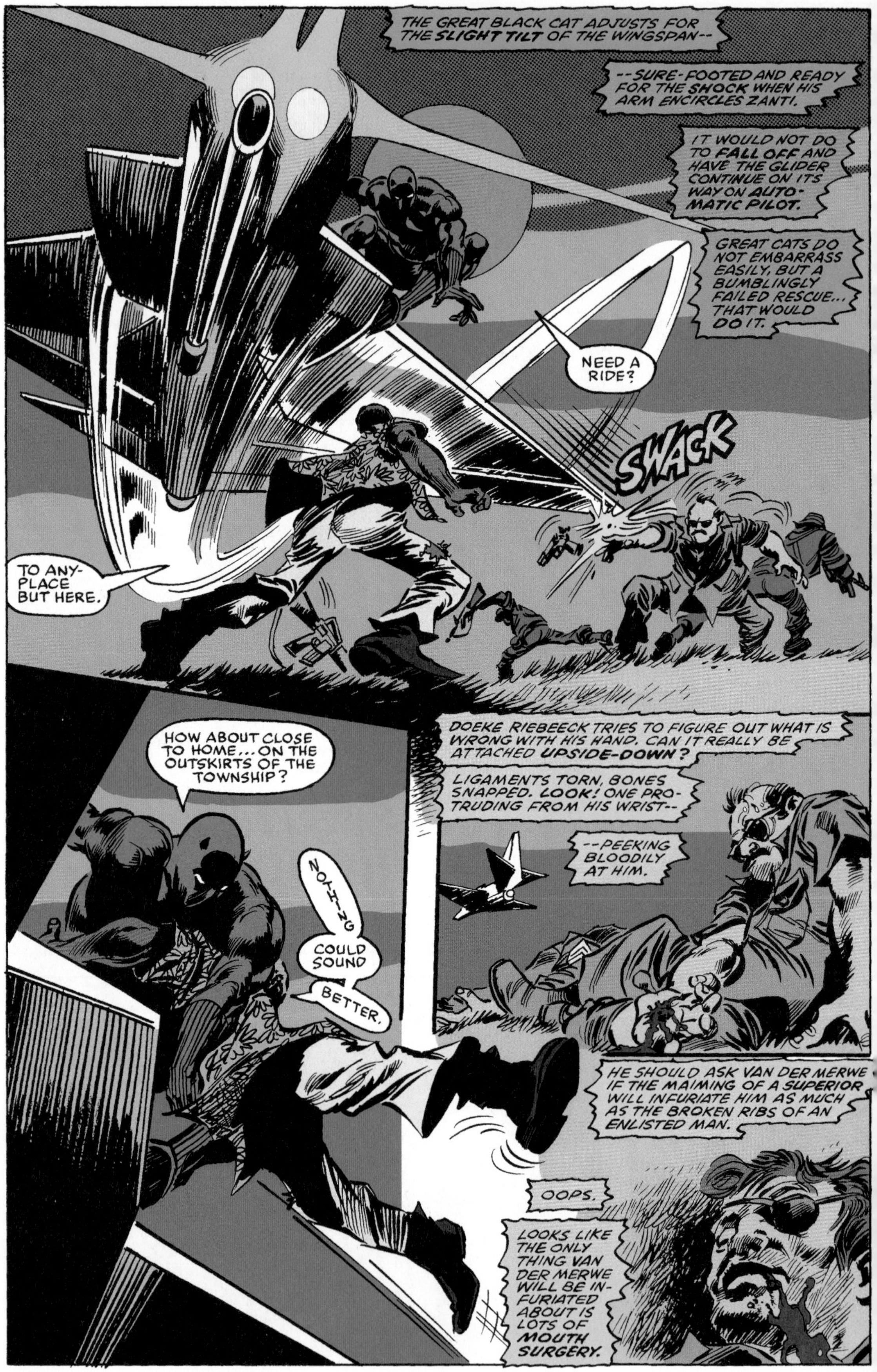
THE GREAT BLACK CAT ADJUSTS FOR THE SLIGHT TILT OF THE WINGSPAN--
--SURE-FOOTED AND READY FOR THE SHOCK WHEN HIS ARM ENCIRCLES ZANTI.
IT WOULD NOT DO TO FALL OFF AND HAVE THE GLIDER CONTINUE ON ITS WAY ON AUTOMATIC PILOT.
GREAT CATS DO NOT EMBARRASS EASILY, BUT A BUMBLINGLY FAILED RESCUE... THAT WOULD DO IT.
NEED A RIDE?
SWACK
TO ANYPLACE BUT HERE.
HOW ABOUT CLOSE TO HOME... ON THE OUTSKIRTS OF THE TOWNSHIP?
NOTHING COULD SOUND BETTER.
DOEKE RIEBEECK TRIES TO FIGURE OUT WHAT IS WRONG WITH HIS HAND. CAN IT REALLY BE ATTACHED UPSIDE-DOWN?
LIGAMENTS TORN, BONES SNAPPED. LOOK! ONE PROTRUDING FROM HIS WRIST--
--PEEKING BLOODILY AT HIM.
HE SHOULD ASK VAN DER MERWE IF THE MAIMING OF A SUPERIOR WILL INFURIATE HIM AS MUCH AS THE BROKEN RIBS OF AN ENLISTED MAN.
OOPS.
LOOKS LIKE THE ONLY THING VAN DER MERWE WILL BE INFURIATED ABOUT IS LOTS OF MOUTH SURGERY.

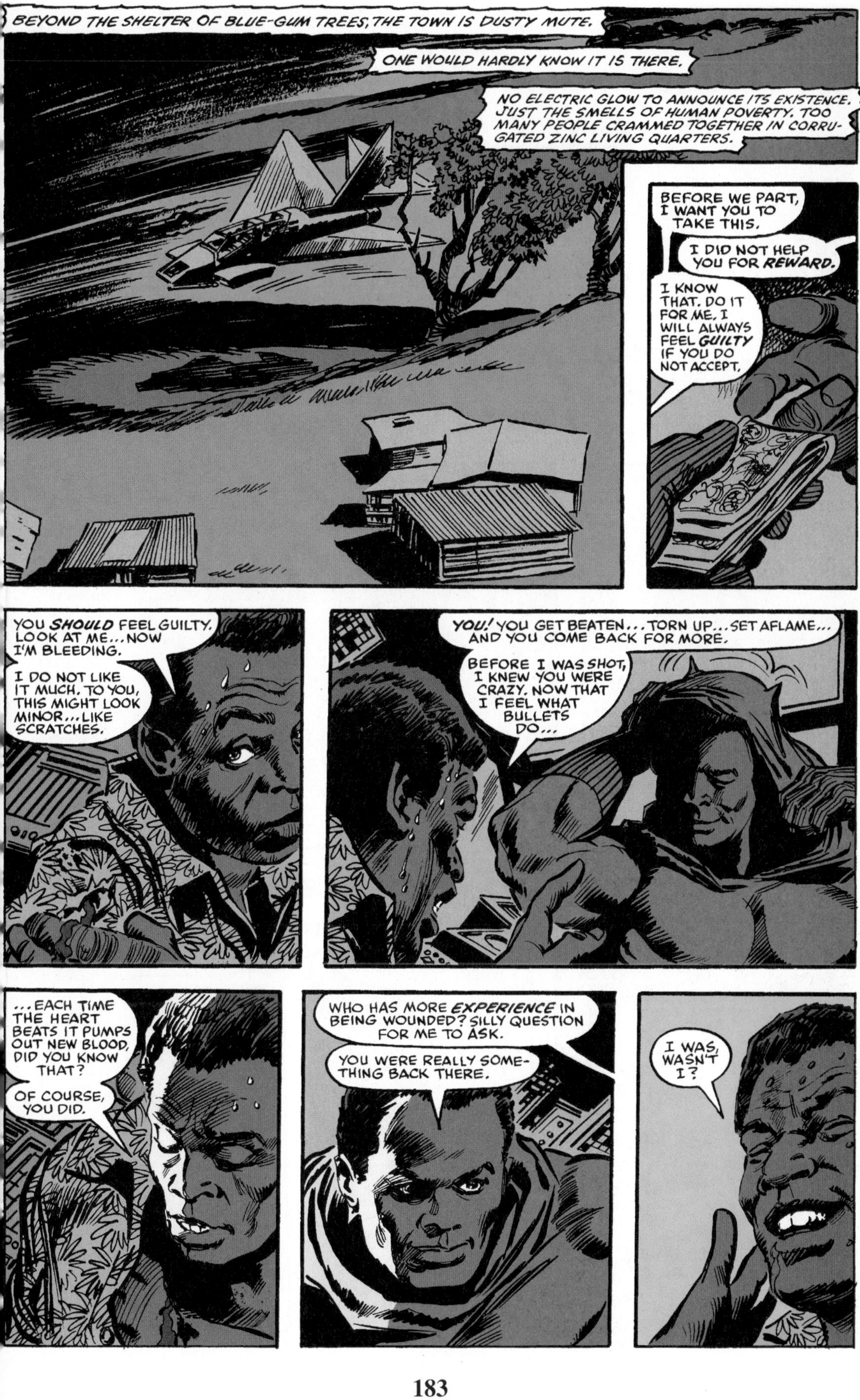
BEYOND THE SHELTER OF BLUE-GUM TREES, THE TOWN IS DUSTY MUTE.
ONE WOULD HARDLY KNOW IT IS THERE.
NO ELECTRIC GLOW TO ANNOUNCE ITS EXISTENCE. JUST THE SMELLS OF HUMAN POVERTY. TOO MANY PEOPLE CRAMMED TOGETHER IN CORRUGATED ZINC LIVING QUARTERS.
BEFORE WE PART, I WANT YOU TO TAKE THIS.
I DID NOT HELP YOU FOR REWARD.
I KNOW THAT. DO IT FOR ME. I WILL ALWAYS FEEL GUILTY IF YOU DO NOT ACCEPT.
YOU SHOULD FEEL GUILTY. LOOK AT ME... NOW I'M BLEEDING.
I DO NOT LIKE IT MUCH. TO YOU, THIS MIGHT LOOK MINOR... LIKE SCRATCHES.
YOU! YOU GET BEATEN... TORN UP... SET AFLAME... AND YOU COME BACK FOR MORE.
BEFORE I WAS SHOT, I KNEW YOU WERE CRAZY. NOW THAT I FEEL WHAT BULLETS DO...
...EACH TIME THE HEART BEATS IT PUMPS OUT NEW BLOOD, DID YOU KNOW THAT?
OF COURSE, YOU DID.
WHO HAS MORE EXPERIENCE IN BEING WOUNDED? SILLY QUESTION FOR ME TO ASK.
YOU WERE REALLY SOMETHING BACK THERE.
I WAS, WASN'T I?

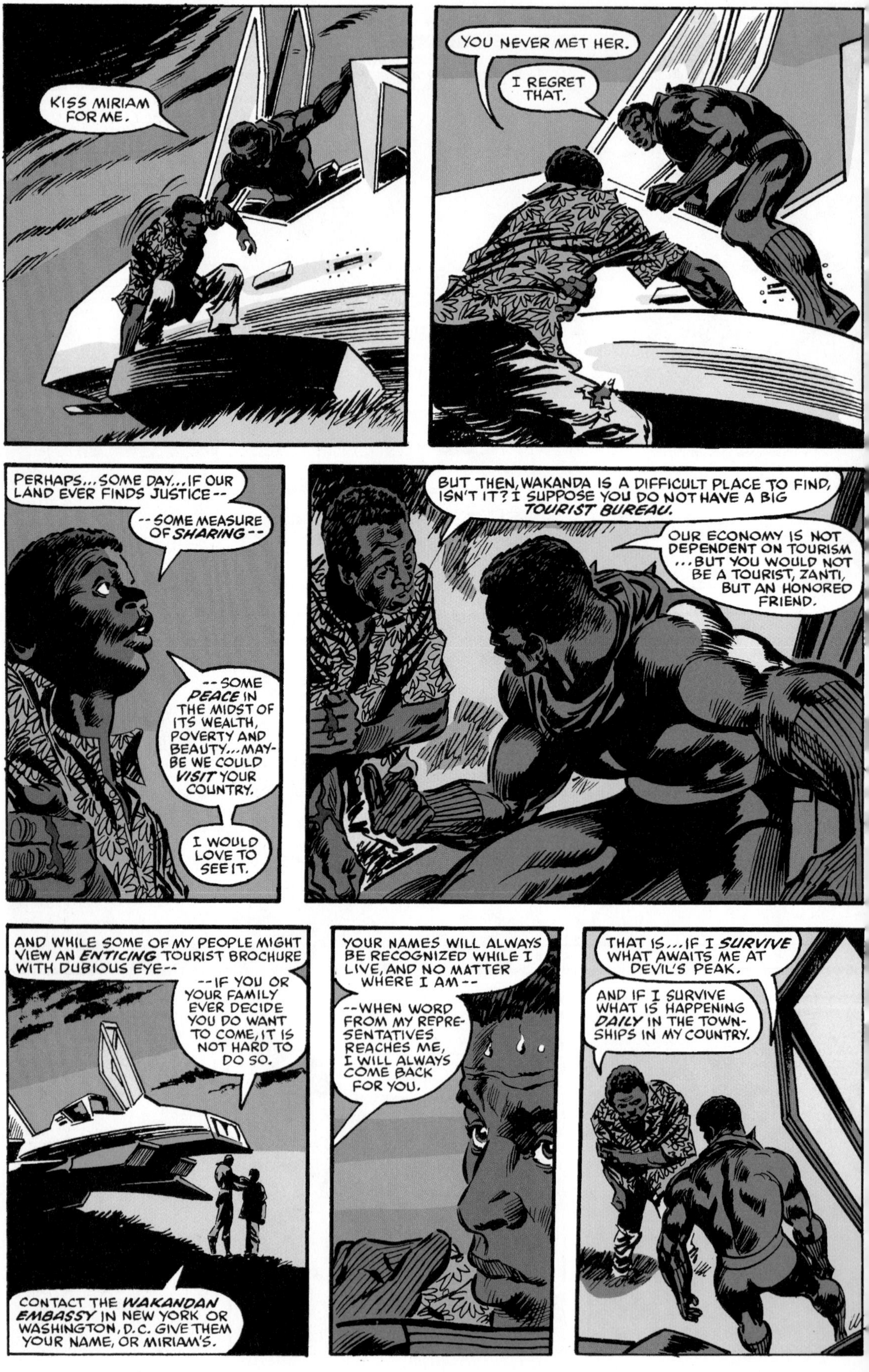

KISS MIRIAM FOR ME.
YOU NEVER MET HER.
I REGRET THAT.
PERHAPS... SOME DAY... IF OUR LAND EVER FINDS JUSTICE--
--SOME MEASURE OF SHARING--
--SOME PEACE IN THE MIDST OF ITS WEALTH, POVERTY AND BEAUTY... MAYBE WE COULD VISIT YOUR COUNTRY.
I WOULD LOVE TO SEE IT.
BUT THEN, WAKANDA IS A DIFFICULT PLACE TO FIND, ISN'T IT? I SUPPOSE YOU DO NOT HAVE A BIG TOURIST BUREAU.
OUR ECONOMY IS NOT DEPENDENT ON TOURISM ... BUT YOU WOULD NOT BE A TOURIST, ZANTI, BUT AN HONORED FRIEND.
AND WHILE SOME OF MY PEOPLE MIGHT VIEW AN ENTICING TOURIST BROCHURE WITH DUBIOUS EYE--
--IF YOU OR YOUR FAMILY EVER DECIDE YOU DO WANT TO COME, IT IS NOT HARD TO DO SO.
CONTACT THE WAKANDAN EMBASSY IN NEW YORK OR WASHINGTON, D.C. GIVE THEM YOUR NAME, OR MIRIAM'S.
YOUR NAMES WILL ALWAYS BE RECOGNIZED WHILE I LIVE, AND NO MATTER WHERE I AM--
--WHEN WORD FROM MY REPRESENTATIVES REACHES ME, I WILL ALWAYS COME BACK FOR YOU.
THAT IS... IF I SURVIVE WHAT AWAITS ME AT DEVIL'S PEAK.
AND IF I SURVIVE WHAT IS HAPPENING DAILY IN THE TOWNSHIPS IN MY COUNTRY.

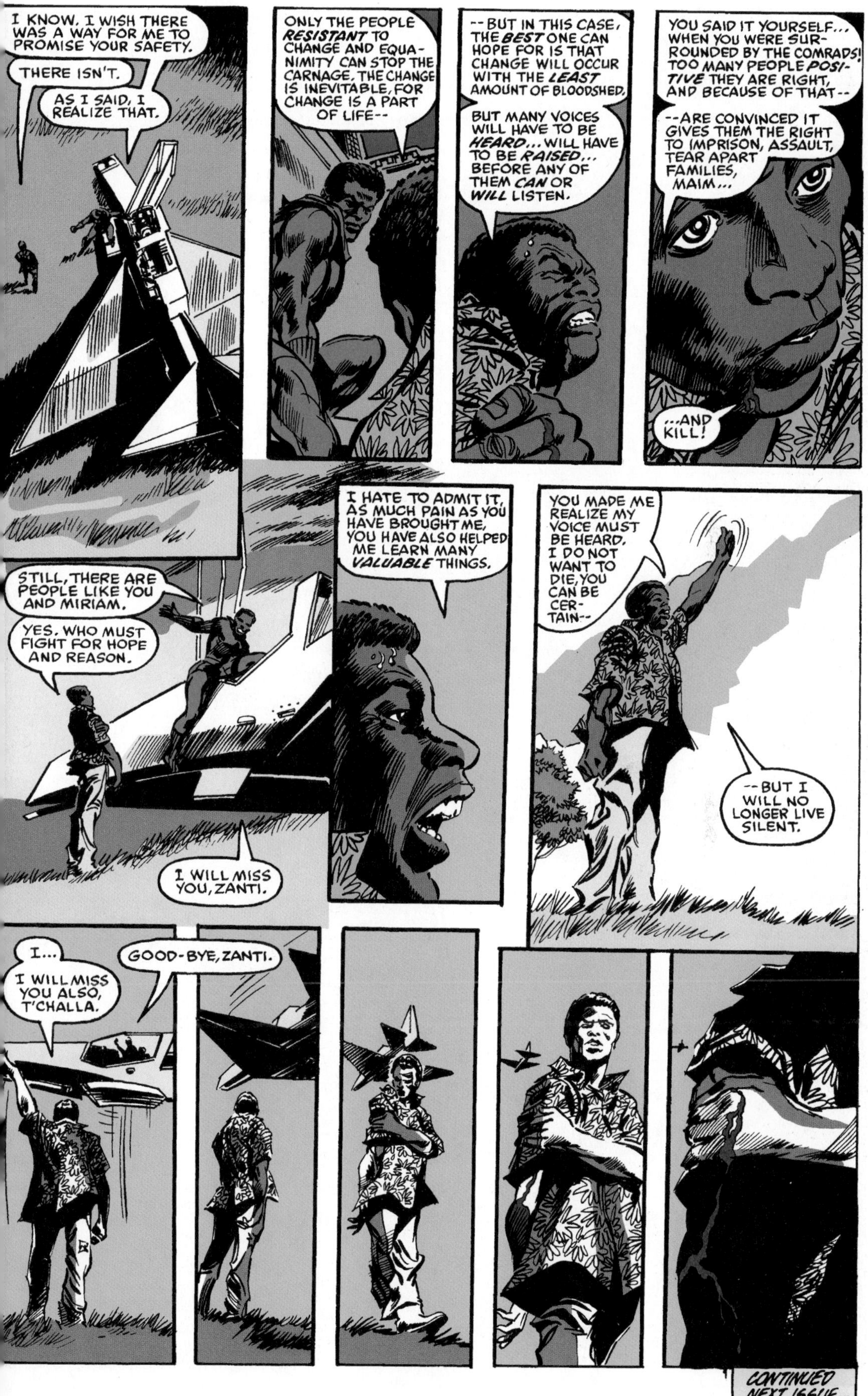
I KNOW. I WISH THERE WAS A WAY FOR ME TO PROMISE YOUR SAFETY.
THERE ISN'T.
AS I SAID, I REALIZE THAT.
ONLY THE PEOPLE RESISTANT TO CHANGE AND EQUANIMITY CAN STOP THE CARNAGE. THE CHANGE IS INEVITABLE, FOR CHANGE IS A PART OF LIFE--
--BUT IN THIS CASE, THE BEST ONE CAN HOPE FOR IS THAT CHANGE WILL OCCUR WITH THE LEAST AMOUNT OF BLOODSHED.
BUT MANY VOICES WILL HAVE TO BE HEARD... WILL HAVE TO BE RAISED... BEFORE ANY OF THEM CAN OR WILL LISTEN.
YOU SAID IT YOURSELF... WHEN YOU WERE SURROUNDED BY THE COMRADS! TOO MANY PEOPLE POSITIVE THEY ARE RIGHT, AND BECAUSE OF THAT--
--ARE CONVINCED IT GIVES THEM THE RIGHT TO IMPRISON, ASSAULT, TEAR APART FAMILIES, MAIM...
...AND KILL!
STILL, THERE ARE PEOPLE LIKE YOU AND MIRIAM.
YES. WHO MUST FIGHT FOR HOPE AND REASON.
I WILL MISS YOU, ZANTI.
I HATE TO ADMIT IT, AS MUCH PAIN AS YOU HAVE BROUGHT ME, YOU HAVE ALSO HELPED ME LEARN MANY VALUABLE THINGS.
YOU MADE ME REALIZE MY VOICE MUST BE HEARD. I DO NOT WANT TO DIE, YOU CAN BE CERTAIN--
--BUT I WILL NO LONGER LIVE SILENT.
I... I WILL MISS YOU ALSO, T'CHALLA.
GOOD-BYE, ZANTI.
CONTINUED NEXT ISSUE...

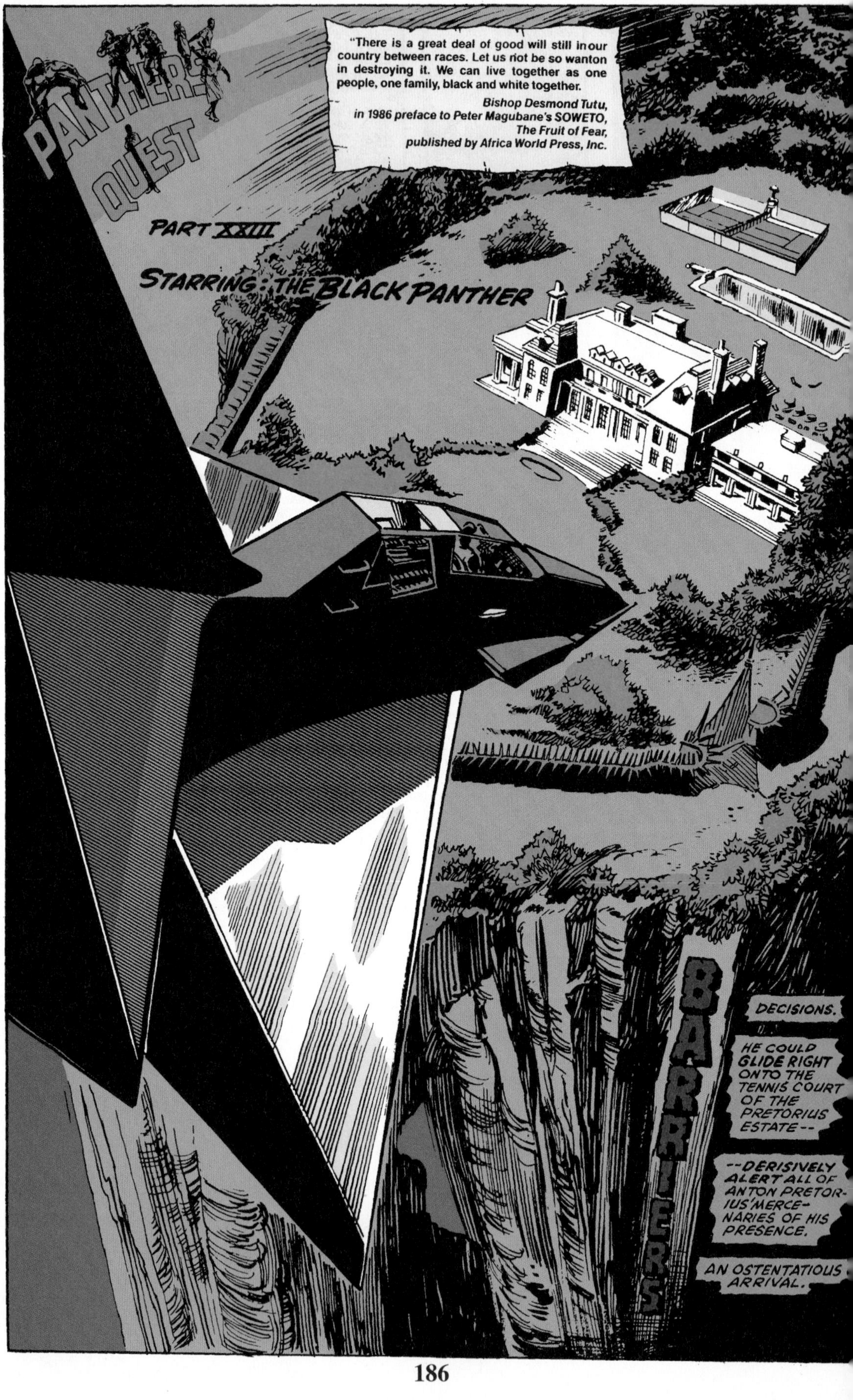
"There is a great deal of good will still inour country between races. Let us not be so wanton in destroying it. We can live together as one people, one family, black and white together.
Bishop Desmond Tutu,
in 1986 preface to Peter Magubane's SOWETO,
The Fruit of Fear,
published by Africa World Press, Inc.
PANTHER'S QUEST
PART XXIII
STARRING: THE BLACK PANTHER
BARRIERS
DECISIONS.
HE COULD GLIDE RIGHT ONTO THE TENNIS COURT OF THE PRETORIUS ESTATE--
--DERISIVELY ALERT ALL OF ANTON PRETORIUS' MERCENARIES OF HIS PRESENCE.
AN OSTENTATIOUS ARRIVAL.

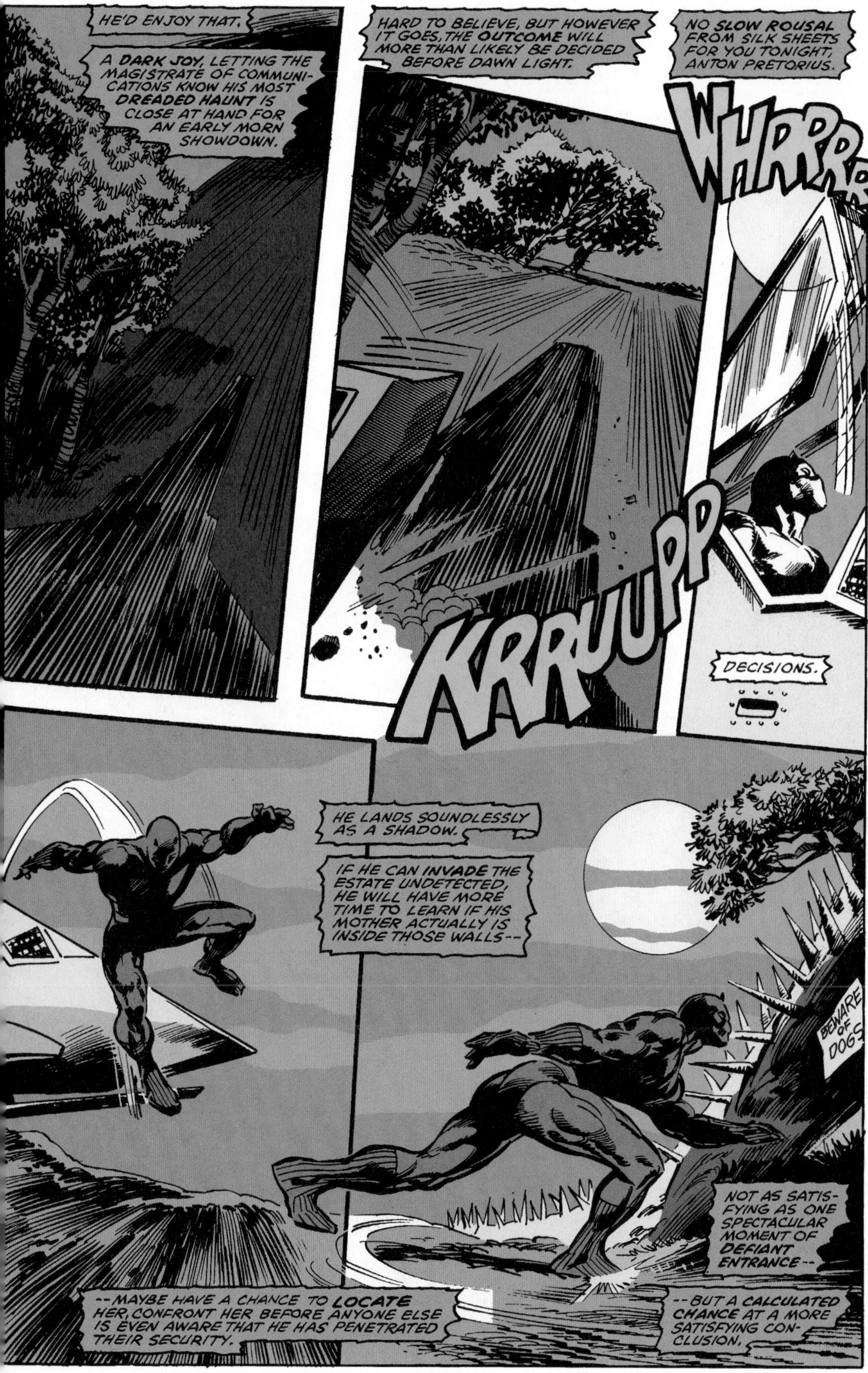
HE'D ENJOY THAT.
A DARK JOY, LETTING THE MAGISTRATE OF COMMUNICATIONS KNOW HIS MOST DREADED HAUNT IS CLOSE AT HAND FOR AN EARLY MORN SHOWDOWN.
HARD TO BELIEVE, BUT HOWEVER IT GOES, THE OUTCOME WILL MORE THAN LIKELY BE DECIDED BEFORE DAWN LIGHT.
NO SLOW ROUSAL FROM SILK SHEETS FOR YOU TONIGHT, ANTON PRETORIUS.
WHRRRR
KRRUUPP
DECISIONS.
HE LANDS SOUNDLESSLY AS A SHADOW.
IF HE CAN INVADE THE ESTATE UNDETECTED, HE WILL HAVE MORE TIME TO LEARN IF HIS MOTHER ACTUALLY IS INSIDE THOSE WALLS--
BEWARE OF DOGS
NOT AS SATISFYING AS ONE SPECTACULAR MOMENT OF DEFIANT ENTRANCE--
--MAYBE HAVE A CHANCE TO LOCATE HER, CONFRONT HER BEFORE ANYONE ELSE IS EVEN AWARE THAT HE HAS PENETRATED THEIR SECURITY.
--BUT A CALCULATED CHANCE AT A MORE SATISFYING CONCLUSION.

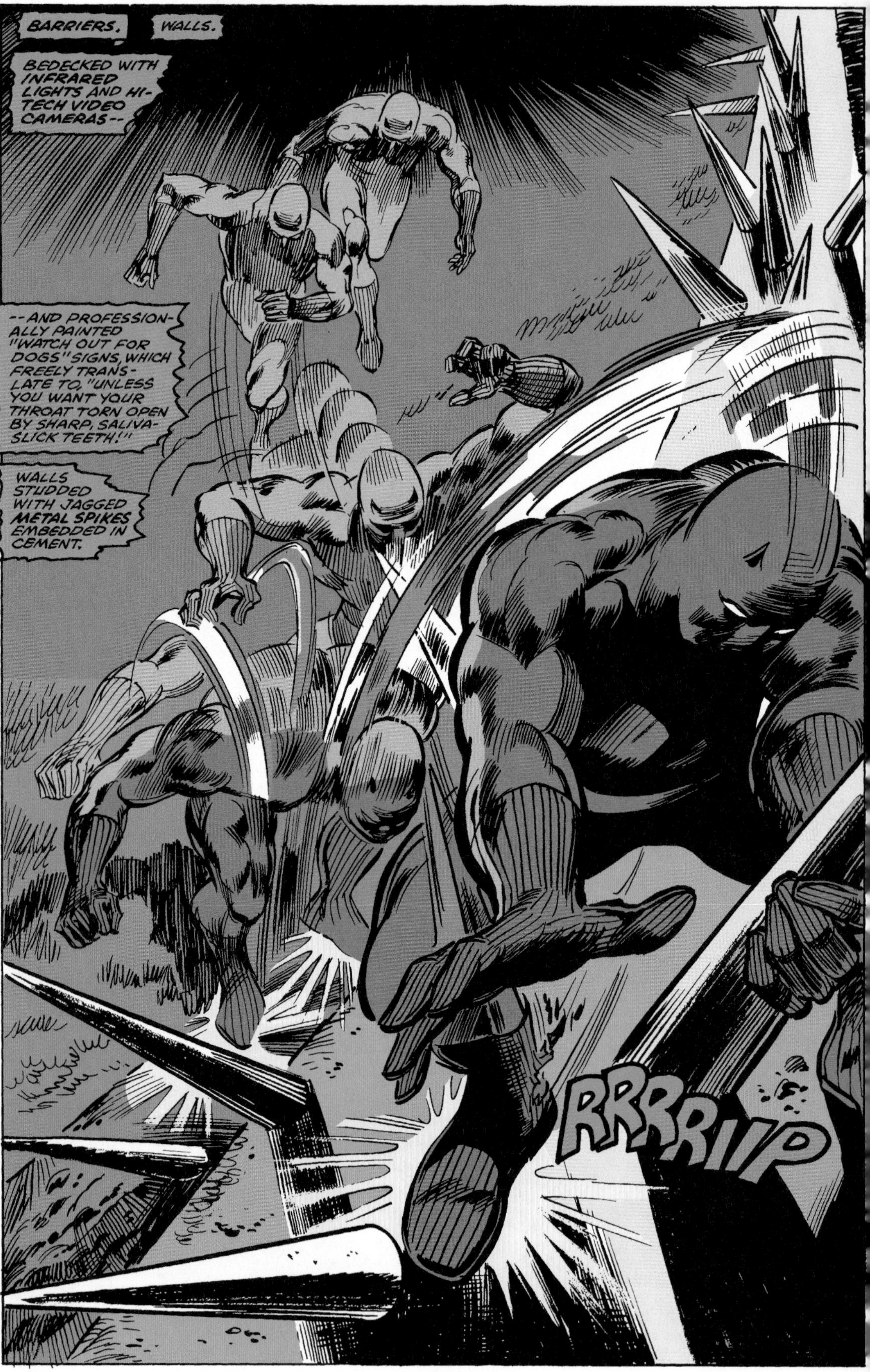
BARRIERS.
WALLS.
BEDECKED WITH INFRARED LIGHTS AND HI-TECH VIDEO CAMERAS--
--AND PROFESSIONALLY PAINTED "WATCH OUT FOR DOGS" SIGNS, WHICH FREELY TRANSLATE TO, "UNLESS YOU WANT YOUR THROAT TORN OPEN BY SHARP, SALIVA-SLICK TEETH!"
WALLS STUDDED WITH JAGGED METAL SPIKES EMBEDDED IN CEMENT.
RRRRIIP

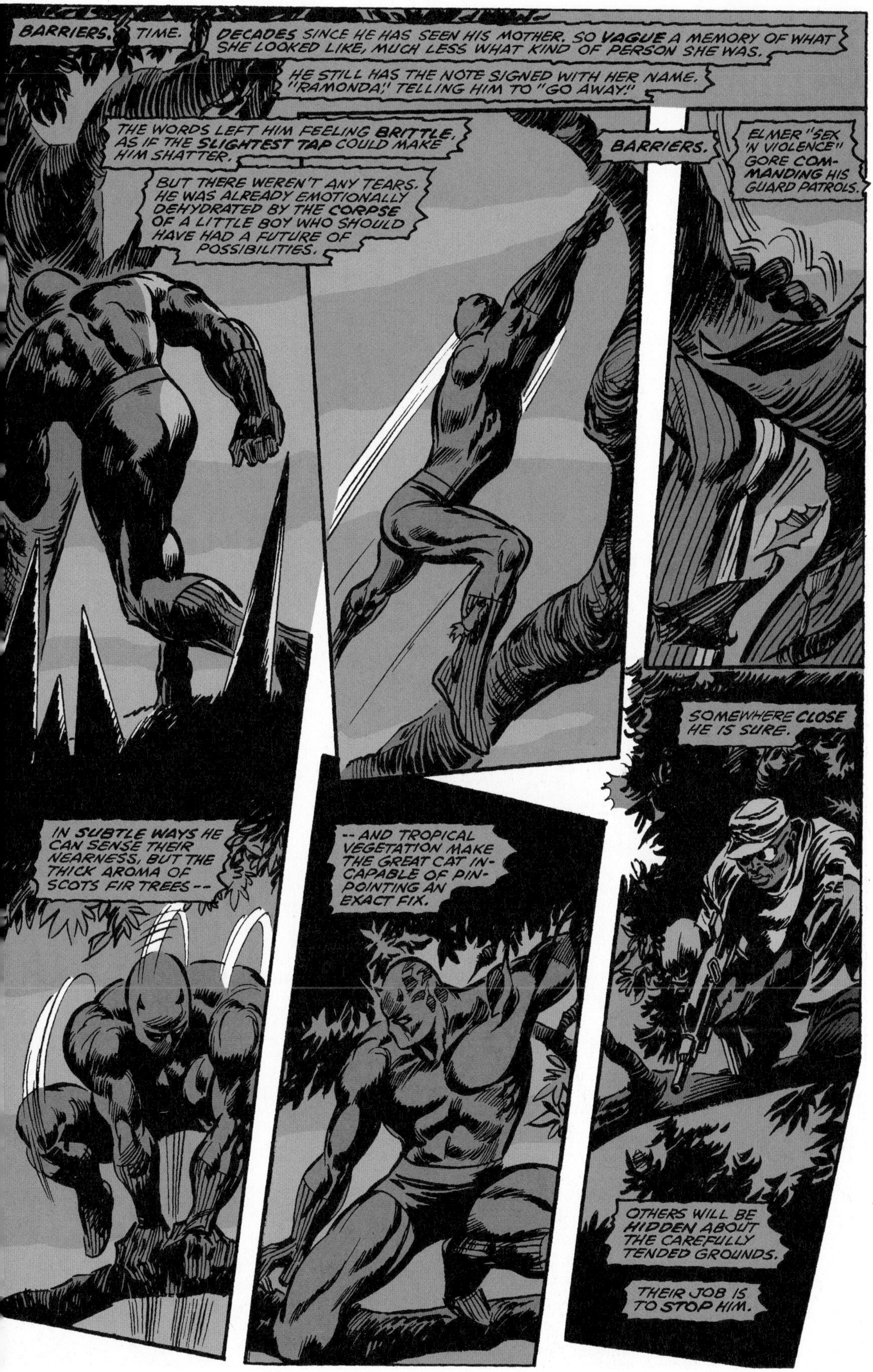
BARRIERS.
TIME.
DECADES SINCE HE HAS SEEN HIS MOTHER. SO VAGUE A MEMORY OF WHAT SHE LOOKED LIKE, MUCH LESS WHAT KIND OF PERSON SHE WAS.
HE STILL HAS THE NOTE SIGNED WITH HER NAME, "RAMONDA," TELLING HIM TO "GO AWAY."
THE WORDS LEFT HIM FEELING BRITTLE, AS IF THE SLIGHTEST TAP COULD MAKE HIM SHATTER.
BUT THERE WEREN'T ANY TEARS. HE WAS ALREADY EMOTIONALLY DEHYDRATED BY THE CORPSE OF A LITTLE BOY WHO SHOULD HAVE HAD A FUTURE OF POSSIBILITIES.
BARRIERS.
ELMER "SEX IN VIOLENCE" GORE COMMANDING HIS GUARD PATROLS.
SOMEWHERE CLOSE HE IS SURE.
IN SUBTLE WAYS HE CAN SENSE THEIR NEARNESS, BUT THE THICK AROMA OF SCOTS FIR TREES --
-- AND TROPICAL VEGETATION MAKE THE GREAT CAT INCAPABLE OF PINPOINTING AN EXACT FIX.
OTHERS WILL BE HIDDEN ABOUT THE CAREFULLY TENDED GROUNDS.
THEIR JOB IS TO STOP HIM.

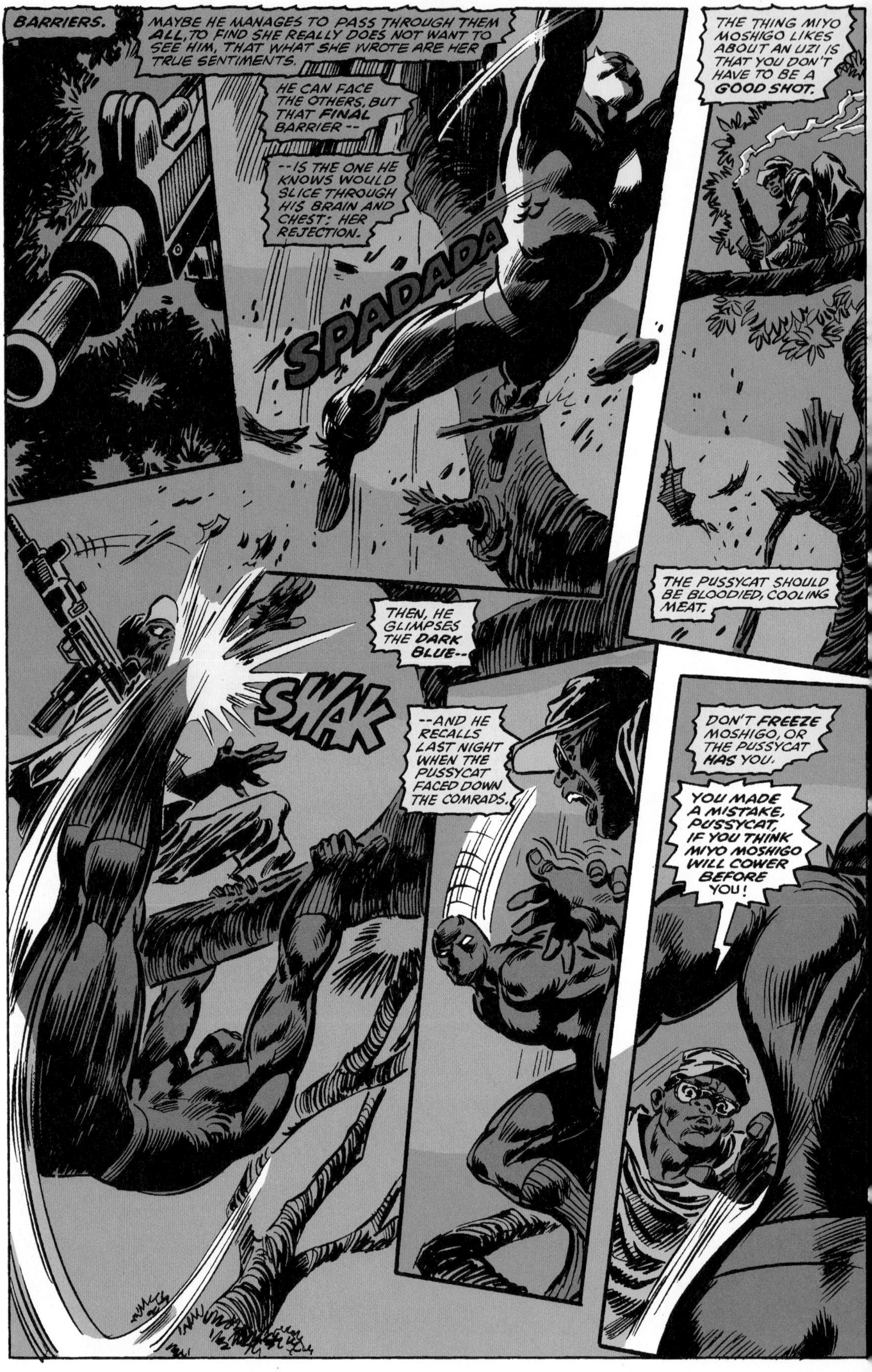
BARRIERS.
MAYBE HE MANAGES TO PASS THROUGH THEM ALL, TO FIND SHE REALLY DOES NOT WANT TO SEE HIM, THAT WHAT SHE WROTE ARE HER TRUE SENTIMENTS.
HE CAN FACE THE OTHERS, BUT THAT FINAL BARRIER --
--IS THE ONE HE KNOWS WOULD SLICE THROUGH HIS BRAIN AND CHEST: HER REJECTION.
SPADADA
THE THING MIYO MOSHIGO LIKES ABOUT AN UZI IS THAT YOU DON'T HAVE TO BE A GOOD SHOT.
THE PUSSYCAT SHOULD BE BLOODIED, COOLING MEAT.
THEN, HE GLIMPSES THE DARK BLUE--
SHAK
--AND HE RECALLS LAST NIGHT WHEN THE PUSSYCAT FACED DOWN THE COMRADS.
DON'T FREEZE MOSHIGO, OR THE PUSSYCAT HAS YOU.
YOU MADE A MISTAKE, PUSSYCAT, IF YOU THINK MIYO MOSHIGO WILL COWER BEFORE YOU!

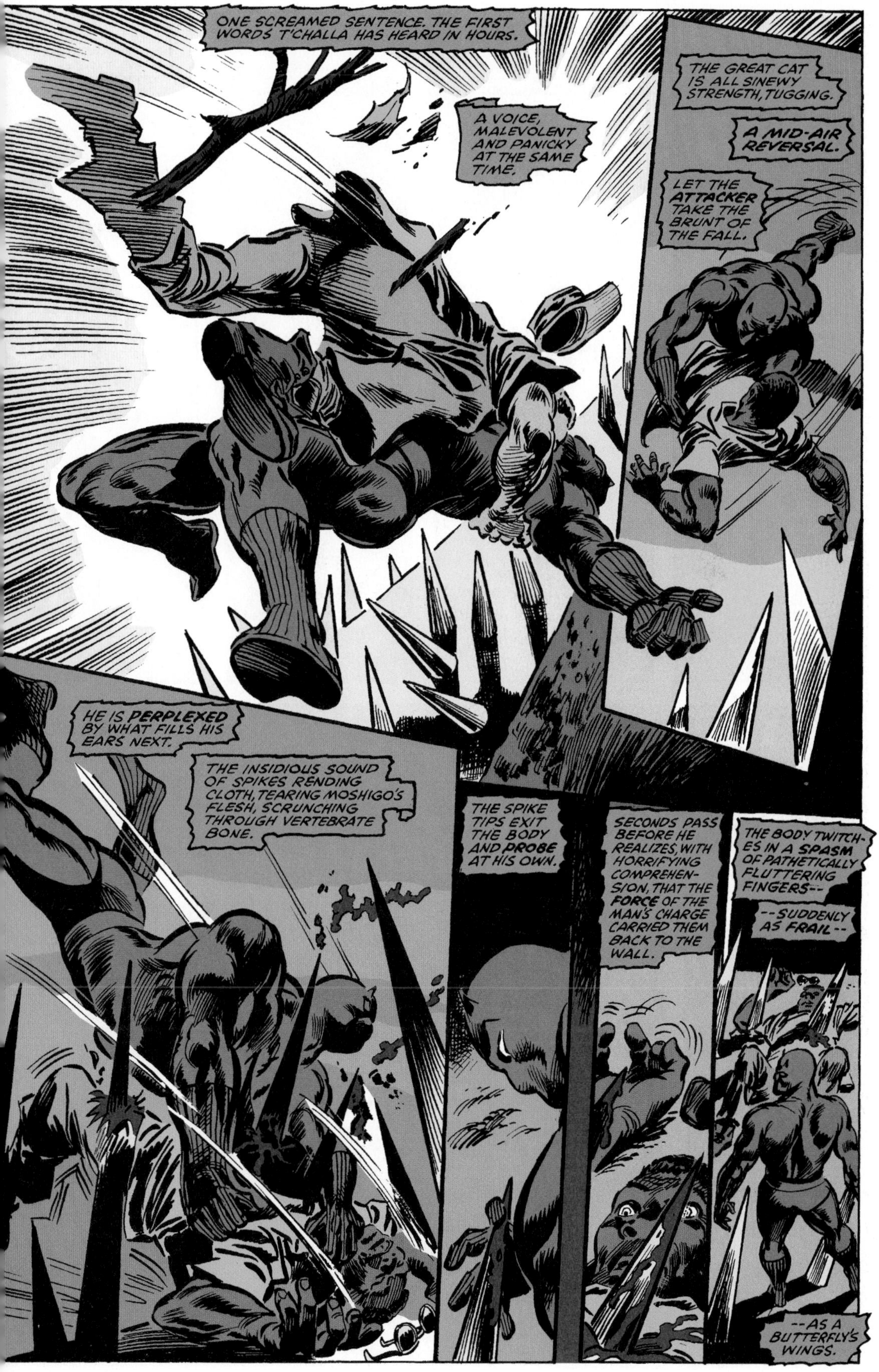

ONE SCREAMED SENTENCE. THE FIRST WORDS T'CHALLA HAS HEARD IN HOURS.
A VOICE, MALEVOLENT AND PANICKY AT THE SAME TIME.
THE GREAT CAT IS ALL SINEWY STRENGTH, TUGGING.
A MID-AIR REVERSAL.
LET THE ATTACKER TAKE THE BRUNT OF THE FALL.
HE IS PERPLEXED BY WHAT FILLS HIS EARS NEXT.
THE INSIDIOUS SOUND OF SPIKES RENDING CLOTH, TEARING MOSHIGO'S FLESH, SCRUNCHING THROUGH VERTEBRATE BONE.
THE SPIKE TIPS EXIT THE BODY AND PROBE AT HIS OWN.
SECONDS PASS BEFORE HE REALIZES, WITH HORRIFYING COMPREHENSION, THAT THE FORCE OF THE MAN'S CHARGE CARRIED THEM BACK TO THE WALL.
THE BODY TWITCHES IN A SPASM OF PATHETICALLY FLUTTERING FINGERS--
--SUDDENLY AS FRAIL--
--AS A BUTTERFLY'S WINGS.

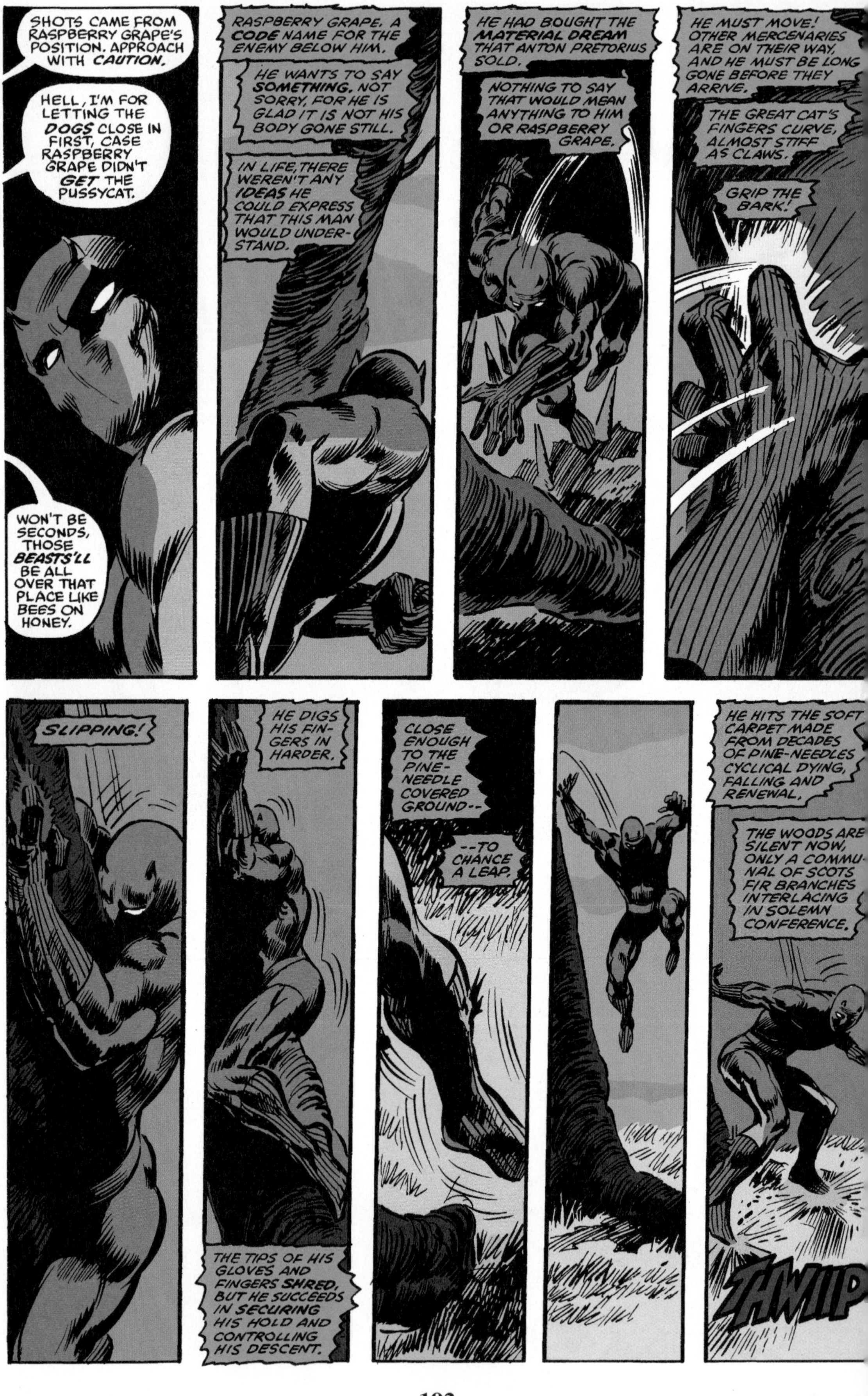

SHOTS CAME FROM RASPBERRY GRAPE'S POSITION. APPROACH WITH CAUTION.
HELL, I'M FOR LETTING THE DOGS CLOSE IN FIRST, CASE RASPBERRY GRAPE DIDN'T GET THE PUSSYCAT.
WON'T BE SECONDS, THOSE BEASTS'LL BE ALL OVER THAT PLACE LIKE BEES ON HONEY.
RASPBERRY GRAPE. A CODE NAME FOR THE ENEMY BELOW HIM.
HE WANTS TO SAY SOMETHING. NOT SORRY, FOR HE IS GLAD IT IS NOT HIS BODY GONE STILL.
IN LIFE, THERE WEREN'T ANY IDEAS HE COULD EXPRESS THAT THIS MAN WOULD UNDERSTAND.
HE HAD BOUGHT THE MATERIAL DREAM THAT ANTON PRETORIUS SOLD.
NOTHING TO SAY THAT WOULD MEAN ANYTHING TO HIM OR RASPBERRY GRAPE.
HE MUST MOVE! OTHER MERCENARIES ARE ON THEIR WAY, AND HE MUST BE LONG GONE BEFORE THEY ARRIVE.
THE GREAT CAT'S FINGERS CURVE, ALMOST STIFF AS CLAWS.
GRIP THE BARK!
SLIPPING!
HE DIGS HIS FINGERS IN HARDER.
THE TIPS OF HIS GLOVES AND FINGERS SHRED, BUT HE SUCCEEDS IN SECURING HIS HOLD AND CONTROLLING HIS DESCENT.
CLOSE ENOUGH TO THE PINE-NEEDLE COVERED GROUND--
--TO CHANCE A LEAP.
HE HITS THE SOFT CARPET MADE FROM DECADES OF PINE-NEEDLES CYCLICAL DYING, FALLING AND RENEWAL.
THE WOODS ARE SILENT NOW, ONLY A COMMUNAL OF SCOTS FIR BRANCHES INTERLACING IN SOLEMN CONFERENCE.
THWIIP

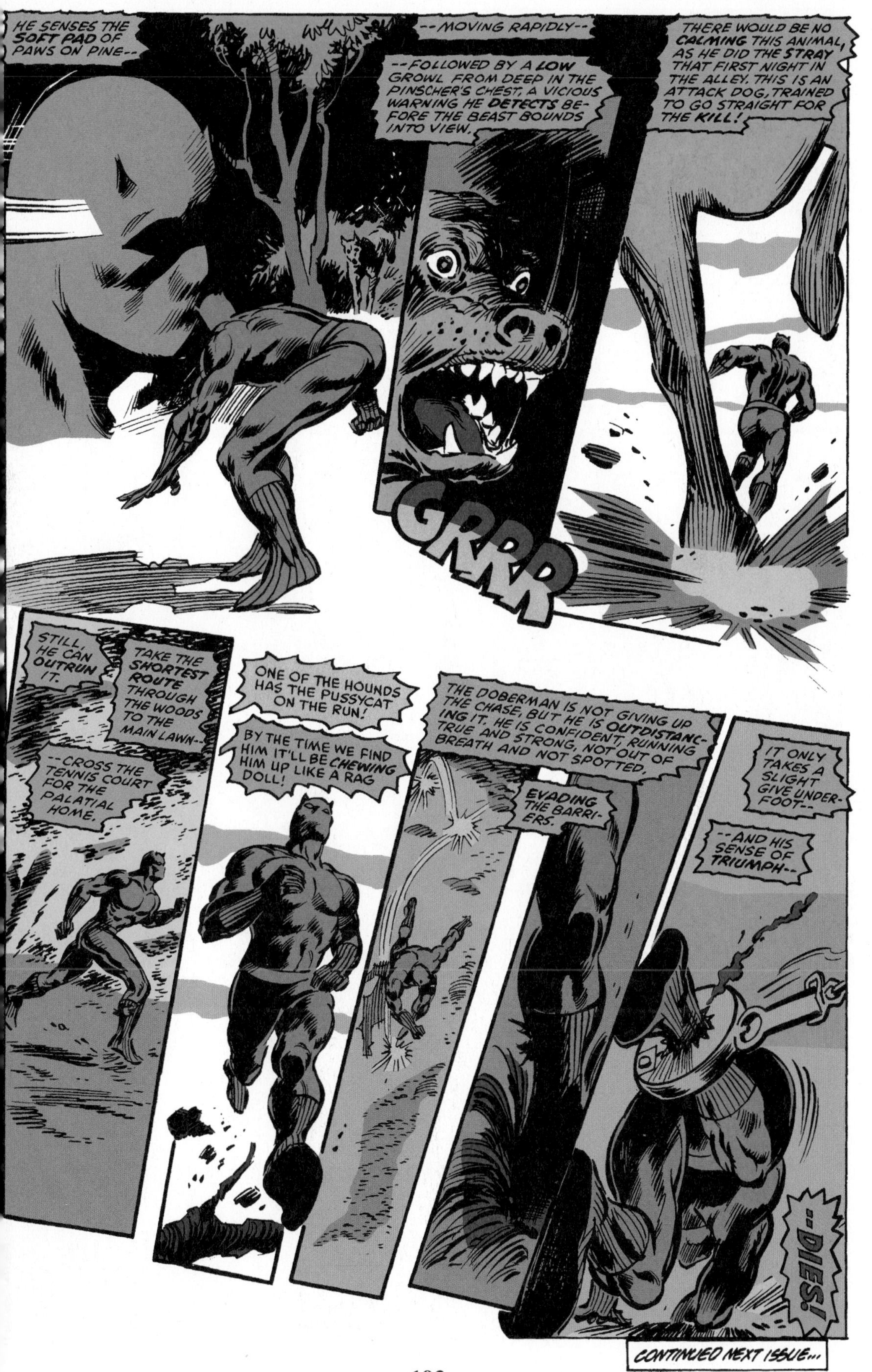

HE SENSES THE SOFT PAD OF PAWS ON PINE--
--MOVING RAPIDLY--
--FOLLOWED BY A LOW GROWL FROM DEEP IN THE PINSCHER'S CHEST, A VICIOUS WARNING HE DETECTS BEFORE THE BEAST BOUNDS INTO VIEW.
THERE WOULD BE NO CALMING THIS ANIMAL, AS HE DID THE STRAY THAT FIRST NIGHT IN THE ALLEY. THIS IS AN ATTACK DOG, TRAINED TO GO STRAIGHT FOR THE KILL!
GRRR
STILL, HE CAN OUTRUN IT.
TAKE THE SHORTEST ROUTE THROUGH THE WOODS TO THE MAIN LAWN--
--CROSS THE TENNIS COURT FOR THE PALATIAL HOME.
ONE OF THE HOUNDS HAS THE PUSSYCAT ON THE RUN!
BY THE TIME WE FIND HIM IT'LL BE CHEWING HIM UP LIKE A RAG DOLL!
THE DOBERMAN IS NOT GIVING UP THE CHASE, BUT HE IS OUTDISTANCING IT. HE IS CONFIDENT, RUNNING TRUE AND STRONG, NOT OUT OF BREATH AND NOT SPOTTED.
EVADING THE BARRIERS.
IT ONLY TAKES A SLIGHT GIVE UNDERFOOT--
--AND HIS SENSE OF TRIUMPH--
--DIES!

CONTINUED NEXT ISSUE...

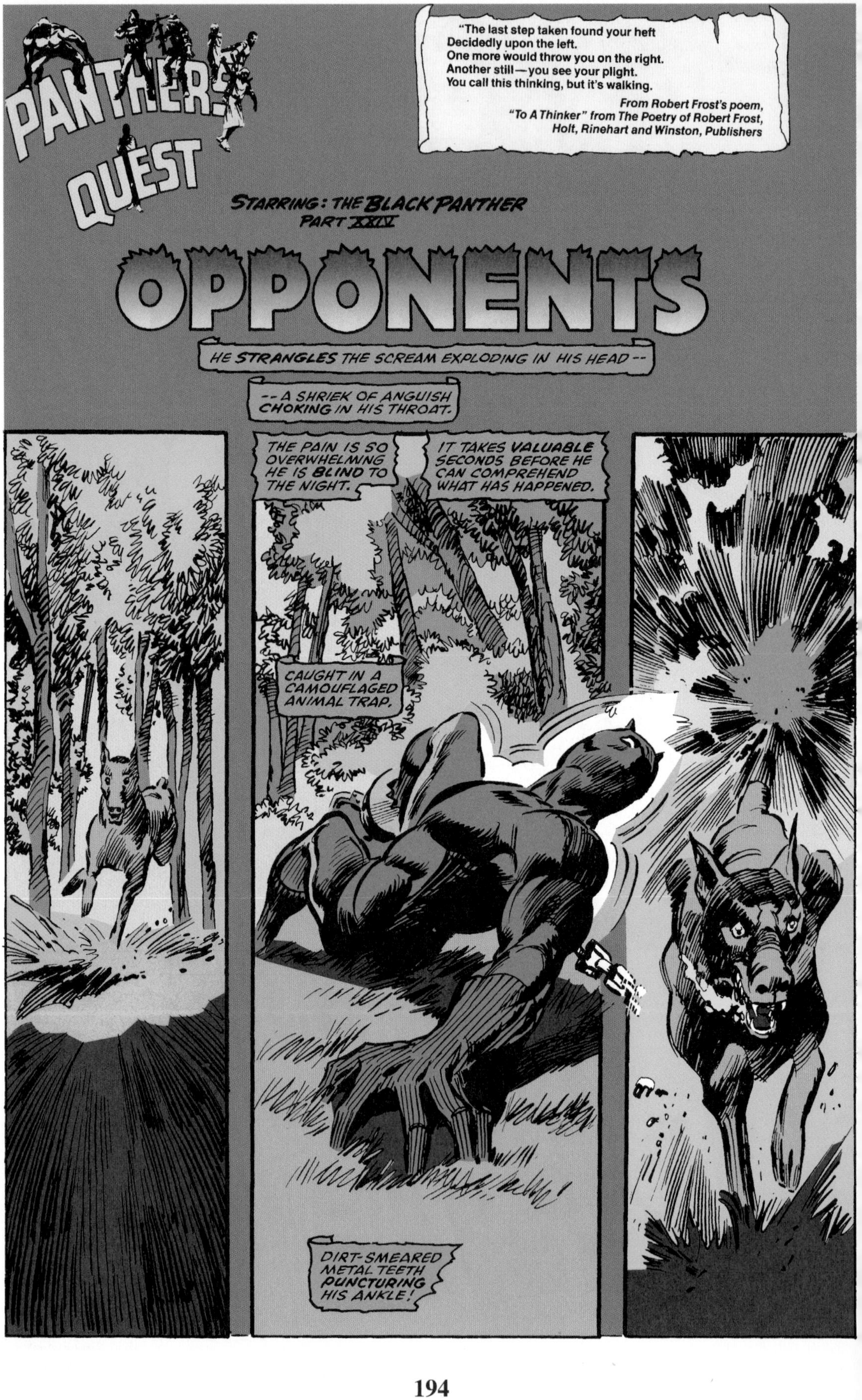
"The last step taken found your heft
Decidedly upon the left.
One more would throw you on the right.
Another still—you see your plight.
You call this thinking, but it's walking.
From Robert Frost's poem,
"To A Thinker" from The Poetry of Robert Frost,
Holt, Rinehart and Winston, Publishers
PANTHER'S QUEST
STARRING: THE BLACK PANTHER
PART XXIV
OPPONENTS
HE STRANGLES THE SCREAM EXPLODING IN HIS HEAD--
--A SHRIEK OF ANGUISH CHOKING IN HIS THROAT.
THE PAIN IS SO OVERWHELMING HE IS BLIND TO THE NIGHT.
IT TAKES VALUABLE SECONDS BEFORE HE CAN COMPREHEND WHAT HAS HAPPENED.
CAUGHT IN A CAMOUFLAGED ANIMAL TRAP.
DIRT-SMEARED METAL TEETH PUNCTURING HIS ANKLE!

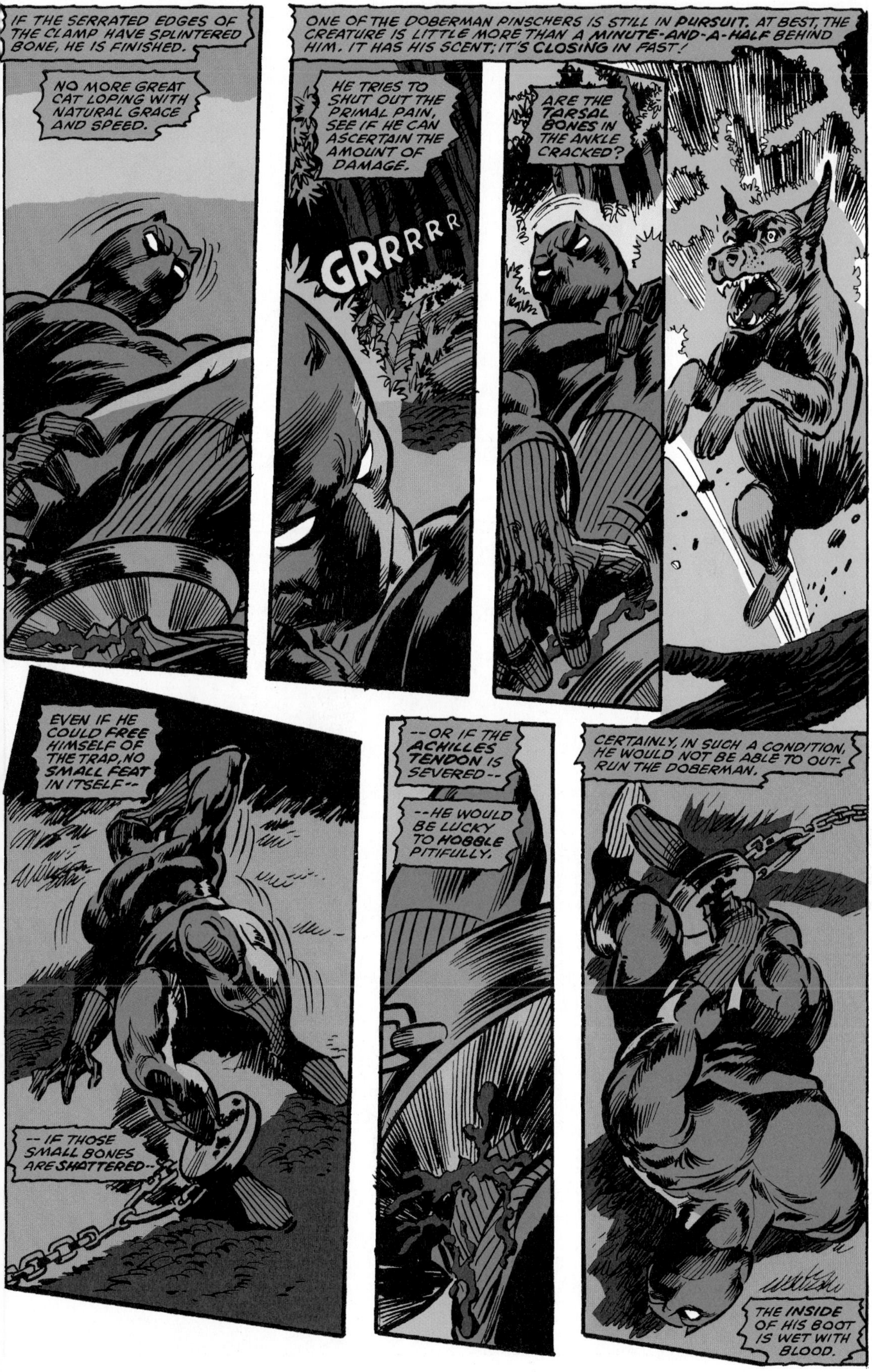

IF THE SERRATED EDGES OF THE CLAMP HAVE SPLINTERED BONE, HE IS FINISHED.
NO MORE GREAT CAT LOPING WITH NATURAL GRACE AND SPEED.
ONE OF THE DOBERMAN PINSCHERS IS STILL IN PURSUIT. AT BEST, THE CREATURE IS LITTLE MORE THAN A MINUTE-AND-A-HALF BEHIND HIM. IT HAS HIS SCENT; IT'S CLOSING IN FAST!
HE TRIES TO SHUT OUT THE PRIMAL PAIN, SEE IF HE CAN ASCERTAIN THE AMOUNT OF DAMAGE.
GRRRRR
ARE THE TARSAL BONES IN THE ANKLE CRACKED?
EVEN IF HE COULD FREE HIMSELF OF THE TRAP, NO SMALL FEAT IN ITSELF--
-- IF THOSE SMALL BONES ARE SHATTERED--
--OR IF THE ACHILLES TENDON IS SEVERED--
--HE WOULD BE LUCKY TO HOBBLE PITIFULLY.
CERTAINLY, IN SUCH A CONDITION, HE WOULD NOT BE ABLE TO OUT-RUN THE DOBERMAN.
THE INSIDE OF HIS BOOT IS WET WITH BLOOD.

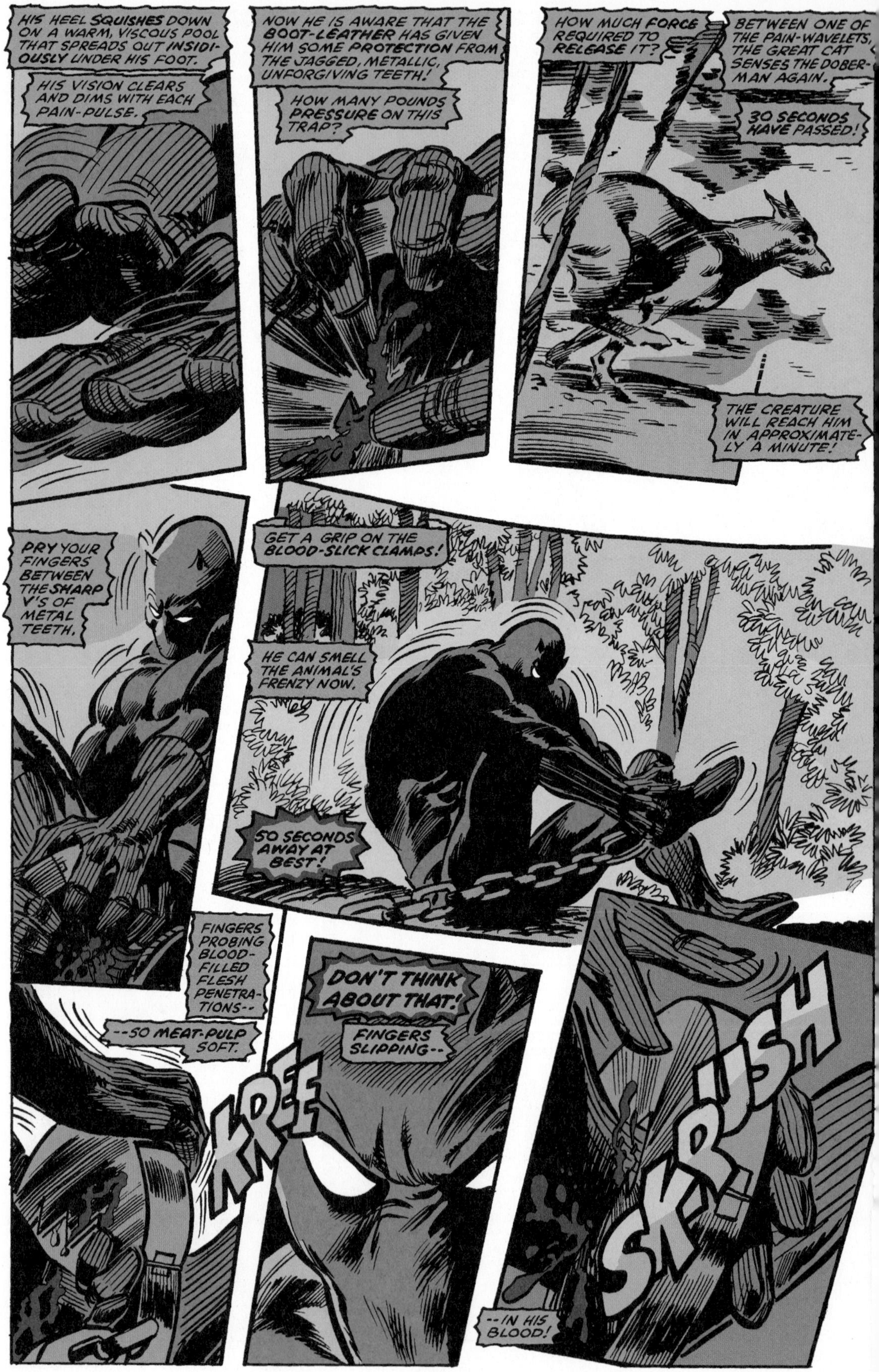
HIS HEEL SQUISHES DOWN ON A WARM, VISCOUS POOL THAT SPREADS OUT INSIDIOUSLY UNDER HIS FOOT.
HIS VISION CLEARS AND DIMS WITH EACH PAIN-PULSE.
NOW HE IS AWARE THAT THE BOOT-LEATHER HAS GIVEN HIM SOME PROTECTION FROM THE JAGGED, METALLIC, UNFORGIVING TEETH!
HOW MANY POUNDS PRESSURE ON THIS TRAP?
HOW MUCH FORCE REQUIRED TO RELEASE IT?
BETWEEN ONE OF THE PAIN-WAVELETS, THE GREAT CAT SENSES THE DOBERMAN AGAIN.
30 SECONDS HAVE PASSED!
THE CREATURE WILL REACH HIM IN APPROXIMATELY A MINUTE!
PRY YOUR FINGERS BETWEEN THE SHARP V'S OF METAL TEETH.
GET A GRIP ON THE BLOOD-SLICK CLAMPS!
HE CAN SMELL THE ANIMAL'S FRENZY NOW.
50 SECONDS AWAY AT BEST!
FINGERS PROBING BLOOD-FILLED FLESH PENETRATIONS--
--SO MEAT-PULP SOFT.
KREE
DON'T THINK ABOUT THAT!
FINGERS SLIPPING--
SKRUSH
--IN HIS BLOOD!

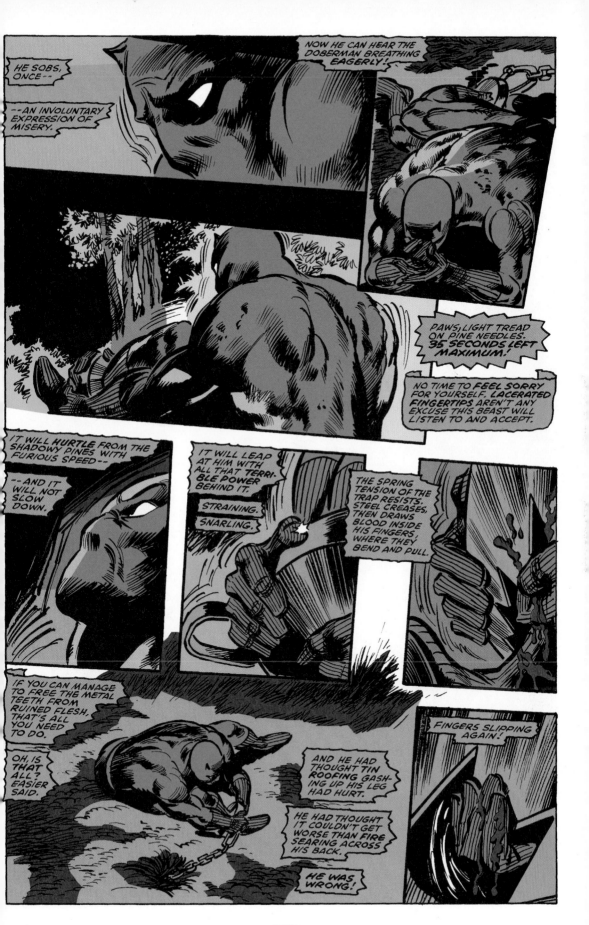

HE SOBS, ONCE--

--AN INVOLUNTARY EXPRESSION OF MISERY.

NOW HE CAN HEAR THE DOBERMAN BREATHING EAGERLY!

PAWS, LIGHT TREAD ON PINE NEEDLES. 35 SECONDS LEFT MAXIMUM!

NO TIME TO FEEL SORRY FOR YOURSELF. LACERATED FINGERTIPS AREN'T ANY EXCUSE THIS BEAST WILL LISTEN TO AND ACCEPT.

IT WILL HURTLE FROM THE SHADOWY PINES WITH FURIOUS SPEED--

--AND IT WILL NOT SLOW DOWN.

IT WILL LEAP AT HIM WITH ALL THAT TERRI-BLE POWER BEHIND IT.

STRAINING.

SNARLING.

THE SPRING TENSION OF THE TRAP RESISTS. STEEL CREASES, THEN DRAWS BLOOD INSIDE HIS FINGERS, WHERE THEY BEND AND PULL.

IF YOU CAN MANAGE TO FREE THE METAL TEETH FROM RUINED FLESH, THAT'S ALL YOU NEED TO DO.

OH, IS THAT ALL? EASIER SAID.

AND HE HAD THOUGHT TIN ROOFING GASH-ING UP HIS LEG HAD HURT.

HE HAD THOUGHT IT COULDN'T GET WORSE THAN FIRE SEARING ACROSS HIS BACK.

HE WAS WRONG!

FINGERS SLIPPING AGAIN!

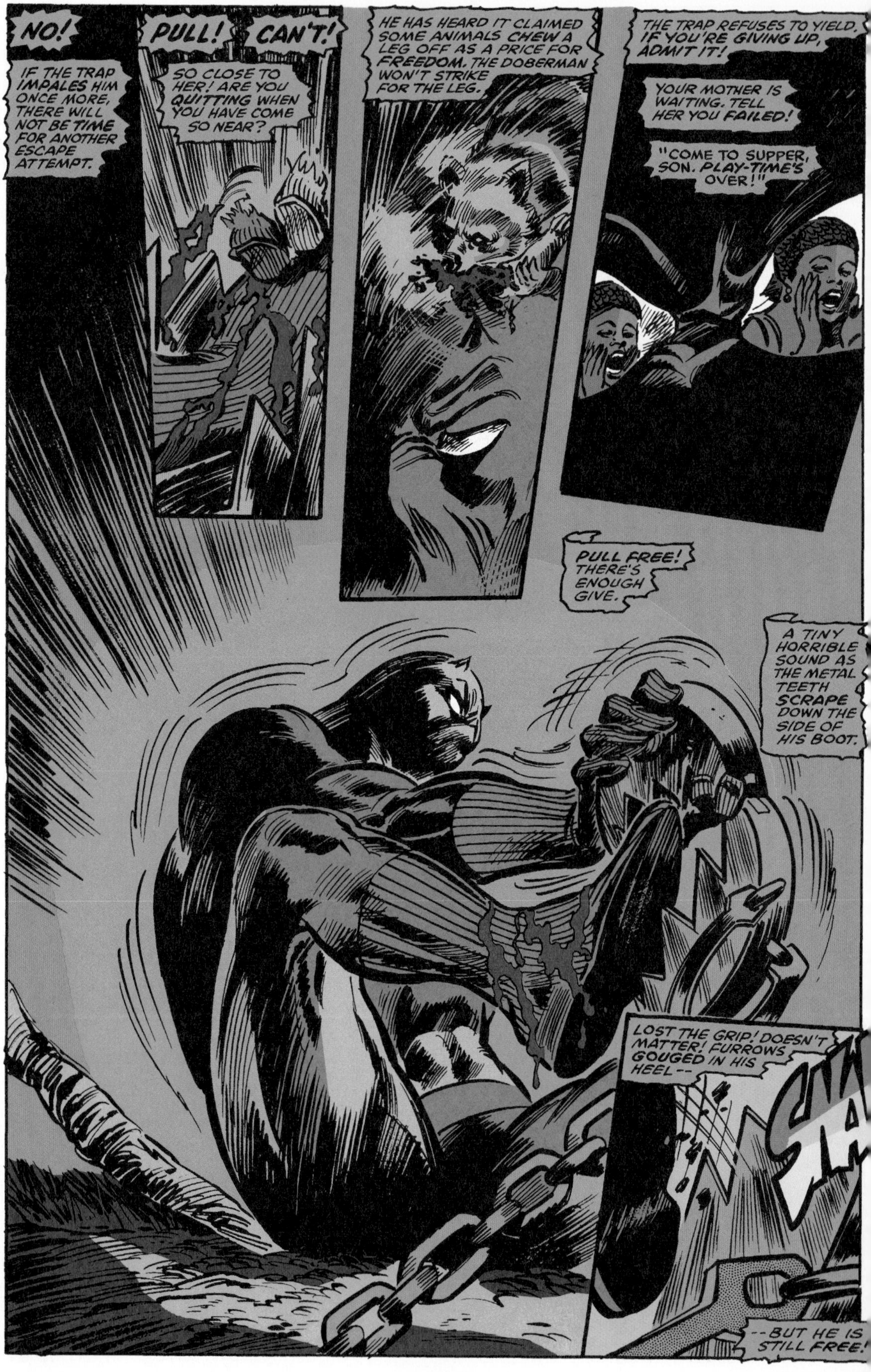
NO!
IF THE TRAP IMPALES HIM ONCE MORE, THERE WILL NOT BE TIME FOR ANOTHER ESCAPE ATTEMPT.
PULL! CAN'T!
SO CLOSE TO HER! ARE YOU QUITTING WHEN YOU HAVE COME SO NEAR?
HE HAS HEARD IT CLAIMED SOME ANIMALS CHEW A LEG OFF AS A PRICE FOR FREEDOM. THE DOBERMAN WON'T STRIKE FOR THE LEG.
THE TRAP REFUSES TO YIELD. IF YOU'RE GIVING UP, ADMIT IT!
YOUR MOTHER IS WAITING. TELL HER YOU FAILED!
"COME TO SUPPER, SON. PLAY-TIME'S OVER!"
PULL FREE! THERE'S ENOUGH GIVE.
A TINY HORRIBLE SOUND AS THE METAL TEETH SCRAPE DOWN THE SIDE OF HIS BOOT.
LOST THE GRIP! DOESN'T MATTER! FURROWS GOUGED IN HIS HEEL--
--BUT HE IS STILL FREE!

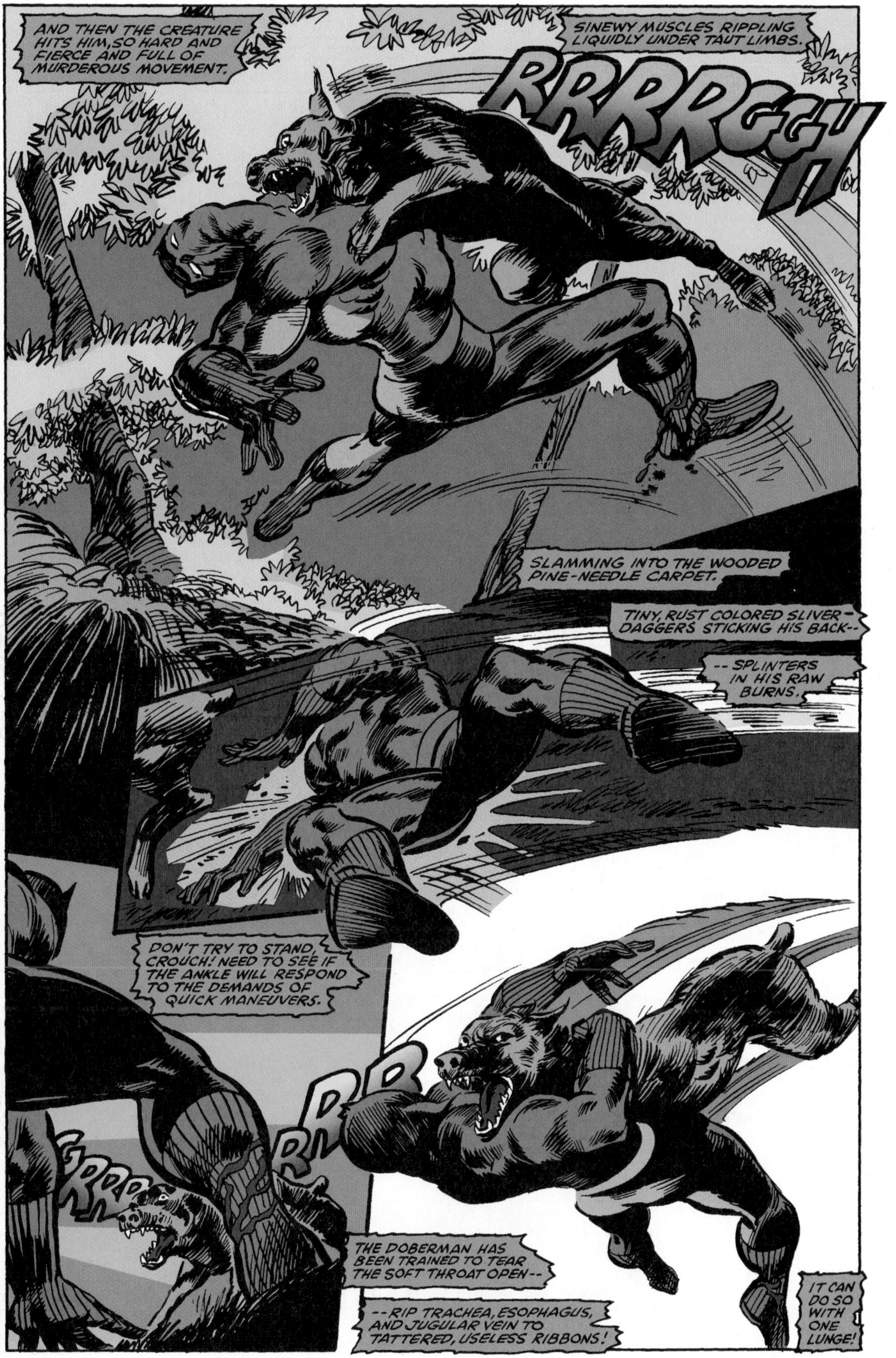
AND THEN THE CREATURE HITS HIM, SO HARD AND FIERCE AND FULL OF MURDEROUS MOVEMENT.
SINEWY MUSCLES RIPPLING LIQUIDLY UNDER TAUT LIMBS.
RRRRGGH
SLAMMING INTO THE WOODED PINE-NEEDLE CARPET.
TINY, RUST COLORED SLIVER-DAGGERS STICKING HIS BACK--
--SPLINTERS IN HIS RAW BURNS.
DON'T TRY TO STAND, CROUCH! NEED TO SEE IF THE ANKLE WILL RESPOND TO THE DEMANDS OF QUICK MANEUVERS.
THE DOBERMAN HAS BEEN TRAINED TO TEAR THE SOFT THROAT OPEN--
--RIP TRACHEA, ESOPHAGUS, AND JUGULAR VEIN TO TATTERED, USELESS RIBBONS!
IT CAN DO SO WITH ONE LUNGE!

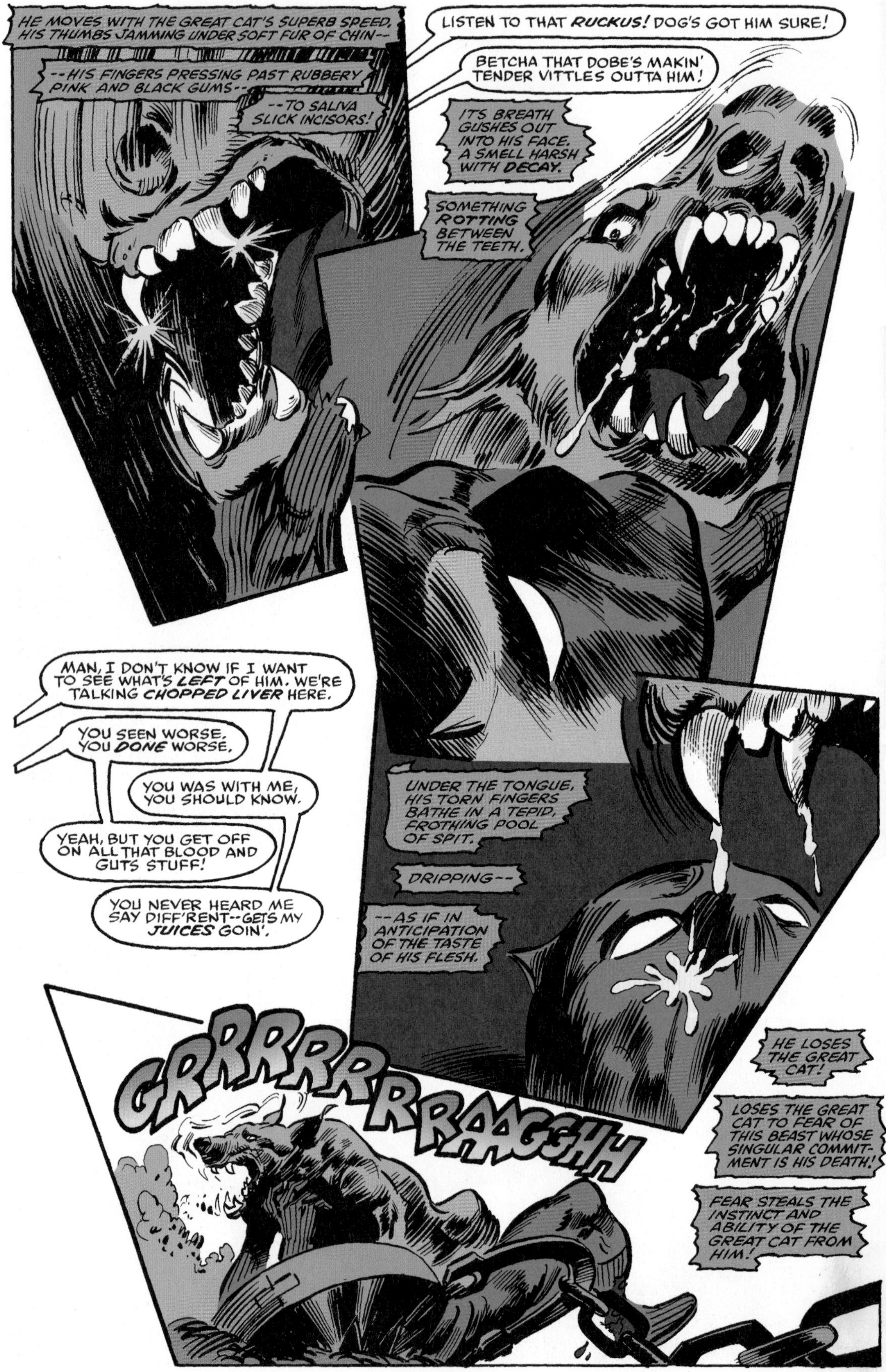

HE MOVES WITH THE GREAT CAT'S SUPERB SPEED, HIS THUMBS JAMMING UNDER SOFT FUR OF CHIN--
--HIS FINGERS PRESSING PAST RUBBERY PINK AND BLACK GUMS--
--TO SALIVA SLICK INCISORS!
LISTEN TO THAT RUCKUS! DOG'S GOT HIM SURE!
BETCHA THAT DOBE'S MAKIN' TENDER VITTLES OUTTA HIM!
IT'S BREATH GUSHES OUT INTO HIS FACE. A SMELL HARSH WITH DECAY.
SOMETHING ROTTING BETWEEN THE TEETH.
MAN, I DON'T KNOW IF I WANT TO SEE WHAT'S LEFT OF HIM. WE'RE TALKING CHOPPED LIVER HERE.
YOU SEEN WORSE. YOU DONE WORSE.
YOU WAS WITH ME, YOU SHOULD KNOW.
YEAH, BUT YOU GET OFF ON ALL THAT BLOOD AND GUTS STUFF!
YOU NEVER HEARD ME SAY DIFF'RENT--GETS MY JUICES GOIN'.
UNDER THE TONGUE, HIS TORN FINGERS BATHE IN A TEPID, FROTHING POOL OF SPIT.
DRIPPING--
--AS IF IN ANTICIPATION OF THE TASTE OF HIS FLESH.
GRRRRRRRAAGGHH
HE LOSES THE GREAT CAT!
LOSES THE GREAT CAT TO FEAR OF THIS BEAST WHOSE SINGULAR COMMITMENT IS HIS DEATH!
FEAR STEALS THE INSTINCT AND ABILITY OF THE GREAT CAT FROM HIM!

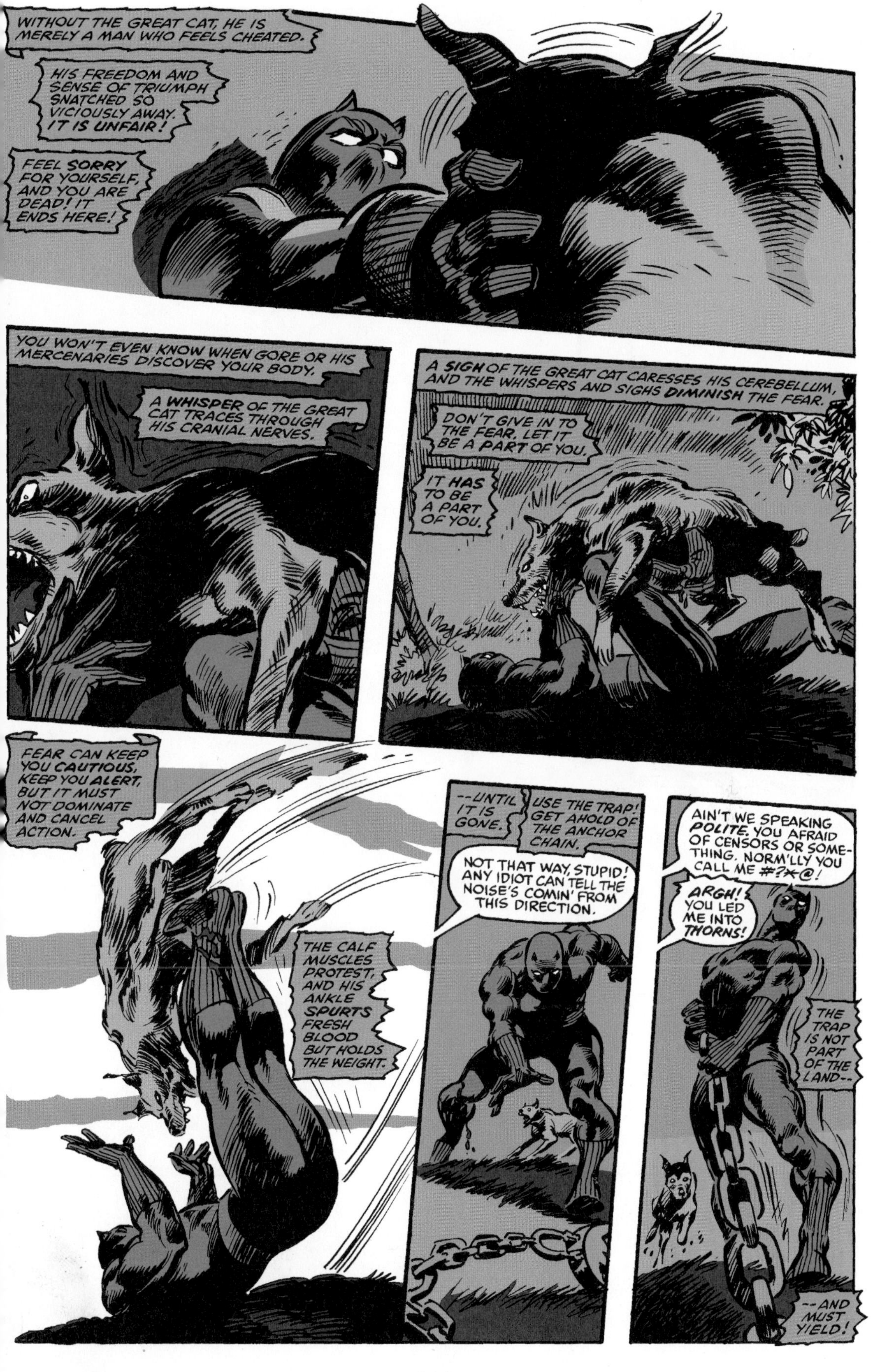
WITHOUT THE GREAT CAT, HE IS MERELY A MAN WHO FEELS CHEATED.
HIS FREEDOM AND SENSE OF TRIUMPH SNATCHED SO VICIOUSLY AWAY. IT IS UNFAIR!
FEEL SORRY FOR YOURSELF, AND YOU ARE DEAD! IT ENDS HERE!
YOU WON'T EVEN KNOW WHEN GORE OR HIS MERCENARIES DISCOVER YOUR BODY.
A WHISPER OF THE GREAT CAT TRACES THROUGH HIS CRANIAL NERVES.
A SIGH OF THE GREAT CAT CARESSES HIS CEREBELLUM, AND THE WHISPERS AND SIGHS DIMINISH THE FEAR.
DON'T GIVE IN TO THE FEAR. LET IT BE A PART OF YOU.
IT HAS TO BE A PART OF YOU.
FEAR CAN KEEP YOU CAUTIOUS, KEEP YOU ALERT, BUT IT MUST NOT DOMINATE AND CANCEL ACTION.
THE CALF MUSCLES PROTEST, AND HIS ANKLE SPURTS FRESH BLOOD BUT HOLDS THE WEIGHT.
--UNTIL IT IS GONE.
USE THE TRAP! GET AHOLD OF THE ANCHOR CHAIN.
NOT THAT WAY, STUPID! ANY IDIOT CAN TELL THE NOISE'S COMIN' FROM THIS DIRECTION.
AIN'T WE SPEAKING POLITE. YOU AFRAID OF CENSORS OR SOME-THING. NORM'LLY YOU CALL ME #?*@!
ARGH! YOU LED ME INTO THORNS!
THE TRAP IS NOT PART OF THE LAND--
--AND MUST YIELD!

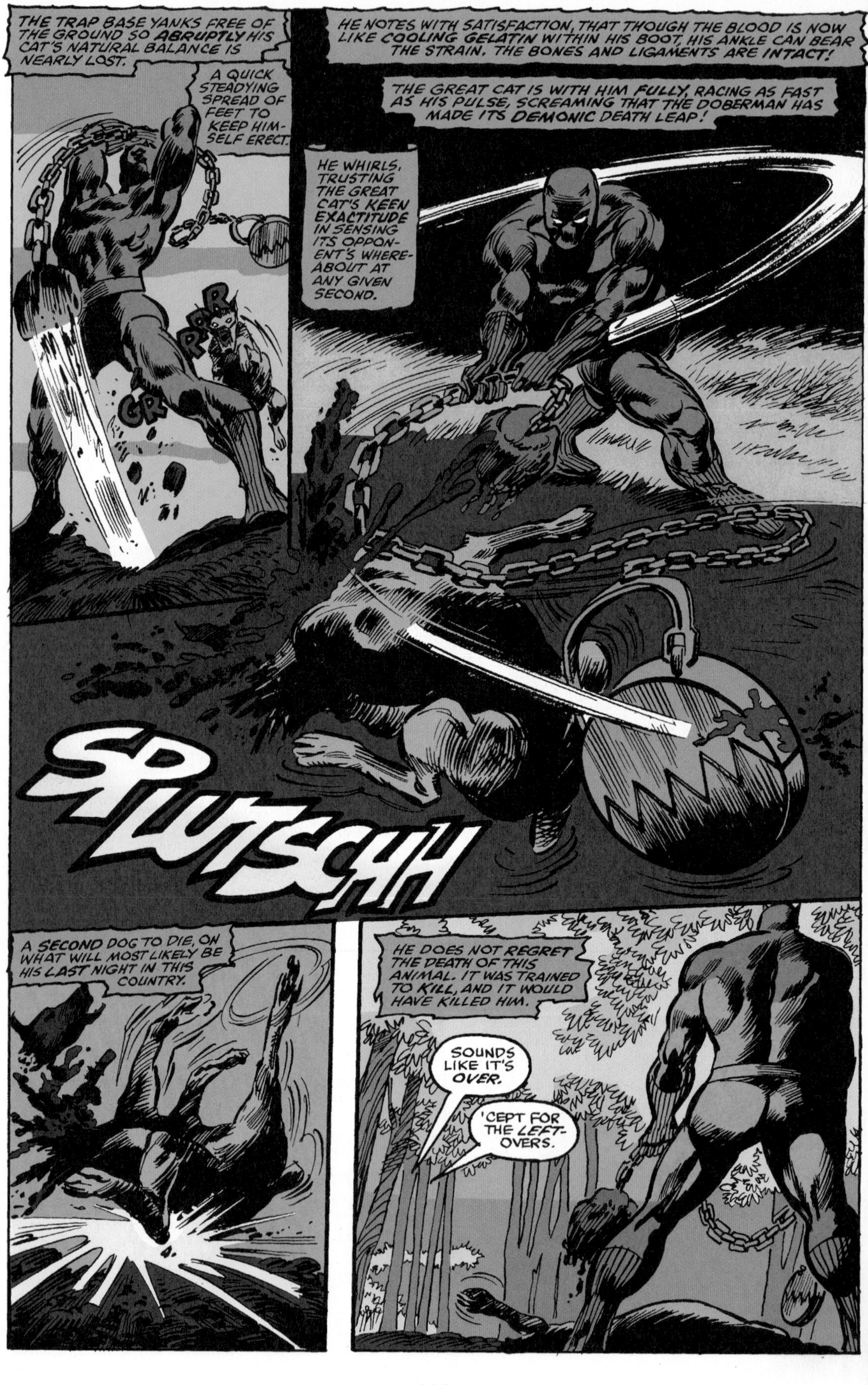
THE TRAP BASE YANKS FREE OF THE GROUND SO ABRUPTLY HIS CAT'S NATURAL BALANCE IS NEARLY LOST.
A QUICK STEADYING SPREAD OF FEET TO KEEP HIMSELF ERECT.
GR
RRR
HE NOTES WITH SATISFACTION, THAT THOUGH THE BLOOD IS NOW LIKE COOLING GELATIN WITHIN HIS BOOT, HIS ANKLE CAN BEAR THE STRAIN. THE BONES AND LIGAMENTS ARE INTACT!
THE GREAT CAT IS WITH HIM FULLY, RACING AS FAST AS HIS PULSE, SCREAMING THAT THE DOBERMAN HAS MADE ITS DEMONIC DEATH LEAP!
HE WHIRLS, TRUSTING THE GREAT CAT'S KEEN EXACTITUDE IN SENSING ITS OPPONENT'S WHEREABOUT AT ANY GIVEN SECOND.
SPLUTSCHH
A SECOND DOG TO DIE, ON WHAT WILL MOST LIKELY BE HIS LAST NIGHT IN THIS COUNTRY.
HE DOES NOT REGRET THE DEATH OF THIS ANIMAL. IT WAS TRAINED TO KILL, AND IT WOULD HAVE KILLED HIM.
SOUNDS LIKE IT'S OVER.
'CEPT FOR THE LEFTOVERS.

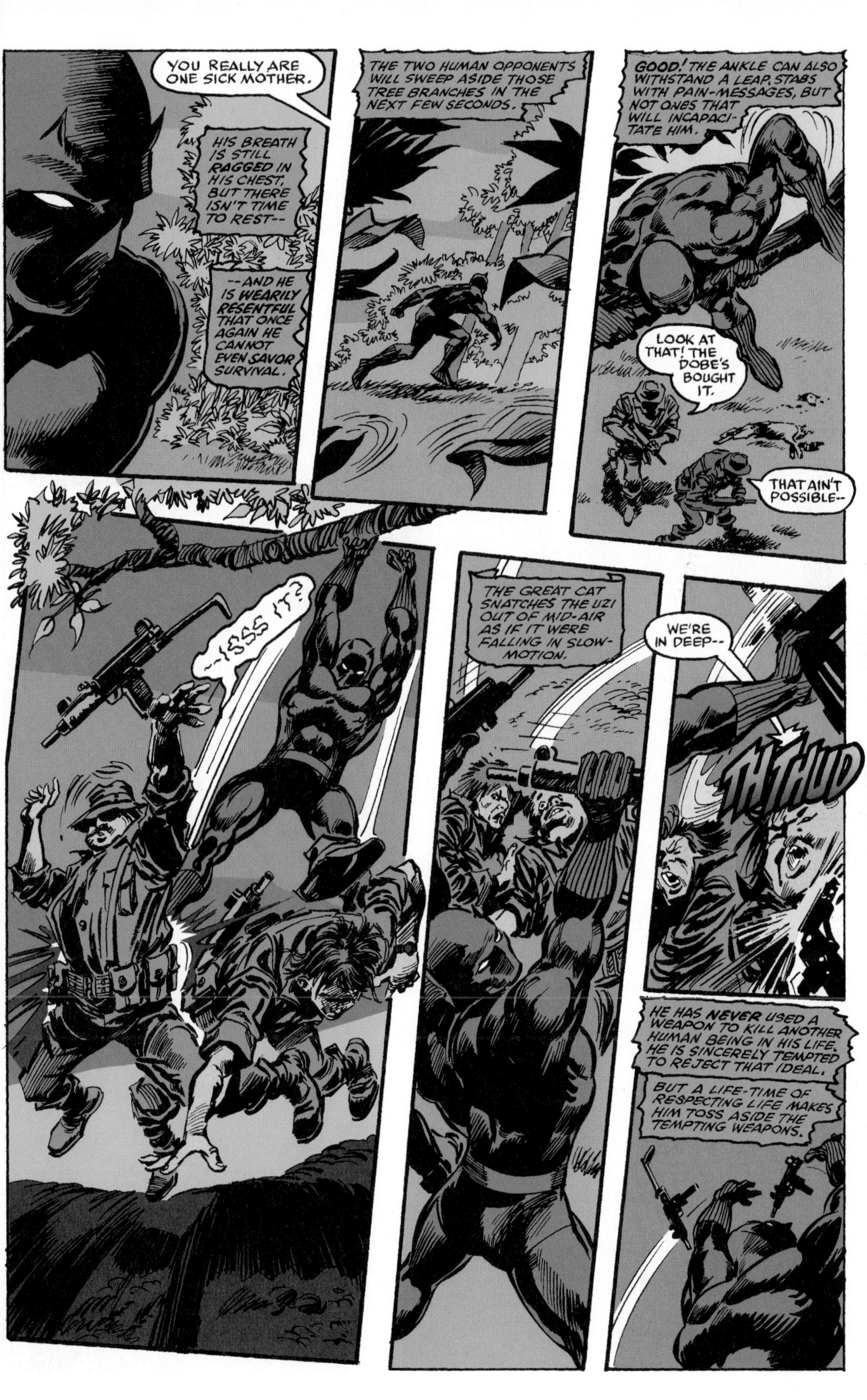

YOU REALLY ARE ONE SICK MOTHER.
HIS BREATH IS STILL RAGGED IN HIS CHEST, BUT THERE ISN'T TIME TO REST--
--AND HE IS WEARILY RESENTFUL THAT ONCE AGAIN HE CANNOT EVEN SAVOR SURVIVAL.
THE TWO HUMAN OPPONENTS WILL SWEEP ASIDE THOSE TREE BRANCHES IN THE NEXT FEW SECONDS.
GOOD! THE ANKLE CAN ALSO WITHSTAND A LEAP, STABS WITH PAIN-MESSAGES, BUT NOT ONES THAT WILL INCAPACITATE HIM.
LOOK AT THAT! THE DOBE'S BOUGHT IT.
THAT AIN'T POSSIBLE--
--ISSS IT?
THE GREAT CAT SNATCHES THE UZI OUT OF MID-AIR AS IF IT WERE FALLING IN SLOW-MOTION.
WE'RE IN DEEP--
THTHUD
HE HAS NEVER USED A WEAPON TO KILL ANOTHER HUMAN BEING IN HIS LIFE. HE IS SINCERELY TEMPTED TO REJECT THAT IDEAL.
BUT A LIFE-TIME OF RESPECTING LIFE MAKES HIM TOSS ASIDE THE TEMPTING WEAPONS.

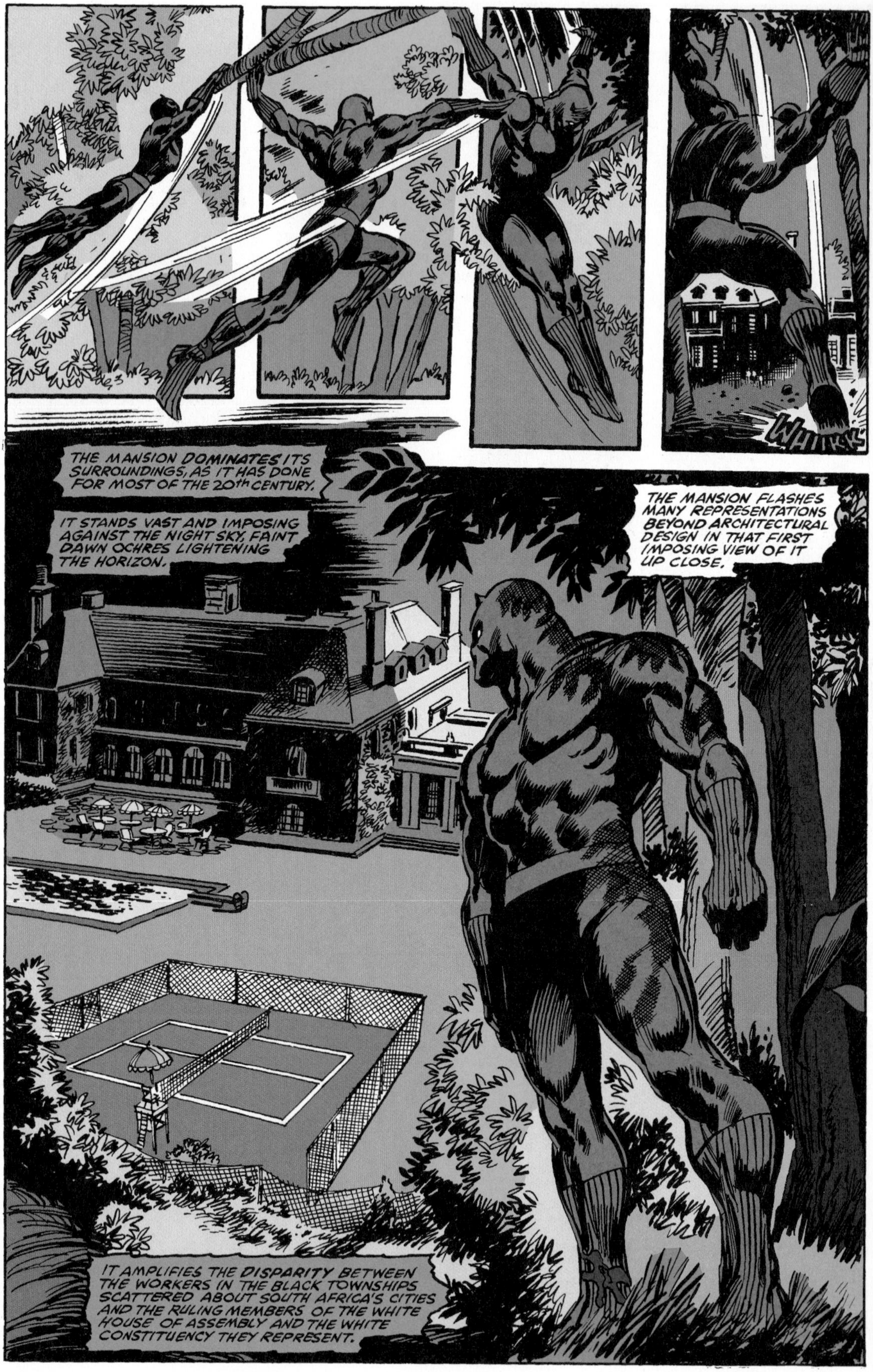
THE MANSION DOMINATES ITS SURROUNDINGS, AS IT HAS DONE FOR MOST OF THE 20th CENTURY.
IT STANDS VAST AND IMPOSING AGAINST THE NIGHT SKY, FAINT DAWN OCHRES LIGHTENING THE HORIZON.
THE MANSION FLASHES MANY REPRESENTATIONS BEYOND ARCHITECTURAL DESIGN IN THAT FIRST IMPOSING VIEW OF IT UP CLOSE.
IT AMPLIFIES THE DISPARITY BETWEEN THE WORKERS IN THE BLACK TOWNSHIPS SCATTERED ABOUT SOUTH AFRICA'S CITIES AND THE RULING MEMBERS OF THE WHITE HOUSE OF ASSEMBLY AND THE WHITE CONSTITUENCY THEY REPRESENT.

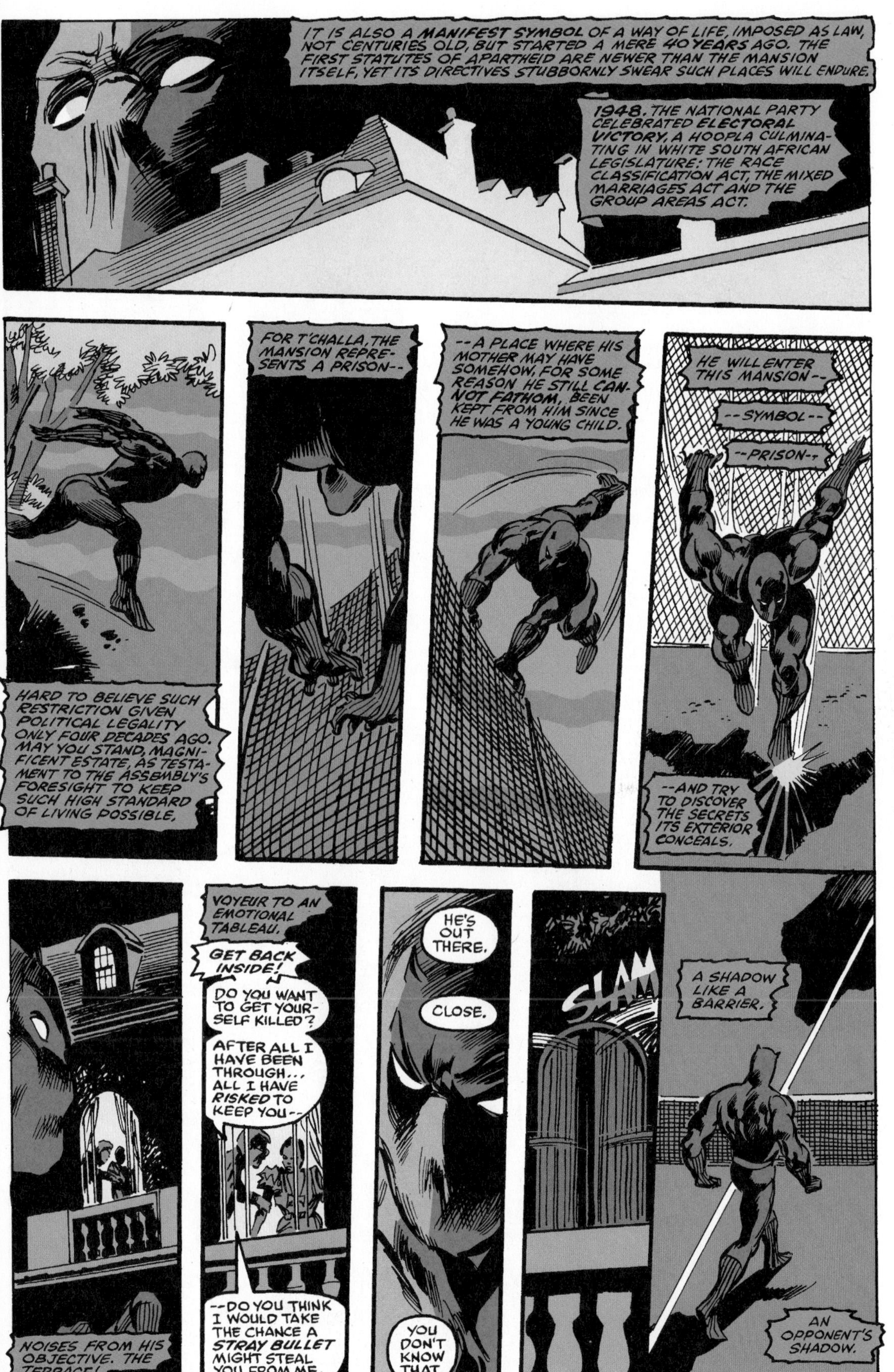
IT IS ALSO A MANIFEST SYMBOL OF A WAY OF LIFE, IMPOSED AS LAW, NOT CENTURIES OLD, BUT STARTED A MERE 40 YEARS AGO. THE FIRST STATUTES OF APARTHEID ARE NEWER THAN THE MANSION ITSELF, YET ITS DIRECTIVES STUBBORNLY SWEAR SUCH PLACES WILL ENDURE.
1948. THE NATIONAL PARTY CELEBRATED ELECTORAL VICTORY, A HOOPLA CULMINATING IN WHITE SOUTH AFRICAN LEGISLATURE: THE RACE CLASSIFICATION ACT, THE MIXED MARRIAGES ACT AND THE GROUP AREAS ACT.
HARD TO BELIEVE SUCH RESTRICTION GIVEN POLITICAL LEGALITY ONLY FOUR DECADES AGO. MAY YOU STAND, MAGNIFICENT ESTATE, AS TESTAMENT TO THE ASSEMBLY'S FORESIGHT TO KEEP SUCH HIGH STANDARD OF LIVING POSSIBLE.
FOR T'CHALLA, THE MANSION REPRESENTS A PRISON--
--A PLACE WHERE HIS MOTHER MAY HAVE SOMEHOW, FOR SOME REASON HE STILL CANNOT FATHOM, BEEN KEPT FROM HIM SINCE HE WAS A YOUNG CHILD.
HE WILL ENTER THIS MANSION--
--SYMBOL--
--PRISON--
--AND TRY TO DISCOVER THE SECRETS ITS EXTERIOR CONCEALS.
NOISES FROM HIS OBJECTIVE. THE TERRACE!
VOYEUR TO AN EMOTIONAL TABLEAU.
GET BACK INSIDE!
DO YOU WANT TO GET YOURSELF KILLED?
AFTER ALL I HAVE BEEN THROUGH... ALL I HAVE RISKED TO KEEP YOU--
--DO YOU THINK I WOULD TAKE THE CHANCE A STRAY BULLET MIGHT STEAL YOU FROM ME.
HE'S OUT THERE.
CLOSE.
YOU DON'T KNOW THAT.
SLAM
A SHADOW LIKE A BARRIER.
AN OPPONENT'S SHADOW.

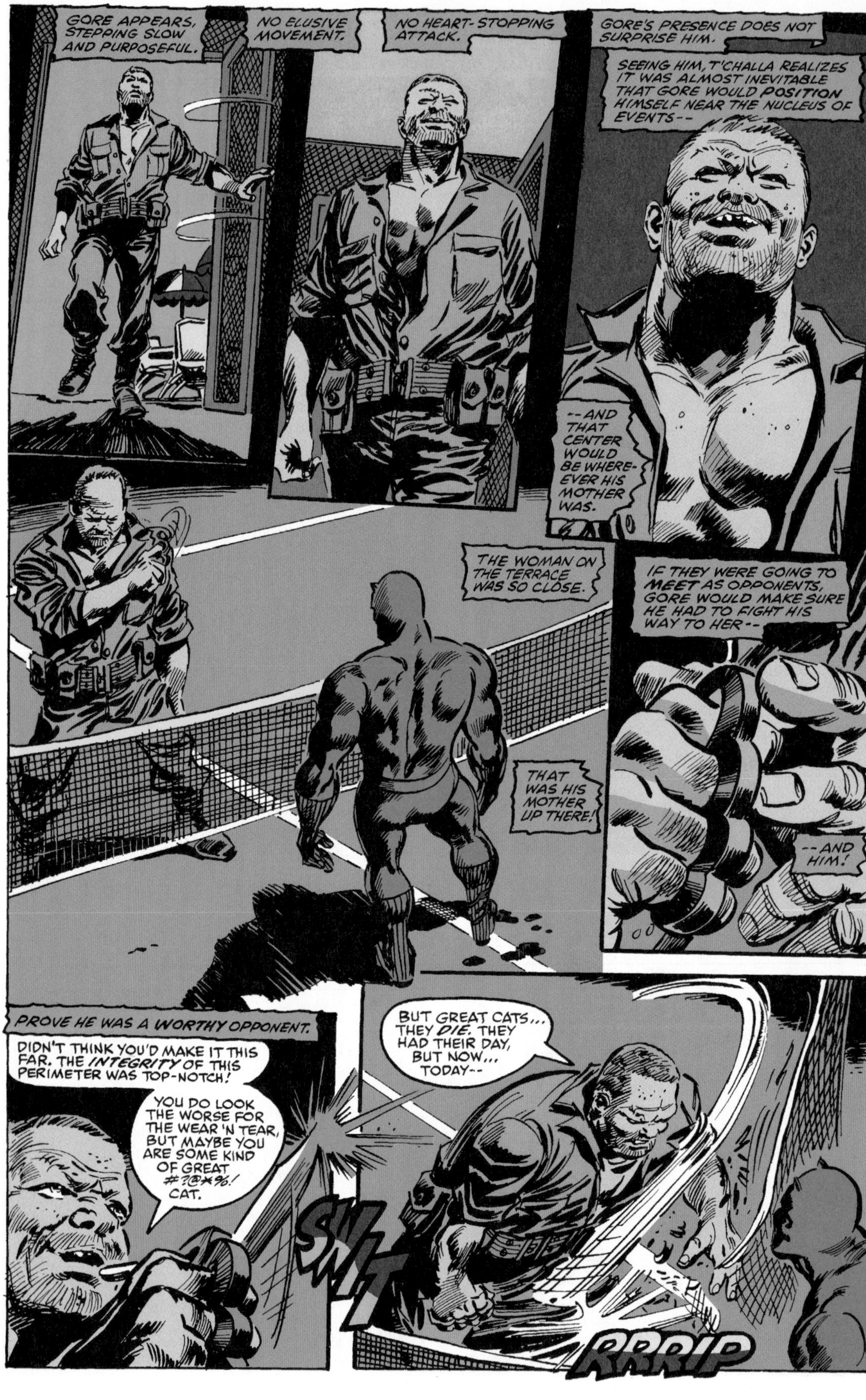
GORE APPEARS, STEPPING SLOW AND PURPOSEFUL.
NO ELUSIVE MOVEMENT.
NO HEART-STOPPING ATTACK.
GORE'S PRESENCE DOES NOT SURPRISE HIM.
SEEING HIM, T'CHALLA REALIZES IT WAS ALMOST INEVITABLE THAT GORE WOULD POSITION HIMSELF NEAR THE NUCLEUS OF EVENTS--
--AND THAT CENTER WOULD BE WHEREEVER HIS MOTHER WAS.
THE WOMAN ON THE TERRACE WAS SO CLOSE.
THAT WAS HIS MOTHER UP THERE!
IF THEY WERE GOING TO MEET AS OPPONENTS, GORE WOULD MAKE SURE HE HAD TO FIGHT HIS WAY TO HER--
--AND HIM!
PROVE HE WAS A WORTHY OPPONENT.
DIDN'T THINK YOU'D MAKE IT THIS FAR. THE INTEGRITY OF THIS PERIMETER WAS TOP-NOTCH!
YOU DO LOOK THE WORSE FOR THE WEAR 'N TEAR, BUT MAYBE YOU ARE SOME KIND OF GREAT #?@*%! CAT.
SNIT
BUT GREAT CATS... THEY DIE. THEY HAD THEIR DAY, BUT NOW... TODAY--
RRRIP

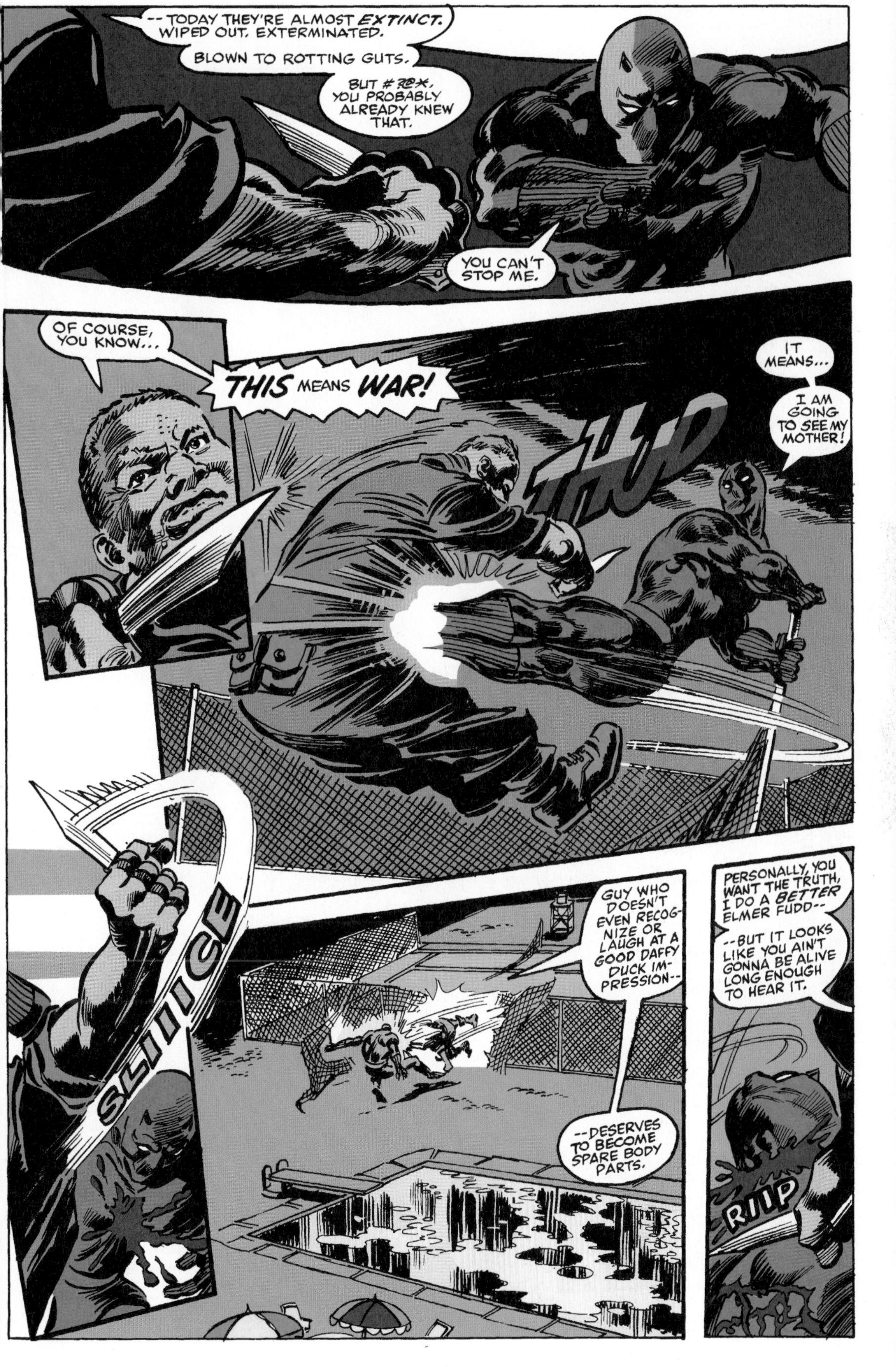
--TODAY THEY'RE ALMOST EXTINCT. WIPED OUT. EXTERMINATED.
BLOWN TO ROTTING GUTS.
BUT #?@*, YOU PROBABLY ALREADY KNEW THAT.
YOU CAN'T STOP ME.
OF COURSE, YOU KNOW...
THIS MEANS WAR!
IT MEANS...
I AM GOING TO SEE MY MOTHER!
THUD
SLIIICE
GUY WHO DOESN'T EVEN RECOG-NIZE OR LAUGH AT A GOOD DAFFY DUCK IM-PRESSION--
--DESERVES TO BECOME SPARE BODY PARTS.
PERSONALLY, YOU WANT THE TRUTH, I DO A BETTER ELMER FUDD--
--BUT IT LOOKS LIKE YOU AIN'T GONNA BE ALIVE LONG ENOUGH TO HEAR IT.
RIIP

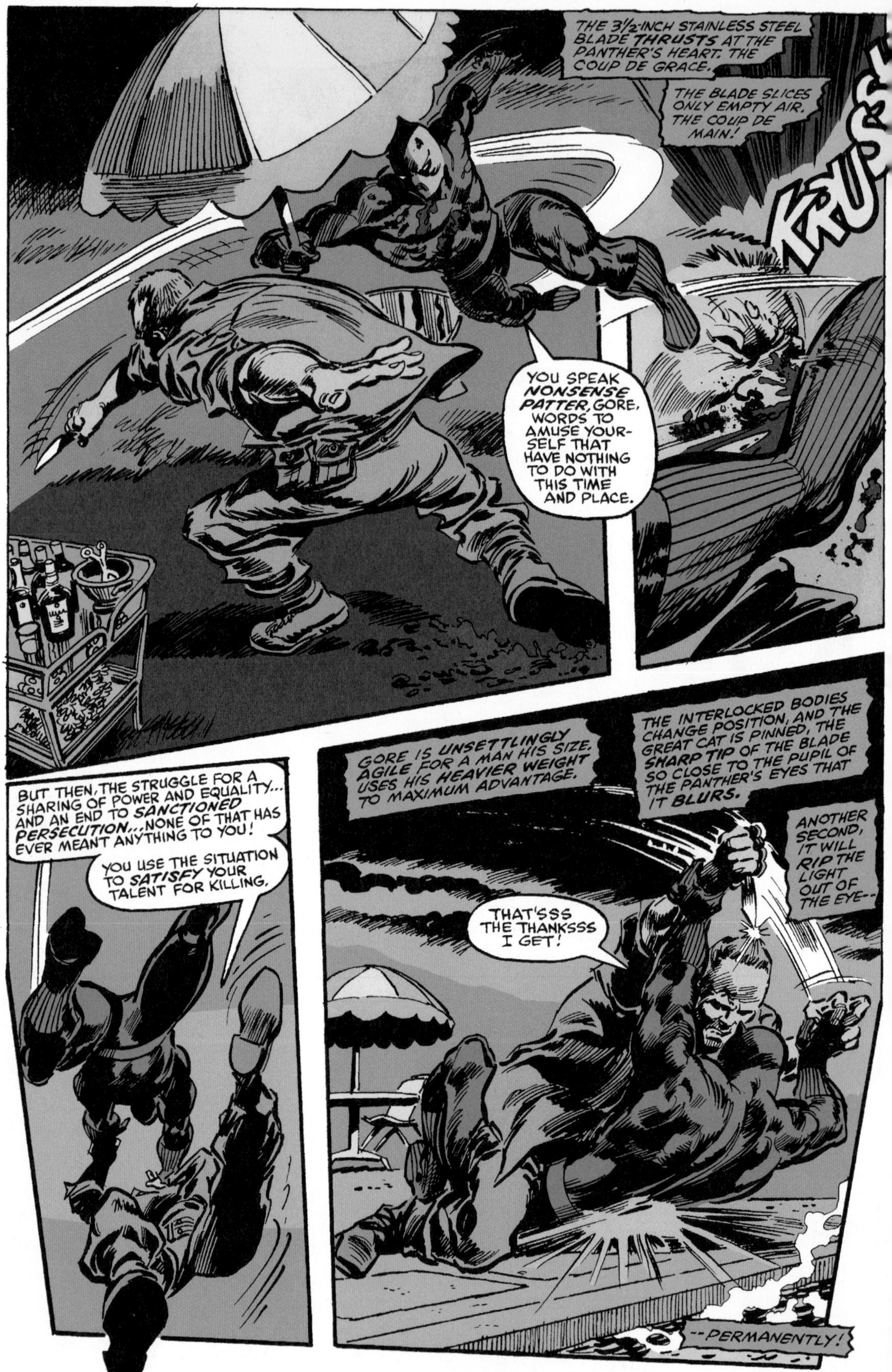
THE 3½-INCH STAINLESS STEEL BLADE THRUSTS AT THE PANTHER'S HEART. THE COUP DE GRACE.
THE BLADE SLICES ONLY EMPTY AIR. THE COUP DE MAIN!
KRUSSS
YOU SPEAK NONSENSE PATTER, GORE, WORDS TO AMUSE YOURSELF THAT HAVE NOTHING TO DO WITH THIS TIME AND PLACE.
BUT THEN, THE STRUGGLE FOR A SHARING OF POWER AND EQUALITY... AND AN END TO SANCTIONED PERSECUTION... NONE OF THAT HAS EVER MEANT ANYTHING TO YOU!
YOU USE THE SITUATION TO SATISFY YOUR TALENT FOR KILLING.
GORE IS UNSETTLINGLY AGILE FOR A MAN HIS SIZE. USES HIS HEAVIER WEIGHT TO MAXIMUM ADVANTAGE.
THE INTERLOCKED BODIES CHANGE POSITION, AND THE GREAT CAT IS PINNED, THE SHARP TIP OF THE BLADE SO CLOSE TO THE PUPIL OF THE PANTHER'S EYES THAT IT BLURS.
ANOTHER SECOND, IT WILL RIP THE LIGHT OUT OF THE EYE--
THAT'SSS THE THANKSSS I GET!
--PERMANENTLY!

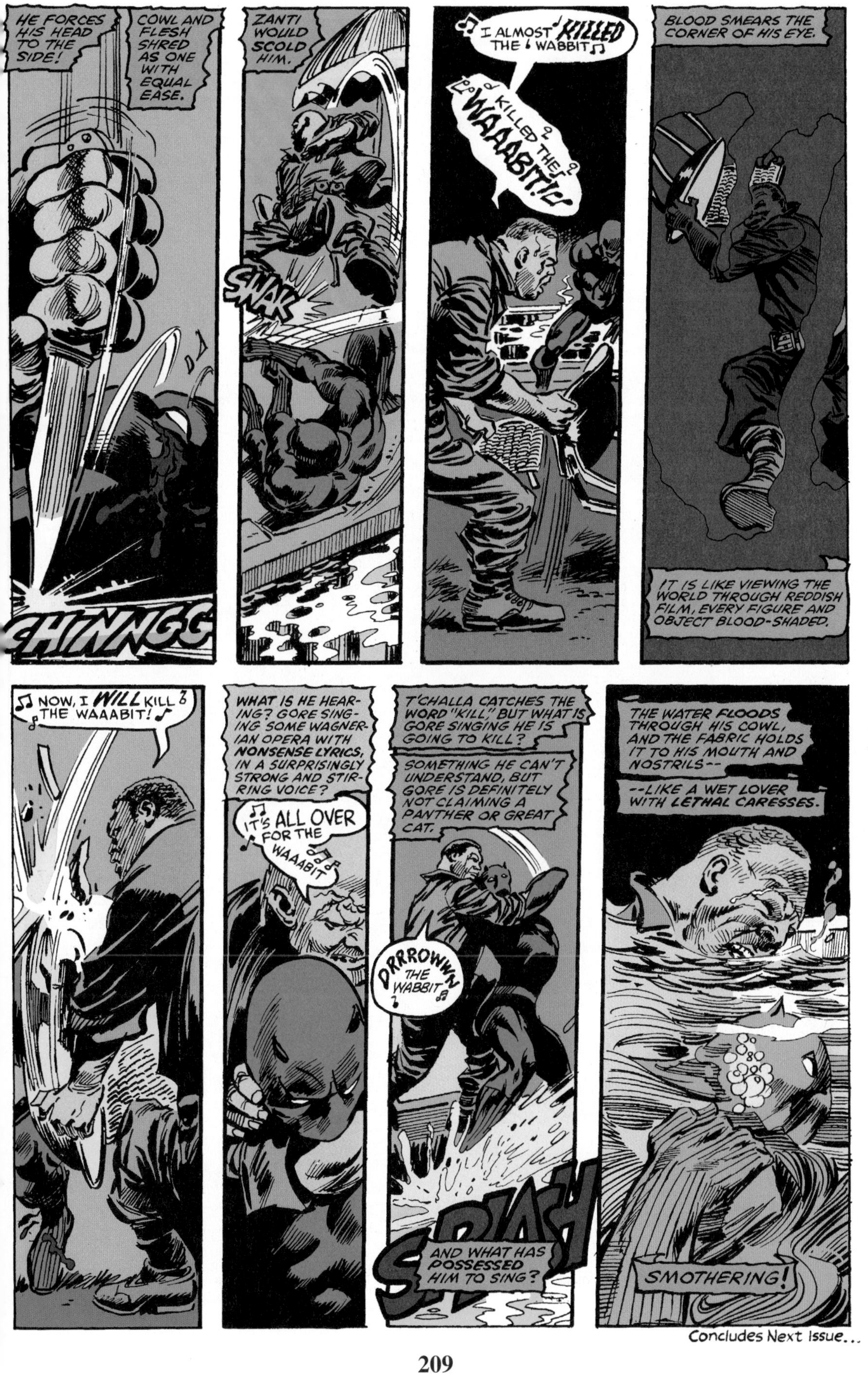
HE FORCES HIS HEAD TO THE SIDE!
COWL AND FLESH SHRED AS ONE WITH EQUAL EASE.
CHINNGG
ZANTI WOULD SCOLD HIM.
SNAK
I ALMOST KILLED THE WABBIT
KILLED THE WAAABIT!
BLOOD SMEARS THE CORNER OF HIS EYE.
IT IS LIKE VIEWING THE WORLD THROUGH REDDISH FILM, EVERY FIGURE AND OBJECT BLOOD-SHADED.
NOW, I WILL KILL THE WAAABIT!
WHAT IS HE HEARING? GORE SINGING SOME WAGNERIAN OPERA WITH NONSENSE LYRICS, IN A SURPRISINGLY STRONG AND STIRRING VOICE?
IT'S ALL OVER FOR THE WAAABIT
T'CHALLA CATCHES THE WORD "KILL," BUT WHAT IS GORE SINGING HE IS GOING TO KILL?
SOMETHING HE CAN'T UNDERSTAND, BUT GORE IS DEFINITELY NOT CLAIMING A PANTHER OR GREAT CAT.
DRRROWWN THE WABBIT
SPLASH
AND WHAT HAS POSSESSED HIM TO SING?
THE WATER FLOODS THROUGH HIS COWL, AND THE FABRIC HOLDS IT TO HIS MOUTH AND NOSTRILS--
--LIKE A WET LOVER WITH LETHAL CARESSES.
SMOTHERING!

Concludes Next Issue...

PANTHER'S QUEST

> "It was strange, he thought, to find himself vaguely on the defensive for what yesterday was accepted necessity. In the years that had passed he had never once considered the possibility that he was wrong. It took her presence to bring about such thoughts. And they were strange, alien thoughts."
>
> —*From the novel, "I Am Legend,"*
> ***by Richard Matheson, 1954.***
> ***Hardbound edition published by Nelson Doubleday.***

STARRING: THE BLACK PANTHER
PART XXV

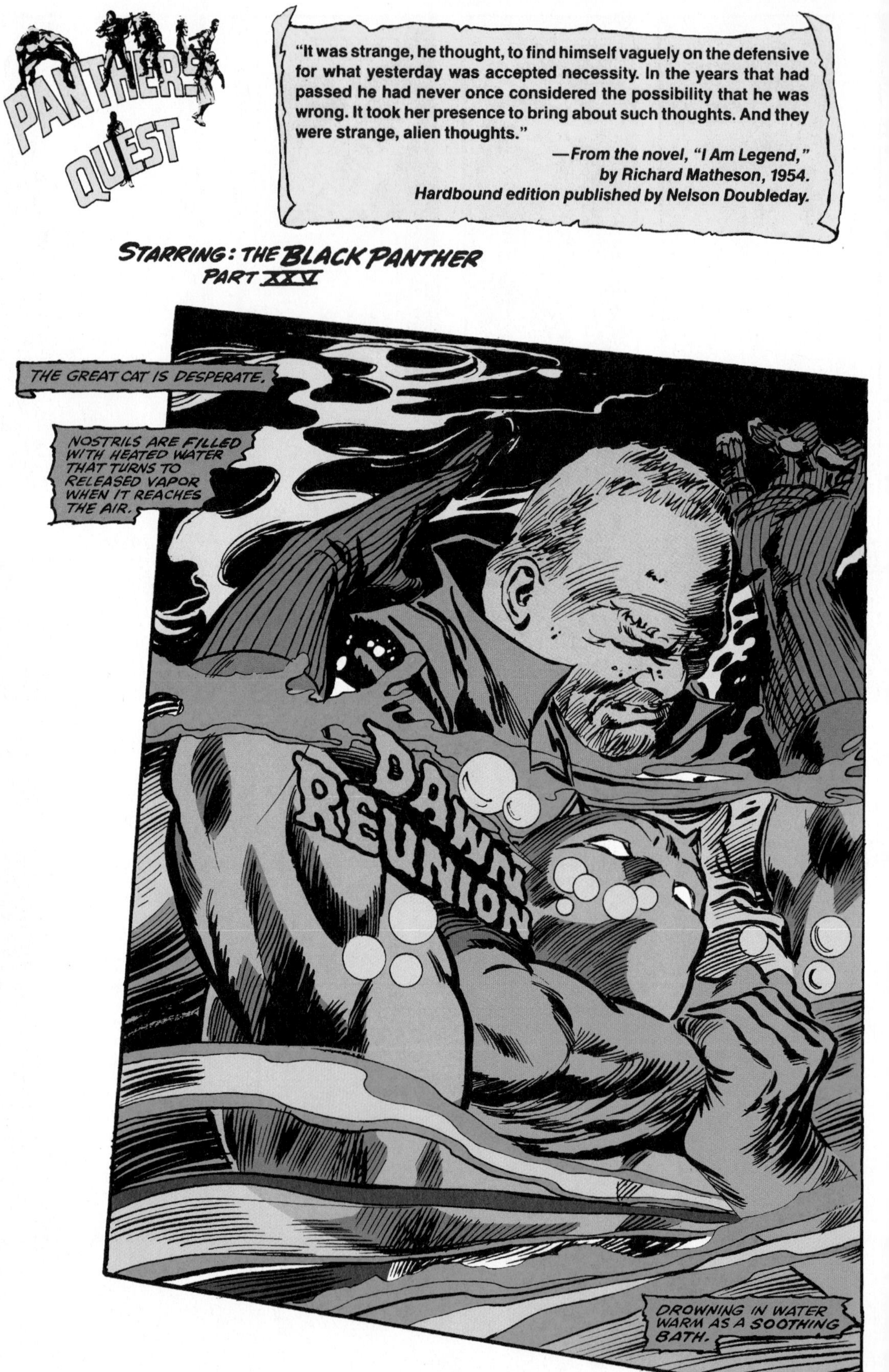
THE GREAT CAT IS DESPERATE.
NOSTRILS ARE FILLED WITH HEATED WATER THAT TURNS TO RELEASED VAPOR WHEN IT REACHES THE AIR.
DAWN REUNION
DROWNING IN WATER WARM AS A SOOTHING BATH.

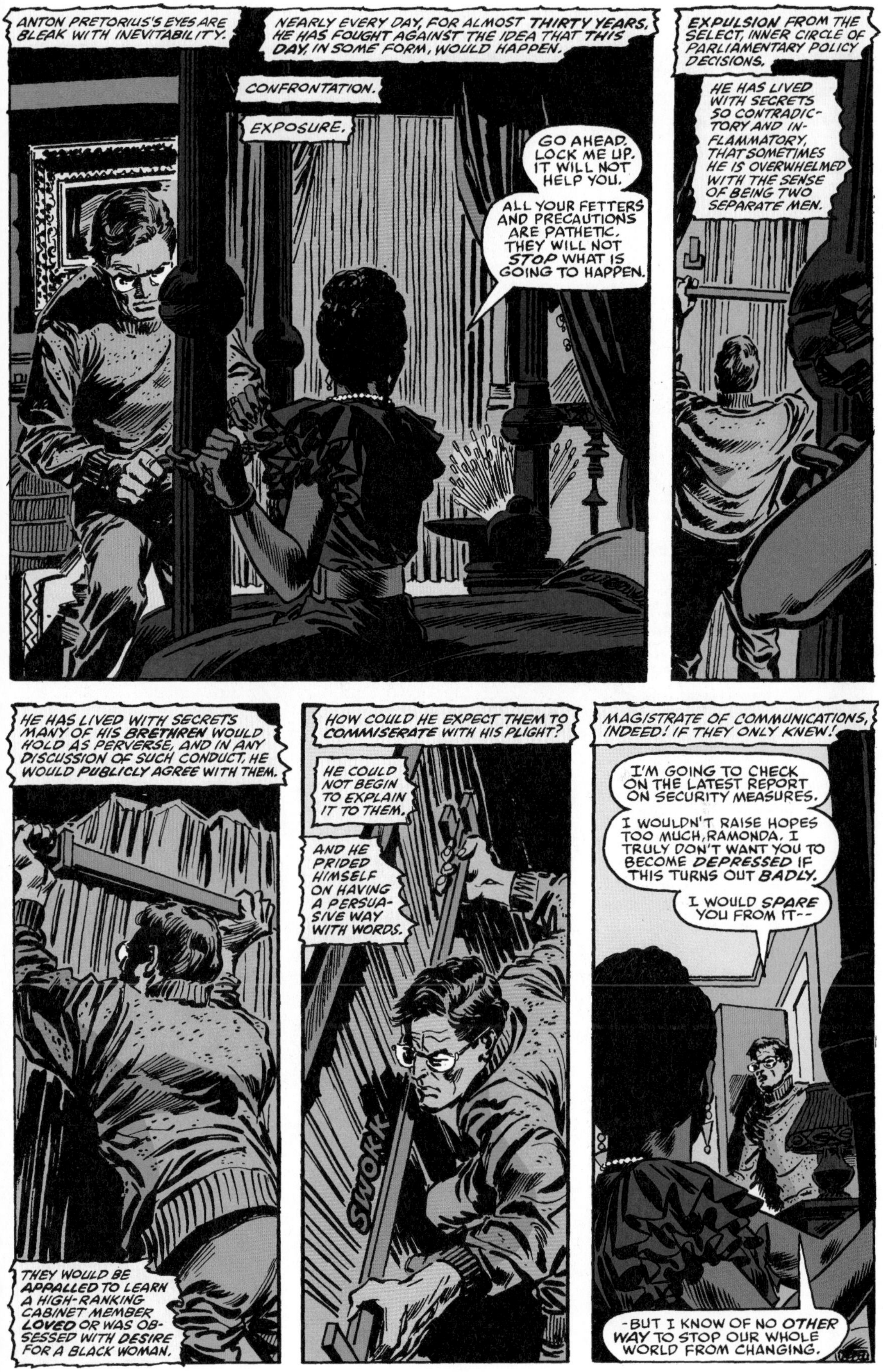
ANTON PRETORIUS'S EYES ARE BLEAK WITH INEVITABILITY.
NEARLY EVERY DAY, FOR ALMOST THIRTY YEARS, HE HAS FOUGHT AGAINST THE IDEA THAT THIS DAY, IN SOME FORM, WOULD HAPPEN.
CONFRONTATION.
EXPOSURE.
GO AHEAD. LOCK ME UP. IT WILL NOT HELP YOU.
ALL YOUR FETTERS AND PRECAUTIONS ARE PATHETIC. THEY WILL NOT STOP WHAT IS GOING TO HAPPEN.
EXPULSION FROM THE SELECT, INNER CIRCLE OF PARLIAMENTARY POLICY DECISIONS.
HE HAS LIVED WITH SECRETS SO CONTRADICTORY AND INFLAMMATORY, THAT SOMETIMES HE IS OVERWHELMED WITH THE SENSE OF BEING TWO SEPARATE MEN.
HE HAS LIVED WITH SECRETS MANY OF HIS BRETHREN WOULD HOLD AS PERVERSE, AND IN ANY DISCUSSION OF SUCH CONDUCT, HE WOULD PUBLICLY AGREE WITH THEM.
THEY WOULD BE APPALLED TO LEARN A HIGH-RANKING CABINET MEMBER LOVED OR WAS OBSESSED WITH DESIRE FOR A BLACK WOMAN.
HOW COULD HE EXPECT THEM TO COMMISERATE WITH HIS PLIGHT?
HE COULD NOT BEGIN TO EXPLAIN IT TO THEM.
AND HE PRIDED HIMSELF ON HAVING A PERSUASIVE WAY WITH WORDS.
SWOKK
MAGISTRATE OF COMMUNICATIONS, INDEED! IF THEY ONLY KNEW!
I'M GOING TO CHECK ON THE LATEST REPORT ON SECURITY MEASURES.
I WOULDN'T RAISE HOPES TOO MUCH, RAMONDA. I TRULY DON'T WANT YOU TO BECOME DEPRESSED IF THIS TURNS OUT BADLY.
I WOULD SPARE YOU FROM IT--
-BUT I KNOW OF NO OTHER WAY TO STOP OUR WHOLE WORLD FROM CHANGING.

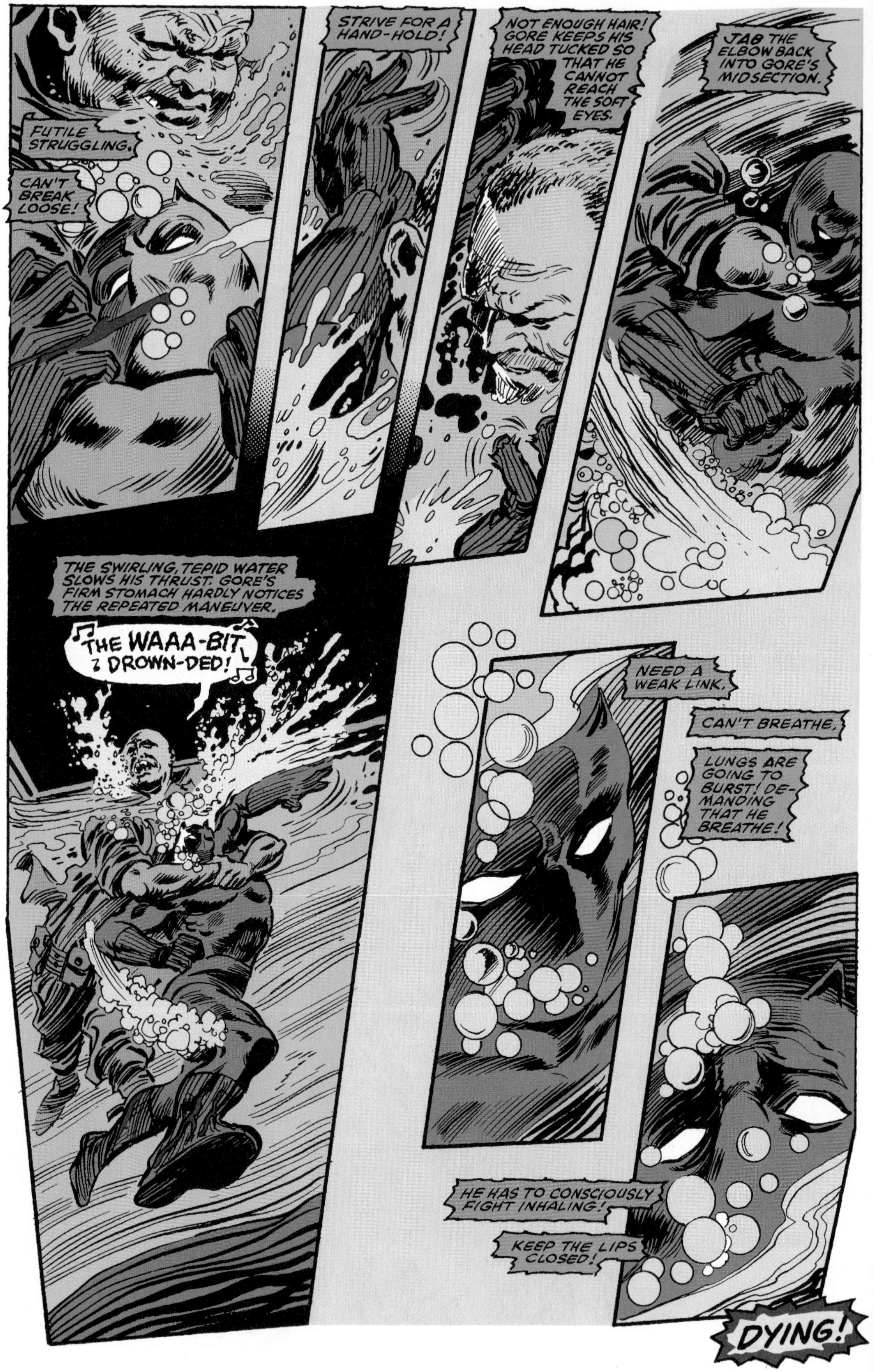
FUTILE STRUGGLING.
CAN'T BREAK LOOSE!
STRIVE FOR A HAND-HOLD!
NOT ENOUGH HAIR! GORE KEEPS HIS HEAD TUCKED SO THAT HE CANNOT REACH THE SOFT EYES.
JAB THE ELBOW BACK INTO GORE'S MIDSECTION.
THE SWIRLING, TEPID WATER SLOWS HIS THRUST. GORE'S FIRM STOMACH HARDLY NOTICES THE REPEATED MANEUVER.
THE WAAA-BIT DROWN-DED!
NEED A WEAK LINK.
CAN'T BREATHE.
LUNGS ARE GOING TO BURST! DE-MANDING THAT HE BREATHE!
HE HAS TO CONSCIOUSLY FIGHT INHALING!
KEEP THE LIPS CLOSED!
DYING!

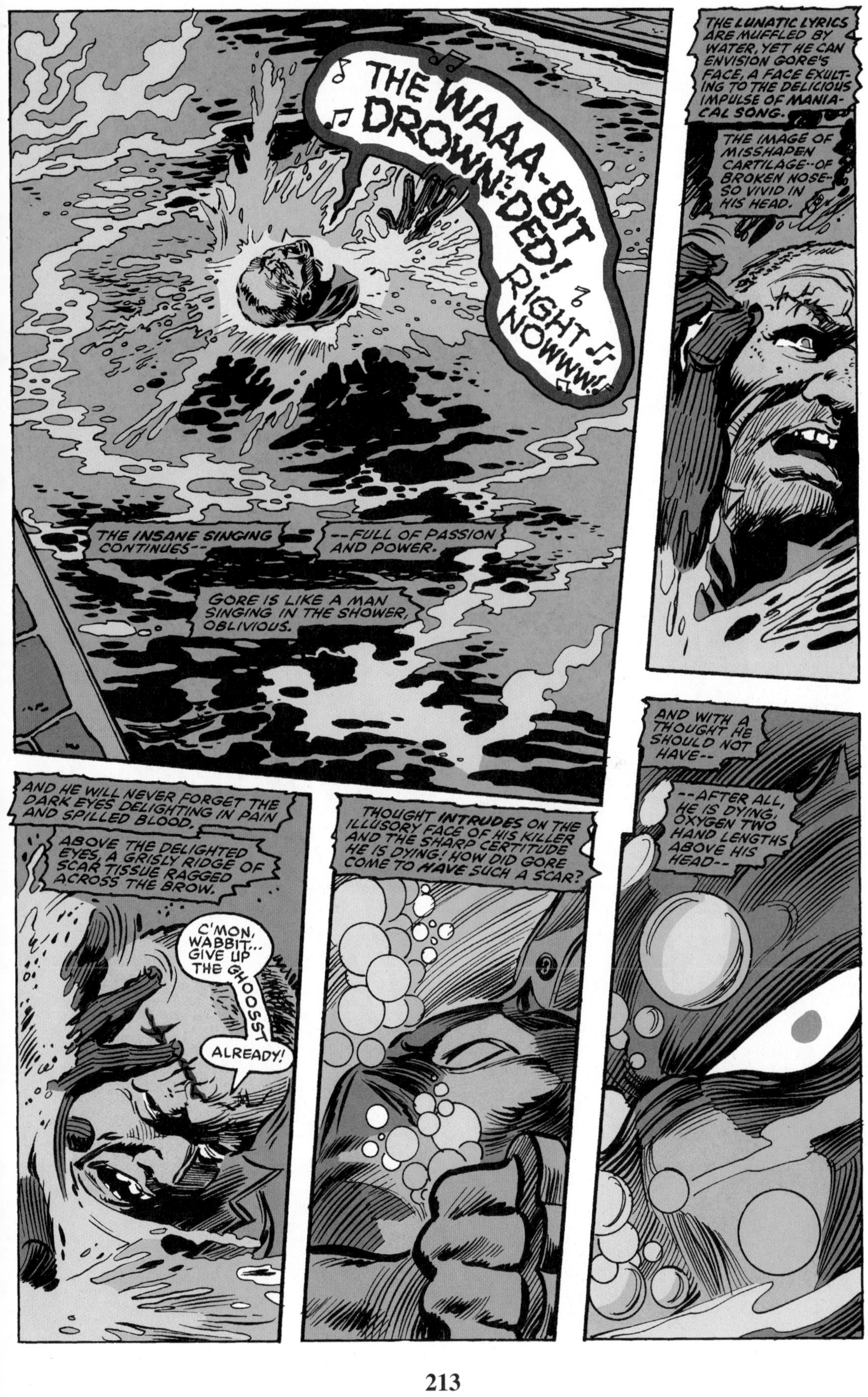
THE WAAA-BIT DROWN-DED! RIGHT NOWWW!
THE INSANE SINGING CONTINUES--
--FULL OF PASSION AND POWER.
GORE IS LIKE A MAN SINGING IN THE SHOWER, OBLIVIOUS.
THE LUNATIC LYRICS ARE MUFFLED BY WATER, YET HE CAN ENVISION GORE'S FACE, A FACE EXULTING TO THE DELICIOUS IMPULSE OF MANIACAL SONG.
THE IMAGE OF MISSHAPEN CARTILAGE--OF BROKEN NOSE--SO VIVID IN HIS HEAD.
AND HE WILL NEVER FORGET THE DARK EYES DELIGHTING IN PAIN AND SPILLED BLOOD.
ABOVE THE DELIGHTED EYES, A GRISLY RIDGE OF SCAR TISSUE RAGGED ACROSS THE BROW.
C'MON, WABBIT... GIVE UP THE GHOOSST
ALREADY!
THOUGHT INTRUDES ON THE ILLUSORY FACE OF HIS KILLER AND THE SHARP CERTITUDE HE IS DYING! HOW DID GORE COME TO HAVE SUCH A SCAR?
AND WITH A THOUGHT HE SHOULD NOT HAVE--
--AFTER ALL, HE IS DYING, OXYGEN TWO HAND LENGTHS ABOVE HIS HEAD--

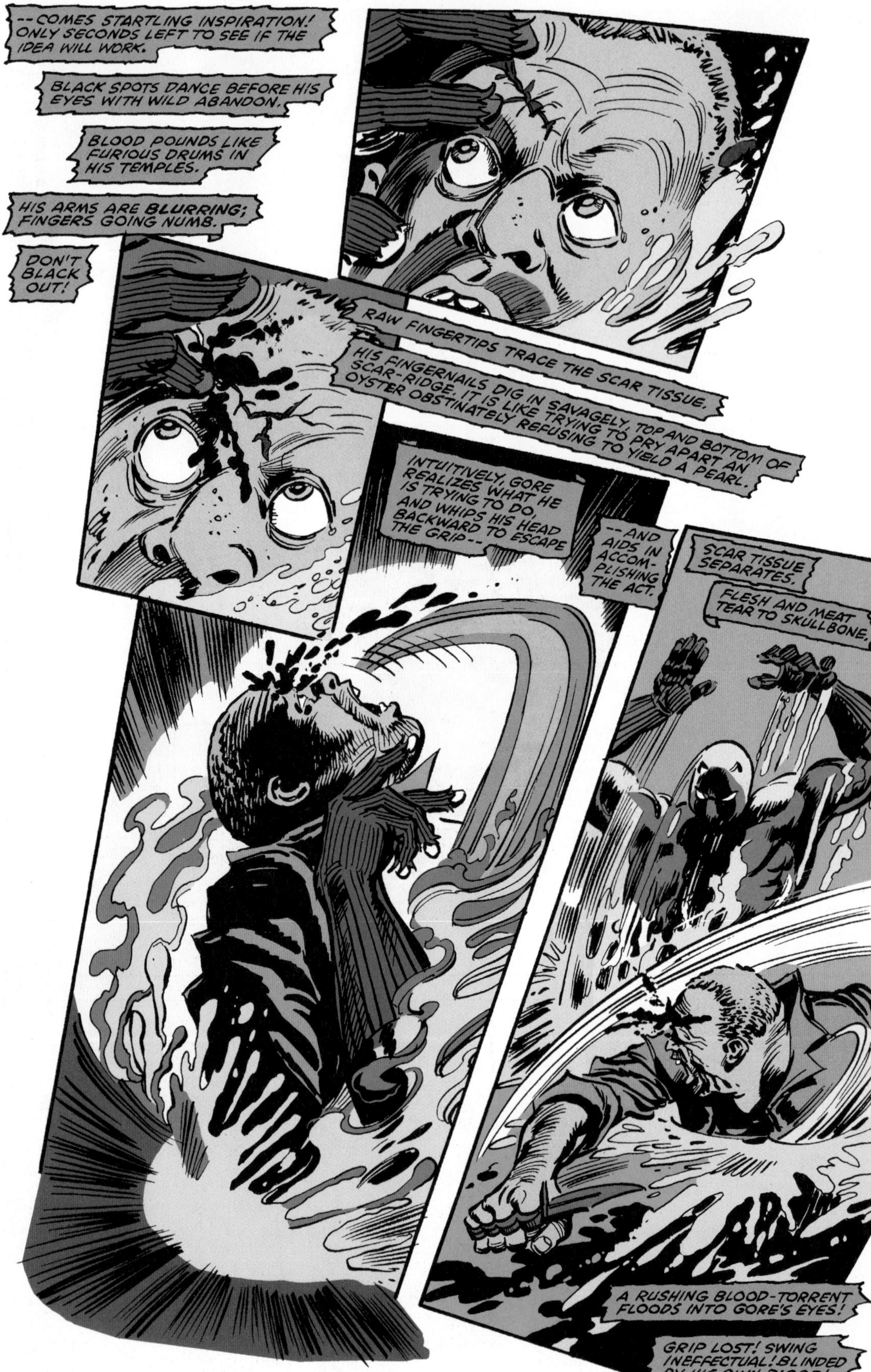
--COMES STARTLING INSPIRATION! ONLY SECONDS LEFT TO SEE IF THE IDEA WILL WORK.
BLACK SPOTS DANCE BEFORE HIS EYES WITH WILD ABANDON.
BLOOD POUNDS LIKE FURIOUS DRUMS IN HIS TEMPLES.
HIS ARMS ARE BLURRING; FINGERS GOING NUMB.
DON'T BLACK OUT!
RAW FINGERTIPS TRACE THE SCAR TISSUE.
HIS FINGERNAILS DIG IN SAVAGELY, TOP AND BOTTOM OF SCAR-RIDGE. IT IS LIKE TRYING TO PRY APART AN OYSTER OBSTINATELY REFUSING TO YIELD A PEARL.
INTUITIVELY, GORE REALIZES WHAT HE IS TRYING TO DO, AND WHIPS HIS HEAD BACKWARD TO ESCAPE THE GRIP--
--AND AIDS IN ACCOMPLISHING THE ACT.
SCAR TISSUE SEPARATES.
FLESH AND MEAT TEAR TO SKULLBONE.
A RUSHING BLOOD-TORRENT FLOODS INTO GORE'S EYES!
GRIP LOST! SWING INEFFECTUAL! BLINDED BY HIS OWN BLOOD!

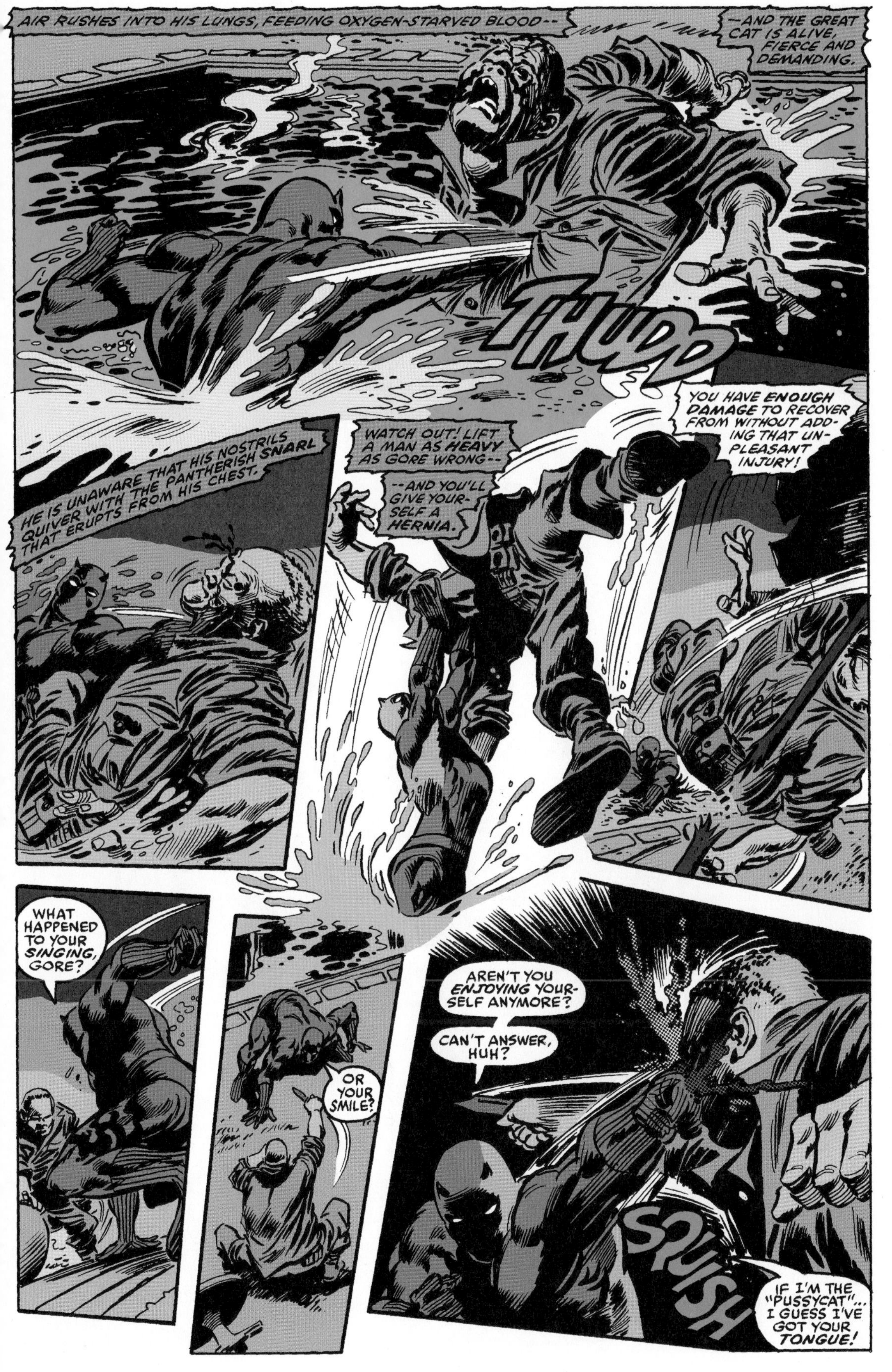
AIR RUSHES INTO HIS LUNGS, FEEDING OXYGEN-STARVED BLOOD--
--AND THE GREAT CAT IS ALIVE, FIERCE AND DEMANDING.
THUDD
HE IS UNAWARE THAT HIS NOSTRILS QUIVER WITH THE PANTHERISH SNARL THAT ERUPTS FROM HIS CHEST.
WATCH OUT! LIFT A MAN AS HEAVY AS GORE WRONG--
--AND YOU'LL GIVE YOURSELF A HERNIA.
YOU HAVE ENOUGH DAMAGE TO RECOVER FROM WITHOUT ADDING THAT UNPLEASANT INJURY!
WHAT HAPPENED TO YOUR SINGING, GORE?
OR YOUR SMILE?
AREN'T YOU ENJOYING YOURSELF ANYMORE?
CAN'T ANSWER, HUH?
SQUISH
IF I'M THE "PUSSYCAT"... I GUESS I'VE GOT YOUR TONGUE!

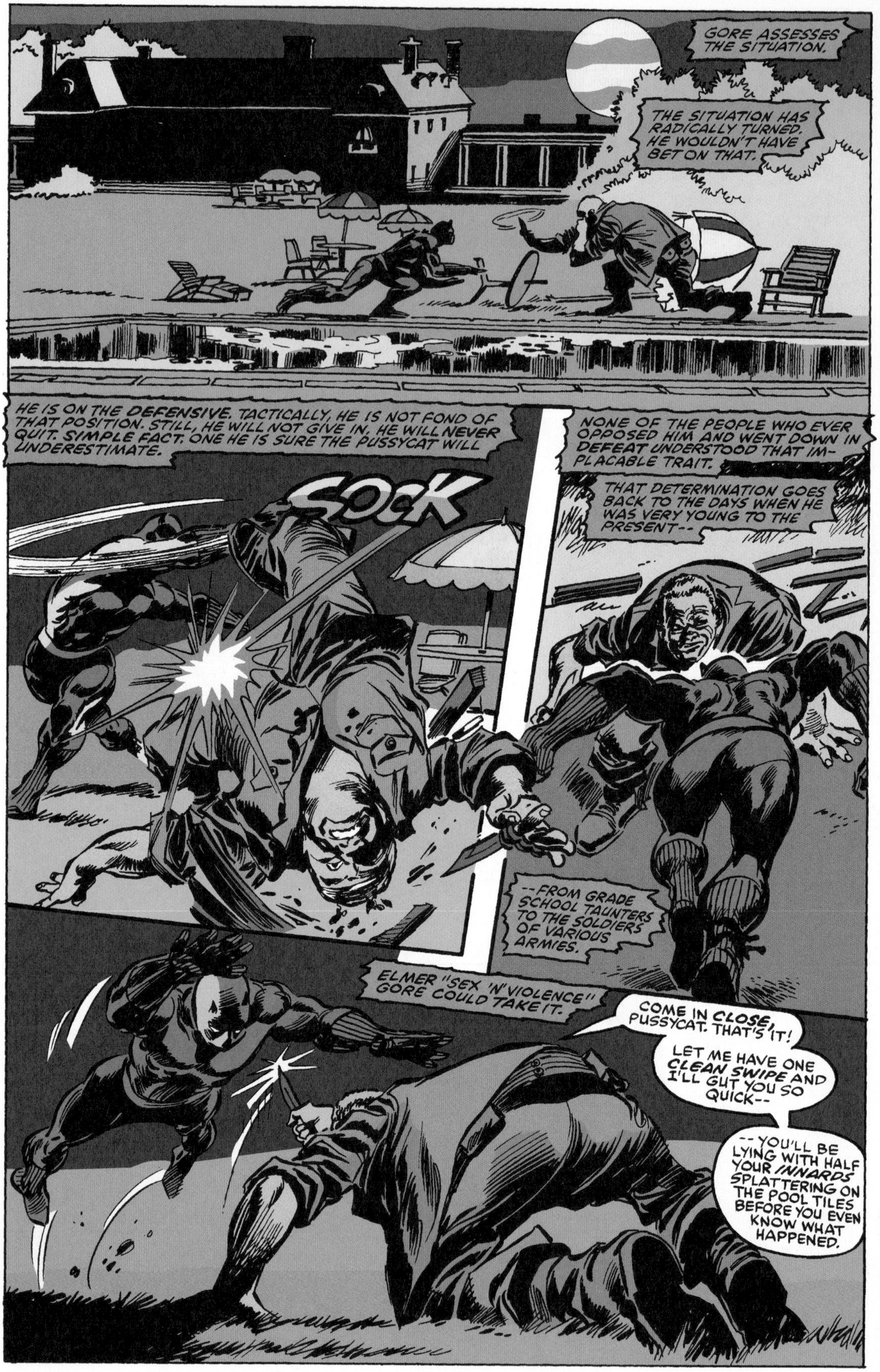
GORE ASSESSES THE SITUATION.
THE SITUATION HAS RADICALLY TURNED. HE WOULDN'T HAVE BET ON THAT.
HE IS ON THE DEFENSIVE. TACTICALLY, HE IS NOT FOND OF THAT POSITION. STILL, HE WILL NOT GIVE IN. HE WILL NEVER QUIT. SIMPLE FACT. ONE HE IS SURE THE PUSSYCAT WILL UNDERESTIMATE.
SOCK
NONE OF THE PEOPLE WHO EVER OPPOSED HIM AND WENT DOWN IN DEFEAT UNDERSTOOD THAT IMPLACABLE TRAIT.
THAT DETERMINATION GOES BACK TO THE DAYS WHEN HE WAS VERY YOUNG TO THE PRESENT--
--FROM GRADE SCHOOL TAUNTERS TO THE SOLDIERS OF VARIOUS ARMIES.
ELMER "SEX 'N' VIOLENCE" GORE COULD TAKE IT.
COME IN CLOSE, PUSSYCAT. THAT'S IT!
LET ME HAVE ONE CLEAN SWIPE AND I'LL GUT YOU SO QUICK--
--YOU'LL BE LYING WITH HALF YOUR INNARDS SPLATTERING ON THE POOL TILES BEFORE YOU EVEN KNOW WHAT HAPPENED.

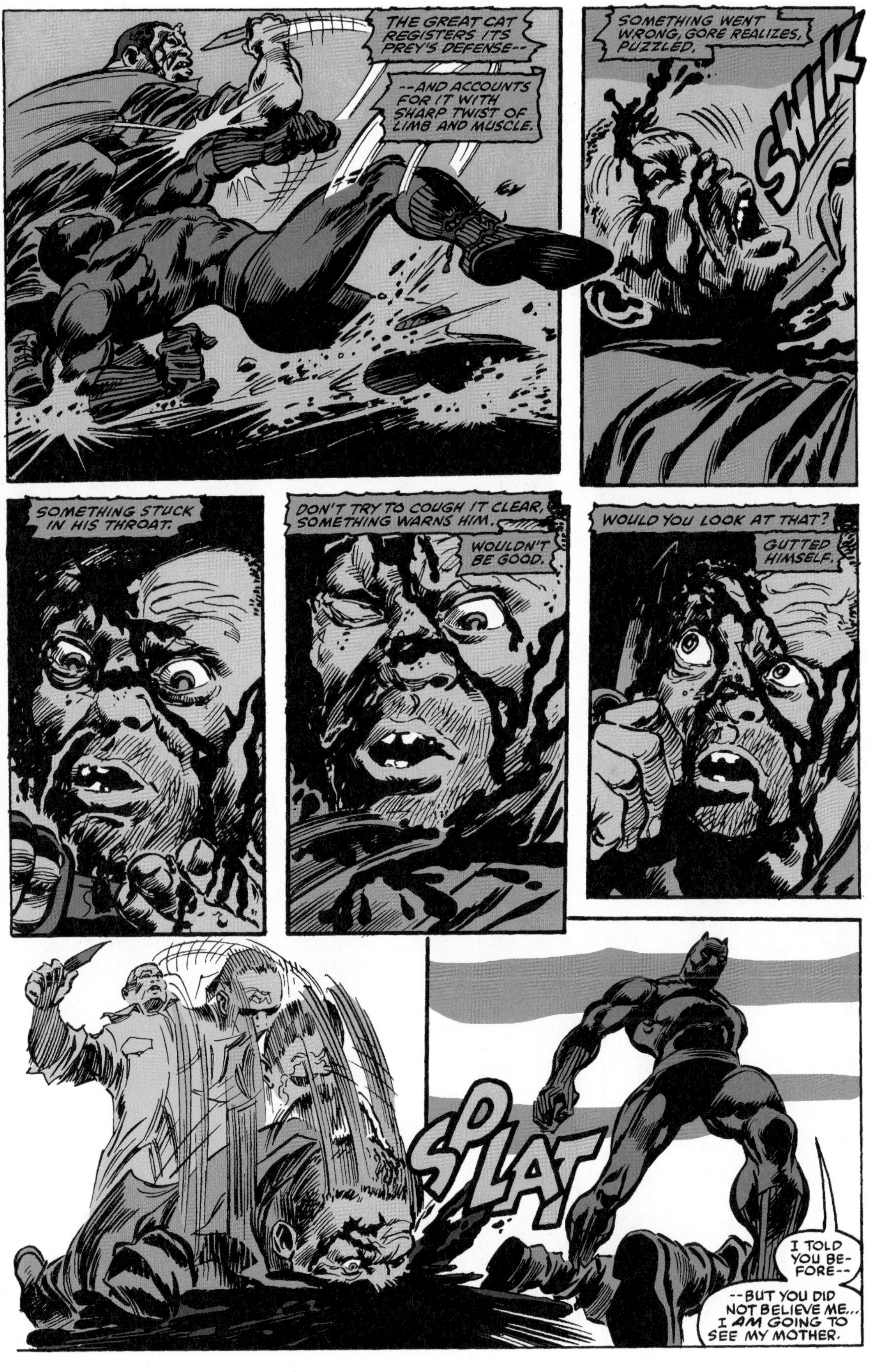
THE GREAT CAT REGISTERS ITS PREY'S DEFENSE--
--AND ACCOUNTS FOR IT WITH SHARP TWIST OF LIMB AND MUSCLE.
SOMETHING WENT WRONG, GORE REALIZES, PUZZLED.
SWIK
SOMETHING STUCK IN HIS THROAT.
DON'T TRY TO COUGH IT CLEAR, SOMETHING WARNS HIM.
WOULDN'T BE GOOD.
WOULD YOU LOOK AT THAT?
GUTTED HIMSELF.
SPLAT
I TOLD YOU BEFORE--
--BUT YOU DID NOT BELIEVE ME... I AM GOING TO SEE MY MOTHER.

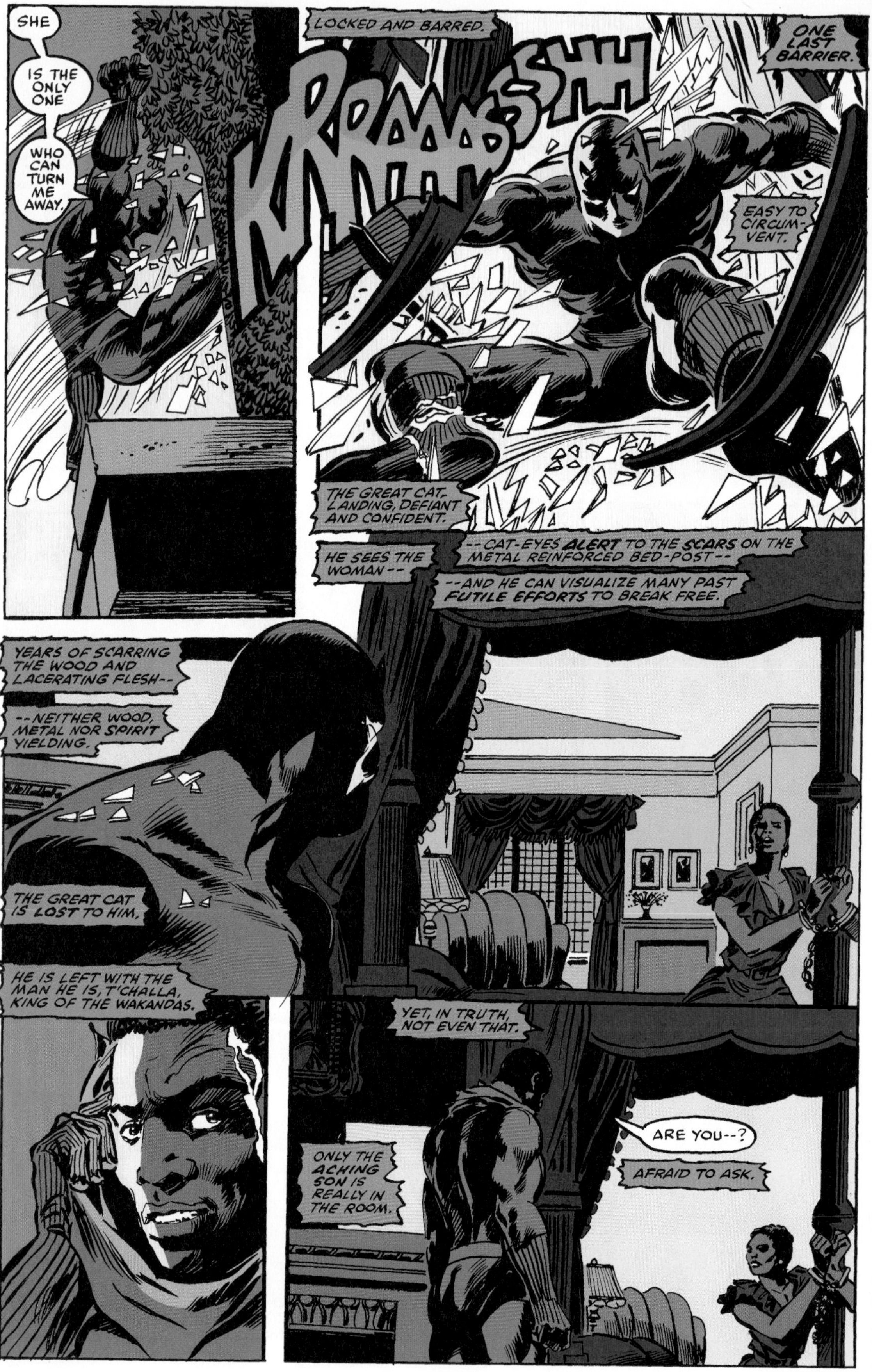

SHE
IS THE ONLY ONE
WHO CAN TURN ME AWAY.
LOCKED AND BARRED.
KRAAASSHH
ONE LAST BARRIER.
EASY TO CIRCUMVENT.
THE GREAT CAT. LANDING, DEFIANT AND CONFIDENT.
HE SEES THE WOMAN--
--CAT-EYES ALERT TO THE SCARS ON THE METAL REINFORCED BED-POST--
--AND HE CAN VISUALIZE MANY PAST FUTILE EFFORTS TO BREAK FREE.
YEARS OF SCARRING THE WOOD AND LACERATING FLESH--
--NEITHER WOOD, METAL NOR SPIRIT YIELDING.
THE GREAT CAT IS LOST TO HIM.
HE IS LEFT WITH THE MAN HE IS, T'CHALLA, KING OF THE WAKANDAS.
YET, IN TRUTH, NOT EVEN THAT.
ONLY THE ACHING SON IS REALLY IN THE ROOM.
ARE YOU--?
AFRAID TO ASK.

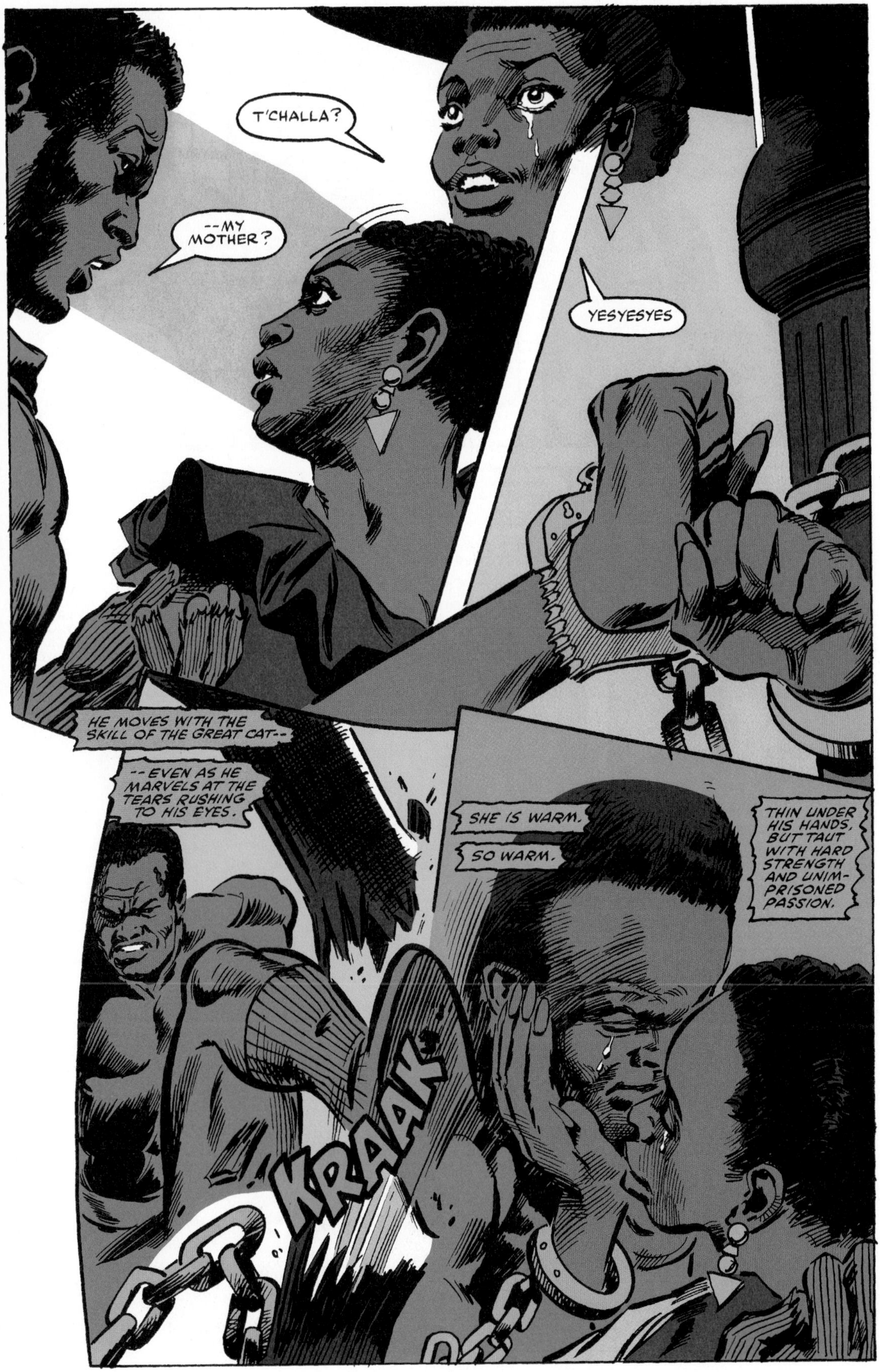
T'CHALLA?
--MY MOTHER?
YESYESYES
HE MOVES WITH THE SKILL OF THE GREAT CAT--
--EVEN AS HE MARVELS AT THE TEARS RUSHING TO HIS EYES.
SHE IS WARM.
SO WARM.
THIN UNDER HIS HANDS, BUT TAUT WITH HARD STRENGTH AND UNIMPRISONED PASSION.
KRAAK

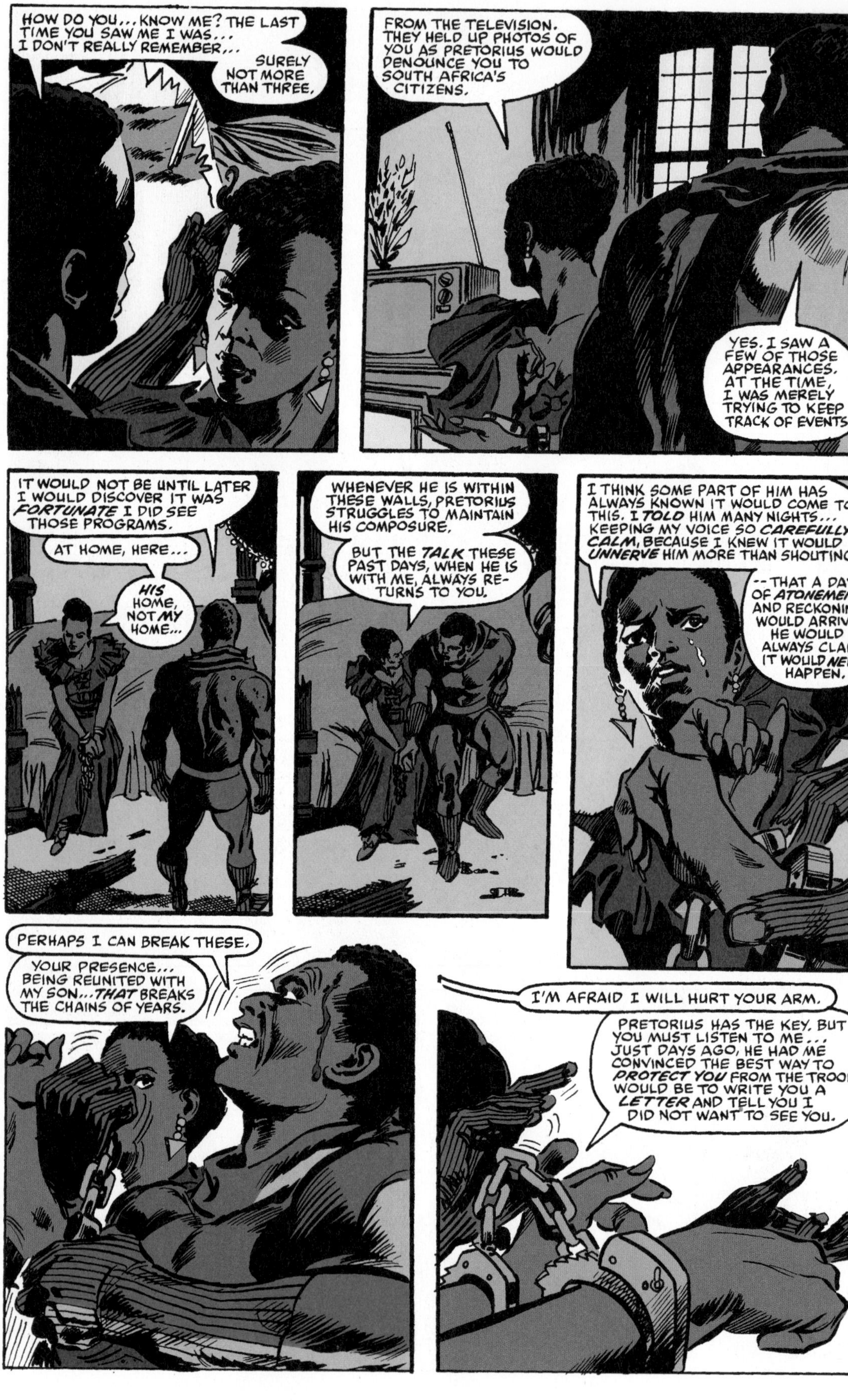

HOW DO YOU... KNOW ME? THE LAST TIME YOU SAW ME I WAS... I DON'T REALLY REMEMBER...
SURELY NOT MORE THAN THREE.
FROM THE TELEVISION. THEY HELD UP PHOTOS OF YOU AS PRETORIUS WOULD DENOUNCE YOU TO SOUTH AFRICA'S CITIZENS.
YES. I SAW A FEW OF THOSE APPEARANCES. AT THE TIME, I WAS MERELY TRYING TO KEEP TRACK OF EVENTS.
IT WOULD NOT BE UNTIL LATER I WOULD DISCOVER IT WAS FORTUNATE I DID SEE THOSE PROGRAMS.
AT HOME, HERE...
HIS HOME, NOT MY HOME...
WHENEVER HE IS WITHIN THESE WALLS, PRETORIUS STRUGGLES TO MAINTAIN HIS COMPOSURE.
BUT THE TALK THESE PAST DAYS, WHEN HE IS WITH ME, ALWAYS RETURNS TO YOU.
I THINK SOME PART OF HIM HAS ALWAYS KNOWN IT WOULD COME TO THIS. I TOLD HIM MANY NIGHTS... KEEPING MY VOICE SO CAREFULLY CALM, BECAUSE I KNEW IT WOULD UNNERVE HIM MORE THAN SHOUTING--
--THAT A DAY OF ATONEMENT AND RECKONING WOULD ARRIVE. HE WOULD ALWAYS CLAIM IT WOULD NEVER HAPPEN.
PERHAPS I CAN BREAK THESE.
YOUR PRESENCE... BEING REUNITED WITH MY SON... THAT BREAKS THE CHAINS OF YEARS.
I'M AFRAID I WILL HURT YOUR ARM.
PRETORIUS HAS THE KEY. BUT YOU MUST LISTEN TO ME... JUST DAYS AGO, HE HAD ME CONVINCED THE BEST WAY TO PROTECT YOU FROM THE TROOPS WOULD BE TO WRITE YOU A LETTER AND TELL YOU I DID NOT WANT TO SEE YOU.

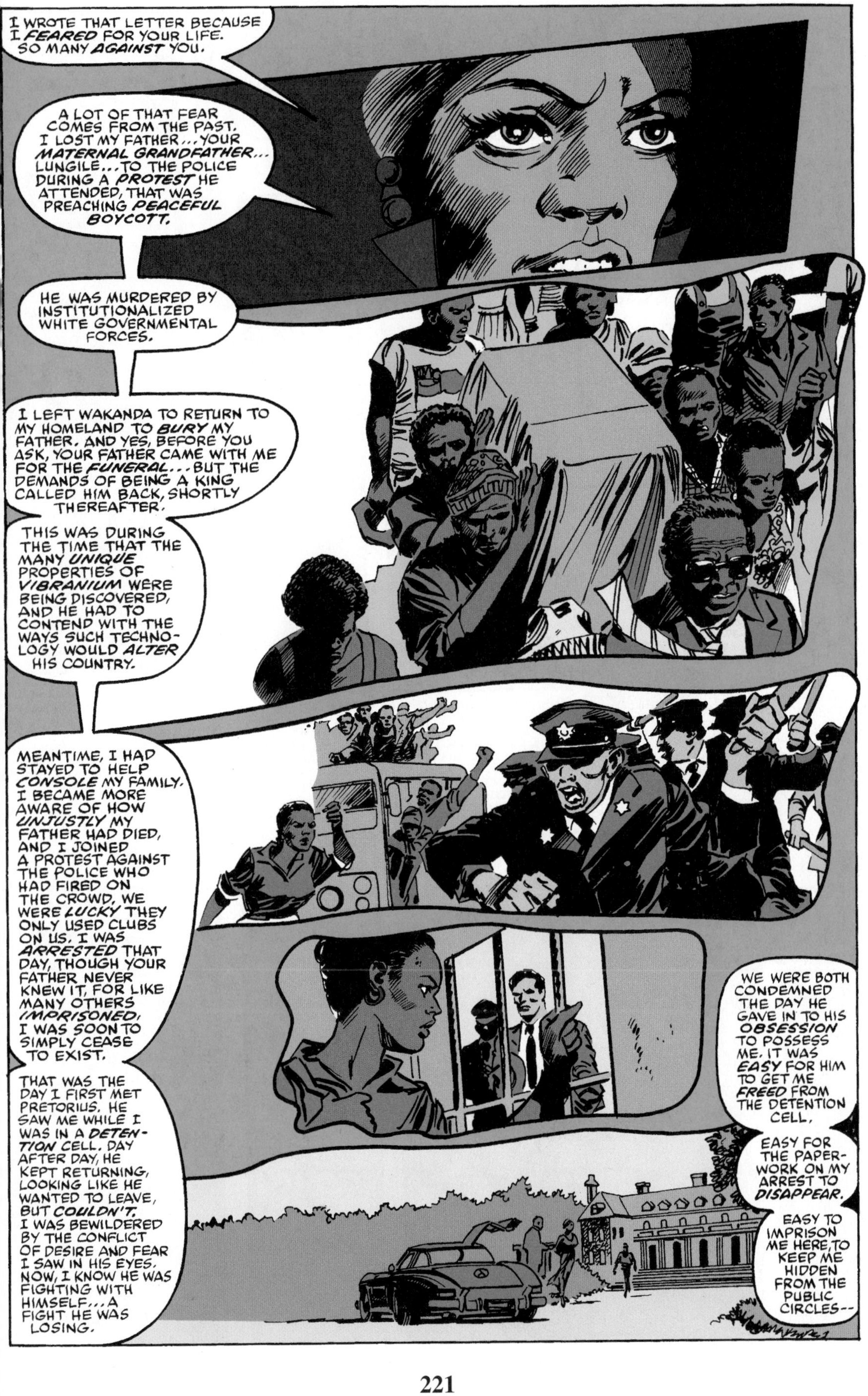
I WROTE THAT LETTER BECAUSE I FEARED FOR YOUR LIFE. SO MANY AGAINST YOU.
A LOT OF THAT FEAR COMES FROM THE PAST. I LOST MY FATHER... YOUR MATERNAL GRANDFATHER... LUNGILE... TO THE POLICE DURING A PROTEST HE ATTENDED, THAT WAS PREACHING PEACEFUL BOYCOTT.
HE WAS MURDERED BY INSTITUTIONALIZED WHITE GOVERNMENTAL FORCES.
I LEFT WAKANDA TO RETURN TO MY HOMELAND TO BURY MY FATHER. AND YES, BEFORE YOU ASK, YOUR FATHER CAME WITH ME FOR THE FUNERAL... BUT THE DEMANDS OF BEING A KING CALLED HIM BACK, SHORTLY THEREAFTER.
THIS WAS DURING THE TIME THAT THE MANY UNIQUE PROPERTIES OF VIBRANIUM WERE BEING DISCOVERED, AND HE HAD TO CONTEND WITH THE WAYS SUCH TECHNOLOGY WOULD ALTER HIS COUNTRY.
MEANTIME, I HAD STAYED TO HELP CONSOLE MY FAMILY. I BECAME MORE AWARE OF HOW UNJUSTLY MY FATHER HAD DIED, AND I JOINED A PROTEST AGAINST THE POLICE WHO HAD FIRED ON THE CROWD. WE WERE LUCKY THEY ONLY USED CLUBS ON US. I WAS ARRESTED THAT DAY, THOUGH YOUR FATHER NEVER KNEW IT, FOR LIKE MANY OTHERS IMPRISONED, I WAS SOON TO SIMPLY CEASE TO EXIST.
THAT WAS THE DAY I FIRST MET PRETORIUS. HE SAW ME WHILE I WAS IN A DETENTION CELL. DAY AFTER DAY, HE KEPT RETURNING, LOOKING LIKE HE WANTED TO LEAVE, BUT COULDN'T. I WAS BEWILDERED BY THE CONFLICT OF DESIRE AND FEAR I SAW IN HIS EYES. NOW, I KNOW HE WAS FIGHTING WITH HIMSELF... A FIGHT HE WAS LOSING.
WE WERE BOTH CONDEMNED THE DAY HE GAVE IN TO HIS OBSESSION TO POSSESS ME. IT WAS EASY FOR HIM TO GET ME FREED FROM THE DETENTION CELL.
EASY FOR THE PAPERWORK ON MY ARREST TO DISAPPEAR.
EASY TO IMPRISON ME HERE, TO KEEP ME HIDDEN FROM THE PUBLIC CIRCLES--

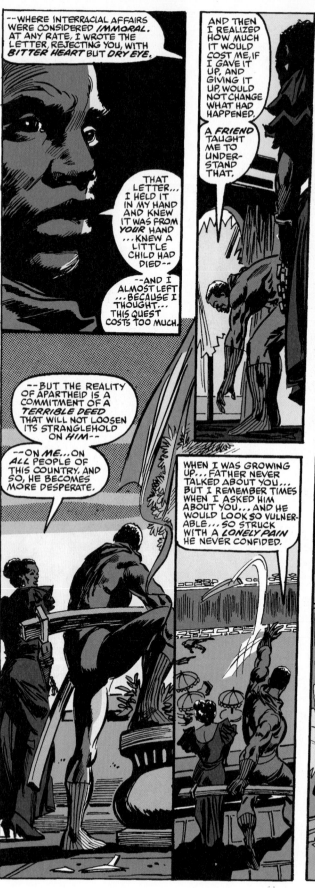

--WHERE INTERRACIAL AFFAIRS WERE CONSIDERED *IMMORAL.* AT ANY RATE, I WROTE THE LETTER, REJECTING YOU, WITH *BITTER HEART* BUT *DRY EYE.*

THAT LETTER... I HELD IT IN MY HAND AND KNEW IT WAS FROM *HIM* HAND ...KNEW A LITTLE CHILD HAD DIED--

--AND I ALMOST LEFT ...BECAUSE I THOUGHT... THIS QUEST COSTS TOO MUCH.

--BUT THE REALITY OF APARTHEID IS A COMMITMENT OF A *TERRIBLE DEED* THAT WILL NOT LOOSEN ITS STRANGLEHOLD ON *HIM*--

--ON *ME*...ON *ALL* PEOPLE OF THIS COUNTRY, AND SO, HE BECOMES MORE DESPERATE.

AND THEN I REALIZED HOW MUCH IT WOULD COST ME, IF I GAVE IT UP, AND GIVING IT UP, WOULD NOT CHANGE WHAT HAD HAPPENED.

A *FRIEND* TAUGHT ME TO UNDERSTAND THAT.

WHEN I WAS GROWING UP... FATHER NEVER TALKED ABOUT YOU... BUT I REMEMBER TIMES WHEN I ASKED HIM ABOUT YOU...AND HE WOULD LOOK SO VULNERABLE....SO STRUCK WITH A *LONELY PAIN* HE NEVER CONFIDED.

COST ME, FOR THE REST OF MY LIFE.

I AM SORRY. I DID NOT WANT TO LOSE MY SON, AS I HAD MY FATHER AND HUSBAND.

YOU SHOULD NOT BE SORRY. HE SHOULD.

WHY DID HE NOT SEARCH FOR YOU? WHY DID THE MENTION OF YOU CAUSE HIM SUCH SORROW?

SPLASH

IN A WAY, PRETORIUS *IS.* HE WOULD DEARLY LOVE TO AVOID ALL THIS--

YOUR FATHER *DID* SEARCH FOR ME, BUT IT WAS AS IF I HAD BEEN SWALLOWED BY THE WORLD. PRETORIUS HAD PICTURES TAKEN OF US...YOU CAN IMAGINE WHAT KIND--

--AND THROUGH SOURCES YOUR FATHER WOULD CONSIDER *RELIABLE* HAD THOSE PHOTOS SURPRISINGLY DISCOVERED. THE STORY ACCOMPANYING THOSE PICTURES WAS THAT I HAD LEFT HIM FOR ANOTHER MAN.

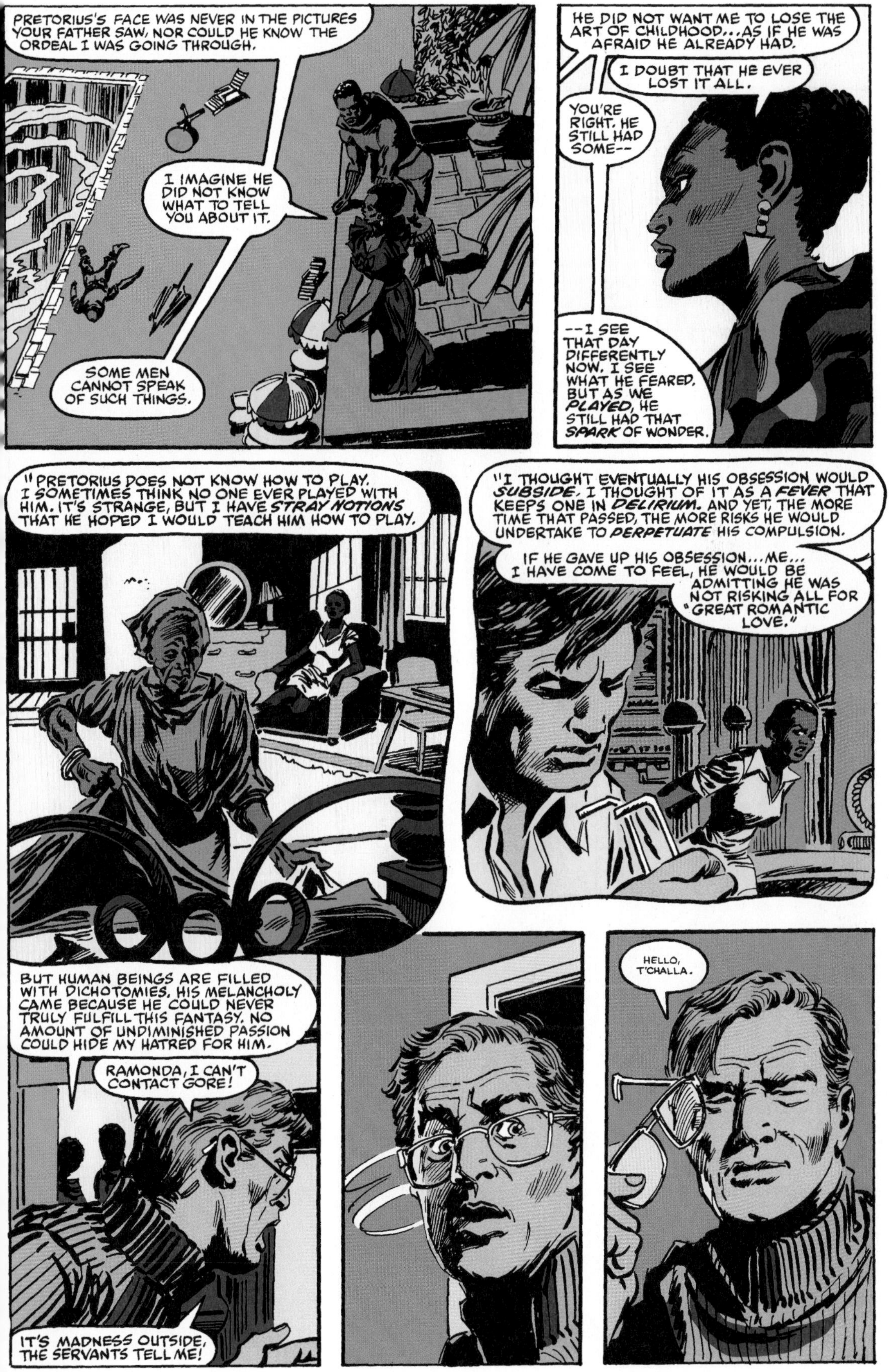
PRETORIUS'S FACE WAS NEVER IN THE PICTURES YOUR FATHER SAW, NOR COULD HE KNOW THE ORDEAL I WAS GOING THROUGH.
I IMAGINE HE DID NOT KNOW WHAT TO TELL YOU ABOUT IT.
SOME MEN CANNOT SPEAK OF SUCH THINGS.
HE DID NOT WANT ME TO LOSE THE ART OF CHILDHOOD... AS IF HE WAS AFRAID HE ALREADY HAD.
I DOUBT THAT HE EVER LOST IT ALL.
YOU'RE RIGHT. HE STILL HAD SOME--
--I SEE THAT DAY DIFFERENTLY NOW. I SEE WHAT HE FEARED, BUT AS WE PLAYED, HE STILL HAD THAT SPARK OF WONDER.
"PRETORIUS DOES NOT KNOW HOW TO PLAY. I SOMETIMES THINK NO ONE EVER PLAYED WITH HIM. IT'S STRANGE, BUT I HAVE STRAY NOTIONS THAT HE HOPED I WOULD TEACH HIM HOW TO PLAY.
"I THOUGHT EVENTUALLY HIS OBSESSION WOULD SUBSIDE. I THOUGHT OF IT AS A FEVER THAT KEEPS ONE IN DELIRIUM. AND YET, THE MORE TIME THAT PASSED, THE MORE RISKS HE WOULD UNDERTAKE TO PERPETUATE HIS COMPULSION.
IF HE GAVE UP HIS OBSESSION... ME... I HAVE COME TO FEEL, HE WOULD BE ADMITTING HE WAS NOT RISKING ALL FOR "GREAT ROMANTIC LOVE."
BUT HUMAN BEINGS ARE FILLED WITH DICHOTOMIES. HIS MELANCHOLY CAME BECAUSE HE COULD NEVER TRULY FULFILL THIS FANTASY. NO AMOUNT OF UNDIMINISHED PASSION COULD HIDE MY HATRED FOR HIM.
RAMONDA, I CAN'T CONTACT GORE!
IT'S MADNESS OUTSIDE, THE SERVANTS TELL ME!
HELLO, T'CHALLA.

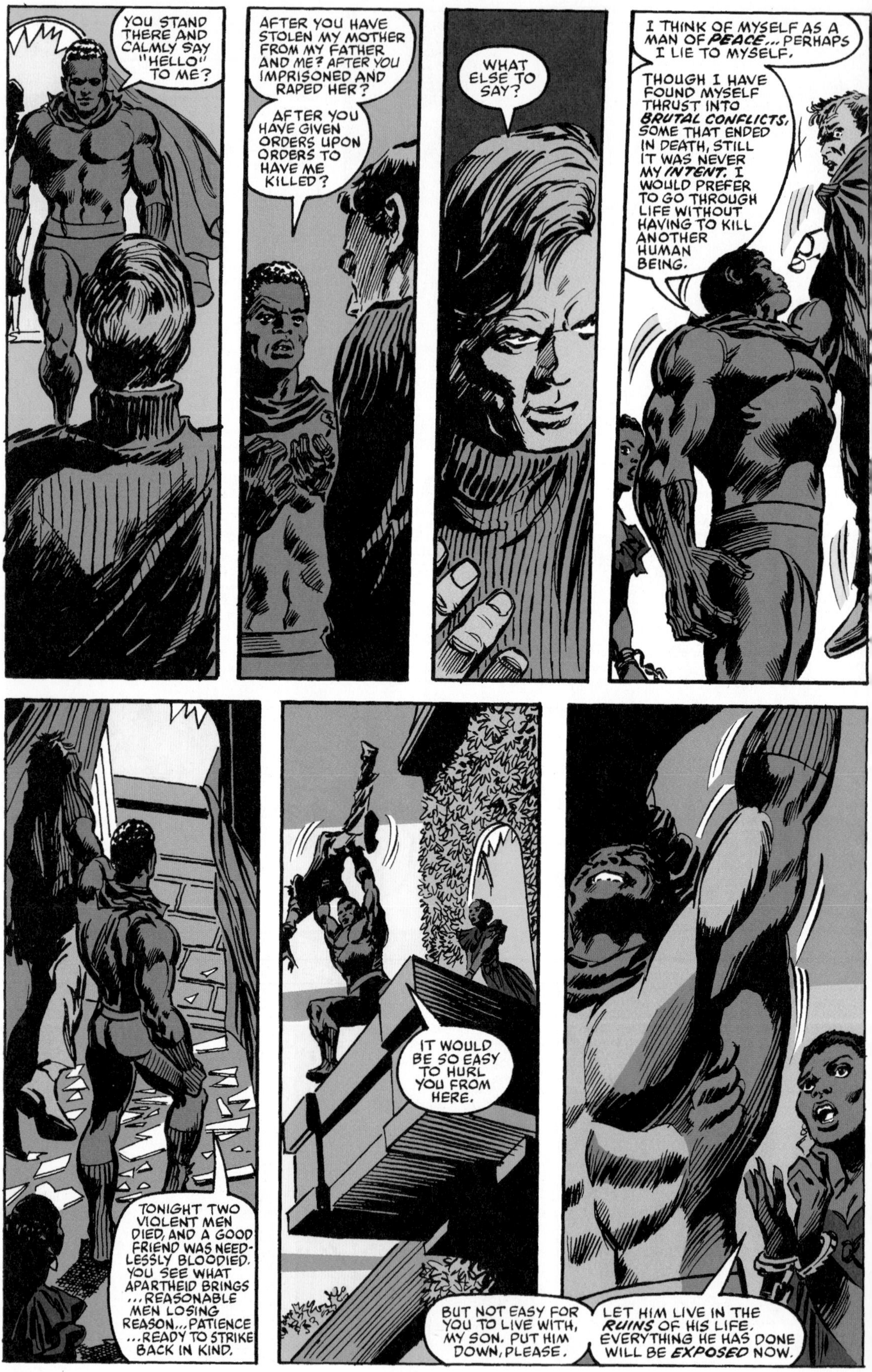
YOU STAND THERE AND CALMLY SAY "HELLO" TO ME?
AFTER YOU HAVE STOLEN MY MOTHER FROM MY FATHER AND ME? AFTER YOU IMPRISONED AND RAPED HER?
AFTER YOU HAVE GIVEN ORDERS UPON ORDERS TO HAVE ME KILLED?
WHAT ELSE TO SAY?
I THINK OF MYSELF AS A MAN OF PEACE... PERHAPS I LIE TO MYSELF.
THOUGH I HAVE FOUND MYSELF THRUST INTO BRUTAL CONFLICTS, SOME THAT ENDED IN DEATH, STILL IT WAS NEVER MY INTENT. I WOULD PREFER TO GO THROUGH LIFE WITHOUT HAVING TO KILL ANOTHER HUMAN BEING.
TONIGHT TWO VIOLENT MEN DIED, AND A GOOD FRIEND WAS NEEDLESSLY BLOODIED. YOU SEE WHAT APARTHEID BRINGS ...REASONABLE MEN LOSING REASON... PATIENCE ...READY TO STRIKE BACK IN KIND.
IT WOULD BE SO EASY TO HURL YOU FROM HERE.
BUT NOT EASY FOR YOU TO LIVE WITH, MY SON. PUT HIM DOWN, PLEASE.
LET HIM LIVE IN THE RUINS OF HIS LIFE. EVERYTHING HE HAS DONE WILL BE EXPOSED NOW.

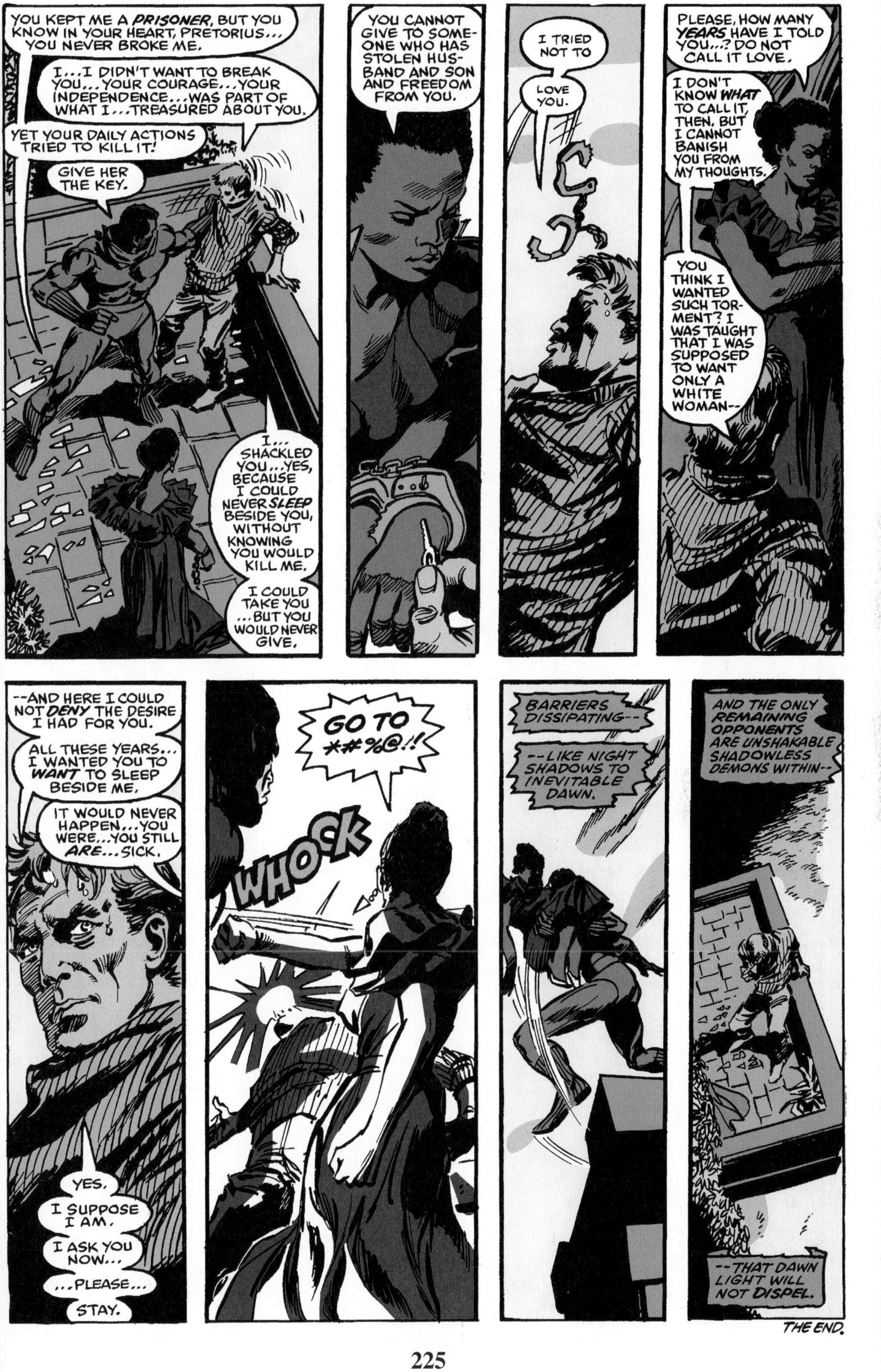
YOU KEPT ME A PRISONER, BUT YOU KNOW IN YOUR HEART, PRETORIUS... YOU NEVER BROKE ME.
I...I DIDN'T WANT TO BREAK YOU...YOUR COURAGE...YOUR INDEPENDENCE...WAS PART OF WHAT I...TREASURED ABOUT YOU.
YET YOUR DAILY ACTIONS TRIED TO KILL IT!
GIVE HER THE KEY.
I... SHACKLED YOU...YES, BECAUSE I COULD NEVER SLEEP BESIDE YOU, WITHOUT KNOWING YOU WOULD KILL ME.
I COULD TAKE YOU ...BUT YOU WOULD NEVER GIVE.
YOU CANNOT GIVE TO SOMEONE WHO HAS STOLEN HUSBAND AND SON AND FREEDOM FROM YOU.
I TRIED NOT TO
LOVE YOU.
PLEASE, HOW MANY YEARS HAVE I TOLD YOU...? DO NOT CALL IT LOVE.
I DON'T KNOW WHAT TO CALL IT, THEN. BUT I CANNOT BANISH YOU FROM MY THOUGHTS.
YOU THINK I WANTED SUCH TORMENT? I WAS TAUGHT THAT I WAS SUPPOSED TO WANT ONLY A WHITE WOMAN--
--AND HERE I COULD NOT DENY THE DESIRE I HAD FOR YOU.
ALL THESE YEARS... I WANTED YOU TO WANT TO SLEEP BESIDE ME.
IT WOULD NEVER HAPPEN...YOU WERE...YOU STILL ARE...SICK.
YES. I SUPPOSE I AM.
I ASK YOU NOW...
...PLEASE...
STAY.
GO TO *#%@!!
WHOCK
BARRIERS DISSIPATING--
--LIKE NIGHT SHADOWS TO INEVITABLE DAWN.
AND THE ONLY REMAINING OPPONENTS ARE UNSHAKABLE SHADOWLESS DEMONS WITHIN--
--THAT DAWN LIGHT WILL NOT DISPEL.
THE END.

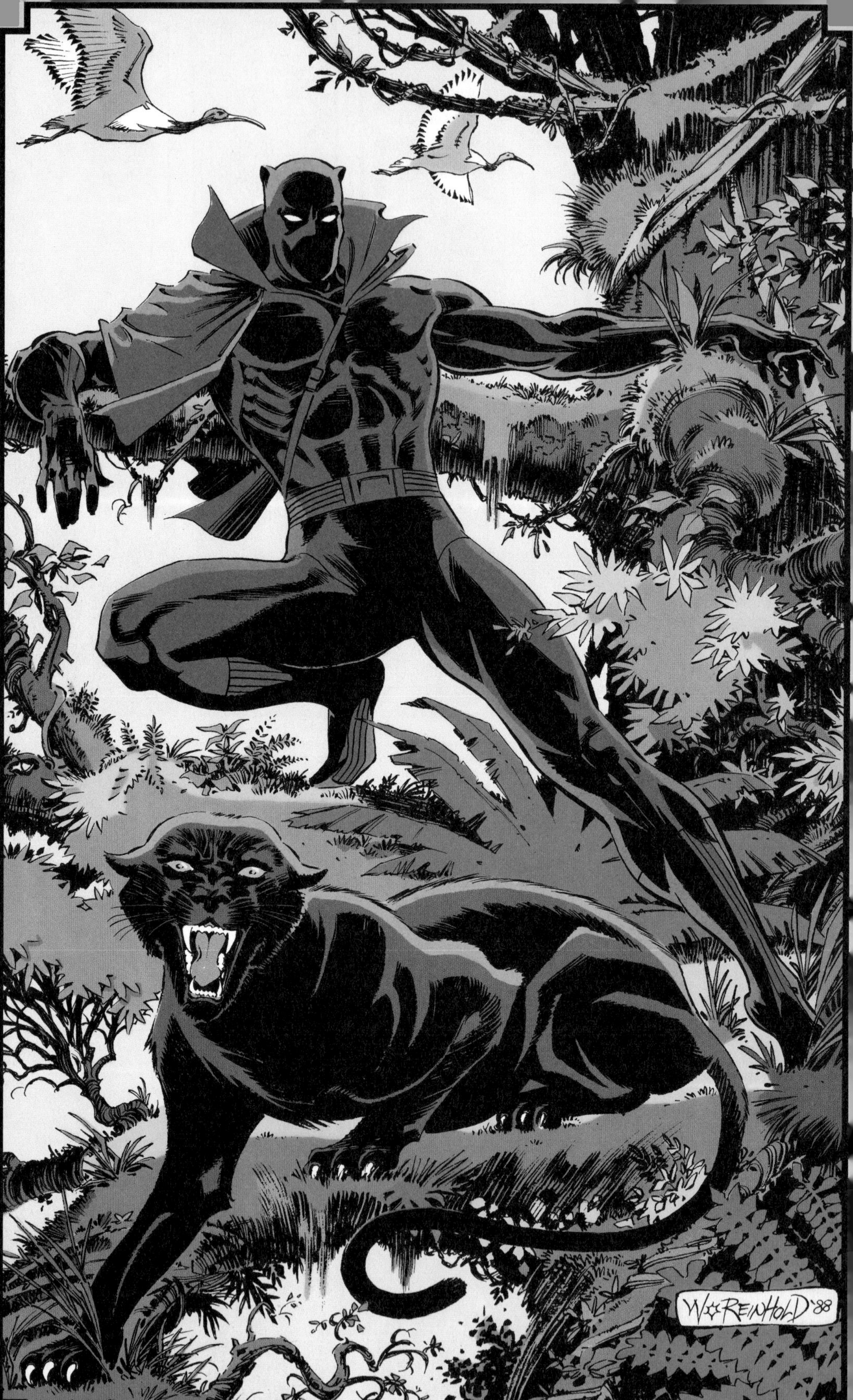
W☆REINHOLD '88

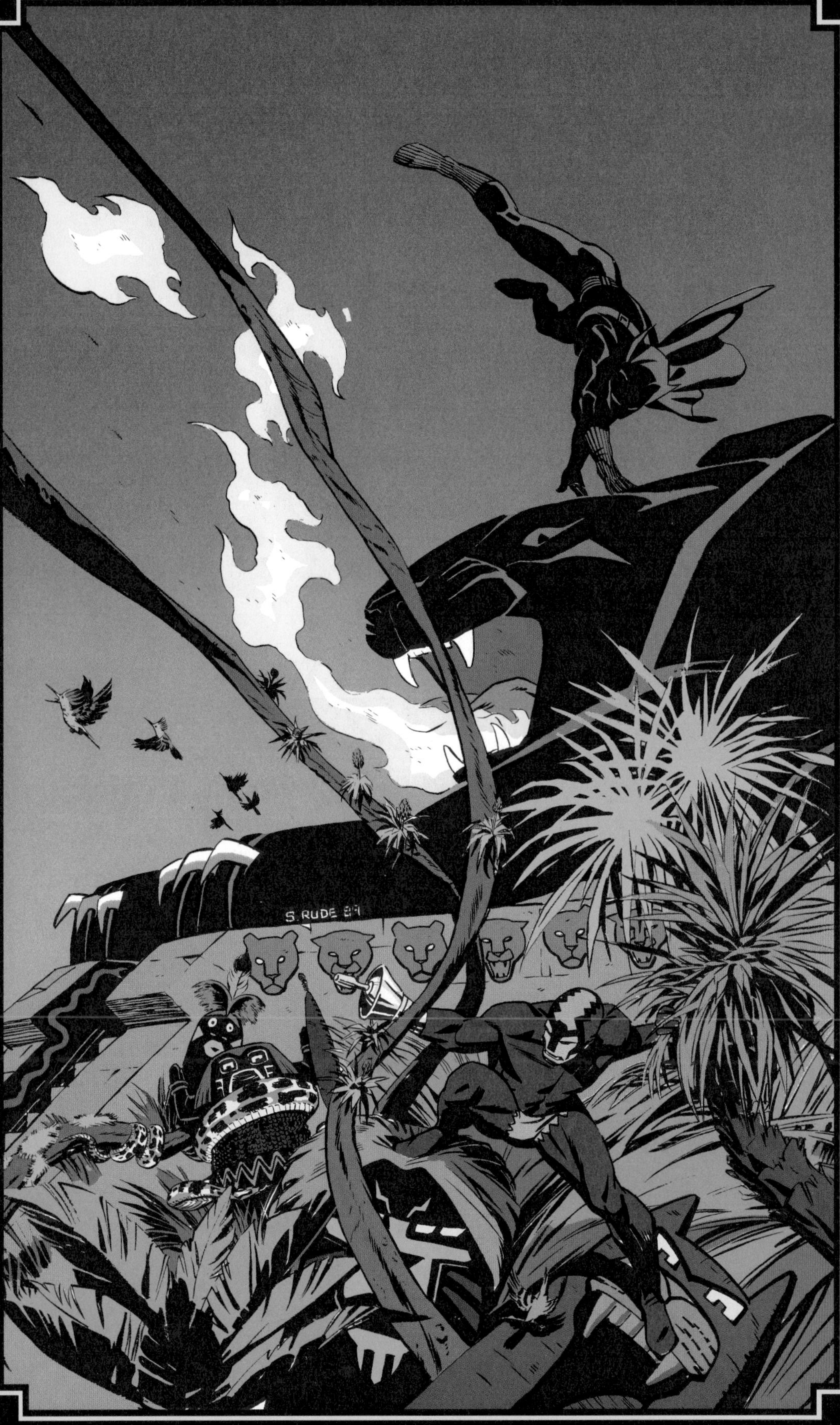
S. RUDE 89

MARVEL FANFARE #45 PINUP BY **STEVE RUDE & STEVE OLIFF**

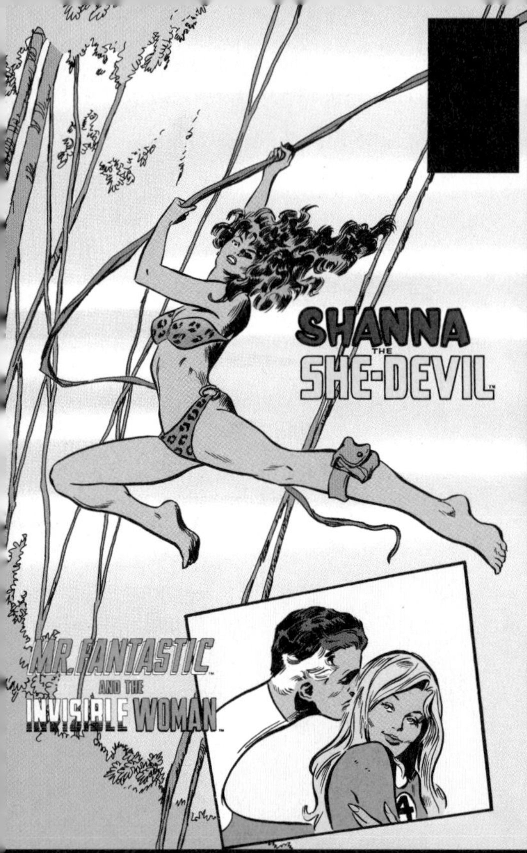
SHANNA THE SHE-DEVIL
MR. FANTASTIC AND THE INVISIBLE WOMAN

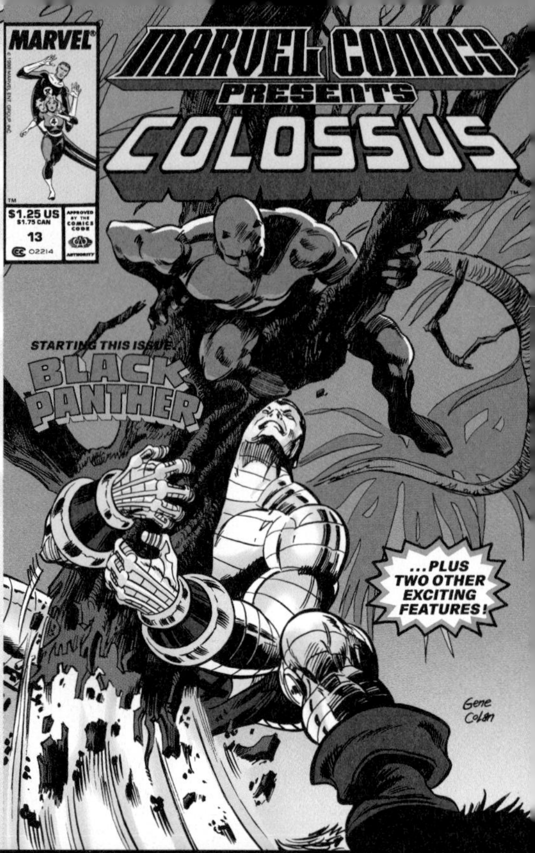
MARVEL
MARVEL COMICS PRESENTS
COLOSSUS
$1.25 US
$1.75 CAN
13
APPROVED BY THE COMICS CODE AUTHORITY
STARTING THIS ISSUE...
BLACK PANTHER
...PLUS TWO OTHER EXCITING FEATURES!
Gene Colan

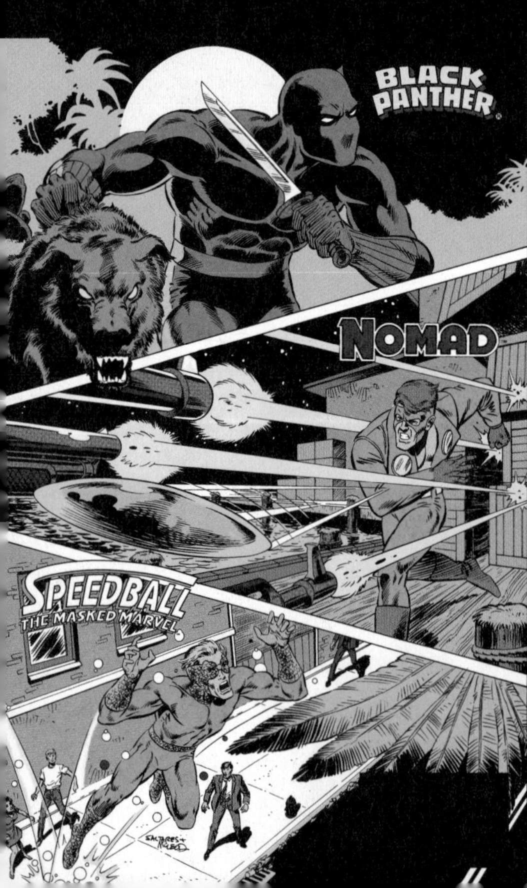
BLACK PANTHER
NOMAD
SPEEDBALL THE MASKED MARVEL

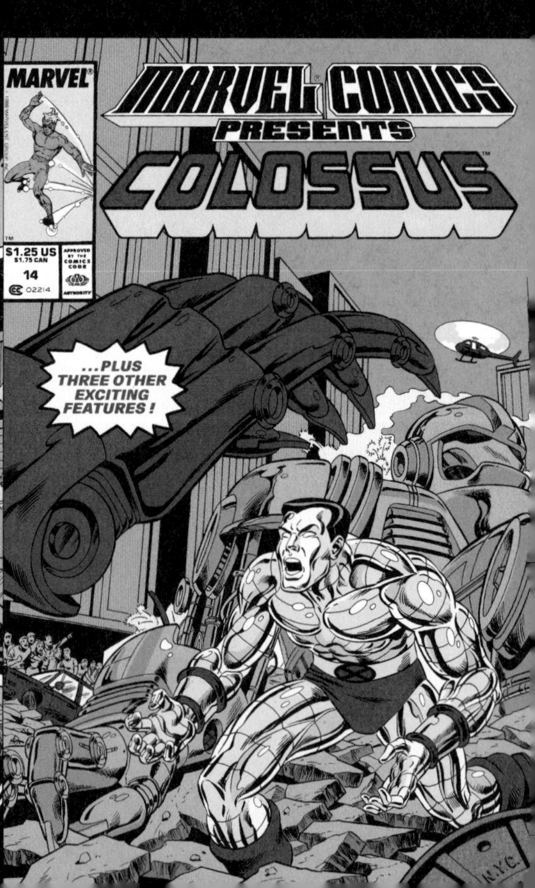
MARVEL
MARVEL COMICS PRESENTS
COLOSSUS
$1.25 US
$1.75 CAN
14
APPROVED BY THE COMICS CODE AUTHORITY
...PLUS THREE OTHER EXCITING FEATURES!

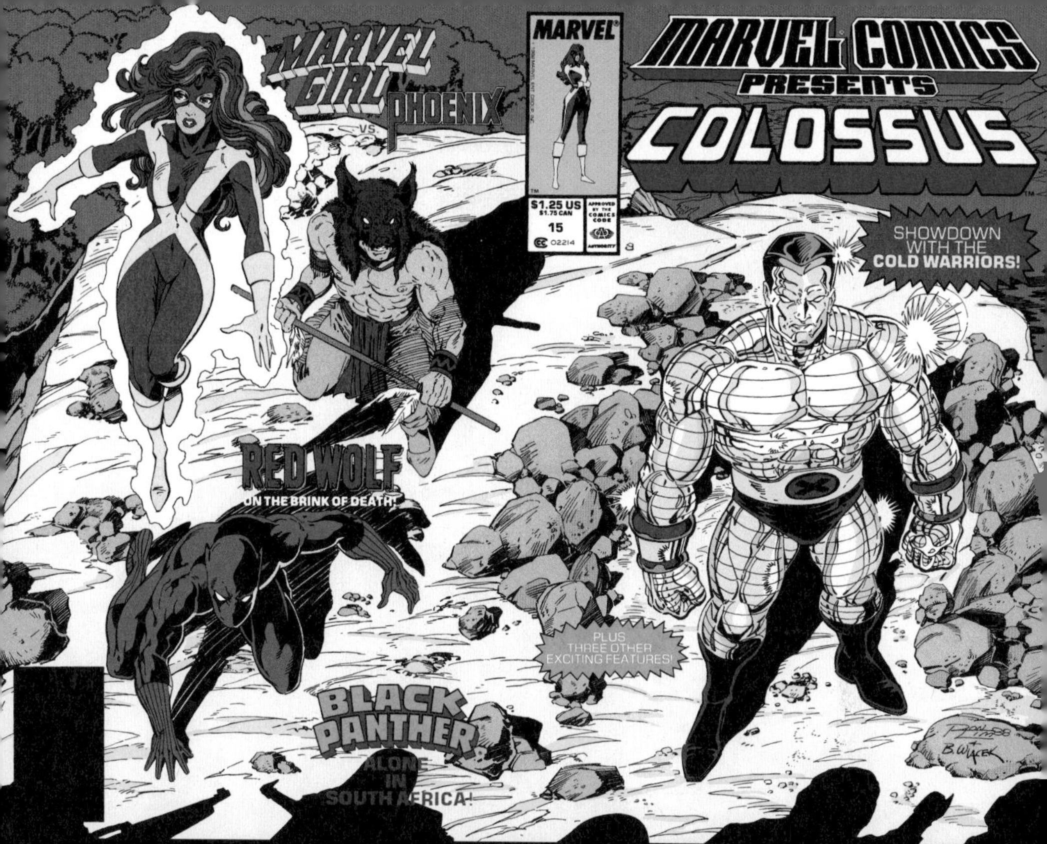
MARVEL GIRL
VS
PHOENIX
MARVEL
$1.25 US
$1.75 CAN
15
APPROVED BY THE COMICS CODE AUTHORITY
MARVEL COMICS PRESENTS
COLOSSUS
SHOWDOWN WITH THE COLD WARRIORS!
RED WOLF
ON THE BRINK OF DEATH!
PLUS THREE OTHER EXCITING FEATURES!
BLACK PANTHER
ALONE IN SOUTH AFRICA!

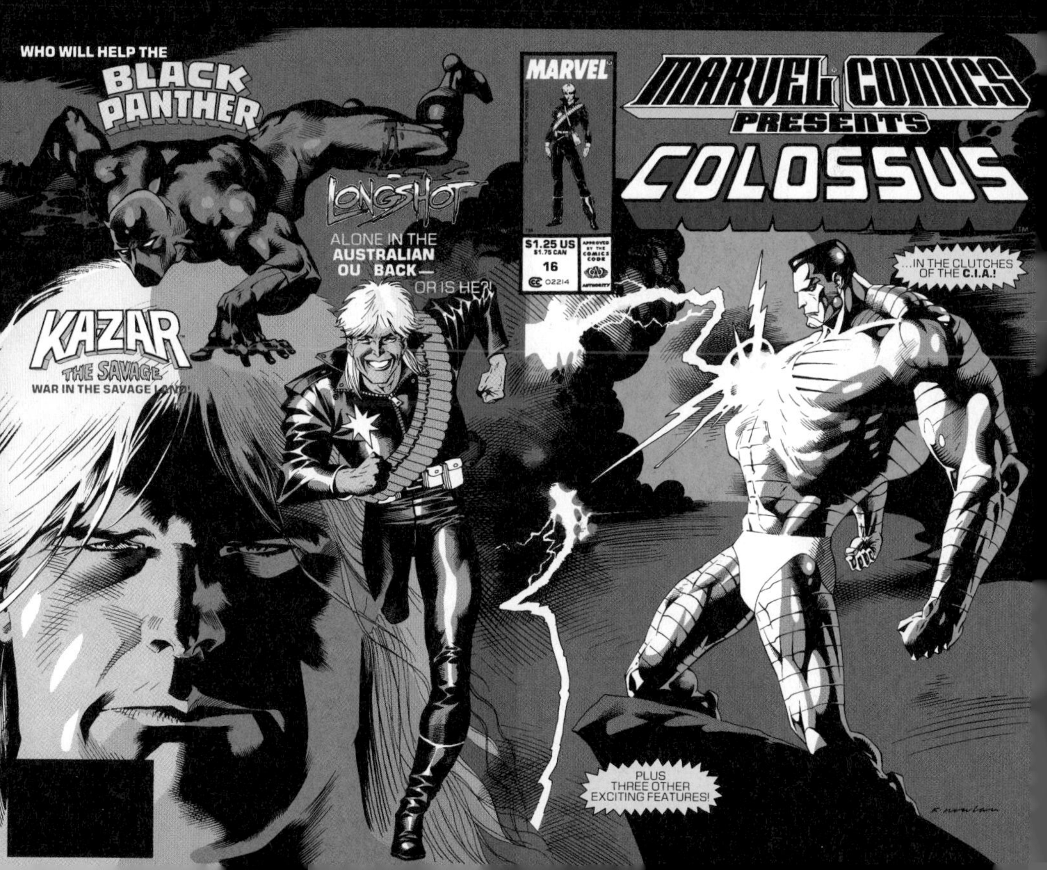
WHO WILL HELP THE
BLACK PANTHER
LONGSHOT
ALONE IN THE
AUSTRALIAN
OU BACK—
OR IS HE?!
MARVEL
$1.25 US
$1.75 CAN
16
APPROVED BY THE COMICS CODE AUTHORITY
MARVEL COMICS PRESENTS
COLOSSUS
...IN THE CLUTCHES OF THE C.I.A.!
KAZAR
THE SAVAGE
WAR IN THE SAVAGE LAND!
PLUS THREE OTHER EXCITING FEATURES!

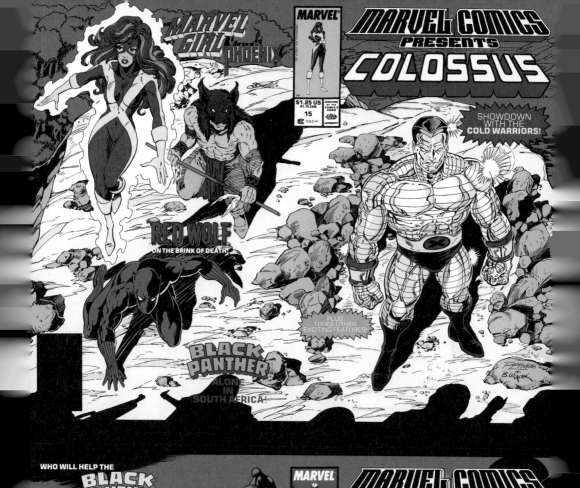

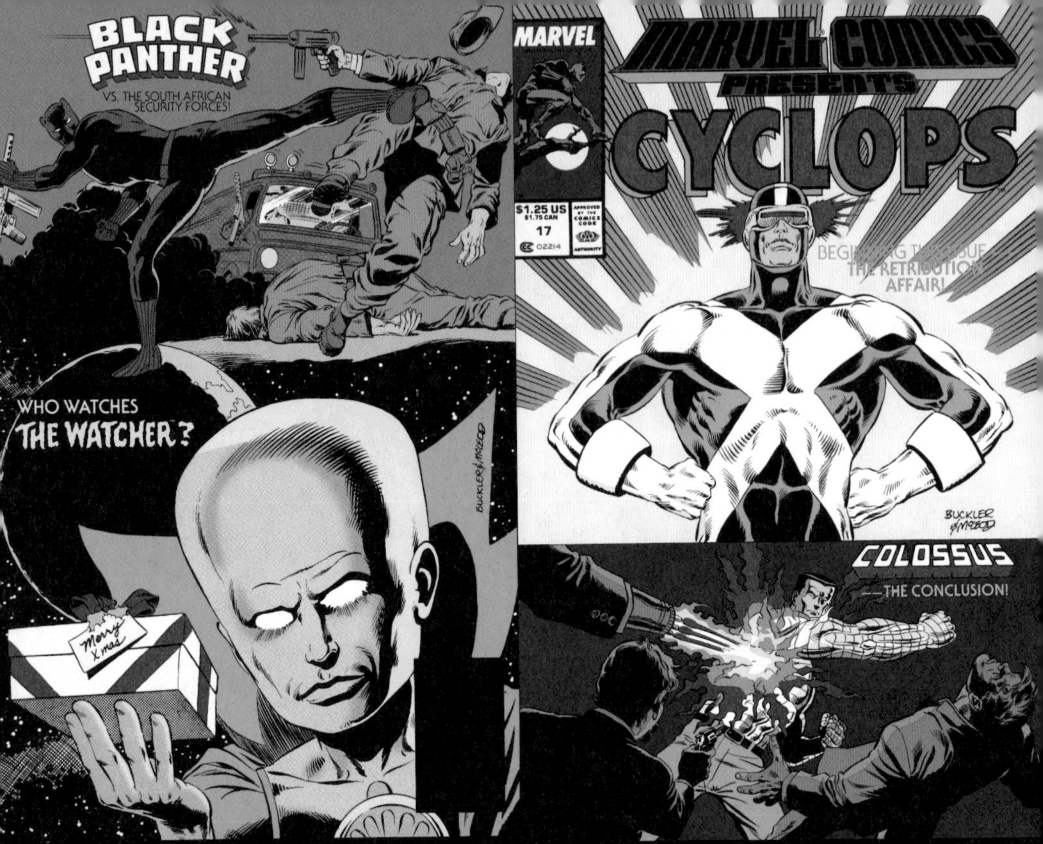
BLACK PANTHER
VS. THE SOUTH AFRICAN SECURITY FORCES!
WHO WATCHES THE WATCHER?
Merry Xmas
BUCKLER & McLEOD
MARVEL
MARVEL COMICS PRESENTS
CYCLOPS
$1.25 US
$1.75 CAN
17
APPROVED BY THE COMICS CODE AUTHORITY
02214
BEGINNING THIS ISSUE
THE RETRIBUTION AFFAIR!
BUCKLER & McLEOD
COLOSSUS
—THE CONCLUSION!

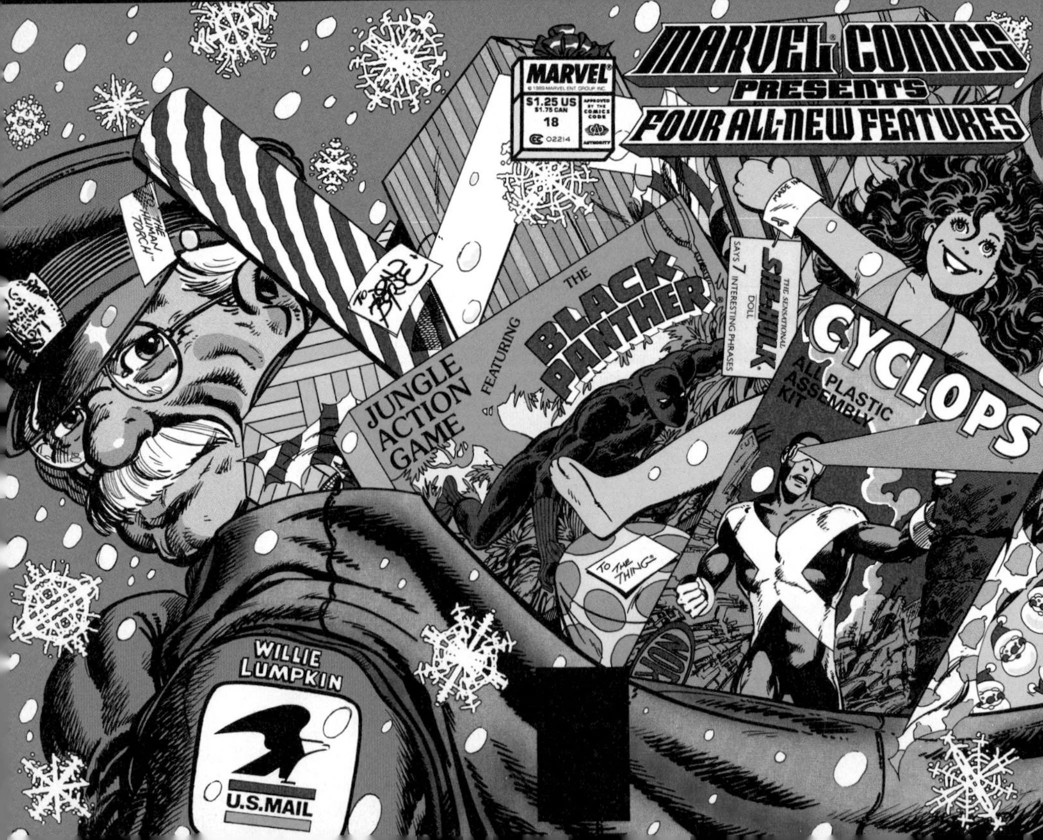
MARVEL
© 1989 MARVEL ENT. GROUP, INC.
$1.25 US
$1.75 CAN
18
APPROVED BY THE COMICS CODE AUTHORITY
02214
MARVEL COMICS PRESENTS
FOUR ALL-NEW FEATURES
THE HUMAN TORCH
JUNGLE ACTION GAME
FEATURING THE BLACK PANTHER
THE SENSATIONAL SHE-HULK DOLL
SAYS 7 INTERESTING PHRASES
CYCLOPS
ALL PLASTIC ASSEMBLY KIT
TO THE THING
WILLIE LUMPKIN
U.S.MAIL

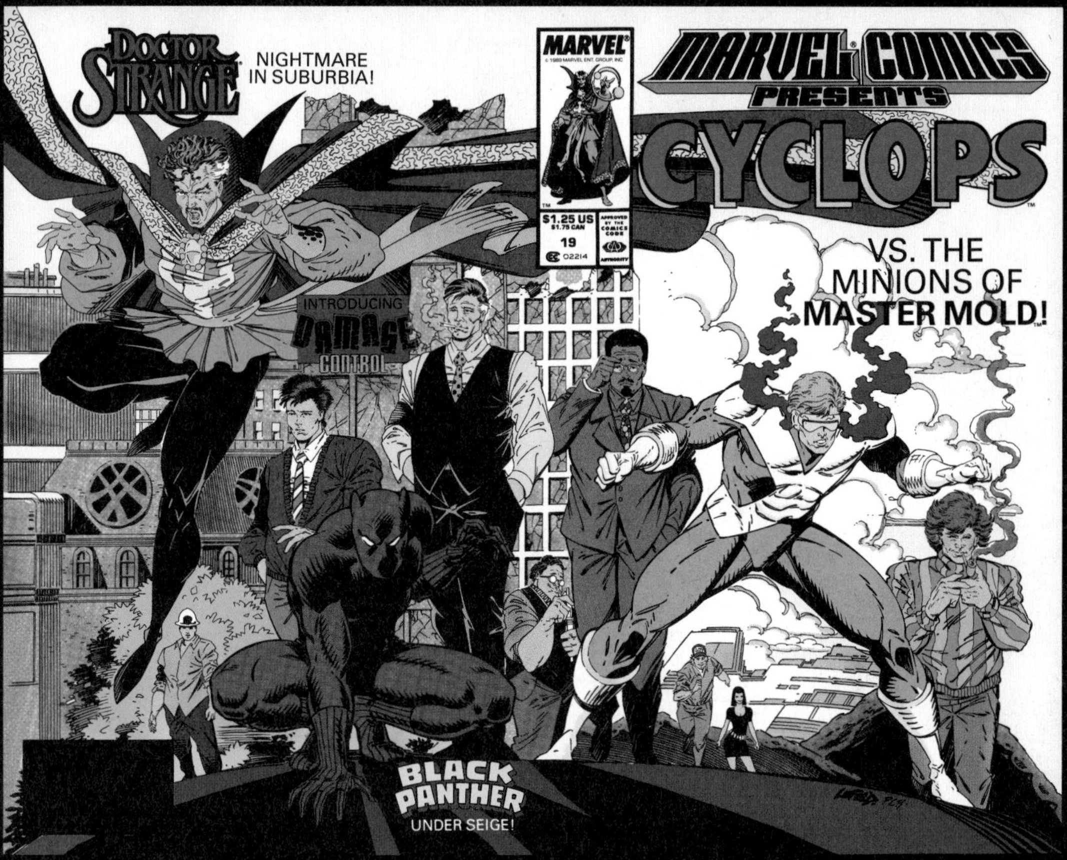
DOCTOR STRANGE
NIGHTMARE IN SUBURBIA!
MARVEL
© 1989 MARVEL ENT. GROUP, INC.
$1.25 US
$1.75 CAN
19
02214
APPROVED BY THE COMICS CODE AUTHORITY
MARVEL COMICS PRESENTS
CYCLOPS
VS. THE MINIONS OF MASTER MOLD!
INTRODUCING DAMAGE CONTROL
BLACK PANTHER
UNDER SEIGE!

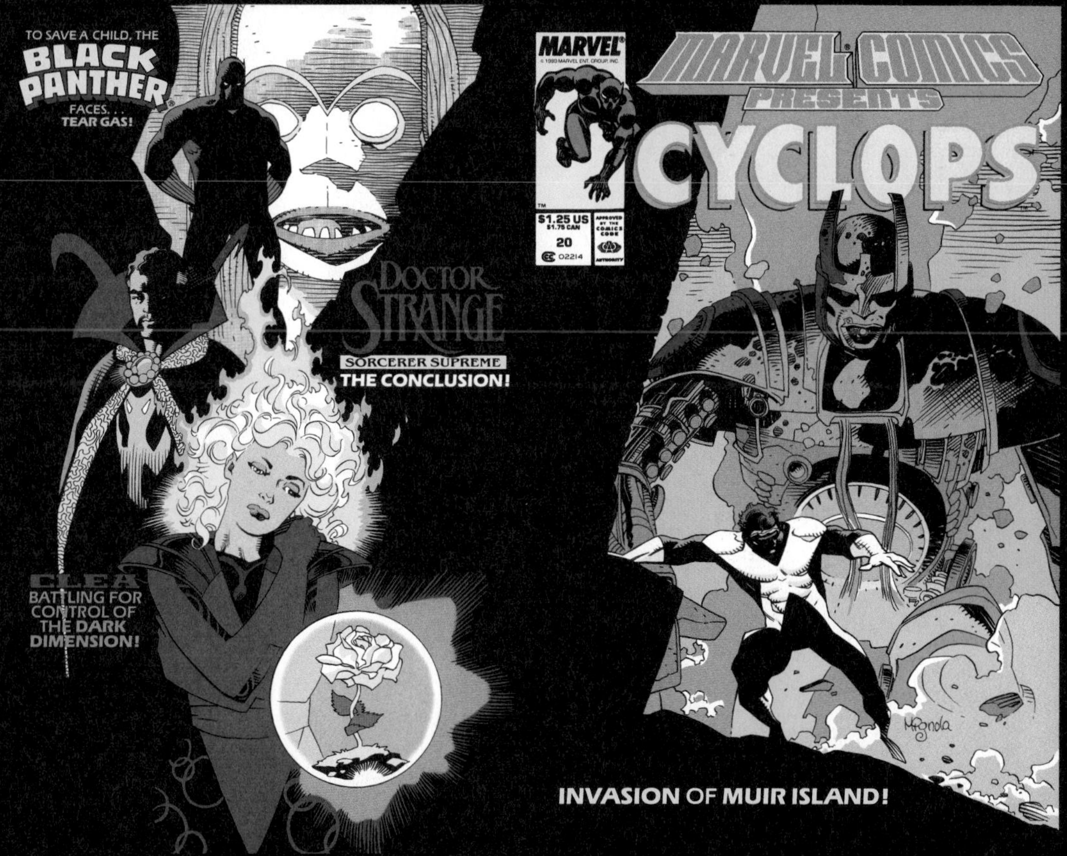
TO SAVE A CHILD, THE
BLACK PANTHER
FACES. . .
TEAR GAS!
DOCTOR STRANGE
SORCERER SUPREME
THE CONCLUSION!
CLEA
BATTLING FOR CONTROL OF THE DARK DIMENSION!
MARVEL
© 1989 MARVEL ENT. GROUP, INC.
$1.25 US
$1.75 CAN
20
02214
APPROVED BY THE COMICS CODE AUTHORITY
MARVEL COMICS PRESENTS
CYCLOPS
Mignola
INVASION OF MUIR ISLAND!

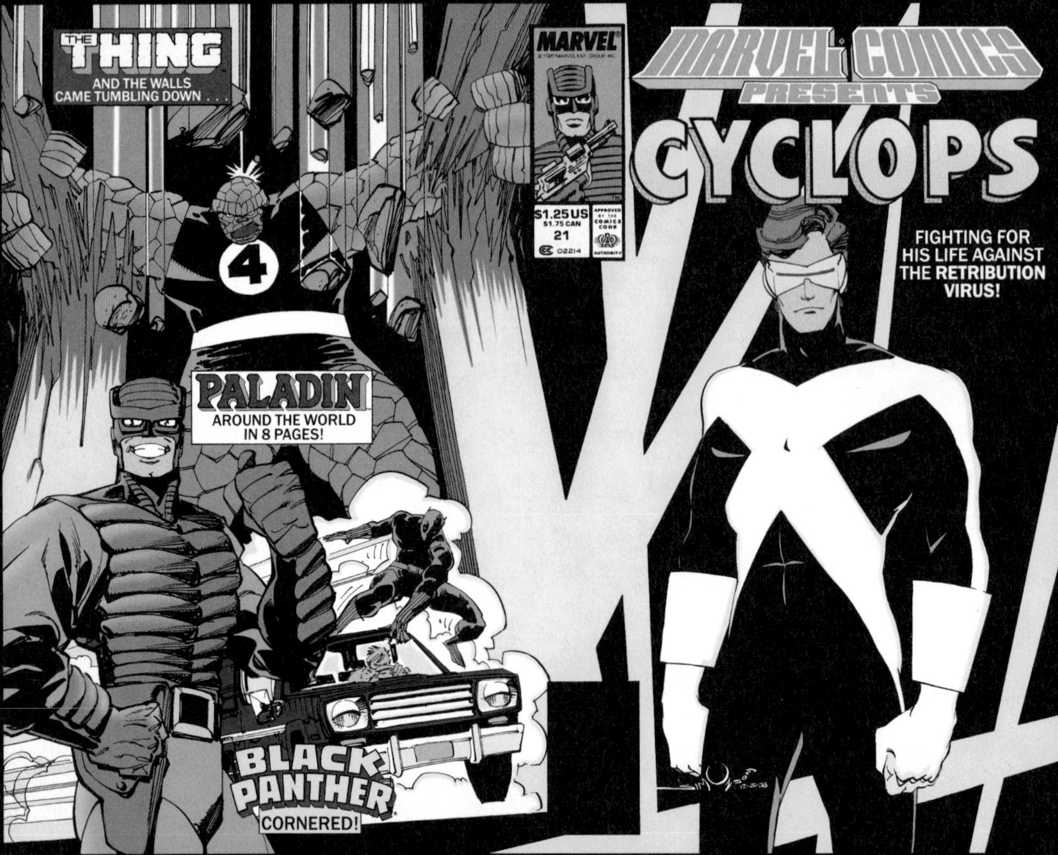

THE THING
AND THE WALLS CAME TUMBLING DOWN . . .
PALADIN
AROUND THE WORLD IN 8 PAGES!
BLACK PANTHER
CORNERED!
MARVEL
$1.25 US
$1.75 CAN
21
02214
APPROVED BY THE COMICS CODE AUTHORITY
MARVEL COMICS PRESENTS
CYCLOPS
FIGHTING FOR HIS LIFE AGAINST THE RETRIBUTION VIRUS!

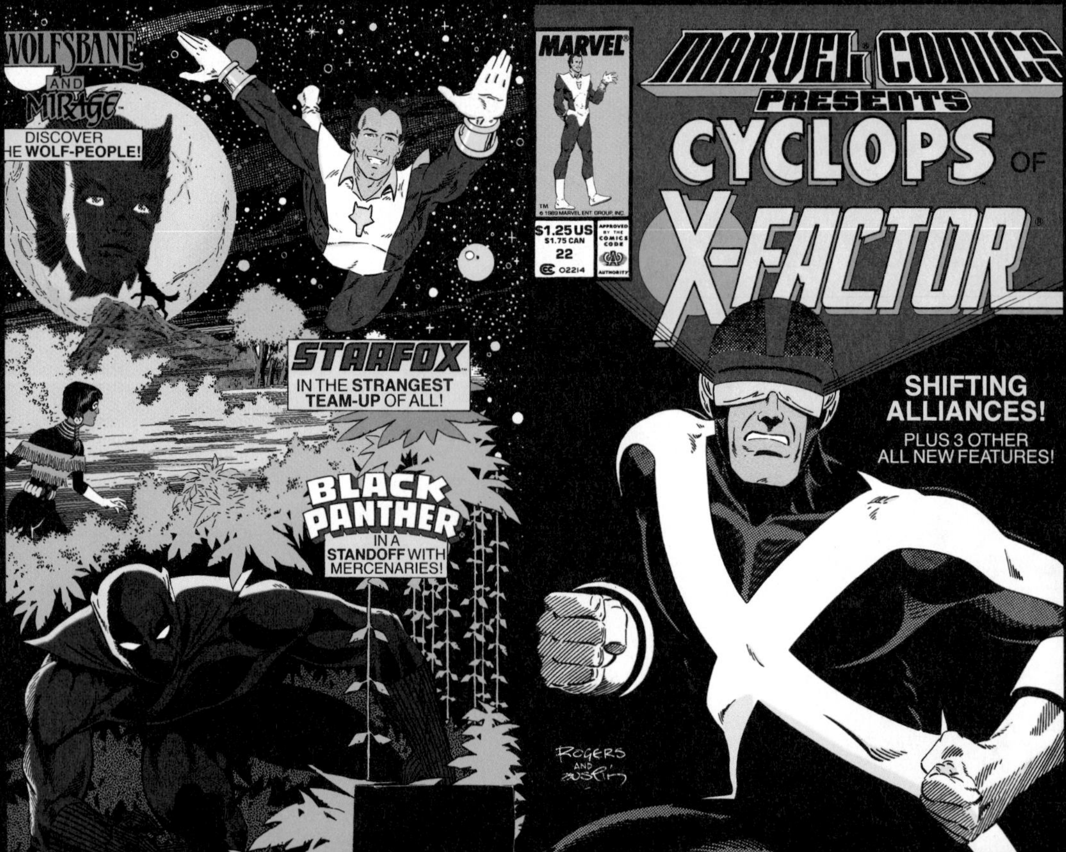

WOLFSBANE
AND
MIRAGE
DISCOVER
HE WOLF-PEOPLE!
STARFOX
IN THE STRANGEST TEAM-UP OF ALL!
BLACK PANTHER
IN A STANDOFF WITH MERCENARIES!
MARVEL
© 1989 MARVEL ENT. GROUP, INC.
$1.25 US
$1.75 CAN
22
02214
APPROVED BY THE COMICS CODE AUTHORITY
MARVEL COMICS PRESENTS
CYCLOPS OF
X-FACTOR
SHIFTING ALLIANCES!
PLUS 3 OTHER ALL NEW FEATURES!
ROGERS AND

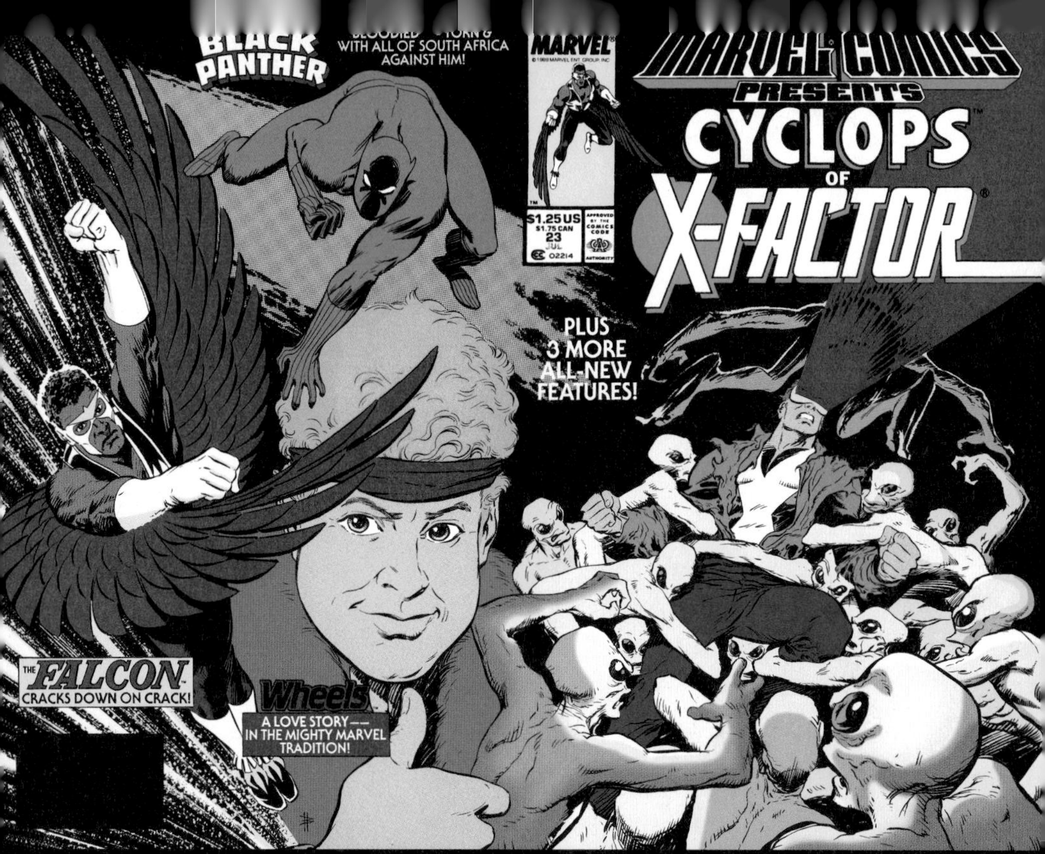

BLACK PANTHER
WITH ALL OF SOUTH AFRICA AGAINST HIM!
MARVEL
© 1989 MARVEL ENT. GROUP, INC.
$1.25 US
$1.75 CAN
23
JUL
APPROVED BY THE COMICS CODE AUTHORITY
02214
MARVEL COMICS PRESENTS
CYCLOPS OF X-FACTOR
PLUS 3 MORE ALL-NEW FEATURES!
THE FALCON
CRACKS DOWN ON CRACK!
Wheels
A LOVE STORY — IN THE MIGHTY MARVEL TRADITION!

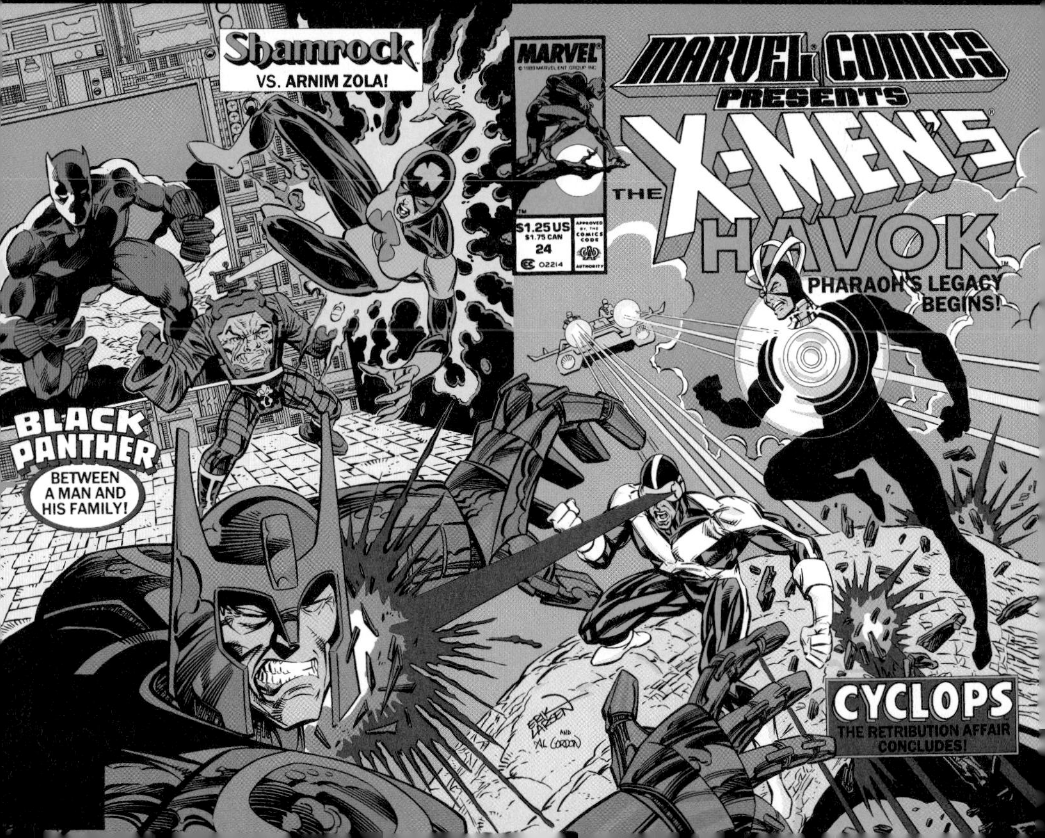

Shamrock
VS. ARNIM ZOLA!
MARVEL
© 1989 MARVEL ENT. GROUP, INC.
$1.25 US
$1.75 CAN
24
APPROVED BY THE COMICS CODE AUTHORITY
02214
MARVEL COMICS PRESENTS
THE X-MEN'S HAVOK
PHARAOH'S LEGACY BEGINS!
BLACK PANTHER
BETWEEN A MAN AND HIS FAMILY!
ERIK LARSEN AND AL GORDON
CYCLOPS
THE RETRIBUTION AFFAIR CONCLUDES!

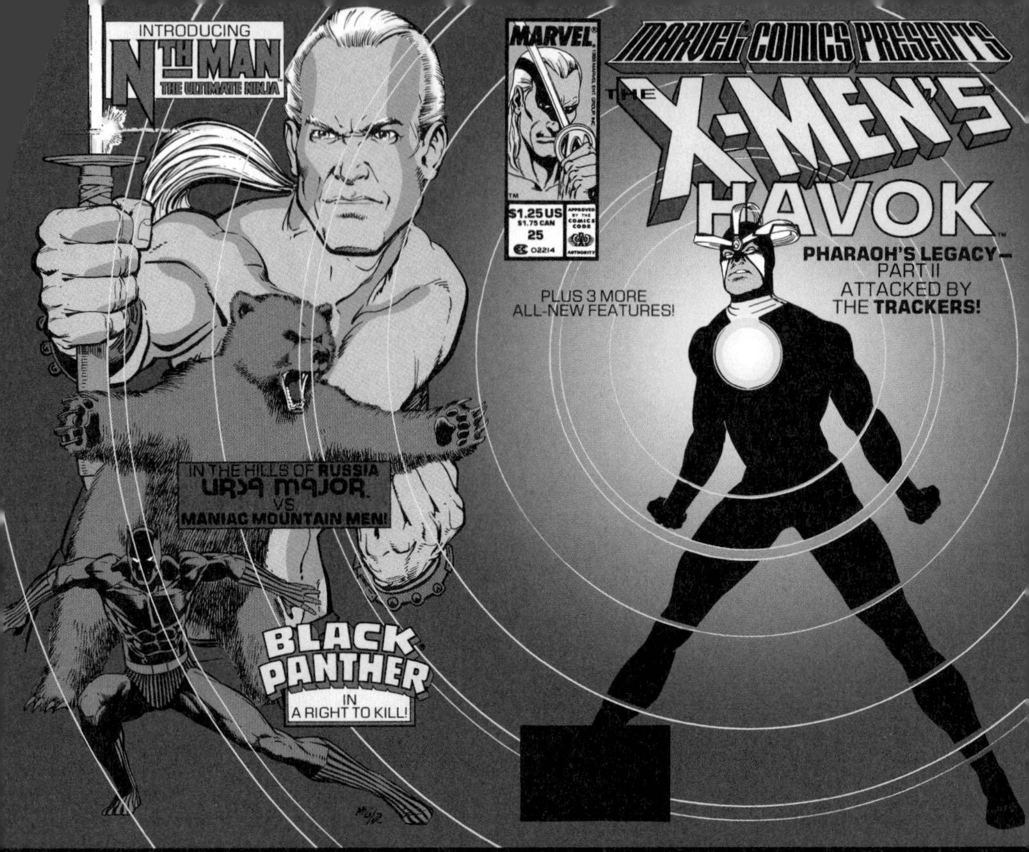
INTRODUCING
NTH MAN
THE ULTIMATE NINJA
IN THE HILLS OF RUSSIA
URSA MAJOR
VS.
MANIAC MOUNTAIN MEN!
BLACK PANTHER
IN
A RIGHT TO KILL!
MARVEL
$1.25 US
$1.75 CAN
25
APPROVED BY THE COMICS CODE AUTHORITY
MARVEL COMICS PRESENTS
THE X-MEN'S HAVOK
PHARAOH'S LEGACY—
PART II
ATTACKED BY
THE TRACKERS!
PLUS 3 MORE
ALL-NEW FEATURES!

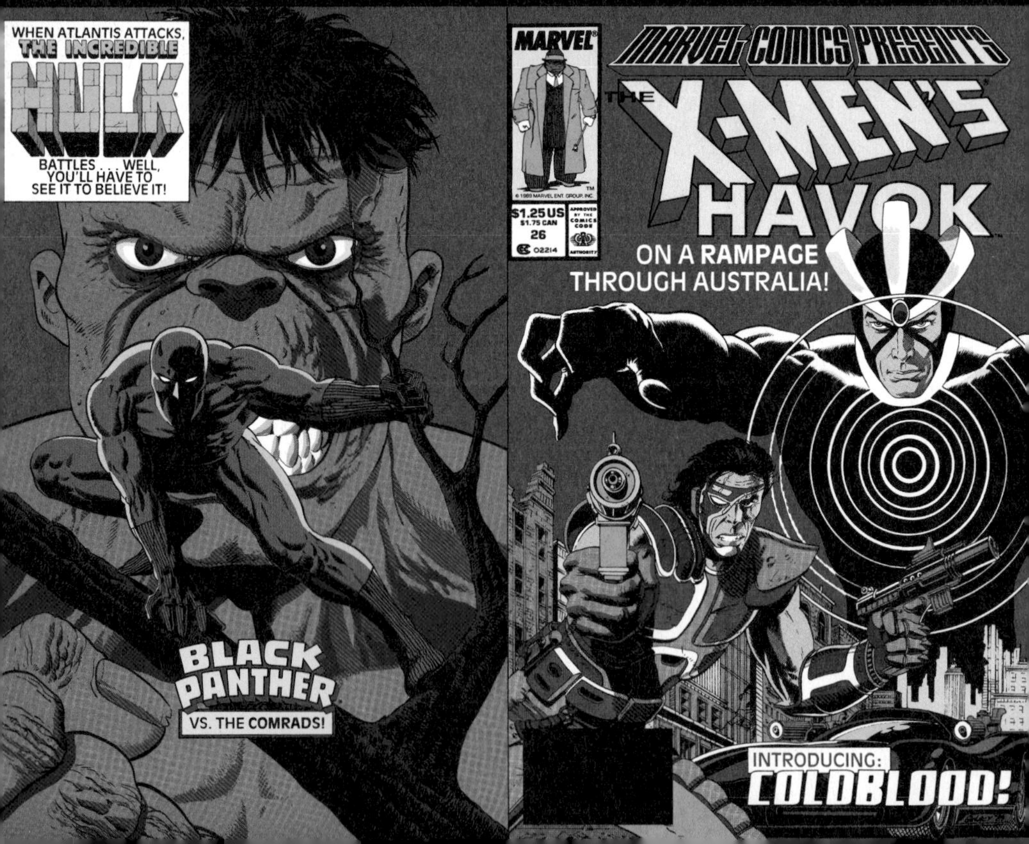
WHEN ATLANTIS ATTACKS,
THE INCREDIBLE
HULK
BATTLES . . . WELL,
YOU'LL HAVE TO
SEE IT TO BELIEVE IT!
BLACK PANTHER
VS. THE COMRADS!
MARVEL
© 1989 MARVEL ENT. GROUP, INC.
$1.25 US
$1.75 CAN
26
APPROVED BY THE COMICS CODE AUTHORITY
MARVEL COMICS PRESENTS
THE X-MEN'S HAVOK
ON A RAMPAGE
THROUGH AUSTRALIA!
INTRODUCING:
COLDBLOOD!

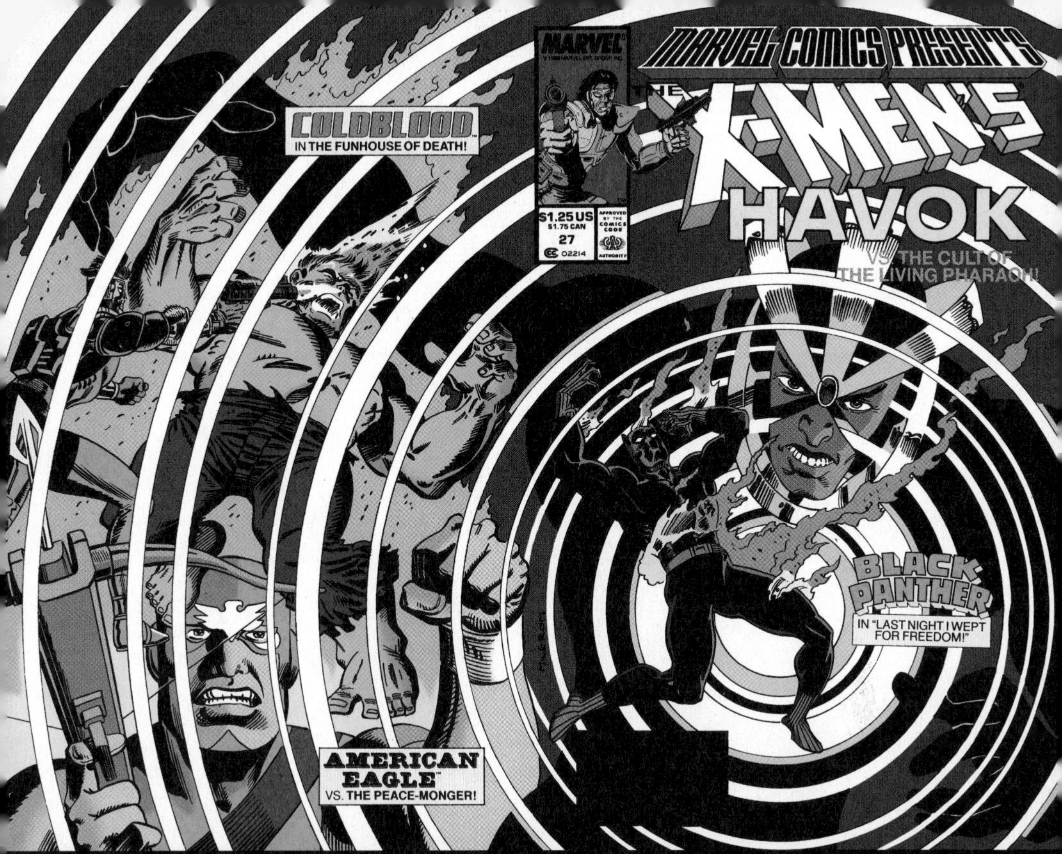

MARVEL
© 1989 MARVEL ENT. GROUP, INC.
$1.25 US
$1.75 CAN
27
APPROVED BY THE COMICS CODE AUTHORITY
02214
MARVEL COMICS PRESENTS
THE X-MEN'S HAVOK
VS. THE CULT OF THE LIVING PHARAOH!
COLDBLOOD
IN THE FUNHOUSE OF DEATH!
BLACK PANTHER
IN "LAST NIGHT I WEPT FOR FREEDOM!"
AMERICAN EAGLE™
VS. THE PEACE-MONGER!

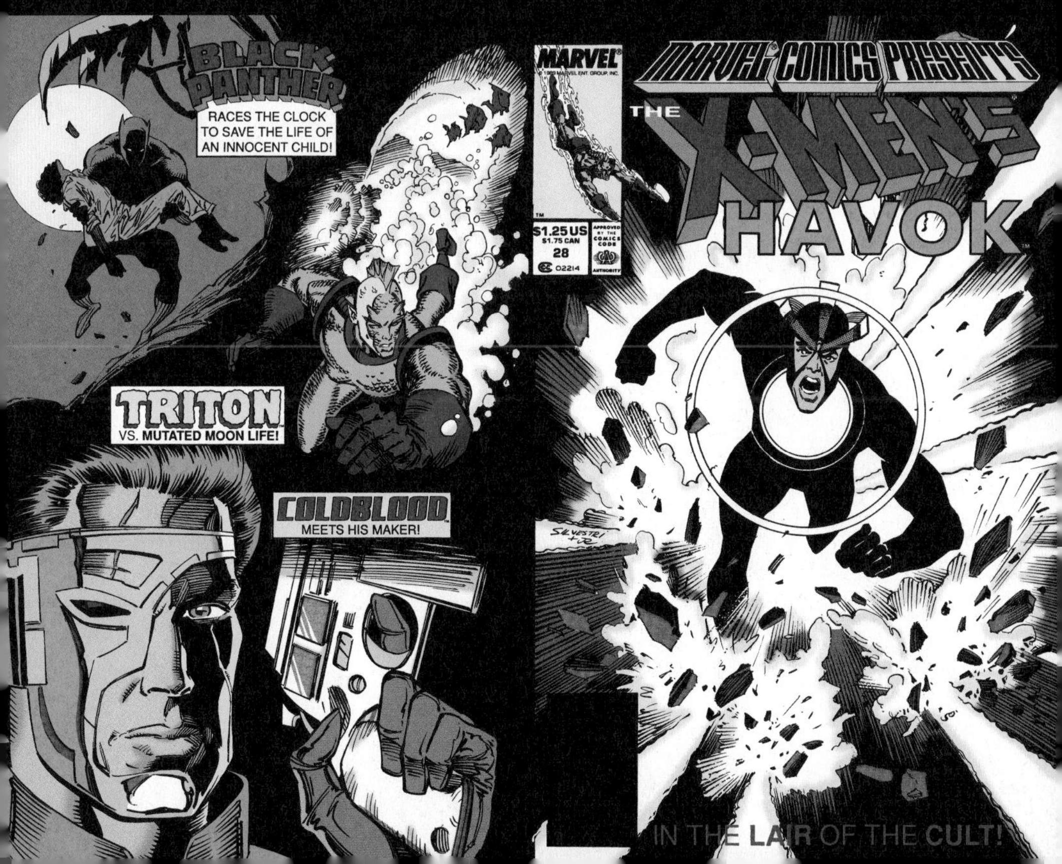

MARVEL
© 1989 MARVEL ENT. GROUP, INC.
$1.25 US
$1.75 CAN
28
APPROVED BY THE COMICS CODE AUTHORITY
02214
MARVEL COMICS PRESENTS
THE X-MEN'S HAVOK
BLACK PANTHER
RACES THE CLOCK TO SAVE THE LIFE OF AN INNOCENT CHILD!
TRITON
VS. MUTATED MOON LIFE!
COLDBLOOD
MEETS HIS MAKER!
IN THE LAIR OF THE CULT!

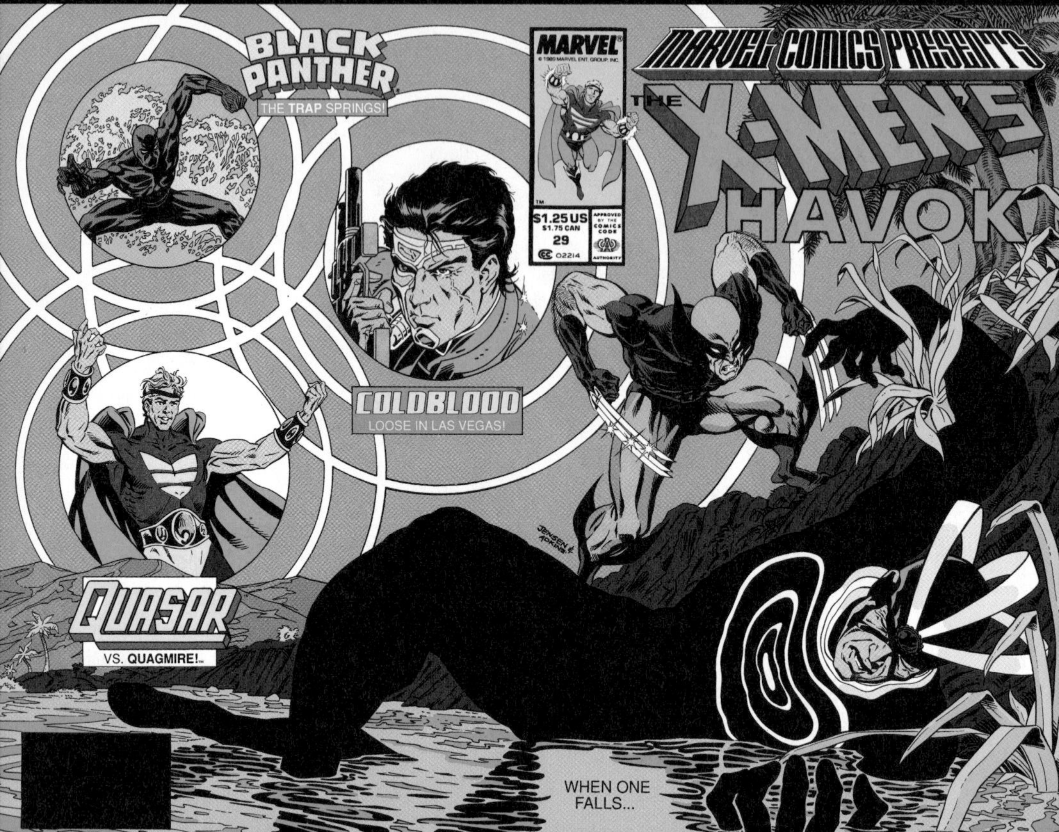
MARVEL
$1.25 US
$1.75 CAN
29
APPROVED BY THE COMICS CODE AUTHORITY
MARVEL COMICS PRESENTS
THE X-MEN'S HAVOK
BLACK PANTHER
THE TRAP SPRINGS!
COLDBLOOD
LOOSE IN LAS VEGAS!
QUASAR
VS. QUAGMIRE!
WHEN ONE FALLS...

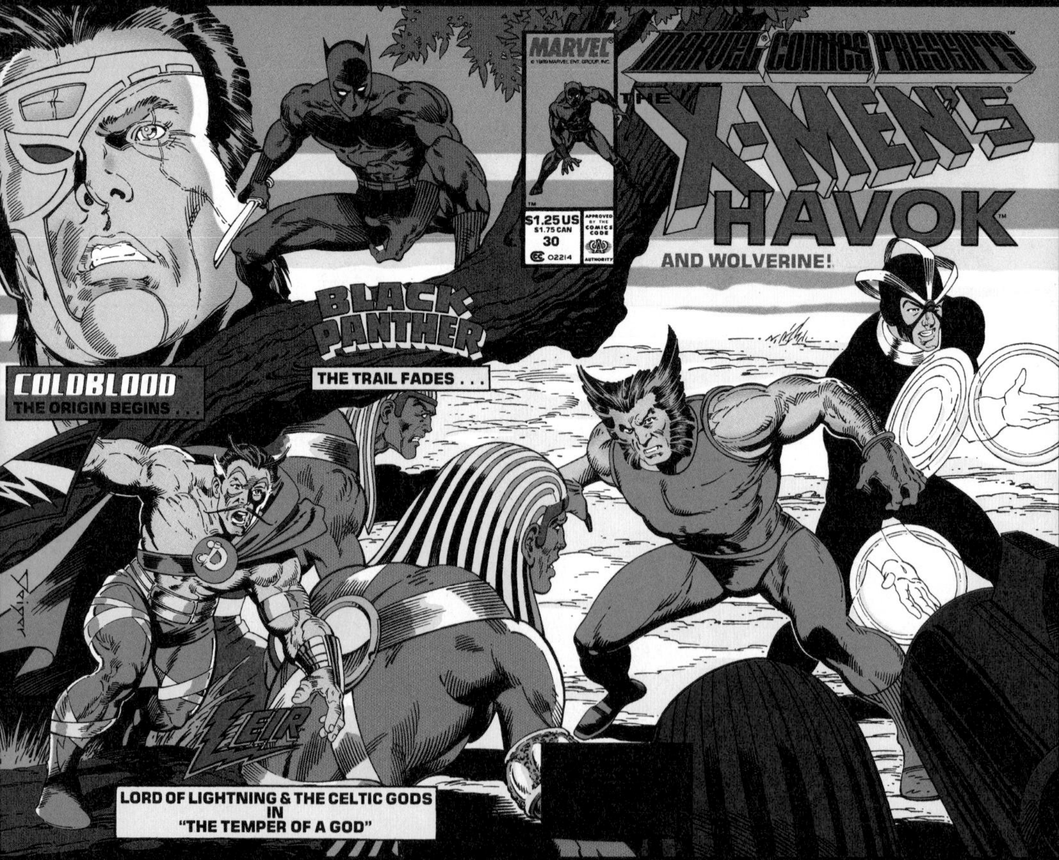
MARVEL
$1.25 US
$1.75 CAN
30
APPROVED BY THE COMICS CODE AUTHORITY
MARVEL COMICS PRESENTS
THE X-MEN'S HAVOK
AND WOLVERINE!
BLACK PANTHER
THE TRAIL FADES . . .
COLDBLOOD
THE ORIGIN BEGINS . . .
LEIR
LORD OF LIGHTNING & THE CELTIC GODS
IN
"THE TEMPER OF A GOD"

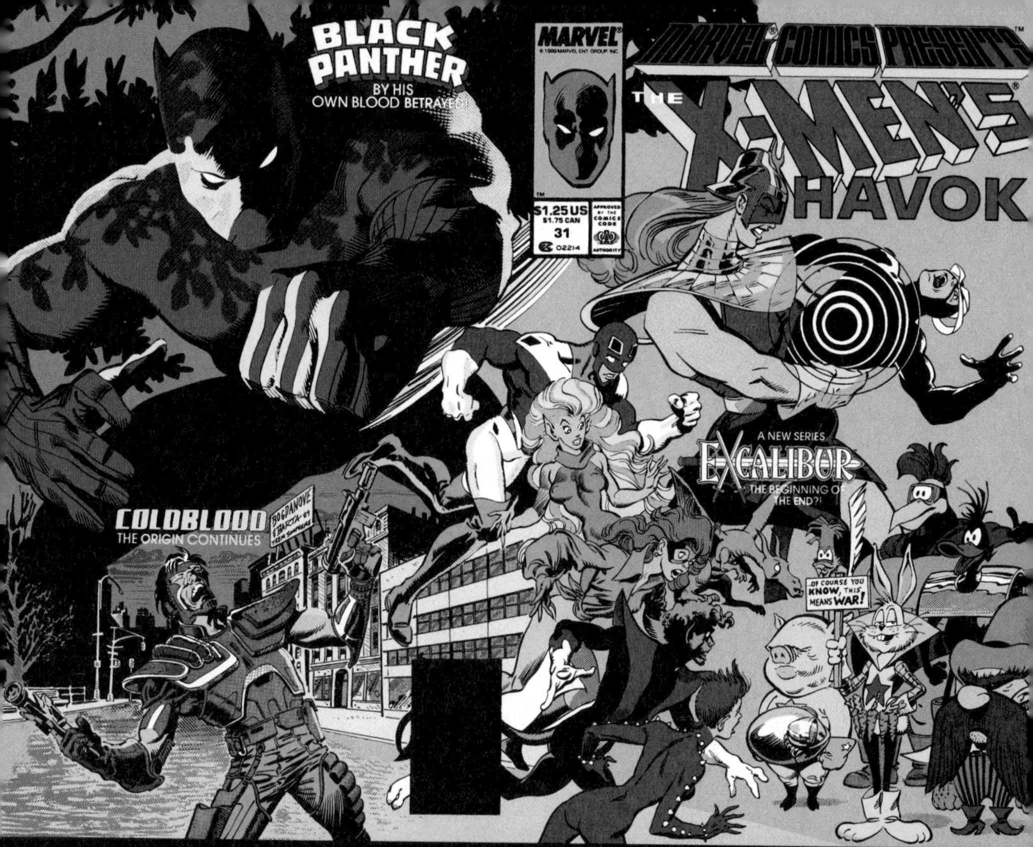
BLACK PANTHER
BY HIS OWN BLOOD BETRAYED!
MARVEL
© 1989 MARVEL ENT. GROUP, INC.
MARVEL COMICS PRESENTS
THE X-MEN'S HAVOK
$1.25 US $1.75 CAN 31
APPROVED BY THE COMICS CODE AUTHORITY
A NEW SERIES
EXCALIBUR
THE BEGINNING OF THE END?!
COLDBLOOD
THE ORIGIN CONTINUES
...OF COURSE YOU KNOW, THIS MEANS WAR!

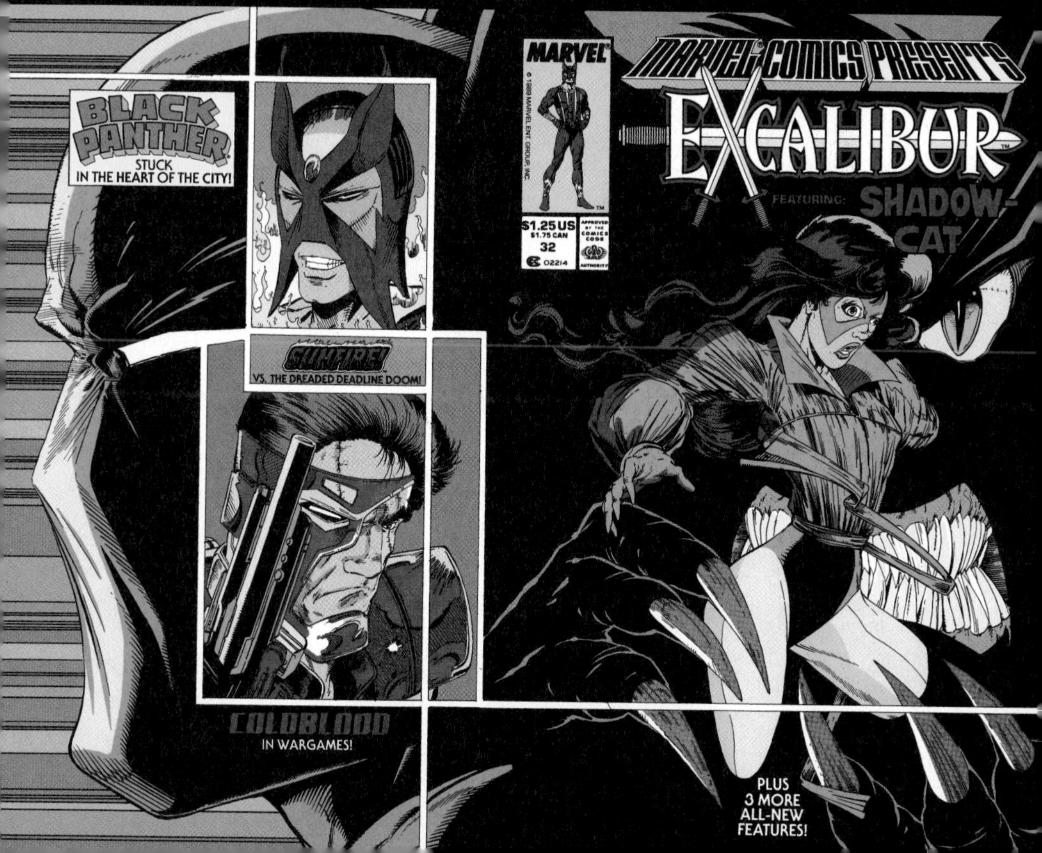
BLACK PANTHER
STUCK IN THE HEART OF THE CITY!
MARVEL
MARVEL COMICS PRESENTS
EXCALIBUR
FEATURING: SHADOW-CAT
$1.25 US $1.75 CAN 32
APPROVED BY THE COMICS CODE AUTHORITY
SUNFIRE!
VS. THE DREADED DEADLINE DOOM!
COLDBLOOD
IN WARGAMES!
PLUS 3 MORE ALL-NEW FEATURES!

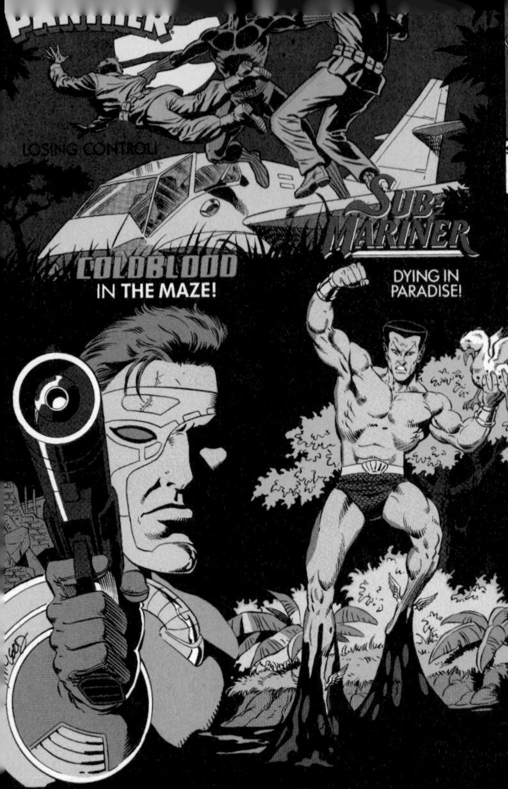
LOSING CONTROL!
SUB-MARINER
COLDBLOOD
IN THE MAZE!
DYING IN PARADISE!

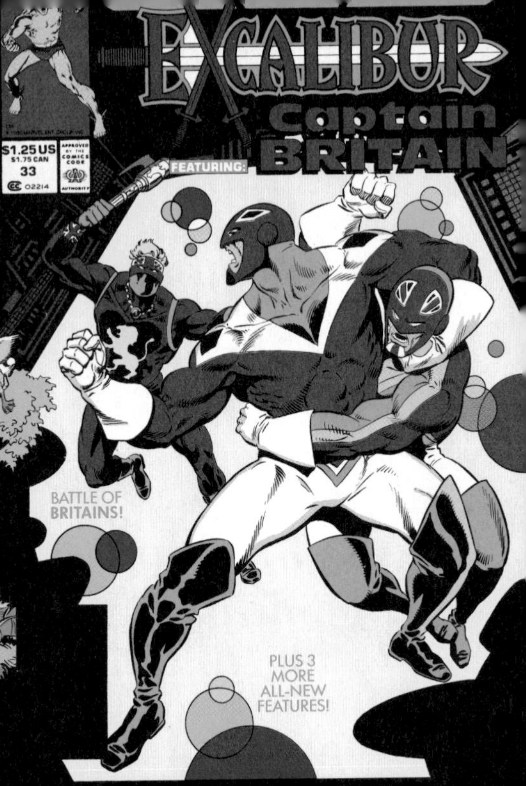
$1.25 US
$1.75 CAN
33
APPROVED BY THE COMICS CODE AUTHORITY
EXCALIBUR
FEATURING: Captain BRITAIN
BATTLE OF BRITAINS!
PLUS 3 MORE ALL-NEW FEATURES!

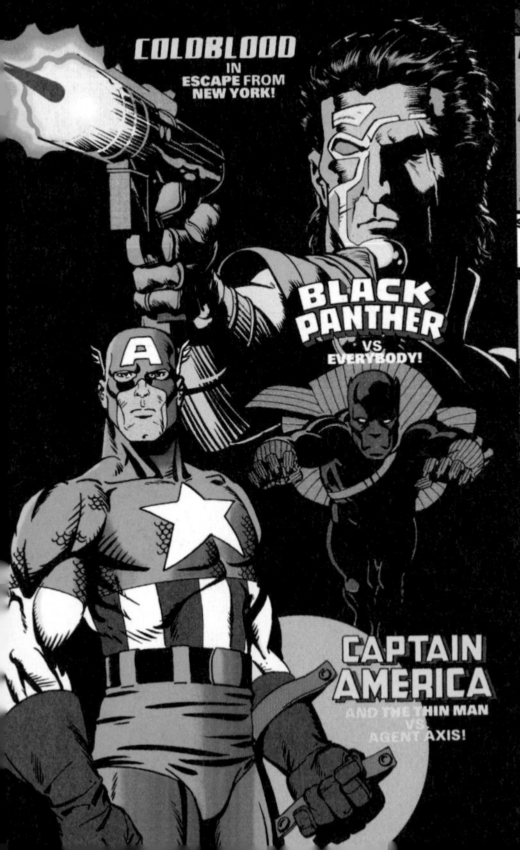
COLDBLOOD
IN ESCAPE FROM NEW YORK!
BLACK PANTHER
VS. EVERYBODY!
CAPTAIN AMERICA
AND THE THIN MAN VS. AGENT AXIS!

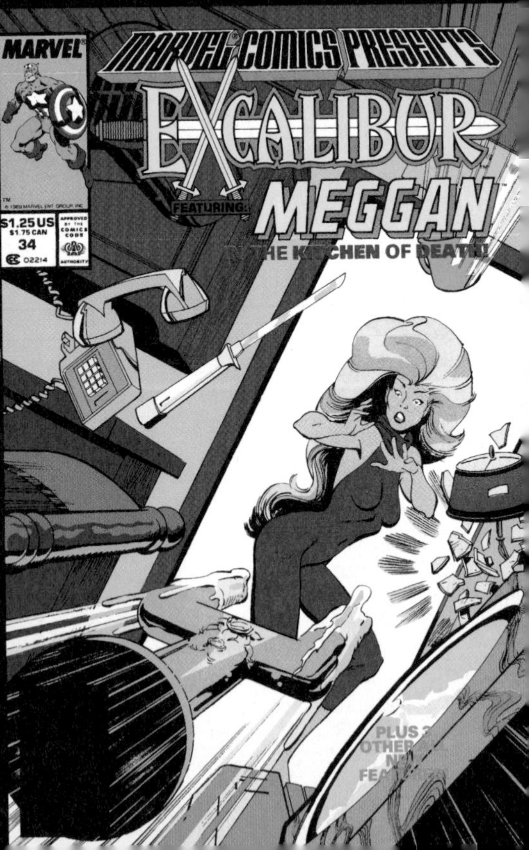
MARVEL
MARVEL COMICS PRESENTS
EXCALIBUR
FEATURING: MEGGAN
THE KI CHEN OF DEATH!
$1.25 US
$1.75 CAN
34
APPROVED BY THE COMICS CODE AUTHORITY
PLUS 3

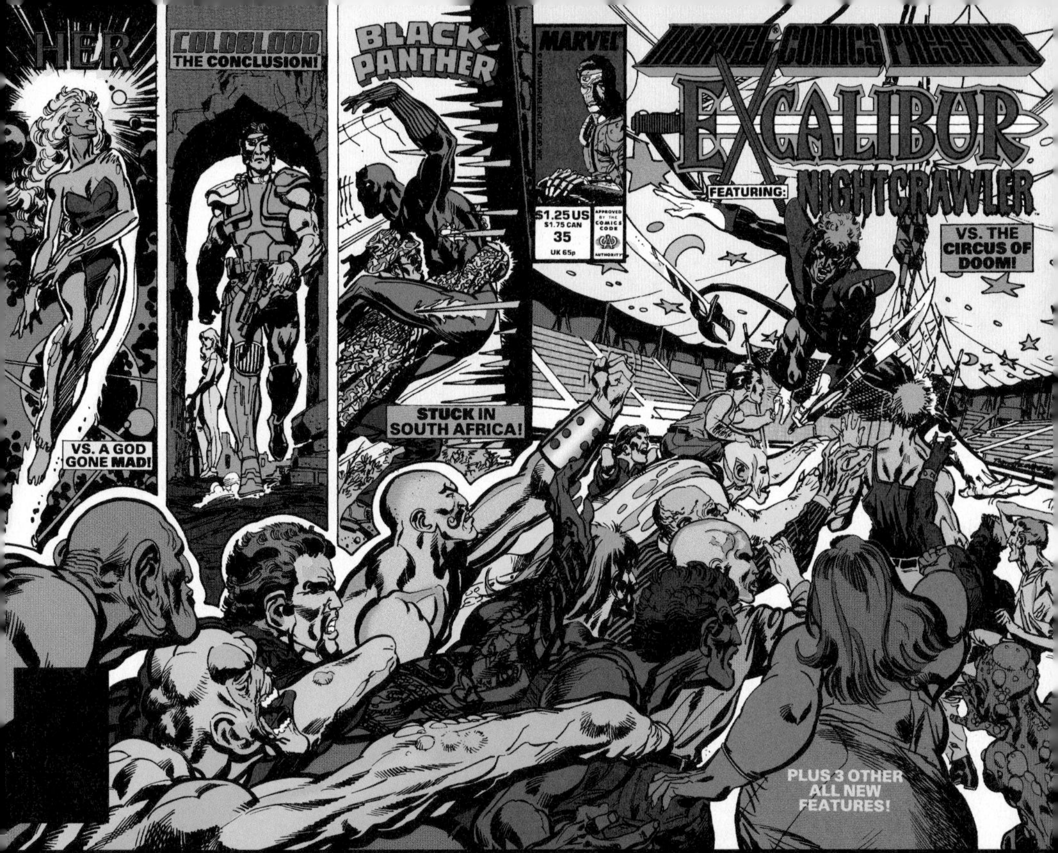

HER
VS. A GOD GONE MAD!
COLDBLOOD
THE CONCLUSION!
BLACK PANTHER
STUCK IN SOUTH AFRICA!
MARVEL
$1.25 US
$1.75 CAN
35
UK 65p
APPROVED BY THE COMICS CODE AUTHORITY
MARVEL COMICS PRESENTS
EXCALIBUR
FEATURING: NIGHTCRAWLER
VS. THE CIRCUS OF DOOM!
PLUS 3 OTHER ALL NEW FEATURES!

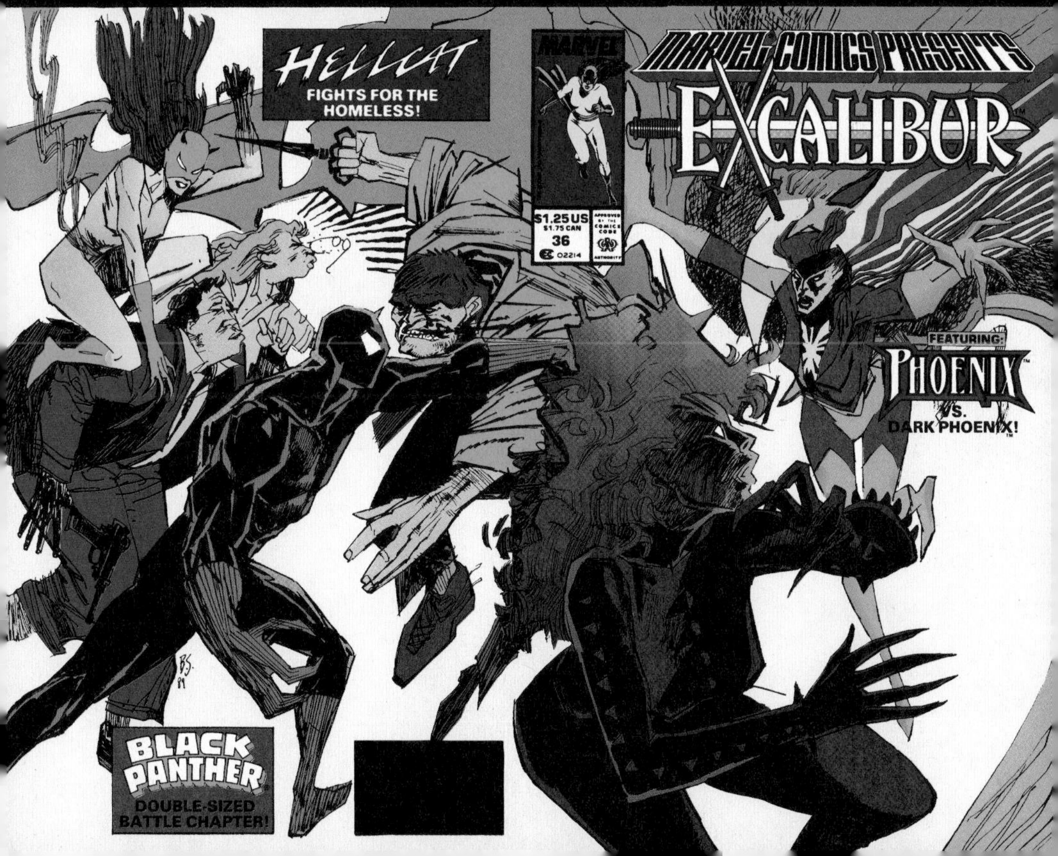

HELLCAT
FIGHTS FOR THE HOMELESS!
MARVEL
$1.25 US
$1.75 CAN
36
02214
APPROVED BY THE COMICS CODE AUTHORITY
MARVEL COMICS PRESENTS
EXCALIBUR
FEATURING:
PHOENIX
VS.
DARK PHOENIX!
B.S. 89
BLACK PANTHER
DOUBLE-SIZED BATTLE CHAPTER!

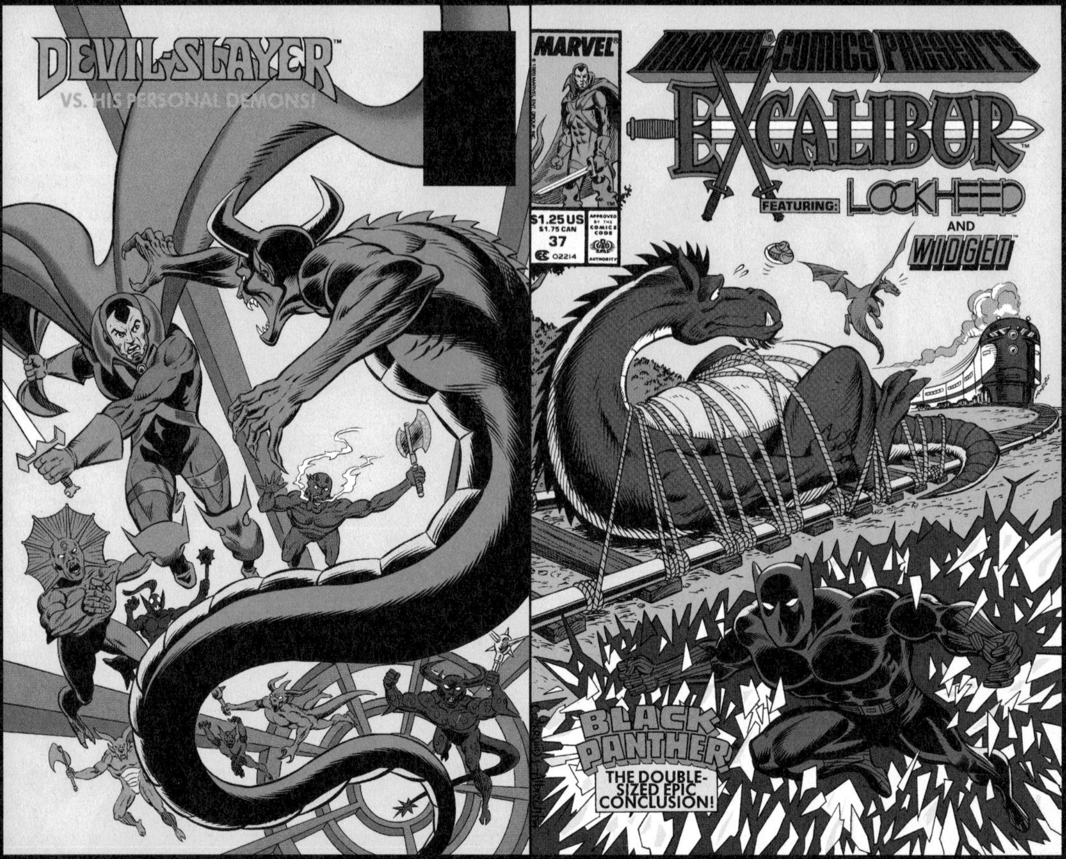
DEVIL-SLAYER™
VS. HIS PERSONAL DEMONS!
MARVEL
$1.25 US
$1.75 CAN
37
APPROVED BY THE COMICS CODE AUTHORITY
02214
MARVEL COMICS PRESENTS
EXCALIBUR™
FEATURING: LOCKHEED
AND
WIDGET™
BLACK PANTHER
THE DOUBLE-SIZED EPIC CONCLUSION!

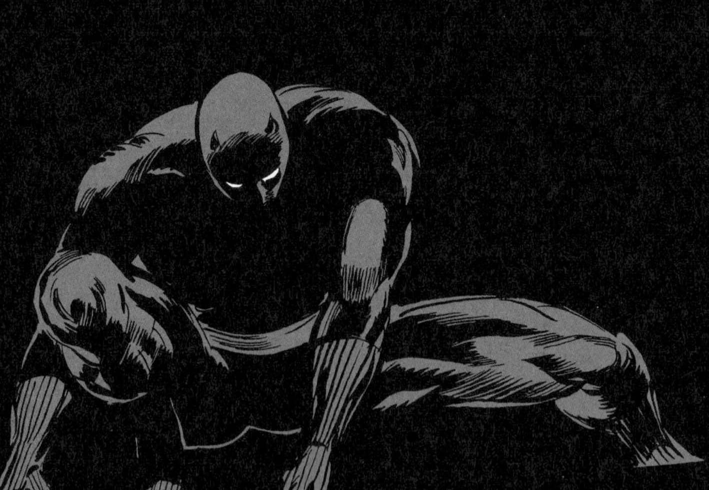